Spies

Spies

THE RISE AND FALL OF THE

KGB

IN AMERICA

John Earl Haynes, Harvey Klehr, and Alexander Vassiliev

with translations by Philip Redko and Steven Shabad

Yale University Press   New Haven & London

Published with assistance from the Mary Cady Tew Memorial Fund.

Designed by James J. Johnson and set in New Caledonia and Bulmer types by
The Composing Room of Michigan, Inc.
Printed in the United States of America by Sheridan Books, Ann Arbor, Michigan.

Library of Congress Cataloging-in-Publication Data

Haynes, John Earl.
    Spies : the rise and fall of the KGB in America / John Earl Haynes, Harvey Klehr, and
Alexander Vassiliev.
        p.   cm.
    Includes bibliographical references and index.
    ISBN 978-0-300-12390-6 (cloth : alk. paper)
    1. Espionage, Soviet—United States—History.   2. Soviet Union. Komitet gosu-
darstvennoi bezopasnosti—History.   3. Spies—Soviet Union—History.   4. Spies—
United States Union—History.   I. Klehr, Harvey.   II. Vassiliev, Alexander.   III. Title.

    UB271.R9H389 2009
    327.124707309'045—dc22

                                                                        2008045628

A catalogue record for this book is available from the British Library.

This paper meets the requirements of ANSI/NISO Z39.48–1992 (Permanence of Paper).

10 9 8 7 6 5 4 3 2 1

To my beloved wife, Janette
—JOHN EARL HAYNES

To women of valor, Susan Kline Klehr and Robin Klehr Avia
—HARVEY KLEHR

To my son, Ken Vassiliev
—ALEXANDER VASSILIEV

Contents

Preface

Is there anything new to be learned about Soviet espionage in America? After more than a decade of fresh revelations, it may seem that we must know most of the details and there is little left to uncover. But new information continues to emerge. In the fall of 2007, after Russian president Vladimir Putin announced a posthumous award to a previously unknown spy, George Koval, credited with enabling the USSR to steal vital atomic secrets, the *New York Times* published a front-page article detailing the remarkable story of his transition from an Iowa-born child of Russian-Jewish (and Communist-sympathizing) parents who moved in 1932 to Birobidzhan, Stalin's artificial Jewish homeland in Siberia, and his transformation into a Soviet spy sent back to the United States who wound up working at the secret Oak Ridge atomic facilities during World War II.[1]

The Koval story illustrates some of the dilemmas faced by anyone attempting to write a factual account of Soviet espionage. The original story relied on Russian claims about the value of the material Koval supplied. Despite a number of clues pointing to his having a less significant role in atomic espionage than the claims boasted, a credulous press inflated his importance, inadvertently echoing his employer. Russian military intelligence, the GRU, has, in recent years, attempted to emulate the public relations offensive that its long-time sister agency and rival, the KGB, embarked on in the 1990s to convince the Russian public and government officials that it had a major role in the military and political successes achieved by the Soviet Union.

When the underlying documentation for a spy story is unavailable, the bits and pieces of information released by governments to placate public curiosity about espionage can be misleading. Official government statements often have more to do with internal bureaucratic factionalism or public relations than the truth. The spies themselves are rarely available to be interviewed and have good reasons to avoid being too specific or entirely candid. And when they do speak through memoir literature they are as prone as autobiographers in other walks of life to romanticize their importance, minimize their mistakes, and pass over unpleasant events with silence or misdirection. Frustratingly, archival information regarding intelligence and counterintelligence activities from the 1930s onward continues to be tightly held and parceled out in a miserly fashion.

For all these reasons, Alexander Vassiliev's notebooks provide a uniquely rich insight into Soviet espionage during the 1930s and 1940s. As Vassiliev explains in his introduction, he had unprecedented access to the archival record of KGB activities in America in that era. Contemporaneous documents, written at the time the events they describe were occurring or shortly afterwards, they also have the virtue of being a record of how the very agency that conducted the spying understood its operations. These official communications are neither the conclusions or guesses, sometimes inspired, sometimes incorrect, of counterespionage organizations dedicated to uncovering the spies; nor the reluctant admissions of suspects minimizing their involvement; nor statements from defectors who may have a personal agenda. Instead, they are the contemporaneous accounts of the successes and failures of the KGB by the KGB itself. They are not public "spin" offered by bureaucratic organizations and officials anxious to demonstrate their value to a public or protect an organization's self-image. Any archival historian knows that even contemporaneous documents can sometimes mislead because their author didn't correctly understand the events he was reporting for some reason, harbored prejudices and assumptions that distorted what was reported, or for self-promotion or self-protection distorted what actually happened. But that danger of misleading is true of all archival records, no matter what the subject, and it is why historians feel more confident when there are multiple documentary sources that corroborate one another and allow one to screen out the misleading outlier. And given the several thousand KGB documents transcribed, quoted, extracted, and summarized in their more than 1,115 pages, Vassiliev's notebooks provide researchers with an abundance of material that offers both internal corroboration and ample basis for corroboration with independent sources.

We traveled to London in the fall of 2005 to meet with Vassiliev after learning that the 1948 "Gorsky memo," introduced as evidence in his libel suit (see the introduction) in Great Britain, was not the only extract of a KGB document in his possession that scholars had not yet examined. A preliminary look at Vassiliev's notebooks made clear how valuable they were, and we quickly decided to find funding to undertake a skilled translation and produce a book based on them.[2]

Despite everything that has appeared in the past decade, the Vassiliev notebooks offer the most complete look at Soviet espionage in America we have yet had or will obtain until the likely far off day when Russian authorities open the KGB's archives for independent research. Material from Communist International (Comintern) and Communist Party, United States (CPUSA) files, while significant and helpful and shedding some light on espionage in the United States, includes only KGB material that made its way to those bodies and represents only a tiny fraction of KGB activities. We dealt with such material in two books, *The Secret World of American Communism* and *The Soviet World of American Communism.* The World War II KGB and GRU cables deciphered by the National Security Agency's (NSA) Venona project and released in the mid-1990s are also a very valuable documentary source, out of which we wrote *Venona: Decoding Soviet Espionage in America.* But the Venona decryptions are only a few thousand cables out of hundreds of thousands sent, and those decoded were random, the result of the few cables out of the total body that were vulnerable to deciphering. Consequently, the subjects of the deciphered messages ranged from the trivial to the important, and often they were only partially decrypted. Even when complete, they were messages boiled down for transmission by telegram, often short, terse, and lacking detail.[3]

In 1992, retired KGB officer Vasili Mitrokhin defected to Great Britain. In the latter part of his career he had been the KGB's archivist and privately made notes on some of the documents that passed through his hands. After he retired in 1984, he secretly typed up his notes into ten manuscript volumes (eight geographical and two case histories), destroying the original notes. When the British Secret Intelligence Service (SIS; also known as MI6) exfiltrated him to the West, he brought with him the ten volumes of transcribed notes and some envelopes of original notes not yet transcribed. These materials formed the basis for two highly valuable books on Soviet intelligence, Christopher Andrew and Vasili Mitrokhin's *The Sword and the Shield* and *The World Was Going Our Way,* as well as a KGB lexicon. Andrew is one of the leading historians of intelligence and Mitrokhin's material is extremely rich, but as valuable as the books are, scholars would like to have the underlying material open for independent review. As of 2008, the SIS and the Mitrokhin family have released only a small portion of the transcribed material or original notes, none of it dealing with operations in the United States. (In any case, only a portion of Mitrokhin's material dealt with American operations, whereas all of Vassiliev's material focuses on American-related subjects.)[4]

In order to facilitate research and allow others to see the basis for our interpretations, we are making available electronic scans of Vassiliev's original handwritten notes, a Cyrillic word-processed transcription, an English-language translation, and a supplementary concordance of cover names and real names, simultaneously with the publication of this book. Alexander Vassiliev gave his original notebooks, along with hard copy of the Cyrillic transcription and English translation, to the Library of Congress, where they are available for research without restriction.

From a historian's point of view, the ideal situation would be for the Russian Foreign Intelligence Service (SVR), successor to the KGB, to open its archive of KGB documents so that researchers could compare Vassiliev's transcriptions and summaries with the originals. We hope that will happen, but it is likely to be in the distant future. The partial and restricted opening that allowed Vassiliev access came at a unique historical moment. Just a year after the collapse of the Communist regime, with economic chaos and inflation threatening pensions and government budgets, the intelligence service responded to a proposal from Crown Publishers, which offered a substantial payment to a pension fund for its retired officers in return for cooperation on a series of books on Soviet intelligence. As part of the agreement that ensued the SVR gave Alexander Vassiliev permission to examine archival records for a book project that teamed a Russian (Vassiliev) and an American (Allen Weinstein) for a book on Soviet espionage in the United States in the 1930s and 1940s. Vassiliev did not sign a document limiting the use he could make of his material or pledging secrecy. The plan was for the Russian partner to produce material from the archives that would be vetted by a declassification committee before being turned over to the American partner for final writing and shaping into a book.[5]

From the beginning the Crown agreement was controversial and engendered anger and resistance within the Russian intelligence community. Many nationalists and hard-line Communists, a substantial element in the intelligence services, perceived it as a serious breach of security and a sale of the national patrimony to the state's enemies. By 1996 Alexander Vassiliev himself felt so threatened by the prospect of a Communist electoral victory, the not-so-veiled warnings of retaliation, and the fear that he might be accused of communicating state secrets because of rumors that his co-author, Weinstein, had ties to American intelligence that he felt it expedient to leave the country. That brief and limited KGB archival opening of the early 1990s ended as Russia stabilized and the SVR regained its authority in the Russian state.

When he moved to Great Britain, Vassiliev left the notebooks behind, fearing they would be confiscated at customs. (In 2001, he had them shipped to him in London.) For this reason, the original notebooks were never seen by his co-author, Allen Weinstein. Consequently, Weinstein wrote *The Haunted Wood: Soviet Espionage in America — The Stalin Era* from summary sanitized chapters written by Vassiliev and approved by an SVR declassification committee (as planned by the Crown agreement), as well as chapters intended for that committee that had not gone through the committee by the time Vassiliev left Russia. Since the policy of the Soviet and Russian intelligence service was and is not to identify any sources or agents who have not themselves admitted to working for it, those summaries generally did not contain the real names behind the cover names. In other cases, Vassiliev left out information, not knowing how it fit into the summary chapters he wrote. These drawbacks did not lessen the importance of *The Haunted Wood*, the first survey of Soviet intelligence in the United States written from KGB archival sources, but they did limit the information it contained.

When we first met with Vassiliev and became aware of what was in the notebooks, we recognized the opportunity to write a more complete, factual, and detailed portrait of Soviet intelligence than ever before was at hand. Not only was it now possible to identify scores of previously unknown or unidentified Soviet spies, but also already told stories could be enriched by the detail provided by the documents recorded in the notebooks. And what a wonderful tapestry the notebooks revealed—an astounding array of characters, some long known or suspected of KGB ties, others never remotely believed to be involved. The following chapters provide fresh revelations about such prominent Americans as Alger Hiss, Ernest Hemingway, J. Robert Oppenheimer, I. F. Stone, Lee Pressman, and Corliss Lamont. But some of the most fascinating characters in this book are previously unknown men and women about whom we have been able to turn up enough information to allow us to glimpse the remarkable diversity and occasionally bizarre backgrounds that led them to work with the KGB. Henry Ware, Stanley Graze, James Hibben and Russell McNutt are not household names, but their stories and their lives are stranger than fiction.

The Venona material not only provided abundant evidence of the espionage activities of more than a hundred Americans who worked for Soviet intelligence, but it also included over a hundred other cover names that American counterintelligence never identified. Many of the mysteries can now be solved; in the pages that follow we identify more than seventy previously unknown Soviet sources. Some of them are obscure men and women about whom we still know little more than their names and where they worked; others are reasonably well known or significant portions of their life stories can be reconstructed. Famous journalists, brilliant scientists, important government employees—their connections with Soviet intelligence reveal a picture that no one has ever before suspected.

Beyond the identities of sources and agents, we can provide an unparalleled glimpse of the real world in which espionage takes place. There is often a vast gulf between the rather spare, bureaucratic, and stilted prose of official communications and the frequently lurid, recreated, and seemingly implausible dialogue used by popular writers on espionage or in autobiographies. Embellished and embroidered, first-person accounts often provoke disbelief or disdain. But the workaday KGB documents Vassiliev saw and copied in Moscow are filled with marvelous human details, sometimes absurd, sometimes tragic, occasionally amusing, and always reminders that espionage is an activity engaged in by human beings with foibles and quirks, and espionage agencies are sometimes efficient, occasionally bumbling, and always staffed by human beings, not automatons.

Some readers may wonder why it all matters. Is the account of Soviet espionage merely of antiquarian interest, a matter of fascination to the handful of scholars who have made it their specialty and the somewhat larger community of spy buffs who delight in learning the details of this secret world? While filling in the blank spots in the historical record is enough of a justification, especially for historians, the question of who worked for the KGB has importance well beyond the purely historical. On this particular topic the need for clarity and completeness is especially significant.

Few eras in American history are as quickly and easily characterized as the one to which an otherwise undistinguished Republican senator from Wisconsin gave his name. Although Joseph McCarthy did not burst into national prominence until 1951, his name is popularly used to characterize the post–World War II years, during which, it is alleged, America was obsessed with the issue of domestic communism in general and the theme of Communist subversion in particular. McCarthy's charges that scores of Americans working for the Department of State (DOS) and other government agencies had cooperated with Soviet intelligence or otherwise served Communist (as opposed to American) interests have been harshly judged by most historians and derided in the popular culture, where the victims of entertainment industry blacklists and campaigns by labor groups and all sorts of associations to expel Communist members have been hailed as heroes or paragons of virtue persecuted by anti-democratic and fear-ridden enemies of free speech and free association.

The debate over the nature of American communism and the fierce reaction it engendered has remained a topic provoking passionate emotions long after most of its principals were dead and the CPUSA itself nearly comatose. In the past decade the fervid, one-sided rhetoric about McCarthyism has been replaced by heated debates as newly opened archives have disgorged long-held secrets. Many of the people profiled in this book insisted to their dying days that their lives had been unfairly blighted by false and rash accusations against them motivated by an unthinking and obsessive anti-communism, a crass desire to tar the New Deal with the Communist brush or to discredit otherwise noble causes with the charge of serving Soviet interests. Others never fell under suspicion. A handful really were falsely accused. Was the hunt for Communist spies in fact a witch hunt, a search for fictional demons, that tells us more about the paranoia and madness of the inquisitors, or was it a rational, if sometimes excessively heated, response to a genuine threat posed by scores of otherwise normal Americans who had decided to assist the Soviet Union? This book supplies the details that enable us to answer these questions based on fact, not emotion.

Just consider that in recent years there have been fervent and angry debates about such symbols of the 1940s and 1950s as Alger Hiss, I. F. Stone, and J. Robert Oppenheimer. President Bill Clinton's nominee to head the Central Intelligence Agency (CIA), Anthony Lake, was forced to withdraw after he publicly doubted Hiss's guilt. A new Web site at New York University is devoted to Hiss's innocence, and so fervid in some circles is the belief in Hiss's innocence that in 2007 *The American Scholar,* the official magazine of Phi Beta Kappa, published a lead article accusing an innocent man, Wilder Foote, a respected American journalist and foreign affairs specialist who worked for the State Department and the United Nations, of being the spy Alger Hiss has been thought to be. Journalists who proudly claimed I. F. Stone as their mentor and model have angrily charged "neocons" anxious to tarnish his legacy with concocting false charges about his ties to the KGB, the better to justify their own support for foreign aggression. And a Pulitzer Prize–winning biography of Oppenheimer ridiculed allegations that he had ever joined the CPUSA, much less cooperated with the KGB. In many ways we still live with the legacy of these questions. Now they can be answered and the cases closed.

As illuminating and detailed as Vassiliev's notebooks are, they are not a complete record of KGB operations in the United States. Although Alexander Vassiliev examined more KGB files about American espionage than any other researcher, he did not have unrestricted access to the KGB's secrets. Limited to two years' work in the archives, he was also constrained by the spy agency's unwillingness to provide certain types of files. Beginning his research with the correspondence files for the 1930s, he initially was able to read the messages sent between Moscow Center and the American station. Many contained references to or comments about agents and potential agents. Requests for the operational or personal files of those agents usually brought results and also reminders of the agency's policy of refusing to confirm the identity of sources who had not themselves admitted their work for the KGB. Although there were occasional inconsistencies—Vassiliev received operational files on such people as Harold Glasser and Victor Perlo, sources named by Elizabeth Bentley and neither of whom ever publicly confessed—his requests for other operational files were rebuffed. For his research on atomic espionage, Vassiliev received the first volume (KGB archival files are usually bound into book-like volumes) of the "Enormous" file, details of the Soviet effort to penetrate the Manhattan Project during World War II, but volume 2 and any subsequent volumes on postwar atomic espionage had not arrived by the time he left Russia in 1996.

If Vassiliev's notebooks represent only a segment of the vast documentation of Soviet espionage in the United States, it is a far richer and more extensive portion than we had before. Combined with other once secret information about Soviet espionage made available in recent years —Comintern and CPUSA records, Federal Bureau of Investigation (FBI) files released under the Freedom of Information Act, the Mitrokhin archive, and the Venona decryptions—they enable us to piece together the most complete picture of KGB activities in the United States ever seen. In this enormous jigsaw puzzle, there are still gaps and a number of missing pieces. Sometimes one part of the puzzle lacks a few jagged pieces here or there. Occasionally, another portion has just the outlines of a figure and lacks identifying details. Blank spots remain, but we have filled in many of the missing pieces.

In addition to obviously not including what Vassiliev did not see, we have not included much of what he recorded in the notebooks. To have discussed everything would have required a book much longer than any publisher, either commercial or academic, would tolerate or almost any reader would wade through. Portions of Vassiliev's notes dealing with the Soviet campaign to gain diplomatic recognition in 1933 or lengthy reports about American diplomacy in the 1940s are of interest and relevance to diplomatic historians but of less significance to a study of espionage. We have only touched on the material in the notebooks about KGB infiltration of anti-Bolshevik Russian exile groups and Ukrainian nationalists. There is ample material for additional books and articles on a variety of specialized interests. Some segments from the notebooks have already appeared in *The Haunted Wood,* of course, and we have occasionally lightly glossed over some topics that volume covered in detail, such as the amazing story of the KGB's bribing of Congressman Samuel Dickstein. By the same token, we have decided not to go over in detail the same ground we have already covered in our own earlier books on Soviet espionage, particularly accounts of Soviet sources about whom the notebooks add only limited substance. Thus, while we have discussed members of the Golos/Bentley network whose names were not discovered in Venona, we have largely avoided repeating in detail the stories of its most prominent and well-discussed members here except when new evidence deepens our understanding of their role or changes our knowledge of their activities.

A word about how this book was produced. Vassiliev made a Russian-language transcription of his handwritten notebooks to facilitate translation. Two translators, with access to both transcription and original, then produced an English-language translation that was double-checked by Vassiliev, who speaks and reads English with facility. John Haynes developed a concordance to enable us to maintain consistency in translating cover names, providing the correct English spelling of American names in the notebooks in phonetic Russian and keeping track of the cast of hundreds of characters, with sometimes two or three cover names and the occasional confusion of spelling garbles in the KGB files. Harvey Klehr and Haynes both wrote preliminary drafts of chapters and, as in all of their previous books, constantly edited and reedited each other's work. Vassiliev then vetted each chapter and made his suggestions and corrections. In all ways this has been a joint and cooperative endeavor.

The chapters that follow revisit some old controversies and tell some new stories. After demonstrating that the argument about whether Alger Hiss committed espionage is now closed, we offer the most complete account yet of the Soviet effort to steal the secrets of the atomic bomb, including the stories of several hitherto unknown atomic spies. That is followed by chapters on the remarkable number of journalists who worked for and with the KGB, including I. F. Stone; the extensive Soviet networks devoted to technical and industrial espionage, in which for the first time we identify previously unknown members of the Rosenberg ring; and surprising KGB sources in the State Department, Commerce Department, and other places. Another chapter looks at the remarkable number of KGB spies within the Office of Strategic Services (OSS), America's wartime intelligence agency. A chapter on KGB couriers examines the often anonymous support personnel, whose devotion and diligence enabled the espionage apparatuses to function. We also discuss several KGB obsessions, occasions when recruitments either failed or did not produce meaningful results despite years of efforts. The book concludes with a look at KGB tradecraft and its problems, examining the obstacles and roadblocks that confronted its operations in the United States. Although it cost the United States a great deal in both resources and secrets, the KGB was far from a smoothly functioning and error-free organization. Its lapses and mistakes deserve, if not just as much attention as its triumphs, at least some recognition.

A number of factors made us confident that the Vassiliev notebooks were indeed genuine notes and transcriptions of authentic archival documents. We are not inexperienced in assessing archival documents. We were the first American historians to examine Communists International and CPUSA records in Moscow after the collapse of the Soviet Union and have written books based upon them. We assisted in opening the Venona decryptions to research in Washington and wrote a book based on those as well. Our eyes have glazed over reading thousands of pages of mind-numbing FBI investigatory files opened by the Freedom of Information Act. Based on our prior research, we have no doubts of the authenticity of the material recorded in Alexander Vassiliev's notebooks.

Apart from the contract with Crown that gave Vassiliev access to KGB files and his indisputable presence at the SVR's Press Office for two years reading files and making notes on them, there is the evidence of the note-

books themselves. They include archival file numbers and, more important, details that could come only from internal KGB documents. Take,
for example, the cover names of agents. In addition to confirming the
identifications of more than a hundred cover names figured out by the
NSA in its Venona decryptions, the notebooks enabled us to correct errors made by American counterintelligence. While American cryptogra-
phers concluded that in addition to "Dir," Mary Price was known as
"Arena," documents copied by Vassiliev make it clear that "Arena" was actually Stanley Graze—and the particulars about "Arena" in Venona match
Graze perfectly.

Numerous cover names that were unidentified in Venona are outed
in the documents Vassiliev saw. We were able to link more than fifty-five
additional people to cover names. In some cases, these were individuals
named by such spies as Elizabeth Bentley but whose cover names were
not identified or did not even appear in the particular messages decrypted
by the Venona project. In other cases the cover names in the Venona decryptions were never linked to real names because too little detail had
appeared in the terse KGB cables to allow NSA/FBI analysts to reach a
conclusion. Many of these previously unknown spies are discussed in this
book. Some of these individuals had been investigated by the FBI or
questioned by congressional committees; others were far more obscure.
In case after case, research confirmed that the careers and activities of
these heretofore obscure people matched what was in the notebooks.
Take just one example. The Venona decryptions provided the cover
names of five of the sources of Julius Rosenberg's technical intelligence
apparatus with sufficient details that they were easily identified: Julius
himself ("Antenna" and "Liberal"), David Greenglass ("Bumblebee" and
"Caliber"), William Perl ("Gnome" and "Yakov"), Joel Barr ("Scout" and
"Meter"), and Alfred Sarant ("Hughes"). One other source, cover-named
"Nil," had earlier had a partially deciphered cover name whose first two
letters were "Tu." NSA/FBI analysts left "Nil"/"Tu" unidentified. Not only
can we now identify this source as Nathan Sussman, a Communist engineer and long-time friend of Julius Rosenberg, but we can also provide
his earlier cover name, "Tuk." There are also a number of KGB messages
that were only partially broken in Venona that Vassiliev copied in toto.
And, of course, there are examples in his notebooks of complete Venona
decryptions, many of which had not yet been released when Vassiliev left
Moscow in 1996. One example is Venona 1251, dated 2 November 1944,
in which New York KGB station chief Stepan Apresyan cabled Moscow
confirming fourteen changes of cover names and proposing alternatives

for eight more of its suggestions. The same list appears in Vassiliev's *White Notebook #1* on page 55.

In the spring of 2006 we convened a small panel of historians, archivists, and retired intelligence personnel with expertise on the KGB to meet with Vassiliev, examine his notebooks, and question him about his methods of work. One retired officer and historian didn't doubt the authenticity of the notebooks, but he did question the accuracy of a KGB report in one document that one of the daughters of Allen Dulles, later head of the CIA, had, like her father, worked for the OSS in World War II. After checking the OSS records in the National Archives and contacting her surviving sister, he reported that Clover Todd (Toddie) Dulles had in fact worked for the OSS in 1944 and 1945, even though there was no mention of it in the published biographies of Dulles and "no one at the archives, or any former OSS officer I know, was aware of this bit of trivia."[6]

We are confident that the unanimous judgment of these scholars and experts that the notebooks are an invaluable and reliable source of information on the KGB will be confirmed as this unique tool for comprehending Soviet espionage in the United States is used over the years.

John Earl Haynes
Harvey Klehr

Acknowledgments

Throwing light on the murky world of espionage is a cooperative endeavor, and we have been fortunate to have had the assistance of numerous people, whom we are delighted to acknowledge. We are grateful to scholars and retired intelligence officers who gave us sage advice and shared information and documents with us as this project developed. They include Ronald Bachman, Włodzimierz Batóg, Raymond Batvinis, Robert Louis Benson, Leonard Bruno, Alan Campbell, John Fox, Leo Gluchowski, David Hatch, Greg Herken, Max Holland, Mark Kramer, Harold Leich, Dan Mulvenna, David Murphy, Eduard Mark, John McIlroy, Stan Norris, Charles Palm, Hayden Peake, Ronald Radosh, Louise S. Robbins, and Steve Usdin. Nancy Reinhold at the Robert W. Woodruff Library of Emory University was an enormous help. The skilled work of Philip Redko and Steven Shabad in translating Alexander Vassiliev's notebooks was not only of great assistance to us but will also benefit other researchers for decades to come.

We are deeply grateful to the Smith Richardson Foundation, which generously provided a grant that enabled us to translate Vassiliev's notebooks, and to our program officer there, Allan Song. Harvey Klehr was able to spend the 2007–2008 academic year as a senior fellow at the Bill and Carol Fox Center for Humanistic Inquiry at Emory University. He is grateful to the center's director, Martine Brownley, and assistant director, Keith Anthony, for creating such a pleasant environment for scholarship.

Working with the editors and staff at Yale University Press is always a pleasure. We are once again indebted to our editor, Jonathan Brent, whose enthusiasm, prodding, and appreciation for the importance of the study of communism is unmatched. That he is the Alger Hiss Visiting Professor at Bard College only increased his well-developed sense of irony and humor as he sheparded this project to completion. We are grateful as well for the work of our copy editor, Bojana Ristich, for her close attention and diligence in noting the flaws that we could not see. We also greatly appreciate the keen eye and patience of Margaret Otzel, senior production editor, who saved us from a number of errors.

Finally, our families deserve medals for enduring several more years of our obsession with cover names, dead drops, and konspiratsia without themselves defecting. We thank Marcy Steinberg Klehr, Ben and Annsley Klehr, Gabe Klehr, Josh Klehr, Aaron Hodes, Erik Benjamin, and Janette, Amanda, and Bill Haynes.

Conventions for Nomenclature, Citations, Cover Names, Quotations, and Transliteration

Nomenclature

This book deals with the activities of the Soviet foreign intelligence service that originated as part of the "Cheka." This agency, while having a continuous organizational history, went through a variety of title changes and was at various times part of a larger entity. For reasons of simplicity and to avoid confusion, the agency in most instances will be referred to as the "KGB," the Committee of State Security, its title from 1954 until the collapse of the USSR at the end of 1991. But readers should keep in mind that its actual title prior to 1954 was as specified below:

December 1917	Cheka—All-Russian Extraordinary Commission to Combat Counterrevolution and Sabotage
February 1922	GPU—State Political Directorate (a section of the NKVD, the People's Commissariat of Internal Affairs)
July 1923	OGPU—Unified State Political Directorate
July 1934	GUGB—Chief Administration of State Security (a section of the NKVD)
February 1941	NKGB—People's Commissariat of State Security
July 1941	GUGB—Chief Administration of State Security (a section of the NKVD)
April 1943	NKGB—People's Commissariat of State Security
March 1946	MGB—Ministry of State Security

October 1947   KI—Committee of Information
March 1953   MVD—Ministry of Internal Affairs
March 1954   KGB—Committee for State Security
October 1991   CSR—Central Intelligence Service
December 1991   SVR—Foreign Intelligence Service

The Soviet armed forces had a separate foreign military intelligence agency that also went through several name changes. For similar reasons of simplicity, Soviet military intelligence will be referred to as the GRU —Chief Intelligence Directorate.

Citation Convention for KGB Archival Documents

The principal sources cited in this book are handwritten transcriptions, extracts, and summaries of documents from the archive of the Russian Foreign Intelligence Service for the KGB and its predecessor agencies. Alexander Vassiliev recorded the documents in eight notebooks, titled by him as *Black, White #1, White #2, White #3, Yellow #1, Yellow #2, Yellow #3,* and *Yellow #4,* as well as some additional loose pages called the Odd Pages. All notebook pages are numbered. Within each notebook, documents are cited to numbered pages in a numbered archival file. The original handwritten notebooks, transcriptions into word-processed Russian, and translations into English are available for research use at the Manuscript Division of the Library of Congress, Washington, D.C., as well as on the Web. The transcriptions and translations are paginated and formatted to match the original handwritten notebooks.

Sample citation. On pages 1–15 of *White Notebook #1* Alexander Vassiliev transcribed large sections of a 30 September 1944 report from Vasily Zarubin to Vsevolod Merkulov entitled "Memorandum (on the station's work in the country)" and cited it to pages 381–445 of volume 1 of archival file 35112. (Most KGB archival records are bound into volumes.) This report is cited as follows:

Zarubin to Merkulov, "Memorandum (on the station's work in the country)," 30 September 1944, KGB file 35112, v. 1, pp. 381–445, Alexander Vassiliev, *White Notebook #1 [2007 English Translation],* trans. Steven Shabad (1993–96), 1–15.

Any subsequent citation to *White Notebook #1* in a chapter will be shortened to: *"White #1."*

KGB cables decrypted by the National Security Agency's Venona project are cited by the message number, sending and receiving stations, and date. Sample: "Venona 628 KGB New York to Moscow, 5 May 1944." The Venona decryptions are available at the National Cryptologic Museum, Ft. Meade, MD, and on the Web.

Convention for Cover Names

Alexander Vassiliev in his notebooks usually recorded cover names inside double quotation marks, but he also often used single quotation marks or none at all. The double quotation mark convention is used in this volume in text written by the authors. However, in the case of text quoted from the notebooks where double quote marks were omitted or single quote marks used, the quoted material is left unchanged. When material is quoted from the notebooks, when a cover name is quoted, the real name behind the cover name will be given in *brackets* upon the *first* occurrence in a quoted passage but not for subsequent occurrences of the cover name in the same passage. All bracketed material in a quotation from Vassiliev's notebooks is an editorial insertion. On the few occasions where passages quoted from the notebooks contained brackets, the brackets have been changed to parentheses.

Convention for Quoted Material

Vassiliev's notebooks contain direct quotes from KGB archival files and his own summaries of material in the files. Quotations from the archival files were recorded in his notebooks inside double quotation marks. Occasionally, the closing quote marks were omitted, but the formatting of the notes usually made the ending point obvious. Note than even in direct quotations, Vassiliev used abbreviations for repetitive names or terms. These abbreviations in a translated form are retained in quotations from the notebooks in this volume. Summaries were recorded without quotation marks in the Vassiliev notebooks.

Readers need to be attentive to what is a quotation of a Vassiliev summary of a KGB archival document and what is a quotation of Vassiliev's direct quotation from an archival document. This volume quotes *from Vassiliev's notebooks.* Thus, when material from a notebook is quoted that is Vassiliev's summary, it is, if brief, inside double quotation marks or, if of sufficient length, in an indented quote *without any quotation marks.* However, when material from a notebook was itself quoted from the archival document and *is in double quotation marks in the notebook,* it is, if brief, inside double quotation marks and single quotations marks. Sample: "'Meanwhile, 'Liberal' [Julius Rosenberg] did not meet with any of his probationers [sources] for 10 days.'" Or, if of sufficient length, the material is in an indented quote with double quotation marks in the indented text. Sample:

"Meanwhile, 'Liberal' [Julius Rosenberg] did not meet with any of his probationers [sources] for 10 days. 'Liberal' and 'Caliber' [David Greenglass] subsequently met at his mother-in-law's apartment, that is, 'Caliber's' mother, b/c 'Liberal's' wife and 'Caliber' are brother and sister. After speaking with 'Caliber' and receiving confirmation of his agreement to send us information known to him about the work being done in camp No. 2 [Los Alamos], 'Liberal' gave him a list of questions to which it would be preferable to get a reply. These were general questions to determine the type of work being done there."

Some of the passages that are not within quotation marks in the notebooks read as if they were direct quotations, and they may be. Readers should keep in mind that Vassiliev wrote the notebooks to assist his research for a book and not with the anticipation that they would one day constitute a primary source. Consequently, they contain notes to himself, marginal annotations, grammatical shortcuts, and abbreviations. Also his conventions for recording certain types of documents changed as he better understood the material. Underscored material in the notebooks when quoted is converted to italic text.

Transliteration

Transliteration of Cyrillic-alphabet Russian names and titles will use the BGN/PCGN system. This system is familiar to many American readers because it is used by major newspapers. In many publications a simplified form of the system is used to render English versions of Russian names, typically converting ё to *yo*, simplifying *-iy* and *-yy* endings to *-y*. That convention will be used here. However, when a name is well established in the literature under a different transliteration system, the more familiar variation will be used.

Supporters of Leon Trotsky referred to themselves as "Trotskyists," while American Communists derisively called them "Trotskyites." The distinction does not exist in the Russian language, but in conformity with American practice, the Russian term is translated as "Trotskyites" when used by American Communists or Russians. In unquoted text the more neutral "Trotskyist" is used.

Introduction

How I Came to Write My Notebooks,
Discover Alger Hiss, and Lose to His Lawyer

ALEXANDER VASSILIEV

In the summer of 1993, I got a buzz from Yury Kobaladze, press officer of the Foreign Intelligence Service (SVR) of the Russian Federation, at my desk at the *Komsomolskaya Pravda,* the daily where I worked as a columnist. I was writing mostly on international topics and espionage, and several days earlier I had published a story that mentioned some operations of the Soviet KGB, SVR's predecessor. Kobaladze invited me to his office at 13 Kolpachny Street, not far from Lubyanka Square, and I gladly accepted. I anticipated some dressing down about my latest article, but it didn't bother me much. I was looking forward to meeting Yury, who had a reputation as a nice person and bon vivant among the Moscow press corps.

When I arrived, Yury made it clear he didn't care much about my article. Instead, he invited me to take part in a book project. Crown Publishers, a subsidiary of Random House, and the Association of Retired Intelligence Officers (ARIO) of the KGB had signed an agreement to publish five books based on top secret archival documents of the KGB. There would be books on the Cuban crisis; the murder of Leon Trotsky; and Soviet espionage operations in the United States, Britain, and West Berlin. Each book was supposed to be written by an American and a Russian author. Crown was to choose the American authors, and Yury was in the process of picking writers on the Russian side. He wanted me to work on the book dealing with Soviet espionage in the United States in the 1930s and 1940s.

My initial intention was to say "No, thank you, I've got to run." I liked writing about espionage and had nothing against Russia's Foreign Intelligence Service, but I didn't want to be involved in "a project" of any special service in any country, even if it was called "a book project." I was quite happy with my professional life at the moment: in addition to being an international columnist for a newspaper with a daily circulation of more than twenty million, I hosted political programs on the first channel, the most heavily watched channel on Russian television. I wasn't a celebrity but intended to become one very soon. To soften my negative answer, I asked if this was a serious project or some kind of "active measure" cooked up by the intelligence service. Yury insisted that the SVR wanted to have a true history of Soviet intelligence operations. There were dozens of books on this subject, all written by Western scholars, all based only on the material available in the West. But that was just a small part of the whole story. If I accepted, I would be receiving real files and researching them. Of course, I would not get everything for the book, but I would be given "a lot." Kobaladze seemed honest. I said I would have to think about it.

There is an alleged Chinese curse, quite popular in the United States: may you live in interesting times. Under Boris Yeltsin all Russians lived in such times. A few people became billionaires while millions of their compatriots were starving. As for me, I could get a chance to read top secret KGB files and be a part of an exciting enterprise. Besides, it wouldn't hurt to have a serious book on my journalistic vitae. Several days later I called Yury Kobaladze back and said I was ready to start.

Things moved quickly. In the fall of 1993 I signed my contract with Crown and met my American co-author, Allen Weinstein. He gave me his book *Perjury* and asked me to be on the lookout for Alger Hiss and Whittaker Chambers in the files. I promised to do so. I quit my TV job. As a columnist, I had flexible hours and the right not to come to the office every day, and I used these privileges with gusto. In early 1994 I started working with the files at the SVR press bureau at 13 Kolpachny Street.

There were two questions to which I had to find answers on my own because I didn't want to make Kobaladze think again about the desirability of the project or his choice of me. First question: why me? I wasn't a scholar, and I had no ties to the SVR, although I had once worked for the KGB. In fact, my life story should have kept Yury from dealing with me.

I concluded, first, that they needed a person with writing experience, which I had, and second, that they needed a person with at least a theoretical knowledge of espionage tradecraft in order both to read the KGB files and to understand them. I could do that since I had the relevant background. Third, as far as I knew, Yevgeny Primakov, then the SVR director, wanted to have civilian writers in the Russian group. By that time I had been a civilian for more than three years. In addition, my personal acquaintance with Primakov probably helped. I had met him in the early 1990s, when he was an adviser to President Mikhail Gorbachev.

Second question: why was the project being done? There were suggestions in the U.S. media that the SVR had agreed to the project for the money. I have never read the contract between Crown and ARIO. I've heard that the American publisher's money was for veteran Soviet operatives, but I don't think it was the huge amount some publications have reported (some people were terribly wrong about the sum I had received). If the SVR had intended to help the veterans, that would have been totally understandable. To put it mildly, the Yeltsin government treated Soviet retirees like garbage—their savings evaporated in "financial reforms," and their pensions gave them just the chance to survive. So why not give Soviet intelligence veterans part of the money received for the books on events in which they had played a major role?

The money factor, however, probably wasn't the main reason for the project. The SVR top brass, or at least some of it, was quite enthusiastic about getting a true history of Soviet intelligence operations, and Primakov was a historian himself. It was hard to believe, but no one had done any historical research in those files before!

And there was another factor that also had to do with Yeltsin's era. After the collapse of the Soviet Union, the Russian special services, which inherited the tasks and methods of the infamous KGB, were not the most popular organizations in the country. Some liberal journalists suggested getting rid of the Foreign Intelligence Service and asking the American CIA to spy for both the United States and Russia since the two countries had become "allies" and their leaders called each other "Boris" and "Bill." At the same time the liberal part of public opinion in Russia wanted to open all the secret files, just as had been done in East Germany.

The book project gave the SVR a chance to tell about its history to the Russian taxpayer and answer the demand to open the files by saying, "But we are opening the files! Just give us time." From various points of view the book project was a brilliant idea, and I was glad to be part of it. But it was so unusual that more than once I thought that if I had been a member of the SVR leadership, I would have opposed it. And I would never

have given access to the KGB secret files to a civilian journalist. Why?
I'm not sure, but perhaps my KGB training was influencing me.

In 1983, at the beginning of my fifth year as a student in the international section of the faculty of journalism at Moscow State University, I
received an offer to work for "a government agency that often sends its
employees abroad." It didn't take me much time to guess what that
meant, and I said, "Yes! Yes!! Yes!!!" It was my dream to be a Soviet spy.

The vetting process started, and I was "clean": no Jews in either my
background or my wife's, no relatives abroad, already a member of the Soviet Communist Party, high marks on exams, three foreign languages, no
dissident inclinations, no dirty jokes about members of the Soviet leadership, no heavy drinking. Plus I was going to get a degree in international journalism, and that profession was considered the best cover for
an intelligence officer. However, my recruiting officers wanted me to
work for a year in the Soviet media after my graduation to get journalistic experience. While a student, I had worked as a freelancer for Soviet
radio, but that wasn't enough, and in 1984 I joined the international department of *Komsomolskaya Pravda*. I worked there for a year, and at
the end of the summer of 1985 I was officially drafted into the Soviet
armed forces as an officer in reserve. That was a cover, and it didn't work;
somehow my colleagues knew where I was going and smiled at me knowingly when I tried to complain how unlucky I was. In the fall of 1985 I became a student at the Andropov Red Banner Institute of the KGB—the
spy school. First of all, they sent us new recruits to the Bolgrad airborne
division for commando training for a month, and after we came back, we
began studying the espionage craft. I believe spies in all major countries
train the same way, so if you are interested in the details, just ask your CIA
friend, and he or she will tell you everything.

Two years later I graduated from the institute and joined the U.S. department of the First Chief Directorate of the KGB. I was on cloud nine:
not only was I going to work in the KGB intelligence directorate, but I
was also going to be an operative in the most elite unit—the American
department!

Then the most boring thirty months of my life started, and I believe
I should thank Aldrich Ames for that. In the mid-1980s Ames, a CIA officer recruited by the KGB, betrayed about a dozen people who were cooperating with the CIA, among them several KGB officers who were
working in various departments having to do with the United States. They
were arrested and most of them executed. The atmosphere in the U.S.
department was very tense. Young officers, including myself, were treated

with the customary respect, but we felt we were not trusted. The exposure and arrest of our colleagues was explained the following way: one of the CIA sources in the KGB lost a lighter that contained a mini-camera. That traitor was promptly found, and the results of his interrogation helped to catch the others. Let it be a good lesson to you, kids.

During the two and a half years I spent in the U.S. department I never heard the name of Aldrich Ames. As a matter of fact, I never heard the name of any KGB source or even that of a significant acquaintance of our officers in Washington, New York, or San Francisco. Having spent five years at Moscow University, a month in a commando unit, and two years in the KGB spy school, I was now shuffling meaningless papers and reading articles about U.S. foreign and domestic policy in readily available American journals. Meanwhile, perestroika and glasnost were taking root in the Soviet Union. During the First Congress of People's Deputies in 1989 the U.S. department almost stopped working; everyone, including our bosses, was listening to live radio broadcasts from the congress. Every day we discussed articles in liberal newspapers and magazines or last night's TV shows, whose authors were saying things unimaginable even a year before. Obviously any place outside the fence of the First Chief Directorate's headquarters in Yassenevo was more exciting, and the most exciting profession was journalism.

As to Mikhail Gorbachev's foreign policy, our analysts were complaining that he didn't care about the information and recommendations provided by the KGB. Gorbachev seemed to be listening only to the Foreign Ministry and its head, Eduard Shevardnadze. At every summit he made concessions, first to Ronald Reagan, then to George H. W. Bush, and Soviet foreign and defense policy was collapsing. I was useless, and the whole KGB intelligence service seemed useless too.

When a young and ambitious intelligence officer spends eight hours a day shuffling stupid papers in "the Forest" (that's what we called the service's headquarters in Yassenevo, on the outskirts of Moscow), he starts thinking about big issues, and it's dangerous. Here is what I thought: suppose I get a chance to spy in the United States. Suppose I even recruit a source in the Pentagon or the State Department (one chance in a million, but I am optimistic by nature). Suppose my source's information goes straight to Gorbachev's desk. Will he take it into account? Will he even read it? I had my doubts. And what will happen to my source? Sooner or later he will get caught (it happens to almost everyone), he will get a prison term, and his family will be destroyed like the families of the KGB officers executed for cooperating with the CIA. And for what? Espionage

is a crime; it destroys innocent people's lives. In 1985–87 I could easily
justify this crime to myself. By the end of 1989 I couldn't.

I began thinking about retirement. The problem was I had never
heard of someone who had retired from the KGB intelligence service of
his own free will before reaching the pensionable age. Apparently there
was no such precedent in the U.S. department. I knew about defectors,
but I had no intention of being one. I wanted to leave quietly and de-
cently. I had no grudge against the service. I respected it—I just didn't
want to be part of it.

Later some of my former colleagues asked me: Were you afraid? No,
I wasn't. It was a calculated risk. I was convinced that if I didn't create a
scandal, the service wouldn't either. Besides, it was 1990, and I could go
to liberal newspapers and tell them my story. The service wouldn't want
such exposure. So one day in February 1990 I wrote a short memo to the
KGB chairman, Vladimir Kryuchkov: "I, Vassiliev Alexander Yurievich,
operative of the First Department of the First Chief Directorate of the
KGB of the USSR, captain, am asking you to dismiss me from the KGB
of the USSR because I do not support the policy of the current leadership of the Communist Party of the Soviet Union and do not consider it
necessary to defend it." My note explained only part of my motives, but
I wanted it to be short and crisp, and I didn't want to get into Dostoevsky-
style discussions with the chairman of the KGB.

I kept this memo in my safe for a couple of days, still thinking about
it. I decided to send it on the day when we were informed that Russian
opposition parties were planning to hold a demonstration at the gates of
our headquarters in Yassenevo and that we were going to get guns to defend it. That was the last straw. I signed my memo and gave it to my immediate boss. Very soon I was called in to see the head of the U.S.
department, a general in the KGB's officer rankings. The general was
calm and polite. He asked why I wanted to leave; I explained my reasons.
He asked if I had any requests of him. I said that since I was going to
continue in my civilian profession—international journalism—I would
appreciate it if I were allowed to travel abroad. The general said there
would be no problems with traveling to socialist countries, but as far as
capitalist countries were concerned, I would have to wait for a few years.
I was astonished: it was 1990—socialism in Europe was dead! Still, I decided to keep mum. I realized I was getting off the hook easily. The
process of my dismissal took several hours. I was led out of the gates of
the headquarters, my pass was taken from me, and I went home.

A week later in the middle of a working day I went to central Moscow to see a new movie. I came out of the subway station at Pushkin Square, took a deep breath of fresh, frosty air, and said to myself, "You are free!" Life in the USSR was coming to a boil. I had missed a lot in "the Forest" behind the fence, but I was going to catch up. The fence went down for me like the Berlin Wall.

I made my first trip as a reporter for the *Komsomolskaya Pravda* in the summer of 1990 to the Black Sea to cover the first all-Union festival of erotica and striptease. My second trip was to Tallin to write a story about a new nightclub called Cockatoo. I covered Richard Nixon's visit to the Central Market in Moscow. To my amazement, traders from Georgia and Armenia immediately recognized him and wanted to give him brandy, fresh meat, and fruit; Nixon accepted a bottle of brandy and some fruit. Then a tipsy Muscovite mistook Richard Nixon for a big muck-a-muck from the Moscow administration and started complaining to him in Russian about the hardships of life in the city. I wish I had asked Nixon his opinion of Alger Hiss, but at the moment I had no idea who Hiss was.

In August 1990 I was sent to South Yemen to report on Soviet fishermen kidnapped by Somali bandits and released thanks to the combined efforts of Soviet diplomats and KGB officers in Aden and Cairo. I got my Soviet foreign passport within twenty-four hours; the country was in such a mess that even the passport system wasn't working. And in September I went to Saudi Arabia for a month to cover Operation Desert Shield. The following year it was Israel, NATO headquarters in Brussels, Afghanistan, and Pakistan. No problems; no looking back.

Ironically, I was meeting people not many KGB intelligence officers could dream of meeting: Shimon Peres and Ariel Sharon in Tel Aviv (I've got Sharon's book with his autograph), Benjamin Netanyahu in Jerusalem (got his book too), and leaders of the Afghan mujahideen in Peshawar (they didn't write books). I went to talk to Gulbuddin Hekmatyar at his military camp in Afghanistan; I believe I was the first Soviet journalist who met Afghan mujahideen on their turf. I played ping pong with one of the nephews of King Fahd in Riyadh and went to see his camels.

After two and a half years of misery in "the Forest" I found happiness in the desert. For a week I was the only Soviet journalist in the international press corps in Dhahran during Operation Desert Shield (got a T-shirt from there—a technician from an American TV crew was doing business on the side). I was going places and meeting people just because I wanted to, with no need to ask permission from KGB mandarins who would spend weeks weighing the pros and cons of every trip and interview.

Then in August 1991 there was a coup attempt in Moscow against

Gorbachev, and I got nervous. I didn't expect anything good from a conservative regime as far as my professional life was concerned, and I was
sure it would strip me of my foreign passport if it won. It lost.

After the failure of the coup, hundreds of my former colleagues retired from the KGB, and I stopped looking like a weirdo and traitor to
them. The KGB itself ceased to exist, and new people came to the top in
"the Forest." In December 1991 Yevgeny Primakov was appointed head
of the Foreign Intelligence Service and Yury Kobaladze its press officer. I
believe it is impossible to overestimate the role of Primakov and Kobaladze in saving the service in the political tempest that followed the August coup and collapse of the USSR. Suddenly it became a must for almost
all Russian journalists to express opinions on every issue concerning the
special services, including those who had no idea of what they were talking about. I expressed some constructive criticisms myself but never suggested disbanding the service or asking the CIA to spy for Russia.

For a while I came under criticism in the Russian liberal media because of my articles on international politics and espionage. One of my
colleagues at the *Komsomolskaya Pravda* even wrote a memo to the editorial board accusing me of being an agent of conservative forces, planted
at the newspaper. After that I went on strike for a month, spending it
making my TV shows. At the same time my stand won me some respect
among espionage practitioners, and it led to that telephone call from Yury
Kobaladze in the summer of 1993.

In 1994 I was even invited to come back to the service as an operative, but I politely refused. I had tasted freedom, and I loved it. However, I must admit I was tempted for about a second because the idea of
serving my country in difficult times wasn't totally lost on me. Besides,
people I met in the SVR press bureau—Yury Kobaladze, Tatyana Samo-
lis, Oleg Tsarev, Boris Labusov, Vladimir Karpov—were the nicest people I had ever met, and the office at 13 Kolpachny Street seemed at the
moment the friendliest place I had ever worked.

Researching the KGB files for the book project turned into a full-time
job. The files were kept in the SVR archives at Yassenevo, and the press bureau employees used to bring them to Kolpachny Street at my request. I
came almost every morning to the bureau to sit in a room with Oleg Tsarev
and Boris Labusov, read, and make notes from the files into my notebooks.
The files and the notebook I was using were kept in the safe of one of the
officers. No one checked what I was writing in the notebooks, and I could
take them home after I filled them out and brought a new one.

There were several books on espionage and a file on the Center for

Democracy, a Washington-based organization headed by my co-author, Allen Weinstein, in the bookcase in the room. Allen, who made several trips to Moscow while the project was under way, liked to talk about his connections in Washington, D.C., particularly about his friendship with James Woolsey, then the CIA director, and SVR officers liked to listen to those stories—hence the file. They suspected Allen of cooperating with the CIA and allowing the agency to use the Center for Democracy as a cover for secret operations. Some of the press bureau employees expressed their concern with his participation in the project, but Yury Kobaladze took a more reasonable stand: if the SVR wanted to go ahead with the books, it didn't matter if CIA people were co-authoring them. However, to be on the safe side they decided to give access to the files only to the Russian co-authors. In the case of Allen Weinstein it didn't matter because he didn't read Russian anyway.

Personally, I didn't care about the nature of Allen's contacts because I had never seen him doing anything suspicious. But some officers' ideas regarding my co-author became a major factor in early 1996.

Apart from the file on the Center for Democracy, the bookcase contained *The FBI-KGB War*, by Robert Lamphere, and *After Long Silence*, by Michael Straight. At home I had Allen Weinstein's *Perjury* and *KGB: The Inside Story of Its Foreign Operations from Lenin to Gorbachev*, by Christopher Andrew and Oleg Gordievsky, which had been published in Russia. That was my historical background in the field of Soviet espionage in the United States when I started my research in the files. Not much. In the late 1980s operatives in the U.S. department had not been encouraged to learn the history of the intelligence activities of their predecessors. One needed special permission to get an old file from the archives and had to explain why it was needed. Believe me, you would not want to explain to the boss why you wanted to know more secrets after some of your colleagues had been executed for high treason.

The same was true with the KGB library at Yassenevo. There were a few Western books on Soviet espionage in a special depository, but to get a book from there we needed permission. And why would one want to read about the "lies of American propagandists and KGB defectors"? In early 1994 my mind was almost a blank slate, and I thought that was good. Starting from scratch gave me a chance to see things with my own eyes.

There are different types of KGB files, but for the purposes of our book I needed primarily two of them: operational correspondence files, which contained all correspondence between the stations and Center as well as many internal documents, and personal files, which contained information on each agent. I asked for the earliest operational correspondence files and got materials from the early 1930s. Later they found some files from the 1920s.

When I opened my first file, I was shocked: it was a total mess. Obviously bureaucracy hadn't been the forte of Soviet operatives of that era. I would find a cable in one file and a response to it in another. Some documents had no dates. Many of them were typed on small pieces of yellowed paper and contained grammar or stylistic mistakes. Apparently Soviet spies of the 1920s and early 1930s were so busy spying they didn't bother to write long documents; the information was often quite sparse. The most important drawback, however, was the lack of a cover sheet listing the people and organizations mentioned in the file; such a cover sheet was an obligatory part of any file in my time. I was initially unhappy about that but subsequently realized how lucky I was that the names of those mentioned in the files were not listed. I attacked the material like any scrupulous journalist: I wrote down any name or cover name in the hope of discovering a story behind it later; I made notes of almost every description of an event or a person. Gradually I noticed that some cover names were mentioned again and again while others disappeared.

In the early stages of my work I struck gold: in one of the operational correspondence files I found a list of agents who could have been betrayed by Elizabeth Bentley, a courier and group handler who defected in 1945 to the FBI. The list was composed by Anatoly Gorsky, a former Soviet station chief in Washington, in December 1948 and contained the names and cover names of American agents who had cooperated with the Soviets. With Gorsky's list and a collection of often-mentioned cover names I was able to ask for personal files.[1]

One of the cover names that appeared in several interesting documents was "Crook." I asked for his personal file and got it. "Crook" turned out to be Samuel Dickstein, a U.S. congressman who had been a paid agent of the Soviet NKVD in the 1930s. That discovery surprised not only American scholars and readers of the book Weinstein and I wrote, *The Haunted Wood*, but it was a big surprise for the SVR too, as no one there knew the service used to have such an agent.[2]

Getting personal files wasn't always easy. Different files on Soviet operations in the United States belonged to different departments, and the issue of my access to them depended on the head of a relevant department. The fact that SVR director Primakov approved the book project in general didn't mean I could get every file I wanted because Primakov left it to the discretion of the department heads. The chiefs of departments

"S" (illegal intelligence) and "T" (scientific technical intelligence) didn't want to have anything to do with the project, and I never received their files. However, the new boss of the U.S. department was quite enthusiastic, and many personal files I needed were under his jurisdiction. As to operational correspondence files, I needed only the permission of the head of the archives department to get access to them.

File distributions were strange in the SVR bureaucracy. Julius Rosenberg's file belonged to department "T," and I couldn't see it, but the files of David and Ruth Greenglass, as well as the "Enormous" file on atomic espionage, were in the U.S. department's domain, and therefore I got them.

Now I should explain why it was so important that the files didn't have cover lists of the persons and organizations mentioned in them. For instance, the SVR didn't want me to see personal files on Julius Rosenberg and Harry Dexter White (in the latter case for unexplained reasons), and preventing my access to them was easy because Rosenberg and White were registered in the archives by their names and cover names. But no one knew what kind of information the operational correspondence files contained because there were no lists, and I never had any problems with receiving those files—and they turned out to be a gold mine. There I found documents on Alger Hiss, Julius Rosenberg, Harry Dexter White, and many more that I wasn't supposed to see.

Sometimes it was difficult to restrain myself from jumping from my chair and screaming, "Yes! I got him! Look what I found!" When Oleg Tsarev and Boris Labusov asked if I had found something interesting, I often sighed and said, "Same old, same old" because I didn't want the SVR to know I was digging too deep. (Sorry, Oleg and Boris, but you know what it's like—you've got much more experience in this kind of thing.) I tried to copy into my notebooks as many documents as possible verbatim since I believed we had a unique chance to tell the story of Soviet espionage in America through the words of operatives and agents. I made summaries of documents I didn't find quite as vivid. In every case I noted file and page numbers.

In 1995 I started writing draft chapters for *The Haunted Wood* on the basis of the material I had collected in my notebooks. The draft chapters were to be vetted by the Declassification Commission (composed of the chiefs of the SVR operational departments relevant to the book project), the head of the archives department, and Yury Kobaladze. I could give the draft chapters to Allen Weinstein only after they had been released by the commission. As far as I know, Yevgeny Primakov asked the Declassification Commission to look at the draft chapters from the point of view of whether the information they contained could damage the current operations of the Foreign Intelligence Service. I didn't see any problems with that since I was writing about the 1930s–1940s and the espionage methods are practically the same in all major intelligence agencies.

There was, however, a more serious obstacle. The SVR has a very simple policy about admitting whether a person had cooperated with it or not: if that person doesn't admit it himself, the SVR will never do so, even if the agent was put in prison. Therefore all requests from journalists and scholars for information regarding hot espionage cases receive the same answer: "No comment." This principle works even if the person in question had cooperated with the Soviet NKVD seventy years ago. By invoking it, the Foreign Intelligence Service assures its future agents that the fact of their cooperation will remain secret.

This principle explains why the SVR reacted as it did to Alger Hiss in 1992. On 3 August 1992 Hiss wrote a letter to General Dmitri Volkogonov, chairman of the Commission for the Accession of KGB and Soviet Communist Party Archives of the Supreme Council of the Russian Federation. Hiss gave a short account of his official career and trials and then wrote the following:

I denied the accusations. Nonetheless, after two trials, I was convicted in 1950 of perjury and sent to prison. Ever since, I have been trying to prove my innocence and clear my name. Thus, I have a direct interest in seeing the KGB and other Soviet Union archives about me, my accuser Whittaker Chambers, and the case. Moreover, it would be an historical injustice if those archives were given to any publisher or other person on an exclusive basis. Whittaker Chambers died in 1961. I am 88 years old and unable to travel to Moscow. I hereby authorize John Lowenthal, director of The Nation Institute project on the Hiss case Soviet archives, to act in my stead. Please let Mr. Lowenthal examine and obtain copies of all documents about me, Whittaker Chambers, and the Hiss case.

It was very touching and very naive—or very clever if the person who wrote this letter knew what kind of reply he would get. Naturally, John Lowenthal had no chance of examining and obtaining copies of Soviet intelligence files. But the Hiss team got what it really wanted. On 25 September 1992, less than two months after the Hiss letter, Dmitri Volkogonov sent John Lowenthal a fax:

Esteemed Mr. Lowenthal, I would like to ask you to convey to Mr. Alger Hiss the following. On his and your request, I looked through the archive of the intelligence services and studied the information which the archive staff gave me. On the basis of a most careful analysis of the data, I can report to you that

Alger Hiss was never an agent of the intelligence services of the Soviet Union. Probably, the old accusations against him are based on misunderstanding or incorrect information.

General Volkogonov was being economical with the truth, and later he admitted that he had never done proper research in the archives.[3]

In a letter of 30 September 1992 Yury Kobaladze wrote as follows to Lowenthal: "In connection with the letter of Mr. Alger Hiss to Yevgeny Primakov dated August 3, 1992, we inform you of the following: In the archives of the Foreign Intelligence Service of the Russian Federation, there is no material indicating that Alger Hiss at any time or in any manner cooperated with the foreign intelligence of Russia or its predecessors." I still don't know why the SVR didn't give its usual "no comment" answer. My guess is that Volkogonov's reply, which preceded Kobaladze's letter by five days, set the general tune. After Volkogonov's letter a "no comment" response would actually have meant the SVR had something on Alger Hiss. Another possible explanation: the SVR didn't have a personal file on Hiss because Hiss was handled by Soviet military intelligence (GRU), and it just didn't know there was material on him in operational correspondence files, which I found later during my research.[4]

The period between Hiss's letter and Kobaladze's—3 August 1992 to 25 September 1992—was very brief. Did Russia's Foreign Intelligence Service stop working and send every operative in "the Forest" to the archives to research the files to satisfy Alger Hiss's and John Lowenthal's curiosity? If not, claiming that someone had "looked through the archive of the intelligence services" is nonsense. The files of the 1930s–1940s are not indexed, and there must be hundreds of them on operations in the United States alone. One can't go down to the archives and ask what they've got because they don't know what they've got. I found some materials on Alger Hiss by researching the files for two years and by reading every page; I found them in different files for different years. Had anyone done it before me? I don't think so.

As for the GRU archives, Serge Schmemann's report in the *New York Times* of 17 December 1992 quoted Volkogonov as saying, "The Ministry of Defense also has an intelligence service, which is totally different, and many documents have been destroyed. I only looked through what the KGB had. All I said was that I saw no evidence." Further the same report added, "General Volkogonov said he was 'a bit taken aback' by the commotion his letter caused. He acknowledged that his motive in writing the letter was 'primarily humanitarian,' to relieve the anguish of a man approaching death." The

Washington Times of 25 November 1992 noted that in testimony before the Senate Select Committee on POW-MIA Affairs "Gen. Volkogonov described the chaotic condition of files of the GRU." The paper also quoted Volkogonov: "You must go through a number of documents page by page . . . literally hundreds of thousands of documents."

Another example on the same subject is the case of Julius Rosenberg. For many years KGB colonel Alexander Feklisov, who had handled Rosenberg in New York in the 1940s, unsuccessfully lobbied the service's chiefs to admit that Rosenberg had cooperated with Soviet intelligence and to acknowledge him as a hero. However, such an acknowledgment would violate one of the basic principles of the Russian espionage agencies. Despite Feklisov's argument that Julius and Ethel Rosenberg would have wanted it themselves, their participation in Soviet espionage in the United States was not officially confirmed by the Russian side because they died in the electric chair without confessing.

I had to find a way around this roadblock. I knew that it would be a shock for the Declassification Commission to see the real names of American agents in my chapters, especially of those who had not confessed. However, the final text for *The Haunted Wood* didn't have to be approved by the commission, and Allen Weinstein could rewrite my chapters anyway. What I needed was the right to use quotations from the KGB documents. I tried to use mostly cover names in my own text when I wrote my chapters. Since many cover names had been identified in the United States, there would be no problem for Allen to understand who was who, and if he had any difficulties, I would help him using Anatoly Gorsky's list and my notebooks.

I could use the real names of Soviet operatives and people like Elizabeth Bentley and Boris Morros. I presented Jacob Golos as an illegal station chief rather than an agent (he was described both ways in the documents) to be able to call him by his name. Writing about Laurence Duggan, I accentuated the fact that he had tried to break with the NKVD several times (that chapter wasn't submitted to the commission anyway). I used Martha Dodd's and Alfred Stern's real names because they went to live in the Soviet bloc and by doing so admitted they had been connected to the Soviets. There was no way to hide Martha from the Declassification Commission under her cover name: the fact that she was the daughter of the U.S. ambassador to Nazi Germany was too important for her story. And I couldn't do it with Samuel Dickstein because I needed juicy quotes showing that "Crook" was a member of the U.S. Congress.

As far as I know, there was a discussion in the Declassification Commission about whether to release the chapter on Dickstein since his role in Soviet espionage had previously been unreported. But the story was amazing, and Dickstein really was a crook! In the end, "pro-book circles" in the commission won, and this chapter, as well as chapters on Martha Dodd, Jacob Golos, Elizabeth Bentley, and the cooperation between the NKVD and the OSS during World War II, were released for publication.

At the time I didn't know what to do with the materials that contained the real names of people like Alger Hiss. I would never have given them to Allen Weinstein to be used in *The Haunted Wood* if I had stayed in Russia. I am sure the SVR realized I would behave sensibly; that's probably why I was able to do my research and even keep my notebooks at home. However, in 1995 it became more difficult for me to work. The mood in the country was changing. President Yeltsin's popularity was plummeting, and the results of the 1996 presidential elections were very uncertain. People in the SVR press bureau were telling me that foreign researchers had lost access to various Russian archives. It was getting increasingly hard for me to obtain new files—I had to wait longer. I already had extensive material in my notebooks, but naturally I wanted more.

I submitted my draft chapter on atomic espionage to the Declassification Commission, and approval was delayed for months. Someone seemed to have decided to turn the screws. It may have been good for my country, but it was certainly bad for my book.

The worst blow came from America: Crown, in financial distress, canceled the book project, and the agreement with ARIO ended. Allen Weinstein, who was the project's adviser on the American side, was informed about the cancellation by fax, and he was furious. I learned the news from Yury Kobaladze, who nevertheless allowed me to continue working in the hope that a new publisher would be found, and I was extremely grateful to him. By this time I had spent almost two years on the project; I had abandoned my television career, and I was losing my clout on the *Komsomolskaya Pravda.* Now the whole project was in jeopardy. According to the Crown-ARIO agreement, the SVR was supposed to declassify a certain number of the top secret KGB documents to support the books. I don't think there was a clear indication of how many documents would be released, but I know that the SVR was prepared to declassify some. I was meticulously transcribing the files under the assumption that other scholars would be able to see copies of those documents—the more documents, the better—and I prepared several lists of documents I thought should be included. But since the Crown-ARIO agreement had been canceled, so was the SVR commitment. In the end I received about fifty more pages of mostly useless papers. The only interesting document was a report by Anatoly Gorsky about his meeting with U.S. secretary of commerce Henry Wallace in October 1945, and we reproduced it in *The Haunted Wood.*

Early in 1996 matters got even worse. In January I was told by Yury Kobaladze that the Foreign Intelligence Service was ending its cooperation and that I would not be receiving new files. A few days later came an incident that changed the life of my entire family. I was sitting in a big room with some officers from the press bureau watching TV news. There was a report about Gennady Zyuganov, leader of the Communist Party of Russia and Boris Yeltsin's main challenger in the presidential elections to be held in June 1996. Zyuganov was campaigning using nationalist and anti-Western slogans, and many Russians, including me, were absolutely sure he would win.

There was a Communist cell in the SVR that held meetings and collected dues. I wasn't sure if it was legal for SVR officers to be members of any political party after President Yeltsin's decree of 1991 about depoliticizing all state organizations, but they never tried hard to cover their activities. As we watched the TV news about Zyuganov, suddenly one of the SVR officers known to be an active Communist turned to me and said, "After the election we are going to deal with you. We'll see what kind of a book you are writing there." I snorted and said nothing. But I started thinking really fast.

As an ex-KGB officer, I had a pretty clear idea how the book project could be spun. On the one hand, I had been invited by the Foreign Intelligence Service to take part in the project. On the other hand, I was copying top secret KGB files in my notebooks and was going to pass my material to Allen Weinstein, a suspected CIA agent. Could I prove that I had not given him classified material? A lot depended on the political atmosphere in Russia. Relaxed rules under Boris Yeltsin made the book project possible, but if Gennady Zyuganov won the 1996 election, his new regime could easily turn me into a traitor. I didn't think Yevgeny Primakov or Yury Kobaladze would be able to help because they themselves would probably come under attack, especially the liberally minded Kobaladze.

I discussed all this with my wife Elena, and we decided to move to the West. We chose Great Britain because I had been there twice before and liked it. I had good connections in the press office of the British Embassy in Moscow. Since my second trip to Britain in 1993 had been organized by the British Foreign Office, I didn't expect problems with visas. I arranged an assignment for myself in Britain as a correspondent for the

Express Gazette, the first Russian tabloid, modeled on the British *Sun* (the London job for the *Komsomolskaya Pravda* was already taken), and we applied for visas. We received them in May and promptly left Russia. To my surprise, Boris Yeltsin won the election, but we decided to stay in London anyway. I have not returned to Russia since, because I am not sure that my work on these files might not be used against me.

I decided not to take my notebooks with me because I was afraid I would be searched at the Sheremetyevo Airport and the notebooks would be seized. I left them with people I trusted. Before our departure I copied all the draft chapters I had written for *The Haunted Wood,* including some that had not been submitted to or cleared by the Declassification Committee, onto floppy discs. I also copied some documents containing the real names of Alger Hiss and Julius Rosenberg. That material and the material Allen Weinstein already had in the United States served as a basis for *The Haunted Wood.*

The Haunted Wood doesn't contain the real names of two atomic agents—"Persian" and "Eric"—although I knew them. It was my deliberate decision not to put the names of Russell McNutt ("Persian") and Bertl Broda ("Eric") in the draft I gave to Allen Weinstein (I didn't know the name of Melita Norwood at the time, though we have her in *The Haunted Wood* as "Tina"). There were two reasons for this. First, my position in London was far from stable. I had to renew my journalistic visa at the British Home Office every year, and to do so I needed a confirmation from the *Express Gazette* that I was still working for it. If someone in Moscow decided to put pressure on the *Gazette,* I wouldn't receive that confirmation. I came to London as a civilian journalist—which I was; I wasn't a defector, didn't want to become one, and therefore couldn't count on any "special attitude" from the British authorities. Second, the future of *The Haunted Wood* didn't look totally certain, especially in view of what had happened with Crown in 1995. People from Random House weren't talking to me, they didn't know what I was going through, and I didn't think they would care even if they did know. In such a situation I didn't want to name names.

There was a moral dilemma too. *The Haunted Wood* didn't have new names; it had new material about people who were already known, and I thought all the characters mentioned under their real names were dead except Michael Straight, who long ago had admitted his contact with Soviet operatives. Those people had become part of the history of the twentieth century, and their stories had to be told sooner or later by somebody. I saw no reason why it shouldn't be me since I had something to tell. With

Russell McNutt and Bertl Broda it was different. In 1996 I had no idea what had happened to them, and I didn't want to do them harm. As far as the history of Soviet espionage in America is concerned, it's important to understand where I come from. I was born and bred in the Soviet Union, and if to most Americans, individuals like Julius Rosenberg, Nathan Gregory Silvermaster, and Theodore Hall are traitors, to me they are still heroes. They helped my country in very difficult times, and I had no reason to disrespect their memory or cause them any trouble if they were alive. Ten years later, when John Haynes, Harvey Klehr, and I started working on this book, I was sure no characters in my notebooks remained alive: Michael Straight had died in 2004; Theodore Hall, perhaps the youngest agent, in 1999; and Alger Hiss, in 1996. Imagine my surprise (and discomfort) when in the fall of 2007 John and Harvey discovered that Russell McNutt was alive and living in North Carolina, age ninety-three, but refused to be interviewed on his activities. McNutt, however, died in February 2008.

After *The Haunted Wood* was published, Allen Weinstein and I had our portion of controversy, even without Russell McNutt and Bertl Broda. The *New Yorker* published our piece on U.S. congressman Samuel Dickstein—in my opinion, one of the most exciting stories in the book. I expected people to talk about the love story of Elizabeth Bentley and Jacob Golos, about the adventures of Boris Morros, or about the crisis in Nathan Gregory Silvermaster's agent group. Instead they cared only about Alger Hiss. I knew Hiss was important—Weinstein told me, but I thought it was mostly Allen's personal interest since he had written a book about Hiss before. Suddenly I found myself in the epicenter of a heated discussion with people attacking my integrity.

Allen and I also had a personal falling out, prompted by my discovery that he had used the Hiss material in a new edition of *Perjury* that appeared prior to the publication of our book. That discovery initiated a brief correspondence with Victor Navasky, editor of *The Nation* and himself a fierce defender of Hiss. In May 2000 I received a letter from an American writer named Susan Butler: "I have found many mistakes and inconsistencies in Weinstein's *Perjury*. The fact that you, his co-author, are highly critical of the finished product, *The Haunted Wood*, bears out my instinctive negative reaction to Weinstein as reliable authority on anything. I would like to discuss both books with you." I answered by e-mail on 8 May 2000: "Frankly speaking, I don't remember my being 'highly critical' of *The Haunted Wood*. How can I be critical of the book for which I did research for 2 years and wrote a draft manuscript? In my opinion, it's an absolutely fantastic book which should be read (at least, bought) by every American."

Butler and I met that same month at the Clifton Pub in St. John's Wood in London. By that time I was well aware of the controversy surrounding Hiss and suspected Butler had an agenda. Yet I was prepared to talk to everyone since I considered myself above the scuffle. Butler probably felt she had started out on the wrong foot and changed her tune. She lavished compliments on me and said everyone had liked *The Haunted Wood,* including Michael Straight, who had a special chapter devoted to him. I was mildly surprised since our story, based on Straight's personal file from the KGB archives, differed from his account in *After Long Silence.* Some time later Butler had a slip of the tongue: she said Michael Straight had said or written something nasty about *The Haunted Wood.* When I reminded her that she had said he liked the book, she quickly explained that he just hated Weinstein! I let it go.

For the next two or three hours Susan Butler interviewed me about my work on *The Haunted Wood,* recording the conversation. Many of her questions dealt with the material we had on Alger Hiss. Later we exchanged several e-mails, and I was astonished by her attitude toward Hiss. On 17 June 2000 she wrote to me: "It is actually not that Hiss transmitted information to the Russians that bothers me and many others. If he did that when U.S. and Soviet interests coincided it is perfectly understandable." That was exactly what I would have said as an ex-KGB officer and ex-Communist, but I didn't expect to hear it from the other side of the Atlantic in 2000. In the same e-mail Butler added, "And things were very different back then. It was President Roosevelt himself who sprung Earl Browder from jail. But if Chambers' charges were true, then Alger Hiss was guilty of lying through two trials, and putting his many supporters through a meaningless charade."

It was time to give a political lecture. I wrote the following on 18 June 2000:

Now about Hiss' "lying through two trials." Frankly speaking, the fact that some people can't accept this idea bewilders me enormously. Hiss was an extremely valuable, experienced and trusted member of the most powerful espionage network in the world. He did what he was supposed to do—he denied everything. The Rosenbergs did it, Colonel Rudolf Abel did it. People who don't do that, people who confess and testify, are called defectors and traitors. If Hiss had testified he would have exposed other American sources and Soviet operatives. He would have become another Chambers. Neither [he] nor the Rosenbergs wanted to do that because they still believed in what they had been doing for many years. As to the fact that Hiss put "his many supporters through a meaningless charade," he probably thought first of all about people he worked with—Americans and Soviets. What he did was absolutely right, and it worked (though it didn't in the case of the Rosenbergs). In my opinion these people should be admired for their commitment to their ideals.

Butler replied:

You see, whether Hiss was or was not an agent, that does not change the fact that he was an enormous help to your country and to mine. And particularly when compared to a character like Chambers, who set things back in the United States so that everyone was afraid to speak, many were put in jail, and we lost the best and brightest who stayed away from government service. I doubt if we would have gone into Vietnam if we had had knowledgeable people in key posts. But still, Hiss shines brighter if what he did he did not as an agent.

The correspondence with Susan Butler certainly expanded my knowledge of political life in the United States. The account of her interview with me that she published in *The Nation* on 15 October 2001 enlightened me about the methods Alger Hiss's supporters used to make their idol "shine brighter." Having promoted me from ex-captain to ex-colonel, Butler wrote the following:

The Haunted Wood was formed under conditions that should be known: The co-authors are not really co-authors. There was the researcher, Alexander Vassiliev, who spent two years in the KGB archives gathering the material, and the editor, Allen Weinstein, who put the book together. Vassiliev had virtually no say on what went into the book. It wasn't supposed to be that way. Vassiliev, an ex-KGB colonel, seems to have been overwhelmed by Weinstein's reputation, his rhetoric and by the prospect that Weinstein kept dangling in front of him of making big bucks from the book. . . . The uneven collaboration unfortunately weakens the book in more ways than one. The heavy anti-Hiss slant is pure Weinstein.

There was a lot in common between me and Alger Hiss's fanatical defenders: we were all saying good things about him. The difference was that I had written an honest book and told people what I had seen in the top secret KGB files; the fanatics didn't want to know, they didn't want other people to know, and they were prepared to destroy everyone who wanted to tell the story.

In February 2001 I received from Butler an article, "Venona and Alger Hiss," by John Lowenthal, published in the journal *Intelligence and*

National Security in autumn 2000. I looked through it and found nasty things about *The Haunted Wood* and me, as well as quotes from Boris Labusov, who by that time had replaced Yury Kobaladze as the head of the SVR press bureau—and I did not pay much attention. I had never heard of John Lowenthal or *Intelligence and National Security* before. So when Butler asked me whether I was going to respond to Lowenthal's allegations, I wrote to her on 4 March 2001 as follows: "Thank you for the article by Mr. Lowenthal. I don't think I will be answering it in any way. I've got nothing to say to people who want to serve as a mouthpiece of the Russian Intelligence Service. On the other hand, I must admit the things he said about me and my work [are] the best advertisement for *The Haunted Wood* I could imagine. I would be much more worried if the Service said they liked the book."

A few months later I went to Amazon.com to see how *The Haunted Wood* was doing and saw among readers' comments a review by the same John Lowenthal; it began with the words "Unreliable and mostly unverifiable." He said that the book, "particularly in its use of KGB archival files, is unreliable and, for the most part, unverifiable. Where it is verifiable at all, it turns out to be wrong." Lowenthal quoted Boris Labusov and touted his own article in *Intelligence and National Security*.

This time I got upset. Lowenthal's allegations at Amazon.com damaged both my credibility and the sales of *The Haunted Wood*, and they had a much bigger impact than an article in some obscure journal. I searched the Web and discovered other unpleasant things. "Venona and Alger Hiss" had been posted on at least two Web sites: that of the British Universities Film and Video Council and one devoted to Alger Hiss at New York University. *Intelligence and National Security* turned out to be a respectable journal, and it placed an extract about *The Haunted Wood* on its own Web site to promote the article. This nastiness was spreading like a cancer. As for John Lowenthal, he wasn't a nobody; he was a former lawyer and friend of Alger Hiss and a politically motivated crusader.

In his article Lowenthal made several allegations that were particularly painful to me since I was the one who had done the research. The first one: "Press officer Boris Labusov was still with the Foreign Intelligence Service when *The Haunted Wood* was published (1999), and I asked him what he thought of it. He said, 'if you want to be correct, don't rely much on *The Haunted Wood*. . . . When they put this or that name in Venona documents in square brackets, it's the mere guess of the coauthors.'"

At the last stage of work on *The Haunted Wood* either Allen Weinstein or the editors decided to replace cover names in the quotations from the KGB files with real names in brackets for the sake of the simplicity of the narrative. I learned about it only when I received copies of the book. I had written draft chapters on the basis of the files, translated them into English, and given them to Allen. He rewrote them, using additional material he had available, and sent them back to me for review. I made my comments and sent them to Allen. However, I never received galleys from the publisher, and I thought replacing the cover names with real names in brackets was a bad idea—it distorted the quotes and opened us to criticism. Yet Lowenthal's saying that it was a "mere guess of the co-authors" was a shameless lie. I had access to agents' personal files that contained their real names, and Boris Labusov knew it since he was sitting in the same room with me and sometimes brought me files from "the Forest." I had also found Anatoly Gorsky's list with cover names and real names. Moreover, a few documents contained real names either in the text or in the margins. (I am much more comfortable with the convention adopted in this book, where the original cover names are retained in quotations and the real names added in brackets on the first occurrence (not replacing the cover name) just so the reader does not get confused as to who is "Pilot," who is "Aileron," and so on.)

The second allegation: "The co-authors, said Labusov, 'were wrong when they put the name of Alger Hiss in the places where they tell about somebody who cooperated with Soviet special services, yes? So we are quite right in saying that we, the Russian intelligence service, have no documents . . . proving that Alger Hiss cooperated with our service somewhere or anywhere.'"

That was a lie too. I found documents mentioning Alger Hiss under his real name in a context that made it clear he had taken part in Soviet espionage. And where did I get the quotations? There could be only one conclusion from what Labusov had said about me: I invented them.

The third allegation, another quote from Labusov: "'Mr. Vassiliev worked in our press service just here in Moscow, but, if he's honest, he will surely tell you that he never met the name of Alger Hiss in the context of some cooperation with some special services of the Soviet Union.'" Now it was about my personal honesty.

The fourth allegation was made by Lowenthal himself: "He [Alger Hiss] got the cover name 'Lawyer' from Weinstein and Vassiliev." Not at all. Hiss got his cover name from Soviet operatives, and I didn't invent it. (In this book we have translated this cover name as "Jurist.") And the allegation was repeated in Lowenthal's review on Amazon.com. By this time *The Haunted Wood* was the most important thing I had done in my professional career. The book had changed the lives of my wife, my son, and myself. We had left our native country. Now someone was saying the book was a lie and I was a liar. I wanted to sue everyone: Lowenthal, *Intelligence and National Security*, Amazon.com, the Foreign Intelligence Service, New York University. I thought Lowenthal had simply fooled the British Universities Film and Video Council, and it probably didn't know what it had gotten into. I didn't want the council's blood. I sent it a letter, and it immediately removed the article from its site.

I couldn't afford a lawyer, and I went to the High Court of Justice in London (only the High Court hears defamation cases in England) to get help and advice. A lawyer there heard my story and said that I had a case. He suggested I get in touch with some legal firms in London since some of them might be interested in handling my case on a no win, no fee basis. I did, and they weren't. I decided to file suit on my own as a litigant in person (in the following two years I learned a lot of new English words). I went to a book shop and purchased some books as guides. I dropped the SVR from my list since the idea of bringing Russian spies to justice seemed a bit supernatural. Where would I send my claim? To the SVR station chief in London? Well, what was his name? Also, I had nothing against Boris Labusov personally. I knew him as a decent man, and I knew he was just doing his job.

I also dropped New York University and John Lowenthal from the suit. The university seemed a difficult case since it was in America, where the defamation law was far more relaxed than in England. As to Lowenthal, I decided to deal with him later, after I finished with Amazon.com, which had a branch in Britain, and Frank Cass, the British publisher of *Intelligence and National Security*. According to the defamation law of England and Wales, the fact that these two had repeated what Boris Labusov had allegedly said didn't give them immunity from prosecution. It would have made my case much more difficult if they had given me a chance to respond to Labusov's and Lowenthal's statements in the same publications, but they hadn't. The journal had never gotten in touch with me, and as far as I could tell from Lowenthal's article, it hadn't talked to Allen Weinstein either.

I started two separate proceedings against Frank Cass and Amazon .com in July 2001. *Intelligence and National Security* then offered me a chance to respond to Lowenthal by writing my own article for it, but I refused because I believed that playing tit for tat with someone like Lowenthal was futile.

I realized I would need my notebooks as evidence during the trial. I asked a person in Moscow I could trust to send them to me by DHL, and I received all eight of them. The litigation took almost two years. At preliminary hearings the defendants managed to get rid of important paragraphs in my particulars of claims, and each hearing I lost cost me several thousand pounds because I had to pay the defendants' legal costs. They were wearing me down financially. All our savings evaporated, and I had to borrow money from my bank.

During the litigation Frank Cass presented a number of documents as evidence, including my correspondence with Susan Butler; correspondence among Alger Hiss, John Lowenthal, Dmitri Volkogonov, and the SVR; and some papers prepared in the process of reviewing John Lowenthal's article for publication in *Intelligence and National Security*. I found useful comments about the journal's partisan and polemical tone and a warning that it "needs to be less pejorative when dealing with its opponents." Several commentators had suggested that Weinstein be asked to respond. Rather late in the proceedings, in August 2002, I received under discovery a transcription of the interview between Lowenthal and Labusov; it showed that the latter's comments were not in fact as straightforward as they looked in the article: Lowenthal was pushing and trying to put words into Labusov's mouth, while Labusov was trying to avoid direct answers, saying "No comment," and constantly recommending that Lowenthal get in touch with me in London. Some answers were unintelligible, at least one was misquoted in the article, and about twenty seconds of the interview were "accidentally erased." The interview was substantially distorted in the article.

At one point Labusov protested to Lowenthal, "You know, you push me to some criminal deed," a comment reminiscent of what General Volkogonov had told the *New York Times* in 1992: "His attorney, Lowenthal, pushed me hard to say things of which I was not fully convinced."

Not surprisingly, John Lowenthal described in his article only the first part of the Volkogonov story, in which Volkogonov "enjoyed unrestricted access to Russia's archives"; he had examined not only the KGB and presidential archives but also the GRU archives and reported that "there, too, no traces of Alger Hiss have been found." The second part of the story, in which the general admitted he had lied because he wanted to be Mother Teresa to Alger Hiss, was omitted.

My strategy was clear: to demonstrate to the jury that the defendant Frank Cass had defamed me and in effect called me a liar by publishing an article written by a fanatical Hiss defender and personal friend relying on distorted comments from the Russian Intelligence Service. Cass had been warned several times by reviewers and editors to tread carefully but had not and had uncritically relied on the word of an employee (Labusov) of an espionage agency whose own principles precluded an honest response, as even Lowenthal had acknowledged in the article.

Frank Cass based its defense on three points. First, it argued "qualified privilege": it "had a moral or social duty" to publish Lowenthal's piece. Second, it asserted that the statements about which I was complaining were "fair comment upon a matter of public interest." Finally, it claimed justification: "the words complained of are true in substance and in fact insofar as they meant and were understood to mean that the presentation of the case against Hiss in *The Haunted Wood* (of which the Claimant was a co-author) was unsound, defective and partisan, and that accordingly the Claimant was an unreliable author." (Those who are interested in the details can find all the documents in the archives of the High Court of Justice in London, Queen's Bench Division.)

In January 2003 Frank Cass's lawyers offered to settle the monetary claim for a little more than £2,000 and promised not to republish the Lowenthal article. Overconfident about winning the case, I rejected the offer. I also wanted an official apology, and Frank Cass wasn't offering that. Plus I wanted to see John Lowenthal face-to-face in court, first as a witness and later as a defendant, and I thought that a settlement would undermine my chances to sue him personally. In addition, I wasn't sure how a settlement in this case would affect my case against Amazon.com. I also turned down a request from Cass for a meeting and a May 2003 offer upping the proposed settlement to £7,500 but still without an apology.

What I should have then done was to ask the court for another preliminary hearing on the subject of malice on the part of Frank Cass. Originally it was part of my claim, but it had been tossed out in a preliminary hearing. With new documentary evidence provided after that earlier hearing, such a claim would, if accepted, require Frank Cass to base its defense solely on justification, making qualified privilege and fair comment moot. The problem was money. By that time I was heavily in debt and didn't know where to get £7,000 or £8,000, which I would have needed to pay the defendant's legal costs if I had lost the hearing again. In any case, buoyed by the two offers of settlement, I believed I could win.

The trial started on 9 June 2003 before Judge David Eady, who specialized in defamation cases, and a jury that consisted of seven women and five men. Unfortunately, I had no right to tell them that Frank Cass had offered to settle twice. I presented my case first, laying out my arguments and being cross-examined by Cass's lawyer, Andrew Monson. I thought I acquitted myself well, explaining the development of the book project, my role, and my research methods. Then, for two days I cross-examined the defense witnesses, including Butler, who admitted that she had praised *The Haunted Wood* in order to "disarm" me and had misquoted me in her article in *The Nation*. John Lowenthal said it had never crossed his mind that Russia's Foreign Intelligence Service in the person of Boris Labusov could have lied to him. That came from a man who in the *Intelligence and National Security* article had written, "The professional involvement of intelligence agencies in deception and disinformation, character assassination and murder, lies, forgeries, and burglaries pervades their institutional culture and dictates their policies of secrecy."

To demonstrate that he had tried to contact me, Lowenthal offered a fax he had sent in 2000 to an address where I had not lived since 1997. I asked him why he hadn't tried to find me through other channels, such as Allen Weinstein or Random House, before writing defamatory statements about me. Lowenthal, who claimed he had written his article over a four-year period from 1996 to 2000, said he was very busy. He admitted that he had written inaccurately when he claimed to have done research in KGB files. Since he did not speak Russian, that was plainly a lie. Moreover, his claim that he had relied on someone else to do the research was also inaccurate; there was no evidence of that.

On the final day of the trial, Friday, 13 June 2003, Judge Eady summed up the case for the jury and instructed it about the procedure for reaching a verdict. It was a long speech, and somewhere in the middle of it I started realizing that I had lost the case. Judge Eady asked the jury members to answer three questions. To the first one—"Do you find that the words are in their context defamatory of Mr. Vassiliev?"—they answered "Yes." To the second one—"If yes, do you find that the defamatory allegations were expressions of opinion or were allegations of fact?" —the answer was "Opinion." And to the third one—"If opinion, were the comments such that an honest person could express them in the light of what Mr. Lowenthal knew at the time his article was published?"— they answered "Yes." So the "fair comment" defense had worked. There was no need to go to the question of justification.

Later the same day Judge Eady gave his verdict on "qualified privilege," and the defendant succeeded here too. The judge also decided that the contents of John Lowenthal's allegations in the article and in his review posted on Amazon.com were similar, and there was no need to have a trial of my case against Amazon; this meant I had lost that case as well. (I didn't dwell here on my case against Amazon because it based its defense mostly on the 1996 Communications Decency Act, claiming the act gave Amazon immunity from prosecution, and the discussions we had were mostly on technical and legal matters.)

When I got back home, I couldn't look my wife Elena in the eye. She was very tired of my literary adventures, which had started ten years before. I felt absolutely devastated. Our son, Ken, was unusually quiet in his room. I didn't follow the reaction to the trial on the Web; I couldn't stand seeing the name of Alger Hiss, even a different name starting with "A" and "H." Much later I tried to find on the Web site of *The Nation* any mention of the trial since its reporter had been present every day in the courtroom. There was nothing. I learned that in September 2003 John Lowenthal died of cancer. I was sure I was through with espionage history. But in 2005 I got interested in Wikipedia and went to its site to check how accurate it was. And I decided to have a look at the article about . . . Alger Hiss!

There were some external links at the end of the article, and one of them led to John Haynes's Web site. I knew John and his co-author, Harvey Klehr, by reputation, and I clicked on the link. I had a look at some pages at his site, and suddenly I saw my handwriting: it was Anatoly Gorsky's list, a copy of which I had presented as evidence during the trial; somehow it had reached John. And there were some comments by David Lowenthal, John Lowenthal's brother, questioning the accuracy of the list. The Alger Hiss cult was still at it! I wrote to John Haynes, correcting David Lowenthal's fantasies about my work at the SVR press bureau. And that's how this book project started. John and Harvey were excited to learn that I now had my original notebooks and convinced that they offered an opportunity to go well beyond what Allen and I had done in *The Haunted Wood* in telling the story of Soviet espionage in the United States.

I know this book will cause new discussions about Hiss, and I don't want to be pulled into them. Alger Hiss is a religion, and there is no point in arguing with people about their religious beliefs. My life is too short, and it certainly didn't get longer after two years of litigation against Frank Cass and Amazon.com. I've told my story, and I don't give a damn about Alger Hiss. Never did.

с. 479   "...Было бы весьма нежелательно противопоставлять анти-
советской и антишпионской кампании американцев
какое-либо эффективное мероприятие с нашей стороны.
В связи с этим р-ра просит расмотреть след. предложение.
Ввиду того, что "Карл" является немцем по происхождению,
если и ушло нам с боем в Кушке "найти" в немецких
архивах дело на "Карла", из к-го было бы видно, что он
является немецким агентом, по заданию гестапо зани-
мался шпионской работой в США и по ее же заданию прошёл
в америк. компартию. Если мы объявим об этом в нашей печати и опубликуем некоторые "документы" к-е можно су-
готовить было, то эффект об этом будь очень большой. За это
сообщение ухватятся не только зарубежные компартии, но и
пресс. печать во всех странах, в результате чего пущен комиссии по расследованию антиамерик. деят-ти, Гранд
жюри и др. органов будут сильно поборраны.
Можно заявить дальше, что "Карл" как агент гестапо хорошо известен комиссии и Гранд жюри и др. америк.
органам, но руководители этих учреждений, будучи вра-
ми оскавителями СССР, компартии и прогрессивного
движения вообще, представили дело так, что "Карл и др.
занимались шпионажем якобы в пользу СССР, а не в
пользу Германии.
Более того, некоторые су беспринцип. руководителей Комиссии, Гранд жюри и др. ведомств сами являлись аген-
тами гестапо, о чём сов. органы, захватившие немецкие
архивы, имеют сообветст-е документы к-е они могут
в случае необходимости опубликовать.

Ответ на ргу инициативу:

Был Рапурб на имя председателя КЧ за подписью П. Федо-
това и К. Кукина, (дек. 1948г.)
                          Дело 43173 т. 2Б

с. 203   "Предложение рук-ра об изготовлении и опублико-
вании в нашей печати док-тов о том что председ. Чемберс
являлся немецким агентом, по заданию гестапо вел
шпионскую работу в США и по заданию немцев прошёл
в КП США, - не может быть принято. Опубликование
подобных "документов" безусловно крайне отрицательно
отразится на нашей бывшей агентуре, возглавляемой Чем-
берсом (Хисс А., Хисс Д., Уайлер, Пиблман, Рено) и др.,
что зная, что они работали на нас и "поверочившись"
в немецких агентов эти люди могут пойти, например,
на сотрудничество с властями, выдать им оставшихся по-
к раниций и т.д.

Кроме того, превращение этих лиц су предполагаемых
агентов сов. разведки в установленных агентов страны,
воевавшей с США, никак не может им помочь с точки
юридич-й точки зрения.
Предложение руг-ров об изготовлении и опублико-
нии док тов изобличающих нек-х руководителей
"комиссии по расследованию антиамер. деят-ти" и Фе-

· ·

CHAPTER 1

Alger Hiss

Case Closed

lexander Vassiliev's notebooks quote KGB reports and cables
from the mid-1930s to 1950 that document KGB knowledge of
and contacts with Alger Hiss and unequivocally identify Hiss as
a long-term espionage source of the KGB's sister agency, GRU,
Soviet military intelligence. Hiss is identified by his real name as well as
by cover names, "Jurist," "Ales," and "Leonard." The material fully corroborates the testimony and accounts of Whittaker Chambers, Hede
Massing, Noel Field, and others, while offering new details about Hiss's
relationship with Soviet intelligence.

No individual is a more potent symbol of American collaboration with
Soviet intelligence than Alger Hiss. From the moment of his confronta-
tion with Whittaker Chambers in 1948, Hiss became the central figure in
a debate that has divided Americans for decades. On the one side stood
those who saw him as the archetype of a generation of young, college-
educated people radicalized by the Depression, drawn to Washington

---

A 1948 KGB headquarters memo listing Alger Hiss as one of "our former agents" who were betrayed by Whittaker Chambers in testimony to the House Committee on Un-American Activities. Courtesy of Alexander
Vassiliev.

during the heady days of the New Deal, and ultimately converted to communism. Intoxicated by their new ideology, they cooperated with Soviet intelligence agencies and eventually betrayed liberalism's commitment to political democracy and aided Stalin's totalitarian state. On the other side are those who regarded Hiss as an innocent victim of anti-Communist paranoia, a New Deal idealist maliciously framed by right-wing provocateurs backed by the reactionary wing of the Republican Party and malign elements of the FBI who were eager to discredit liberalism and taint the New Deal and the Democratic Party with treason.[1]

The Hiss-Chambers case riveted the nation as it moved from the halls of Congress to the federal courtroom, where Hiss was convicted of perjury for lying about providing government secrets to Chambers, a self-confessed Soviet agent handler. Not only was Hiss a seeming model of the New Deal establishment—elite prep school, Johns Hopkins University, Harvard Law School, protégé of Felix Frankfurter, law clerk to Oliver Wendell Holmes, and president of the Carnegie Foundation for International Peace—but he also had occupied important posts in the government, rising from an obscure lawyer for the Agricultural Adjustment Administration (AAA) to become a senior diplomat, director of the State Department's Office of Special Political Affairs, attending the 1945 three-power Yalta Conference as an adviser to President Roosevelt, and presiding at the founding conference of the United Nations. In addition to these achievements, he was an elegant, handsome, charming, and distinguished-looking man.

That so obvious an exemplar of the reigning American liberal establishment might have been a Soviet spy in the 1930s and may have continued to serve Soviet interests into the 1940s seemed incredible. Nevertheless, the evidence demonstrating that Hiss had long been living a lie was substantial. Many people could discount Whittaker Chambers's testimony about his relationship with Hiss as delusional or a provocation, but they could not so easily dismiss the documents he produced. When he broke with Soviet intelligence in 1938, Chambers kept materials given to him by Hiss. Some were summaries or quoted extracts of State Department documents written in Hiss's hand or typed on a Hiss family typewriter while others were photographs of State Department documents with Hiss's office stamp and his handwritten initials. In addition, government investigators uncovered documentary evidence supporting claims made by Chambers about the used car Hiss secretly donated to the Communist Party and financial transactions between him and Hiss.

Chambers's account of their friendship much more closely matched the documented facts than Hiss's story of a short-lived, distant relationship. Supporting witnesses also testified to Chambers's activities as the courier and supervisor of a network of Soviet sources.

Following Hiss's conviction in 1950 his supporters began a campaign that continues to this day to assert his innocence. Over the years they have generated many theories to account for the evidence that convicted him, ranging from an FBI conspiracy to a plot engineered by a sexually spurned homosexual (Chambers). Despite massive evidence to the contrary, some have maintained that not only is there no convincing evidence that Hiss was a spy, but also that Chambers was a fantasist who invented his own work for the Soviets. In the 1990s, one Hiss defender, his lawyer, John Lowenthal, briefly persuaded former Soviet Army general and military historian Dmitri Volkogonov to claim that a search of Russian archives had found no evidence to support the charge that Hiss had been a Soviet agent or that Chambers himself had been one. Faced with skepticism and questions about how he could make such sweeping statements in light of the contrary evidence, Volkogonov quickly retracted his statements, noting that he had been allowed to see only KGB material selected for him by agency officials and had not asked for information from Soviet military intelligence files, despite the fact that Chambers and, presumably, Hiss had worked for the GRU. Volkogonov told the *New York Times,* "The Ministry of Defense also has an intelligence service, which is totally different. . . . I only looked through what the KGB had . . . [but] the attorney, Lowenthal, pushed me hard to say things of which I was not fully convinced."[2]

Although Soviet intelligence archives themselves remained largely closed to research after the 1991 collapse of the USSR, other Soviet-era archives were opened. Files from the archives of the Comintern supported key elements of Chambers's story about the existence of a covert American Communist Party apparatus headed by Josef Peters. Decrypted World War II KGB cables from the National Security Agency's Venona project corroborated Chambers's identification of mid-level government officials as secret Communists and Soviet spies. Few of the cables the Venona project decoded were from GRU, but one 1945 KGB cable reported contact with a GRU source, cover-named "Ales," whom American security officers judged was "probably Alger Hiss." Finally, Allen Weinstein and Alexander Vassiliev's *The Haunted Wood* (1999) cited specific KGB archival documents that explicitly named Hiss as a Soviet agent.

After a brief period of silence and confusion, Hiss's defenders re-grouped and went on a counteroffensive. A new Web site dedicated to the proposition that he had been framed emerged, hosted at New York University. Critics attacked *The Haunted Wood* on the grounds that only the authors had access to its underlying documentation, parsed the Venona project's "Ales" message, and offered elaborate and convoluted interpretations of why "Ales" might not be Hiss that were published in prestigious academic journals and promoted by left-wing journals of opinion such as *The Nation*.

Vassiliev's Notebooks and the Hiss Case

The earliest references to Hiss in the documents in Vassiliev's notebooks recount a mid-1930s imbroglio involving Hiss, two KGB State Department sources (Laurence Duggan and Noel Field, discussed in chapter 4 below), and KGB operative Hede Massing. The situation developed as follows. Duggan joined the U.S. State Department in 1930, rose rapidly, and became head of the Latin American Division in 1935. Alerted to his Communist sympathies by party contacts, Peter Gutzeit, head of the KGB's legal station, reported in October 1934 that he had met with Duggan and was impressed with his willingness to assist the Soviet cause. While the Latin American Division was not of major interest to the Soviets, Gutzeit noted that through Duggan the KGB could "'gain access to Field—an analyst in the Euro. division of the State Department with whom D. [Duggan] is on friendly terms,'" and Europe was Moscow's chief intelligence target.[3]

Noel Field, born in 1904, had spent much of his childhood in Europe but returned to the United States to attend Harvard. He joined the Department of State as a foreign service officer in 1926, became radicalized in the late 1920s, and began to read CPUSA literature and associate with party members. His increasingly left-wing inclinations were known in the State Department and blocked his hopes for a foreign diplomatic post. In frustration, he shifted from its diplomatic service to its professional and scientific service, whose staff focused on technical foreign relations issues. Field became a specialist in American interaction with the League of Nations.

In 1935 Hede Massing, who had been cultivating Laurence Duggan and his wife Helen Boyd, approached and quickly recruited Noel Field, given the cover names "17" and "Ernst" in KGB communications. ("Cultivating" was the KGB's term for getting to know and developing a recruit.) Massing was Austrian-born but had spent several childhood years in America before returning home. Radicalized after World War I, she married Gerhart Eisler, a leading figure in the German Communist Party and later the Comintern. Her second husband was Julian Gumpertz, a publisher of Communist literature, with whom she traveled to New York in 1926 and mingled with radical American literati. At the end of the 1920s she married Paul Massing, a fellow Communist and a leading figure in the Institute for Social Research, a center of Marxist social thought at the University of Frankfurt in Germany. In 1929 Ignace Poretsky, a senior GRU officer, recruited her for intelligence work. After a hiatus in Moscow, she began to receive assignments in 1931. The Nazis arrested Paul Massing after Hitler seized power, and Hede was sent to the United States in late 1933. Posing as a newspaperwoman, she developed extensive contacts in left and liberal circles in Washington and New York. Released from Nazi prison in 1934, Paul became a minor celebrity in the anti-fascist world. He left Germany, rejoined Hede, and also entered Soviet service. In the meantime, Poretsky had shifted from GRU to KGB, increasingly the dominant Soviet intelligence agency, and the Massings moved with him.[4]

By Field's own account, he provided the Soviets with significant quantities of State Department material in 1935 and early 1936. But he continued to feel frustrated in his State Department assignment, and in April 1936 he took a post with the League of Nations and moved to Switzerland. Before he left, however, his naiveté regarding espionage tradecraft brought about the first entanglement of Alger Hiss with the KGB.[5]

Field had become a friend of Alger Hiss shortly after Hiss moved to Washington in 1933 and became part of the group of radicalized young professionals drawn to the nation's capital by the New Deal's promise to reconstruct American economic life. Hiss left a Wall Street law firm to take a position with AAA, where he was part of a secret Communist caucus called the "Ware group" since it was organized by the CPUSA's agricultural specialist, Harold Ware. Hiss later left AAA to take a post with the U.S. Senate's Committee on Investigation of the Munitions Industry, chaired by Senator Gerald Nye. From there he moved briefly to the Justice Department but then in September 1936 took a salary cut to take a position at the Department of State, where he remained until the end of 1945. In Whittaker Chambers's account, in 1935 Josef Peters sought to connect selected members of the party's Washington underground to Soviet intelligence. Chambers, a former writer at the *Daily Worker* and editor of the party's literary magazine, *New Masses,* had been assigned to covert work in the early 1930s and worked with Peters and on various assignments for both GRU and the KGB. He related that by early 1936 Hiss was functioning as part of a Washington network of sources recruited via the CPUSA with Chambers as the network's link to the professional officers of Soviet military intelligence.[6]

Hiss, not yet holding a sensitive position himself and not yet attuned to the need for caution, approached his friend Noel Field in early 1936 and attempted to recruit him for his GRU-linked apparatus. While Hiss was indiscreet, Field's reaction compounded the problem. Hede Massing described what happened in an April 1936 report to the KGB quoted at length in Vassiliev's notebooks:

"Our friend Ernst [Field], the day before he left for Europe, related to me the following incident, of which he himself will give a detailed account to our friends overseas. Roughly a week before his departure from Washington, he was approached by Alger Hiss. A. [Alger Hiss] informed him that he is a Communist, that he has ties to an organization working for the Sov. Union; and that he is aware that Ernst has ties as well; however, he fears that they are not robust enough and that his knowledge is probably being misused. Then he bluntly proposed that Ernst give an account of the London conference. Because they are, as E. ["Ernst"/Field] puts it, close friends, he did not refuse to discuss this topic with him, but he told Alger that he had already delivered a report on that conference. When A., whom, as you probably recall, I met through E., insisted that he would like to receive that report himself regardless, E. said that he would have to contact his 'connections' and ask their advice. Within a day, having 'thought it over,' A. said that he would not insist on receiving the report himself, but that he will have to ask E. to speak with Larry and Helen [Duggan] about him and to tell them who he is and give him (A.) access to them. Once more, E. said that he had already established a connection with Larry and Helen, but A. insisted that E. would have to speak with them regardless, which E. did. He spoke with Larry about A., and of course about himself as well, telling him 'in what situation they found themselves,' 'that their main task at present is the defense of the Sov. Union,' etc., etc., and 'that each of them has to use his advantageous position in order to provide assistance in this matter.' Larry seemed upset and frightened and said that he had not gone so far yet, that some time would pass before he would be able to take such an irrevocable step, and that he is still hoping to do some work of a conventional sort, reorganizing his department and trying to achieve some kind of results in this regard, etc. Obviously, judging by what E. said, he gave no promises and did not prod A. to take action of any kind; instead, he politely backed down. A. also asked E. a whole series of oth. quest-s, e.g., who would be his successor, what kind of a person he is, and whether E. would want to establish his connection with him. He also asked him to help him in getting into the State Department, which E. apparently did.

When I pointed out to E. what a terrible lack of discipline he had shown and what a danger he had created for the value of his use and for the whole enterprise by linking three people with each other, he acted as if he did not understand. He believed that 'because A. had been the first to show his cards, he did not have a reason to keep everything secret, moreover, because A. had said that he 'is doing this for us' and because he is living in Washington and therefore cannot meet with Larry more often than I myself can, and finally, because I intend to leave the country for a while, he thought the best thing would be to establish contact between them."

In the above KGB document Hiss is identified by his real name. There is no parsing or convoluted argument that can be advanced to avoid the unambiguous identification of Alger Hiss in a 1936 KGB document by his real name as "a Communist, that . . . has ties to an organization working for the Sov. Union."[7]

A letter to Moscow Center from Boris Bazarov, head of the KGB's illegal station, summarized the damage done by Field's actions:

"The outcome is that '17' [Field] and Hiss have, in effect, been completely deprived of their cover before '19' [Duggan]. Evidently, '19' also clearly understands the identity of 'Redhead' [Massing]. And more than a couple of months ago, Redhead and Hiss also got exposed to each other. Helen Boyd—'19's' wife, having been present at almost all of these meetings and discussions, is undoubtedly clued in as well, and now knows as much as '19' himself. . . .

I think that in light of this incident, we should not accelerate the cultivation of '19' and his wife. It seems that apart from us, the persistent *Hiss* will continue his initiative in that direction. 19's wife will be arriving in NY any day now. Redhead will meet her here for a purely friendly meeting. Upon 17's departure from Washington, Helen expressed a great desire to see Redhead again. It is possible that Helen will tell Redhead about her husband's frame of mind."

A Moscow Center annotation on the letter specified Hiss's cover name, "A. Hiss—'Jurist,'" and noted that Hiss was an attorney in Washington. Likely "Jurist" was Hiss's GRU cover name because the KGB had little reason to provide its own for someone who reported to GRU.[8]

The Center, Moscow's KGB headquarters, was not pleased by these developments. For security reasons no intelligence agency wants its different networks to know of each other and even less to intermingle with networks belonging to other agencies of its government. The KGB's networks, however, did get entangled on several occasions with those of GRU because both had extensive operations in Washington and tended to recruit from the same pool of CPUSA members or those close to the party. Moscow Center quickly expressed its irritation to its New York station:

"We fail to see for what reason Redhead [Massing] met with 'Jurist' [Hiss]. As we understand it, this took place after our directive stipulating that 'Jurist' is the neighbors' [GRU's] man and that it is necessary to stay away from him. Experiments of this sort could have undesirable consequences. We strongly urge you to arrange it so that none of your people undertakes anything without your consent. This applies in particular to Redhead, bearing in mind her shortcomings, as manifested in her 'impetuousness.' Now for the question—how to get out of this mess. 17 [Field] departed, this isolates him to a certain extent, and Jurist will gradually forget about him.

Now with regard to how to save 19 [Duggan] and his wife. 19 could be of interest, considering his position in the 'Surrogate' [State Department]; his wife as well, considering her connections. To refuse to cultivate them means going down the path of least resistance. Therefore it is essential that we skillfully smooth over the emerging situation and steer both of them away from Jurist. As a last resort, 19 could say that 'he is helping the local fellowcountrymen [Communists] and that the latter suggested to him that he not get involved with anyone else.' We are to blame for the fact that 17, being already our agent, was left in the hands of Redhead, who is ill-suited to handle either an agent or even herself."[9]

Stung by the Center's criticism, Iskhak Akhmerov, an officer of the illegal station, forwarded an explanation of what had happened and defended Massing's meeting with Hiss as occurring before Moscow had informed the New York station that Hiss was already a GRU agent:

""Redhead" [Massing] met "Jurist" [Hiss] on only one occasion during the entire time of her stay in this country, in the winter. She went to this meeting at the behest of Cde. Nord [Bazarov]. After you informed us that he (i.e., "Jurist") has ties with the neighbors [GRU], we did not meet with him. . . . After meeting with "Redhead" and speaking with her in our 17's [Field's] apartment, "J." no doubt informed his superiors about the meeting. By random coincidence, an operative at our fraternal organization [CPUSA], who is connected to "Jurist," knew "Redhead" well since the time that the latter was connected with the fraternal line. When it proved absolutely necessary, we occasionally went through "Redhead" to solicit help from this fraternal operative, who is known to us as "Peter" [Josef Peters]. This "Peter" is the same fraternal operative whom I described to you orally when I was home [in Moscow]. When the need arises for us in cases involving only certificates of naturalization, we resort to this "Peter" for help.

This same Peter, during one of his rare meetings with "Redhead," said the following: 'In Wash-n you stumbled across my buddy (meaning "Jurist"), you had better keep your hands off him, etc. . . .' And apparently Peter, when suggesting in turn to "Jurist" that he not develop ties with Redhead, handled it rather ineptly, i.e., in such a way that Jurist more or less understood "Redhead's" identity."[10]

In the late 1940s and early 1950s three participants in this episode provided independent corroboration of this incident. The accounts by Hede Massing, Noel Field, and Whittaker Chambers, however, were based on their memories of events twelve to fifteen years earlier. Vassiliev's notebooks offer contemporaneous KGB documentation that corroborates all of the main elements of the story the three provided.

Hede Massing in testimony at the second Hiss trial (1949–50) and in her 1951 memoir related that Boris Bazarov, her KGB superior, instructed her to meet with Hiss and evaluate him. Massing stated that in the fall of 1935 she met Hiss at Noel Field's apartment, a meeting confirmed in Akhmerov's 1936 report above. She wrote that after dinner she and Hiss bantered about whose apparatus Field would join; neither one admitted which organization employed them. She also related Field's report of his indiscreet response to Hiss's recruitment effort and of the severe chastisement she received from her KGB superiors for what had happened. Whittaker Chambers also testified about the incident at the Hiss trials and in his memoir, stating that Hiss had reported his meeting with Massing (confirming Akhmerov's prediction to Moscow that Hiss "no doubt informed his superiors about the meeting"), as well as his attempt to recruit Field and Field's response that he already worked for a Soviet network.[11]

Noel Field, unlike Chambers and Massing, remained a committed Communist his entire life. In 1949 he toured Eastern Europe looking for employment to avoid returning to the United States and being drawn into the Hiss trials. Unfortunately for him, Stalin was purging the new Communist regimes, and the KGB needed a Typhoid Mary who could be used to infect those marked for removal with the bacillus of betrayal of the Communist cause. Field was arrested and forced to confess to having been an American superspy who used his position in Switzerland at the League of Nations and later as director of Unitarian war relief in World War II to recruit refugee Communists, later the leaders of the postwar Communist regimes of Hungary, Czechoslovakia, Poland, and East Germany, as agents of American intelligence. Those implicated in Field's coerced confessions were arrested, imprisoned, and a number executed. After Stalin's death in early 1953, East European Communist authorities sought to undo the damage done to their regimes by the absurd purge by rehabilitating those falsely accused. Hungarian security police (and later the security authorities of other East European Communist regimes) asked Field, in prison in the Hungarian People's Republic, to provide an uncoerced, accurate account of his activities to assist not only in his own rehabilitation but also that of those falsely accused in his earlier confessions.

When Noel Field and his wife were formally released from Hungarian prison in 1954, all that was publicly stated was that they had been rehabilitated. Meeting with Western reporters in 1955, Field passed off his imprisonment as a mistake and announced he was seeking political asylum in Communist Hungary. He even denied being a Communist, although in 1961 he would admit in a memoir to having been a party member from the 1930s onward. In return for his public cooperation, security police provided him with a private villa, servants, and a highly paid post with a government agency. He remained faithful to the Soviet cause, never returned to the West, and died a loyal Communist in 1970.[12]

Publicly, in accord with the Communist position on the subject, Field denied that either he or Hiss had anything to do with Soviet espionage. But what he secretly told Hungarian security police was very different. The transcripts of his rehabilitation interviews were not made public until the 1990s, after the collapse of the Hungarian Communist regime. In them, Field explained that in 1935 Paul and Hede Massing recruited him for Soviet intelligence and that Hede was his regular liaison with the KGB. In the course of discussing his espionage work for Massing, Field stated the following:

Alger Hiss wanted to recruit me for espionage for the Soviet Union. I did not find the right words and carelessly told him that I was already working for the Soviet intelligence. . . . I knew, from what Hiss told me, that he was working for the Soviet secret service. I drew the conclusion that Chambers was Hiss's upper contact in the secret service, too. Later, it became certain, first when in Chambers' flat they found the secret material obtained by Hiss, and then when Chambers' testimony made it clear that he knew of the conversation between Hiss and myself, when Hiss tried to recruit me into the secret service. . . .

We made friends with Alger Hiss, one of the top officials of Roosevelt's New Deal. Through our gatherings we discovered that we were Communists. In the summer of 1935, Alger Hiss tried to persuade me to render services to the Soviets, which led me to commit the unforgivable indiscretion of telling him he had come too late. At that very moment, I notified Hede [Massing] about the event. She loaded me with the worst reproaches. She did not know what her boss would say to that, with whom, by the way, I never got acquainted. A little later, she told me that I had done greater damage than I would believe, and that because of me the whole work had to be reorganized. . . . Our misfortune was that not only had the Massings become traitors, but so had Hiss's connection—Chambers.

Field's secret testimony conformed to Massing's and Chambers's testimony at the Hiss trials and in their memoirs, as well as the documents quoted in Vassiliev's notebooks, with the exception that Field in 1954 remembered Hiss's approach having been in 1935 while the documents demonstrate that it was early 1936.[13]

Yet another brush with GRU in 1938 once again brought Alger Hiss to the KGB's attention. This brief incident involved Michael Straight (cover name "Nigel"). Recruited by Soviet intelligence in England while at Cambridge University, Straight (discussed in chapter 4) used his family's social and political connections to President Roosevelt to obtain a post by 1938 as an assistant to Herbert Feis, the State Department's chief adviser on international economic affairs.

At the KGB's urging, Straight brushed aside contacts by secret Communists in Washington, who had heard about his activities in England and were anxious to enlist him in the cause. However, Iskhak Akhmerov, his KGB contact, became more alarmed when Straight took notice of Alger Hiss. Akhmerov informed Moscow:

"Through his job, N. ["Nigel"/Straight] unfortunately made contact with Hiss. N. had told me previously that he was an interesting employee with a senior post, etc. That Hiss, as he said, was very ideologically progressive. I am not betraying any interest in him, but at the same time I'm not telling him not to meet with him. If I tell him that, then he will figure out that Hiss is a member of our family.

There is anoth. danger: that the fraternal's [CPUSA's] or neighbors' [GRU's] station chief (I don't know for sure who Hiss is connected with) might instruct Hiss to work on recruiting N-l, considering that fraternal workers already approached him once through [Solomon] Adler. I am confident that N-l won't take this bait and that he will refuse if they try to recruit him, but still, if this happens, N-l will learn Hiss's nature. It is possible that they might send a diff. recruiting agent to N-l. I am writing about all this for your information and to see if, when you have a chance, you could influence the neighbors' station chief if he decides to work on recruiting N-l through Hiss. If Nikolay [Gutzeit] worked on recruiting 19, the same way the neighbors may try to approach N-l. Enclosed with this mailing is N's note about his meeting with Hiss."

Possibly due to Akhmerov's warnings, Straight and Hiss did not get entangled, and there was no repeat of the Hiss-Field snarl.[14]

In 1938 Akhmerov reported another incident involving Hiss. He periodically met with Josef Peters (chief of the CPUSA's underground) to seek CPUSA assistance for various KGB tasks. In July Akhmerov reported:

"During one of our earliest conversations, Storm [Peters] blurted out that Hiss was a member of the fraternal [CPUSA] organization who had infiltrated the Surrogate [State Department] and was then transferred to the neighbors [GRU]. He told me this when I was hunting for Hiss. During one of our conversations, Nikolay [Gutzeit] told me that it was possible the neighbors were not currently connected with Hiss, apparently in connection with certain difficulties of an organizational nature."

The "difficulties of an organizational nature" that led to Hiss's temporarily losing his connection with "the neighbors" are clear in retrospect. In April 1938, Whittaker Chambers dropped out of Soviet espionage. Not knowing if Chambers had gone to American authorities (he hadn't), GRU temporarily deactivated the sources of Chambers's network (including Hiss) and withdrew Boris Bykov, Chambers's contact, from the United States.[15]

In addition to documentation of these KGB-GRU entanglements involving Hiss, there are additional details about the KGB's awareness of Hiss's status as a GRU agent in the 1930s. In November 1936, Bazarov sent to Moscow a copy of the just-released State Department directory. In a cover note he pointed out, "'You will find 11 [David Salmon] at the start of the directory, along with 19 [Duggan].'" ("11"/Salmon and "19"/Duggan were the two leading KGB sources at the State Department at the time.) Bazarov also said, "'You will not find the neighbors' 'Jurist' in the photograph directory because he has worked there only since September.'" And indeed Hiss had begun work at the State Department in

September 1936. With a touch of envy, Bazarov also wrote that Duggan "'reported that J. ["Jurist"/Hiss] is the one who has everything important from every division on his desk, and must be one of the best-informed people at the Surrogate [State Department].'" Bazarov's envy is clearer in another letter to Moscow where he noted his station's limited penetration of the State Department and remarked, "We need a suitable recruiting agent. We don't have one. There was 'Jurist' [Hiss] . . . , but the neighbors snatched him up, as you informed us. (Indeed, if we had J-st, no one else would really be needed)."[16]

The KGB New York station sent a letter to Moscow in September 1938 explaining that "we are continuing to look for means of approach to four persons in the State Department," describing them as "progressive people who regard our country approvingly." One of the four named was "Robert Hiss." There were only two Hisses at the Department of State at the time: Alger Hiss and his brother Donald. One or the other was probably intended, but whoever wrote the letter misremembered the first name. This is also a letter from the legal station, whereas it had been the illegal station under Bazarov and Akhmerov that was more familiar with Alger Hiss.[17]

During World War II, Alger Hiss appears incidentally in several KGB documents by or about several of its American sources. Victor Perlo, an economist with the War Production Board, was a leading figure in a CPUSA-based espionage apparatus consisting of Communists who worked in a wide variety of U.S. government agencies. By the fall of 1944 the KGB assumed direct control of his network from Elizabeth Bentley. As part of the process, it revetted the members of the group. Normally such background reviews were done prior to or around the time of initial recruitment, but in this case they were done retroactively due to the network's having been delivered intact to the KGB via CPUSA.

As part of Victor Perlo's own revetting, he was asked to provide a list of persons *not* in his own apparatus but who, nonetheless, he had reason to believe "work with intelligence" (meaning work with *Soviet* intelligence) and had a present or past connection with a Soviet intelligence agency. Perlo prepared a list in English that was in KGB files and that Vassiliev copied into his notebooks. Dated 15 March 1945, it included fourteen people and the agency for which they worked and specified if they had a current connection with a Soviet agency, if they had worked with Perlo at some point, and whether they knew Perlo had a Soviet connection. Among the fourteen Perlo listed were Alger Hiss and Donald Hiss:

List of people who, according to "Raid's" [Perlo's] information, work with intelligence, except for those with whom he currently works on a regular basis. From 15.03.45

	Agency	Present connection	Did I ever work with?	Does he know I have a connection?
Irving Kaplan	FEA	Has	No	Yes
Bela Gold	FEA	Has	No	No
Gregory Silvermaster	Treasury Procurement	Has	No	No
George Silverman	Army Air Forces	Think he has	Yes	Yes
Alger Hiss	State	-//-[ditto]	No	Don't know
Donald Hiss	-//- (may have left)	Don't know	Yes	Yes
Charles Flato	Property Disposal Board	None	Yes (dropped)	Yes
Charles Seeger	Pan American Union	None	Yes (dropped)	Yes
Joseph Gillman	WPB	Think none	No	Probably
Herbert Schimmel	Senator Kilgore	Yes, with Blumberg	No	Probably
Frank Coe	Treasury	Yes	Yes	Yes
David Weintraub	UNRRA	Think so	No	Yes
Van Tassel	Senator Murray	Yes, probably with Schimmel	No	No
Henry Collins	Think at Senate	Don't know	Yes	Yes

Perlo thus became the fourth participant in Soviet espionage (after Whittaker Chambers, Hede Massing, and Noel Field) who identified Alger Hiss as a fellow Soviet agent.[18]

Harold Glasser and "Ales"

Harold Glasser, a senior Treasury Department official, was one of the most valuable members of Perlo's apparatus. In order to assist in gauging the reliability and potential of agents, the KGB often asked its most valued sources to prepare autobiographies. Vassiliev's notebooks contain lengthy extracts from the one Glasser wrote in December 1944. He stated that he joined the Communist Party in 1933 while teaching at People's Junior College in Chicago. In 1936 he joined the Treasury Department as an economist and steadily moved up the ranks of the bureaucracy. He also became a member of the Communist Party's clandestine organization in Washington. Josef Peters judged Glasser suitable for more serious espionage work. The opportunity came when Whittaker Chambers's GRU apparatus turned to Peters for assistance in 1937. Chambers later wrote that his contact, Boris Bykov, "fumed" that one of Chambers's sources, Harry Dexter White, then assistant director of Treasury's Division of Monetary Research, should have been providing much more material than he actually was. Bykov was also frustrated because White was only a sympathizer and did not respond to orders like committed CPUSA members. Chambers explained: "I went to J. Peters, who was in Washington constantly in 1937. . . . I explained the problem to him and asked for a Communist in the Treasury Department who could 'control' White. Peters suggested Dr. Harold Glasser, who certainly seemed an ideal man for the purpose, since he was White's assistant. . . . Peters released Dr. Glasser from the American Communist underground and lent him to the Soviet underground. Glasser soon convinced me that White was turning over everything of importance that came into his hands."[19]

Glasser described his relationship with Chambers's network and what followed after Chambers's desertion in his KGB autobiography:

"I first met "Karl" [Chambers] in 1937, around May. He and I met on a more or less regular basis until the fall of 1939. During this time, I met with him on average once a month. The meetings each lasted two or three hours. He knew everything about me: my past, my activities, my friends, etc. In the summer or fall of 1939 (though I am not entirely sure of the date), "Karl" did not show up for our regular meeting, and I never saw him again. He was replaced by a self-styled successor . . . who tried to approach me in June 1940. He said his name was "Paul" [Maxim Lieber], but because I was preparing to go abroad, the matter ceased on its own."

"Karl" is not directly identified in the notebooks, but Chambers in his 1952 autobiography noted that his pseudonym in the underground in the 1930s was "Carl." Additionally, the pseudonym he used in an essay that he gave to a journalist in 1938 after his defection was "Karl." Chambers's account of his relationship with Glasser fits with Glasser's account of his relationship with "Karl." The only discrepancy is that Chambers dropped out of Soviet intelligence in April 1938, rather than in "the summer or fall of 1939" as Glasser remembered in his 1944 autobiography. But chronological errors of that sort are common in memoir literature, and Glasser even told the KGB, "I am not entirely sure of the date."[20]

"Paul," described by Glasser as claiming to be "Karl's" successor, was Maxim Lieber. "Paul" was not directly identified as Lieber in Vassiliev's notebooks, but Chambers in *Witness* wrote that Lieber was the agent the CPUSA and GRU chose to hunt for Chambers after his defection and that in the underground Lieber's cover name was "Paul." Born in Poland, Lieber became a naturalized U.S. citizen and a successful literary agent in the 1930s, representing such highly popular writers as Erskine Caldwell. He was also a secret member of the CPUSA and carried out various tasks for Chambers's espionage network. In 1948 Lieber admitted to FBI agents that he and his family had shared a summer cottage with the Chambers family in 1935 but refused to further discuss his role and invoked the Fifth Amendment rather than answer questions before a grand jury. After a hostile examination by the House Committee on Un-American Activities in 1951, during which he once again invoked the Fifth Amendment, Lieber hastily fled to Mexico. Fearing extradition to the United States, in 1954 he moved to Poland, where Communist authorities provided for his housing and support, and his wife was given a post teaching English at Warsaw University. He did not return to the United States until 1968.[21]

In addition to forwarding Glasser's autobiography, handwritten in English, to Moscow, Anatoly Gorsky, then Washington KGB station chief, also sent a summary in which he wrote that "Karl" earlier had been a GRU station chief who also used the cover name "Steve" when reporting on "Richard" (the cover name of Harry Dexter White). Gorsky, however, was confused. "Karl" and "Steve" were separate persons and neither had been a GRU station chief, as Moscow Center, after checking with GRU, pointed out in a memo to him correcting his summary: ""Karl" (Robert Tselnis) had worked with the neighbors [GRU], but had subsequently refused and threatened to betray probationers [agents] he knew about to the Amer. authorities. "Pol" had also worked with the neighbors. "Steve" is "Storm"; we do not use him at present." "Steve" was Josef Peters, who also had the KGB cover name of "Storm." "Steve" was one of several pseudonyms that Peters used in the underground. Chambers, for example, noted Peters's use of "Steve" in *Witness*. Hope Hale Davis, another Washington Communist, also remembered Peters as "Steve" in her memoir of her activities in the party underground.[22]

Glasser in his autobiography had written that he had been contacted by "Paul." Both Gorsky in his summary and Moscow Center in its reply substituted a variant Russian spelling of the name Paul, one that is rendered "Pol" when transliterated into the Latin alphabet. Phonetically the difference between "Paul" and "Pol" is minor, and in any case, it is clear that Glasser's "Paul" is the same person as Gorsky's and the Center's "Pol." Moscow Center confirmed that "Pol" was a GRU agent but did not further identify him. As noted above, other evidence identifies "Pol" and "Paul" as Maxim Lieber.[23]

As for "Karl," Moscow Center's report said that "Karl" had also been a GRU agent but one who had dropped out ("refused") and threatened to go to American authorities. This conforms to Glasser's memory that "Karl" had at some point disappeared and to Chambers's account that in the late spring of 1938 he dropped out of Soviet espionage and warned GRU that he had kept documents that would compromise its operations and that he would deliver them to American authorities if he or his family were harmed.[24]

The Center also reported that "Karl" was also known as "Robert Tselnis." This name does not occur anywhere in FBI investigatory files, congressional hearings, or the literature on Soviet espionage and the CPUSA. It is likely a hitherto unknown pseudonym used by Whittaker Chambers; he is known to have used a number during his covert work: Adams; Carl; Charles; Bob; David Breen; Lloyd Cantwell; Arthur Dwyer; Hugh Jones; Karl; John Kelley; Harold; and Charles Whittaker. Robert Tselnis may just be one more of that long list. But possibly it was simply an error in reporting by GRU to the KGB. In any event, no real "Robert Tselnis" can be found. Other KGB documents also confirm Whittaker Chambers's identification as "Karl." In late December 1948 the KGB Washington station cabled Moscow with a plan to discredit "Karl," who was described as having given damaging testimony to the House Committee on Un-American Activities and a U.S. grand jury about Soviet espionage in connection with the Alger Hiss case. It was Whittaker Chambers, not "Robert Tselnis," who testified to the House Committee on Un-American Activities about the Hiss case in the late summer and fall of 1948 and to the grand jury investigating the Hiss case in October and December. Additionally, an internal KGB evaluation of the Washington station's suggestion dispensed with the cover name and referred to "Karl" as "the traitor Chambers."[25]

A further direct confirmation that "Karl" was Whittaker Chambers was a December 1948 KGB memo authored by Anatoly Gorsky, the same man who as chief of the KGB Washington station informed Moscow about Glasser's relationship to "Karl" in December 1944. In 1948 Gorsky was a senior official at Moscow Center, then headquarters of the Committee of Information (KI), a short-lived merger of KGB foreign intelligence with the foreign intelligence arm of GRU. Gorsky's memo listed a large number of Soviet sources, agents, and officers in the United States who had been compromised or exposed by defectors from both the KGB and GRU. Leading Gorsky's list was "Karl—Whittaker Chambers." The memo listed twenty-one persons, "Karl's group," compromised by Chambers's defection and included Alger Hiss and Harold Glasser.[26]

Additionally, Elizabeth Bentley in a statement to the FBI in December 1945 identified Glasser as having been one of her sources via the Perlo apparatus, and an October 1944 KGB document on Bentley's sources listed "'Ruble,' . . . Former GRU source." "Ruble" was Glasser's KGB cover name. (The ruble was the Soviet monetary unit, thus the cover name was a wordplay on Glasser's status as a Treasury Department official.) This October 1944 KGB memo, Glasser's December 1944 KGB autobiography, and Gorsky's December 1948 document establish that "Ruble"/Glasser had been in the late 1930s part of a GRU apparatus, "Karl's group," managed by Chambers, and after Chambers's defection, Maxim Lieber ("Paul"/"Pol") had attempted to reconnect with members of the network, unsuccessfully in Glasser's case because he was about to leave for nearly two years on a Treasury Department assignment to Ecuador.[27]

Glasser's connections to Alger Hiss were not ended, however. After his return from Ecuador and reconnection to Soviet intelligence through the Perlo group, Glasser refocused KGB attention on his one-time colleague from Chambers's 1936–38 GRU apparatus. This is best understood by examining 1945 documents about "Ales" in both Vassiliev's notebooks and the deciphered KGB cables of Venona.

"Ales" was Hiss's GRU cover name in 1945. "Ales"/Hiss was a GRU source, and while aware of his status, the KGB had no direct contact with him until March 1945. That changed, likely triggered by a 3 March 1945 cable signed by the chief of foreign intelligence, General Pavel Fitin, with an urgent order for the KGB's illegal station chief, Iskhak Akhmerov:

At the forthcoming meeting with Albert [Akhmerov], pass on to him on our behalf the following task. Jointly with Robert [Gregory Silvermaster], take all requisite steps to obtain in good time and pass on to us information about the composition of the delegation to the forthcoming conference which is in Babylon . . . what tactics the delegation intends to adopt, whom it is counting on for support, what blocs have been prepared already and formed, how far there will be a united line for the representatives of the Anglo-Saxon world and so on. As the information comes in pass on to the Center by telegraph without delay.

"Babylon" was the cover name for San Francisco, so the upcoming founding conference of the United Nations was the subject. Akhmerov was an illegal officer and not on the staff of a Soviet diplomatic office such as the embassy in Washington or the consulates in New York and San Francisco. Illegal officers operated under false identities and posed as ordinary persons. Moscow Center did not communicate directly with them; thus the instruction in the cable that the order was to be passed to Akhmerov at a "forthcoming meeting." The 3 March cable went to the legal KGB station at the Soviet consulate in New York. From there it would have been delivered to Akhmerov at a regularly scheduled meeting, where messages were passed between the legal station and his illegal station. Akhmerov was then working at a fur and hat shop in New York. In any event, it would be a day or two at least, and perhaps a week or more, before the instructions reached Akhmerov.[28]

Fitin's order was high priority, so the American station likely moved quickly to produce results. As the cable had suggested, one route was through "Robert," the cover name for Gregory Silvermaster, an economist with the War Assets Division of the Treasury Department. Silvermaster led a CPUSA-based network of government officials that had come to the KGB via Jacob Golos and Elizabeth Bentley, just like the Perlo group, and included one highly placed source, Harry Dexter White, recently promoted to assistant secretary of the treasury, who was a senior adviser to the American delegation to the UN conference. Akhmerov, KGB liaison with Silvermaster, made the necessary arrangements, and at the San Francisco conference White met covertly with a Soviet intelligence officer, provided information on the American negotiating strategy, and offered advice on how the Soviets might defeat or water down positions being advanced by his own government (see chapter 4).[29]

As useful as White might be (and was), Anatoly Gorsky realized that potentially there was an even better source, Alger Hiss, a Soviet agent reporting to GRU. Hiss had joined the State Department's Office of Special Political Affairs in May 1944 and had become its director in March 1945; it was this office that supervised U.S. preparations for the founding of the United Nations. Normally, the KGB would leave alone a source known to report to GRU, but given the urgency of General Fitin's 3

March order, Gorsky ignored this policy and on 30 March reported by cable that one of his officers had been in direct contact with "Ales":

As a result of a conversation of "Pya" with Ales, it turns out:

1. Ales has been continuously working with the neighbors since 1935.
2. For a few years now he has been the director of a small group of probationers of the neighbors, for the most part drawn from his relatives.
3. The group and Ales himself are working on obtaining only military information, materials about "the Bank"—the neighbors allegedly are not very interested and he doesn't pass it regularly.
4. In recent years, Ales has been working with Pol repeat Pol who also meets with other members of the group on occasion.
5. Recently Ales and his whole group were awarded Soviet medals.
6. After the Yalta conference, back in Moscow, one very high-ranking Soviet worker allegedly had contact with Ales (Ales implied that it was Comrade Vyshinsky) and at the request of the military neighbors he conveyed to him their thanks, etc.

This 30 March message was deciphered by the Venona project, and "Pya" was a garbled decryption that the chief NSA code breaker eventually decided was "A" for "Albert"/Akhmerov. "Ales" was not identified directly in this cable as Alger Hiss. A footnote to the cable prepared by FBI and NSA analysts concluded that "Ales" was "probably Alger Hiss." Additional details about "Ales" in documents in Vassiliev's notebooks make the identification certain.[30]

The pool of the possible candidates for "Ales" is a small one because of statement number 6 in the message: "*6. After the Yalta conference, back in Moscow, one very high-ranking Soviet worker allegedly had contact with Ales.*" With the defeat of the Nazis certain, President Franklin Roosevelt, Prime Minister Winston Churchill, and General Secretary Joseph Stalin met at Yalta in the Crimea in early February 1945 to negotiate an agreement for the occupation of Germany and other liberated nations. When the conference ended, most of the American delegation returned home via the Middle East. A contingent from the American embassy in the Soviet Union returned to Moscow but stayed there. "Ales," however, was back in the states in March in time to meet a KGB officer. Only a small party, led by Secretary of State Edward Stettinius, went from Yalta to Moscow to finish a few details of the conference and returned to Washington by March. Aside from support staff (and "Ales" was not plausibly someone in that category), the Stettinius party included only four State Department officials who could possibly have been "Ales": Stettinius himself, senior diplomat and adviser on European affairs H. Freeman Matthews, Stettinius's press aide Wilder Foote, and Alger Hiss.[31]

While all four men satisfy statement number 6 in Gorsky's 30 March cable, only Alger Hiss matches any of the other five statements, and he matches *all five*:

"*1. Ales has been continuously working with the neighbors since 1935.*" The evidence that Hiss had begun work for GRU ("the neighbors") in the mid-1930s is overwhelming. It led a jury to convict him in 1950 and was reaffirmed by every court that examined the case thereafter and is supported by the leading scholarly accounts of the case.[32]

"*2. For a few years now he has been the director of a small group of probationers of the neighbors, for the most part drawn from his relatives.*" In 1948 Chambers produced typed and handwritten material he had hidden a decade earlier from his final months before he dropped out of Soviet espionage. He recalled that Priscilla Hiss retyped many of the documents her husband stole from the State Department. Technical examination by both prosecution and defense experts established that most of the material was typed on a typewriter owned by the Hiss family in the mid-1930s. One of the document specialists hired by the Hiss defense went even further, advising defense lawyers that on the basis of the strong and weak hits of the typing pattern, the documents had been typed by Priscilla and not Alger.[33]

Chambers also implicated Hiss's brother: "Donald Hiss never at any time procured any documents. Nevertheless, he was a member of the apparatus which I headed." Donald Hiss transferred to the State Department from the Department of Labor in November 1937, shortly before Chambers dropped out of Soviet espionage, and remained there until the end of World War II. When Chambers met with Assistant Secretary of State Adolf Berle in September 1939 and identified several dozen persons as active in the Communist Party's covert operations in Washington and implied possible espionage links, he included Donald and Priscilla along with Alger Hiss. Victor Perlo included Donald Hiss on his list of people with connections to Soviet intelligence.[34]

"*3. The group and Ales himself are working on obtaining only military information, materials about "the Bank" — the neighbors allegedly are not very interested and he doesn't pass it regularly.*" When the GRU dominated Soviet foreign intelligence operations in the 1920s and 1930s, its networks sought political and strategic information as well as more narrowly defined military intelligence. But as the KGB established its supremacy in foreign intelligence in the mid-1930s, GRU's jurisdiction was steadily narrowed, and it had to get its agents to produce more strictly military information within its jurisdiction. In the fall of 1945 Alger Hiss made an extraordinary proposal that the State Department create a new "special assistant for military affairs" linked to his Office of Special Political Affairs, an office devoted to handling UN-related matters, with little discernible need for military information. Moreover, when security officers belatedly began to look closely at Hiss in 1946, they discovered that he had used his authority to obtain top secret reports "on atomic energy . . . and other matters relating to military intelligence" that were outside the scope of his Office of Special Political Affairs.[35]

"*4. In recent years, Ales has been working with Pol repeat Pol who also meets with other members of the group on occasion.*" "Pol," as noted above, was Maxim Lieber, the former participant in Chambers's 1930s apparatus whom GRU detailed to pick up the pieces of Chambers's network after his defection. Lieber invoked the Fifth Amendment to avoid testifying about his relationship with Chambers and Hiss. The files of Hiss's legal defense team demonstrate that at the time of his trial, a Communist Party contact met with Lieber and conveyed a message to Hiss's lawyers that Lieber "does know Hiss but does not propose to admit it."[36]

"*5. Recently Ales and his whole group were awarded Soviet medals.*" In April 1945 General Fitin sent a memo to Vsevolod Merkulov, head of the entire KGB, reviewing the extensive work that "Ruble"/Glasser had done for the KGB and stating the following:

"According to information received from 'Vadim' [Gorsky], the group of agents of the military 'neighbors' to which 'Ruble' [Glasser] had previously belonged was recently decorated by the USSR. 'Ruble' learned about this from his friend 'Ales,' who is the leader of this group.

In light of 'Ruble's' committed work for the USSR over the course of 8 years and the fact that, because he was transferred to our station 'Ruble' was not decorated along with the oth. members of 'Ales's' group, I think it would be expedient to recommend him for the Order of the 'Red Star.' I ask for your approval."

This passage not only confirms the 30 March cable that "Ales" and his group were awarded Soviet medals, but also adds that Glasser had been working with "Ales's" group, providing further confirmation that "Ales" was Hiss. Additional corroboration is in Elizabeth Bentley's lengthy November 1945 deposition, which described Harold Glasser's role in the Perlo group:

Referring again to Harold Glasser, I recall that after his return from his assignment in Europe, probably in Italy, for the United States Treasury Department, Victor Perlo told me that Glasser had asked him if he would be able to get back in with the Perlo group. I asked Perlo how Glasser happened to leave the group and he explained that Glasser and one or two others had been taken sometime before by some American in some governmental agency in Washington, and that this unidentified American turned Glasser and the others over to some Russian. Perlo declared he did not know the identity of this American, and said that Charley Kramer, so far as he knew, was the only person who had this information. Sometime later I was talking with Kramer in New York City, and brought up this matter to him. At this time Kramer told me that the person who had originally taken Glasser away from Perlo's group was named Hiss and that he was in the U.S. State Department.

Bentley's statement that Glasser had been on loan to an espionage network headed by Hiss fits with Fitin's memo that Glasser had been working with "Ales's" GRU group and that the latter had been decorated.[37]

While Alger Hiss fits all six characteristics for "Ales" given in the 30 March cable, Stettinius, Matthews, and Foote meet only the travel itinerary of "Ales." There is no evidence linking any of the three to even a single other item.

There is another Gorsky cable to Moscow Center regarding "Ales" in Vassiliev's notebook, dated Monday, 5 March 1945, just two days after the Saturday, 3 March, cable arrived from Moscow with its order to find sources for the upcoming UN conference. This cable has the appearance of a quick response to Moscow's order, intended to show that the American station would swiftly deal with Moscow's request and suggesting the option of going outside existing KGB sources to contact "Ales," the GRU agent.

Two of the early sentences of the 5 March cable appeared to shrink further the pool of candidates for "Ales" and actually appeared to exclude Alger Hiss: "Particular attention—to 'Ales.' He was at the Yalta Conference, then went to Mexico City and hasn't returned yet." After leaving Moscow, Stettinius's party, including Matthews, Hiss, and Foote, did not return directly to the United States but went on to Mexico City for the Chapultepec conference of hemispheric foreign ministers starting on 21 February. Matthews, a European specialist, and Hiss, responsible for preparing for the upcoming UN meeting, were not needed. Both left the conference early, getting back to Washington at the end of February, while Stettinius and Foote remained in Mexico City until the conference ended on 8 March.[38]

Superficially, this appears to remove Matthews and Hiss as candidates for "Ales," leaving only Stettinius and Foote. But the statement actually indicated that Anatoly Gorsky *thought* "Ales" was still in Mexico City as part of the American delegation. If one looks at the totality of the evidence, the most sensible conclusion is that Gorsky simply did not know that "Ales" had returned early. Gorsky *could have known* that Hiss had returned. Hiss had spoken on a public affairs radio program, and two newspaper stories on the program mentioned him, although in neither case was he given headline treatment because more prominent diplomats, including the acting secretary of state, Joseph C. Grew, were speaking on the program. But that Gorsky *could* have known is simply to state a possibility and is not the same as his *actually knowing.* Hiss was not at this time a prominent figure. He was a senior DOS official but one at the third or fourth level of the hierarchy and as yet little known to the press or public. Not until he presided over the opening sessions of the UN founding conference in San Francisco in May 1945 did he make an impression on the national media. Nor, for that matter, was "Ales" an agent whom the KGB would have reason to track. He was a GRU source of whom the KGB was aware simply because one of its agents, Glasser, had worked with "Ales." Aside from Glasser's association with "Ales," Gorsky and the KGB had had no contact, regular or otherwise, with "Ales" and no reason to pay attention to his movements.[39]

It would have been easy for Gorsky to have assumed on 5 March that Hiss was still in Mexico City. We do not know precisely when Gorsky saw Moscow Center's 3 March cable with its order that information on the upcoming UN conference be sent to Moscow "without delay," but the earliest was Saturday, with Sunday more likely since it had to be deciphered, and he had to compose his reply, get it ciphered, and send it on the way on Monday, 5 March. With all his responsibilities as a KGB station chief in wartime, balancing the time demands of his cover job as a senior embassy diplomat with his other job directly overseeing the KGB Washington station and supervising the KGB stations in New York and San Francisco, as well as the illegal station headed by Akhmerov, it is likely that he simply assumed "Ales" was still in Mexico City with Secretary Stettinius.

In any case, the 5 March cable has more to say of "Ales" than the single item that Gorsky thought he was still in Mexico City. These other attributes of "Ales" revealed in the cable all point straight at Alger Hiss:

Our only key to him—"Ruble" [Glasser]. "Ruble" is going on assignment himself (Italy). . . . It is difficult to oversee "Ales" through him. "We spoke with

'Ruble' several times about 'Ales.' As we have written already, 'Ruble' gives 'Ales' an exceptionally good political reference as a member of the Comparty. 'Ruble' reports that 'Ales' is strong and strong-willed, with a firm and decisive nature, completely aware that he is a Communist in an illegal position, with all the ensuing consequences. Unfortunately, it seems that, like all local Communists, he has his own ideas about secrecy. As we already reported to you, 'Ales' and 'Ruble' used to work in 'Karl's' [Chambers's] informational group, which was affiliated with the neighbors. When the connection with 'Karl' was lost, 'Ruble' backed out, while 'Ales' entered into a connection with 'Pol' [Lieber]. He told 'Ruble' about this himself a year and a half ago, when he asked the latter to meet with 'Pol' in order to continue work."[40]

Gorsky's description of the relationship of "Ruble"/Glasser with "Ales" fits Hiss and only Hiss. Most important, Gorsky stated, *"'Ales' and 'Ruble' used to work in 'Karl's' informational group, which was affiliated with the neighbors.'"* As already noted, "Karl" was Whittaker Chambers; the "informational group which was affiliated with the neighbors" was Chambers's 1936–38 GRU apparatus. Both Hiss and Glasser were members of Chambers's group. The other three candidates for "Ales" (Stettinius, Matthews, and Foote) never had any link to Chambers's apparatus. Stettinius and Foote were neither living nor working in Washington during the 1936–38 period when Chambers's apparatus, which was Washington-focused, was in operation, while Matthews was only occasionally in Washington during a series of foreign diplomatic assignments. Additionally, once again "Pol"/Lieber is linked to "Ales," and Maxim Lieber had ties to Hiss but to none of the other candidates for "Ales."

Gorsky noted that Glasser gave *"'Ales' an exceptionally good political reference as a member of the Comparty.'"* Again, Hiss's links to the Communist Party are well documented, while there is no evidence of any CPUSA links for the others. Glasser had a documented relationship with Alger Hiss, telling the FBI he had known Alger since 1938 and had a close personal relationship with Donald Hiss. In contrast, there is no evidence that he had a personal relationship with Stettinius, Foote, or Matthews. In January 1945 Glasser prepared a list of his close contacts at the KGB's request. Of the thirty-one persons he listed, all but three are known to have been active members of the Washington Communist underground. Of the four "Ales" candidates, only Alger Hiss appeared.[41]

There is one final "Ruble"/Glasser document in Vassiliev's notebooks that references "Ales." In April 1945, Gorsky reported that "Ruble," still the KGB's only link to "Ales," had delivered an alarming report:

"An FBI agent informed Stettinius that one of their agents had seen a batch of documents that were delivered in a suitcase to NY to be photographed. Afterwards, they were returned to Washington within 24 hours. These documents included a polit. report and important cipher communications. Based on the nature of the documents, only 3 people had access to them. One of these people was 'Ales.' The FBI agent said that in the next 72 hours they would conclusively identify who had been responsible for leaking these documents. According to Stettinius, the FBI agent had told him that operations of this sort involving documents have been going on for 18 months now, and that 'hundreds upon hundreds' of documents had been removed as a result." Stettinius asked the FBI agent whether these documents ended up at 'PM' [*PM* newspaper] to which the latter replied: "'No, much further left than that.' Toward the end of his conversation with "*Ales*" on this subject, Stettinius told him: 'I hope it isn't you.'"

The incident referred to was the *Amerasia* case, where hundreds of stolen OSS and State Department documents were found at the offices of *Amerasia,* a journal published and edited by a secret Communist, Philip Jaffe. Hiss himself corroborated this incident reported by Glasser in 1945 to the KGB, telling his chief attorney in 1949 "that he was at the San Francisco Conference in 1945 when the Amerasia scandal broke and that Stettinius told him that he had seen some of the papers taken from Jaffe . . . and that they included papers from Stettinius's office and from Hiss's office." (The FBI soon established that Emmanuel Larson and John Service at the State Department and Andrew Roth at the Office of Naval Intelligence were the principal sources of the stolen documents, and attention turned away from Hiss.)[42]

Another reference to "Ales" in this period was also likely related to the *Amerasia* case. Moscow Center cabled Gorsky on 29 May 1945 to warn that it had received information that American counterintelligence had stepped up its activities, noting, "the incidents with 'Hare' and 'Ales' are yet another confirmation of this." "Hare" was Maurice Halperin, chief of the Latin American Division of the Research and Analysis section of the OSS and a productive Soviet agent. There is no indication what trouble Halperin faced, but the *Amerasia* investigation and the suspicion it threw on "Ales" clearly worried Moscow.[43]

The final reference to "Ales" in Alexander Vassiliev's notebooks comes in a KGB Washington cable to Moscow in June 1945: "Vadim [Gorsky] reported that he established a connection with M. at the beginning of June. Several years ago, M. worked as a courier between "*Peter*" ("Storm") and the latter's people. M. knows "A." through this work."[44] The cable is part of the KGB file for "Mole," the cover name for Charles Kramer, a productive source who came to the KGB via the Perlo group. ("M." was Vassiliev's abbreviation in this note for "Mole.") "Peter" and "Storm" were both cover names for Josef Peters. Here Gorsky was reporting that in the 1930s Kramer had worked as a courier between Peters and various members of the Washington Communist underground. Gorsky also noted that "M. knows 'A.' through this work." Vassiliev made a marginal notation in his notebook for this message, "'Ales'—Hiss," indicating that "A." was his abbreviation for "Ales" and that "Ales" was Hiss. Kramer was a member of the Ware group and would have known both Hiss and Peters.

Aside from Vassiliev's annotation, "Ales" is not explicitly identified as Alger Hiss in Vassiliev's notebooks, but the overwhelming weight of the evidence of "Ales's" characteristics described by the documents in the notebooks, particularly "Ales's" relationship with "Karl"/Chambers and "Ruble"/Glasser, points to Alger Hiss and only Alger Hiss as the Soviet spy "Ales."

Finality: The Trial and Conviction of "Leonard"

The final set of KGB documents involving Hiss comes from the period after his exposure by Whittaker Chambers. These documents unambiguously designate Alger Hiss as a Soviet spy, albeit under a new cover name.

By late 1948 Soviet intelligence operations in the United States were in disarray. Beginning in 1945 a series of defectors—Igor Gouzenko, Elizabeth Bentley, Louis Budenz, Hede Massing, and Whittaker Chambers—identified Soviet intelligence officers and scores of their American agents and sources. The KGB and GRU hastily withdrew their most experienced and skilled professional officers from the United States and Canada, put existing networks and sources "on ice," severed contact with exposed agents, stopped recruitment of new sources, and devoted much of their efforts to damage control (see chapter 9).

No espionage case had a higher profile than that of Alger Hiss. By the end of 1948 it had become a media firestorm with dueling congressional testimony by Chambers and Hiss, grand jury investigations, subpoenas and libel suits, and the melodramatic retrieval of microfilm of stolen State Department documents from a hollowed-out pumpkin on Chambers's Maryland farm—all culminating in Hiss's indictment for perjury. The relentless media coverage impressed the American public with

the threat of Soviet espionage more than anything that had surfaced up
to that time. Thrashing about for a way to minimize the damage, the KGB
Washington station suggested to Moscow Center forging documents and
then having someone

"'find' a file on 'Karl' in the German archives revealing that he is a German
agent, that he worked as a spy for the Gestapo in the U.S. and, on a mission
from them, had infiltrated the American Comparty. If we print this in our
newspapers and publish a few 'documents' that can be prepared at home, it
would have a major effect. This report would be seized upon not only by foreign Comparties, but also by the progressive press in all countries, and, as a
result, the position of the Committee on the investigation of Un-American
Activities, the Grand Jury, and other agencies would be seriously undermined.

   We could also claim that 'Karl' was known to the Committee, the Grand
Jury, and oth. American agencies as a Gestapo agent, but that because the leaders of these institutions were vehement opponents of the USSR, the Comparty,
and the progressive movement in general, they had represented the matter as if
'Karl' and others had been spying for the USSR rather than Germany."[45]

   Moscow Center quickly rejected the plan, pointing out that it would
likely demoralize the very agents the KGB wanted to protect:

"The station's proposal to manufacture and publish documents in our newspapers about the fact that the traitor Chambers is a German agent, conducted
espionage work in the USA on assignment from the Gestapo, and on German
instructions, infiltrated the CPUSA—cannot be accepted. The publication of
such 'documents' would undoubtedly have a very negative effect on our former agents who were betrayed by Chambers (A. Hiss, D. Hiss, Wadleigh, Pigman, Reno) and oth., because, knowing that they had worked for us, but having 'turned' into German agents, these people could, for example, choose to
cooperate with the authorities, give them candid testimonies, etc. Moreover,
the transformation of these individuals from alleged Sov. intelligence agents
into established agents for a country that had been at war with the USA would
certainly not help them from a purely legal standpoint."

Two senior officials prepared this December 1948 negative report for the
chairman of the KI, as the KGB was then termed. These Soviet intelligence officers, using real names, designated as "our former agents" Alger
Hiss, Donald Hiss, Julian Wadleigh, Warren Pigman, and Franklin Reno.
All five were persons Chambers identified as part of his GRU-linked apparatus of 1936–38. This Moscow Center's report also eschewed using

the cover name "Karl" and in plain text referred to "the traitor Chambers."[46]

Late in 1948 the KGB's foreign intelligence directorate prepared a summary damage assessment for the agency's leadership on the state of intelligence work in America. The report noted, "Intelligence work in the USA was completely deactivated in November/December 1945 and did not resume until September 1947," and placed the chief blame on the "betrayals of Gouzenko, "Karl" [Chambers], "Myrna" [Bentley], and "Buben" [Budenz], as well as of "Berg" and "Art" [Alexander and Helen Koral], lamenting that "these traitors handed over 62 of our former agents to Amer. authorities, which is to say, practically our entire network in the USA that was working on the polit. line."[47]

A 1948 memo by Anatoly Gorsky, entitled "Failures in the USA (1938–1948)," provided the details. ("Failure" was KGB jargon for any agent or operative who had been exposed to hostile counterintelligence or otherwise compromised.) Gorsky listed the cover names and real names of the Soviet officers and American sources compromised by the defectors. He began his recapitulation with twenty-one officers and sources exposed by Whittaker Chambers:

Failures in the USA (1938–48)

"Karl's" group:

1. Karl—Whittaker Chambers, former editor in chief of "Time" magazine. Traitor.
2. Jerome—Barna Bukov (Altman), our former cadre employee. Currently in the USSR.
3. Leonard—Alger Hiss, former employee of the State Dept.
4. Junior—Donald Hiss, former employee of the Dept. of the Interior
5. 104th—Henry A. Wadleigh—former employee of the State Department
6. 118th—F. V. Reno—former employee of the Aberdeen Proving Ground
7. 105th—Henry Collins, former employee of Department of Agriculture, at pres., director of the American-Russian Institute in NY
8. 114th—William W. Pigman, former employee of the Bureau of Standards
9. "Storm"—Joseph Peters (a.k.a. Isadore Boorstein), former member of the Central Committee of the CPUSA
10. "Vig"—Lee Pressman, former legal adviser of the Congress of Industrial Organizations
11. 116th—Harry Azizov, former employee of a steel-smelting company in Chicago
12. 101st—Peter MacLean, journalist and photo reporter, not used since '37

13. 103rd—David Carpenter, newspaper employee
14. 107th—Felix Inslerman, place of employment unknown
15. 113th—Harry Rosenthal, employee of an insurance company in Philadel-
    phia
16. 115th—Lester Hutm, former employee of the Frankford Arsenal
17. "Ernst"—Noel Field, former employee of the State Dept.
18. "Rupert"—V. V. Sveshnikov, former employee of the War Dept.
19. "Richard"—Harry White, former assistant to Sec. of the Treasury Morgen-
    thau, died in '48
20. "Aileron"—G. Silverman, former chief of the Planning and Statistics Divi-
    sion of the AAF
21. "Ruble"—Harold Glasser, former director of the Monetary Division of the
    Dept. of the Treasury.

Gorsky's report unambiguously designated Alger Hiss, by his real name, as a Soviet agent betrayed by Whittaker Chambers. It also noted that by this time, December 1948, Hiss had a new cover name, "Leonard." Gorsky was also correct about the extent of the damage wrought by Chambers's defection. Under questioning by the FBI, Chambers identified as involved in Soviet espionage almost everyone Gorsky named as potentially compromised.[48]

The final KGB document in Vassiliev's notebooks that deals with Alger Hiss, dated 16 March 1950, was a plan to reestablish a vigorous Soviet intelligence presence in the United States. In the course of laying out what needed to be done, it included a summary of the setbacks of the late 1940s. One of those specified was "the trial of the GRU GSh VS agent "Leonard," the chief of one of the main divisions of the State Department and a member of "Karl's" group, ended in his conviction at the beginning of 1950." ("GRU GSh VS" was the Chief Intelligence Directorate of the General Staff of the Armed Forces—that is, Soviet military intelligence.) Not only was "Leonard" identified as Alger Hiss in Gorsky's December 1948 memo, but Hiss was also the only former State Department official tried and convicted in 1950. "Leonard" was Alger Hiss, and Hiss was a Soviet spy.[49]

Hiss and History

Any reasonable person will conclude that the new documentation of Hiss's assistance to Soviet espionage, along with the massive weight of prior accumulated evidence, closes the case. Given the fervor exhibited by his loyalists, it is unlikely that anything will convince the remaining die-hards. But to serious students of history continued claims for Hiss's innocence are akin to a terminal form of ideological blindness. The evidence from a myriad of sources—eyewitnesses and written documents, public testimony and private correspondence, fellow spies and Soviet intelligence officers, decrypted cables and long-closed archives—is overwhelming and conclusive. Alger Hiss worked for the GRU in the 1930s and 1940s. The KGB hoped to use him in mid-1945. He was identified in Soviet intelligence documents by his real name and three different cover names, each of which is clearly and demonstrably linked to him. KGB officers and CPUSA underground leaders knew him as a member of the Soviet apparatus. Several of his fellow agents, including Noel Field, Hede Massing, Charles Kramer, Victor Perlo, and Harold Glasser, identified him as an agent in confidential communications that made their way back to Moscow. And its own damage assessments confirm that Soviet intelligence knew that Alger Hiss belonged to it. Case closed.

с.170   Фотографии Зимберд и семьи.

Показания Д. Грингласс на процесс Д. Руденберг 9.3.50.

с.178 [Д.Г. не знал, что работал над бомбой, в ноябре 44г. ему сказала жена эту согласившись на Руденберг]

[Дело "Ида" ("Лея") 861/91 т.1]

с.15   М-В → Ц 7.12.44

"Либерал" провёл беседу с Осой о её помощи наш. делу согласилась выполнить поручения, к-е будут исходить от Л-ла и также, как и Л-л, высказала уверенность, что К. согласится на помощь.

Перед её отъездом Л-л встречался с ней два раза и провёл с ней инструктаж в соответствии с нашими указаниями.

Оса должна сперва выяснить у К. его взгляд на возможность информировать заинтересованную в работе к-в нашего дела и его участии в ней. Если К. сочтёт это возможным, тогда она должна будет ему передать, что этим в-сом интересовался Л-л и выяснить у него род и пути помощи."

с.16   Сообщение "Л-ла" об "Осе" 5.12.44

"The following is a record of the conversation held by Julius, Ethel and Ruth.

First of all, Julius inquired of Ruth how she felt about the Soviet Union and how deep in general did her Communist convictions go, whereupon she replied without hesitation that to her Socialism was the only hope of the world and the Soviet Union commanded her deepest admiration.

Julius then wanted to know whether or not she would be willing to help the Soviet Union. She replied very simply and sincerely that it would be a privilege. When Ethel mentioned David, she assured us that it was her judgment such was also David's understanding.

Julius then explained his connections with certain people interested in supplying the Soviet Union with urgently needed technical information it could not obtain through the regular channels and impressed upon her the tremendous importance of the project upon which David is now at work. Therefore she was to ask him the following kind of questions:
1) How many people were now employed there
2) What part of the project was already in operation if any. Were they encountering any

· ·

CHAPTER 2

Enormous

The KGB Attack on the
Anglo-American Atomic Project

I n 1950 Klaus Fuchs, a senior physicist working on the British atomic bomb project, confessed to authorities that he had been a Soviet spy when he worked at Los Alamos in 1944 and 1945 as part of a British contingent assisting the American atomic bomb program, the Manhattan Project. That same year the FBI arrested David Greenglass, who confessed to being a Soviet source when he was at Los Alamos working as a skilled machinist in the workshop that built special components for the implosion-design plutonium bomb. For decades most historians thought that was the end of the story. There were dissenters: some on the left insisted that Greenglass had confessed to crimes he hadn't committed while some on the right suspected that Robert Oppenheimer, scientific chief at Los Alamos, had been a key Soviet source. However, until the 1990s a scholarly consensus limited Soviet atomic espionage to Fuchs and Greenglass.

In a startling 1994 memoir, however, a former KGB officer, Pavel Su-

---

Report by Julius Rosenberg, written in the third person and in English, on his and Ethel Rosenberg's meeting with Ruth Greenglass to recruit her to Soviet espionage, supplying questions for her to ask David Greenglass about Los Alamos. Courtesy of Alexander Vassiliev.

doplatov, implicated Manhattan Project scientists Oppenheimer, Enrico Fermi, and Leo Szilard in espionage. In a heated and highly public response, prominent scientists, journalists, political figures, and historians criticized Sudoplatov's memory, evidence, and motives. The American Physical Society, the leading physicists' professional organization, denounced the book and demanded that the U.S. government repudiate its claims. The FBI does not usually make statements on historical controversies, but in response to pressure from Representative Les Aspin (D-WI), it issued a letter stating that it possessed no evidence to support the allegations against the scientists. Hans Bethe, a Nobel Prize–winning physicist who had worked at Los Alamos, insisted that there was nothing new to be learned about Soviet nuclear espionage, emphatically stating, "Fuchs's espionage was enough to account for all the information that came from Los Alamos to the Soviets, both oral and in the form of copied secret documents. No additional moles were needed."[1]

Sudoplatov's allegations received a deserved battering, but the view that Soviet atomic espionage was a closed question did not last either. The assertion that Fuchs's espionage explained everything evaporated in 1995 when the NSA (America's cryptologic agency) released World War II KGB cables decoded by its Venona project that identified a major but hitherto unknown atomic spy: Theodore Hall, a physicist who had worked on the plutonium bomb at Los Alamos (discussed below). The Venona decryptions also included the code names of several additional atomic spies that the NSA and FBI could not identify.

The KGB designated its World War II atomic intelligence project "Enormous," and Vassiliev's notebooks demonstrate that it was aptly named. There was a very great deal more to the story of Soviet atomic espionage than the recently uncovered Hall and the long-known Fuchs and Greenglass. KGB memos and messages recorded in the notebooks identify three additional unknown atomic spies. They also show that Robert Oppenheimer was *not* a KGB source (neither was Fermi or Szilard) and that the course of Soviet atomic intelligence in the United States was far more complicated than the traditional narrative or its dissident alternatives had suggested.[2]

"Fogel" and "Persian": The Unknown Atomic Spy

The decoded KGB cables released in 1995 not only exposed Theodore Hall as a previously unknown Soviet source at Los Alamos but also identified, although only with a cover name (first "Fogel," later changed to

"Persian"), another source providing information on the Manhattan Project facility at Oak Ridge, Tennessee. The cover names occurred in four KGB cables in 1944. The messages made clear that "Fogel" was engaged in atomic espionage, appeared to have technical knowledge, and provided information about Oak Ridge. But the deciphered portions had little detail about "Fogel"/"Persian" himself, and NSA/FBI analysts footnoted him as "unidentified."

The unidentified atomic spy generated speculation that "Fogel"/"Persian" might be Robert Oppenheimer or Philip Morrison (a Manhattan Project scientist with Communist ties). Much of the confusion stemmed from disinformation provided by retired KGB officers in the early 1990s. The truth about "Fogel"/"Persian" is less sensational but more fascinating. He was not a high-profile scientist but an obscure engineer. However, he was also the first significant source the KGB developed within the Manhattan Project. Further, he was recruited by none other than Julius Rosenberg, who thus recruited not just one atomic source (the long-known David Greenglass) but *two* atomic spies.[3]

The Vassiliev notebooks contain a February 1944 message from the KGB New York station to Moscow Center about its new source, "Fogel": "A good friend of "Antenna's" [Rosenberg's]—Russ McNutt ("Fogel"). Civil engineer. F. asked A. where he should work. A. suggested 'Kellogg.' F. got a job at 'Kellex,' a subcontractor of 'Kellogg.' Fogel—fellowcountryman [Communist]. He is on Dies's list. F. has an idea of where his information goes, but this doesn't bother him. So far, neither F. nor A. has any idea what kind of factory F. is helping to build." Kellex, a subsidiary of M. W. Kellogg company, signed a contract in December 1942 to design, supervise the construction of, and procure the equipment for the K-25 uranium gaseous diffusion plant at Oak Ridge. A 1945 KGB memo discussing the sources on the technical intelligence (XY) line summarized McNutt's contribution: "'Persian'—Russell McNutt. B. in 1916 in the USA. A civil engineer at the 'Kellex' company. Married, 1 child. A fellow-countryman [Communist]; his father—a longtime fellowcountryman, a close friend of 'Helmsman's' [Browder's]. He is well-to-do. Gave materials on equipment used for 'Enormous.' + A floor-plan of camp No.1 [Oak Ridge]."[4]

Russell McNutt's father, Ernest, was a Kansas newspaperman and radical whose acquaintance with Earl Browder (chief of the CPUSA until mid-1945) went back to the founding of the Communist Party. Browder was Kansas-born and -raised and a radical activist opposing American involvement in World War I (he was imprisoned for impeding the draft). Ernest was a founder and state secretary of the Communist Labor Party in Kansas in 1919. During the 1920s, however, he pretended to moderate his politics. Ernest eventually owned seven small newspapers, publishing in Kansas, Oklahoma, Texas, and other Midwestern states. In 1939 a former CPUSA member from Kansas testified before the U.S. House Special Committee on Un-American Activities (the Dies Committee) that Ernest was a secret member of the state Communist Party's executive board, although he had run for the office of state printer in 1938 as a Democrat. He also identified Ernest's sons, Waldo and Russell, as concealed Communists. Waldo had appeared at the first American Youth Congress (AYC) gathering in 1934 as a delegate from the Rocky Mountain Young Men's Christian Association and a leading figure in the caucus dominated by the Communists that seized control of the organization; he became chairman of the AYC in 1935. In an interview decades later, Gil Green, head of the Young Communist League (YCL), identified Waldo McNutt as a secret member of the Communist Party.[5]

Russell A. McNutt, Waldo's brother, was born in La Cygne, Kansas, in 1914 (not 1916 as the KGB memo stated). He studied civil engineering at Kansas State University for one year, transferred to Brooklyn Polytechnical Institute, and graduated in 1940, after three years as an evening student, working during the day for the federal Works Progress Administration. He was employed as an assistant engineer for the Borough of Manhattan until 1942. McNutt then worked briefly for Republic Steel and the Chemical Construction Corporation. He began work at Kellex in November 1943.[6]

Russell McNutt and Julius Rosenberg first met after Julius called Waldo, then manager of a Communist-dominated consumer cooperative in New York City, to inquire about farms that took people as summer guests. At that time Ernest McNutt (Waldo and Russell's father) had a farm in Haddam, Connecticut, and rented rooms and served meals to summer guests who came for hiking in the area. Russell told FBI agents in 1951 that he had encountered Julius at the farm several times and even drove him there from New York once.[7]

Julius Rosenberg connected McNutt to the KGB in February 1944. Despite more than two years of effort, at that point the KGB had not developed a single source in the Manhattan Project. A grateful Moscow Center told its New York station chief: "'A bonus in the amount of $100 has been allotted out of the 2nd quarter estimate for 'Antenna's' initiative in acquiring an agent to cultivate 'Enormous.' We leave at your discretion the best form in which to give it to 'Antenna'—cash sum, gift, etc.'"[8]

Russell McNutt worked on structural designs for concrete water-cooling flumes and other major facilities of the K-25 gaseous diffusion plant at Oak Ridge. Most of the time, he worked out of the company's New York office, but he made occasional trips to Tennessee. Two deciphered KGB cables reported on his activities. In February 1944 a long, technical report, largely unrecovered by American cryptanalysts, noted that "Fogel" had provided information on "Enormous." One of the fragments of decoded text referred to "80 pounds for the neutralization of weak. . . ." On 16 June 1944, Stepan Apresyan, chief of the KGB New York station, informed Moscow that he had dispatched by diplomatic pouch the layout of a Manhattan Project plant, clearly facilities at Oak Ridge, obtained from "Fogel." In an analysis of intelligence work conducted in 1944 by the KGB New York station, Moscow hailed "'Persian's' recruitment" as one of the year's main achievements.[9]

Although there were several messages in Alexander Vassiliev's notebooks indicating that the KGB planned to transfer liaison with McNutt from Rosenberg to Harry Gold, there is no evidence that ever occurred. Gold later cooperated with the FBI and identified many of his sources but never McNutt or anyone resembling him. A listing of agents in March 1945, after Rosenberg's sources had been reassigned in a security move, showed that Anatoly Yatskov had been assigned to supervise "Persian" and held his first meeting with McNutt on 11 March 1945.[10]

Over time, however, McNutt turned out to have less commitment and value than originally believed. He was working at a Kellex design office in New York City, a useful source for information on the massive uranium separation plant that the company was building at Oak Ridge. But the KGB wanted sources on the spot with access to information about the machinery and technical operations under way inside the facilities. McNutt, to the KGB's consternation, refused an offer from Kellex to move to Oak Ridge. The KGB New York station reported that he did not want to leave his comfortable apartment in New York for a place where there was no housing for his family, including his child, nor did he want to abandon the summer vacation business he had started with a fellow Communist, one that had required a $20,000 investment and that he was assisting in managing. At Moscow Center senior officer Andrey Graur wrote on the New York cable, "Can't we persuade Persian to go work at the camp? We would cover the necessary additional payments."[11]

The Center promptly cabled New York to meet with McNutt to emphasize how much it wanted him to take the job transfer and urged the

New York station to "appeal to Persian's [McNutt's] sense of civic duty and explain to him that by moving to Camp-1 [Oak Ridge], he would have an opportunity to be of great benefit to our common cause." To assuage his financial concerns, KGB promised to pay him whatever he needed and urged him to have one of his relatives take over the summer lodge business. Yatskov met McNutt every two weeks from March until May; he reported that he continued to provide Kellex design information but also confessed failure in persuading McNutt to move to Oak Ridge:

"Persian [McNutt] refused to go to Novostroy [Oak Ridge] in connection with his wife's illness. At pres., in addition to the fact that his wife's health has not improved, Persian's trip is also impossible because the company is no longer renewing its proposal, and Persian cannot bring it up himself b/c, people usually only agree to travel to Novostroy, which doesn't give any advantage, only if there is no alternative. In the March–April period, Persian worked on standard computations for water supply and ventilation and did not have any interesting materials at his disposal. It was only at the last meeting, on May 8th, that he gave a plan indicating equipment location in building K-302 (the reference on a key plan), four pages of blueprints, and a supplement to the plan."

McNutt's insistence on staying in New York limited his usefulness for Soviet intelligence, and, as with all members of the Rosenberg network, the KGB lost touch with him after Elizabeth Bentley's defection in late 1945 triggered the withdrawal of most of the officers who had handled technical intelligence. But when the KGB recontacted Julius Rosenberg in May 1948 to reestablish their earlier relationship, Moscow Center listed McNutt as one of his former agents that it wanted Rosenberg to revive.[12]

David Greenglass had first met McNutt in 1946, when he and Rosenberg discussed McNutt's becoming the South American representative of the small machine parts business that they had started with other relatives. (McNutt did move to Caracas in 1947 to pursue business opportunities and obtained a job with Gulf Oil. He remained abroad until 1949.) Greenglass also recalled that Rosenberg asked him to deliver an envelope containing $1,000 to McNutt. Rosenberg was an investor in one of McNutt's postwar business ventures, an effort to develop a forty-acre site in Westchester County, New York, as a planned community through McNutt's company, Industrial Planners and Designers. (The venture was not successful.) Although the FBI investigated McNutt after

Rosenberg's arrest and concluded that he was at the least a Communist sympathizer and possibly a party member, he was never publicly identified or named during the case. Despite a number of contradictions between McNutt's account of his postwar relationship with Rosenberg and Greenglass's account, the FBI concluded that "no information positively identifying him as a member of the Julius Rosenberg espionage network has been developed to date." By his own silence and willingness to face execution rather than cooperate with the government, Rosenberg shielded the first of his two atomic espionage recruits from arrest and prosecution.[13]

Other members of the Rosenberg espionage apparatus faced prison, years of investigation, or public obloquy, or they fled to the Soviet Union. But Russell McNutt emerged unscathed and publicly unassociated with Soviet espionage. He went on to a successful career as an engineer, both in the United States and abroad. By 1974 he was a vice-president of Gulf-Reston, the Gulf Oil subsidiary that was developing the planned community of Reston, Virginia. He eventually became chief engineer of Gulf Oil and traveled the world for the company. In 2007 the last surviving Soviet spy on the Manhattan Project was retired and living at the Blue Ridge Country Club, a luxurious Lee Trevino–designed golf course and resort in the Blue Ridge Mountains of North Carolina that he had developed and built. When contacted, he recalled Julius Rosenberg, but the ninety-three-year-old former spy claimed to no longer remember anything else about his past association with him and declined an interview. He died in February, 2008.[14]

The Elusive Target: J. Robert Oppenheimer

As famous as Russell McNutt was obscure, J. Robert Oppenheimer was the chief technical architect of the Manhattan Project. Hailed as an American scientific hero after the detonation of atomic bombs over Japan and an influential voice in public and bureaucratic debates about nuclear weapons early in the Cold War, he was humiliated after losing his security clearance amid charges that he was either a spy or a concealed Communist. For more than a half a century Oppenheimer has been denounced as the most damaging Soviet spy inside the Manhattan Project or defended as an honorable man undone by false and politically motivated charges. KGB documents demonstrate that he was not a spy, although not for lack of KGB effort.

A leading theoretical physicist at the University of California, Berkeley, Oppenheimer had joined the atomic bomb project in early 1942, and his impressive performance persuaded project leaders that he might be the man to direct the principal secret facility that would actually build the device. In the fall of 1942 General Leslie Groves, military commander of the Manhattan Project, overruled skeptics who pointed to Oppenheimer's lack of a Nobel Prize and administrative experience and made him the scientific leader of the project and director of its Los Alamos, New Mexico, site. Oppenheimer turned out to be an inspired choice, able to manage the individualistic, egotistical, and prickly scientists unaccustomed to military ways. He was able to coordinate the scientific effort, manage the egos, and work out a *modus vivendi* between the soldiers and scientists that brought the atomic bomb project to a successful conclusion. Almost all historical assessments of the Manhattan Project have judged his role to be one of the key factors in its success.

When General Groves chose Oppenheimer as the project's scientific director, most senior scientists welcomed or at least acceded to the choice. Army security officers, however, were appalled. Robert Oppenheimer had been an ardent Popular Front liberal and ally of the Communist Party from the late 1930s until early 1942, and his sympathy for the Communist cause had been strong enough to withstand the Nazi-Soviet Pact of August 1939. Army security and FBI agents also were aware that he and his wife socialized with Steve Nelson, San Francisco Bay Area CPUSA leader and, to the certain knowledge of security officers, a conduit between the Communist Party and Soviet intelligence. Oppenheimer's wife, Katherine, had been a Communist and married to Joseph Dallet, a full-time Communist functionary who had died while serving as a political commissar with the International Brigades in the Spanish Civil War. Security officials also thought it likely that his younger brother, Frank Oppenheimer (also a physicist), and Frank's wife were concealed Communists, and a number suspected that Robert was one as well. (Frank vehemently denied Communist Party membership until 1949. He then admitted he had joined the party in 1937 and remained a member until 1941.) General Groves understood the basis for the concern, but he judged Oppenheimer the man for the job of scientific director and trusted him. He overrode military security and ordered that Oppenheimer be given the appropriate clearances for access to all atomic bomb project information.

After the end of the Manhattan Project, Oppenheimer briefly returned to the University of California before he became director of the Institute for Advanced Study at Princeton, New Jersey. He also continued to be one of the chief advisers to the U.S. government on nuclear weapons development. Doubts about his loyalty persisted and were exacerbated by harsh personal conflicts between Oppenheimer and other nuclear scientists, military officials, and civilian policymakers over development of the hydrogen bomb. In 1954 the Atomic Energy Commission (AEC) held a hearing on whether his security clearance should be revoked. During the AEC proceeding Oppenheimer admitted to a series of friendships with Communists, membership in Communist front groups, the signing of letters and petitions supporting Communist causes, and regular donations of large sums of money (he had considerable private means) to party causes through Isaac Folkoff, a veteran California Communist. (Folkoff, American security officials knew, also had ties to Soviet intelligence.) He insisted there was nothing sinister in these activities and, further, that he had long since changed his views. He adamantly denied ever being a secret member of the Communist Party.

Evidence that has accumulated over the years indicates that Oppenheimer had lied and had been a secret member of the Communist Party and active in a secret Communist faculty club at the University of California as late as 1941. FBI telephone taps and listening devices in the early 1940s overheard senior officials of the San Francisco Bay Communist Party refer to the Oppenheimer brothers as members of the party but no longer active. Also confirming his membership are three other items: first, an unpublished memoir by Gordon Griffiths (a historian and fellow member of the U.C. Berkeley faculty Communist club) in which Griffiths discussed his and Oppenheimer's participation in the Communist unit; second, the private journal of Barbara Chevalier about her late husband Haakon Chevalier, a professor of French literature, in which she wrote of her husband joining the U.C. Berkeley Communist club at the same time as his close friend Robert Oppenheimer; third, a 1964 Haakon Chevalier letter to Oppenheimer indicating that in his forthcoming memoir Chevalier would confirm that they had both been members of the Berkeley faculty Communist club. (Oppenheimer replied that he would publicly repudiate Chevalier, and when his book appeared, Chevalier instead said they had been members of a Marxist discussion group rather than a party unit.) The evidence also indicates that after 1941 Oppenheimer's political attitudes shifted. He counseled junior scientists to abandon Communist activities, and by late 1943 Oppenheimer was assisting Manhattan Project security officers in identifying and removing security risks from the project.[15]

An episode that contributed most directly to Oppenheimer's loss of his security clearance began in August 1943, when he informed Manhattan Project security officers that he had indirect information that someone had approached several scientists with requests to provide sensitive information to the USSR. Pressed for details by General Groves, Oppenheimer after considerable delay changed his story: the approach had been made to his brother Frank, who had then consulted him. According to Oppenheimer's new version, his friend Professor Haakon Chevalier had asked Frank to provide atomic bomb secrets in early 1943, and Oppenheimer had then personally rebuked Chevalier for the suggestion. Chevalier told Oppenheimer that he had been approached by George Eltenton, a chemical engineer who had worked in the Soviet Union. Eltenton asked Chevalier to act as an intermediary to feel out a number of Manhattan Project scientists about privately sharing information (a polite euphemism for spying) with the USSR.

Oppenheimer had difficulty explaining to General Groves why he had not reported the incident until months later and why his initial report had been inaccurate. He also explained some things to Groves about his brother Frank's role and asked Groves not to share the information with Army security. Oppenheimer also provided information to Army security about several young scientists at the University of California, Berkeley, including Giovanni Rossi Lomanitz, Joseph Weinberg, and David Bohm, whom he knew to be close to the Communist Party and whose ideological loyalties raised questions of their trustworthiness. (All were excluded from Manhattan Project work.) To complicate matters more, in 1946 Oppenheimer gave a third version of the incident to the FBI, stating that only he had been approached by Chevalier and leaving his brother Frank entirely out of the story.[16]

Chevalier, for his part, denied Communist loyalties and said that he had only casually mentioned to Oppenheimer that George Eltenton had raised the sharing of information with the USSR with him but that he, Chevalier, had rejected the suggestion at once. It is now clear that Chevalier was a concealed Communist and so was Eltenton, whom U.S. security officers observed meeting on several occasions in 1942 with Peter Ivanov, a GRU officer operating out of the Soviet consulate in San Francisco. The FBI questioned Eltenton in 1946. He admitted that at the request of Ivanov he had asked Chevalier to approach Oppenheimer and urge him to give the Soviets information about his scientific work. Unlike Chevalier, Eltenton did not attempt to pass off his activities as trivial, admitting to the FBI that he had a contact at the Soviet Consulate and that the information from Oppenheimer was to be transmitted by concealed microfilm. Eltenton said that Chevalier reported back that Oppenheimer had refused to cooperate, and he, Eltenton, so informed Ivanov.[17]

Deciphered KGB cables released in the mid-1990s provided very little information about Oppenheimer and Soviet espionage. His name appeared in several messages in clear text when various Soviet sources reported on which scientists were supervising various aspects of the Manhattan Project. These are reports *about* him by Soviet spies, not reports *from* him. None suggested any compromised relationship with Soviet intelligence.[18]

Two messages contain the cover name "Veksel," whom NSA/FBI analysts identified as Robert Oppenheimer. These mentions also were benign or ambiguous. In any case, documents recorded in Vassiliev's notebooks make it clear that this is one of the few cases where NSA/FBI analysts erred in an identification: "Veksel" was Enrico Fermi, not Robert Oppenheimer.[19]

The documents in Vassiliev's notebooks, however, contain a great deal of information about Oppenheimer, the KGB's high hopes that he might be recruited, and its ensuing lengthy pursuit of him. The KGB had a small station operating out of the Soviet consulate in San Francisco. In December 1942 the San Francisco station chief, Grigory Kheifets (officially Soviet vice-consul), sent Moscow information on a Communist scientist known to Louise Bransten. The latter was a wealthy San Francisco political activist and so close to Kheifets that she was frequently referred to as his mistress. The FBI, which closely monitored her activities during World War II, described her as "the hub of a wheel, the spokes thereof representing the many facets of her pro-Soviet activities, running from mere membership in the Communist Party . . . to military and industrial espionage and political and propaganda activities."[20]

Bransten's scientist acquaintance was Alfred Marshak, a prominent geneticist at the University of California, Berkeley, described as "devoted to us and honest," who had ties to both Ernest Lawrence and Robert Oppenheimer, and "might be of interest." (Lawrence, a Nobel Prize winner, was a close colleague of Oppenheimer and a leading Manhattan Project physicist.) Late in January 1943 Moscow Center told Kheifets, "The neighbors [GRU] have been cultivating Robert Oppenheimer since June 1942," but "his recruitment does not seem possible." This may have been a reflection of the fact that GRU officer Ivanov had heard from Steve Nelson that Oppenheimer had been distancing himself from his earlier Communist connections as his involvement with the Manhattan Project increased. It may also have reflected the failed effort initiated by Ivanov to approach the Oppenheimer brothers via Eltenton and Chevalier, although possibly this occurred later in 1943. In view of Moscow Center's message that GRU was already attempting to approach Oppenheimer, Kheifets apparently dropped his notion of using Marshak to approach the physicist.[21]

But Moscow Center's frustration with the lack of progress in penetrating the Manhattan Project grew. In July 1943 it rebuked the KGB New York station: "'In the presence of this research work, vast both in scale and scope, being conducted right here next to you, the slow pace of agent cultivation in the USA is particularly intolerable. Instead of grabbing onto the smallest opportunities and developing them further, you are not even following the specific courses of action that were suggested to you on the basis of reports that you yourself sent over.'" In August Pavel Fitin, chief of KGB foreign intelligence, summarized atomic intelligence in a report to KGB chief Merkulov. Fitin allowed that "'the state of agent cultivation of this problem and its outlook continues to be unsatisfactory, especially in the USA.'" He then offered a solution: take over GRU's atomic sources and prospects:

"1. The material received from our agents shows that work on the investigation of a new, extremely powerful energy source—'Enormous'—is being conducted at a very intensive pace in the USA and England and is growing ever larger in scale. This problem has received a great deal of attention, it has been allotted extensive scientific and material support, and is being worked on by a large contingent of leading physicists. As a result even now, despite wartime conditions, exceedingly interesting and important results have been achieved, especially in the USA. This problem has major national economic significance, and the application of these works' results will be most significant primarily in the postwar period. A specific issue is the application and use of the results for military technology, namely for the manufacture of uranium bombs. . . . The special laboratory at the Academy of Sciences, established at our request by a GKO [State Defense Committee] resolution for the purposes of expediting our leading scientists' work on 'Enormous' and realizing the results of the works of English and Amer. scientists through the use of agent materials we have obtained, is still in its organizational stage. The organizational pace is entirely unsatisfactory and the project is taking a very long time to get going.

2. Despite certain achievements by a section of the intelligence operation in obtaining information on the work being done in England and the USA

on 'Enormous,' the state of agent cultivation of this problem and its outlook continues to be unsatisfactory, especially in the USA. As you know, both we and the GRU NKO [Soviet military intelligence] are working simultaneously on the agent cultivation of this problem. . . . By simultaneously cultivating the same narrow, and at the same time authoritative, circle of scientists and specialists as the GRU, we are essentially doubling our work. This creates unhealthy competition at work; the same people are cultivated and recruited (May, Henry Norman—in London; Oppenheimer—in San Francisco and oth.), which leads to useless expenditure of time and energy and could inevitably lead to the exposure of our intentions, plans, and intelligence activities, and ultimately even to exposures. Therefore, I think it would be expedient to consolidate efforts to cultivate this problem in the 1st Directorate of the NKGB USSR [KGB foreign intelligence] and to give it all available GRU agents."

In November 1943 Moscow Center notified Vasily Zarubin, New York KGB station chief: "It is proposed to have agents on 'Enormous' handed over from the neighbors [GRU] to us." Anticipating this, Moscow pointed out: "Charon [Kheifets] has a possible means of approach to Oppenheimer" and noted also that a West Coast KGB source, "Erie," knew Oppenheimer. "Erie" was Paul Nahin, a chemist working for the Union Oil Company in California.[22]

In February 1944 Moscow Center prepared a report summarizing where "Enormous" stood. Somewhat more positive than in the prior year, it noted that at long last the KGB had added some sources in America's Manhattan atomic project to those it had in Britain's "Tube Alloys" project. But Robert Oppenheimer was not among the new sources, only on a wish list of prospects:

"Of the leads we have, we should consider it essential to cultivate the following people: 'Chester'—Robert Oppenheimer, b. 1906, an Amer. Jew, secret member of the fellowcountryman org. [CPUSA], a professor at the U. of California, works on 'En-s' ["Enormous"] in the field of rapid neutrons; he oversees the construction of the Califor. cyclotron. In view of the special significance and importance of the work he does, he is supposedly kept under special security, and as a result the fellowcountryman organization received orders from its center to break off relations with 'Ch.' to avoid his exposure. 'Ch.' is of great interest to us. The fact that he is a fellowcountryman, as well as his friendly attitude toward our country, gives us reason to expect that his cultivation will yield positive results."

Not only was the KGB *not* in contact with Oppenheimer in February 1944, but it also didn't have anyone close enough to him to provide accurate information about his work. He was a theoretical physicist, and it was his colleague, Ernest Lawrence, who presided over the cyclotron. Nor was there any indication that the KGB understood that Oppenheimer was by that time the director of the Los Alamos facility. It also had his birthdate wrong (1904, not 1906). Nor was the KGB even certain as to whether GRU had succeeded in contacting him and had received no background briefing on what GRU had learned about him: "'According to our information, the neighbors [GRU] have been cultivating 'Ch.' ["Chester"/Oppenheimer] since June 1942. If 'Ch.' has been recruited by them, it is essential to make his transfer over to us official. If he has not been recruited, obtain all available materials on 'Ch.' from the neighbors and begin actively cultivating him through the means of approach available to us.'" The report also suggested approaching Oppenheimer through Louise Bransten and Alfred Marshak, the same people who had been cited in 1943 and who had, for whatever reason, not gotten the job done. It did suggest a third possible contact, Olga Neyman. Neyman was the Russian-born wife of a leading theoretical statistician and professor of mathematics at the University of California, Berkeley. The KGB had recruited her in London in 1935. This report also suggested that the KGB's American officers "'begin cultivating 'Ch.'s' brother—'Beam' [Frank Oppenheimer], also a professor at the U. of California and a member of the fellowcountryman organization, though politically he is closer to us than 'Ch.'''" Essentially, however, this February 1944 report indicated that the KGB was no closer to contacting Oppenheimer than it had been earlier.[23]

Moscow Center had been unhappy with Kheifets's performance as San Francisco station chief for some time. In 1944 it recalled him to face scathing assessments of his work: "'The facts indicate that for almost a year 'Charon' [Kheifets] has done nothing concrete.'" He was accused of failing to make progress on scientific/technical intelligence and specifically faulted for not actively cultivating Marshak and Frank Oppenheimer. A memo prepared in March 1944 for the new San Francisco station chief, Grigory Kasparov, tasked him to "undertake active cultivation of individuals working on 'Enormous'" and listed several prominent Berkeley scientists as possible targets, among them Robert and Frank Oppenheimer. Again, Oppenheimer remained simply on the KGB's wish list with no evidence of contact. Nor had that changed by June 1944, when Moscow Center sent another harshly worded complaint about the limited success of the effort to obtain atomic intelligence. Moscow told the new KGB New York station chief, Stepan Apresyan: "'In the entire time that we have worked on "E" ["Enormous"], in spite of our constant reminders to implement various measures and a number of absolutely concrete suggestions—where to work, what to work on—we have nothing besides "Fogel" [McNutt]. "Rest" [Fuchs] does not count, b/c he was sent to you fully formed. We cannot consent to such a situation in the future.'" Again, there was no indication of any progress in approaching Robert Oppenheimer.[24]

In July 1944 Pavel Fitin sent a review of "Enormous" to KGB chief Merkulov that reported that Kheifets had "cultivated" Frank Oppenheimer. "Cultivation" in KGB tradecraft vocabulary was a term encompassing gathering background material and "feeling out" an individual either indirectly through intermediaries or directly. Often KGB officers used contacts in the CPUSA for indirect cultivation, and Fitin had noted that the lead to Frank Oppenheimer had been provided by Isaac Folkoff, the veteran California Communist leader. KGB officers under diplomatic cover, such as Kheifets, vice-consul at the Soviet consulate in San Francisco, directly cultivated individuals that they met in the course of diplomatic activities and at social events. Cultivation might result in a judgment that the target would be hostile or was otherwise inappropriate for recruitment as a source. If, however, the judgment was that he was likely to respond positively, then a direct recruitment contact would follow. Fitin's report had no details on the extent of contacts with Frank Oppenheimer, saying only "the cultivation was conducted by 'Charon' [Kheifets]." Aside from the cultivation of his younger brother, however, Fitin reported no progress on contacting Robert Oppenheimer: ""Chester" [Oppenheimer] was cultivated by the neighbors [GRU], and as a result the issue of recruiting him for us became moot, which we reported to "Charon" [Kheifets] on 15.01.43. Since Enormous has been turned over to us, he must now be actively cultivated." This was Fitin's mid-1944 view of what should be done and reflected the reality that up to that point KGB officers in America, particularly Kheifets, had failed to achieve contact with Oppenheimer.[25]

Oppenheimer remained an elusive target. A plan of action on "Enormous" approved by Fitin on 5 November 1944 excoriated the American station for recruiting only one agent working on the project—Russell Mc-Nutt—whose access was limited. (The KGB New York station had lost touch with Fuchs at this point.) Most of the valuable atomic intelligence, Fitin noted, was coming from England. Perhaps in part due to Moscow's frustration with the lack of success in obtaining atomic information, the KGB reorganized its apparatus in the United States. A Moscow Center cable on 10 November 1944 appointed senior KGB officer Leonid Kvasnikov to head a semi-independent scientific/technical intelligence sector with its own budget within the KGB New York station.[26]

The cable appointing Kvasnikov reminded him of the "importance of 'Enormous,' which interests Cde. Petrov personally." "Petrov" was the cover name in KGB communication for the much feared Lavrenty Beria, head of the People's Commissariat for Internal Affairs, who would in December formally take over supervision of the Soviet atomic bomb program. Moscow Center suggested: "Renew ties with "Ernst" [Nahin] through "Huron" [Darling], with the aim of using him to cultivate "Chester." "Chester"—Robert Oppenheimer, an Amer. Jew, a secret member of the fraternal, works in camp "y" [Los Alamos] on the development of the atomic bomb." The KGB, however, had been unable to get Darling, who worked in Detroit, to renew ties with Manhattan Project scientists in nearby Chicago, and nothing resulted from this suggestion that Darling go to the West Coast, where Nahin worked.[27]

In addition, Kvasnikov, despite having been given responsibility for atomic intelligence, didn't at that time have a clear picture of the leadership of the Manhattan Project. He queried Moscow in mid-December 1944 for additional information on Robert Oppenheimer and George Kistiakowsky because David Greenglass had mentioned them in one of his reports. (Having lost touch with Fuchs, the KGB's only source at Los Alamos then was Greenglass.) Moscow responded, "'All we know about them is that they work at Camp-2 [Los Alamos], and that O. [Oppenheimer] is a major authority who oversees the work at Camp-2.'" (Kistiakowsky, a physical chemist, directed the "implosion department" that designed the vital implosion trigger for the plutonium bomb.) By March 1945, however, Kvasnikov was able to report substantial progress. The KGB New York station was by that point running five sources on "Enormous." Three were at Los Alamos—Klaus Fuchs (back in contact), Theodore Hall (a recent "walk-in"), and David Greenglass—and two at Oak Ridge—Alfred Slack (just hired) and Russell McNutt. As for Robert Oppenheimer, there was no progress to report. He wasn't on the list of sources, he was still on the wish list, and Kvasnikov could only note that the KGB New York station would "work on the possibility of approaching Oppenheimer."[28]

Although the KGB New York station had gotten nowhere with approaching Oppenheimer as of March 1945, what of the San Francisco station? In July 1945 Semen Semenov, back in Moscow after several years as the senior technical/scientific intelligence officer of the KGB New York station, prepared a report on Kheifets's leads at the time the latter had departed from San Francisco in late July 1944. The contents suggest the report was based on Semenov's review of Kheifets's reports and on Kheifets's own defense of his tenure at San Francisco. On the Oppenheimer brothers, the report stated:

2. "Chester" is Robert Oppenheimer, a U.S. cit., born 1906, a secret fellow-countryman [Communist], a professor at the Univ. of Calif., works on the Enormous problem in the field of fast neutrons and is construction chief of the Calif. cyclotron. The lead for Chester was provided by Jack [Olga Neyman] and Uncle [Folkoff]. Cultivation was done by Charon [Kheifets] through Uncle and Map [Bransten]. Chester is close friends with "Lion" [Holland Roberts], who has a strong influence on Chester.
3. "Beam" is Frank Oppenheimer, a U.S. cit., a prof. at the Univ. of Calif., a radio expert. The lead came from Uncle, the cultivation done by Charon. Beam is a friend of Lion. Cultivation can be done through Uncle and Lion. Contact through Uncle.

This report indicated a variety of things. It reflected Kheifets's and Semenov's limited understanding of whom and what they were dealing with. Frank Oppenheimer was not a "radio expert" but a physicist who dealt with radiation. And it repeated earlier faulty information that Robert Oppenheimer was "construction chief of the Calif. cyclotron" while not appearing to know that Oppenheimer was director of the laboratories at Los Alamos and the single most important scientist in the Manhattan Project.[29]

As with Fitin's July 1944 report, this July 1945 report noted that Kheifets had cultivated Frank Oppenheimer. It went on to suggest that the cultivation be renewed through Folkoff of the CPUSA and Holland Roberts. Roberts was a professor of education at Stanford University. Likely neither Kheifets nor Semenov knew that in 1944 Stanford had not renewed his contract (he was untenured), an action possibly reflecting disquiet with his radical political activity. He then joined the Communist-aligned California Labor School in San Francisco. In any event, while the report stated that Roberts had been "prepared for recruitment as a talent-spotter, background-checker, and recruiter," the recruitment had not taken place before Kheifets departed, so nothing further had been done to use Roberts to approach Frank Oppenheimer. This July 1945 report stated that Robert Oppenheimer had been recommended to Kheifets by Folkoff and Olga Neyman and cultivated indirectly by Folkoff and Louise Bransten up to the time of Kheifets's departure (July 1944). Semenov recommended attempting to renew the cultivation through Isaac Folkoff.

The most striking part of Semenov's report, however, was his declaration: "Since Charon [Kheifets] left, no work on XY has been done in the Western U.S." Semenov's report, consequently, was not only a summary of how KGB scientific/technical intelligence (the "XY" line in KGB terminology) stood on the West Coast in July 1944 but also where it stood in July 1945. And with reference to Robert Oppenheimer, this indicated only preliminary indirect cultivation through old Communist Party colleagues with not only no recruitment, but also no direct contact with the KGB.[30]

The dearth of technical intelligence work from the KGB San Francisco station can be explained by poor leadership and the press of other business. Kheifets hadn't been very effective at it; his replacement, Grigory Kasparov, had been transferred to Mexico City less than six months after taking over; and Kasparov's replacement, Stepan Apresyan, was a junior officer who had become acting New York station chief in 1944. Apresyan had had a difficult time in New York, and at his new post he concentrated on political intelligence and was consumed with preparations, both diplomatic and espionage-related, for the founding conference of the United Nations, held in San Francisco from April through June 1945. In these circumstances, the small San Francisco station pushed technical/scientific intelligence to the side. In his July 1945 report, Semenov urged establishing a dedicated XY section as part of the KGB San Francisco station and possibly one in the KGB's even smaller substation in Los Angeles as well.[31]

In the latter half of 1945 Robert Oppenheimer continued to be on the KGB's wish list, not its agent list. Fitin again reviewed the KGB's work on "Enormous" for Merkulov in August 1945, crediting his agency with some success: "'Active agent cultivation of the problem of E. ["Enormous"] in the USA was begun in 1942. Since then, a network of agents, with very interesting and important opportunities through their official jobs, has been created within the NY station's organization. Distributed among the most important centers of work on 'En-s,' these agents give extremely valuable information, both on the substance of the scientific research and on the progress of research.'" Fitin's memo named the KGB's principal sources, and Oppenheimer was not among them. In September Leonid Kvasnikov and Andrey Shevchenko, leading XY line officers at the KGB New York station, sent a review of New York station activities on "Enormous" operations to Merkulov. They reported that they had sent Byron Darling to meet with Joseph Weinberg, the Berkeley physicist and one-time Oppenheimer protégé in hopes of using him as a link to Oppenheimer. Darling met with Weinberg in New York in early October 1945, and Weinberg told him that "'he does not see 'Yew' [Oppenheimer] at all these days'" and, moreover, Oppenheimer "'had changed and was losing his left convictions.'"[32]

Oppenheimer was also the subject of a lengthy October 1945 report written by Charles Kramer, a KGB source on the staff of U.S. Senator Harley Kilgore. Kramer had attended a Washington breakfast in late September at which Oppenheimer discussed with Senator Kilgore pending legislation dealing with control of atomic energy in the postwar environment. This was an intense political controversy at the time, with the U.S. military supporting continued Pentagon control over nuclear weapons production and tight federal government control over nuclear power and other atomic research. A vocal section of leftists and liberals, however, was attempting to minimize the military's role and pushing for the United States to relinquish control to an international body that would include the USSR in its governing structure and would share American nuclear secrets with the world. A number of junior and some senior Manhattan Project scientists vigorously supported the proposal to internationalize control of nuclear energy and hoped that Oppenheimer, then at the peak of his prestige, would support their views. Kramer's report of Oppenheimer's views was not one to please the Soviets:

"Oppenheimer is playing a curious role in the entire atomic energy discussions now going on inside and outside of government. As noted last week, his central position seems to be that nations must arrive at profound political collaboration in the atomic age or face disaster. This is the theme which he seems to propound publicly to most groups and individuals. At the same time he has consistently supported the War Department and its scientific henchmen, Vannevar Bush and James B. Conant in their attempts to rush through the warlike May-Johnson Bill to set up an Atomic Energy Commission for so-called 'purely domestic aspects' of atomic energy, even though most of his fellow workers on the atomic bomb disagree violently with the bill and all of them desire that greater consideration be given to the bill before rushing it through to passage.

At present a wide breach is developing between Oppenheimer and the younger scientists who have to date practically worshipped him not only for his scientific acumen but for his political sagacity as well. Last week, before the hearings reopened on the May-Johnson Bill in the House Military Affairs Committee, O-r was striving desperately to maintain a united front of the scientific workers, particularly the top level of physicists, to prevent any open break with the War Department and the Administration on its desire to get the bill put

through quickly. He was unsuccessful, as you have seen from the newspapers—
two associates, Dr. Leo Szilard and Dr. H. L. Anderson, came out openly
against the bill, while O-r and Arthur Compton came out supporting the bill,
although with some amendments in O-r's case. O-r's position (as explained by
some of his opponents and as have been gathered from his own remarks) is that
the present research work would go to pieces unless something immediately is
done to continue the work on atomic energy. He thus separates the so-called
'domestic' problems from the foreign or international problems, and says that
the United States must continue its work in atomic energy, even with the May
Johnson Bill's imperfections, even though the international political problems
are not taken care of. At the same time he argues publicly that the international
aspects, that is, the political relations with other countries, is of more decisive
importance than the domestic ones, and repeat the warning that we must learn
to live with other nations or be destroyed. Under questioning by Senators Ful-
bright, Magnuson and Kilgore, in public hearings last Wednesday, he even said,
This may not only be the last war, but the last victory, meaning that no nation
would survive an atomic war. But when a group of younger scientists testified at
the same hearings that we must perform a miracle in political science and international relations if we are to consider any developments in, or attempt to keep
atomic energy research secret, O-r termed their view in effect as political
naiveté. While the bulk of the younger physicists and other scientists are opposed to the May-Johnson Bill, and are opposed to secrecy, O-r seems to take
his stand with those scientific bureaucrats who want to keep it secret under the
terms of the May-Johnson Bill."

Kramer evaluated Oppenheimer as a liberal "'in need of conversation
and guidance from the 'right kind of people.'"[33]

Vassiliev's notebooks also contain notes on a plan of action prepared
for KGB chief Merkulov to expand the number of agents working on
Enormous. This plan is undated, but the context in the notebook suggests the fall of 1945, likely in October. It was authored by Lev Vasilevsky,
formerly the KGB station chief in Mexico City but in 1945 an officer back
in Moscow, and approved by General Fitin, head of KGB foreign intelligence. Vasilevsky noted: "'We have done no work in the western USA on
'Enormous,' or on the XY line as a whole, since the start of 1944, owing
to the absence of operatives there who could be entrusted with this matter.'" Echoing Semenov's suggestions of July for dedicated XY line sections, Vasilevsky urged setting up a new operations center on the West
Coast that would focus on work at the University of California, and he
listed three targets for the new technical intelligence section: Ernest
Lawrence and the still elusive Oppenheimer brothers.[34]

Nothing came from any of the plans, however. The defection of Gouzenko, Bentley, and Budenz in the fall of 1945 devastated KGB operations. The KGB withdrew most of its senior field officers, ambitious plans for new recruitment were put aside, and the depleted KGB stations focused on damage control. Oppenheimer remained on a KGB list, but not as a prospective recruit. In February 1950, following Fuchs's arrest, Andrey Raina, a senior officer in Moscow Center, drew up a plan of operational measures to deal with the developing furor in the United States over atomic espionage. One of his goals was to find

ways to discredit certain leading reactionary scientists working on the atomic problem in the USA and England. . . . "To look into the possibility and advisability of discrediting the Amer. scientists: a) Urey, Grosse, and Smith, who are currently working on the atomic problem. b) The designer of the first atomic bomb, Opp-mer [Oppenheimer]. . . . c) Reactionary scientist and defector Gamow, who left the USSR in 1933. d) The prominent, Hungarian-born scientist from U. of Chicago, Szilard. . . . e) The head of the general physics division at the Eng. atomic center, the German fascist Skinner."[35]

More than a score of KGB archival documents, spanning the period from 1942 to 1950 and quoted or summarized in Vassiliev's notebooks, directly or indirectly indicate that Robert Oppenheimer was not a KGB source and was never in communication with a KGB officer. This point requires some emphasis because of the continuing controversy over whether he was or was not a Soviet spy. Both Army security and the FBI were suspicious of Oppenheimer due to his Communist ties and subjected him to intense scrutiny, but neither agency found evidence to conclude that he was cooperating with Soviet intelligence. No charges were brought or even proposed. A minority of security officers, however, disagreed. In 1953, for example, William Borden, earlier staff director for the congressional Joint Committee on Atomic Energy, sent a letter to J. Edgar Hoover that reviewed the evidence and concluded: "The purpose of this letter is to state my own exhaustively considered opinion, based upon years of study, of the available classified evidence that more probably than not J. Robert Oppenheimer is an agent of the Soviet Union." While most historians have concluded that Oppenheimer was innocent of espionage, a minority have felt he either was a spy or might well have been one. In recent years those suspicious of Oppenheimer have received support from two sources.[36]

One was the already mentioned memoir of KGB general Pavel Sudoplatov. Sudoplatov had a long career in the KGB, overseeing assassinations of Soviet defectors among other tasks, and in 1945 and 1946 heading a KGB department that depersonalized the KGB's atomic intelligence to remove information that might identify the sources before it was forwarded to Igor Kurchatov, scientific chief of the Soviet bomb program. Sudoplatov was closely associated with Lavrenty Beria, and when Beria fell from power in 1953, Sudoplatov was imprisoned for fifteen years for his role in KGB tests of lethal poisons on live prisoners. With the assistance of his son and American journalists Jerrold and Leona Schecter he published his memoir, *Special Tasks,* in 1994. Covering his long career in Soviet internal security and foreign intelligence (he joined the original Cheka in 1921), the book was welcomed by many historians for the light it shed on obscure matters, such as the 1938 assassination of exiled Ukrainian nationalist leader Yevhen Konovalets (personally carried out by Sudoplatov).

But, as noted above, Sudoplatov's chapter on atomic espionage created a sensation and was hotly contested. He flatly stated that "Oppenheimer, Fermi, Szilard . . . were often quoted in the NKVD files form 1942 to 1945 as sources for information on the development of the first American atomic bomb" and that "they agreed to share information on nuclear weapons with Soviet scientists." Sudoplatov claimed that Kheifets met Oppenheimer twice, once on 6 December 1941, when Oppenheimer first informed him of American interest in the uranium problem, and later in order to report to Moscow that scientists were planning to move to a new site to conduct research. Sudoplatov wrote that early in 1943 Italian physicist Bruno Pontecorvo informed the KGB that Enrico Fermi was prepared to hand over information. Sudoplatov credited Elizabeth Zarubin (KGB officer and wife of KGB station chief Vasily Zarubin) with traveling frequently to California, where she cultivated Oppenheimer's wife; persuaded Oppenheimer himself to recruit Klaus Fuchs to work at Los Alamos; and solicited Oppenheimer, Fermi, and Szilard to help "us place moles in Tennessee, Los Alamos and Chicago." The information from Los Alamos was transmitted via a covert KGB station operating out of a drugstore in Santa Fe, New Mexico, near Los Alamos. In total, according to Sudoplatov, Oppenheimer passed along five classified reports.[37]

The first point that needs to be taken into account is that *Special Tasks* was a memoir, written by a man in his late eighties about events that took place forty years earlier and during which he played no direct role but was a staff officer at Moscow Center. While memoirs are a valuable source of information, historians know that in relying on them, one must keep in mind such problems as poor memory, errors about details, embellishment, self-service, sensationalism, and outright deception. Critics also quickly noted obvious mistakes and flaws in the story. Among other errors, Sudoplatov gave Oppenheimer and Fermi a shared cover name, "Star," but when the Venona decryptions were released in 1995, it was clear that cover name actually belonged to Saville Sax, Theodore Hall's courier. Historians of the Manhattan Project also found that Oppenheimer had nothing to do with Fuchs's assignment to Los Alamos. Nor was there independent evidence that Elizabeth Zarubin had ever met Katherine Oppenheimer. While there is some evidence to suggest that the KGB might have had a covert safe house in Santa Fe in the late 1930s as a way station for its operations against the exiled Leon Trotsky in Mexico (assassinated by a KGB agent in 1940), there is no indication that this facility, if it existed, remained in use during the Los Alamos atomic period. There is a great deal of detail available about the travels of such couriers as Saville Sax, Harry Gold, and Lona Cohen, all of whom made careful and risky journeys to New Mexico to collect information from KGB sources at Los Alamos. Harry Gold, for example, made a full confession of his activities. But nothing indicates that these couriers stopped at a Santa Fe drugstore.[38]

The Schecters, who had assisted in writing Sudoplatov's memoir, added new specifications to the indictment of Oppenheimer in a new book, *Sacred Secrets*, in 2002. They dropped Sudoplatov's claim that Oppenheimer's cover name was "Star" and agreed that it was "Chester," a cover name that first appeared in Weinstein and Vassiliev's 1999 *Haunted Wood*. They wrote that Kitty Harris, a Canadian Communist and veteran KGB agent, had located two old KGB covert agents in California, one of whom was close to the Oppenheimer family. Through one of them, they asserted, Elizabeth Zarubin had recruited Robert Oppenheimer. And, they added, Elizabeth Zarubin arranged for atomic secrets to be funneled through the drugstore in Santa Fe to Kitty Harris, assigned to the KGB's Mexico City station, thus bypassing the New York station. This convoluted system allowed the Schecters to account for the absence of Venona traffic to support their story. Except it didn't. Elizabeth Zarubin was an officer of the KGB New York station and wife of its station chief. Her activities would have been known to the KGB New York station and routinely reported to Moscow. Additionally, the Venona project deciphered a number of KGB cables between Moscow Center and its Mexico City station. No corroboration of the Schecters' narrative can be found in the Venona traffic or in Vassiliev's notebooks.[39]

The Schecters reproduced a single KGB document to support the charge that Oppenheimer had supplied information to the KGB, a memo to Beria from Merkulov dated 2 October 1944. Reporting on the efforts to garner atomic information, Merkulov claimed that important information had been gleaned via Grigory Kheifets: "In 1942 one of the leaders of scientific work on uranium in the USA, Professor R. Oppenheimer, while being an unlisted member of the apparatus of Comrade Browder, informed us about the beginning of work." The memo went on to credit Oppenheimer, at Kheifets and Browder's request, with providing "cooperation in access to research for several of our tested sources, including a relative of Comrade Browder." The Schecters provided no explanation of where they got the document and cite no archival source.[40]

It is, nonetheless, possible that the document is genuine. If genuine, it contains information that, in light of Vassiliev's notebooks and the Venona decryptions, greatly embellishes the status of KGB atomic intelligence at that time. Its claim that Oppenheimer, while a secret member of the CPUSA in 1942, informed the Soviets about the beginning of work on an atomic bomb is congruent with Steve Nelson's claim to Joseph Weinberg (discussed below) that Oppenheimer had told him about the preliminary atomic bomb research being done at Berkeley prior to Oppenheimer's joining the Manhattan Project. The claim that Oppenheimer had enabled Soviet sources to gain access to atomic research may be an exaggerated comment on the number of Communists hired to work on "Enormous." In its early stages Oppenheimer had been indifferent to the Communist background of his protégés at the Radiation Laboratory at Berkeley; it was, after all, a background he shared. But Oppenheimer began to distance himself from his old CPUSA ties and counseled his younger colleagues to do so as well. And in 1943 he identified those who were still active in Communist affairs to Army security, resulting in their exclusion from participation in the project. There is no evidence that a relative of Browder's ever worked on the Manhattan Project.

Points in the document and in the discussion of Oppenheimer in *Sacred Secrets* are contradicted by numerous KGB documents quoted in Vassiliev's notebooks. In 1944 Moscow Center recalled Kheifets from San Francisco; the reason was stated in several KGB documents already quoted and summed up in a Pavel Fitin note of November 1944: "Kheifets recalled from the U.S. for failing to cope with his job." Kheifets arrived back in Moscow in August and wrote a report defending his work, dated 9 September 1944, one month before the Merkulov memo to Beria produced by the Schecters. In his report he discussed his contacts in the scientific community in the San Francisco area. At no point does he even hint he ever met directly with Robert Oppenheimer and notes only having heard about Oppenheimer's left-wing politics and pro-Soviet inclination from Louise Bransten and George Eltenton. He discusses his cultivation of Stanford professor Holland Roberts because he believed Roberts was a friend of Oppenheimer. He specifically notes: "'Lion' [Roberts] prepared a meeting with 'Chemist' [Oppenheimer] for me, but for various reasons the meeting fell through." Kheifets suggested an excuse for his lack of contact with Oppenheimer, noting that the link to Robert and Frank Oppenheimer had been via the CPUSA but that Isaac Folkoff, the party's West Coast liaison with the KGB, had told him that after the Oppenheimer brothers joined the Manhattan Project, "due to their special military work, the connection with them was suspended." Kheifets also refers to the KGB's belief that GRU might have been cultivating Oppenheimer and that he "was supposed to be turned over to us. This matter, however, has not moved forward."[41]

By Kheifets's own statements, he had *not* had contact with Oppenheimer before leaving San Francisco in late July 1944, contradicting Sudoplatov's claims and the Merkulov document the Schecters produced from an unidentified source. And what of the complex scheme by which Kitty Harris, working with Lev Vasilevsky, chief of the KGB Mexico City station, used old KGB contacts in California to connect Elizabeth Zarubin with the Oppenheimers? It was Vasilevsky who authored the late 1945 Moscow Center action plan (discussed above) that declared one of the KGB goals as contacting the Oppenheimer brothers. If his subordinate, Harris, had already done so when Vasilevsky had been running the Mexico City station, he would not have included this goal in his plan.[42]

The claim advanced by Sudoplatov and supported by the Schecters that Oppenheimer had direct contact with the KGB and actively assisted Soviet atomic espionage was based on one man's memory (an inherently weak source) and sparse documentation with no provenance. It is not only not corroborated by the ample KGB documentation in Vassiliev's notebooks and in the Venona traffic, but it is also directly and repeatedly contradicted. Additionally, Sudoplatov's allegations about Enrico Fermi and Leo Szilard are also unsupported. The extensive material in Vassiliev's notebooks about the KGB's Enormous project does not show any contact, or even attempted contact, with Szilard. The KGB did attempt to reach Fermi, but Vassiliev's notebooks show that the American agent chosen for the task, Byron Darling, never carried out the mission.

On the evidence, Oppenheimer's ties to the Communist Party up through 1941 were very strong. He was not simply a casual Popular Front liberal who ignorantly bumped up against the CPUSA in some of the arenas in which it operated. He was, in fact, a concealed member of the CPUSA in the late 1930s and appears to have dropped out of the party in early 1942. Until he went to Army security officials and General Groves in 1943, Oppenheimer's attitude toward possible Communist espionage came very close to complete indifference. It was as if at some point in the first half of 1943 his views had changed sufficiently that he realized that there actually was a serious security issue involved. Even then, it appeared he wanted only to give security officials enough information to neutralize the problem but not enough to expose associates to prosecution for what they already might have done. (They were, however, excluded from the project.) This paralleled a shift in his political views in which he increasingly distanced himself from the CPUSA and its ideology. While the weight of the evidence argues overwhelmingly against Oppenheimer as an active Soviet source, there is one matter that cannot be ruled out. The possibility exists that up to the time he reported the Chevalier approach to security officials in mid-1943, he may have turned a blind eye to the conduct of others whom he had reasonable grounds to suspect, a passivity motivated by his personal and political ties to them.

Throughout his life Oppenheimer declined to provide a detailed or accurate accounting of his relationship with the CPUSA in the late 1930s and early 1940s and of his knowledge of Communists who worked on the Manhattan Project. It was this unwillingness to speak honestly about his ties to the Communist movement that ultimately gave his critics the ammunition that led to Oppenheimer's loss of his security clearance in 1954. With what is known in 2008, it is clear that in 1954 Oppenheimer was not a security risk, and his continued possession of a security clearance and advice on nuclear issues were in America's interest. But those making the decision in 1954 did not have the benefit of what is now known. What they had to contend with was clear evidence that Robert Oppenheimer had in the past and in sworn testimony before the Atomic Energy Commission knowingly lied about his past relationship to the Communist Party. That they would decide to deny him a security clearance under those circumstances was understandable. On the more important question of espionage, however, the documents recorded in Vassiliev's notebooks add evidence of such quality and quantity that the case for Oppenheimer's innocence of the charge of assisting Soviet espionage is overwhelming: the case is closed.

The KGB's "Enormous": Frustration and Success

The stories of Russell McNutt and Robert Oppenheimer were part of the complicated and convoluted story of the KGB's pursuit of atomic information. Moscow received definite word of the existence of the American atomic bomb program in March 1942. For the next two years Soviet intelligence pursued a variety of leads and prospects, none of which yielded significant results. Ultimately, however, it succeeded. The USSR detonated its first nuclear bomb on 29 August 1949, at least two years before Western intelligence had predicted. The Red bomb was a copy of the American "Fat Man," the plutonium implosion bomb dropped on Nagasaki on 9 August 1945, and a dramatic demonstration of the greatest triumph of Soviet intelligence.

Nuclear physics had made great strides in the 1920s and 1930s, and by the late 1930s leading scientists in several nations realized that the enormous energy released by the splitting of the atom could potentially fuel a weapon of staggering destructiveness. Germany, Great Britain, France, and the Soviet Union possessed highly talented nuclear physicists capable of designing an atomic bomb. Building a working weapon, however, was more than a matter of scientific talent. It required an astoundingly large investment of industrial, engineering, and technological resources in research and development to figure out what theoretical approaches could be realized in a practical form. Equipment, devices, and massive industrial facilities had to be designed, built, redesigned, and rebuilt before success was achieved. France's nascent atomic energy program came to a halt with the country's defeat and occupation in 1940. Nazi Germany, possessing some of the world's most talented nuclear physicists, started an atomic project, but with its industrial resources strained by more immediate war needs, the program made only limited progress. Similarly, the USSR established a project, but with its resources fully mobilized for conventional military requirements, the Soviets had little more than a scientific office preparing plans for a postwar effort. Great Britain established an atomic program but quickly realized that it could not divert sufficient industrial resources from its other war commitments to get very far. While the Soviets turned to espionage, Britain finessed the difficulty by temporarily merging its effort with the American atomic bomb program, the Manhattan Project. During World War II, the United States was the sole nation with industrial, engineering, and technological resources of sufficient depth that it could not only supply its own armed forces with everything they needed but also supply, through Lend-Lease, significant additions to the British and Soviet war effort *and* make the staggering investment necessary to produce the working atomic bombs that ended the war against Japan in 1945.

The KGB's "Enormous" supplied the Soviet atomic project with about ten thousand pages of technical papers from the British and American atomic programs. The relationship between intelligence and the Soviet atomic program was so close that Igor Kurchatov, its scientific head, reviewed the intelligence product supplied by the KGB and provided detailed technical follow-up questions to be raised with its sources. Atomic espionage allowed the Soviet bomb program to skip much of the research and development phase and move swiftly to final engineering and production. It did not have to go down blind alleys, resort to expensive and time-consuming trial-and-error, or experiment with impractical approaches; all of that had already been done by the Manhattan Project. The result was a huge savings in time and resources for the Soviet bomb program. The saving of resources was particularly important given that Soviet infrastructure had been badly damaged by the war and that the postwar reconstruction effort severely strained Soviet industrial capabilities.[43]

That the first Soviet bomb was a plutonium bomb triggered by implosion was itself a demonstration of the advantage that espionage provided the Soviet bomb program. Scientists initially assumed that the most direct way to a working bomb was through splitting the uranium atom. And the first atomic bomb used in combat, the "Little Boy" dropped on Hiroshima on 6 August 1945, was a uranium bomb. But Manhattan Project scientists and engineers quickly realized that producing uranium bombs raised a very practical problem. Uranium in nature consists largely of two isotopes, U-238 and U-235. More than 99 percent is U-238, useless as the fuel for an atomic bomb because it is too stable—not "fissile" in technical terms. A fission chain reaction required a concentrated amount of U-235, sometimes termed enriched uranium or bomb-grade uranium. The technical barriers to separating U-238 from U-235 to produce enriched bomb-grade uranium were daunting but were ultimately overcome by the Manhattan Project. Another major problem, however, remained. Despite investment of tremendous engineering and industrial resources, all of the methods to extract U-235 were extremely time-consuming and would severely limit the number of bombs that could be manufactured. If atomic bombs could be constructed using only U-235, while one could be (and was) prepared for use in late summer 1945, it would be 1946 before a second uranium bomb was ready.

American and British scientists, however, worked out a substitute for U-235: plutonium. Plutonium does not occur in nature. It was first created in 1941 by chemist Glenn Seaborg, who used a cyclotron at the University of California, Berkeley, to bombard easily available uranium U-238 with neutrons and produce the first artificial element: plutonium. Manhattan Project scientists soon discovered that plutonium could be produced in significant quantities in uranium-fueled nuclear reactors and in only a fraction of the time needed to produce U-235 enriched uranium. Plutonium was highly fissile, even more so than U-235, and could easily be stimulated to produce a fission chain reaction.

However, another problem quickly appeared. Plutonium was, in fact, too fissile. "Little Boy," the uranium bomb, had a simple triggering method. One mass of highly enriched uranium was shot down a barrel (as if in a rifle), using conventional explosives, at tremendous speed at a target at the end of the barrel that also consisted of highly enriched U-235. When the two collided, the energy generated by the collision stimulated the U-235 to become "critical"—that is, to fission and set off a chain reaction that produced a nuclear explosion. In the case of the "Little Boy" bomb, the explosive force was equivalent of about fifteen thousand tons of TNT.

Plutonium was so fissile, however, that the gun-type design was unworkable. When a mass of plutonium was fired at a plutonium target, a chain reaction began so rapidly when the two came together that most of the fuel was blown apart before the reaction had spread to all of the plutonium. The result was a "fizzle," a premature explosion perhaps enough to blow up a city block, but not the massive blast envisioned. The technical breakthrough developed at Los Alamos was an implosion design. Instead of the firing of one mass at another, a single plutonium hemisphere was completely encased by conventional explosives. The encasing explosive was set off simultaneously all around the hemisphere, configured in a shaped charge, sometimes called an explosive lens, that directed most of the force of the explosion inwardly in a uniform fashion, squeezing all of the plutonium simultaneously with great energy and turning it critical. The resulting chain reaction affected all of the plutonium, and a full nuclear explosion resulted. In the case of the "Fat Man" bomb used against Nagasaki, the explosion was the equivalent of twenty-one thousand tons of TNT. As a result of espionage, the Soviet bomb program skipped the Manhattan Project's hard-learned lessons on the practical limitations of a uranium bomb and went directly to a plutonium bomb with its implosion trigger.[44]

Did it matter that the Soviet Union got the atomic bomb two to four years sooner than it otherwise would have? Historical what-ifs are always speculative. But Joseph Stalin's, rather than one of his less aggressive successors', having the atomic bomb may have helped precipitate the Korean War. In the spring of 1949 Kim Il Sung, the Communist dictator of North Korea, asked Stalin's agreement to an invasion of South Korea but was refused; Stalin cited the uncertainty of success and the risk of American intervention. Without massive Soviet military support (weaponry, munitions, vehicles, supplies, and military technicians), North Korea was incapable of attacking the South. But in August 1949 the USSR exploded its first atomic bomb, and in early 1950 Stalin informed Kim that he was now willing to support an invasion. He cited several reasons for his shift in position, and one was a lessened risk of American intervention due to Soviet acquisition of the atomic bomb. Said Stalin: "The prevailing mood [in the United States] is not to interfere. Such a mood is reinforced by the fact that the USSR now has the atomic bomb." Stalin's judgment was wrong. The North Korean attack brought swift American intervention, and the war produced four million casualties, including more than thirty thousand American dead, several hundred thousand Chinese dead, and more than a million military and civilian war dead in the two Koreas. Several million people were wounded, and the peninsula suffered horrific physical devastation.[45]

Early Soviet possession of the atomic bomb also had important psychological consequences. When the USSR exploded a nuclear device in 1949, ordinary Americans as well as the nation's leaders realized that an exceptionally cruel despot with a history of mass murder had just gained the power to destroy entire cities with a single bomb. This perception was not merely unsettling; it was deeply frightening and colored the early Cold War with the hues of the apocalypse. While the Cold War never lost the potential for a civilization-destroying conflict, Stalin's death in March 1953 noticeably relaxed Soviet-American tensions.[46]

Often in the history of espionage it is difficult to tell if the information gained made a significant difference in ensuing events. With Soviet atomic intelligence, however, one can be reasonably certain that it changed history.

The History of Soviet Atomic Intelligence

Part of the history of Soviet atomic intelligence has been well documented, with some Soviet sources inside the Anglo-American atomic project revealed in the 1940s and others only a few years ago. In 1943 an FBI listening device recorded Joseph Weinberg, a young nuclear physicist at the University of California, discussing the atomic program with a Communist Party official. Security officials quickly removed Weinberg from the Manhattan Project. In 1944 the FBI observed Clarence Hiskey, a senior chemist at the Manhattan Project facility at the University of Chicago, meeting covertly with a Soviet intelligence officer operating in the United States under a false identity. He, too, was removed from the project. In September 1945 Igor Gouzenko, a Soviet military intelligence cipher officer, defected in Canada. He brought with him GRU documents that revealed widespread Soviet espionage in Canada. One of those identified was Allan Nunn May, a young British physicist who in 1944 had been sent to work at the Anglo-Canadian Chalk River nuclear laboratory, a facility supporting the Anglo-American bomb project. May was arrested, confessed, and was imprisoned.

Most important was the arrest of Klaus Fuchs, a scientist who was part of the British contingent working at Los Alamos..Fuchs had been part of the scientific team that worked on designing the implosion detonation method that made a plutonium bomb practical. After the war he had returned to Britain to a senior position in the British atomic program. In 1949 the American Venona project deciphered KGB cables that identified Fuchs as a Soviet spy, and the British Security Service (MI5) confronted him. He confessed, pled guilty, and was imprisoned in 1950. Fuchs's confession led to the identification of his American courier, Harry Gold. Confronted, Gold confessed and fingered another Soviet spy at Los Alamos, David Greenglass. A far less important figure than Fuchs, Greenglass was, nonetheless, not without value. Part of a U.S. Army engineering unit, he worked as a skilled machinist preparing model implosion lenses and triggering devices for the plutonium bomb, a practical complement to Fuchs's more theoretical contribution. Confronted, Greenglass also confessed.

Another major Soviet source became public in 1995, when KGB cables deciphered by Venona were opened for research. Theodore Hall, a young physics prodigy, graduated from Harvard in 1944 at the age of eighteen. He was immediately recruited by the Manhattan Project and sent to Los Alamos, where he was assigned as a junior scientist to the team working on the plutonium bomb. Hall was also a secret Communist and volunteered to spy for the KGB. The decrypted cables allowed the FBI to identify Hall as a spy, but when confronted in 1951, he denied everything. For security reasons, the cables could not be used in a court for criminal prosecution, and since the FBI was unable to find other compelling evidence, Hall escaped prosecution. When Venona publicly identified him as a Soviet source in 1995, an unrepentant Hall confirmed his assistance to the Soviets.

Vassiliev's Notebooks and "Enormous"

In addition to Russell McNutt, Alexander Vassiliev's notebooks identify two other unknown Soviet atomic sources, one who provided information on the key issue of uranium isotope separation and a second with access to the British atomic program in England. Scientists and others are also identified who, while not themselves directly involved in the atomic bomb project, attempted to recruit colleagues who were. In addition to documenting the KGB's futile pursuit of Robert Oppenheimer, the notebooks detail its frustration with its ineffectual recruitment in 1942 and 1943 and its ultimate success beginning in 1944, when its sister service, GRU, handed over Klaus Fuchs and Theodore Hall volunteered his assistance. The notebooks also document that several scientists regarded as security risks and fired from the program at the FBI's instigation and subsequently treated as victims of irrational paranoia in some historical accounts were, in fact, Soviet sources or Soviet sympathizers who were candidates for KGB recruitment. Additionally, Vassiliev's notebooks show that the confessions of Fuchs and Greenglass were partial, and both held back the full extent of their espionage. Finally, the notebooks provide the first start-to-finish story of the KGB's attack on the Manhattan Project.

"Enormous" in Great Britain: Cairncross, Broda, May, and Norwood

Britain's atomic bomb project began in 1940, more than a year before the American Manhattan Project. In a retrospective report written in 1945, Pavel Fitin, chief of KGB foreign intelligence, noted that Soviet sources in England were the first to provide Moscow with atomic intelligence. Further, their intelligence revealed not only Britain's progress on the atomic bomb but also, due to Britain's partnership, that of the United States:

"There is highly valuable info. coming in from the London station regarding scientific work on 'En-s' ["Enormous"]. The first materials on 'En-s' were received at the end of 1941 from the source 'Liszt.' The materials included valuable and top secret documents, both on the substance of the problem of 'E-s' and on measures taken by the Brit. gov't to organize and develop work on the problem of atomic energy. These materials served as a starting point for laying down the groundwork and organizing work on the problem of atomic energy in our country. Because Amer. and Canadian work on 'En-s' is sent to E. as part of a tech. information exchange, the London station sends materials covering the state and progress of work on 'En-s' in three countries: England, the USA, and Canada."[47]

"Liszt" was John Cairncross. An ardent young Communist at Cambridge University in the mid-1930s, he was spotted by Anthony Blunt and Guy Burgess, already KGB contacts. After graduation in 1936 Cairncross joined the Foreign Office, and Burgess completed his recruitment as a KGB source. In addition to the Foreign Office, he also held posts with the Treasury and Britain's Secret Intelligence Service (SIS or MI6). In 1941 Cairncross was in an excellent position to keep the Soviets informed about Britain's atomic bomb project: he was then working as secretary to Lord Maurice Hankey, a cabinet member and head of a committee that reviewed Britain's atomic program.

In addition to Cairncross, Fitin cited two other valuable sources in Britain, "Quid" and "Tina." "Quid" was a 1945 cover name; earlier it was "Eric." "Eric" appeared in a number of deciphered Venona messages as a key Soviet atomic spy in Great Britain, but British authorities were unable to identify "Eric's" real name. Unidentified atomic spies often generate speculation, and in the case of "Eric" one candidate advanced was Sir Eric Rideal, a prominent British scientist. The speculation was wrong: "Eric" was Engelbert (Bertl) Broda, a refugee Austrian physicist who had arrived in Britain in 1938, after his country's annexation by the German Reich. A talented physicist, he found haven at Cambridge University and by 1942 was working at the Cavendish Laboratory assisting Hans Halban, a physicist working on atomic reactors and controlled chain reactions and a major participant in the British atomic project. (Halban, a scientist in the French atomic program, had fled the continent in 1940 in front of the advancing German Army, carrying in his luggage much of France's supply of the scarce "heavy water" used in nuclear reactors.) Broda was also a secret Communist and a close friend of Austrian-born Edith Tudor Hart (cover name "Edith"), a veteran KGB courier and talent spotter. In December 1942, KGB's London station reported the following:

"'Edith' [Hart] sent us a detailed report through Mary [unidentified] on the results and status of work on enormous, both in England and in the USA. 'Eric' [Broda] had given her this report on his own initiative to pass to the fraternal [Communist Party]. The materials will be sent out in the near future. According to additional information that has been gathered, 'Eric'—who since Jan. 1942 has been Professor Halban's assistant in a special division (devoted to enormous) of the central laboratory on explosives in Cambridge—is completely informed about all the work being done on 'Enormous,' both in England and in the USA, b/c he has access to Amer. materials on enormous that the English had received as part of an information exchange. . . . Eric is a long-time fellowcountryman [Communist] who understands the need for such work."[48]

Impressed with the report and Broda's volunteering it, the KGB London station, with Moscow Center's agreement, arranged for Hart to press Broda for more. London reported:

"We instructed 'Edith' [Hart] to conduct a preliminary conversation with him and get him to agree to meet with our comrade. During the conversation between 'Edith' and 'Eric' [Broda], the latter was initially hesitant and said that he had to think about it and that he does not see any need to meet with someone, b/c he has already written down everything he knows about 'Enormous.' Later in the same conversation, 'Eric's' attitude changed, and he said that he hopes the person he meets will not be an Englishman, b/c English comrades are generally very indiscreet. And, in the end, once 'Edith' had told him that everything had been properly arranged, 'Eric' said that he would be happy to meet with our comrade."

In January 1943 Broda met with a KGB officer, and the London station told Moscow:

"'Eric' [Broda] met 'Glan' [unidentified KGB officer] cordially and carried himself with great ease and friendliness, although it was obvious that he was nervous. He carefully verified all of the rendezvous terms. At the outset of the meeting, 'Eric' said that he had only been notified of the meeting the day before and therefore was unprepared for a serious discussion about 'Enormous.' Because 'Glan's' primary objective was to strengthen ties with 'Eric,' obtain his direct consent to work with us, and determine the course of this work, 'Glan' did not press him for information right away and instead set about achieving the aforementioned objectives. The first conversation with 'Eric' lasted over an hour and a half. As a result of the conversation, 'Eric' gave his full consent to work with us. During the conversation, nothing was called by its proper name, but 'Eric' knows who it is he agreed to work for. . . . 'Eric' reports that in their field of work, the Americans were significantly ahead. As part of a tech. information exchange, their laboratory receives bulletins from the Americans on the progress of work on 'Enormous' in America. Owing to the nature of his work, 'Eric' has access to these bulletins, and the info. he gives us reflects Amer. achievements in this field as well as English ones."

Broda agreed to meet a KGB courier every two or three weeks to provide reports and technical information on the atomic project.[49]

The KGB relationship with Broda went well, and in August 1943 Moscow referred to Broda as "at pres., the main source of info. on work being done on E. ["Enormous"], both in England and in the USA." In 1944 the London station reported that Broda's access to British and American technical data had further increased, explaining:

One of 'Eric's' [Broda's] colleagues went to Canada for a while and gave him his personal key to the library containing reports on 'En-s' ["Enormous"]. . . . "We made 'Eric' a copy of the key and arranged contact terms that allowed us to contact him in London three times a week without any prior arrangement. In accordance with these terms, on arriving in London on one of the agreed upon days, 'Eric' was supposed to mark a page of a phone book inside a designated phone booth. After entering this phone booth at a fixed time and finding the mark he had made, we would go out to meet him at the appointed place and time. . . . As a result, we were able to receive from 'Eric' all available Amer. reports of the second batch, as well as oth. interesting mater-s [materials] on 'En-s'. . . .

'Eric' continues to work willingly with us, but he still balks at even the slightest hint about mater. assistance. We once gave him more than he asked to cover his expenses. He was displeased by this and said that he suspects we want to give him a certain kind of help. He asked us to give up any such thoughts once and for all. In such circumstances, we fear that any gift from us as a token of appreciation for his work will make a negative impression. 'Eric' is completely selfless in his work with us and extremely scrupulous when it comes to anything that could be seen as 'payment' for his work."

Among the specific information Broda was credited with delivering were Miles Leverett and Tom Moore's plans for one of the Manhattan Project's early nuclear reactors. (Leverett and Moore, lead engineers at the Metallurgical Laboratory at the University of Chicago, designed larger and more practical reactors to replace the first experimental reactor built by Enrico Fermi.) The plans he delivered were described as including "all the necessary information to build a plant, and [it] is exceptionally valuable."[50]

In 2007 the British Security Service opened its investigative files on Engelbert Broda. They showed that the Security Service had become aware of Broda's Communist association as early as 1939 and had advised caution to Britain's Department for Scientific and Industrial Research (DSIR) when he was offered employment at the Cavendish Laboratory. DSIR disregarded the warning. The Security Service kept an intermittent watch on Broda thereafter but never detected his contacts with the KGB documented in Vassiliev's notebooks.

In 1947 Broda resigned from the Cavendish Laboratory and returned to his native Austria and a career as a professor of physical chemistry at the University of Vienna. The Security Service's suspicions about Broda increased when physicist Allan Nunn May, imprisoned as a Soviet spy in 1946, refused in 1949 to provide the name of his recruiter to a Security Service interrogator but said the man who had recruited him into espionage had done so in Britain shortly before he, May, left for Canada and was no longer within reach of British authorities. MI5 thought the man in question was Broda, then beyond its reach in Austria, because of the close association of Broda and May at Cambridge University. This suspicion increased when May was released from prison in 1952 and within a few months married Hildegarde Broda, Engelbert's former wife. Eventually the Security Service concluded: "We feel sure that BRODA was engaged in espionage during the war, although we have no proof of it." Vassiliev's notebooks provide the proof that the Security Service was unable to find. Broda died in Austria in 1983.[51]

Allan Nunn May himself likely was the subject of a cable from "Vadim" (Anatoly Gorsky, then KGB London station chief) to Moscow Center, dated 29 November 1942. Vassiliev's summary of the cable states: "Three young scientists are leaving for Montreal to conduct work on nuclear fission. Their work will be overseen by Professor Chadwick, who is in England. These scientists are illegal fellowcountrymen. In view of this, Vadim proposed recruiting one of them with giving rendezvous terms in Canada."[52] "Illegal fellowcountrymen" in this context was KGB jargon for secret members of the Communist Party, not that such membership was illegal under British law (it wasn't).

Allan Nunn May was part of the British atomic program at Cambridge University and also a secret member of the Communist Party of Great Britain (CPGB). In late 1942 British authorities decided to send him to the atomic laboratory at Chalk River, Canada, and he arrived there in January 1943. This itinerary fits with his being the one of the three picked by the KGB for recruitment. While he worked chiefly in Canada, May also visited American atomic facilities. His role as a Soviet spy was revealed when Igor Gouzenko defected in September 1945, carrying documents that identified May. Security officials allowed May to return to the United Kingdom, placed him under surveillance, and arrested him in March 1946. He quickly confessed and pled guilty to a charge of violating Britain's Official Secrets Act. Sentenced to ten years in prison, he was released in 1952 after his term was reduced for good behavior.

The only anomaly in the fit between Allan Nunn May and "Vadim"/Gorsky's November 1942 cable and plan to recruit a young British scientist on the way to Canada is that May reported to GRU rather than the KGB in Canada. Possibly the KGB did not have sufficient assets in Canada to maintain contact with May and turned him over to GRU, which had extensive Canadian networks. In addition, General Fitin in an August 1943 report on atomic intelligence noted sources who had been "cultivated and recruited" by both GRU and the KGB and referred to "May, Henry Norman" in Britain. Probably Fitin was referring to two persons, a "May" (likely Allan Nunn May) and a "Henry Norman," but possibly "May, Henry Norman" was an error on Fitin's part for "May, Allan Nunn." In either case, if GRU had been cultivating May in Great Britain before he left for Canada, it may have made an independent approach to him, so its taking him over in Canada makes more sense.[53]

In addition to Broda, General Fitin in 1945 identified "Tina" as a major atomic intelligence source in Great Britain. "Tina" was Melita Stedman Norwood, a fervent Communist who had been recruited for espionage against Britain in the mid-1930s, working chiefly as a courier between British sources and KGB officers. She was employed at the same time as a secretary in the British Non-Ferrous Metals Research Association, not then a Soviet espionage target. But once the British atomic program got under way, it became one of the agencies employed by the British government for atomic research. Norwood used her position as secretary and personal assistant to the director of the association to steal and copy much of the technical data produced by the British program, as well as copies of reports received from the Manhattan Project in the United States. For example, in 1945 KGB London station reported "the second removal of documents via "Tina" [Norwood]. 20 new reports were obtained, as well as a scientific correspondence among specialists working on these questions at the institute. As a result, all the materials on E. ["Enormous"] that were in "Tina's" office—over 35 reports and a scientific correspondence—have been obtained. In the fall, we intend to organize a new removal, using specially prepared keys to the safe where materials are kept. By that time, new materials and reports will have accumulated." Melita Norwood's role as a Soviet source inside the British atomic program became public in 1999 with the publication of Andrew and Mitrokhin's *The Sword and the Shield.* Norwood was still alive and still a Communist. She told reporters, "I did what I did not to make money, but to help prevent the defeat of a new system which had at great cost given ordinary people food and fares which they could afford, a good education and health service," and "in the same circumstances I know that I would do the same thing again."[54]

The KGB's sources in Great Britain were important not only for information about Britain's Tube Alloys atomic project but also because they acted as conduits in 1942 and 1943 for reports about the Manhattan Project at a time when KGB efforts in the United States were falling far short of Moscow's hopes.

"Enormous" in America: Frustration, 1941–43

The first KGB message out of America regarding atomic intelligence noted in Vassiliev's notebooks came early, in November 1941. Senior KGB officer Pavel Pastelnyak sent a ciphered telegram to Moscow with news that a team of American scientists headed by Columbia University chemist Harold Urey (winner of the Nobel Prize in 1934) was visiting London to discuss their work on "'an explosive of enormous power.'" The news had come from Emil Conason, a Communist medical doctor in New York who was friendly with Davrun Wittenberg, described as Urey's assistant. (Wittenberg has not been independently identified, and the spelling of his name in English is uncertain.) Conason vouched for Wittenberg's reliability and noted that Wittenberg's wife had been a Communist and his mother still belonged to the party. Conason told the KGB that Wittenberg was not a man given to exaggeration, despite having said the explosive was potentially so powerful that an airplane dropping it might need to fly hundreds of miles to avoid being damaged. Pastelnyak asked that the information be checked in London. The KGB London station via Cairncross verified that Urey, along with George Pegram, one of America's most influential science administrators, had visited London on a mission dealing with Uranium-235 but was unable to learn any details about the trip.[55]

Four months later Moscow sent the New York station an urgent message about a new high-priority intelligence task, stating that scientists "'in England, Germany, and the USA are frantically working to obtain Uranium-235 and use it as an explosive to make bombs of enormous destructive power, and to all appearances, this problem is quite close to its practical solution. It is essential that we take up this problem in all seriousness.'" It listed Urey and ten other senior American scientists thought to be working on the atomic problem and instructed the KGB New York station to seek contact with them or access to their work. But the KGB was never able to establish productive contact with any of them. The scientists were Harold Urey, Peter N. Bragg, Glenn Fowler, Aristid Grosse, John Dunning, Alfred O. Nier, Robert Van de Graaff, George Gamow, Davrun Wittenberg, E. T. Bute, and Tramm (first name unknown).[56]

Attempts to gain access to Urey and his work through Conason's relationship with Wittenberg foundered. A frustrated Moscow Center complained in 1943: "All in all, there is a lot of talk about "Invalid" [Conason] and "Sarin" [Wittenberg], but nothing has been done." Given Conason's ineffectiveness, the KGB also had one of its veteran technical sources, William Malisoff, make an attempt. The Russian-born Malisoff ran his own company in New York, United Laboratories, which carried out technical intelligence tasks for the KGB. He held a PhD from Columbia and knew both Urey and Wittenberg. But Wittenberg rebuffed his attempt to discuss nuclear fission during a meeting, and this approach also came to nothing.[57]

In addition to Malisoff and Conason, the KGB attempted to use another Russian-born scientist, "Catalyst," to approach one of its priority atomic targets. "Catalyst" was unidentified, although he was described as having daughters living in the Soviet Union and having worked on radioactive substances at a German university in the 1930s in association with Moscow Center's real target: another refugee Russian chemist, Aristid Viktorovich Grosse. Grosse by the early 1940s had established a worldwide reputation as a leading physical chemist and was on Moscow's priority list along with Harold Urey. (Grosse later worked at the Manhattan Project's gaseous diffusion plant, K-25, at Oak Ridge.) Moscow Center suggested that a New York station officer approach "Catalyst" and tell him that if he "'successfully obtains information and materials that interest us, we can provide material assistance to his daughters.'" Moscow Center thought "Catalyst" might be able to appeal to Grosse because Grosse's brother, living in Shanghai, China, had twice asked for permission to return to the USSR and gain Soviet citizenship, once implying that Aristid also was interested. Moscow Center suggested meeting with Grosse, giving him a letter from his brother that the KGB had obtained, and telling him "that such a move could only be possible after the war, and for now he should demonstrate his best intentions toward us"—that is, assist Soviet intelligence.[58]

It does not appear, however, that "Catalyst" or any other KGB agent made such an approach to Grosse (given the cover name "Neutron"). Grosse visited Moscow in late 1942 as part of an American scientific delegation discussing the wartime production of artificial rubber and related matters. Moscow Center informed its New York station that in discussions with Soviet officials in Moscow, Grosse had spoken with "great reserve" and did not indicate that any sort of covert contact was established or even attempted. But it still held out some hope that an approach might be made in the United States. Eventually, however, Moscow Center gave up, in November 1943 instructing the KGB New York station: "Clearly, there is no need to focus on 'Neutron' [Grosse]. More interesting opportunities have come up."[59]

Yet another refugee Russian scientist of interest to the KGB was George Gamow. Born in the Ukraine, Gamow had made a worldwide reputation for his work on radioactivity and quantum mechanics. After two foiled plots to escape the USSR, he secured an invitation to a conference in Europe in 1933 and defected along with his wife. He began teaching at George Washington University in the District of Columbia in 1934 and became an American citizen in 1940. (Although Moscow thought Gamow was working on the Manhattan Project, he was not. While he was consulted by project scientists on some matters, American military security insisted that although he was a defector from the USSR, the fact that he had also been a Red Army officer was simply too much of a risk for him to be included in the project.) "Catalyst" knew Gamow, but as with Grosse, there is nothing to suggest that he ever approached Gamow. In September 1945, however, a Soviet diplomat in Washington who was assisting the KGB succeeded in meeting Gamow with the help of a mutual Russian acquaintance. Gamow, who had been savagely denounced by the Soviets when he defected, was startled at meeting a Soviet official, but the diplomat carefully kept the conversation on Russian literature and matters that might arouse Gamow's nostalgia for his native land. He succeeded in winning an invitation to Gamow's home, and Leonid Kvasnikov, the KGB officer overseeing the matter, had high hopes that the diplomat could prepare Gamow for a meeting with a KGB officer. However, as with Grosse, these hopes led to nothing. By 1950 Gamow was on a KGB list of "leading reactionary scientists working on the atomic problem in the USA and England" who were to be discredited by a KGB disinformation program.[60]

Frustration: "Quantum"

Deciphered KGB cables released in the mid-1990s contained both real names and cover names. Often Venona project analysts were able to identify the real names behind cover names. But there remained, nonetheless, more than 175 cover names of Americans who were assisting Soviet espionage that were never linked to real names. One of the most intriguing was "Quantum." Only three deciphered KGB cables mentioned "Quantum." All three dealt with his meeting with a senior Soviet diplomat and two KGB officers at the Soviet Embassy in Washington in June 1943. Thereafter "Quantum" disappeared from sight. What made "Quantum" interesting was that the messages showed he had handed over complex chemical equations on the gaseous diffusion method for separating bomb-grade U-235 from unwanted U-238 and had received a $300 payment (more than $3,500 in 2008 dollars).[61]

"Quantum" appeared to be a scientist or engineer of some sort and senior enough to warrant a meeting with a high-ranking Soviet diplomat. But beyond that and the fact he was in Washington in June 1943, there were no clues to his identity. NSA/FBI footnotes to the "Quantum" messages simply stated "unidentified." Candidates for "Quantum" have ranged from George Gamow, to Louis Slotin (a Canadian physicist with Communist ties in his youth who died in a plutonium accident at Los Alamos in 1946), to Bruno Pontecorvo (an Italian physicist who worked at the atomic research laboratory at Chalk River during World War II and who defected to the USSR in 1950).

All of the speculation was wrong. Vassiliev's notebooks identify "Quantum": he was Boris Podolsky, a scientist never suspected of any association with Soviet intelligence. Born in Russia in 1896, Podolsky had immigrated to the United States in 1911. After receiving his PhD in physics from the California Institute of Technology, he returned to the USSR from 1930 to 1933, working as director of theoretical physics at the Ukrainian Physio-Technical Institute. Back in America in 1933, he took a post at the prestigious Institute for Advanced Study at Princeton. In 1935 Podolsky co-authored with Albert Einstein and Nathan Rosen one of the most famous theoretical articles ever written on quantum mechanics. After a quarrel with Einstein, Podolsky left Princeton to become a professor of mathematical physics at the University of Cincinnati.[62]

The KGB did not seek out Podolsky. Instead, an early 1942 Moscow Center report stated: "'Podolsky. He approached the embassy with a proposal to go to the Soviet Union to work on the problem of Uranium-235.'" The KGB gave Podolsky the cover name "Quantum," and a KGB New York station memo in May 1943 designated him as its "only" source on "Enormous" at the time.[63]

Podolsky was not only then the New York station's only source, but he was also a difficult one. He met Vladimir Pravdin, a senior KGB officer, and Semen Semenov, a specialist in scientific intelligence. Realizing that Podolsky had a very high opinion of the worth of his knowledge, Pravdin posed as a Soviet official newly arrived from the USSR:

"In order to establish definitively the results of his theoretical investigations into this problem, he was invited in April to the 'Factory' [Amtorg] building, where he was interviewed by 'Twain' [Semenov] and 'Sergey' [Pravdin]. The latter was introduced as Vasily Ivanovich Ognev, recently arrived from the Soviet Union, supposedly with instructions to meet with Quantum [Podolsky] and find out what exactly he would like to report. Initially, he refused to report his findings here altogether and thought it possible to report them only in the Soviet Union, grounding this in a desire to keep his findings secret and expressing distrust that we would preserve this secrecy and his connection with us. When asked if there was someone here, then, whom he could trust to receive his report on his current findings, b/c otherwise a trip to the Soviet Union would be out of the question, he agreed to pass materials only to 'Grandfather,' in person."

In 1944 "Grandfather" was the cover name for the Soviet consul general in New York. In 1943, however, it appears, but is not certain, that "Grandfather" was the Soviet ambassador in Washington.[64]

The encounter scheduled with "Grandfather" took place in June 1943 at the Soviet Embassy in Washington. A KGB cable reported that "Quantum" delivered a technical paper to "Grandfather's deputy," "Grandfather" himself being absent. Semenov was also present and reported: "Quantum [Podolsky] declared that he is convinced of the value of the materials and therefore expects from us a similar recompense for his labor—in the form of a financial reward." Semenov judged the material of value and gave Podolsky $300 on the spot.[65]

The KGB New York station transmitted the material Podolsky handed over in a lengthy three-part cable that set out the chemical equations underlying the gaseous diffusion uranium separation. The cable itself was unusual. Normally complex technical information went to Moscow via diplomatic pouch. While such material took weeks to reach Moscow, the formatting of telegraphic cables did not lend itself to complex and lengthy chemical equations and posed difficult problems for the cipher officers who had to encode them. Long international cables were also exceedingly expensive. Possibly the lack of success by the KGB New York station in producing significant atomic intelligence up to that point caused it to rush this prized information to Moscow. Gaseous diffusion, developed at the Manhattan Project's affiliate at Columbia University, was highly secret, and how "Quantum"/Podolsky got access to the formula that expressed one of the variant methods to do it is unknown. He was never employed by the Manhattan Project, and none of its activities were pursued at the University of Cincinnati, where he taught. However, he was a respected senior physicist and had done some work in gaseous diffusion (although not on uranium), so possibly scientists working on uranium separation had consulted him and shared with him some of the results coming out of the work at Columbia.[66]

The KGB had referred Podolsky's request to return to the USSR to work on the uranium problem to higher authorities and recorded: "'At the echelon [high Soviet leadership] it was decided that there was no need to bring 'Quantum' [Podolsky] into our country. Therefore, we have to use him where he is.'" The Soviet Union had a number of talented theoretical physicists, and adding another was not a priority. What Soviet authorities wanted was not theoretical skill (Podolsky's strength) but experimental data and technical results on the American atomic bomb project, something that Podolsky had little opportunity to obtain at the University of Cincinnati. The KGB urged him to seek a post with more access to the sort of information it wanted, and Moscow Center even authorized financial incentives. But Podolsky remained at the University of Cincinnati. By November 1943 Moscow Center's patience was exhausted, and it told the KGB New York station: "'Quantum' does not seem reliable." And with that there were no more references to "Quantum." Podolsky continued to teach at the University of Cincinnati until 1961, when he moved across town to Xavier University. He died in 1966.[67]

Frustration: Clarence Hiskey

In late March 1942 Zalmond Franklin, a veteran KGB courier, had dinner with Clarence Hiskey in New York. The two had known each other in the mid-1930s at the University of Wisconsin, where both had been active in the Communist Party. Franklin, born in 1909 in Milwaukee, had worked as a laboratory technician for the Department of the Interior before going to fight in Spain in 1937 with the Communist International Brigades. After he returned, he began working for the KGB New York station doing courier work, surveillance, and various espionage tasks. Hiskey, born Clarence Szczechowski in Milwaukee in 1912, had graduated from the University of Wisconsin in 1935 and remained to earn his PhD in chemistry in 1939. After teaching at the University of Tennessee and working as a chemist for the TVA, Hiskey transferred to Columbia University. In 1942 he joined the Substitute Alloy Material Laboratory, a Manhattan Project facility, where he worked with Harold Urey's gaseous diffusion uranium separation project.[68]

Franklin had never heard of the atomic bomb (few people had) and was certainly unaware that Hiskey was working on it. He had run into Hiskey on the subway and accepted a dinner invitation from his old party comrade because he was considering entering the armed forces, knew Hiskey had a reserve commission from college, and wanted advice about getting a military assignment in bacteriological warfare. (Franklin's laboratory training included bacteriological work.) In a report to the KGB New York station, Franklin explained that he had had dinner with Clarence and his wife and added:

"When I left to go home Hiskey decided to walk me to the subway. Our conversation on the way is what leads to the reason for this report. It came about in this manner: Hiskey remarked: Imagine a bomb dropped in the center of this city which would destroy the entire city. I scoffed at that but pricked up my ears because I have known Hiskey never to have been given to making spectacular and ridiculous claims. That [I] scoffed at him seemed to make him angry with the result that he said more than he intended to say.

There is such a bomb he stated very emphatically—I'm working on it. I asked him if it was a 'death ray' or gas. He, still angry at my unbelieving tone, said it was a radioactive bomb.

Talking very rapidly now, he told me plenty: The essential points are as follows: 1. That the Germans were far ahead on this bomb. 2. That his research, together with a number of the leading chemists and physicists, were working with desperate haste. 3. The radioactive bomb has not been perfected in their laboratory but considerable progress has been made. 4. The Germans may be advanced sufficiently to be ready to use it. 5. That if desperate, the Germans may use it even before perfection has been reached. 6. The big problem with this bomb is one of control. It is expected that this bomb will melt down buildings within a very large radius—perhaps even hundreds of miles. But radioactivity is still considerable of a mystery and there is no telling what properties the radioactivity suddenly released will impart to such stable substances as concrete—and how long this character will be imparted. In other words, Hiskey claims that the only reason the Germans have not as yet used the bomb is because they fear that a vast area will be made unavailable to them too. 7. The scientists in the Columbia research lab have advanced far enough to be planning on trying it out in some vast desert area. Hundreds of miles will be blocked off. 8. Much of the work consists of finding a defense for this bomb. 9. A great fear exists among those who know of the bomb—it may truly destroy millions of people at a crack. 10. It does not weigh more than a thousand bombs—that is, the bomb will need not weigh more than that to do untold destruction. Hiskey was sorry he told me about this and swore me to silence. I said that I hoped the Soviets knew about this —he said he hoped so too."[69]

Franklin's report was dated 28 March 1942, perhaps arriving at the desk of Vasily Zarubin (KGB New York station chief) nearly the same day he received Moscow Center's 27 March letter that scientists "'in England, Germany, and the USA are frantically working to obtain Uranium-235 and use it as an explosive to make bombs of enormous destructive power'" and telling the KGB's operatives, "'It is essential that we take up this problem in all seriousness.'" It must have seemed providential to Zarubin that at the same time Moscow declared atomic intelligence to be a high priority, one of the station's American agents had handed in a report of long-standing friendly contact with a scientist working on the project who was an ardent Soviet sympathizer and who had volunteered a description of the very issue that Moscow wanted pursued.[70]

Zarubin swiftly sent a ciphered telegram to Moscow on 1 April summarizing the Franklin-Hiskey conversation. He proposed recruiting Hiskey but noted that while Hiskey had joined the CPUSA in 1936, it was not known if he was still a member. His wife, Marcia Sand, had been expelled from the party as "'a gossip.'" In a response to New York on 5 April, Moscow Center noted that Hiskey's description of the work being done on U-235 was accurate but overly optimistic about what had been achieved. Emphasizing that the issue "'is of great interest to us,'" the Center posed a series of questions to which it wanted answers. How was the U-235 being extracted from uranium, what progress was being made on the shell for the bomb, what was the primer, how were workers protected from radioactivity during production, what was the status of the German research, and what kind of practical factory work was being done?[71]

Franklin had a second encounter with Hiskey, having dinner at the latter's apartment in late April. His report was sent to Moscow:

"I had dinner with Clarence and his wife and spend the evening with them at their home. At no time did Clarence bring up the subject of his work and following instructions, I did not mention the subject. The time previously that he discussed the thing with me, his wife was not present and so it may be that he did not mention it this time because his wife was present the entire evening. However I feel that he will not raise the subject again on his own volition. Chances are he regrets having done so in the first place. Clarence asked me if I wanted to take a job on the project. I told him I would be interested and asked him about pay, etc. He said that he could get me in at once remarking that an opening existed in the bacteriological phase of this work. But then he reminded himself of my political background. He recalled that in my University days—at that time Clarence was one of the leading faculty Comrades—the underground—I was actively known as a Communist, that I was one of the organizers of the University YCL and that this information was down on paper in the University records. He went on to say that the FBI made a most thorough checkup of all workers on this project and that it would be dangerous for me, as far as the job was concerned, to face such an investigation. And in view of that he felt that perhaps it would not be good for him to recommend me inasmuch as if the FBI finds out my past then it will not look good for him. He suggested that I apply for the job on my own. I told him I would think it over.

In reference to the work that I would be doing if I had the job, Clarence stated that I would not see the results. Only the leading personal get to see the results. He stated further that some 16 Universities were now taking up the problem of this particular radioactive bomb. (He just said 'problem'—did not mention the word 'bomb.')"[72]

For the next two years the KGB tried to cultivate Hiskey through Franklin, an ultimately futile effort. Part of the problem, as the KGB New York station reported, was that the Manhattan Project transferred Hiskey

"[to] the University of Chicago, where the work and equipment from Columbia U. are being transferred. For this purpose, a new laboratory building was built at the University of Chicago, and three old buildings were cleared out. 'Ramsay' [Hiskey] is leaving for Chicago, where it seems he will be director of operations. He was allotted 1.5 million dollars by the government and allowed to pick his own workers. On that last subject, 'R.' ["Ramsay"] was given a special briefing on caution, meaning the possibility that their work could be infiltrated by agents from Germany or from us, or by fellowcountrymen. For instance, shortly after 'Ramsay' hired a certain Tom Silverberg, who was subsequently taken into the army, where he is currently studying at the Air Force school, an agent from Hut [the FBI] came to see 'Ramsay' and informed him that apparently Silverberg was one such agent (Silverberg is in fact a fellowcountryman [Communist]) and that 'Ramsay' should be careful in his choice of assistants. 'Ramsay' offered 'Chap' [Franklin] to come work with him in Chicago on his recommendation.

'Ramsay' told 'Chap' the following about his position in the fellowcountryman organization: After moving from Wisconsin, R. did not get transferred to the University of Tennessee organization. Upon arriving in Tyre [New York], Ramsay was paid a visit by Rose Olsen's husband, a fellowcountryman, who told R. that because of the great importance of his work, 'Ramsay' should stay away from fellowcountryman activities and conduct himself accordingly."

(Rose Olsen was a pseudonym likely used by Rosalyn Childs, wife of Jack Childs, a leading figure in the CPUSA's underground organization.)[73]

Moscow responded, observing that it was "essential to find a good opportunity to plant someone into the U. of Chicago," but the KGB New York station did not have any resident agents in the Chicago area. And Moscow Center warned against using Franklin, since with his background he was vulnerable to an FBI security check, but suggested that he should recommend someone else to Hiskey. By the end of November 1943, it had hit upon a candidate. Moscow instructed the KGB New York station to "introduce 'Huron' to Ramsay [Hiskey] through Chap [Franklin]. Huron is personally acquainted with employees at the U. of Chicago, including Fermi."[74]

The cover name "Huron" also appeared in five KGB cables deciphered by the Venona project. The messages indicated that "Huron" was a scientist and had some connection with Soviet atomic intelligence, but, like "Quantum," he was not identified by American counterintelligence. And just as in "Quantum's" case, the connection to atomic espionage encouraged speculation about the identity of yet another unknown scientist spy. Candidates suggested included Bruno Pontecorvo (also suggested for "Quantum") and Ernest Lawrence. Again, the speculation was wrong. "Huron" was Byron Darling, who had received a PhD at the University of Michigan in 1939 and had taken a position as a research physicist at the U.S. Rubber Company in Detroit in 1941. He had become a secret member of the CPUSA probably in the late 1930s and had begun assisting the KGB in 1942. His KGB recruiter, technical intelligence specialist Semenov, wrote that "Huron" was "a lead from the fellowcountrymen [CPUSA]," who had a PhD in physics and specialized in synthetic rubber. Semenov described Darling as "'Politically mature, stead-fast, should be trusted. While studying and working at the univs. of Chicago and Michigan, acquired connections among scientific circles in the field of physics. The connection of greatest interest is the Italian professor Fermi, who was involved in 'Enormous' while working at Columb. Univ. Currently, according to "Huron," Fermi works at the University in Chicago.'"[75]

In early 1944 Moscow reiterated the need to introduce Darling to Hiskey via Franklin but warned that it was dangerous to involve Franklin in the Manhattan Project since he had come under investigation by counterintelligence on a recent trip to Canada. Still, it did "'not object to his strengthening his ties with 'R' ["Ramsay"/Hiskey], as we intend to take advantage of this relationship to introduce our man to 'R.'" In a report to KGB chief Merkulov in February 1944 two senior officers, Gayk Ovakimyan and Andrey Graur, discussed Hiskey's conversations with Franklin and explained that their relationship "'allows us to use 'Ramsay' without his knowledge in order to plant our man through him on 'Chap's' recommendation.'" Since Franklin was "exposed" to American counterintelligence, it was necessary to have Darling become Hiskey's contact, have Franklin limit himself to maintaining friendly relations with Hiskey to learn about other scientists who might be of interest, and cultivate Hiskey "as someone who is of interest to us for the purpose of contracting him in the future."[76]

In March 1944 the KGB New York station informed Moscow that Bernard Schuster had learned that Hiskey had been in touch with the Chicago Communist Party. (Schuster was the CPUSA's liaison with Soviet intelligence on the East Coast.) By this time Leonid Kvasnikov, who had supervised KGB technical intelligence at Moscow Center from 1940 to 1943, had arrived in the United States to take personal charge of KGB scientific espionage. He proposed using these Communist Party connections to inform Hiskey that he would be approached "'by a trusted individual, whose purpose will be to learn about certain matters having to do with the work being done in his department. A password will be arranged with this person so that 'Ramsay' can identify him.'" He suggested sending Semenov, who would pose as a local Communist. After gauging Hiskey's access and "'his attitude toward us,'" the KGB would decide whether to use Darling as his liaison.[77]

A May 1944 KGB New York cable responded to a Moscow Center query about Kvasnikov's plan: "the object of Echo's [Schuster's] trip is as follows: Olsen is district leader of the Fraternal [Communist Party] in

Chicago. Olsen's wife, who has been meeting Ramsay [Hiskey], is also an active Fellowcountryman [Communist] and met Ramsay on the instructions of the organization. At our suggestion Echo can get a letter from Olsen with which one or other of our people will meet Ramsay and thereafter will be able to strike up an acquaintance." "Olsen" was not identified, but it likely was the cover name or the Communist Party name of Morris Childs, at that time the head of the CPUSA district 8 (Illinois). The message stated that Childs's wife had been cultivating Hiskey, and the KGB wanted to use the relationship to put one of its agents in contact with him.[78]

In July 1944 the KGB New York station reported a follow-up to this May message. It told Moscow that Schuster had passed along copies of two letters that had been sent to Hiskey by "Victor" (unidentified) and "Rose Olsen." Rose, however, was probably not Morris Childs's wife but his sister-in-law, Rosalyn Childs. Rosalyn's husband, Jack Childs, was a full-time CPUSA functionary who worked for the party underground and had previously warned Hiskey not to associate openly with the CPUSA so as not to endanger his position in the Manhattan Project. (It is possible that the KGB New York station had confused Jack's wife Rosalyn with Morris's wife in the May message. Rosalyn, a Comintern staffer in the 1930s, was active in the CPUSA underground with her husband, while Morris's wife was much less active in party affairs, overt or covert.) The letters assured Hiskey that its bearer was a reliable friend and asked the scientist to acquaint him with his work.[79]

On 18 September 1944 the KGB New York station sent a cable responding to several inquiries from Moscow, one of which was the status of the approach to Hiskey, explaining that its intermediaries in the matter, Bernard Schuster and Joseph Katz (one of the KGB's veteran American agents), were currently out of New York, while Rosalyn Childs, at that point designated by the cover name "Phlox," and her husband had traveled to "Ramsay's area" (Chicago) but had not yet returned. Finally, the KGB New York station told Moscow in December 1944: "'Dick' [Schuster] was directly in touch with 'Phlox's husband' [Jack Childs] and not with 'Phlox' [Rosalyn Childs] herself. The intention of sending the husband to see Ramsay [Hiskey] is explained by the possibility of avoiding a superfluous stage for transmitting instructions." Here the New York station was conveying its decision to Moscow that Jack Childs would make the approach to Hiskey.[80]

No agent of the KGB New York station, however, was able to carry through with these plans to contact Hiskey in Chicago. In March 1945, the KGB New York station admitted: "We still do not have a definitive outcome in the cultivation of Ramsay [Hiskey]. For six months we have been unable to get the necessary people sent to him through Echo [Schuster]. We gave 200 dollars for such a trip back at end of 1944, but to this day we have not seen any results." In July 1945 Kvasnikov informed Moscow that Schuster had not been able to contact Hiskey even with the assistance of Morris Childs and that he had decided to try to use Zalmond Franklin once again. Moscow was not pleased and in August blasted the KGB New York station for its "'poor work'" and "'inexcusable delay in 'Ramsay's' [Hiskey's] cultivation'" and pointedly reminded the New York station: "'Top priority tasks: 1. To finish cultivating "Ramsay."'"[81]

The KGB New York station continued to attempt to contact Hiskey but reported that Franklin had been unable to connect. And finally, Alexander Vassiliev's notebooks record: "In November, Chap learned from his comrade that Ramsay—is in Alaska, where he had been sent after being discharged from work on Balloon." ("Balloon" was by late 1945 another KGB cover name for the atomic bomb.) The pursuit of Hiskey ended.[82]

In time the KGB likely learned that all its maneuvering to contact Hiskey since April 1944, and probably some time earlier, had been a complete waste of time. Unbeknownst to the KGB, by the spring of 1944 Clarence Hiskey had become a source for "the neighbors," Soviet military intelligence. Exactly when and under what circumstances GRU recruited him is unknown. But recruit him it did. After that point, probably under GRU orders, he had politely avoided the KGB's attempts to approach him. But while the KGB remained in the dark for more than a year, American counterespionage did not.

Arthur Adams was a veteran GRU officer who had been in and out of the United States in the 1920s and 1930s. On his last mission he arrived from Canada in 1938 with a false Canadian passport. Identified by the FBI by 1944 as a Soviet intelligence officer, he was kept under surveillance and in April 1944 was observed meeting covertly with Clarence Hiskey. The FBI informed the Army, which oversaw Manhattan Project security. A covert meeting was in itself insufficient for a criminal indictment, but Army security was in any event more interested in eliminating a security threat than prosecuting a spy. Hiskey, although he had not been called to duty due to his work on the Manhattan Project, held a commission as a reserve U.S. Army officer. The Army lifted his exemption and dispatched him to an American base in the Northwest Territories in

Canada (not Alaska, but not far away). Apparently not realizing that his induction had been prompted by FBI surveillance (or by his acting very foolishly), before leaving, Hiskey contacted John H. Chapin, a chemical engineer with whom he had worked at the Substitute Alloy Material Laboratory at Columbia University, and arranged for him to meet with Adams. Security officials, however, observed that encounter as well, and when later questioned, Chapin admitted that Hiskey had told him that Adams was a Soviet agent; he denied, however, actually passing any secrets to him. Hiskey also put Edward Manning, a technician working at the Chicago Metallurgical Laboratory, in touch with Adams. Confronted by security officers, Manning admitted to meeting with Adams seven times but denied that he had actually passed any information to him. As with Hiskey, authorities had insufficient evidence for criminal charges and contented themselves with neutralizing Manning and Chapin by excluding them from the project.[83]

The KGB, however, knew none of this at the time. It continued to attempt to contact Hiskey in Chicago, not realizing until the fall of 1945 that "Ramsay" had been removed from the Manhattan Project in late April 1944 and had spent the rest of the war at a remote Army base in Canada.

Frustration: Darling and Weinberg

The KGB's plans for Byron Darling ("Huron") were not limited to his serving as a conduit to Clarence Hiskey; it wanted him to approach Enrico Fermi, the leading scientist at the Manhattan Project's Chicago facility. On 21 March 1945, Fitin directed Leonid Kvasnikov of the KGB New York station to send Darling to Chicago to "renew acquaintance" and "reestablish contact" with Fermi and Hyman Goldsmith, another physicist working at the Metallurgical Laboratory. While Darling had no compunction about providing information from his own work for U.S. Rubber, he was more reluctant about serving as a recruiter for such an eminent scientist as Fermi. On 1 April KGB officer Anatoly Yatskov met with Darling and grumbled: "'Huron' [Darling] has as yet done nothing to renew his acquaintance with Fermi. He has not written to Goldsmith or to Fermi himself. His explanation was that he thinks he can't look for a new job now and that it would be better for him to stay at his rubber company, because if he leaves the company, he will inevitably be drafted into the army and ultimately end up in the army and nowhere else. He explained that there are people on the enlistment committee where he is registered who have long had a bone to pick with him and didn't pack him off to the army only at the company's insistence.'"[84]

Darling stayed at U.S. Rubber but was more helpful in facilitating the KGB's contact with an old graduate school colleague and fellow Communist from the University of Wisconsin, Joseph Weinberg. Born in 1917 in New York to Jewish immigrants from Poland, Weinberg grew up in a Communist milieu. Described as a brilliant student, he graduated from the City College of New York (CCNY), moved to Wisconsin for his master's degree, and then migrated to the University of California, Berkeley, in 1939 to study with J. Robert Oppenheimer for his PhD, obtained in 1943.

On 29 March 1943, an FBI wire tap on the telephone of Steve Nelson (chief of the CPUSA in the San Francisco Bay Area) picked up someone named "Joe" telling Nelson's wife that he had urgent and important information and would come to the house to wait for Nelson's arrival. FBI listening devices collected most of the conversation in the subsequent meeting. "Joe," later identified as Weinberg, and Nelson discussed "the professor," presumably Robert Oppenheimer. Nelson acknowledged that Oppenheimer earlier had told him in general terms about the atomic project but had recently become more reticent. Weinberg indicated that Oppenheimer was also becoming increasingly uncomfortable with his young, radical graduate students, like Weinberg himself. Nelson pressed Weinberg for information about "the project" and asked for a copy of what had already been produced. Weinberg was hesitant, noted that he expected that he would be moving to the new site where work on the bomb would be conducted, and was concerned that his membership in the CPUSA since 1938 might cause him problems. Nevertheless, he offered a verbal description of the research work being undertaken on the atomic bomb, and the two discussed methods of future contact. Nelson cautioned Weinberg against writing anything down. The next day Nelson called the Soviet consulate and arranged to meet "at the usual place" with Peter Ivanov, a GRU officer operating under diplomatic cover at the consulate. Six days later the two rendezvoused on the grounds of a San Francisco hospital.[85]

By June 1943 the FBI informed military security officers about Weinberg's meeting with Nelson. They raised the matter with Oppenheimer, and in August he informed Weinberg the latter would not be moving to Los Alamos to take a role in the atomic bomb project. During a series of encounters Oppenheimer berated several of his former graduate students for their Communist political activities. Weinberg then mailed a package that the FBI intercepted; it contained a plea that Nelson and Bernadette Doyle (another Bay Area CPUSA official) not communicate with him and not mention his name. Spooked by the rebuff from Oppenheimer and frightened by the dismissals of several of his Communist friends from the Berkeley Radiation Laboratory, Weinberg had decided to lay low. He remained at Berkeley, teaching Oppenheimer's course on quantum theory but with no role in the Manhattan Project.[86]

There is no indication that the KGB had any idea that American security officers had identified Joseph Weinberg as a security risk and had isolated him from the Manhattan Project. Consequently, the New York station continued to regard him as a candidate for recruitment, although it was not until September 1945 that it notified Moscow that it was prepared to move to formal recruitment. In a report on "Enormous" sent to KGB chief Merkulov, Leonid Kvasnikov and Andrey Shevchenko noted that they were cultivating Weinberg and his wife through Darling: "Method [Joseph Weinberg] fills in for "Yew" [Oppenheimer] at the Univ. of Calif. and is a close friend of his. "Method" and "Idea" [Mrs. Merle Weinberg] are fellowcountrymen [Communists] who were brought into that fold by Huron [Darling]. Huron intends to meet with Method in Sept. or Oct. in NY or Detroit during the latter's vacation. The plan is to find out whether it is possible to obtain assistance from Method as well as from "Yew" himself."[87]

Darling met with Weinberg in New York on 5 and 6 October, and the New York station sent a detailed report to Moscow:

"The conversation was held first in a restaurant and subsequently in a park. Earlier, Huron [Darling] had already discussed the question of the balloon [atomic bomb] in the context of the int'l situation. He continued it here and concluded that it was essential for our country to obtain the secret of balloon construction. In conversation, he noted that 'Method' [Weinberg], who is involved in the balloon project and knows a lot of people who work there, has the resources to do something about this. Having correctly assessed the polit. situation and agreed that the USSR should have its own balloons, he argued, however, that in view of the strict measures to protect secrecy, it was impossible to pass materials across the border; that there was clearly a great danger of damaging relations between our country and the USA, and that if the USSR knew about the existence of such plans, it would prohibit taking any steps in that direction; that there could always be a provocateur among the accomplices who would get everyone exposed, b/c no one can be trusted; that a number of progressive scientists were taking part in the project who understand and stay abreast of the polit. situation, and they (or at least one of them—added 'Method') would not allow the balloon to be used against our country. . . .

During their conversation, Method said that he himself does not work on the balloon, and that he does not see 'Yew' [Oppenheimer] at all these days. Moreover, he tried to create the impression, as though inadvertently, that 'Yew' had changed and was losing his left convictions. Nevertheless, Huron is inclined to argue that the phrase 'or at least,' which Method let slip several times during the conversation, refers specifically to 'Yew.' Method noted that he has no ties with anyone and at the same time affirmed, in confirmation of his views, that a number of progressive scientists work there who hold the same views as himself.

One of the interesting points in the conversation was the idea, expressed by Method, where he noted that it would be better—and entirely possible— to move the 'brains' themselves that created the balloon to Moscow, rather than sending over information. To Huron's objection that it would be impossible for a scientist like that to leave, considering the security measures in place, Method countered that there was at least one person who would agree to leave the country behind and work in the USSR, after first getting sick and leaving work on En-s ["Enormous"]. Huron did not go any further into these matters; he believes that this scientist is 'Yew.' All this creates the impression that Method continues to maintain contact with 'Yew' and that the views he expressed to Huron may, in part, express 'Yew's' own point of view."

Kvasnikov and Darling optimistically and erroneously concluded that Weinberg remained in close touch with Oppenheimer and that his views reflected those of his one-time mentor. Likely because of its suggestion that some American Manhattan Project scientists, possibly Oppenheimer himself, might be willing to defect to the USSR, an annotation on the report noted that a copy was forwarded to Lavrenty Beria, then supervising the Soviet atomic bomb program.[88]

There are no more mentions of Weinberg in Vassiliev's notebooks. Perhaps the KGB finally realized that, once a promising source, he had been excluded from the Manhattan Project, was under security scrutiny, and was no longer a trusted Oppenheimer associate. Darling's value to the KGB also quickly deteriorated. A KGB officer reported that on 7 October 1945, on his way home after his meeting with Weinberg, Darling was detained by FBI agents for three days after he had noted surveillance at the railroad station. Although the FBI had told Darling that it was simply a mistake because "they had suspected he was an escapee from a mental institution," the KGB wasn't taking any chances and suspended meetings between Anatoly Yatskov (Darling's contact) and his agents. There is no record of any further contacts with Darling.[89]

Darling left Detroit in 1946 and worked at short-term positions at the University of Wisconsin and Yale University until he won a physics professorship in 1947 at Ohio State University, where later he also worked on a U.S. Air Force research project. The House Committee on Un-American Activities twice called him to testify in 1953, the first time in Washington, the second in Columbus, Ohio. At both hearings he took the Fifth Amendment to questions about communism and espionage. Suspended by Ohio State after the first hearing, he faced a university disciplinary committee. Instead of taking the Fifth Amendment, he lied, asserting that he had never belonged to either the CPUSA or "any organization which, to my knowledge or belief, was affiliated or connected with the Communist Party," and defended his refusal to answer questions under oath. He was fired. He moved to Canada and held a professorship at Laval University for the rest of his professional career. He never admitted his Communist loyalties or his cooperation with Soviet intelligence. Several historical accounts of the era have treated Darling as an innocent man persecuted by witch hunters.[90]

Frustration: Martin Kamen

When former KGB San Francisco station chief Grigory Kheifets returned to Moscow in August 1944 to face accusations of inefficiency, he prepared reports on his tenure emphasizing the positive. A September report, for example, proudly noted that just days prior to his departure from San Francisco he met with a new prospect with connections to the Manhattan Project:

"Doctor Kamen is a PhD in chemistry. Lawrence's closest colleague at the laboratory (cyclotron). A chance acquaintance by "Map" [Louise Bransten] through the line of the American-Russian Inst. Kamen is 32–35 years old. Born to Russian parents in Chicago, also graduated from the university there. According to the comments of experts, "Dorin" [Eltenton] in particular, he is a brilliant chemist and the best informed on the cyclotron's operations. According to "Dorin," Kamen knows the secret of the special formula of neutron flow. I have maintained a friendly relationship with Kamen. He is a big Russian vodka lover and when there's no vodka, he also likes top brands of American whiskeys. In connection with my departure he passed along semi-official scientific anthologies as a present for the USSR's scientific institutions. Shortly before that he gave similar material to "Map" to send to the Union through the American-Russian Institute. To secure the contact, a letter of thanks should be sent to K. from the appropriate scientific institution and a present sent. "Gift" [Kasparov] maintains personal contact with K."[91]

Martin Kamen was everything that Kheifets described and more. He was a close associate of Ernest Lawrence, and while not a CPUSA member, Kamen was an ardent pro-Soviet fellow traveler, accounting for his association with the American-Russian Institute and Louise Bransten, secret CPUSA member and Kheifets's intimate companion in San Francisco. That Kamen would at his own initiative deliver "semi-official scientific" information to Kheifets and Bransten as gifts to the Soviet Union marked him as a prospect for KGB cultivation. And Kheifets noted that his successor as San Francisco KGB station chief, Grigory Kasparov, already had established contact with Kamen. Kamen, in fact, was a more desirable prospect than Kheifets realized. Kheifets didn't appear to know it, but Kamen was also working at the Manhattan Project laboratories at Oak Ridge.

However, by the time Kheifets wrote his report about his new prospect, Kamen had been rendered useless. One of the reasons Kheifets made so little progress against "Enormous" was that American counterintelligence had identified him as a Soviet intelligence officer at least by 1943. As Soviet vice-consul in San Francisco, Kheifets was immune from arrest. But mindful of the Manhattan Project activities across the bay at Berkeley, both FBI agents and military security operatives dogged his every step. (Surprisingly, Kheifets does not appear to have realized that he was subject to other than routine American security surveillance.) So intense was surveillance that operatives of the FBI and Army security stumbled over each other when Kheifets, accompanied by Grigory Kasparov, took Martin Kamen to lunch at the Fish Grotto in San Francisco on 2 July 1944. The FBI agents got through the door of the restaurant first and procured a table in close proximity to the one where Kamen lectured to the two Soviet diplomats/intelligence officers all through the meal. The noise level in the restaurant prevented them from clearly understanding what Kamen was saying, but they heard enough to record that he was discussing radiation and atomic research. They also observed Kamen giving the Soviets a thick sheaf of papers.

Kamen later testified to Congress about the incident and admitted discussing radiation, but only the latest research about the medical use of X-rays, particularly with cancer, then a cutting-edge medical technology. He insisted the documents he gave the Soviets dealt with scientific research but were unclassified and denied providing any information on the Manhattan Project. He also confirmed that Louise Bransten had introduced him to Kheifets. Kheifets's September 1944 report corroborates Kamen's story. For that matter, the FBI agents' notes only partly contradicted his version. They included indications that Kamen had also spoken about Oak Ridge and Washington (site of the Hanford facility) and of an atomic pile, as nuclear reactors were then termed. But what they were able to hear and note down was so intermittent that it was not sufficient to establish if Kamen had spoken of those matters only in passing or in detail. Kamen, for his part, denied that he had even mentioned these matters casually. In any event, Kheifets's September summary of the relationship with Kamen does not indicate that he betrayed classified information to the Soviets or had a knowing relationship with Soviet intelligence. Given that Moscow Center was then accusing Kheifets of failing to make progress on "Enormous," he could have been expected to boast about any bomb-related information that Kamen had provided.[92]

From the point of view of security personnel, whether Kamen had or had not delivered classified information when meeting with two Soviet officials at the Fish Grotto was irrelevant. Their goal was to prevent any unauthorized leak from occurring, not to catch a spy after the deed was done. A scientist who met privately with Soviet diplomats, particularly KGB officers, and was motivated by pro-Soviet fervor to give them advanced technological information, even if it was unclassified, had acted in an irresponsible fashion and was a security risk. Martin Kamen, the prospect Kheifets proudly described to Moscow Center in his September report, was fired from the Manhattan Project on 12 July, ten days after lunching with Kheifets and Kasparov.

Frustration: Alfred Slack

In February 1945 a KGB New York station report on its agent network included a new source at the Manhattan Project facility at Oak Ridge, Tennessee, from whom it had every reason to expect considerable productivity:

"Bir"—*Al Slack.* Chemical engineer. At camp No. 1 [Oak Ridge] since Dec. '44. Before that—at an explosives factory, and before that—at the Eastman Kodak film factory in Rochester, NY. With us since '38. Valuable materials.

Married. Bir uses his wife's aunt to deliver urgent summonses and confidential reports to Arno [Harry Gold]. The aunt does not know the true nature of this correspondence (she lives in Brooklyn). The cover story of Arno and Bir's connection—a wish to jointly open a private business after the war. Bir used to be in the CP but later left. Before "Bir" joined camp No. 1, Arno would go see him once every month and a half to two months.[93]

Alfred Dean Slack had been a highly productive industrial spy for Soviet intelligence since the late 1930s (see chapter 6). He had assisted in recruiting other engineers and technicians into industrial espionage, and the KGB had found his material of considerable value and given him generous cash bonuses for his work. His productivity had continued to the fall of 1944, when he was employed at the Holston Ordnance Works in Kingsport, Tennessee, and he supplied Harry Gold, his KGB contact, with samples of RDX, a powerful new explosive. But after he got a job in late 1944 at the Clinton Engineering Works, the chief employer at the Oak Ridge complex, he appeared to have ceased supplying material to Gold. Exactly why is not clear.

After Gold was arrested in 1950, he identified Slack as one of his sources. FBI agents confronted Slack, and he quickly confessed that he had provided Gold with technical information from 1940 to 1944, receiving a payment of $200 per report, but denied supplying anything atomic-related. By his account, at their last meeting, when he was still employed at Holston Ordnance, he had told Gold that he had obtained a new job at a very secret government facility at Oak Ridge (Slack said he thought at that point that the facility was involved with poison gas) and was severing his links to the KGB. Gold had a slightly different version. Slack did not break the contact; instead, Gold had later received instructions from Semen Semenov to cease his connection with Slack. Gold said that he had no contact with Slack after he went to Oak Ridge and no knowledge if Slack had supplied any information on Oak Ridge to another KGB courier. Lacking any evidence to challenge Slack's account, the government decided to charge him only with his admitted espionage prior to his job at Oak Ridge. He was convicted in September 1950. Federal prosecutors, in light of Slack's quick confession, asked for a ten-year sentence. But Judge Robert L. Taylor, noting that American soldiers in Korea were then fighting and dying in combat with Communist troops, rejected leniency and sentenced Slack to fifteen years in prison.[94]

Slack's claim that he did not supply information on Oak Ridge was probably true. It is unlikely that the February 1945 KGB report of Slack supplying "valuable materials" could be a reference to him providing atomic-related material because he had only very recently started work at Oak Ridge. It almost certainly reflected his much longer career as a productive but non-atomic industrial spy. Alfred Slack was yet another frustration for KGB hopes for atomic intelligence.

Breakthrough

The year 1944 was one of transition for the KGB's "Enormous" project. Despite significant success in Great Britain, the KGB had been unable to recruit any important sources in the United States in 1942 or 1943. Its chief targets on the Manhattan Project continued to elude it in 1944. But several unexpected sources suddenly gave it entree to key atomic facilities. Russell McNutt, handed over by Julius Rosenberg in February 1944, was the first unexpected gift out of the blue. That same year, the KGB received information from a mysterious source mentioned in an August 1944 Moscow Center message chastising its New York station:

"The fact that you received material on 'En-s' ["Enormous"] from a source unknown to us shows first and foremost that your work in that area is unsatisfactory and that you are not discovering or using available resources, instead leaving the unraveling of this problem to chance. We find the nonchalance, or indifference, with which you informed us of this material and the circumstances in which it was obtained (only a few lines, not even in the letter itself but in the list of supplements to it) quite shocking. If someone chose to take a step as risky as bringing this top secret document to the factory [Amtorg], how could you disregard this person and not take every possible step to identify the unknown individual? We attach a great deal of importance to this whole affair; the anonymous person's material is extremely interesting, and information we received from oth. sources corroborates its content. Therefore, take all possible steps to identify the person in question. Report your results immediately."[95]

Neither the original report that raised Moscow Center ire nor any follow-up appears in Vassiliev's notebooks. What was this all about? In Andrew and Mitrokhin's *The Sword and the Shield,* also based on KGB archival material, there is the following passage:

In April 1943, a month after the opening of Los Alamos, the New York residency reported an important source on the MANHATTAN project. An unknown woman had turned up at the Soviet consulate-general and delivered a letter containing classified information on the atomic weapons program. A month later the same woman, who again declined to give her name, brought another letter with details of research on the plutonium route to the atomic bomb. Investigations by the New York residency revealed that the woman was an Italian nurse, whose first name was Lucia, the daughter of an anti-fascist Italian union leader, "D." At a meeting arranged by the residency through the leaders of the Friends of the USSR society, Lucia said that she was acting only as an intermediary. The letters came from her brother-in-law, an American scientist working on plutonium research for the DuPont company in Newport while completing a degree course in New York, who had asked his wife Regina to pass his correspondence to the Soviet consulate via her sister Lucia. The scientist—apparently the first of the American atom spies—was recruited under the codename MAR; Regina became MONA and Lucia OLIVIA.

According to Andrew and Mitrokhin, "Mar" became by the end of 1943 a Soviet source at the DuPont laboratory at the Manhattan Project facility at Hanford, Washington.[96]

While there are certain overlaps between the story in *The Sword and the Shield* and the passage on the anonymous walk-in discussed in Vassiliev's notebooks, there are major differences as well. Chiefly, in *The Sword and the Shield* the walk-in resulted in the recruitment of a scientist in the Manhattan Project by the end of 1943, but the walk-in in the Moscow Center message transcribed in Vassiliev's notebooks remains unidentified and unrecruited in August 1944. Nor is there any mention or even hints of the existence of "Mar," "Mona," or "Olivia" in Vassiliev's notebooks. This remains one of the mysteries of "Enormous."

A Gift from the Neighbors: Klaus Fuchs

The third 1944 source on American atomic research came to the KGB via its "neighbors," Soviet military intelligence. Klaus Fuchs had joined the Communist Party of Germany (KPD) while a student at Kiel University in 1932. After the Nazi seizure of power in 1933, he fled to France and then to Great Britain, where he earned advanced degrees in physics at the University of Bristol and the University of Edinburgh. He remained a steadfast Communist, although generally avoiding open political activity. Under threat of a German invasion in 1940, British authorities briefly interned German nationals as enemy aliens, and Fuchs was sent to Canada. On review British authorities judged him not to be a security threat; he was released and returned to Britain. He applied for British citizenship, and it was granted in 1942.[97]

In mid-1941 Rudolf Peierls, also a refugee from Germany, a senior physicist, and one of the driving figures behind the creation of the British atomic bomb program, recruited Fuchs to join Tube Alloys. Shortly after learning what work he was doing, Fuchs contacted Jurgen Kuczynski, a fellow refugee from Germany and a leader of the exiled KPD in Britain and asked to be put in touch with the Soviets. Kuczynski delivered Fuchs's request and vouched for his Communist loyalties to the KPD's contact at the Soviet Embassy in London. A GRU report sent to the KGB summarized what happened next:

"F. [Fuchs] was recruited for intelligence work in England in Aug. 1941 by our operative, former military attaché secretary Cde. Kremer, on a lead from Jurgen Kuczynski (brother of our illegal station chief in England, 'Sonya' [Ursula Kuczynski]). The latter was living in London at the time and was one of the senior workers of the German Comparty in England; Kremer knew him through offic-al connections. F. agreed to work on an ideological basis and did not accept payment.

While working for us, F. passed us a number of valuable materials containing theor-cal calculations for splitting the uranium atom and creating an atomic bomb. In July 1942, the connection with F. was temporarily interrupted due to Kremer's departure for the USSR. On 22.10.1942, 'Sonya' informed our worker that her brother, J. Kuczynski, had told her that in July 1942, a physicist by the name of F. had lost contact with a representative of the Sov. Emb-ssy's milit-ry department who called himself Johnson. 'Sonya' also reported that at Kuczynski's suggestion, she already established contact with F., received materials from him, and asks us to indicate whether she should continue to maintain contact with him and accept mater-als from him. On our instructions, Sonya continued to maintain contact with F. . . . F. has shown himself to be a hardworking and conscientious agent who worked solely for ideological reasons."

Ursula Kuczynski Beurton, Jurgen's sister, was an experienced intelligence agent who had worked on GRU operations in China and Switzerland before moving to London on the basis of her marriage to Len Beurton, a British veteran of the Communist International Brigades.[98]

Fuchs supplied information from the British bomb project to GRU until late 1943, when he was sent to the United States with other key British scientists to assist the Manhattan Project. Initially Fuchs worked on gaseous diffusion uranium separation at a Kellex facility in New York City. In August 1944 he was transferred to Los Alamos, where he worked in the Theoretical Physics Division as part of a team assigned to the problem of how implosion could be used to trigger a plutonium bomb.

Once in the United States, Fuchs's contact with Soviet intelligence shifted from GRU to the KGB. Fuchs first came to the attention of the KGB in November 1943, when Engelbert Broda, the Austrian physicist and KGB source, identified Fuchs as a secret Communist who was working on the British atomic bomb project. Since Fuchs was German, KGB London officers queried Jurgen Kuczynski about him but reported that Kuczynski was surprisingly uncommunicative "and acted so strangely as to automatically suggest" to the KGB officers that Fuchs was already working for another branch of Soviet intelligence. The KGB checked with GRU, and GRU chief General Ivan Ilichev informed the KGB's Fitin in late November:

K. Fuchs—physicist, German émigré, German CP member, currently lives in Birmingham, England, where he works on uranium problems at a phys. laboratory at the U. of Birmingham.

K. F. has been a source of ours since Aug. 1941, when he was recruited on the recommendation of Jurgen Kuczynski. In connection with the laboratory's relocation to America, it is expected that F. will go there as well. Be informed that we have taken steps to set up a connection with F. in America. More detailed information will be reported when Fuchs is handed over to you.

This was a time when the KGB was pressing GRU very strongly to hand over its atomic intelligence sources.[99]

Not until January 1944 did Soviet military intelligence get around to providing a report on Fuchs:

"Over the course of working with us, F. [Fuchs] has passed us a number of theor. calculations for splitting the atom and creating a uranium bomb. We sent the mater-als to the Representative of the State Committee of Defense USSR, Cde. Kaftanov, and later to the Vice-Chairman of the Council of People's Commissars USSR, Cde. Pervukhin. The mater-ls received a high assessment. [Shipment dates: 22.9.41, 30.9.41, 26.5.43, 17.6.43, 12.7.43, 16.9.43, 28.10.43]. . . . F. did not receive regular remuneration from us. He was occasionally given individual gifts. When he was given a gift of money, F. did not turn it down. Because a group of Eng. scientists working on creating a uranium bomb were transferred to the USA, F. went there as well at the start of November 1943."

In an amusing coincidence, GRU also wrote: "'In April 1943, F. [Fuchs] gave a lead for recruiting an Austrian scientist in England named Broda . . . , a physical chemist by specialization. Broda is an active member of the Austrian Comparty. He works on fast neutrons at Cambridge, and before that he worked on slow neutrons with a scientist named Halban. . . . When he gave the lead, F. expressed a desire not to take part in this recruitment himself and to remain incognito for Broda. We have not recruited Broda.'" Broda, as noted above, had suggested that the KGB recruit Fuchs. GRU also provided the KGB with arrangements it had made for a rendezvous with him in New York, as well as contact information for his sister, Kristel Heineman, who lived in Cambridge, Massachusetts.[100]

Fitin immediately transmitted this information to the KGB New York station with orders to contact Fuchs as quickly as possible:

"'Rest' [Fuchs] was recruited by the neighbors [GRU] in August 1941 on the recommendation of a senior worker of the fellowcountryman [Communist] organization in Germany. He worked on an ideological basis. He did not receive regular pay from the neighbors. Occasionally, gifts were made. When offered a monetary gift, however, he would not turn it down. In accordance with an agreement between the Island [UK] and the Country [USA], reached in the second half of last year, when a special delegation from the Island came to the Country, a number of leading scientific workers from the Island have moved to the Country, including Chadwick, Frisch, Oliphant, Peierls, et al. At the beginning of November, 'Rest' went there as well. . . . As an agent, 'Rest' is a major figure with considerable opportunities and experience in agent work, which he acquired over two years of work with the neighbors. Once you have determined his position in the Country and his opportunities at the initial meetings, you can immediately switch over to practical work receiving information and material."

Fitin also sent the rendezvous information GRU had provided, along with critical remarks about the "neighbors'" tradecraft:

Rendezvous in NY—to establish a connection with "Rest" [Fuchs]. Meeting place: . . . at the front door of Henry Street Settlement, in Henry Street, Down Town, East End, Jewish Quarter, NY. Time: at 16.00 on the 1st and 3rd Sat. of every month, starting in Jan. '44. Recognition signals: "Rest" will be holding a green book and a tennis ball. Our man will be wearing gloves. He will be carrying a third glove in one of his hands.

OUR MAN: *What is the way to the China Town?*
"REST": *I think the China Town is closed at 5 o'clock.*

Meeting place—a well-known Jewish philanthropic center.
"Note: From our point of view, the rendezvous is very poorly conceived. Periodically showing up on certain days and waiting around in the same place for a person carrying objects as unusual as the ones indicated could easily at-

tract anyone's attention. Nevertheless, we are obliged to follow the accepted rendezvous terms."

If you are unable to establish a connection by 1.04.44, then go through his sister, Heineman, who lives on 144 Lake View Avenue, Cambridge, Massachusetts. Married, she and her husband—fellowcountrymen. Password:

OUR MAN: *I bring you greetings from Max.*
SHE: *Oh, I heard Max had twins!*
OUR MAN: *Yes, seven days ago.*

Moscow specifically suggested Harry Gold, a veteran KGB liaison with American technical sources, as "the most suitable handler for 'Rest' [Fuchs]."[101]

Gold met with Fuchs in New York on Saturday, 5 February 1944, and wrote:

"We were both at the appointed place on time at 4:00 P.M.: he had the green book and the tennis ball and I had the four gloves. I greeted him and he accepted my offer of a walk. We strolled a while and talked. He is about 5 ft., 10 in., thin, pale complexioned, and at first was very reserved in manner; this last is good. K. [Klaus] dresses well (tweeds) but not fancily. After a ride on the subway, we took a taxi and went to eat. As I kept talking about myself, he warmed up and began to show evidence of getting down to business. For instance, I would say that I had felt honored at having been told to meet him, and he said that he 'could hardly believe it' when he had been told that we would like him to work with us (this was in England, of course). The following developed about K.: He obviously has worked with our people before and he is fully aware of what he is doing. Also, he is apparently one of us in spirit. K. has only been here since September, but he expects to be here for at least the duration; he may be transferred out of New York, but it is not very likely—in any case he will be able to let us know in plenty of time. He is a mathematical physicist and a graduate of the Universities of Bristol and Edinburgh; he is most likely a very brilliant man to have such a position at his age (he looks about 30). We took a long walk after dinner, and he explained the 'factory' [Manhattan Project] setup."

Fuchs went on to describe the Manhattan Project's major lines of research on uranium separation—electronic at the University of California and gaseous diffusion at Columbia University—and practical bomb work to be carried out at "Camp Y," which Fuchs thought was somewhere in New Mexico. Although the work was being conducted in "'water-tight compartments,'" Fuchs agreed to "'furnish us with everything'" in his division "'and as much of the other as possible.'"[102]

Three weeks later Kvasnikov cabled Moscow with the news that Fuchs had turned over a report on his own work on "Enormous." Three weeks after that, Harry Gold explained that at his 11 March meeting in Manhattan, Fuchs, after providing another fifty pages, had asked how his report had been received. When Gold said there was only one flaw, the absence of a more detailed context and how his work fit in with the overall project, Fuchs was "'not very pleased'" because he had already done this with his British contact and he was concerned that taking such documents might endanger him "'if such explanatory material were found in his possession, b/c his work here has nothing to do with such materials. Nevertheless, he agreed to give us what we need as soon as possible.'" In a report to Moscow Kvasnikov sniffed that "it is obvious that in their work with 'Rest,' the neighbors [GRU] did not guide him or report any conclusions based on his materials."[103]

At the end of March, Gold and Fuchs met on the Grand Concourse in the Bronx and had dinner together. Fuchs complained that the Americans were withholding information from the British scientists and British authorities might send him back to Great Britain by July. The other option was that he might be sent to Los Alamos, but he could not guarantee that possibility. On 4 May they met in Long Island City, and Fuchs promised to find out the details about the three-week trip Rudolf Peierls, his boss, had just taken to Los Alamos, the key site where the bombs were actually being built. In early June, Fuchs handed over another report but thought his tenure in America was coming to an end. Wrangling between the two countries over the British decision to build its own diffusion plant had sparked plans to send the British scientists home. He thought he had only about six more weeks in America. On 15 June Gold gave him specific questions to answer and heard that the situation remained uncertain.[104]

Moscow was delighted with Fuchs's intelligence; at last the KGB had a highly placed source within the Manhattan Project, but remained critical of his handling by the New York station. Even though it acknowledged receiving regular reports he had provided, Moscow complained that the reports did not have sufficient information from Gold about the personal relationship between the two, about Fuchs's personality, his place of work, where he lived, the cover story to account for their meetings, and "'terms of contact for 'Rest' [Fuchs] in case the connection is suddenly lost.'"[105]

The Center's fears proved prescient. The KGB New York station learned in July that Fuchs was probably moving to England and instructed Gold to arrange future communications, but Fuchs did not show up for a scheduled meeting in New York on 5 August. Gold was too busy to come to the next meeting, and Fuchs was not present at the next scheduled one (he had arrived at Los Alamos on 14 August and had no way to contact Gold). When Gold went to Fuchs's apartment in New York, he was told that Fuchs had left for England. Gold tried to find Fuchs through his sister but was unable to contact her. Informed by cipher telegram on 29 August that contact with Fuchs, the only high-level source in the Manhattan Project, had been lost, Moscow Center was outraged: "'The liberty taken by Goose [Gold] (failure to appear at a meeting) is outrageous. A stern warning and reprimand must be made to Anton [Kvasnikov] and Goose for losing contact with such a source, and as a result a search for R. ["Rest"/Fuchs] that violates the rules of covert work is beginning.'" The New York station defended Gold, reminding Moscow that he frequently missed meetings due to his job responsibilities and that such occurrences could not be fully anticipated. Only providing a more flexible cover for Gold "'that would take up as little of his time as possible and allow him to use most of his time for our work'" would resolve the problem.[106]

In late September 1944 Gold traveled to Boston and went to the home of Fuchs's sister. The Heineman family, he learned, was away on vacation. He returned in late October, waited for a period when her husband was out, and introduced himself with the verbal recognition signals arranged earlier. She told him that she thought her brother had returned to England, but she had not heard from him. Gold came back in early November to see if she had heard anything and reported: "'I arrived in the morning and again went out to Camb. [Cambridge], laden with candy and a book ("Some of My Best Friends Are Soldiers" by Margaret Halsey). She had very good news: Rest [Fuchs] had called from Chicago and had said that he was there on business from New Mexico, where he is stationed—he did not go to "Ostrov" [Britain] after all. Further, he will be home to Cambridge for two weeks during Christmas. So I can see him then. I was so overjoyed that I stayed for lunch.'" Gold arranged to return in a month or so. When he did, on 7 December, Kristel Heineman told him there was still no word about exactly when Fuchs would arrive, but in a phone call he had also told her that in addition to visiting the Heinemans in Boston, he might have to go to New York for a day or so. Gold judged this indicated that "'Klaus expected us to get in touch with him. I gave her a small piece of paper with the message for him carefully printed out, and Mrs. Heineman said she would give it to Klaus as soon as he would arrive.'" Gold's instructions were for Fuchs to call the telephone number of "Hudson" [unidentified] with news of his arrival.[107]

Christmas of 1944 came and went, and there was still no word of Klaus Fuchs. Moscow Center proposed that Gold go back to Boston more frequently, but Kvasnikov pointed out that such meetings might raise suspicions with Kristel Heineman's husband, whom the KGB did not want to involve. Fuchs finally arrived in Boston during the second week of February and called the number Gold had left for him. Anatoly Yatskov got the news and promptly went to Philadelphia to inform Gold. On Monday, 19 February, Gold arrived in Boston and Fuchs was there, but Mrs. Heineman warned him that her husband was home and a visitor from the British Consulate was expected. He went back to Philadelphia and returned on Wednesday. Gold's report read as follows:

"This time the trip was a complete success. I arrived again at the sister's home at exactly the same time in the morning, and K. [Klaus] welcomed me most warmly. After distributing the gifts I had for the children and K's sister—as well as the opera wallet for K.—we went back into Boston while K. bought some small items for his friends in Santa Fe, and of course we talked while he explained the situation to me.

It is this: 1. He was not granted a leave at Christmas and so was unable to come to Boston till now. The traveling time took away six days so that all he was really left was just a day over a week. K. was due to leave Thursday night. 2. Since he is supposed to make a written report on all people he meets (and in fact even on those at work who speak of the project outside of the actual working hours and outside of their own particular field), he did not want his brother-in-law to meet me—particularly since the man from the Brit. Consulate was supposed to visit K. either Monday or Tuesday. But for some reason, which K. does not know, this man did not come—which is probably just as well. 3. K. said that he had made a very careful check and was certain that he was not being watched.

We returned to Cambridge about 1 o'clock and had a very fine lunch with K's sister. Then we went upstairs and K. outlined the setup at the camp to me: a) When he went there in August, there were only 2,500 to 3,000 people. Now it has expanded to 45,000! b) The work being carried on is the actual manufacture of 'factory' bombs. Employed there are physicists, mathematicians, chemists, engineers: civil, mechanical, electrical, chemical, and many other types of technical help, as well as a U.S. Army Engineer Detachment. c) They are progressing very well and are expected to go into full-scale production in about three months—but K was hesitant about this date and said he would not like to be held to it. d) The area is about 40 miles N.W. from Santa Fe and covers the grounds of Los Alamos Ranch, a former Ranch School.

R. ["Rest"/Fuchs] is allowed only one day a month off to go shopping in Santa Fe (as are all others), and we made a date for the first Saturday in Santa Fe. I am to get off the bus station at Shelby and San Francisco and set my watch by the large clock on San Francisco. Then I am to meet him at 4 P.M. on the Castillo St. Bridge crossing Santa Fe River. The waiting time is 10 minutes. If we do not meet, the same procedure is to be repeated month after month. Should a substitute have to come (though he would very much prefer me), he is to be identified as follows: the man will have a yellow pencil between two blue ones in his lapel, and he will be carrying a copy of Bennett Cerf's *Try and Stop Me*. K will say to him, 'How is your brother Raymond?' and the answer will be, 'Not well, he has been in the hospital for two weeks.' The final identification is to be by means of two sections of paper torn in a jagged pattern, one of which K has. K was really prepared and gave me a bus schedule and a map of Santa Fe—he advises me not to go directly there but to a nearby city such as Albuquerque. He also gave me the material which I submitted, and we parted at 3:30 P.M.

My attempt to give him money was unsuccessful—but I did not offend him as I led up to the subject very delicately. He says that he is making all he needs. K does, however, want one thing: when we enter Kiel and Berlin in Germany, he wants the Gestapo Headquarters there searched and his dossier (which is very complete) destroyed before it should fall into other hands. This, I told him, we would try to do if at all possible."

On the last item, the KGB New York station also suggested that the Red Army be alerted to look out for Emile Fuchs, Klaus's father, who was believed to be in a Nazi labor camp and might need special assistance.[108]

After analyzing documents that Fuchs had given Gold, Fitin cabled Kvasnikov that the material was "of great value, contains information for the first time about the electromagnetic method of separation." While delighted by the renewal of ties with Fuchs (with the new cover name of "Charles"), the Center peppered New York with questions; exactly where did Fuchs work at Los Alamos and what did he do, what had he been doing in Chicago and whom had he seen, why was the next meeting not until June, why not use Kristel Heineman as the contact to alert the station to any alterations in Fuchs's plans rather than the KGB New York station plan to use Lona Cohen, a young American KGB agent? Kvasnikov replied that the June meeting was at

"Ch.'s ["Charles"/Fuchs's] request, motivated both by a need for meeting near the Preserve [Los Alamos] as rarely as possible in the interest of security, and because, by that time, Ch. will have the results of the work on preparing the 'En-s' ["Enormous"] device for a test device, which they plan to conduct at anoth. location. The decision to use Leslie's [Lona Cohen's] address to receive a letter from Ch., and the refusal to use Ant's [Kristel Heineman's] address for this purpose, was made because Arno's [Gold's] frequent trips to see Ant, just to find out whether there was any information from Ch., could not have remained inconspicuous to Ant's husband. Not only is the latter not close to us, but in 1944, Ant had been planning to divorce him. Therefore, a more reliable and simple path was chosen—using Leslie's address, and this was the one given to Ch. If necessary, Ch. will send a letter to this address, not under his own name, but under an assumed name. Thus, Ch.'s identity will not be revealed to L."

As for Fuchs's work, Kvasnikov reported: "Ch. is in charge of work on the internal explosion, i.e., the primary explosion, which is necessary to start the chain reaction. He works jointly with Kisti [Kistiakowsky] on the staff of Camp-2's [Los Alamos's] theoretical group under Peierls."[109]

Anatoly Yatskov also reported that he had asked Gold to ascertain if Fuchs had a girlfriend. Gold replied that the subject had not been discussed and he doubted Fuchs would talk about such matters. Yatskov was mulling over the possibility of using a woman "'to play the part of an official 'sweetheart,'" who could visit him "'on a regular basis and meet him without fear of arousing suspicion on the part of authorities if their liaison were discovered.'" Gold promised to raise the issue at his next rendezvous and also to learn about the rules pertaining to bachelors at Los Alamos and their relationships with women. Andrey Graur, a senior KGB officer in Moscow, sternly denounced this suggestion, along with the informality of Yatskov's report. He lectured Yatskov that it was "unacceptable" to raise the woman question, although it was unclear whether out of concern for propriety or fear that it would offend Fuchs. Yatskov responded respectfully that he had no intention of meddling in Fuchs's private life or even providing a girlfriend for him; he was only exploring the creation of a "'fictitious liaison'" that would, in any case, have to be approved by Moscow. The discussion with Gold had been conducted "'in a purely businesslike and completely respectable and straightforward tone, and was not reminiscent in form of that somewhat overly familiar style in which my report had been written.'" That report had been a "'running commentary'" for Leonid Kvasnikov, his superior at the KGB

New York station and had inadvertently been sent to Moscow "'in an un-polished form.'"[110]

When Yatskov met with Gold at the beginning of March and learned that his veteran agent handler was suffering from constant sore throats, he decided, "'It would be a good idea to take advantage of the dry climate in New Mexico to treat his ear, nose, and throat equipment,'" as well as meet with Fuchs. They agreed that Gold would locate a sanatorium and take his mother along with him. Yatskov reasoned that her presence "'would make the trip itself seem entirely peaceful and domestic. . . . Ob-viously, he should take his vacation in the first half of June, which is when the meeting with Ch-s ["Charles"/Fuchs] is scheduled.'" Moscow ap-proved the plan, and Gold left for Colorado with his mother in late May, planning to take an excursion to Santa Fe to meet Fuchs in early June. (In his discussions with the FBI after he confessed, Gold never mentioned that his mother accompanied him on his trip west, perhaps to avoid in-volving her; he remained devoted to her until her death in 1947.) A re-port from New York on 13 June conveyed the good news to Moscow that Gold had received "very interesting information."[111]

Meeting Klaus Fuchs had not been Gold's only assignment on his June trip. Officers at the KGB New York station had made a fateful de-cision shortly before Gold left, one that would end up contributing to the destruction of key parts of its espionage network in the United States. By this point the KGB New York station had three sources at Los Alamos: Fuchs, Greenglass, and Theodore Hall. While it evaluated Fuchs's ma-terials as "the most valuable" of the three, the KGB wanted all the infor-mation it could get out of Los Alamos, and sending couriers to New Mex-ico was not all that easy. Consequently, shortly before Gold left for Colorado and New Mexico, Anatoly Yatskov informed him that he needed to go to Albuquerque after meeting Fuchs in Santa Fe to pick up mate-rials from a second source, David Greenglass. (Greenglass, a soldier, was a skilled machinist working at Los Alamos as part of a U.S. Army de-tachment. His wife, Ruth, had an apartment in Albuquerque, and David was able to get there on weekend leave.)[112]

Igor Gouzenko's defection in September led the New York station to increased security concerns and a temporary cessation of contacts with Gold's sources. New York, however, cabled Moscow asking for permission to allow Gold to make his scheduled meeting with Fuchs on 19 Septem-ber and received approval, not least because it had to arrange a password for a meeting in England, where Fuchs expected to return after the end of the war. Gold left on 14 September, again accompanied by his mother. After a stopover in a resort town in Arizona where he left her, he took a train to Albuquerque and a bus to Santa Fe. Gold described "'conditions in the vicinity of the Preserve [Los Alamos] as far more tense than they had been during his trip there in June. The local residents, proud that their state has the honor of developing and testing the first balloon [atomic bomb], are particularly wary of people from out of state.'" As for the meeting itself, Gold wrote:

"For the first time since I have known him Charles [Fuchs] was late—by fifteen minutes. But he did come along in a car and picked me up. We drove out into the mountains beyond S.F. [Santa Fe], and he explained the reason for his tardiness by telling that he had great difficulty in breaking away from his friends at Zapovednik [Los Alamos]. He said, further, that we had made an error by choosing to meet in the evening in SF [Santa Fe] and that it would have been better to have come together in the afternoon when everyone was busy shopping. In fact, Charles said, it was very bad for me to come to SF in any case but that we would not have foreseen this since the last meeting. He was very nervous (the first time I have seen him so), and I was inwardly not too calm myself. His first remark had been, 'Well, were you impressed?' I answered that I was even more than impressed, and in fact was even somehow horrified. Charles said that the test shot had far exceeded expectations but that these had been purposely toned down because the results of the calculations showed them to be so incredible. Charles was present at the test shot, some 20 miles away.

As regards the future, Charles says that a research institute will be established in "Ostrov" [Britain], but that he will most likely be here till at least the beginning of the year. He agreed, however, that it was a good idea for making an arrangement for meeting in Ostrov. The city is London; the place Mornington Crescent, along the Crescent; the date is the first Saturday of the month after which Charles returns, and so on the first Saturday of each month thereafter; the time 8 o'clock in the evening; Charles is to carry a copy of Life magazine, our man is to carry three books tied together with a stout twine and held by a finger; Charles's remark is: 'Can you tell me the way to Harward Square?' (Charles is to speak first); our man's remark is 'Yes, but excuse me a minute—I have an awful cold' (and our man is to blow his nose into a handkerchief).

Charles gave me the material, which is excellent and fully covers everything. He dropped me off in the outskirts of SF. The next meeting will be in the city of Charles's sister, probably in November or December. I am to keep in touch with her so as to be advised when. After a few bad moments of waiting for the bus, I left SF with no mishaps."

The material Fuchs handed over included a detailed technical description of the pure uranium bomb dropped on Hiroshima.[113]

Yatskov met with Gold on 12 November and imposed additional security measures. Fuchs was to leave his materials at his sister's and Gold would collect them later, avoiding any direct contact. This was, it turned out, Gold's last contact with Soviet intelligence for nearly a year. The Soviets received news via Kim Philby (a KGB source within the British Secret Intelligence Service) on 20 November that within a week Allan Nunn May, betrayed by Igor Gouzenko, would be detained for questioning. Although May was actually just kept under surveillance (he was arrested in May 1946), the reverberations of Gouzenko's defection and news that Elizabeth Bentley had likewise proven unreliable severely curtailed Soviet espionage activities for many months.[114]

Julius Rosenberg Delivers a Second Source

Russell McNutt eventually disappointed the KGB by his refusal to move to the Manhattan Project facility at Oak Ridge, Tennessee. But Julius Rosenberg's second atomic recruit made up for that by working at the heart of the Manhattan Project: Los Alamos. The KGB New York station cabled Moscow Center on 20 September 1944: "'Liberal' [Rosenberg] has recommended Ruth Greenglass, his wife's brother's wife, for the role of caretaker of the safe-house apartment. Young Communist League member since 1942, a typist for the electricians' union. According to "L.'s" description, an able and smart young woman. Her husband is David Greenglass, a mechanic, drafted into the army, is at a factory in Santa Fe. Fellowcountryman [Communist]. "May" [Apresyan] requests approval to bring both Greenglasses into the fold, with a view to sending her to live with David after she is recruited." A follow-up cable the next day added that Greenglass was not at just any factory in Santa Fe but at an "Enormous" facility and that Ethel Rosenberg also vouched for Ruth's reliability. Not surprisingly, Moscow responded on 3 October that "the possibility of utilizing" the Greenglasses "is of interest to us" and assigning them cover names. Ruth became "Wasp," and David was "Bumblebee," the latter changed to "Caliber" when it was noticed that "Bumblebee" was already assigned to someone else. Impressed that he had not only passed on information from one source in the Manhattan Project but had also produced a second potential source, Moscow praised Rosenberg, warned the KGB New York station that "carelessness with him could have serious consequences for our entire operation," and instructed the station:

"In the interest of using 'Liberal' [Rosenberg] as effectively as possible on 'E' ["Enormous"], familiarize him with the main points of this problem," —that is, explain the nature of the atomic bomb project.[115]

In a series of conversations at the Rosenbergs' apartment in November shortly before she left for New Mexico to visit David, Ruth Greenglass agreed to "cooperate with drawing in" her husband. The KGB New York station sent Moscow a detailed report written in English by Julius (partially in the third person) about his and his wife's recruitment interview with Ruth:

"The following is a record of the conversation held by Julius, Ethel and Ruth. First of all, Julius inquired of Ruth how she felt about the Soviet Union and how deep in general did her Communist convictions go, whereupon she replied without hesitation that to her Socialism was the only hope of the world and the Soviet Union commanded her deepest admiration.

Julius then wanted to know whether or not she would be willing to help the Soviet Union. She replied very simply and sincerely that it would be a privilege; when Ethel mentioned David, she assured us that it was her judgment such was also David's understanding. Julius then explained his connections with certain people interested in supplying the Soviet Union with urgently needed technical information it could not obtain through the regular channels and impressed upon her the tremendous importance of the project upon which David is now at work. Therefore she was to ask him the following kind of questions. 1) How many people were now employed there. 2) What part of the project was already in operation, if any; were they encountering any difficulties and why; how were they resolving their problems. 3) How much of an area did the present setup cover. 4) How many buildings were there and their layout; were they going to build any more. 5) How well guarded was the place.

Julius then instructed her under no circumstances to discuss any of these things inside a room or indeed anywhere except out-of-doors and under no circumstances to make any notes of any kind. She was simply to commit to memory as much as possible. Ethel here interposed to stress the need for the utmost care and caution in informing David of the work in which Julie was engaged and that for his own safety all other political discussion and activity on his part should be subdued. At this point we asked Ruth to repeat our instructions which she did satisfactorily."[116]

The New York station chief cabled Moscow center on 15 December 1944 that Ruth had returned with welcome news:

Anton [Kvasnikov] reports that Wasp [Ruth Greenglass] is back from a visit to her husband. Caliber [David Greenglass] told her that he had given some thought to the question of covering the work being done in Camp-2 [Los Alamos], and now he expressed his willingness to do so. He reported that the camp leadership was openly taking measures to keep information on En-s ["Enormous"] from falling into Russian hands. The progressive constituent among the camp's workers is very displeased with this. According to Caliber, he knows people who find it necessary to keep the main ally—the Sov. Union —informed about the work being done.

Caliber will be in NY in the middle of January. In view of this, Liberal [Rosenberg] said that he wants our worker to contact Caliber in order to conduct a personal conversation, basing this on a lack of knowledge about the problem. He says he is firmly convinced that Caliber would be glad to have such a meeting. . . . Anton has inquired about the possibility of such a meeting. If it is impossible, he intends to put together a questionnaire for Liberal. He therefore asks that we give him a list of the questions that interest us most.[117]

The Center sent along a list of questions, ranging from physical descriptions of Los Alamos to information on its employees, including those who were "progressives." In New York on leave from 30 December to 18 January, Greenglass met with Julius, confirmed his willingness to work for the Soviets, and handed over a description of Los Alamos. A report sent to Moscow in February 1945 explained:

"He (Caliber [David Greenglass]) was in Tyre [New York] from December 30th to January 18th and obtained the leave to which he was entitled. During the first five days of his stay in Tyre, no one contacted him. Meanwhile, 'Liberal' [Rosenberg] did not meet with any of his probationers for 10 days. 'Liberal' and 'Caliber' subsequently met at his mother-in-law's apartment, that is, 'Caliber's' mother, b/c 'Liberal's' wife and 'Caliber' are brother and sister. After speaking with "Caliber' and receiving confirmation of his agreement to send us information known to him about the work being done in camp No. 2 [Los Alamos], 'Liberal' gave him a list of questions to which it would be preferable to get a reply. These were general questions to determine the type of work being done there.

'Caliber' holds the rank of sergeant. He works at the camp as a mechanic and carries out various tasks assigned by the leadership. The actual place where 'Caliber' works is a factory that manufactures various devices for measuring and studying the explosive force of various explosive substances in their various forms (lenses). Test explosions are set off at testing areas ('C' calls them *sites*). In order to gain access to one of these areas, one needs a special pass. 'C.' says that he has observed that there are at least four sites to which they send various materials and things (see 44 pp. materials). As far as we can tell, these testing areas are the sites of the research and selection of explosive substances that will impart the necessary velocity to 'Enormous's' neutrons to obtain fission (explosion). It seems to us that 'Caliber' himself does not know all the details of this project. At the end of his report, he lists individuals whom he thinks of as progressive and pro-Soviet.

At the end of February, as soon as she gets her RR ticket, 'Wasp' [Ruth Greenglass] will move permanently to Albuquerque, which is home to most of the wives of the workers in the camp. In Albuquerque, 'Wasp' intends to find a job as a secretary. She is a typist/stenographer. She intends to live there for 6–7 months and return to Tyre for the birth of her child. Before she leaves, we will get a material and oral password from her, in case the need should arise to contact her. When she arrives at her destination and finds an apartment, she will inform us of her address in a letter to her mother-in-law. We think that having 'Wasp' in Albuquerque will give us the opportunity to make a more careful study of the kinds of work and people that exist in the camp, and if 'Caliber' has valuable information, she could come to Tyre and report it to us."

After he began cooperating with the FBI in 1950, David also claimed that toward the end of his leave, he met Julius and they entered a car with a mysterious man he assumed to be Russian who questioned him about his work. Alexander Feklisov later confirmed that this was Anatoly Yatskov.[118]

When originally notified of the possibility of recruiting the Green-glasses, Moscow had cautioned New York not to have Julius Rosenberg directly involved and suggested using Harry Gold. The New York station responded by warning General Fitin: "We consider it risky to concentrate all contacts on Enormous to Arno [Gold] alone." It was a warning that Moscow, eager to collect as much information about the Manhattan Project as quickly as possible, tended to ignore, but in the case of Green-glass it did agree that it was safer to have Julius continue as intermediary since they were relatives and their meetings would appear to be normal family affairs. In late February, in response to Julius Rosenberg's firing by the Signal Corps and concern he might be the object of American security interest, Moscow suggested Kvasnikov transfer Russell McNutt to Gold's control. Although no direct response is in the Vassiliev files, Kvasnikov clearly had doubts, because he assigned Yatskov, not Gold, to meet with McNutt. He was not as cautious a few months later when he received word that Ruth Greenglass had written a letter hinting that David had information ready to be conveyed to the Soviets. The original plan, discussed in January 1945, when David had been in New York on furlough, was that Ann Sidorovich would serve as a courier. She was unavailable for some reason—perhaps related to Julius's dismissal and Soviet concerns that contact be made by someone unconnected to Rosenberg's network. In any case, Kvasnikov asked Moscow's consent to have Gold, already scheduled to visit Fuchs in Santa Fe in June, also pick up Greenglass's materials in Albuquerque. Moscow agreed.[119]

Gold made the trip. In a report he wrote for the KGB he noted that he arrived at the Greenglasses' apartment on 2 June 1945, but

"By that time it was 8 o'clock and they had left for the whole evening—he came home for the weekend. Therefore, so as not to seem too anxious, and b/c it was already too late to leave 'S.' ["Sernovodsk"/Albuquerque], I came back the next morning. I identified myself, and they gave me a very warm welcome. 'D' [David Greenglass] asked me to come back in the latter half of the day, b/c he had very important material for me. He said that they had not been expecting me for another two weeks, but that he would get the material ready in a few hours, as was understood. I left them a considerable sum of money, which they were both happy to receive. . . . I met with 'D' in the afternoon, received the materials from him."[120]

Gold's trip, Kvasnikov told Moscow, "went well. Very interesting information was received from all the probationers [sources]." A few weeks later he was less enthusiastic about Greenglass's material: "'Although it does contain some information, Caliber's [Greenglass's] material is unqualified and far from polished. We believe this is a result of, on the one hand, Caliber's insufficient qualifications, and on the other hand, the unexpectedness of Arno's [Gold's] visit to him, when he did not have materials ready.'" While he never handed over anything as valuable as that provided by Klaus Fuchs and Theodore Hall, both well-trained, brilliant physicists, Greenglass was not without value. In one report Kvasnikov explained about the information given by all three—"for the most part they mutually overlap"—giving the KGB additional reassurance that it was not being fed disinformation or exaggerated misinformation. A summary of a KGB New York station report on Greenglass's material read: "1. Report on a scientific experimentation center for preparing a uranium bomb, with a general floor plan and sketches of individual buildings attached—4 pp., 5 sketches. 2. Material on the preparation of a uranium bomb; calculations and information regarding a structural solution to the problem of a uranium bomb; information on an electro-magnetic method for obtaining the element Uranium-235. 33 pp. (Assessment: highly valuable.) 3. On the problem of obtaining Uranium-235. 4. Description of the atomic bomb. 22 pp." It was an impressive list of materials from an Army sergeant with only a limited technical education.[121]

The next scheduled meeting was in New York, when Greenglass (once more on leave) met with Julius Rosenberg on 20 September 1945 and gave him a written description of the bomb that was promptly turned over to Anatoly Yatskov. Moscow Center was sufficiently impressed to authorize a payment of $300 to the Greenglasses. Yatskov also met briefly with Greenglass on the next day and reported to Moscow:

"'Caliber' [David Greenglass] and 'Wasp' [Ruth Greenglass] came to Tyre [New York]. In the present mailing, we are sending you Caliber's materials on the balloon [atomic bomb]. On September 21st, Aleksey [Yatskov] met with Caliber in Tyre. The meeting was very short, because Caliber was supposed to have been home that evening (it was the eve of his departure) and had gotten out of the house only for a short time. During the conversation, it was established that Caliber works in the Preserve's [Los Alamos's] subsidiary workshops, which manufacture instruments and devices for Preserve and, occasionally, parts for the balloon. For instance, the detonator for the fuse of the balloon's explosive substance was manufactured in their workshops, and Caliber gave us a model of such a detonator. Caliber does not have access to the balloon itself or to the main workshops. He compiles the information he gives us about the balloon on the basis of what he hears from his friends who work on the Preserve and who belong to the personnel that has access to scientific materials (the so-called 'red button personnel.' Caliber belongs to the 'blue button personnel,' i.e., the subsidiary personnel).

Caliber has been instructed to compile detailed profiles of people he thinks would be suitable for recruitment to our work. In addition, he was assigned to gather samples of materials that are used in the balloon, such as tuballoy, explosive substances, etc. Materials occasionally end up in Caliber's workshop. The next meeting with Caliber (or rather, with his wife, "Wasp") is scheduled for December 21 in Sernovodsk [Albuquerque]. We think Leslie [Lona Cohen] is a suitable candidate for making the trip there. We asked for approval of this trip by telegraph."[122]

Cohen's trip to Albuquerque, however, was canceled. Increased worries about counterintelligence activity prompted Lavrenty Beria himself to order a temporary halt to the KGB's contacts with its most valuable agents linked to atomic intelligence, including Greenglass, and she never made the trip. (The others named in Beria's order were Klaus Fuchs, Theodore Hall, Julius Rosenberg, and Harry Gold.) The next report on Greenglass was not until 3 June 1946, when the KGB noted that he had been demobilized in March, moved back to New York in April, and gone into business with Julius Rosenberg. Greenglass also asked for KGB advice about where to use his GI Bill benefits for college education.[123]

Greenglass's request for advice came during the period when KGB operations were being pulled back. Feklisov had visited Julius in December 1946 to inform him that operations were shutting down for an indefinite period. In a report on his work in the United States, written in February 1947, Feklisov praised David and Ruth Greenglass as "'young, smart, able and politically developed people who believe strongly in the cause of communism and are full of desire to do everything in their power to provide as much assistance to our country as possible. They are indisputably people who are devoted to us.'" He urged that they be recontacted through Julius Rosenberg "'at the very first opportunity'" with "'the goal of educating this young couple into qualified agents and making them securely covert in the country.'" He thought they should be separated from Julius and that the KGB should "'move them to some other city that has our agents, whom they could work for. "Caliber" [David Greenglass] and "Wasp" [Ruth Greenglass] will obviously need our finan. assistance in the future in connection with the birth of their baby (expected in 1946).'"[124]

A "Fellowcountryman" Walks In: Theodore Hall

The New York station of the KGB was in bad odor with Moscow in the early fall of 1944. The Center had repeatedly made clear that obtaining information about "Enormous" was the major priority of its intelligence work in America, but the New York station had fallen well short of Moscow's expectations. Several promising leads had fizzled or were in abeyance. It knew that a number of the scientists working on the project were Communists, but they could not be reached, were already under American security scrutiny, or were too nervous to help. The most useful source, Klaus Fuchs, had been recruited in Great Britain by GRU and handed to the American station, but the New York station had lost touch with him by August 1944 and was not even sure he was still in the United States. Russell McNutt had been recruited, but after a brief flurry of excitement, it became obvious that while he supplied some useful material, his unwillingness to move to Oak Ridge diminished his value. Julius Rosenberg had not yet identified his brother-in-law David Greenglass as a possible recruit.

At this low point, a volunteer walked through the door. Theodore Hall was a physics prodigy. Raised in New York, he had graduated from Harvard at the age of eighteen in 1944 and had immediately been recruited to work at Los Alamos. Despite his youth and lack of an advanced degree, Hall's brilliance earned him the status of a junior scientist working on the plutonium bomb. Hall was also drafted into the U.S. Army as a private while at Los Alamos, where he spent the remainder of the war working in his same scientific post on the plutonium bomb. After he was exposed by the release in the mid-1990s of the Venona decryptions, which provided a general outline of his recruitment and assistance to the Soviet Union, Hall confirmed the story of his approach to the Soviets via Sergey Kurnakov, a military writer for *Soviet Russia Today*, *Russky Golos*, and other Communist-aligned journals.[125]

Vassiliev's notebooks contain Kurnakov's detailed account of his contact with Hall, written on 23 October 1944, the day after Hall handed him a report on what was going on at Los Alamos. Hall had arrived in New York on leave from Los Alamos and quickly contacted his Harvard roommate, Saville Sax, also a young Communist. The two decided to locate a Soviet representative to whom they could pass Hall's information. Reluctant to go directly to the consulate, which presumably would be under FBI surveillance, Sax went to CPUSA headquarters but was unable to persuade anyone to take him seriously. Hall had better luck. On a visit to Nikolai Napoli, the head of Artkino, a company that exhibited Russian films, he explained "he wanted to speak with someone about an important military issue." Napoli, in fact, had assisted Jacob Golos, head of the CPUSA's covert organization, and had some knowledge of people linked to Soviet intelligence. He refused to accept any information himself but suggested Hall talk to Kurnakov. Hall recognized the name from articles he had read about Red Army operations and made his way to the *Russky Golos* office.[126]

Kurnakov had a brief conversation with Hall and apparently learned that he was concerned about some kind of special military weapon on which he was working. On Sunday, 22 October, Hall called him at his home and expressed an interest in meeting again. They met at Kurnakov's apartment and talked on general matters for nearly an hour. Kurnakov prepared a detailed report on their conversation:

"T. H. [Theodore Hall] 19 years old. He is a 'wonder boy.' Graduated from Towsend Harris High School . . . at fourteen (in 1940. Studied for two years at Queens College), and in 1942 he transferred to Harvard University, from which he graduated this year with a 'B.S.' (Bachelor of Science) in theoretical physics. . . . He had been a member of the Young Communist League and the 'Student League' at Queens College. At Harvard, he did organizational work in the Steelworkers' Union (USW) at the Bethlehem Steel factory in Fall River, Mass. Already at Queens College his feelings toward the Young Communist League had begun to cool, because he couldn't stand the 'narrow-mindedness of the leadership.' I was unable to detect his current polit. bent, although . . . he has 'long-range' doubts. For instance, he is troubled by the idea that when Communism has made everyone's life good, people will lose the incentive to fight, and their interests will be reduced to the level of small-scale personal ambitions. In short—people will go into spiritual atrophy when nothing is left to 'save' a mankind that has already been saved. I asked him how he had reacted to the 'turning points' of the Party line—1939, 1941, and 1944. He says that he had come to terms with both the pact and the attitude toward the war."

Kurnakov wrote that although Hall came from a Jewish family, "'he does not look Jewish'" and described him as tall, thin, "'a pale and slightly pimply face, carelessly dressed; you can tell his boots haven't been cleaned in a long time; his socks are bunched up around the ankles.'" He diagnosed him as "'obviously neurasthenic'" but "'witty and somewhat sarcastic. . . . In conversation he is as sharp and agile as a rapier.'"[127]

As the conversation went on, Hall became more nervous. "'When he finally started biting his nails,'" Kurnakov produced a newspaper clipping about American development of missiles and asked if that was what concerned him. Hall said, "'No, it's much worse than that.'" At that, Kurnakov elicited the story of how Hall had come to find him. Concluding that he really was a physicist despite his obvious youth and had been active in the left-wing movement and that simply promising to put him in touch with an official Russian representative would be awkward, Kurnakov bluntly asked for his story:

"He told me that the new secret weapon was an 'atomic bomb' of colossal destructive capacity. I interrupted him: Do you understand what you are doing? What makes you think you should reveal the USA's secrets for the USSR's sake? He replied: The S.U. is the only country that could be trusted with such a terrible thing. But since we cannot take it away from other countries—the USSR ought to be aware of its existence and stay abreast of the progress of experiments and construction. This way, at a peace conference, the USSR—on which the fate of my generation depends—will not find itself in the position of a power subjected to blackmail."

Hall then explained the principles of the bomb, "'took out a neatly written report,'" and gave it to Kurnakov. "'Show this to any physicist,'" he instructed, "'and he will understand what it's about.'" While he didn't know the structure of the bomb itself, he could find out. Hall also provided a list of the scientists working on the atom bomb and described the conditions at Los Alamos.[128]

Kurnakov now faced a dilemma. How could he be sure this was not some kind of FBI sting or provocation? He concluded, however, that since Hall had been hoping to have a Soviet official present, if he was a provocateur, he would not have produced his written report until someone more important than Kurnakov could be entrapped. Kurnakov also had his wife go outside and look for signs of surveillance; she had seen none. Still, as soon as Hall left, Kurnakov walked around in his neighborhood to lure away anyone watching, while his wife removed Hall's report from the apartment. He was also concerned that as a KGB agent (not a professional officer), he had no authority to accept such sensitive material without approval. But, he reasoned, the importance of this information and the urgency of ensuring that Hall, who was returning to Los Alamos (where he would be very hard to reach) in just a few days, had a contact justified his assumption of risk. Kurnakov promised Hall that he would contact him in the day or so before he left.

Worried that Kurnakov had not taken him seriously, Hall sent Saville Sax to the Soviet Consulate the next day with a copy of the report he had already handed over. Sax devised a cover story to explain the trip in case he was questioned by American counterintelligence: he was inquiring about the fate of family relatives still in the Soviet Union. Referred to Anatoly Yatskov, he elicited immediate interest. Yatskov arranged to meet with Sax and Hall the next day, 26 October, unaware that Hall had already met with Kurnakov. When the latter called Hall to arrange another meeting and learned what was planned, he worried that the Soviet diplomat might be tailed to the meeting and advised Hall not to go but to send Sax by himself. Kurnakov himself surreptitiously observed the meeting and was relieved to see no surveillance. With the permission of the KGB New York station chief, Kurnakov obtained a photograph from Hall and set up preliminary future meeting arrangements.[129]

It took the New York station almost two weeks to send news to Moscow of its new source on "Enormous." The delay may have been occasioned by its concern that Hall, a walk-in about whom it had no prior knowledge, was an FBI plant or just a fantasist. During the interim, it likely investigated both Hall and Sax via its contacts with the CPUSA; the ciphered telegram to Moscow contained details about Sax's Communist family, including his mother's work for Russian War Relief. The message also noted that Hall was "'characterized by political development, broad-

mindedness, and exceptionally sharp intelligence.'" Because of his im-
minent return to Los Alamos "'urgent measures were adopted.'" Kvasnikov recommended that Sax be used as the courier with Hall instead of
involving yet another person. Moscow Center expressed great interest, assigned cover names—"Mlad" and "Star"—to Hall and Sax, approved the
measures taken, ordered Yatskov to train Sax in conspiratorial methods,
suggested cutting Kurnakov out of this important project (probably to increase security), and demanded detailed information about both Hall and
Sax.[130]

Early in December 1944, Kvasnikov telegraphed Moscow the names
Hall had supplied of scientists working on the atom bomb—the cable, deciphered in 1946, was one of the earliest read by American cryptanalysts
in the Venona project—and a brief account of Hall's odyssey. He also
sent Kurnakov's report of his meetings by diplomatic pouch and a longer
explanation written by the station of the events that led to this unexpected
intelligence windfall. In late January 1945 Kvasnikov informed Moscow
that Hall had been inducted into the U.S. Army but kept at Los Alamos.
He also noted that Kurnakov was upset that he had been cut out but that
Yatskov, an experienced professional officer, had been assigned to supervise Sax and the contact with Hall. While Kurnakov had expressed great
confidence in Sax, Yatskov was not so sure he was the appropriate person
to use as a courier. The station had asked Bernard Schuster, its CPUSA
liaison, to check on Hall and Sax, as well as Sax's mother. By 1 February
1945, when it listed its American sources and agents, the New York station included "Mlad"/Hall and "Star"/Sax, although it noted that Hall had
only been "with us since Oct. '44. He has not been tested at work yet, nor
has he been studied." But the information he had given Kurnakov in October had already proven exceedingly valuable. When Merkulov wrote a
report for Beria on 28 February, he included specific details about Los
Alamos and discussed such matters as the plutonium implosion concept
that likely came from Hall because Klaus Fuchs had not yet reestablished
contact with the KGB.[131]

The KGB's frustration with its lack of access to the Manhattan Project was over. Evaluating the station's progress report, Pavel Fitin, chief of
KGB foreign intelligence, affirmed: "'The information we received from
'Mlad' [Hall] about 'Preserve' [Los Alamos] and the work that is being
done there confirms that 'Mlad'—as a probationer [source]—and 'Star'
[Sax]—as a courier—are of great interest to us.'" In fact, their potential
was so great that Fitin reprimanded the station for not sending Kurnakov's entire report of his meeting with Hall "'by telegraph in its en-

tirety at that time'" rather than by slower diplomatic pouch. Fitin liked the idea of using Sax as a courier, suggested that he transfer to the University of New Mexico, and urged that he "'be provided with all possible support to ensure the success of his studies and his graduation from the university.'" Several weeks later, in late March, Kvasnikov sent news that Hall had sent Sax a letter asking for a meeting and he was setting it up for mid-April. Moscow approved the rendezvous.[132]

Sax took a bus both ways between Boston and Albuquerque, forgoing a faster and more comfortable train on the grounds that a bus fitted better with his cover as a prospective college student. In a ciphered telegram on 11 May, Kvasnikov reported to Moscow that the trip had been a success. When he arrived, Sax had been questioned by government agents who asked about his citizenship and draft status. Both types of questions were "'brief and superficial.'" Sax explained that he was in town to check out the university, to which he was considering applying. After receiving Hall's original handwritten notes, he copied them onto a newspaper with milk to make them invisible to the naked eye and burned Hall's handwritten originals in case of a search. A cable transmitted a few weeks later reported that Hall had provided a list of what each Manhattan Project facility was doing and described the various methods of uranium separation. While the initial report concluded that the results Sax brought back were "satisfactory," a later message complained about Sax's decision to copy Hall's material: "'As we informed you by telegraph, the contents of Mlad's [Hall's] report that Star [Sax] brought over were written out in milk on newspaper. Aleksey [Yatskov] had to work hard to make out what it said and transcribe it. Given how much work we have, such a method of transmitting materials is extremely undesirable. He was unable to make out some of the words, but there weren't many of them, and the material was on the whole very valuable.'"[133]

It was not until the end of June that Sax disclosed a problem that he had not bothered to report earlier. Hall had told him that early in 1945, he had been talking to Roy Glauber, a fellow young physicist and friend from Harvard with whom he shared a room at Los Alamos. Glauber had grumbled that the British and American governments were keeping news of the atomic bomb from the Russians "'and added that, given the opportunity, he would inform our representatives about the project.'" Intelligence tradecraft (and common sense) dictated that the appropriate response from a covert source would have been to shrug off the comment and do no more than report it to the KGB in case it wished to attempt a follow-up. Instead, Hall "'hinted that he had taken some steps in this direction and, in turn, asked what Roy intended to do, practically speaking, to realize his wish. Roy got scared, started taking back everything he had said, and two weeks later he even moved out of Mlad's [Hall's] room and has since stopped being his friend.'" Despite the incident, Hall was sure that Glauber would not go to the authorities because he was a leftist, although he was "'incapable of taking decisive action when there is risk involved. The fact that he moved out of Mlad's [Hall's] room shows that he wants to stay away from 'dangerous acquaintances.'"" Kvasnikov attributed the incident to Hall's "'inexperience and youth'" and thought it demonstrated the need to have direct contact with him "'in order to conduct a detailed tutorial on the principles of our work and of personal conduct.'" He had also decided to use Lona Cohen as the courier for the next trip in July to pick up Hall's materials. Kvasnikov feared that Sax might be under surveillance since Hall corresponded with him, thought that his previous cover story that he was a prospective student looking at a school would not work a second time, and felt Cohen had a perfect excuse for a trip to New Mexico since she had a doctor's note suggesting a long vacation. She had already bought a ticket for Denver, leaving 14 July, but was as yet unaware of her assignment.[134]

Moscow was outraged at the possibility that so valuable a source might have been compromised. It lamented "the complete inadequacy of Aleksey's [Yatskov's] work with the agents on cultivating Enormous." Moscow Center warned of the "impossibility" of setting up meetings between Hall and a professional Soviet officer due to the danger of exposure. It approved Cohen's use as a courier, however: she was an American and a non-professional agent of the KGB, and her meeting with Hall was much less of a risk.[135]

Despite Moscow's concern, Hall's judgment was right: Glauber never reported the conversation. A very truncated version of "the Grauber incident"—so called because the deciphered cable in which it was mentioned misspelled his name—became available to American code breakers and the FBI. Whatever Glauber, who became a Nobel Prize–winning physicist at Harvard, told the FBI, he professed ignorance to journalists once the Venona documents became public; claimed to have no memory of what could have prompted the KGB's worry; and denied he had any idea that Hall might have been a spy.[136]

Lona Cohen made only one trip to New Mexico to meet with Hall. She was chosen in part because as a young woman, she would be less conspicuous than Sax, and Hall himself had suggested such a tactic. Originally scheduled for July, the meeting had been pushed back to August at

Hall's request, and she had lingered in Las Vegas, taking the long bus trip to Albuquerque to meet Hall at the University of New Mexico campus on 18 August. The delay meant that the station was unable to give Moscow any advance warning about the dropping of atomic bombs on Japan (Hiroshima—6 August, Nagasaki—9 August). While Harry Gold had met Greenglass and Fuchs in June, that was prior to the Trinity test of the plutonium bomb on 16 July, before its use against Japan had been decided, and Gold was not scheduled for another meeting until mid-September.[137]

Moscow Center was not pleased that it first learned about the use of the atom bomb from reading the American press. It sent an angry missive to New York reproaching the station for its long delay in understanding "'the significance that the echelon [high Soviet leadership] attaches to our work'" on the atomic bomb and complaining that "'an event as important as the announcement by the Amer. gov't of the creation of an atomic bomb went unnoticed by the station, and our inquiries went unanswered, at the same time as we were receiving very interesting info. in this regard from elsewhere.'"[138]

Theodore Hall was supposed to visit New York in October on leave; the KGB scheduled a meeting with him. There is nothing in Alexander Vassiliev's notebooks to indicate that the meeting took place. On 27 October 1945 Moscow cabled New York that intensified FBI surveillance required a temporary cessation of contact with the "most valuable agents" on "Enormous," including Hall. Hall remained at Los Alamos until he was discharged from the Army in June 1946.[139]

The KGB's Postwar Atomic Intelligence

After years of frustration and dead ends in trying to penetrate the Manhattan Project, the KGB's American station in New York had struck pay dirt in 1944. Through Julius Rosenberg it had recruited Russell McNutt and David Greenglass, via GRU it had gained access to Klaus Fuchs, and Ted Hall had simply presented himself as a spy. For two years Fuchs and Hall, supplemented by McNutt, Greenglass, and Allan Nunn May (along with Broda and Norwood in Britain), allowed the KGB to produce a cornucopia of information on the Manhattan Project. But in 1946 these productive sources began to dry up. Klaus Fuchs remained an active agent, but he returned to Great Britain in June 1946. Theodore Hall left Los Alamos to pursue an advanced degree in physics at the University of Chicago. Once demobilized, David Greenglass had no access to atomic-related material. Russell McNutt's usefulness had ended after he refused requests to move to Oak Ridge. Clarence Hiskey, Joseph Weinberg, and other young scientists at Berkeley whom the KGB had cultivated were under FBI scrutiny and effectively neutralized.

The agency had anticipated the need to find new recruits shortly after Hiroshima and Nagasaki and expressed high hopes for continued success. In a message to Leonid Kvasnikov, the Center reminded him, "'We are faced with the absolutely urgent task of intensifying and expanding our work on 'E.' ["Enormous"], which is of great national importance to our country.'" It stressed, "'We think that the agent situation in this regard is exceptionally favorable,'" citing "'reports about the fact that among the workers who are actively participating in the work, there are people who have openly stated their goodwill toward us and expressed the opinion that our country should be informed about the results achieved in work on 'E.''" Among the top priorities for Soviet intelligence were "'obtaining new leads'" and setting up several safe houses in the Midwest and West to reduce the need for "'group handlers and couriers'" to travel cross country.[140]

That same month Fitin sent Merkulov a report concluding more was involved than military parity with the United States in the KGB's atomic intelligence program: "'The actual use of an atomic bomb by the Americans signifies that they have completed the first stage in an enormous research project on the problem of releasing intra-atomic energy. This event inaugurates a new era in science and technology and will undoubtedly lead to the speedy development of the entire problem of Enormous—using inter-atomic energy not only for military purposes, but also throughout all of modern economics.'" It was, Fitin argued, incumbent on the USSR to stay abreast of American progress in every area of atomic research. This effort was hindered, however, by the need to freeze contacts with many agents in late 1945 and 1946 due to defections that identified KGB officers and put numerous sources at risk.[141]

"Relative's" Group

In 1947 and 1948 the KGB began to reestablish ties and reactivate old sources. Several cryptic messages recorded in Vassiliev's notebooks deal with a new group of agents with some connection to atomic research. At the end of January 1947 one message gave instructions that when he had completed his work at the "Seminary," "Godsend" should return to Los Alamos and that "Intermediary" was also available. "Seminary" was probably the University of Chicago. "Intermediary" worked at Amtorg in New York. His group included "Relative," "Godsend," "Godfather," and "Nata," all unidentified. Four months later Moscow indicated that "Relative's" group had been created in 1945, "had hardly been used for work, and has not been compromised in any way." A KGB officer had met once with "Relative" and "Godsend" but they were put aside in September 1945, although contact was retained through "Intermediary." The group had "a workshop in NY, set up with our money," and the message noted that "Relative," "Godsend," and "Godfather" were brothers. Moscow Center instructed the KGB Washington station (which had replaced the New York station as the center of the KGB's American work toward the end of World War II) to remove "Intermediary" from contact with "Relative" and his brothers because of some evidence of FBI interest in "Intermediary" and substitute KGB officer Nikolay Statskevich. Nothing more, however, appeared regarding this group.[142]

"Nick's" Group

Moscow Center also ordered a second initiative. A June 1948 Moscow Center cable discussed assignments for reviving the American stations, including this note: "Instructions were given to renew ties with 'Nick's' group: Pony, Sandy, and Tunic." "Nick" was Amadeo Sabatini, an American Communist and International Brigades veteran who became a KGB agent and courier in the late 1930s, servicing technical sources during World War II (see chapter 7). On hearing that KGB officer Nikolay Statskevich had revived contact with "Nick"/Sabatini in October 1948 and that he had "agreed to begin working with us again," Moscow Center stated that his assignment was "to create a group on 'Enormous.'" "Pony," "Sandy," and "Tunic" are unidentified cover names, appear only this single time in Vassiliev's notebooks, and nothing is known of their identity or their connection with the American atomic program.[143]

"Liberal's" Group

When the KGB renewed contact with Julius Rosenberg in 1948, he was still in touch with the two atomic spies he had recruited, Russell McNutt and David Greenglass. But by that time neither had any connection with the American atomic program. However, Rosenberg was also still in contact with Alfred Sarant. During World War II Sarant had been a productive source of military electronic intelligence, but in 1946 he resigned from Bell

Labs, married, and moved to Ithaca, New York, where he planned to enter Cornell University and get an advanced degree. He got a support job working with Cornell's cyclotron and hoped that Cornell faculty and former Manhattan Project physicists Hans Bethe, Richard Feynman, and Philip Morrison (a Communist) would help him enter the graduate program in physics. Possibly this old technical source could become a new atomic source, and Julius Rosenberg might be able to recruit a third atomic spy.[144]

Things Fall Apart

By October 1948 Moscow Center was concerned that its attempt to revive atomic espionage in the United States was faltering. Moscow Center lectured Boris Krotov, the senior KGB officer in New York at the time:

"The policies adopted by the alpinists [Americans] in this matter are clearly indicative of their firm intention to maintain a complete monopoly on "Enormous" and to use the balloon [atomic bomb] for the purposes of aggression against us. According to our information, the alpinists are implementing an extensive program of research work and theoretical investigations on "E." and frantically working to improve models of balloons they already have and to create new models. However, we did not properly cover this important branch of work during the period of deactivation, and it is still not being covered to this day. Moreover, our opportunities for receiving information about 'E.' were significantly cut down by the fact that certain athletes [sources] who had previously worked in that field (Mlad [Theodore Hall], Caliber [Greenglass], Godsend [unidentified]) switched to different jobs for reasons beyond their control, and some of them (Kemp [unidentified] and oth.) had their identities completely revealed.

As a result, we don't have essential information at present about the actual status of work on "E." in the alpinists' country, and consequently, our work in that field must be deemed unsatisfactory. This appraisal forces us to carefully analyze the situation that has arisen in our network and to eliminate this serious flaw in our work as quickly as possible. It is completely obvious that we need to start by creating a network of new athletes, b/c without such a network, we will be unable to carry out the tasks that have been put before us by the leadership." Use Caliber, Yakov [William Perl], Volunteer [Morris Cohen], and Liberal [Julius Rosenberg]. + Mlad. We need leads.[145]

But it does not appear that the leads came.

Hopes that Amadeo Sabatini/"Nick" might organize a group of agents devoted to "Enormous" came to nothing. In 1949 Sabatini developed throat cancer, and, in addition, that same year Venona decryptions allowed the FBI to identify him as a longtime KGB courier. Confronted by the FBI, he gave a partial account of his earlier activities. While he disclosed nothing about his new assignment to pursue atomic intelligence, his identification by the FBI put an end to that venture. He died in 1952. Possibly the unidentified "Godsend," who had once worked at Los Alamos, was able to reenter the American atomic program, but considering the disarray into which KGB espionage fell, this seems unlikely. Whatever hope the KGB harbored that Alfred Sarant might be able to approach some of the nuclear physicists at Cornell University evaporated in 1950, when the FBI identified him as a member of Julius Rosenberg's World War II espionage network. Sarant escaped FBI surveillance and fled to Mexico, from where the KGB covertly moved him to Communist Czechoslovakia and finally to the Soviet Union. But if the KGB's hopes for new atomic sources came to nothing, what of the old?

The Berkeley Prospects Indicted

During World War II, the FBI and military security had neutralized any prospects the KGB or GRU had of using Robert Oppenheimer's young Communist protégés by excluding them from the Manhattan Project. But the government wasn't finished with them. By August 1945 the FBI considered bringing an espionage case against Joseph Weinberg, but the effort was complicated by the Army's reluctance to embarrass either Oppenheimer or Ernest Lawrence, his former bosses at the Radiation Laboratory, and its difficulty in using in court the most damning evidence, which had been gathered by warrantless wiretaps and bugs. The FBI questioned Weinberg in September 1946, and he denied meeting with or even knowing Steve Nelson, a declaration that only confirmed his guilt in the eyes of FBI agents who had listened to their conversation through concealed listening devices. The Justice Department, however, opposed prosecution because of evidentiary problems under America's judicial rules of what evidence could be presented in court.

Two years later, in late August 1948, the U.S. House Committee on Un-American Activities began taking testimony about wartime espionage at Berkeley's Radiation Laboratory. Steve Nelson, at that point a senior CPUSA official, took the Fifth Amendment, while Joseph Weinberg again denied ever meeting or talking to Steve Nelson. During another round of hearings, brought face-to-face with Nelson, Weinberg repeated his lies, but since those who knew about his Communist ties refused to testify, he continued to escape prosecution. Identified only as "Scientist X" when the House Committee on Un-American Activities released a report on atomic espionage, Weinberg remained in limbo, teaching at the University of Minnesota while the FBI tried to find admissible evidence to prove that he had committed perjury. One grand jury refused to indict him in 1950; two years later, buttressed by testimony from ex-Communists Paul and Sylvia Crouch that put him at a party meeting in California, a case was prepared through which Weinberg was indicted in May. In the ensuing trial the judge dealt a fatal blow to the prosecution by refusing to allow the transcript of his conversation with Nelson to be entered into evidence. In March 1953, Weinberg was acquitted. His academic career, however, was over. Having been fired from the university, he took a job with an optics company.[146]

FBI listening devices in Nelson's residence had not only overheard Weinberg discussing the atomic bomb but had also in October 1942 overheard another young Berkeley physicist, Giovanni Rossi Lomanitz, tell Nelson he was working on a highly secret weapon, a reference to the atomic bomb project then in its very early stages. Nelson indicated prior knowledge of the project and advised Lomanitz to be discreet and to consider himself an undercover member of the CPUSA. Military security officials immediately excluded Lomanitz from the Manhattan Project. In 1949 he was called to testify before Congress about atomic espionage and was indicted for contempt after uncooperative testimony but acquitted. David Bohm, who had ignored Oppenheimer's 1943 advice to cut his ties with communism, had also been excluded from work at Los Alamos. In 1949 he refused to answer congressional committee inquiries about his relationship to the CPUSA and was indicted for contempt but acquitted. Bohm moved to Brazil in 1951 and in 1954 applied for and became a Brazilian citizen. He later lost his belief in communism and asked for and got an American passport, stating that he had not intended to repudiate his American citizenship when he became a Brazilian citizen. He also admitted to American authorities that he had been a CPUSA member while at the Berkeley Radiation Laboratory during World War II.[147]

Alfred Marshak was a Berkeley geneticist involved in radiation research and knew Oppenheimer but was closer to Ernest Lawrence. But KGB hopes that he would provide access to either physicist were disappointed. Nonetheless, Grigory Kheifets claimed some success with him. Although not part of the Manhattan Project, Marshak was the lead investigator on a war-related research project at the Berkeley Radiation Laboratory, and in September 1944 Kheifets reported: "'Marshak refrained from any scientific exchange with us due to his pledge for the time that he worked at the laboratory to protect industrial secrets. Marshak has left the laboratory and considers himself freed from all pledges. So he passed a portion of his work to "Map" [Bransten] for us. He is currently working on the rest of the material and expects to finish the preparation of these materials this October.'"[148]

What Kheifets did not know, and Marshak himself did not understand at the time, was that Army security had identified Marshak as likely a Communist. Rather than fire him, however, security officials had simply terminated his project. Subsequently the navy declined his application for a commission, and after the war he had trouble getting a passport or finding employment involving his specialization in radiation. In a 1952 letter to Ernest Lawrence he explained that it was not until 1948 that he "recognized the specific reasons for the termination of the osrd [Office of Scientific Research and Development] project in Berkeley for which I was the responsible investigator." He lamented, "I realized now that I allowed myself to become involved in affairs which were of no immediate concern to me and which later had a devastating effect on my career."[149]

Weinberg, Lomanitz, Bohm, and Marshak all escaped prison, but they were subjected to an ordeal (a public one for the first three) that likely discouraged others in the postwar years who might have been inclined to assist Soviet atomic intelligence.

Theodore Hall after the War

After his discharge from the Army and Los Alamos in 1946, Theodore Hall enrolled in the PhD program in physics at the University of Chicago. Given the withdrawal of KGB officers from the United States in 1946, Hall was without Soviet contact. Additionally, his own research interests shifted to medical uses of radiation and away from subjects relevant to nuclear weapons. In 1947 Hall married and confessed his past activities to his bride. A fellow radical, she fully accepted his work. Later that year the two, eager to advance the Communist cause they shared, joined the CPUSA and participated in its public activities.

Hall might have concluded that his espionage career was over, but the Soviets had other ideas. In 1947 Moscow decided to renew contacts with Morris and Lona Cohen, noting that she had served as Hall's courier. At the end of April 1948 came an order to use them to renew ties with Hall, who was finishing his graduate work, and encourage him to get a job at Los Alamos. The KGB may have been receiving information about Hall from Sax; there is some indication that late in 1947 the latter, then living in Chicago, traveled to New York and returned with at least $1,000 from the Soviets.[150]

By October 1948 the Russians had received news that both Hall and Sax were active publicly in Communist causes, and they were not pleased. Their "activities on their own while they were deactivated have resulted in a significant weakening of their position. The advisability of their use is called into question." Part of the blame was placed on the Cohens, who had not been in regular contact with them and had failed "to get Mlad [Hall] to stop working for progressive organizations" or from joining the CPUSA. Even worse, the KGB had learned that the FBI was investigating Hall's wartime work at Los Alamos and that the wives of both Hall and Sax knew about their work for the KGB.[151]

Vassiliev's notebooks do not contain any more documents on Theodore Hall; in the final year of Vassiliev's work on the research project that produced his notebooks, the flow of files from the KGB's archives slowed, and he never received the second volume of the KGB's "Enormous" file, which focused on post–World War II operations. American journalists Joseph Albright and Marcia Kunstel maintain that after the KGB revived contact with him, Hall helped to recruit two scientific colleagues working at the Hanford, Washington, plutonium facility, but the basis for that claim is weak.[152]

In the spring of 1950, just before American cryptanalysts broke a Soviet cable that named him as a spy, Hall once again decided to end his espionage career. By the time the FBI began to investigate him, Hall was again active in left-wing activity and not in regular contact with the KGB. His fortuitous decision likely saved him from prosecution. The FBI could find no evidence of his current involvement in espionage, and both he and Saville Sax stonewalled during FBI interviews. With KGB cables deciphered by the Venona project unavailable for use in court, the FBI did not have enough other evidence to bring a criminal indictment, and it put his case aside. He was, in any case, no longer a security threat. Not only had he been identified by the FBI, but also his research interests had turned to radiobiology and the medical uses of X-rays. In 1962 he moved to Great Britain to take a position as a biophysicist at the Cavendish Laboratory at Cambridge University. After the release of the Venona decryptions in the mid-1990s made his espionage for the Soviet Union public, he released a statement reaffirming his view that the United States had been and continued to be a threat to the world and expressing no regret for his assistance to Stalin's Soviet Union. He died in 1999 at the age of seventy-four.[153]

Klaus Fuchs after the War

Klaus Fuchs had been the KGB's most important source on the Manhattan Project. A dedicated Communist, brilliant physicist, and assigned to a key post at Los Alamos, he had been in an ideal position to provide Moscow with crucial information. In mid-1946 Fuchs left the United States and returned to Great Britain. To the Center's consternation, Fuchs did not show up at the prearranged rendezvous in London in August 1946, leaving the KGB with no clue as to his whereabouts.

Not only was Fuchs out of touch, but also there had been no word from Gold as to the whereabouts of the final batch of Los Alamos material that he was supposed to pick up from Fuchs's sister, Kristel Heineman, in December 1945. And it was proving hard to reestablish contact with Harry Gold. Sent a signal for a meeting, he missed two rendezvous before Yatskov managed to meet him in the Bronx in December 1946. Gold reported that he had last visited Kristel Heineman in April 1946, but she told him that her brother had not left any papers for him; he also recalled seeing a July article in the *Herald Tribune* that Fuchs had been arrested for espionage in London. (There was no such article; Gold may have seen a story on the espionage conviction of Allan Nunn May in Britain and confused him with Fuchs.) In more dangerous news, Gold explained that after he had lost his job, he had gone to work for Abraham Brothman as his chief chemist, violating, an angry Yatskov noted, "'our express directive not to meet'" with him. Brothman had been a longtime Soviet industrial spy, and Gold had been his liaison with the KGB. A repentant Gold admitted "'that he made a serious mistake and is prepared to make up for it at any price.'" He promised to quit Brothman's company. Yatskov was upset because if Brothman, who had been named by Elizabeth Bentley (Jacob Golos and Bentley had been Brothman's link with the KGB for a period), were confronted by the FBI and confessed, he might expose Gold. The KGB considered trying to persuade Gold to go underground or move to another part of the country and to work out a plausible story to tell the government if he were questioned. But Yatskov and other KGB officers were being withdrawn from the United States in the wake of the Bentley and Gouzenko defections, and there was no follow-through.[154]

Fuchs, meanwhile, had been unable to make the prearranged meeting in Britain but was, nonetheless, anxious to reestablish contact with Soviet intelligence. He approached Jurgen Kuczynski's wife, asking for help in getting in touch with the Russians. She contacted Hans Siebert, now in charge of German Communists in Britain. Siebert met with a KGB officer in late September, provided Fuchs's address, word that he was working at a top-secret installation, and a warning that while he was not under suspicion, meetings would be difficult to arrange. The KGB was uneasy about the contact via the Kuczynskis; although Jurgen had provided it information beginning in 1941, he had never been formally recruited and had been cut loose in 1943 due to concerns that British counterintelligence might be suspicious about him. When he had been recontacted in December 1945, he had rebuffed the KGB on the grounds that he wanted to work exclusively on German matters. Finally "'he agreed to cooperate in the future only under strong pressure, but in all this time he has not given any valuable material, getting away with reports of low value.'" Moreover, the KGB noted that KPD leaders in Britain had criticized Kuczynski "'as someone with reactionary views who does not agree with the decisions of the Tehran Conference of the Big Three regarding the need to disarm G. [Germany] and destroy its military and industrial potential created by the Nazi regime.'" Suspicious that he might be a double agent, the KGB cut off contact with him after August 1946.[155]

Worried that it might be risky to meet directly with Fuchs, the KGB authorized another German Communist, Hanna Klopstock, to tell Fuchs that he "has not been forgotten, and the connection will be renewed whenever this becomes possible." After some delays because Klopstock's ill child prevented her from meeting with Fuchs, she finally delivered the message on 19 July 1947. She set up a meeting for Saturday, 27 September 1947, at a pub, with follow-up meetings to take place every three months. Klopstock's report read:

"I had the appointment with K. [Klaus] on the 19th of July at 2:30. He came with his little own car and we went through Richmond took several turnings until we came out in the open country and took a walk in the park. There I informed him and have given him the messages and also the guide words. I also informed him of the meeting on September, Saturday, the 27th at 8 o'clock, Public Bar opposite Wood Green Tube Station, every 3rd months, so the next meeting would be on the 27th of December 1947. K. should enter the Public Bar, take a table in the corner and drink something. His contact would have a glass of beer, approach the table and would say: 'Stout is not so good. I generally take lager.' K. would answer: 'I think Guinness is the best.' After that conversation K. would leave the Bar and go outside. His contact would follow him and ask him: 'Your face looks very familiar to me.' K. would say: 'I think we met in Edinburgh a year ago.' His contact would then answer: 'Do you know big Hannah?' K. would carry the Tribune with the letters well in sight and your contact would carry a book in a red cover."[156]

Alexander Feklisov, former KGB New York station officer newly assigned to London, met Fuchs as arranged. The KGB London station report to Moscow Center read:

"After a careful checkup in the city in which Korobov [KGB officer Nikolay Ostrovsky] and Jack [unidentified KGB officer] took part, Callistratus [Feklisov] got in our oper. car [operational car] at the prearranged location and, in the next 35 minutes, checked out additionally in the car, which was driven by Boris [unidentified KGB officer]. There were no signs of surveillance during the checks in the buses, on foot, or in the car. Call-s ["Callistratus"/Feklisov] arrived at the meeting area 30 minutes before and familiarized himself with the streets and park that had been chosen for conducting the conversation with the athlete [source]. The meeting itself took place precisely at the agreed-on time. When C-s entered the bar, the athlete was already there, sitting at a table and drinking beer, and there were several other people sitting next to him. After exchanging the first half of the oral password, they both went outside, one after the other with a short interval, where the second half of the oral password was exchanged." (C-s began the conversation by asking after the health of his father, brother—who suffers from tuberculosis—sister, and nephews. C. ["Charles"/Fuchs] discussed work being done on E. in England. Progress has been very insignificant.)

"In the middle of November, a delegation of skier [British] scientists to which Ch. was appointed a member will go to the alpinists [Americans] to take part in the aforementioned conference. According to the current plan, the delegation should stay there only five days before returning to the island [Britain]. We think that C's inclusion in this delegation speaks to the fact that C. enjoys the skiers' trust. When asked whether he could meet with our man in Tyre [New York] during his stay in the alpinists' country, C. said that he would rather not meet with our man during this brief trip. He said he was afraid that after the May incident, the alpinists would be keeping a close watch on all scientists working on enormous who were coming into their country from the island. He is also unsure whether he will be able to notify his sister during this trip. Therefore, we did not arrange with him to have any mater-al passed through his sister." (He described the working principle of the hydrogen bomb that Fermi and Teller were working on at U. Chicago.)

"At the end of the conversation, Call-s thanked him once more for helping us and said that although we knew about his refusal in the past to accept mater. assistance from us, the situation had now changed: He was going to support his father completely, his sick brother needed his help, the costs of living had risen sharply; therefore we thought we might offer him our help as an expression of our gratitude. Afterwards, Call-s handed Ch-s two packets of a hundred pounds each. Ch. took them. After a brief silence, he said: 'We were given May's case to read, and it said that Sov. intelligence officers always try to give money to foreigners who pass them info., so as to morally bind them to continue working for them. But I am not afraid of that. On the contrary, I will take the money you're offering in order to prove my loyalty to you.' He then asked how much money Call-s had given him, and when Call-s named the amount, he returned 100 pounds, saying that it would be obvious if such a large sum came into his possession."[157]

It was the first of six meetings the two held. The KGB asked Fuchs to try to ascertain during his American trip information "'on the current state of Amer. work in the field of atomic reactors and new types of atomic bombs.'" At a brief meeting with Feklisov in London on 13 March 1948, he passed this information along, including data on "'a hydrogen super-bomb.'" Fuchs continued to provide the Russians with details about atomic weapons and the now independent British atomic bomb program through 1948 and 1949. In his autobiography Feklisov claimed he handed over "ninety extremely sensitive documents." Fuchs missed several meetings in May 1948, leading two KGB officers to write a report for Beria and Molotov warning that he might have come under investigation and asking for permission to devise a plan to bring him out of Britain to work in a Soviet institution. That was not the only concern. A KGB officer wrote Feklisov in April 1948 that he had just found out that Fuchs's original recruiter had been questioned by British counterintelligence. It is likely this is a reference to Ursula Kuczynski, "Sonya," who had been approached by the Security Service in September 1947 and learned that MI5 knew of her work in Switzerland for Soviet intelligence, although it remained in the dark about her activities in Britain.[158]

Fuchs did show up for a meeting in July and explained that work on a new reactor had prevented him from getting away. At later meetings he reported that the British were receiving intelligence about Soviet construction of an atomic installation near Sukhumi and that British intelligence may have been in contact with a Soviet scientist. Feklisov then pressed Fuchs, the Soviet spy within the British atomic program, to help identify the British spy within the Soviet program. Fuchs promised he would do what he could to identify whoever was assisting British intelligence inside the USSR but that his pursuing information on this subject might call attention to himself. By early 1949 security concerns grew even more intense. The arrests of Judith Coplon and Valentin Gubichev in New York on 4 March led Moscow to tell the London station that "'the Echelon'" (higher Soviet authorities) regarded its practice of conducting meetings with agents outdoors (Coplon and Gubichev had used that procedure) as a "'foolish working method that does not guarantee the safety of our people and athletes [agents].'" Instead, the Center suggested giving Fuchs funds to buy a car and conduct meetings in it, arrange meetings at a girlfriend's apartment, or arrange for a KGB illegal officer to be his contact (Feklisov was a legal officer working under Soviet diplomatic cover in London). Reporting on his last meeting with Fuchs on 1 April 1949, Feklisov informed Moscow that Fuchs did not have a steady girlfriend and that Fuchs had observed that due to his "situation" (that is, his intelligence activities) "'this is why I try not to fall too deeply in love.'" Feklisov got the impression that the women with whom he spent time were prostitutes, whose apartments would not be secure. Fuchs delivered a verbal report and made arrangements to provide written materials at the next scheduled meeting, on 25 June, with a backup date of 2 July. But he did not show up on either date, and there were no more contacts before the KGB's worst fears were confirmed when British authorities announced Fuchs's arrest on 3 February 1950.[159]

Moscow had premonitions that Fuchs, still its most valuable atomic intelligence source, was in danger. Concerned that Harry Gold's knowledge of Fuchs's espionage in the United States represented a vulnerability, in 1949 the KGB decided to seek him out and persuade him to leave the United States to protect Fuchs. Its concern was that Gold's ill-advised connection to Abraham Brothman, exposed as a technical spy by Elizabeth Bentley in late 1945, might lead to Gold's exposure and, if he broke, then it would lead to Fuchs. Ivan Kamenev, a KGB officer operating out of New York, met with Gold in September 1949 and learned that the KGB's fears about Gold's connection with Brothman were well based. Gold had not immediately left Brothman's company, as he had promised Yatskov in December 1946. Instead, he remained there until 1948. Even worse, Gold also told Kamenev that the FBI had questioned Brothman about his relationship with Jacob Golos and Elizabeth Bentley in May 1947. Brothman had told agents that Gold had been the person who introduced him to Jacob Golos but that their discussions had been entirely about innocent commercial matters. Although Gold had twice been questioned—once before a grand jury—before he testified, he had coordinated his story with Brothman and had insisted that his relationship with Brothman and Golos was purely business. Gold had even allowed the FBI to look at materials he had in his apartment and was convinced that he had assuaged any suspicions it had.[160]

Not fully persuaded, Kamenev urged him to plan on leaving the country, but Gold was reluctant. At another meeting, on 24 October 1949, he agreed to consider fleeing but did not commit to anything because he had never been followed or subjected to a follow-up investigation. The KGB upped its incentive, offering to provide for his father if Gold agreed to leave the United States (his mother had recently died). The New York station told Moscow:

"A's ["Arno's"/Gold's] interrogation and his mother's death left a deep imprint and affected his morale, otherwise it would be difficult to explain the 'memory lapses' regarding past events and the fact that he had been forced to put out of his mind the thought of everything that had happened to him. Time has undoubtedly wiped out the feelings of fear, b/c the interrogation was not followed by immediate punishment, and he was given a chance to work without hindrance or persecution; his moral state, though, has changed nevertheless. We have no doubt that A. has remained a loyal athlete [agent] to us and a steadfast man to the extent that he can, but considering everything that has happened to him recently, it is difficult to foresee how he would behave at an interrogation if the union were to launch a further inquiry into this affair."

A third meeting was scheduled for 5 February 1950. But after Fuchs's arrest was announced on 3 February, the KGB's first assumption was that Gold had betrayed him. Moscow Center ordered the KGB New York station to find out if Gold was free or under arrest. The New York station sent an operative unknown to Gold to the planned 5 February meeting, not to make contact but to observe if Gold came and if he were under surveillance. Gold appeared and waited. The Soviet observer saw no obvious sign he was being watched but departed without making contact.[161]

A report to Stalin a few days later recounted Fuchs's valuable service to the Soviets, explaining that he had been the source of information on the planning and assembly of the atomic bomb while he had worked at Los Alamos and data on the hydrogen bomb, reactors, isolation of plutonium, theoretical calculations on explosions, and data on American testing of bombs after he returned to Britain. The report also summarized Kamenev's efforts to persuade Gold to leave America and the reasons the KGB believed he had betrayed Fuchs. An internal report on 5 February concluded that Fuchs could not have been betrayed by other people who had been peripherally involved but emphasized the need to investigate

further since there was worry that Fuchs could betray others and lead to
further collapses of agent networks. Left unsaid but clearly in the minds
of KGB officers was that if Gold had been the source of Fuchs's failure
—or if Gold were betrayed by Fuchs—the agents with whom he had
worked were at risk, most obviously David Greenglass and, through him,
Julius Rosenberg and his large network of engineer spies.[162]

On 6 February, senior KGB officer Andrey Raina wrote another assessment, concluding that the most likely scenario was that Gold had betrayed Fuchs. And in a letter to the New York station dated 23 February
1950, Moscow announced that it had "'very serious suspicions'" that he
was the guilty party. But it also decided to investigate Ursula Kuczynski
and her brother Jurgen, as well as Fuchs's father and sister. Ursula
Kuczynski, however, fled Britain after Fuchs's arrest and arrived in East
Germany in early March, which removed her from the suspect list. On 28
February Raina ordered the KGB Berlin station to launch an investigation of Jurgen Kuczynski, Hans Siebert, and Hanna Klopstock. Raina focused on Siebert because of his ties to Noel Field, a former Soviet agent
whom the KGB had convinced itself was an American superspy who had
subverted the loyalties of Communists throughout the Eastern Bloc.[163]

The KGB desperately tried to figure out what to do. TASS, the Soviet
news agency, published a statement in early March calling the charge that
Fuchs had passed information to the Soviet Union "a blatant lie" and declared that Fuchs was "unknown" to the Soviets. There was debate about
how to handle Fuchs's trial, how to deal with his father, and whether to
hire a better lawyer for him. By early April, the KGB concluded that
Fuchs had given the British "'all the information he knew about our work
and about people of ours who were connected with him through work'"
and learned that both prosecution and defense lawyers had spoken of
Fuchs's doubts about the Soviet Union's postwar policies. Moscow grew
concerned that his confession would be used "'to sow doubt in our active
agents' minds and to shake their devotion to our cause. . . . In this resulting extremely unfavorable period for conducting our work, there is
the danger that under the influence of the strengthening anti-Sov. campaign, some of our agents who are not constantly working to raise their
polit. level, and because of insufficient educational work with them in the
past, could change their polit. views. There is also the danger that under
the influence of a policy of intimidating and persecuting progressive elements, some of our less resolute agents could refuse to continue working with us.'" The FBI, meanwhile, had been frantically attempting to
track down Fuchs's American courier, questioning the Heinemans, and

poring over Fuchs's confession. To its great irritation, however, not until after Fuchs was sentenced did British officials permit the FBI to interview him. Meanwhile, Gold had already come under FBI suspicion due to his ties to Brothman. FBI agents began questioning him on 15 May, and after Fuchs identified Gold's picture as the courier he had known as "Raymond," the pressure increased. Gold confessed on 22 May 1950.[164]

One week later, Valerian Zorin, deputy minister of foreign affairs and in 1950 also chairman of the Committee of Information (the KGB of that era), wrote a memo to Stalin explaining what Soviet intelligence thought had happened:

"As a result of checking and investigating the circumstances surrounding the failure of our agent Ch-s ["Charles"] (form-r chief of the Theoretical Physics Division at the Eng. atomic center in Harwell, Klaus Fuchs), the following has been established: The Amer. decryption service worked for a long time on one of the telegrams from New York's MGB station (subsequently the KI), dating from 1944–45, during Ch-s's stay in the USA. Unable to decode this telegram in its entirety, the Americans sent it in 1949 to Eng. counterintelligence, which was able to decode it completely and ascertain that Ch. was a Sov. intelligence agent who had passed us important information about work at Amer. and Eng. atomic centers, where he worked.

This cipher telegram was processed using a one-time pad that had been used for a different cipher telegram, which is what allowed counterintelligence to decode its text. The investigation that was conducted revealed that during the war, there had indeed been a vast cipher telegraph correspondence between our station in NY and the center about Ch-s's intelligence work; there had been transmitted a summary of mater-als received from him on the atomic bomb, and one of the telegrams even mentioned his last name and detailed information about him. Our experts allow for the possibility that the English have decoded telegrams of ours that were processed with a used one-time pad.

From documents we obtained by agent means from French counterintelligence, it is known that when the English arrested Ch., he confessed to having collaborated with Sov. intelligence, described the main points of his work with us in the USA and England, and gave testimony about his intelligence contacts; in particular, he gave the address of our agent in Paris, 'Mars' [unidentified], and of our agent in London, 'Ref' [unidentified], which he had been given in 1947 in case he needed to contact us.

On the basis of Ch-s's testimony, on 24 May of this year, in Philadelphia, USA, Harry Gold—our longtime agent 'Arno'—was arrested; he had received mater-als from Ch. on the atomic bomb in 1944–45, and we stopped using him to receive mater-al in December 1945. At the beginning of 1950, in the

interest of preventing employees of the Committee of Info. from being compromised, we recalled Feklisov, an employee of the London station who had
handled agent Ch., and Kamenev, an employee of the New York station who
had handled agent Arno. At pres., there are no Sov. workers in England or the
USA whom these agents might know. Measures have also been taken to get
out from the USA four agents who had previously been connected with Arno
and who are threatened with failure if the latter confesses."

Zorin's analysis was largely accurate. The American Venona project had
deciphered KGB cables from 1944 and 1945 that pointed to Fuchs as a
Soviet source. The FBI in 1949 had turned the information over to the
British Security Service, which then confronted Fuchs. Zorin did not
identify the four American agents the KGB was attempting to get out of
the United States, but two of the obvious candidates were David Greenglass and Julius Rosenberg.[165]

Zorin's correct identification of deciphered cables as the culprits in
Fuchs's arrest did not prevent Soviet internal politics from causing re-
consideration later. In June 1953 Lavrenty Beria lost the struggle to succeed Stalin and was arrested and accused of being a British spy. A draft
report to be sent by the head of KGB foreign intelligence to the Council
of Ministers asserted "'the reasons for Fuchs's failure have not been precisely identified to this day'" and noted the central role Beria and his
longtime associates such as Vsevolod Merkulov had played in atomic intelligence. The draft suggested: "'In view of the uncovering of a criminal
link between the traitor Beria and foreign intelligence services, it would
be desirable to question Beria and his accomplices additionally as to
which information regarding the most valuable scientific-technical intelligence agents and materials obtained from them on atomic energy, jet
aviation and radar, etc. was passed to foreign intelligence services.'" However, other officers thought the evidence too thin, and the report was not
sent. Beria, Merkulov, and other Beria cronies were, in any case, executed. Nonetheless, some KGB officers refused to give up on the notion
that Harry Gold had betrayed Fuchs. For example, Alexander Feklisov
throughout his life believed that Gold, not the KGB cables deciphered by
Venona, had led the FBI to Fuchs.[166]

As the extent of the disaster unfolded, with Fuchs's arrest leading to
Gold's arrest, and Gold's arrest leading to the arrest of David Greenglass,
and his arrest leading to the arrest of Julius Rosenberg and the uncovering of his extensive espionage apparatus, the KGB's anger at Fuchs grew.
A disgusted London station reported in December 1950 that it had

learned that Fuchs had asked to be allowed to keep his British citizenship, that there had been little solid evidence against him, and, consequently, that he had confessed of his own accord and not under serious pressure of prosecution. Leonid Kvasnikov, then a senior KGB officer at Moscow Center, fumed and wrote on the London report that Fuchs "has undergone total degeneration."[167]

Based solely on his confession, Fuchs's trial went swiftly, and he was sentenced to fourteen years in prison and loss of his British citizenship. Released in 1959 after serving nine years of his sentence, he was allowed to emigrate to Communist East Germany. After reaffirming his loyalty to communism, Fuchs became one of the German Democratic Republic's leading atomic physicists, served as deputy director of its Institute for Nuclear Research, and was awarded membership on the central committee of the SED, East Germany's ruling Communist Party.

Eventually Soviet anger at Fuchs cooled as it better appreciated the value of his work for the Soviet Union and the difficulties of his position in 1950. In 1960 the KGB arranged an invitation for him to visit the Soviet Union to meet with Soviet nuclear scientists. During his visit he was kept under close surveillance. After determining that he appeared to be sincerely pro-Soviet, Kvasnikov and another KGB officer met with him at Moscow's Peking Restaurant, then one of the city's premier eating spots. Kvasnikov reported: "'We began the conversation by expressing our gratitude to B. ["Bras"/Fuchs] for the great help he had rendered to the Sov. Union during a difficult time.'" In the conversation that followed, Fuchs explained why he had confessed: "'According to B., this action had been prompted by serious polit. ambivalence and by doubts as to the correctness of Soviet policies, which he had begun feeling under the influence of bourgeois propaganda and his detachment from sources of truthful information. Specifically, this ambivalence and doubt manifested themselves in the fact that at that time, B. came to the conclusion that the Sov. Union had violated the principles of democracy and was treating the People's Democracies unjustly. The consequence of these mistaken views was his opinion that his collaboration with us was a mistake.'" Fuchs went on to say he later realized that he had made ideological errors in losing his faith, and thus his decision to emigrate to East Germany when he was released. He told Kvasnikov that "'our positive assessment of his past work had given him greater satisfaction than 'any decoration,' as he put it.'" For the KGB's part, Kvasnikov wrote: "'As we parted ways, we thanked B. once more for helping us in the past, wished him success in his future life and work, and told him that in the future he can turn to us for friendly support if he ever has any problems.'"[168]

The KGB kept a friendly eye on Fuchs and in 1965 tried, unsuccessfully, to get the Soviet Academy of Sciences to make him an honorary member. (Alexander Feklisov, then deputy chief of the KGB's training institute, initiated the action. Soviet scientists opposed honoring Fuchs, fearing it would reduce the importance of their role in building the Soviet bomb.) Fuchs died in 1988, and in 1989 the KGB successfully petitioned the Central Committee of the Communist Party of the Soviet Union to posthumously award him the "Order of Friendship among Nations."[169]

David Greenglass after the War

As part of its revival of old networks in March 1948 Moscow Center instructed the KGB New York station to meet with Julius Rosenberg and obtain a report on the status of his agent network; "'we are especially interested in what Dave ('Caliber') currently has at his disposal, and whether he is ready to begin working with us.'" Moscow also asked New York to find out if Greenglass could go back to work at Los Alamos or, alternatively, set up safe houses in the New York area. A KGB New York station letter to Moscow in early August reported that Greenglass was in business with Rosenberg. As instructed, KGB officer Gavriil Panchenko had suggested that Greenglass try to rejoin Los Alamos but also asked if Greenglass's links to Rosenberg might be a problem in view of the Signal Corps' having fired Julius because of his radical associations. Rosenberg assured Panchenko that Greenglass already had been through security checks without difficulty and noted that his brother-in-law "'had kept a small amount of plutonium in a lead box'" as a souvenir from Los Alamos but on Julius's orders had thrown it into the East River. (A sample of U-238 that Greenglass had kept was not thrown away but forwarded to Moscow in 1948.) Panchenko suggested to Julius that he assign both Greenglasses to assist in photographing William Perl's heavy volume of materials on jet propulsion at one of the network's safe houses in New York.[170]

By the end of 1948, Moscow concluded that even if Greenglass could get a Los Alamos job, "'his limited education and area of specialization'" would preclude a position that would yield significant information. "'He could be far more useful as a courier'" or assistant for Julius Rosenberg.

Another option the KGB New York station suggested was for Greenglass to attend the University of Chicago and renew friendships with four Los Alamos veterans whom Greenglass had identified as sympathetic to the CPUSA and who were either studying or teaching there. Moscow Center responded that the four were "of great interest" and assigned them cover names. The New York station cabled Moscow in June 1949 that it wanted Greenglass to enroll at Chicago to study physics, cultivate his old friends with the aim "'of using them for our work in the future,'" and "'seek out people whom we could recruit for our work.'" He needed to be discreet: "'under no circumstances should he talk to anyone about our work or try to recruit anyone for our work.'" Every two months he would prepare a report, photograph it, and give it to Ethel Rosenberg, who would serve as a courier and store it in Julius's apartment until it could be passed along to the KGB. The KGB was agreeable to paying all of Greenglass's educational and living expenses plus $125 a month. This ambitious plan did not go anywhere. In late August 1949 Julius Rosenberg told the KGB New York station that he had discussed the issue with Greenglass, who had "'neither the opportunity nor the desire to enroll'" at Chicago. He had applied but not been admitted, and, in any case, his wife, expecting a baby, had flatly refused to leave New York.[171]

Rosenberg met Panchenko on 11 October 1949 and reported that Greenglass had obtained a temporary job at the Arma Corporation in Brooklyn, working nights. If the KGB was interested, he could make copies or reconstruct from memory the devices Arma was manufacturing for the U.S. military. While Greenglass was hoping to get a job at the Synchromatic company, which did atomic-related work, his work at Arma involved "manufacturing radar stabilizers for tank guns. He has access to secret projects." A later report to Moscow explained that the stabilizer "'would keep the gun constantly trained on the target regardless of the oscillations of the tank itself during movement in battle.'" The model was already undergoing testing; Greenglass "'offered to take the camera with him and copy out all the blueprints at work.'" The station more cautiously proposed that he do a sketch from memory and have Julius photograph it. The stabilizer was of interest to Moscow, which also offered to pay Greenglass's costs to attend New York University's engineering school. (Greenglass's willingness to undertake additional espionage tasks in 1949 diverges from his later statements to the FBI that minimized his continued assistance to Soviet intelligence after his having left Los Alamos.)[172]

Amid all these grandiose plans, a specter was haunting the KGB. Harry Gold, the KGB accurately feared, was increasingly vulnerable and could expose both David and Ruth Greenglass. In September 1949 the Center told New York that the Greenglasses needed a cover story for their meeting with Gold in Albuquerque. If there were no witnesses, they should deny it ever took place. Even before Gold implicated them, however, David got an unpleasant visit from the FBI in late January 1950. The agents claimed to be investigating some unaccounted-for uranium from the shop where Greenglass had worked at Los Alamos. He denied any knowledge of the matter and they went away. He waited a week to make sure he was not under surveillance and then told Rosenberg, who informed the KGB New York station. Panchenko assured Rosenberg that the Americans had no proof that Greenglass had collaborated with the KGB. Nonetheless, the KGB officer also briefed him on how he should instruct the Greenglasses to behave if the FBI came back, canceled Julius's regularly scheduled meetings with the KGB, and replaced them by communicating through "dead drops" and meeting in person only after use of a prearranged signal.[173]

The KGB pondered whether the FBI's interview with Greenglass had anything to do with Fuchs's recent arrest in Britain or was simply part of a general investigation of all former Los Alamos employees. Whatever the reason, it feared that Greenglass would remain a person of interest and his ties to Rosenberg would be discovered, possibly leading to "'a thorough investigation'" of Rosenberg's network of engineer spies. David and Ruth Greenglass had to "categorically deny involvement in intelligence work or passing anyone materials of any kind. The competitors do not have information about the work of W. ["Wasp"/Ruth] and C. ["Caliber"/David], but they could set up a trap. Proceed with caution."[174]

By April 1950 Moscow feared that what had once seemed a secure as well as a highly successful intelligence operation had become a house of cards that was about to be blown down. Klaus Fuchs had been arrested, confessed, tried, and imprisoned. Even if Harry Gold had not betrayed Fuchs, it feared that Fuchs had given up Gold as part of his confession (he had). In either case, Gold, whose cover name was changed from "Arno" to "Mad," could lead the FBI to David and Ruth, now called "Zinger" and "Ida," and endanger Julius Rosenberg, now labeled "King," and his entire network. The price of the decision in mid-1945 to save a separate courier run by having Harry Gold pick up espionage material from Greenglass in Albuquerque as well as from Fuchs in Santa Fe was going to be heavy. Additionally, while one set of FBI agents was following up the information Fuchs had provided in his confession, another was attempting to attach real names to the cover names in the KGB cables that were being deciphered by code breakers of the National Security Agency's Venona project. For example, one deciphered cable about "Liberal" stated "Liberal's" wife of five years was named Ethel and was twenty-nine years old. Another cable identified Ruth Greenglass by her real name and noted that she was married to the brother of "Liberal's" wife. As soon as Julius Rosenberg came to the attention of the FBI agents working on Venona, his identification as "Liberal" was a certainty. In total, Venona cryptanalysts eventually deciphered twenty-one messages that discussed Julius Rosenberg's work as a leading Soviet agent-handler.[175]

In April 1950 Moscow Center warned the New York station about the risks that flowed from Fuchs's confession: "There are threads leading from Charles [Fuchs] to Zinger [David Greenglass], Ida (Wasp) [Ruth Greenglass], and King (L-l) [Liberal/Julius Rosenberg]. It is possible that Mad (Arno) [Gold] will fail or turn traitor." In view of these risks, Moscow advised:

"In the case of Zinger and Ida [David and Ruth Greenglass], what the competitors [FBI] have on them is not only their clear and incontrovertible involvement in our work, but also evidence that they passed secret materials on the atomic bomb to us. On this basis the competitors will exert strong pressure on Z. and Ida, using intimidation and other means, even to the point of arresting them, and eventually will compel them to give testimony, with all of the concomitant implications for King, his group, and all of our work in the country. (Discuss with King the possibility of Z. and I. leaving the country.)"[176]

On 25 April the KGB New York station sent a letter to Moscow reporting that family complications had delayed Greenglass's departure. Ruth, pregnant, had been badly burned in a kitchen fire and had only recently returned home after ten weeks in the hospital. Because Ruth had a rare blood type, David had made a radio appeal for blood, and Panchenko saw mention of it in the newspapers. Since he did not know David's last name, however, he had not connected it to Julius's brother-in-law and never realized how it would complicate and delay the plan to exfiltrate the Greenglasses. He asked Rosenberg to let David know that "'if he agrees to leave the USA, we would take upon ourselves all the expenses related to the move, see to it that he gets settled in the new place, and take responsibility for looking after his relatives who remain in this country.'" Rosenberg interjected that the Russians would have to "'make a good Communist of him.'" Startled, Panchenko asked if David "'was a bad Communist. King [Rosenberg] replied that lately, Zinger [Greenglass] has been reading practically none of the Party publications and that clearly his education needed to be supplemented.'"[177]

Panchenko met with Julius Rosenberg again on 23 May 1950. Julius reported that Greenglass had finally agreed to leave the country, but it would take three months since Ruth had just given birth and was still in precarious health. They discussed various options, ruling out France, since it would require a passport, and leaning toward Mexico. Unbeknownst to them, FBI agents had already tracked down Harry Gold, who was arraigned the same day Panchenko and Rosenberg met; his arrest was announced in the press the next day. Time was running out. When it learned of Gold's arrest, the station proposed that the Greenglasses leave for Mexico quickly, in the next two or three weeks. That same day Moscow agreed and sent detailed instructions on travel arrangements, contact routines, and cover stories. It told the New York station:

"Despite all their family difficulties, Ida [Ruth Greenglass] and Zinger [David Greenglass] need to leave the country as soon as possible, b/c if they remain in the country, it will inevitably lead to their arrest. Therefore, they should be advised to prepare for departure immediately. If need be, their preparations can be covered as a trip to a summer house in view of Ida's poor health. At the same time, their preparations should obviously not be publicized.

If it is not possible for Zinger to bring his entire family with him, we must recommend that he leave only with Ida and the newborn and leave the eldest with their parents. They should not free up their apartment in NY.

If extraordinary circumstances arise that prevent Ida from leaving, Zinger should leave without her and explain to Ida that if he does not leave NY, it would have direful consequences for Z. and his family."

Moscow directed that the New York station supply Julius with $10,000 (more than $85,000 in 2008 dollars) to facilitate the departures. Another long memo went to the KGB Mexico City station about required legal papers and secret housing. More telegrams ordered the KGB station in Sweden to check on transit from Mexico; considered the possibility of their going into hiding in the United States; cautioned against discussing anything involving the Greenglasses and the Rosenbergs indoors, where FBI listening devices (much feared by the KGB) might be present; and suggested other security measures.[178]

On 1 June 1950, Julius Rosenberg met with his KGB contact and conveyed the welcome news that Greenglass had agreed to flee the United States and would be ready to leave on 15 June. It was too late. Gold had confessed and begun to cooperate with the FBI. His account of the soldier from Los Alamos from whom he had obtained a report sparked a massive operation that quickly zeroed in on David Greenglass. (Gold had not known Greenglass's real name.) Gold identified a picture of him on 4 June, and Greenglass was quickly placed under surveillance. On 9 June a highly agitated Julius Rosenberg spoke with his KGB contact, who relayed the following:

"During the day on Wednesday, June 7th, K. ["King"/Rosenberg] had stopped by to see Z-r ["Zinger"/Greenglass]. As he was approaching Z-r's house, K. discovered that on the opposite side of the street, across from Z-r's doorway, was a car—D-45-25 (or W-45-25, K. does not remember the first letter of the license plate). According to K., there were three men sitting in the car and constantly looking in the direction of Z-r's doorway, which seemed suspicious to K. K. surmised that Z. was under surveillance, but he nevertheless went into Z-r's house. According to K., during the conversation Z-r informed K. by note that he has, in fact, been under surveillance since June 7th, and moreover, it was constant surveillance.

When he left Z-r's house, K. saw a truck on the corner, with a sign on the side that said 'Acme Construction Company.' At first, K. did not give this truck a second thought. To verify that Z-r was under surveillance, K. walked by Z-r's house on the evening of the same day. The automobile and truck were in the same places they had been during the day; moreover K. saw that two people had gotten out of the automobile, who then walked over to the truck and sat in the back. As he walked by Z-r's house that evening, K. also noticed that there was someone standing on each of the four corners by Z-r's house; in K's opinion, these were undoubtedly counterintelligence agents.

During his conversation with Z-r that day, K. had warned Z-r about the danger he was in, and once more mentioned to Z-r that if he was arrested, he should not say a thing about his operational activities. According to K., Z-r assured him that under no circumstances would he say a word about his intelligence activities. As a result of discovering the surveillance, K. and Z. came to the conclusion that leaving at present was out of the question. K. informed Z. that Z. should calmly stay at home and do nothing, and that his departure for Mexico would now depend on whether there was any surveillance present."

Julius had already given Greenglass $6,000 to finance preparations to leave the United States, and the KGB advised him to send his wife Ethel to the Greenglass apartment to retrieve all but $1,000 since the presence of $6,000 would be hard to explain.[179]

Greenglass was picked up for questioning on 15 June and arrested early the next morning. Moscow sent a cable to New York on 13 July asking if it should try to secure a lawyer for him. New York doubted it could find anyone as prominent as O. John Rogge, whom the family had already hired. But when Moscow Center learned that Rogge was arranging for his client to assist the prosecution, it decided he was a government agent and ordered the KGB New York station to find a new lawyer. This notion, however, was quickly reconsidered as impractical and canceled. After his testimony in the Rosenberg trial, David Greenglass was sentenced to fifteen years in prison. (Rogge's deal allowed Ruth Greenglass, who also cooperated, to avoid prosecution altogether.) By American standards that seemed a stiff sentence for a cooperating witness, but Leonid Kvasnikov, more used to harsher Soviet practices, commented that it was part of a plan "to show that the court spares those who cooperate with it."[180]

Julius Rosenberg was questioned the same day Greenglass was arrested and then released. But the Greenglasses' decision to cooperate with the government provided more than enough evidence to charge him. Julius was arrested on 17 July 1950, his wife a month later. They admitted nothing and rejected prosecution offers of leniency in exchange for a confession and identification of other Soviet spies. They were convicted in 1951 and in April sentenced to die.

The New York station immediately prepared a lengthy letter for Moscow with a proposal to try to save them. Almost every tactic and talking point later used by the Rosenberg defense was laid out in this KGB proposal. The passionate and emotional language suggests not only the gratitude and loyalty KGB officers felt for the Rosenbergs, but also their shock that the American legal system had decided to punish espionage so severely—the latter a surprising view considering that the USSR routinely executed spies.

The first suggestion offered by the New York station was to use the Soviet and foreign press, but the letter noted that "'it would be preferable to publish articles about the trial first and foremost in the non-Communist press.'" It listed eighteen different themes that could be emphasized, including depicting the trial as an exercise in "'coarse anti-Soviet propaganda and a crusade against the CPUSA'"; an effort to frighten Americans; an effort to "'shift the blame for war in Korea off of the gov't. and onto Jews and Communists'"; or an attempt by reactionaries to turn America in a fascist, repressive direction, contrasting the death sentences with lenient sentences for such Axis spies as Tokyo Rose and Axis Sally, as well as arguing that the trial was motivated by "'the hatred against all things progressive,'" symbolized by the ability of "'gangsters, grafters, and murderers'" like Mafia boss Frank Costello to "'command respect and become national heroes,'" "'while a mother of two is sentenced to die by electric chair . . . because of some villainous brother's slanderous denunciation,'" pointing to pre-judgment of the court, the immorality of the sentence, the absurdity of being "'charged with passing secrets, which, as scientists have admitted, do not exist,'" and deploring that David Greenglass, supposedly the man who actually passed information, got the lightest sentence.[181]

In addition to the press campaign the letter considered ways to refute David and Ruth Greenglass's testimony, since they had provided key evidence used to convict the Rosenbergs. Because the KGB was sure that neither David not Ruth had been "'psychologically prepared for such a harsh sentence,'" it recommended letters to their mothers, pleading that they persuade David "'to publicly retract his testimony'" since he had already received his sentence. The KGB counseled that the letters could not appear to have been written by Communists or Russians but should seem to come from the Rosenbergs' friends and should be hand-delivered to prevent American authorities from interfering (one suggestion was to use a "street urchin" to deliver them). Among the points the letters should emphasize was that if he had "'even an iota of conscience,'" David must be ashamed before his sister, Julius, and his mother, "'who, if she is an honest woman, will also turn her back on him, as people once turned their back on Judas when he sold Christ for 30 silver pieces. He must also be ashamed before honest Amer-s, who will spit whenever they speak his name.'" But it was not too late "'to fix his mistake and deserve to be called a man and to look people straight in the eye'" by openly confessing "'that the reason for his false testimony was a desire to save himself and his wife, that he cannot live in peace after such a sentence, and that before God and all honest men, he rescinds his testimony.'" The KGB New York station also thought that lethal threats against the Greenglass family should be part of the theme: "'The letter has been written by Z-r's ["Zinger"/Greenglass's] Amer. friends, who could turn out to be his sworn enemies, and who never forget the bad or the good. . . . The only reward for mitigation of his sentence was at the cost of the lives of his sister and King [Rosenberg], the only reward for betrayal is death. Neither Z-r, nor his wife, nor their children, nor their parents will live a moment longer.'"[182]

David Greenglass did not withdraw his testimony. While the Rosenbergs were awaiting execution, the government offered them the opportunity to avoid death if they confessed and cooperated. Neither did. They were executed on 19 June 1953. Greenglass was released from prison after serving ten of his fifteen-year term.

"Enormous"

Despite the disappointments and setbacks of the postwar era, by any reasonable standard the KGB's Enormous project had been an outstanding success. The KGB supplied the Soviet atomic program during its early years with thousands of pages of high-level technical information that allowed the USSR to detonate a bomb in a remarkably short time and at only a fraction of the cost of the Manhattan Project. If spies such as Alger Hiss gave the USSR an invaluable window into American foreign policy decision making, Klaus Fuchs, Theodore Hall, David Greenglass, Russell McNutt, Boris Podolsky, Engelbert Broda, Melita Norwood, and Allan Nunn May offered technological and scientific information that saved untold billions of rubles and years of scientific experiments and blind alleys. That the Soviet Union would develop an atomic bomb was never in doubt. That it would obtain one so quickly with only minimal strain on its postwar reconstruction and that it would be a replica of that built by the United States was a product of Soviet espionage.

The consequences of "Enormous" were enormous. The shock of the Soviets' atomic test of 1949 produced fear and insecurity in the United States. Not only did it ramp up the hunt for the atomic spies believed to have made the feat possible, but it also seemed to demonstrate that no American secret was safe from betrayal. And the fallout was not limited to more investigations, charges and countercharges, and increased security regulations. Confident that his possession of atomic weapons neutralized America's strategic advantage, Stalin was emboldened to unleash war in Korea in 1950.

с. 57 Через "Шагнал" получаем отраву сухую, эфирную-х "Шагнал"
стекло, оружие. Связан с "Federal Laboratory".

с. 81 Согласно указанию Центра, А/214 ликвидован. А/214.

с. 83 В связи с английской кампанией:
Возможно из организаций русских амер-цев совращался с
русским уехал из Европы. Совраблавгос получили
обещание об руководители земляческих орган-й, но оно
не выполнено.
Письмо от 7.01.36.

с. 90 "Игла" переведен ломкость на агент-е отношения. "Игла"
Юберто получил от него общий вид и размеры но-
вейшего истребителя фирма Нортроп (для д у поставку).

с. 91 В к. леда 35 г. этот самолёт лечу (видимо, узла в меру). даёт
в комиссии
х Мая

с. 113-115 На "Зеро" в защ-ме вошла нелегалка "Рыжая" "Зеро",
и попыталась её завербовать. Напер-говорил, чтобы он "Рыжая"
её не трогал, но "Рыжая" не выполнил. Директиву Нужд.
жена Петра
Д. 3511/2 т.5 с. 330
Письмо от 13.04.36.

с. 128 "Игла" перешел на фирму ломких и. Работает над "Игла"
проектированием сверхскоростного будущего прибора,
"Игла" разрабатывает все оружие для неба.

с. 212 "Блин"/по наводке "Либерала"/ - Исидор Финкштейн, "Блин"
комментатор Нью-Йорк пос.

с. 236 "Отношение Иглы к работе замечательное. Все наши "Игла"
поручения он выполняет точно и аккуратно. Работой весьма
доволен и неоднократно выражал свои беспокойные чувства по от-
ношению к сов.союзу. Недавно он обратился к Эдуарду
с просьбой разрешить ему двухнедельный отпуск, что посвящает
и сделал. Это характерно для Иглы и подчёркивает его дисци-
плинированность и серьёзность."

с. 277 Годовщина и поездка в Европу. Рассказано Бонн "Борт" "Шедия"
в Герм-и: был, химшин, в концерне и.Г. Фарбениндустри,
неудивляла, знает посла США Додда.

Письмо от 20.5.36.

с. 283 Отношения с "блином" вошли в русло нормальной "Блин"
оперативной работы." По командировке губы вызвал
в Вашингтон. Связь в госдеп, конгрессе. Знает Принца. Принц

с. 285 "Блин" сообщил, что в Берлине в кач-ве корреспон-
дента Херстовского агентства "Юниверсал Сервис" работает, другиесь
Karl von Wiegand. Ему было приказано поддерживать отношения с Гитлером, т.к. это якобы выгодного всем, что
германская пресса покупала информацию агентство.
Между Херстом и герм. промышленностью - сделка на поставку Херстом оружия против себя.

CHAPTER 3

. . . .

The Journalist Spies

A 1941 internal KGB summary report broke down the occupations of Americans working for the spy agency in the prior decade. Twenty-two were journalists, a profession outnumbered only by engineers (forty-nine) and dwarfing economists (four) and professors (eight). Unlike engineers, scientists, military personnel, or government officials, journalists rarely had direct access to technical secrets or classified documents, but the espionage enterprise encompasses more than the classic spy who actually steals a document. The KGB recruited journalists in part for their access to inside information and sources on politics and policy, insights into personalities, and confidential and non-public information that never made it into published stories. Certain journalistic working habits also lent themselves to intelligence tasks. By profession journalists ask questions and probe; what might seem intrusive or suspect if done by anyone else is their normal modus operandi. Consequently, the KGB often used journalists as talent spotters for persons who did have access to sensitive information and found them useful in gather-

---

Identifies Isidor Feinstein (later known as I. F. Stone) as a KGB agent recruited in 1936 and engaged in "normal operational work." Courtesy of Alexander Vassiliev.

ing background information for evaluating candidates for recruitment. The flexibility of their work also made them desirable as couriers and agent handlers, the liaisons between KGB professional officers and their American sources. There was also much less risk that a journalist having contact with a government official or engineer would attract the attention of security officials than would a KGB officer under Soviet diplomatic cover. And even if security officials did notice a meeting, it was much easier to provide a benign explanation for contact with a pesky American journalist than with a Soviet diplomat. Additionally, the KGB could use journalists for "active measures," the planting of a story in the press or giving a slant to a story that served KGB goals.[1]

The KGB cables, letters, and reports transcribed or summarized in Alexander Vassiliev's notebooks document the relationships between the KGB and a surprising array of American journalists, some of whom have never been suspected of clandestine contact with Soviet intelligence and others whose status has been the subject of bitter and long-standing debate.

I. F. Stone: The Icon

When new information about KGB operations began to emerge in the 1990s, no individual case generated as much controversy or outrage as that of I. F. Stone. By the time he died in 1989, I. F. Stone had been installed in the pantheon of left-wing heroes as a symbol of rectitude and a teller of truth to power. But charges about connections with the KGB have been swirling about for more than a decade. Until now, the evidence was equivocal and subject to different interpretations.

Born Isidor Feinstein in Philadelphia in 1907 to Jewish immigrants from Russia, Stone dropped out of the University of Pennsylvania to become a journalist. After several years as the youngest editorial writer for a major metropolitan newspaper, the *Philadelphia Inquirer*, he moved to the *New York Post* with instructions from its owner, J. David Stern, to transform it into a champion of New Deal liberalism. Stone was, however, more than just a New Deal liberal. His sympathy for Soviet communism was obvious. In June 1933 he declared that a "Soviet America" was "the one way out that could make a real difference to the working classes" and insisted that FDR's New Deal was not reforming America but leading it to fascism, a view that then reflected the position of the CPUSA.[2]

In New York, Stone also became a contributor to the *Nation* and the

New Republic and a familiar presence in the city's left-wing, Popular
Front intellectual scene. Although he had briefly been a member of the
Socialist Party in the early 1930s, he soon had a reputation as a fervent
pro-Communist, although he never joined the CPUSA. His biographer
conceded that he had a romantic view of communism and viewed "party
members as lined up on the correct side of historical developments, unlike fascists or even members of the smaller left-wing sects." While occasionally critical of aspects of Stalin's purges, he felt that because of the
battle against fascism it was too important to risk fracturing the Popular
Front by openly denouncing Stalin or the Soviet Union. He fervently supported the Loyalist cause in Spain from 1936 onwards. He was a signer
of the statement, published just days before the Nazi-Soviet Pact, defending the USSR and its progress toward democracy and denying it
shared any commonalities with Nazi Germany.[3]

After Stern finally fired him for his excessively pro-Soviet views, Stone
moved to the *Nation*. Briefly shaken by the Nazi-Soviet Pact, he mo-
mentarily pulled back from his Communist alliances, writing an angry
denunciation of the agreement and taking part in a short-lived effort by
several other disillusioned Popular Fronters and ex-Communists to build
a new radical group critical of the CPUSA as a tool of Soviet foreign policy. When in 1940 he moved to *PM,* the left-wing daily edited by Ralph
Ingersoll, however, Stone reverted to his earlier attitudes and became a
stalwart of its pro-Communist faction. His uncritical support of Soviet
and Communist policies continued through the Stalin era. In 1952, for example, he wrote *The Hidden History of the Korean War,* where he promoted the falsehood that it was South Korea that had sparked the war by
invading the Communist North. After *PM* folded, he wrote for its left-
wing successor and, when it also went under in 1953, started his own
muckraking newsletter, *I. F. Stone's Weekly,* which gained a wide audience on the political left. Although he was occasionally critical of aspects
of Soviet policy, it was not until the mid-1950s that he lost his illusions
about the Soviet regime, writing a denunciation that cost his newsletter
a substantial portion of his Old Left, pro-Communist readership. In the
1960s, however, *I. F. Stone's Weekly* regained its leftist audience, particularly during the Vietnam War era, when his angry condemnation of
American foreign policy found a receptive audience among both the old
pro-Soviet left and the younger New Left. Stone learned classical Greek
in his retirement and wrote a book on Socrates and Athens, part of his
life-long obsession with issues of dissent. When he died in 1989, his reputation as a fiercely independent curmudgeon seemed secure.

The first report of Stone's possible ties to the KGB came in 1992, when Oleg Kalugin, a retired KGB general, told a British journalist: "We had an agent—a well-known American journalist—with a good reputation, who severed his ties with us after 1956. I myself convinced him to resume them. But in 1968, after the invasion of Czechoslovakia . . . he said he would never again take any money from us." Herbert Romerstein, a former staff member of the House Committee on Un-American Activities, quoted an unidentified KGB source as saying that the journalist in question was Stone. The British journalist then reinterviewed Kalugin, who admitted that he had been referring to Stone but denied that Stone was a controlled agent. In his later (1994) autobiography, Kalugin characterized Stone as a fellow traveler "who had made no secret of his admiration for the Soviet system" before the mid-1950s. He wrote that when he was asked to reestablish contact with Stone, KGB headquarters in Moscow "never said that he had been an agent of our intelligence service, but rather that he was a man with whom we had regular contact."[4]

Kalugin's careful parsing of Stone's exact relationship to the KGB and hints of an earlier relationship made the discovery of Stone-related materials in the KGB cables deciphered by the Venona project in the mid-1990s the occasion for another uproar. Four cables mentioned Stone. Two were entirely benign. A GRU message from 1943 merely reported that someone with GRU connections had been in Washington and talked with several correspondents, including Stone. A KGB message dated December 1944 mentioned Stone along with several other journalists who had contacts with military leaders. The other two, both from 1944, were more suggestive. In all the KGB messages, Stone had the cover name "Pancake." By itself, that did not indicate that he worked for the KGB. Many individuals, like President Roosevelt and Prime Minister Churchill, were given cover names; they were as much a convenience for cipher officers (who could avoid having to laboriously use a "spell table" to cipher a Latin alphabet name) as for security.

On 13 September 1944, the KGB New York station sent a message to Moscow that Vladimir Pravdin, a KGB officer working under cover of a TASS correspondent, had been futilely trying to contact "Pancake" in Washington, but he had been refusing to meet, citing his busy schedule. Samuel Krafsur, "Ide," an American KGB agent who worked for TASS in the same building as Stone's office, had tried to "sound him out but Pancake did not react." A 23 October 1944 message then reported that Pravdin had succeeded in meeting with Stone:

P. ["Pancake"/Stone] said that he had noticed our attempts to contact him, particularly the attempts of Ide [Krafsur] and of people of the Trust [USSR Em-
bassy], but he had reacted negatively fearing the consequences. At the same
time he implied that the attempts at rapprochement had been made with insufficient caution and by people who were insufficiently responsible. To
Sergey's [Pravdin's] reply that naturally we did not want to subject him to unpleasant complications, Pancake gave him to understand that he was not refusing his aid but one should consider that he had three children and did not
want to attract the attention of the Hut [FBI]. To Sergey's question how he
considered it advisable to maintain liaison P. replied that he would be glad to
meet but he rarely visited Tyre [New York].

While Stone earned a good living, the message added, "he would not be
averse to having a supplementary income."[5]

Taken together, these messages were suggestive but not conclusive.
The KGB wanted to establish a covert relationship with Stone and was
willing to pay him, but what exactly it had in mind was left unstated. Another implication was that Stone feared a connection with the KGB could
attract FBI attention and jeopardize his career but otherwise was not
averse to dealing with it. There was no firm evidence that Stone had
agreed to cooperate with the KGB, although taken with Kalugin's revelation that he had been ordered to reestablish contact with Stone in the
1960s, it was clear that Stone must have had some understanding of who
was cultivating him.

The controversy about Stone continued to simmer in the ensuing
decade, fueled in part by charges by conservative columnist Robert
Novak and polemicist Ann Coulter that he was a paid agent and a Soviet
spy. In 2006 a new biography of Stone hysterically charged that "neocons" had launched these slanderous attacks on Stone since they "have a
vested interest in portraying Stone as a paid Kremlin stooge because he
remains an icon to those who despise all that the far right espoused." Putting aside the matter that the paleo-conservatives accusing Stone of
spying would recoil at being referred to as neo-conservatives, Myra
MacPherson also attempted to demonstrate that there was no reason to
assume "Pancake" was Stone; that even if he was, he had done nothing
more than meet with a Soviet correspondent; and that his only reason for
doing so reluctantly was because the nefarious FBI was terrorizing anyone who dared meet with a Russian.[6]

MacPherson's book set off another round of accusations. Paul Berman, a left-wing anti-Communist writer, dismissed her whitewashing of

Stone, noting that the weight of Stone's own writing showed that he had a long history of glorifying the Soviet Union until the 1950s and that just because he had no access to official secrets and did not steal anything did not mean that the KGB would not value his cooperation. General Kalugin, reinterviewed, remained enigmatic about Stone's precise relationship but added that he had first been in contact with the KGB in 1936. Eric Alterman, a one-time Stone protégé and prominent left-wing polemicist, called the Stone-KGB stories "smears," "phony," and "pathetic," dismissing the whole contretemps as "an almost entirely bogus controversy over whether Stone ever willingly spied for the Russians or cooperated with the KGB in any way. He did not."[7]

KGB archival documents tell a different story. The first mention of Stone comes in a KGB New York station report of 13 April 1936 noting "'Pancake' ('Liberal's' lead)—Isidor Feinstein, a commentator for the New York Post." "Liberal" was Frank Palmer, part of the same New York community of pro-Communist radical journalists as Stone. He had also been an agent of the KGB New York station for several years, and this note indicated that Palmer had suggested to his bosses that they look at Isidor Feinstein (as Stone was then known). The New York station further reported in May 1936: "Relations with "Pancake" [Stone] have entered 'the channel of normal operational work.' He went to Washington on assignment for his newspaper. Connections in the State Dep. and Congress." By stating that its relationship with Stone had entered "'the channel of normal operational work,'" the KGB New York station was reporting that Stone was a fully active agent. Over the next several years, documents recorded in Vassiliev's notebooks make clear, Stone worked closely with the KGB.[8]

Stone assisted Soviet intelligence on a number of tasks, ranging from doing some talent spotting, acting as a courier by relaying information to other agents, and providing private journalistic tidbits and data the KGB found interesting. In May 1936, for example, the KGB New York station told Moscow: ""Pancake"[Stone] reported that Karl Von Wiegand works in Berlin as a correspondent for the Hearst agency 'Universal Service.' He had been ordered to maintain friendly relations with Hitler, which was supposedly dictated by the fact that the German press was buying the agency's information. Hearst is in a deal with German industry to supply the latter with a large consignment of copper. Wiegand does not agree with Hearst's policy. He turned to Pancake's boss for advice." Commenting on Stone's work as a KGB talent spotter and recruiter, the KGB New York station reported: ""Pancake" established contact with Dodd. We wanted to recruit him and put him to work on the State Dep. line. "Pancake" should tell Dodd that he has the means to connect him with an anti-Fascist organization in Berlin." William A. Dodd, Jr., was the son of the U.S. ambassador to Germany and an aspiring Popular Front activist with political ambitions. The KGB did recruit him, and Stone briefly functioned as his intermediary with the KGB, providing him with a contact in Berlin when he went to join his father at the embassy. Stone also passed on to the KGB Dodd's information, picked up from the American military attaché, about possible German military moves against the USSR and the name of a suspected pro-Nazi embassy employee.[9]

There is only one additional reference to I. F. Stone's cooperation with the KGB in the 1930s, a note listing him as one of the New York station's agents in late 1938. The next reference to Stone was a 1944 KGB report on Victor Perlo, head of a network of Soviet sources in Washington during World War II; it noted, "In 1942–43, R. ["Raid"/Perlo] secretly helped "Pancake" [Stone] compile materials for various exposés by the latter." (Perlo was at that time a mid-level economist at the Advisory Council of National Defense.) Similarly, a 1945 report about Stanley Graze, a secret Communist and a valued KGB source, noted that in 1943 Graze's wife had been ""'Pancake's' [Stone's] personal secretary, maintaining ties with the latter's informants in government agencies.'" These 1944 and 1945 notes do not indicate that Stone was an active KGB agent or even in direct contact with it after 1938, and given Stone's initial anger over the Nazi-Soviet Pact, it is likely that he broke relations with the KGB in late 1939. Still, Stone had quickly reverted to a pro-Soviet position and, as his links to Victor Perlo and Mrs. Stanley Graze demonstrate, remained in intimate touch with the Communist underground in Washington in World War II and continued to be viewed by the KGB in a benign light.[10]

In this context, Vladimir Pravdin's October 1944 approach to Stone noted above was not an initial recruitment attempt but an effort to *reestablish* the agent relationship that the KGB had had in 1936–38. It is still not completely clear if this attempt was successful or not. There is only one other document in Vassiliev's notebooks that bears on this question. The Soviets knew little about Harry Truman when he succeeded to the presidency, and in June 1945 Moscow Center told Pravdin, then chief of the New York KGB station, "'Right now the cultivation of Truman's inner circle becomes exceptionally important. This is one of the Station's main tasks. To fulfill this task, the following agent capabilities need to be put to the most effective use: 1. In journalistic circles—"Ide," "Grin," "Pancake" . . . "Bumblebee." Through these people focus on covering the principal newspaper syndicates and the financial-political groups that are behind them; their relationships with Truman, the pressure exerted on him, etc.'" Of the four journalists listed, "Ide"/Samuel Krafsur and "Grin"/John Spivak were unambiguously recruited KGB agents. However, "Bumblebee"/Walter Lippmann was not a KGB agent. Instead, he knew Pravdin only as a Soviet journalist with whom he traded insights and information. As for Stone, given Pravdin's effort to rerecruit him in 1944, he could not have been under the illusion that the Soviet was a normal journalist. Still, with Lippmann's inclusion in the list, this message is ambiguous in regard to Stone's relationship to the KGB at that time and does not have enough detail to warrant a firm conclusion.[11]

It is clear that Stone consciously cooperated with Soviet intelligence from 1936 through 1938—that is to say, he was a Soviet spy—but it is unclear if he reestablished that relationship in 1944–45. That Stone chose never to reveal this part of his life strongly suggests that he knew just how incompatible it would be with his public image as a courageous and independent journalist. His admirers, who have so strenuously denied even the possibility of such an alliance, need to reevaluate his life and reconsider some of the choices he made.

Hemingway, the Dilettante Spy

The mere fact that Ernest Hemingway toyed with Soviet intelligence is one of the more surprising revelations in the KGB files. Although the future Nobel Prize winner never provided any significant information to the KGB, he was in contact with several of its agents for a few years and remained an object of interest into the 1950s.

While principally a novelist, Hemingway also wrote as a journalist, providing topical essays and reports on contemporary events that appeared in newspapers and magazines. After the Spanish Civil War broke out, he traveled to Madrid with press credentials from the North American Newspaper Alliance to cover the conflict. Once there, he grew close to the Communist movement and cooperated with party front organizations in the aftermath of the war. Although the CPUSA was unhappy with his portrayal of International Brigades' chief Andre Marty in the novel *For Whom the Bell Tolls*, Hemingway's fame and willingness to cooperate on selected issues ensured that he remained close to the CPUSA.

Early in 1941 Hemingway and his new wife, Martha Gellhorn, were preparing to leave for a trip to China. Gellhorn had secured an assignment from *Colliers* magazine, and Hemingway reluctantly agreed to accompany her. The left-wing newspaper *PM* contracted to run his stories. More significant, Hemingway spoke to Harry White, chief of the Treasury Department's Monetary Division, who asked him to report secretly to him on relations between the Chinese Communists and the Kuomintang, the Chinese transportation system, and the condition of the Burma Road. Hemingway agreed. During his four-month odyssey, he met with Lauchlin Currie (White House aide on a mission in China) at a dinner in Hong Kong, interviewed Nationalist China's leader Chiang Kai-Shek and his wife in Chungking, and met secretly with Communist leader Chou En-Lai. Upon his return he wrote reports for White and met with an official in the Office of Naval Intelligence. A later historical account of the trip noted that if White really was a Soviet spy, "Hemingway's information very well could have ended up in the Kremlin."[12]

White assuredly was a Soviet source (see chapter 4), but any link with Soviet intelligence Hemingway might have had through White would have been indirect and unknowing. What has not been previously known, however, is that Hemingway had been in *direct* contact with Soviet intelligence before leaving for China. Moscow Center received a report from Jacob Golos, the KGB's liaison with the CPUSA, stating: "'A few days ago I found out that Ernest Hemingway is traveling to China via the Soviet Union. He may apply for an entry visa to the Soviet Union. He was in New York for only one day and I couldn't meet with him. I arranged with him that our people will meet with him in China and show him the stamps that he gave us. We must attempt to meet with him in China or the Soviet Union by using the password that was arranged with him previously. I am sure that he will cooperate with us and will do everything he can.'" Golos didn't state who arranged the password and picked up the stamps that Hemingway handed over. (One possibility would be John Herrmann, an old Hemingway drinking buddy and friend who had himself worked for the CPUSA underground in Washington for several years in the 1930s.)[13]

Although there is no evidence that Hemingway did any actual work for the KGB, his brushes with the clandestine world were apparently intoxicating. He remained infatuated with espionage for the next several years. Upon returning to Cuba, he organized a crew of his drinking and fishing pals and former Spanish Civil War veterans to spy on pro-German elements on the island, even obtaining some funds from the American ambassador to pay for the operation. Later derisively named "the Crook Factory" by Gellhorn, this motley crew outfitted a fishing boat with light weapons and trawled offshore looking for U-boats. While it afforded the writer an opportunity to indulge in fantasies that he was a secret operative, J. Edgar Hoover (then supervising American intelligence in Central and South America) was not impressed, telling subordinates that Hemingway was "the last man, in my estimation, to be used in any such capacity."[14]

Moscow was more hopeful. Hemingway received a cover name, "Argo," and in November 1941 Moscow Center instructed the KGB New York station: "'Look for an opportunity for him to travel abroad to countries of interest to us.'" Hemingway met with KGB officers four more times, and Moscow remained hopeful. But as a KGB summary of 1948 shows, J. Edgar Hoover's dismissal of Hemingway as a dilettante would have been better advised:

"'Argo'—Ernest Hemingway (*Ernest Hemingway*), year of birth: 1898, born in Duke Park, Illinois (USA), American citizen, secondary education, a writer. During the First War of Imperialism, he was a correspondent in the French and Italian armies' medical units.

In 1937, while in Spain, 'Argo' wrote in defense of the Popular Front in his articles and appealed for help for Republican Spain, sharply criticizing isolationists in Congress and the U.S. State Department. 'Argo' insisted that the U.S. lift the embargo on the importation of arms into Repub. Spain. . . .

In 1941, before he left for China, 'Argo' was recruited for our work on ideological grounds by 'Sound.' Contact was not established with 'Argo' in China. In Sept. 1943, when 'Argo' was in Havana, where he owned a villa, our worker contacted him and, prior to his departure for Europe, met with him only twice. In June 1943, the connection with 'Argo' was once more renewed in London, where he had gone as an Amer. correspondent with the Allied Army in the field for the magazine 'Colliers.' This connection was soon interrupted, b/c 'Argo' left for France. When 'Argo' returned to Havana from France in April 1945, we met with him once. We could not maintain a connection with 'Argo' in view of our worker's urgent summons out of the country. Since then, there have been no attempts to establish a connection with 'Argo.'

Our meetings with 'Argo' in London and Havana were conducted with the aim of studying him and determining his potential for our work. Throughout the period of his connection with us, 'Argo' did not give us any polit. information, though he repeatedly expressed his desire and willingness to help us. 'Argo' has not been studied thoroughly and is unverified. We have a material password for renewing ties with 'Argo.'"

(The "material password" would have been the stamps Hemingway earlier gave Golos.) Despite all these meetings and promises of cooperation since 1941 Hemingway had actually delivered nothing as of 1948. In light of this, sensibly, the American station listed Hemingway in 1949 as among earlier American sources with whom it had *not* renewed contact.[15]

But that did not end the matter. In the late 1940s the combination of crippling defections, the FBI's aggressive posture, and intense public hostility toward communism devastated the KGB's once flourishing espionage networks in America. In 1950 Moscow Center pressed its American station to look into renewing ties to agents and sources long ago deactivated or abandoned as useless. One of these was Ernest Hemingway. In August it told the KGB Washington station: "'We remind you that 'Argo' was recruited for our work on ideological grounds in 1941 by 'Sound' but that he has been studied little and has not been verified in practical work. We have a material recognition signal for renewing ties with 'Argo,' which we will send you in case the need should arise.'" But in October the New York station reported that although Hemingway continued to maintain ties with Joseph North, a CPUSA official active in the party's cultural/intellectual work, "'It is said that he allegedly supports the Trotskyites and that he has attacked the Sov. Union in his articles and pamphlets.'" After that nothing more about Hemingway appeared.[16]

Ludwig Lore

Ludwig Lore had been a prominent American Communist during the early 1920s. A native of Germany, he came to the United States in 1903 and by 1919 was executive secretary of the German branch of the Socialist Party and editor of *New Yorker Volkszeitung*, its newspaper. Converted to communism by Leon Trotsky in 1917, he was a member of the first National Executive Committee of the Communist Labor Party, but his colleagues considered him too moderate and removed him. As leader of a faction of the Workers Party (as the CPUSA was then called), Lore was attacked by Moscow as a Social Democrat and Trotsky supporter. The party expelled him in 1925 for "Loreism," but he continued to regard himself as an independent Communist and part of the broader radical movement. He gave up his editorship of the *Volkszeitung* in 1931 to become a freelance journalist; in 1934 he joined the editorial staff of the *New York Post* and wrote a daily column, "Behind the Cables." Lore's column focused on foreign affairs (its title referring to Lore's promise to provide the real story that lay behind the international cables that brought foreign news to America) and emphasized the menace of Nazism to world peace.[17]

While GRU had had extensive operations in the United States in the

1920s, the KGB's presence had been much smaller, and the early 1930s were a period of both learning and expansion. In these years there were as yet only a few professional KGB officers with experience operating in the country or possessing adequate language skills and understanding of American culture. While it might appear counterintuitive, the KGB and GRU in the late 1920s and early 1930s recruited a number of persons expelled by the CPUSA. Those expelled often considered themselves good Communists and saw working for Soviet intelligence as a path back into the Communist movement. Lore was one of these and worked for the KGB's illegal station in the mid-1930s under the code names "Leo" and "10."

In a report written early in January 1935, "Leo"/Lore was described as a talent spotter, recruiter, and agent handler who was responsible for four sources. He had recruited "Gregor," who was supplying economic information early in 1934. He also recruited and handled "Willy," a key source in the State Department. "Willy" (David Salmon) headed the State Department's Communications and Records Division and provided copies of reports sent by American diplomatic personnel overseas (see chapter 4). During 1934 Lore recruited another State Department source, "Daniel," who provided "very valuable" copies of stenographic records of the conversations of high-ranking officials with foreign ambassadors. Additionally, Lore recruited "Albert," described as employed by an unidentified police agency in New York. The KGB New York station also assigned Lore liaison duties with Thomas Schwartz, a former German consul living in New York who had become a KGB source. None of these sources appear to have been primarily motivated by ideology; they all received generous payment for their work, as did Lore himself. Lore was the sole link to several of his sources, picked up the information they produced, and delivered the KGB's stipend.[18]

Valentin Markin, chief of the KGB's illegal station, died in New York in August 1934 either in an accident or a street crime. In the ensuing reorganization of the station, Moscow Center began to express concerns about "Leo." One Moscow analytic report was "inclined to doubt the existence of the agents Daniel and Albert" and observed about "Daniel" that "Leo [Lore] handles the connection. The station chief and his assistants have not met with the agent. We checked DOS's directory. The division he works in wouldn't bring him into contact with the documents that are sent to us." The Moscow Center analysts ventured that likely all the material actually came from "Willy"/Salmon, who did have such access. High-ranking KGB officers wondered if Lore had invented

"Daniel" and "Albert" "'with the aim of increasing his compensation.'" He received $350 a month, while "Daniel" got $500 and "Albert" $400. "Willy"/Salmon meanwhile collected $500 every month, and his product was judged genuine. Moscow Center suspected that Lore was taking a portion of Salmon's authentic material and attributing some of it to his fictitious "Daniel," pocketing his stipend. It concluded that Markin's replacement "needs to get to the bottom of this."[19]

"Gregor" and Schwartz, two authentic Lore contacts and ones with whom KGB officers had had direct communications, were broken off from Lore and liaison transferred to a Soviet officer in September 1934. Moscow Center instructed Boris Bazarov, Markin's replacement, to verify if "Daniel" existed. Yet the KGB New York station moved very slowly with its investigation of Lore's suspected fraud. In July 1936 a report noted that the New York station had direct contact with a senior State Department official, Laurence Duggan, and used him to find out more about Salmon. Duggan verified that Salmon existed and had access to State Department archives. His officer's direct discussion with Duggan also convinced Bazarov that Lore had been providing some misleading information about Duggan.[20]

Discovering Lore's deception, however, did not solve the KGB's problem. Lore was still the only contact with Salmon, and Salmon was providing very useful information at a time when the only other State Department source, Laurence Duggan, was of as yet limited utility due to his focus on South American matters not of priority to Moscow and his fear of exposure, which made him reluctant to provide documents in quantity. A direct KGB approach to Salmon was risky because the KGB did not understand the basis of Lore's relationship with him. Salmon might become alarmed if approached directly and be lost as a source entirely or even go to security officials. Moscow was particularly concerned to learn that Lore had gone to see Duggan, ostensibly for aid in getting a visa for his nephew, a surgeon from Germany. It ordered Bazarov "to do everything possible to keep '10' [Lore] from having contact with '19' [Duggan]." Moscow did not want a potentially valuable source like Duggan to drift into the orbit of a mercenary it no longer fully trusted. But Bazarov noted that ensuring the two did not connect was likely to prove difficult, since any admonition might alert either one to the other's link with Soviet intelligence.[21]

Possibly reflecting the as yet limited number and capacity of the professional KGB officers at his command, Bazarov, despite his mistrust of Lore, continued to use him. But by early 1937, Moscow Center had had enough. It lectured Bazarov that his suggestion that Lore be used to cultivate several of the State Department leads that Laurence Duggan had suggested was unacceptable: "'Even though many of 19's [Duggan's] leads are known to 10 [Lore], it is nevertheless to our disadvantage to have 10 recruit them, because that would mean having to depend on him even more. 10 will just keep them for himself, rather than pass the connection on to us. Therefore we consider it necessary to refuse to have 19's opportunities or leads realized through 10.'" Moscow Center was increasingly convinced that Lore had ties to the hated Trotskyists and was enraged by the increasingly anti-Stalinist tone of his public lectures and newspaper columns, telling the KGB New York station: "Leo's [Lore's] anti-Soviet speeches must be stopped." It ordered Bazarov to insist on direct meetings with Salmon and "Daniel" and to place them under surveillance. The illegal station chief replied that he had assigned "six people and three cars" for the surveillance and asked Hede Massing and her husband Paul, veteran Soviet agents, to investigate Lore's activity. In her 1951 autobiography, Massing reported being assigned to surveil Lore in early 1937. There is no report on exactly how or when the KGB cut its ties with Lore, but there is no mention of him after April 1937. Vassiliev's notebooks, however, also contain excerpts from the 1984 book *Station Chief Gold*, an internal KGB summary of the career of its illegal officer, Iskhak Akhmerov, used as an instructional textbook at the Andropov Red Banner Institute, a KGB training school when Vassiliev was a student there. One passage indicates that in 1937 Akhmerov saw to it that "shady agents and those without prospects, such as 'Leo' [Lore] and his group, had to be weeded out. Suspicion of fraud."[22]

Interestingly, after the KGB cast Lore out, GRU considered picking up some of the pieces. His GRU superior told Whittaker Chambers that Lore had been connected to a Soviet intelligence apparatus but "something stupid" had happened. He instructed Chambers to talk to Lore and see if he would hand over any of his former contacts. (Chambers was unclear about the date, but it appeared to have been in 1937.) Chambers met with Lore; the two got along well and reminisced about Russians with whom they had worked. But despite months of friendly conversations and promises, Lore never gave Chambers any contacts. GRU was not the only agency that approached Lore. Later the FBI did so as well, and he gave it a partial account of his knowledge of Soviet networks in the United States but avoided recounting his own work as a Soviet spy or the sources he recruited, such as David Salmon, in the State Department. One Soviet agent he did identify, however, was Whittaker Chambers, and it was Lore's information that led the FBI to its first interview with Chambers in 1941. Lore died in 1942.[23]

Robert Allen

Unlike Lore, Robert S. Allen had no history of involvement with Communist causes. Born in Kentucky in 1900, he served in the army during World War I by lying about his age. He graduated from the University of Wisconsin, joined the Ku Klux Klan to write an exposé, and at the time of Hitler's abortive coup was studying in Munich, where his reporting enabled him to become a foreign correspondent and then Washington bureau chief for the *Christian Science Monitor.* A hard-nosed reporter with a large dose of skepticism about American intervention in Latin America and angered by his paper's refusal to publish damaging inside stories about Washington, Allen recruited Drew Pearson, a neophyte reporter for the *Baltimore Sun,* and they anonymously wrote *Washington Merry-Go-Round,* published in 1931, a sensational and nasty exposé of the Hoover administration. It sold over 180,000 copies. After the authors were identified, both were fired from their jobs. They quickly produced a sequel in the fall of 1932, *More Merry-Go-Round,* and capitalized on their fame by starting a syndicated newspaper column the following year. Although Pearson was smooth and conciliatory and Allen abrasive and bullying, their styles meshed, and the column, carried by Scripps Howard, became a powerful force in American journalism. Both men were ardently pro-Roosevelt and sympathetic to liberals in the administration like Harold Ickes and Sumner Welles, who frequently fed them inside gossip and leaks. Unbeknownst to his partner, for a time Allen was also providing information to Soviet intelligence.[24]

In January 1933 a KGB New York station message called Moscow Center's attention to reports it was sending

"that came from the newly recruited source Sh/147, who in our opinion is of great interest.

Robert Allen . . . is a journalist by trade. In 1931 he wrote the book "Washington Merry-Go-Round," in which he described official Washington. The characters he depicts in the book are a reflection of the pettiness and emptiness of many of Washington's current Republican congressmen and Cabinet members. When this essentially malicious lampoon of unscrupulous Washington politicians was published, Hoover insisted that he be fired from the magazine where he was working. In 1932 he released a second book of the same type. He personally knows most of the lawmakers and Cabinet members and also has extensive contacts in all of the departments. He personally knows Moley, Roosevelt's chief adviser, and also knows Roosevelt himself, as well as the Democratic majority leader in the Congress. Sh/147 is a valuable contact, especially bearing in mind Roosevelt's future administration."

New York noted that it had put Allen on a $100-a-month stipend ($1,600 in 2008 dollars).[25]

The notes about Allen's supplying the KGB with information were dated January and February of 1933. He provided political gossip about potential appointments to the incoming Roosevelt administration, including the news that Sumner Welles would be appointed undersecretary of state (he actually became an assistant secretary), accounts about the Japanese fortifying Pacific islands, and information attributed to Senator William Borah about FDR's plans for diplomatic recognition of the USSR. There is no indication that ideological fervor motivated him. Whether he simply needed the money or even knew exactly with whom he was dealing is not clear from the documents in Vassiliev's notebooks, although the references to him as a recruited source are unambiguous; nor was Allen a naïf who would have misconstrued his covert paid relationship with gentlemen interested in information on matters of military and diplomatic interest to the USSR. Since he had no official access to government secrets and supplied no government documents, he was violating no law that existed at the time. (In 1938 enactment of the Foreign Agents Registration Act criminalized covert relationships with agencies of a foreign power.) Given the lack of any reference to him after the first two months of 1933 it is likely the relationship did not last more than a few months. There is no indication of whether he or the KGB ended their association.[26]

John Spivak and Frank Palmer

Two other journalists assisting the KGB in the early 1930s were John Spivak and Frank Palmer. Neither man ever openly admitted his Communist affiliation, much less his work for Soviet intelligence, but both were KGB agents who provided valuable material about potential enemies and suggested possible recruits to the KGB.

Born in Connecticut in 1897, John L. Spivak started his journalism career as a police reporter. By the end of World War I, he was working for a Socialist paper, covering labor unrest in West Virginia and ferreting out company spies. He quickly made a career for himself as an investigative journalist, muckraker, and exposer of far-right extremism. Spivak achieved some fame in 1932, when he published *Georgia Nigger,* an exposé of abusive conditions in the mostly black prison labor chain gangs of the deep South. He began to investigate anti-Semitism in 1934 and, after consultation with contacts at the Anti-Defamation League (ADL), visited Frank Prince, an expert on anti-Semitism hired by Jewish organizations and a consultant to the U.S. House Special Committee on Un-American Activities, called the "McCormack-Dickstein Committee" by the press. Spivak used his tips to launch investigations of pro-fascist groups throughout the country, many involving wealthy or politically connected individuals. His subsequent articles in the Communist-aligned *New Masses* (collected and published as *Plotting America's Pogroms*) garnered additional attention. Spivak passed some of his information to Prince, who gave it to the McCormack-Dickstein Committee. He later published exposés of intrigues by agents of imperial Japan in the United States (*Honorable Spy*) and of the populist anti-Semite Father Charles Coughlin (*Shrine of the Silver Dollar*).[27]

Throughout his long career as a journalist Spivak always denied being a Communist, insisting that he was an independent motivated by anti-fascism. But the FBI was convinced by December 1945 that he was a secret member of the CPUSA and carried out a variety of covert tasks for the party, as well as for Jacob Golos, the CPUSA's liaison with Soviet intelligence. In 1952 former CPUSA official John Lautner identified Spivak as a secret member of the party's security apparatus. Evidence of his secret Communist ties caused some researchers in retrospect to question Spivak's role in the "Whalen documents" forgery. In 1930 New York police commissioner Grover Whalen announced to the press that he had obtained a trove of internal documents from the New York offices of Amtorg, a company that functioned as the semi-official international trade agency of the Soviet Union. They revealed that dozens of Amtorg's staff were Soviet spies and that Amtorg was little more than a front for Soviet intelligence. Within a few days of Whalen's production of the documents, however, Spivak proved that they were forgeries (rather crude ones) and even identified the New York printer who had prepared the fake documents, although who had commissioned the printer to do so remained unclear. Spivak's demonstration discredited Commissioner Whalen and also tended to rebut widespread rumors that Amtorg was a front for Soviet espionage. The speed with which he revealed the forgeries convinced some skeptics that Spivak knew they had been foisted on the police to embarrass them.

The argument that the Whalen forgeries had been a clever Communist plot to discredit naive anti-Communists rather than an incompetent anti-Communist plot to taint Amtorg with espionage was plausible. However, that view is likely mistaken. A KGB officer in New York reported on the Whalen documents in three messages in May and September of 1930 and also sent Moscow Center copies of the forgeries, the notes taking up more than three pages. The messages indicated no prior knowledge of the forgeries by the KGB or any connection with their production or link to Spivak's exposure of them. Instead, these internal KGB communications displayed indignation at the forgeries and speculated that they had been prepared by exiled anti-Bolshevik Russians or were "closely tied to the crusading campaign against the USSR launched by the Pope." If the KGB was unaware of the forgeries, it is unlikely that any Soviet or Communist agency was involved. Although not to the extent suggested by the Whalen forgeries, the KGB, GRU, and Comintern did use Amtorg as a cover for covert operations. It is unlikely that any of these agencies would have launched a preemptive disinformation attack without consulting the other agencies that might be affected. It is also unlikely that the CPUSA would have considered initiating such an operation, which affected Soviet interests, without informing Soviet authorities.[28]

At the same time that he was working to ferret out Nazi sympathizers, Spivak was, however, cooperating with the KGB. There is no indication when he became a source, but one 1935 report suggests he had been providing information on Trotskyists as early as 1932. A 1948 KGB memo also underscored his use against the Trotskyist target: "'Grin'—John Spivak, journalist, used on the Trotskyites until '41."[29]

The KGB also kept an eye on the activities of German intelligence in the United States, and Spivak's investigation of pro-Nazi groups proved useful for that task. His work on American anti-Semitism in 1934 and 1935 enabled Spivak to funnel the KGB details about Nazi financing of German-allied groups and connections between native fascists and the German government. One report noted that "Grin" was "a popular, widely known journalist, a Jew." Many of his sources, including Treasury Secretary Henry Morgenthau's niece, Josephine Pomerance, worked with him "'without knowledge of his connection to us.'" (In other words, Pomerance thought she was only assisting an anti-Nazi journalist and was unaware of his link to Soviet intelligence.) The KGB also noted that Spivak "receives materials from Prince" (the ADL and McCormack-Dickstein Committee consultant), who told him "that he is the only journalist to whom he is willing to give the numerous materials he has about the Nazis." Another Spivak source, cover-named "Zero," worked for the U.S.

Committee on Investigation of the Munitions Industry (the Nye Committee) and gave him numerous documents on chemical arms, munitions production, and technical data on specific weapons: she "'doesn't even know that she works for us.'" She was valuable enough, however, that the KGB decided to end the indirect relationship and "'in the next few days we will be taking 'Zero' from 'Grin' and including her in our network.'"[30]

Despite Moscow's earlier interest in his material, by mid-1935, it rethought his usefulness, concluding that Spivak's "potential has gone down, because the Nazis are reorganizing their work in light of the Dickstein Committee's activities and have taken several of their people out of the USA." One of Spivak's contacts, a detective cover-named "Courier," tried unsuccessfully to blackmail him, raising fears that he might be exposed as a Soviet agent. On the other hand, Moscow mused about trying to recruit Spivak's contact, Frank Prince, who had information about the flow of German money into the United States, for propaganda work. By August 1935 Moscow had concluded that Spivak was no longer particularly valuable and ordered him deactivated. One positive result of his work had been "Zero's" recruitment; she was turned over to William Weisband, one of the KGB's several American agent handlers and couriers (see chapter 7).[31]

Spivak went to Europe in October 1935 to investigate Nazi activities abroad. Before leaving, he obtained contacts from high officials in the CPUSA. In Germany he worked closely with Martha Dodd (see chapter 8). Whether or not he informed Soviet intelligence of his investigations or turned over data on German underground organizations is not clear, but at some point the KGB renewed its contact with him, and a 1941 KGB memo listed him among the New York station's most valuable agents. However, he was again soon deactivated for unspecified reasons. But in 1943 a Moscow Center report directed that KGB officers reestablish a connection with Spivak "'with whom we haven't worked for the last two years.'" He was to be used to gather information on the subjects he had targeted in the past: "'Gestapo agents on U.S. territory, in particular, agents working in Ukrainian and White Guard organizations. Materials on the work of Japanese intelligence organizations in the USA.'"[32]

Elizabeth Bentley told the FBI in 1945 that while she had never met Spivak, she knew that Jacob Golos had used him extensively. Golos had paid his traveling expenses and sent him to Mexico and California on assignments dealing with Japanese espionage and to Texas to investigate Representative Martin Dies, the fiercely anti-Communist chairman of the House Special Committee on Un-American Activities. After Golos's death, one of her KGB contacts, Iskhak Akhmerov, spoke to her about Spivak's assistance. In Venona's decrypted KGB cables there are three messages dealing with Spivak. In May 1944 he reported something about Soviet defector Victor Kravchenko, and he visited the Soviet Consulate to convey a letter to KGB officer Alexander Feklisov from Joe North, editor of the *New Masses*, asking for financial assistance.[33]

Spivak continued to undertake covert tasks for the Communist Party in the early 1950s. In April 1953 he and another secret party operative, Leon Josephson, burglarized the law office of O. John Rogge, David Greenglass's attorney, stealing documents later published in the Communist press to discredit Greenglass. During that decade he wrote frequently under various pseudonyms, but by the time he wrote his autobiography, *A Man in His Time*, in 1967, he ended the book criticizing the socialist world (that is, the Communist bloc) for being "far from socialism," suggesting that he had drifted from party circles. Settling in Pennsylvania, he died on 30 September 1981.[34]

Frank Laverne Palmer was at least as valuable to the KGB as Spivak. Never an open Communist, he gave Soviet intelligence entree to the somewhat wider world of left-wing politics and enabled it to recruit several promising sources. Born in Corning, New York, in 1893, the son of a rail freight conductor, Palmer completed a few years of college in Colorado and found work as a printer before becoming editor of the *Colorado Union Advocate* in 1922. In 1927 he joined other left-wing trade union figures such as James Maurer (Socialist and president of the Pennsylvania Federation of Labor) and John Brophy (United Mine Workers' leader) as part of an American trade union delegation to the USSR. Upon their return, they co-authored a positive report, *Russia after Ten Years*, brought out by International Publishers, the CPUSA's publishing arm. Palmer secretly joined the CPUSA sometime after this trip.[35]

In the 1930s Palmer served as managing editor of Federated Press, a left alternative to the Associated Press whose clients were mainly trade union newspapers, and served as the chief editor of the radical journal *People's Press*. He was also a KGB agent. His journalistic duties provided him access to a variety of matters of KGB interest. For example, in October 1935 during a trip to Washington, he "found out information from an employee of the Committee on Investigation of the Munitions Industry, without the latter's knowledge, about the DuPont company's system of espionage." A friend, "Mary" (this may be simply her real name rather than a cover name) was slated to provide him entree to some State Department employees, and he intended to take advantage of the close relationship between Mary and her cousin, Congressman Maury Maverick, to keep up to date on congressional affairs. When Moscow decided that it wanted to plant someone close to right-wing newspaper magnate William Randolph Hearst, it sent this memo: "'It would be desirable to gain an insider to Hearst who would be on close terms with the managing head of that concern. Find out in detail what, specifically, 'Liberal' [Palmer] could do to that end.'"[36]

Palmer was particularly useful in work directed against other left-wing organizations because Federated Press reporters covered their activities and had access to inside information about them. For example, he was part of the KGB's anti-Trotsky offensive in the United States. Several memos from 1935–36 show that he provided details on people close to American Trotskyist leader James Cannon:

"Liberal" [Palmer] gave information about Louis Francis Budenz, who used to be the editor of the magazine "Labor Age" (where "Liberal's" wife worked). . . ."Liberal's" conclusion: There are 3 or 4 people with information that is of interest to us, all of whom are on close terms with Cannon and familiar with current events in Europe. Everyone else—out of the loop, they know whatever is known to the general public. "Bearing in mind 'Liberal's' potential, we are conducting work with him on identifying the persons surrounding Muste . . . , Cannon, and other Trotskyite 'leaders' here, who, while not in leadership positions, are nevertheless up to date on Trotskyite organizational activities."[37]

Palmer's journalistic access to left-wing organizations also assisted his role as a talent spotter. In addition to recruiting I. F. Stone, his most notable success was the aforementioned Louis Budenz, a veteran left trade union activist and journalist. In the early 1930s Budenz was an associate of Abraham J. Muste in the American Workers Party (AWP), a small independent Marxist group. But when Muste led the AWP into a merger with the Trotskyists, Budenz, impressed by the CPUSA's shift toward what became know as its "Popular Front" stance, joined the Communist Party. Like Palmer, he also assisted the KGB's anti-Trotskyist operations. He quickly became part of the CPUSA's senior leadership and rose to the position of managing editor of the *Daily Worker.* However, in 1945 he reverted to the Catholicism of his youth and became a fierce anti-Communist polemicist.

Although his veracity was often challenged after his well-publicized denunciations of former associates, the documents quoted in Vassiliev's notebooks confirm Budenz's often-doubted participation in Soviet espionage. A 1948 memo on the damage done to Soviet intelligence by defectors included Budenz as one of the renegades and identified five participants in Soviet intelligence who were potentially exposed to American authorities by Budenz. One was Grigory Rabinovich, a doctor and KGB officer sent to the United States in the 1930s under Russian Red Cross cover to supervise penetration of the American Trotskyist movement. The other four were Americans who had worked for the KGB. One was Palmer, and the memo noted that he had assisted in recruiting Budenz. The others were Zalmond Franklin, a veteran KGB courier, and two people, Robert Menaker and Sylvia Caldwell, deeply involved in the KGB's anti-Trotsky operations (see chapter 8).[38]

When the KGB was rebuilding its American operations in 1933, Palmer was listed among its "former sources" with whom contact needed to be (and in his case was) renewed. Two of his earlier recruits were also noted: "Through "Liberal" [Palmer]—Art. Kallet (mechanical engineer at the National Bureau of Standards, and E. F. Schink, director of the trade organization, Technic Research." In 1932 Kallet and Schink had authored 100,000,000 Guinea Pigs: Dangers in Everyday Foods, Drugs, and Cosmetics, a huge best-selling book that marked the advent of the modern consumer movement. Both Kallet and Schink had backgrounds as engineers, and in 1933 Kallet joined Schink's young organization, Consumer's Research, which tested consumer products for safety, effectiveness, and reliability. ("Technic Research" in the quote above was likely a KGB officer's translation garble of an attempt to render "Consumer's Research" into Russian.)[39]

The brief note in the 1933 document does not indicate whether Kallet and Schink were helpful after Palmer was reactivated. But Kallet remained close to Communist Party activists. By late 1934 relations between Kallet and Schink had soured. Schink grew increasingly unhappy with demands by Consumer's Research employees for higher wages and union recognition. And he came to suspect that a faction dominated by secret Communists was attempting to take control of the organization he had founded. In September 1935 the workers went out on strike. Schink and his supporters retaliated with strikebreakers, armed guards, and charges that the strikers were "reds." Kallet orchestrated a "public trial" of Schink for betraying the workers, and he and the fired strikers went on to create a new organization, Consumers Union. Arthur Kallet became director and Frank Palmer a member of the board. (Kallet was also a contributing editor to People's Press, the radical newspaper edited by Palmer.)[40]

There were signs that the KGB had become dissatisfied with Palmer's work in 1935. One memo complained that he and John Spivak were "crossing paths and could expose one another." The memo described Palmer as a "failed agent, since people approach him on their own initiative." ("Failed" in this case meant his links to Soviet intelligence were known to too many people.) The memo stated that consideration had been given to deactivating Palmer and Spivak, and they were to be "excluded from the estimate for '36," indicating that no funds would be included for their secret stipends.[41]

Despite these misgivings, however, the KGB continued its relationship with Palmer. While still with Federated Press, in 1937 Palmer moved to Chicago to help start a Communist-aligned newspaper, the *Midwest Daily Record*, where he worked closely with its managing editor, Louis Budenz. (Whether it was at this time or earlier that Palmer linked Budenz to the KGB is unclear.) A KGB report noted that one of its officers visited him there, and "thanks to Liberal [Palmer], one of the workers in London was given a cover (he was sent a reporter card and an official letter with credentials." Sometime later that year, Palmer broke politically with the CPUSA for unspecified reasons but appeared to have continued his association with KGB. A 1941 Moscow Center report on intelligence activities in the United States listed "Liberal" as "connected with us at present" and among the twenty-two "most valuable" agents of the KGB American station, but there were no details about his activities. However, sometime in 1941 or early 1942 the KGB lost contact with Palmer. In mid-1942 the KGB New York station located him, but for unspecified reasons Moscow Center "gave instructions not to re-establish the connection." Shortly afterwards, the cover name "Liberal" was transferred to a new agent, Julius Rosenberg, and Palmer was not mentioned for the remainder of World War II. Although the KGB deactivated Palmer, he remained in good standing. As noted, Moscow Center's 1948 memo on KGB assets exposed by defectors listed Palmer as among those compromised by Louis Budenz's 1945 defection. It also, however, suggested that Soviet intelligence was no longer in touch with Palmer, noting that his place of employment was "unknown."[42]

While Louis Budenz identified many Communists in his testimony, his only public mention of Frank Palmer was as a defender of the CPUSA's civil liberties. He may, however, have informed the FBI of Palmer's role because his one-time recruiter apparently cooperated with the FBI to some extent. Investigating Budenz's charge that Bernard Schuster had been in charge of anti-Trotskyist work in New York from 1936 to 1938, J. Edgar Hoover ordered his agents to show Schuster's photograph to "Frank Laverne Palmer who was instrumental in launching Louis Budenz into his Soviet espionage activities." A follow-up message made reference to Palmer's FBI file, and its title designation indicated that he had been investigated for espionage. Another FBI report noted that Palmer had admitted engaging in espionage for the Soviets between 1931 and 1938 and working with KGB officer Iskhak Akhmerov. He was never tried, he never testified to a congressional committee, no one ever publicly accused him of espionage, and his role in Soviet espionage has gone unnoticed by historians.[43]

George Seldes and Bruce Minton

I. F. Stone's Weekly was modeled on an earlier iconoclastic periodical of independent left journalism that started publishing in the 1930s: In Fact, the brainchild of George Seldes, a radical journalist for more than eighty years. Like Stone, Seldes and his In Fact co-founder, Bruce Minton, had unacknowledged links to the CPUSA and Soviet intelligence. Born in New Jersey to immigrant Russian parents in 1890, Seldes worked as a war correspondent beginning in 1917 and covered the Soviet Union in the early 1920s. But Soviet authorities expelled him and several other re-porters when they discovered they were evading censorship regulations. Moving to Italy, Seldes filed press reports that implicated the Mussolini regime in political assassination, and Fascist officials booted him out of Italy as well. The left-wing slant of his work as a correspondent for the Chicago Tribune increasingly angered its publishers, and he resigned in 1928 to write You Can't Print That, a harshly critical study of press bias and censorship. Other exposés followed, and he also covered the Span-ish Civil War for the New York Post. Returning to the United States in 1940, Seldes launched In Fact in partnership with Bruce Minton. The publication eventually gained more than 175,000 subscribers. It com-bined muckraking articles, including the first on the link between ciga-rettes and cancer, with left-wing polemics about the dangers of fascism. In Fact lost much of its audience in the early Cold War and ceased pub-lication in 1950, but Seldes continued to turn out a stream of books. He testified in executive session before Senator Joseph McCarthy's Senate in-vestigating committee in 1953. He published his autobiography, Witness to a Century, when he was 96 and died in 1995 at the age of 104.[44]

Seldes was unequivocal when he appeared before Senator McCarthy's committee. Pressed about membership in the CPUSA, he vehemently denied it and also denied Louis Budenz's charge that he was under Communist Party discipline. When he and Minton had started the magazine in 1940, he claimed he had no idea that his partner was a Communist and found out only when the party publicly announced his expulsion in 1945. Seldes presented himself as a critic of the Soviet Union and blamed the demise of *In Fact* on his increasingly anti-Soviet writings after World War II; "I began writing a series of articles against Moscow. The result was that many of my readers, whom I realize must have been Communists, canceled subscriptions." Assuaged by Seldes's agreement that North Korea was an aggressor and his denials of party membership, McCarthy did not bother to have him testify in public.[45]

Seldes lied. He had been a member of the CPUSA. In the spring of 1940, the KGB New York station informed Moscow:

"In order to activate our station's political work, particularly in view of the beginning of the presidential reelection campaign (activization of the internal political life of the USA), we have decided to identify, through 'Sound' [Golos], the most qualified, proven American newspaper workers, who have interesting connections and resources for covering the behind-the-scenes activities of political party leaders as well as of individual financial groups, Roosevelt's administration, individual departments, etc. The head master of the local fellow-countrymen [Communist Party] recommended the two aforementioned individuals through Sound: Robert Miller and George Seldes. The former has only just applied for membership in the organization (meaning a secret enrollment), while the latter is a longtime fellowcountryman [Communist], who is listed on a special register. . . . They both run independent newspaper agencies (financially well-off and independent), which we could put to successful use."

"The head master of the local fellowcountrymen" at the time was Earl Browder. Jacob Golos ("Sound") was the CPUSA liaison with Soviet intelligence. "Special register" was a term for a secret roll kept by the CPUSA for Communists whose party membership was not through the usual party organization (that, too, was secret). Such members were not assigned to party units and were kept isolated from other recruits, and only a small number of senior party officials knew of their membership.[46]

While there is no further mention of recruiting Seldes, his partner, Bruce Minton, was recruited and actively used. Minton continued to work openly on party projects while editing *In Fact,* serving as an editor of the CPUSA's literary journal, *New Masses.* As for his work with Seldes, the KGB New York station informed Moscow that it had been told this was CPUSA work: "On assignment from Browder, he issues the bulletin 'In Fact' together with Seldes." Minton was, however, more than just a secret Communist journalist; he was deeply enmeshed in the Communist Party underground and was one of its links to the KGB.[47]

Minton had been born Richard Bransten into a wealthy California family. He married an even wealthier woman, Louise Rosenberg, heiress to a San Francisco produce fortune, and dabbled in the movie industry as a screenwriter. After their divorce, he moved east and assisted in editing *New Masses* under the name of Bruce Minton. He had joined the CPUSA during the San Francisco dock strikes of 1934, which is when he probably met Nathan Gregory Silvermaster, who served as a courier for Earl Browder during that period. When Silvermaster arrived in Washington in 1935, on Browder's advice he dropped public Communist activity and confined his open political activities to conventional liberal causes. Just before going to prison on a fraudulent passport charge in 1940, Browder gave Golos permission to approach Silvermaster in order to expand CPUSA intelligence activities in Washington. Golos, in turn, assigned his old friend Minton as liaison to Silvermaster and the group of mid-level government officials, all secret Communists or ardent Soviet sympathizers, he was assembling.[48]

In a report he wrote on Minton, Golos listed "Bruce's primary contact —Gregory Silvermaster, an economist at the Treasury Department." While he juggled his work for the *New Masses* and *In Fact,* Minton also collected material that Silvermaster had accumulated from his contacts and fellow agents in the government and carried it to New York for Golos, who then passed it on to the KGB New York station. Beginning in mid-1941, a steady stream of material reached Moscow through Minton. From July through October 1941 seven reports were received from "Informator" (Minton's cover name) detailing what senior officials in Washington knew about a wide array of topics. In July the KGB New York station told Moscow it had received from Minton reports "On the average number of bombers used by Britain for nighttime and daytime raids on Germany in the three weeks preceding 13 July of this year. . . . On the Japanese government's order regarding the departure of Japanese families on a private basis from the U.S. . . . On the export of German currency, in the millions, to the U.S." In August it received a Minton report on statements Washington officials had received from the U.S. military attaché in London: "'1) German troop morale in the area of Pskov is poor; 2) the British have requested information from their military mission in Moscow to use in planning their calculations for a two-to-three-year war; 3) the Germans recently sent from West. Europe four groups of long-range bombers with a full bomb load for raids on Moscow; 4) the British Air Ministry believes that the bombers attacking Moscow are flying out of airfields situated 250 miles west of Smolensk.'" Minton also reported:

At lunch on 31 July Knox proposed a wager that the Germans would occupy Moscow, Leningrad, Kiev, and Odessa by 1 September. Morgenthau took the wager. On 1 August he announced this to his colleagues. Sullivan (Morgenthau's deputy, a conservative) backed Knox. Consul General Foley sided with Morgenthau. Colonel Gunter said that Soviet commanders are well trained but "unpolished," like the French. He argues that the Germans will soon break through in the south and north from Smolensk and will encircle Moscow. He obviously obtained this information from his friend, the German attaché in Washington.

Minton also forwarded reports received by senior American officials on FDR's policy on assistance to the USSR and Morgenthau's positive influence on him, opposition from the War Department to sending war materiel to the USSR, evaluation of Soviet anti-aircraft defenses, German plans to develop its navy, FDR adviser Harry Hopkins's private impressions from his trip to Moscow, the discussion in the American cabinet meeting prior to presidential special envoy Averell Harriman's departure for Moscow, the position of Secretary of Commerce Jesse Jones on financial assistance to the USSR, and more. Minton was the courier for these reports, and likely all of them originated with the CPUSA-based network led by Gregory Silvermaster.[49]

In late 1941 the KGB sent Vasily Zarubin to the United States to take charge of its American operations. On 27 November 1941 Moscow Center sent a cable to him in New York summarizing its view of the chief networks available to him and what should be done with them. (Zarubin was then in transit, apparently not reaching New York until January 1942.) Reflecting satisfaction with the reports it had been receiving, Moscow Center stressed the need to develop Minton and Silvermaster's group due to its access to "Cabinet departments and the White House." Moscow Center sent the following information to Zarubin:

""Informator's" [Minton's] and "Pal's" [Silvermaster's] group. This group, besides these two sources, consists of the following: "Jurist" [Harry Dexter White], "Peak" [Frank Coe], "Polo" [Ludwig Ullmann] and "Sachs" [Solomon Adler], and the courier, "Pal's" wife.

"Informator," as a courier, requires meticulous work in training him to get accustomed to systematizing the materials he processes and teaching him the operational techniques of meetings, obtaining materials, and receiving verbal messages. Continue to use him on the communications line with "Pal" and simultaneously groom him as a future deputy station chief.

"Pal." Future use of him should be directed toward studying the possibility of recruiting [Lauchlin] Currie and thereby infiltrating Roosevelt's immediate inner circle. Simultaneously with intensifying the cultivation of opportunities for obtaining information directly from his workplace, give him the assignment to get as close as possible to Currie.

"Jurist" represents the most valuable source from this group. His capabilities, thanks to his proximity to Morgenthau, are very substantial. We should focus our work with him on obtaining important documented and verbal information. In this regard it is essential to train the source to transmit exactly what he has heard and to extract from his interaction from Morgenthau's inner circle information that is of most interest to us. Simultaneously study and cultivate both Morgenthau's connections and his own.

"Peak," "Polo," and "Sachs" are of value because of their official positions but have not yet made use of their capabilities. While studying them, it is essential to orient the sources toward doing everything they can to strengthen their positions in the department, especially since "Peak" in the past has already been somewhat compromised as a 'Red.'"[50]

Early in 1942, Moscow referred to this group as "'Informator's' [Minton's] group" and listed Silvermaster as one of his agents. But Moscow Center had decided on taking a different direction. The memo directed the KGB New York station toward "'gradually deepening our work with individual members of the group'" and ordered that to "'protect the covert work and eliminate the complexity of the whole system, the group should be broken down into separate teams.'" Golos would become the chief intermediary with Silvermaster's group and, consequently, Minton was to be

"completely excluded from this group and is switched over for use as a talent spotter and background checker, while letting him continue to prepare candidates he has identified for contracting. This needs to be done tactfully, with the explanation made to him that he has done important and valuable work, but the situation requires a reorganization. In order for this transition not to be painful for "Informator" [Minton], one or two of "Sound's" [Golos's] connections should be transferred to him, and he should be used to study journalistic circles and acquire new agents. For example, communications with "Cautious" [Julius Joseph] and his wife can be transferred to "Informator" so that he can further study them."

(The KGB New York station, however, did not shift Joseph and his wife to Minton. They remained linked to the KGB through Golos via Elizabeth Bentley.)[51]

Minton did have successes as a talent spotter. Shortly after Maurice Halperin, a secret Communist, arrived in Washington in 1941 to take a senior analytic position with the Office of the Coordinator of Information (OCI; predecessor to the Office of Strategic Services—see below), he contacted Minton and asked how he could be reconnected to the CPUSA. Realizing the sensitivity and intelligence potential of Halperin's position, Minton consulted Golos, and he arranged for Halperin to meet Bentley and begin a career as one of the KGB's most productive sources.[52]

Still, the KGB's decision to remove him as liaison with Silvermaster's apparatus was reinforced by an August 1942 report that Minton was "widely known in W. [Washington] as a fellowcountryman [Communist], works in the open, and is considered the chief mouthpiece of the fellowcountrymen," not a reputation the KGB wanted for a courier to its espionage sources. Additionally, in mid-1943 Golos, the KGB's chief conduit to the CPUSA, wanted to break his ties with Minton, upset by some unspecified act. In December 1943, Moscow ordered the New York station to "'deactivate agents without future prospects,'" and specified several, one of whom was Minton. With that, he disappeared from further mention in Vassiliev's notebooks.[53]

Along with his wife, the humorist and short-story writer Ruth McKinney, Bruce Minton moved to Hollywood in 1944 to work as a scriptwriter. Both were expelled from the Communist Party in 1946, accused of a left-wing ideological deviation. They moved to Europe during the Hollywood blacklist era. He committed suicide in London in 1955.

Walter Lippmann and Mary Price

Even as it exploited a host of journalists with Communist ties to provide information, entree, and cover, the KGB was anxious to learn what more mainstream and establishment journalists knew. The most prominent, and one of its major targets, was Walter Lippmann. One of the doyens of American establishment journalism, Lippmann had evolved from a pre–World War I young, socialist-leaning intellectual to a consummate insider and highly respected commentator on the world of Washington and high government policy. His extensive contacts within the government provided him with copious background information, much of it off-the-record and too sensitive to publish, knowing that while it would assist him to write his opinion columns, it would not appear directly in his newspaper writings. By the early 1940s Lippmann was a man of firm liberal but non-radical views, and while not hostile to the USSR, neither was he particularly sympathetic. Later in the Cold War he came to urge respect for a Soviet sphere of influence but on the basis of a calculated realism rather than any sentimentality about Soviet goals. There was no chance that the KGB could recruit Walter Lippmann as a source. Nonetheless, anxious to gain access to the information that came to his attention, the KGB set out to develop sources close to him, and in 1941 Golos found one—Lippmann's secretary.

Mary Price was a North Carolina native, born in 1909, who had graduated from the University of North Carolina, Chapel Hill, in 1930. She went to work at the *New York Herald Tribune* in 1939 and was assigned to work as Lippmann's secretary and stenographer. She was also a secret Communist, having joined the party sometime in the 1930s. Golos recruited her for covert work in 1941 and assigned Elizabeth Bentley to serve as her contact and courier. For two years in both New York and Washington Price rifled her boss's files, stole copies of his correspondence, and prepared summaries of his conversations and telephone calls, all of which she turned over to Bentley.[54]

A November 1941 report from Price dealt with a matter of KGB interest: Lippmann's relationship with William Donovan, then chief of the Office of the Coordinator of Information, a hurriedly established agency from which would grow America's World War II intelligence agency, the Office of Strategic Services, and its war propaganda arm, the Office of War Information (OWI). In addition to sending a copy of a stolen Lippmann-Donovan letter, the KGB New York station said:

(We are sending "Dir's" [Price's] reports on Lippmann. We are starting a file on him called "Hub.") "Lately Lippmann has significantly cut back on his newspaper work. He has spent a lot of time on correspondence, phone conversations, and personal discussions with certain political figures, obviously putting his main emphasis on participation in the behind-the-scenes activities of various Amer. circles. In addition, he is studying issues involving the presentation of other propaganda broadcasts on the radio. . . . He was allocated a special short-wave radio for listening to foreign radio broadcasts. Obviously, one of the areas of his cooperation with Donovan is precisely this type of activity."

A report on KGB operations in the United States prepared in 1941 noted that Price had provided information on secret talks between the British government and agents of Henri Pétain's Vichy regime in France, while a 1942 report cited information on American Far Eastern policy.[55]

Price continued to spy on her boss on behalf of the KGB throughout 1942, although she considered resigning. Moscow Center commented: "'You write that you are 'holding her back' through "Sound" [Golos] from quitting her job. Since she attributes quitting her job to getting married, it seems problematical to us that you would be able to 'hold her back' for long. Is it possible to give her an opportunity to get married quickly and still keep her in her current job.'"[56]

Price did not get married, but her romantic interests found another outlet that eventually complicated KGB activities. Her sister, Mildred, was also a CPUSA member who worked for the China Aid Council. At the end of 1941, a young, well-connected New York lawyer who was secretly a member of the Communist Party, Duncan Lee, became legal adviser to Russian War Relief. At the same time, he was on the executive board of the China Aid Council. Mary Price met Lee through her sister and informed Golos in 1942 that he would be joining his law firm's former boss, William Donovan, at the newly organized Office of Strategic Services. Golos asked her to develop him as a source. A biography of Lee, prepared by Golos, noted: "'A while ago, we had instructed "Dir" [Price] to find someone new, and when "Koch" [Lee] was transferred to Wash., her sister told her about him. Mildred gave him a good reference. She gave him "Dir's" address, and when he arrived in Wash. he came to see her and stayed at her apartment for two days while looking for an apartment for himself. "Dir" discussed "Koch" with her sister, who assured her that he was a reliable person. "K." wants to work with us and provide us with any info. he can get.'"[57]

Initially Price met with Lee regularly to pick up material. But late in 1943 Price asked Bentley to take over the duty of meeting with Lee, and she did so. It was not until months later that Bentley learned what had motivated the request. Washington station chief Gorsky reported:

Dir [Price] met K. ["Koch"/Lee] through her sister, Mildred, in the spring of 1942 and recruited him for secret work, ostensibly for the fellowcountryman organization. At the same time, D. ["Dir"/Price] began an intimate relationship with K., which she did not tell us about until very recently. Dir held meetings with K. in one of two locations—at her place, or at his apartment; moreover, the meetings took place in the presence of K's wife, who knew about her husband's secret work. In the fall of 1943, D. refused to work with K. As it later turned out, the reason for this was that K's wife had found out about K and D's intimate relationship and had had fits of jealousy in front of the latter.

Although D. broke off her connection with K. on our line, she continues to
have a personal relationship with him. When he comes to NY, K. occasionally
stays at D's apartment. According to D, she is in love with K. and has not lost
hope that she will marry him when the latter divorces his wife. K. has not said
anything to Myrna [Bentley] about his intimate relationship with D, which is
characteristic of him.

The Lees reconciled, however, and there was no divorce.[58]

The stress of covert work, illness, and her affair with Duncan Lee had
taken its toll on Price. The New York station reported that she had symp-
toms of tuberculosis and that Lippmann was increasingly unhappy with her
work. She resigned in April 1943 and left to recuperate in Mexico. Once
she returned to the United States, Soviet intelligence fully expected Price
to resume her intelligence work. She applied for jobs in the State Department and OSS. The KGB New York station told Moscow: "We think that
with the assistance of "Imperialist" [Lippmann], who has shown an interest in setting "Dir" [Price] up at the above institutions, she will succeed in
getting a job there. "Dir's" past activity in the progressive labor-union movement, however, may be an obstacle. D. is currently undergoing a background check, the results of which will be known in a few weeks."[59]

Meanwhile, Golos continued to use Price as a recruiter. The KGB
New York station and Golos had had their eye on Michael Greenberg, a
China specialist and assistant to presidential aide Lauchlin Currie, then
the deputy administrator and day-to-day head of the Foreign Economic
Administration (FEA):

"'Re "Yank" [Greenberg]. We have reported to you about him several times as
valuable contact. As "Page's" [Currie's] secretary, he can provide interesting
information. With this mail we are sending materials Nos. 2414 and 2485,
which contain valuable facts about the political situation in China. . . ."Dir"
[Price], who has returned from the "Countryside" [Mexico], came to "Yank"
on "Sound's" [Golos's] recommendation (they are good acquaintances) and on
behalf of the fellowcountrymen [Communist Party] asked him to supply her
with information. "Yank" agreed.'"

British-born, Greenberg had become a secret Communist while a student at Cambridge University in the 1930s. He immigrated to the United
States in 1939 and became editor of *Pacific Affairs*, a journal published
by the Institute of Pacific Relations. His tenure caused one trustee to
complain that Greenberg had imposed a pro-Communist slant on the
journal. In 1942 he became a China specialist for the Board of Economic

Warfare (BEW; later merged into the Foreign Economic Administration). Elizabeth Bentley identified him as a source; she said she never met directly with Greenberg but received his information via Mary and Mildred Price. (Greenberg became a naturalized American citizen during this period, so his cover name, "Yank," represents a bit of KGB humor.) At the end of World War II, Greenberg succeeded in transferring to a position in the Department of State, but resigned abruptly in 1946, an act likely triggered by Bentley's defection. Questioned by the FBI in 1947, he admitted knowing the Price sisters but denied ever turning over any information. Shortly afterwards, he returned permanently to England.[60]

As for Mary Price, she did not get a new job at the State Department or the OSS and pressed for release from her covert work. Bentley supported her and resisted KGB efforts to take direct control of her troubled agent. Earl Browder also wanted to withdraw Price from espionage and use her for party work. Eventually, the KGB agreed, and Price became director of the Legislative and Educational Department of the Communist-dominated United Office and Professional Workers of America, a small Congress of Industrial Relations (CIO) union, in 1945. In 1946 she moved to North Carolina to serve as secretary-treasurer of the North Carolina Committee of the Southern Conference for Human Welfare and ran for governor on the Progressive Party ticket in 1948.[61]

Having lost its covert entree to Walter Lippmann in 1943, the KGB took steps to recover some part of it. It used Vladimir Pravdin, whose cover job as a TASS correspondent concealed his role as deputy chief of the KGB New York station in early 1944. Pravdin met with numerous journalists, and the New York station reported, "'Contrary to all expectations, the person with whom 'Sergey' [Pravdin] succeeded in achieving the biggest results in the task of establishing a good relationship'" was Lippmann. He attributed this to Lippmann's desire "'to have connections with responsible representatives of our circles in the Country [USA]. He views the acquaintance with "Sergey" [Pravdin] precisely in this light, and naturally he is attempting to use the acquaintance with him to determine our viewpoint on various issues of international politics. He is doing this, of course, very subtly, with the utmost tact. It should be recognized that, by attempting to draw "Sergey" into making candid comments, "Imperialist" [Lippmann] is sharing his own information with him.'" What Lippmann was not aware of was that the man with whom he was trading confidences was not a senior journalistic colleague but an experienced intelligence officer. Pravdin saw the relationship as an opportunity to elicit indiscreet remarks about sensitive American matters to which Lippmann's privileged relationship with senior government officials gave him access.[62]

Bernard Redmont

Bernard Redmont was born in 1918 in New York to immigrant parents. He attended CCNY, where he edited the student newspaper, served in ROTC, and joined the left-wing American Student Union. After obtaining an MA from Columbia Journalism School in 1939, he traveled to Europe and was in the USSR when the Nazi-Soviet Pact was announced. He lived in Mexico, serving as a stringer for several papers, before returning to the United States. After Pearl Harbor, he moved to Washington to become a news writer for the Coordinator of Inter-American Affairs (CIAA).[63]

His friend, William Remington, introduced him to Elizabeth Bentley, whom he claimed he innocently knew as Helen Johnson, a reporter for *PM,* the left-wing New York newspaper, whom he briefed several times and gave publicly available materials. In her initial statement to the FBI, however, Bentley revealed a detailed knowledge of Redmont's background and career at odds with his claim that he barely knew her and insisted that he supplied confidential material from his CIAA office along with cable intercepts. She said that Golos judged Redmont's material to be of low value. Redmont joined the Marines in the summer of 1943 and was wounded while serving as a combat correspondent during a landing on the Marshall Islands. Mustered out of the service in the summer of 1944, he returned to the CIAA. According to Bentley, he telephoned and suggested a meeting. But the KGB was then phasing Bentley out of her liaison role, and she never met with him again. She told the FBI she assumed the KGB had assigned someone else to contact Redmont but noted that in the spring of 1945 Joseph Katz mentioned to her that the KGB had no further need for him.[64]

While Redmont always denied any Communist affiliation, Ann Moos Remington later testified to a U.S. grand jury that she and her ex-husband had been close friends of the Redmonts and that both couples were Communists. William Remington had testified to a congressional committee that Bernard was a Communist, but he later repudiated that statement and apologized for it while trying to persuade Redmont to testify for him during his perjury trial. An FBI wiretap on the Redmont phone in 1946 recorded a conversation between Joan Redmont and Helen Scott (herself a Soviet source) in which Joan jokingly referred to her son, Dennis Foster Redmont, as William Foster's (chief of the CPUSA) "namesake."[65]

Redmont might have escaped trouble, since Bentley had barely mentioned him publicly, except that he agreed to testify on behalf of Remington in his perjury trial. He was immediately fired by his boss, William Lawrence, publisher of *U.S. News and World Report.* He moved to France, where he worked for a series of newspapers and, ultimately, Westinghouse Broadcasting Group. In 1976 he became Moscow bureau chief for CBS. Five years later, he returned to the United States to teach and then served as dean of the College of Communication at Boston University, resigning in 1986 after a disagreement with BU president John Silber over plans to train exiled Afghan journalists to cover the Soviet occupation.

Redmont continued to hew to the position that Bentley was a fantasist, linking her to "pathological liars, cranks, seekers of attention or publicity, or paid purveyors of tales and innuendoes." He insisted that he had been a victim of hysteria: "Tens of thousands of us, who in some way had not conformed, who had joined the wrong organizations, or had the wrong acquaintances, or had been denounced, anonymously or not, by informers, crackpots or self-styled patriots, were caught in the gears."[66]

The evidence is, however, that Bernard Redmont, distinguished American journalist and dean of a college of journalism, was the fabricator, not Elizabeth Bentley. An October 1944 KGB report lists his real name and cover name ("Mon") and identifies him as one of Bentley's sources. A January 1945 report again lists him as a Bentley contact with his real name and "Mon" cover name and adds that he had a Communist Party name of "Berny," that he worked in the press department of the CIAA, and that he had become an inactive source. In December 1945 the KGB station in London informed Moscow Center that Kim Philby had turned over a copy of Bentley's 1945 FBI statement given to British SIS. The KGB report listed forty-one KGB sources Bentley had identified to the FBI, adding their KGB cover names (which Bentley had not known). The last one on the list was, "41. Bernard Redmont (Mon)." A 1948 report, again giving his real name and "Mon" cover name, listed him among the Soviet intelligence contacts exposed by Bentley's defection. He may have been a minor source, but documentary evidence is that he was a source.[67]

William Dodd, Jr.

I. F. Stone assisted in recruiting William Dodd, Jr., as a KGB agent in 1936. Initially Dodd provided the KGB with inside information from the U.S. Embassy in Berlin. Once his father's ambassadorship ended, Dodd returned to the United States, worked as a journalist for a time, and then

challenged an incumbent member of Congress, Howard W. Smith, for
the 1938 Democratic nomination in Virginia's eighth district. Dodd ran
as an ardent New Deal supporter and as part of a White House effort to
replace conservative Democrats with liberals. Eager to have one of its
agents in the House of Representatives, the KGB New York station gave
Dodd $1,000 (nearly $15,000 in 2008 dollars) for his campaign.

In August 1938 Peter Gutzeit, chief of the KGB New York station,
notified Moscow Center that the funds had been delivered to Dodd and
a receipt obtained. Moscow had suggested that subsidizing Dodd would
be just the first step of a broader effort to secretly sponsor congressional
candidates, but Gutzeit warned Moscow that these plans might be highly
expensive:

"Implementation of the plan arising from the tasks you formulated in your last
letter will require, as has already been stated, enormous amounts of money.
These amounts are far greater than our current expenses. The funding of congressmen's election campaigns, the payment of journalists, the upkeep of newspapers, all of this adds up to costs that are impossible to calculate in advance.

The expenditure on a congressman, for example, can vary from case to
case. It's impossible to say in advance how much it will cost us to be able to
buy the pens of popular journalists. It is very difficult to determine even approximately the sum required to purchase a newspaper. In addition, the nature
of all of this work is such that it's impossible to know in advance the limits of
the spending, just as it's impossible to say in advance whether one journalist is
needed or ten. Whether one newspaper is needed or two, etc. So I frankly
state that I am completely at a loss in determining even approximately an estimate of future expenses. Whether these expenses will be 500,000 doll. or
1,000,000 doll. a year, I cannot say, because of the aforementioned considera-
tions. A resolution of this question should be up to you. The question of how
much funding will be allocated for this work for our country must be raised at
the appropriate levels. And then, based on that sum, we will structure all of
our calculations."

Dodd ran an energetic campaign, and press coverage in liberal-leaning
newspapers such as the *Washington Post* suggested that it was a tight
campaign and he had a chance. But in the primary Smith swamped Dodd
by a three-to-one margin. Whether it was Gutzeit's sensible skepticism or
Dodd's loss, nothing more was heard of Moscow Center plans of becoming a significant player in American electoral politics.[68]

The relationship with Dodd, however, continued. In 1939 the KGB
New York station reported that he had passed on inside political gossip
from prominent New Deal members of Congress (Senator Claude Pep-

per of Florida and Representative John Coffee of Washington), provided documents his father had kept from his ambassadorial tenure, and agreed to work as the intermediary between the KGB and Helen Fuller, a woman employed in the Department of Justice whom it hoped to develop into an informant on FBI activities. The KGB also continued to support Dodd's political ambitions, including his idea to purchase a weekly newspaper, the *Blue Ridge Herald,* in the eighth district as a base for a second attempt to unseat Representative Smith. Moscow Center allocated $3,500 for the venture ($52,000 in 2008 dollars), but the KGB New York station wanted at least $5,000 and assured Moscow: "'The direction of the newspaper will depend entirely on us. We will work out every detail of the newspaper's agenda with 'President' [Dodd]. It should not be too left-wing, and it should not be pro-Soviet—nor, it goes without saying, should it be anti-Soviet. A moderately liberal local newspaper with a direct connection to liberal Washington journalists and their participation in this little newspaper.'" For whatever reason, Dodd did not purchase the *Blue Ridge Herald* and did not run against Smith in 1940. The KGB also temporarily cut contact with him in May 1940, when his liaison was recalled to Moscow and the undermanned station was unable to provide a substitute.[69]

A year later Moscow Center urged that Dodd, then with the left-wing journal *American Week,* be reactivated, and the KGB New York station reestablished contact through Zalmond Franklin. Moscow Center clearly had high hopes for Dodd. A proposed budget for a revived American illegal station set a monthly stipend for him at $200. But plans to revive the illegal station in 1941 were aborted when the designated station chief died in transit. The KGB New York station continued contact via Franklin and thought that Dodd and his sister, Martha Dodd Stern, had provided some interesting information from an interview with Secretary of State Cordell Hull. Dodd also raised the possibility that he might get a position as a journalist assigned to Moscow on behalf of the North American Newspaper Alliance and *Harper's* magazine, but the KGB saw nothing to its advantage in the suggestion and it was dropped.[70]

In January 1942 Moscow told Vasily Zarubin, newly arrived chief of the legal station, that Dodd's potential had not been realized:

"For the past two years we have made unsuccessful attempts to use "President" [Dodd] in various areas of work. . . . Even though "President" has communicated with us for a long time, he remains a rough-edged probationer [agent] and requires a good deal of work both to teach him agent skills and to instill brutal discipline and the rules of covert work in him." (The aim is to turn him into a journalist-commentator. To direct his appearances in the press and on the radio so as to earn him a more solid position and reputation. In order to detach him from "Liza" [Martha Dodd Stern], arrange a trip for Pr. somewhere abroad (except for Home [Moscow]).[71]

In 1942 Dodd managed to get a position of mild interest to the KGB: assistant editor for the Foreign Broadcast Monitoring Service (FBMS), a wartime arm of the Federal Communications Commission (FCC). The FBMS provided American intelligence, diplomatic, and military services with translations and summaries of foreign radio broadcasts. However, by then Dodd's political past had begun to catch up with him. The Dies Committee called him to testify in 1943. Dodd unreservedly disavowed any sympathy for communism or links with the CPUSA, but his testimony was confused and often lacking in credibility. He admitted he had authored a 1938 essay in *Champion*, journal of the YCL, but claimed he had no idea that it was a YCL publication. He admitted he had been active in the American League for Peace and Democracy in the late 1930s but denied that it had been Communist-aligned. He denied he had given his permission to be listed on the call for a 1941 national conference of the League of American Writers (by that point an obvious Communist front) but admitted he had attended the conference. Urged on by Representative Dies, a subcommittee of the House Appropriations Committee headed by Representative John H. Kerr (D-NC) investigated a number of government employees, including Dodd, for possible Communist ties. Dodd testified to the "Kerr Commission" and once again denied any sympathy for communism while delivering rambling and incredible testimony about his past association with Communist-aligned groups. Congress in 1943 voted to attach a rider to the FCC's appropriations bill prohibiting salary payments to three named individuals, including William Dodd, Jr.[72]

The Congress, however, was not the only body that found Dodd's testimony unacceptable. KGB New York station chief Zarubin forwarded the Kerr subcommittee report on Dodd's testimony and told Moscow:

"As the report makes clear, "President" [Dodd] conducted himself in a foolish and sometimes disgraceful manner during the interrogations, especially when the questions pertained specifically to the fellowcountrymen [CPUSA] and the USSR and its system. "Vardo" [Elizabeth Zarubin], as we have reported to you, spoke with "President" before the investigation and interrogations began and gave him specific instructions on how to conduct himself so as, on the one hand, not to become confused and not get stuck, and on the other, to emerge with dignity from this affair and not denigrate the "fellowcountrymen" and the USSR. "President" evidently got terribly scared and hoped to keep his job if he would slander the fellowcountrymen and the USSR.

A great deal has been written in the press on "President's" case and a big ruckus has been raised. Because of this, and also because P. did almost nothing for us, we have not been meeting with him in the past few months. He was very frightened by the investigation and avoided meetings himself. . . . Based on the foregoing, President for the moment should be considered deactivated. The question of his future use can be settled once and for all after his situation is clarified."[73]

Dodd and the others named in the 1943 appropriations rider were, in effect, fired by Congress. Years later the U.S. Supreme Court held that the rider was a bill of attainder prohibited by the Constitution, and Dodd received back pay but not reinstatement. Meanwhile, however, he was out of a job and under a cloud. In 1945 he prevailed on his Soviet friends to give him a job as a reporter for TASS. Moscow Center was not pleased. While it had given up on William Dodd as a productive agent, it still had hopes for his sister, Martha Dodd Stern, and her wealthy husband, Alfred Stern. Moscow feared that William's connection to TASS would compromise Martha, and she not only agreed but also wanted her brother fired. Dodd, for his part, argued that in light of the Dies Committee and Congress's actions against him, if he lost his TASS position, he was unemployable. The KGB was unmoved, and TASS fired him. The KGB never renewed contact with him.[74]

Overseas Correspondents

A 1943 KGB report reviewing earlier activity that needed to be reinforced noted the work of four "journalists recruited and sent to Euro. countries: "Eagle," "Yun," "Paul," "Leopard."" There were no indications of the identity of "Leopard," but two of the other three can be confidently identified and one likely so.[75]

The most active of these overseas journalist sources was "Paul." (This KGB "Paul" is a different person from GRU's "Paul"/"Pol" discussed in chapter 1.) In 1941 one Moscow Center message noted having received "through "Paul"—information on the German army's military operations in territories in Norway, France, and other occupied countries + a description of France's naval armaments. Through Paul—descriptions of a large number of Amer. dip. workers in territories in G. and occupied countries." Another 1941 memo, a Moscow Center evaluation of American intelligence, said that "Paul" had been recruited in 1940 and had supplied "a word-for-word translation of a confidential report by the director of the Washington office of "United Press" on the policies of the Amer. government vis-à-vis the Japanese. 2. "Paul"—on French-American negotiations on the question of installing American navy and air force bases on the island of Martinique and on French naval forces in the West Indies." The same memo described "Paul" as "(currently in England)—a journalist. Secret member of the CPUSA. Valuable materials and leads. He has major connections. Could be an information agent, talent-spotting agent, and a recruiting agent." Not surprisingly, Moscow Center put "Paul" on its 1941 list of the "most valuable" agents in the United States.[76]

"Paul" was probably Peter Rhodes. Rhodes was unambiguously a KGB agent. Jacob Golos had met with him, and an October 1941 KGB memo, using his real name, reported: "'*Peter Rhodes.* Peter has been hired for a government job and is traveling to London in three weeks as head of the information office, which will supply information to the president, Donovan, the 2nd Department [Army intelligence, G-2], naval intelligence, and the FBI. Peter has been given the right to hire employees for the aforementioned office. This is a pretty good find for us. Sound [Golos] has been told to get a password and his address in London from him.'" Elizabeth Bentley later identified Rhodes as a member of Golos's network and said that in 1945 she had learned that KGB contact with Rhodes had been lost and the KGB asked her to restore it via Rhodes's wife, who, however, brushed Bentley off. A deciphered KGB cable also documented KGB attempts to restore contact with Rhodes in 1945. As will be seen, Rhodes's Communist background and journalistic assignments also conform closely to those described for "Paul." Taken together the evidence indicates that "Paul" was Rhodes.[77]

Peter Rhodes was born in the Philippines of parents whose citizenship was unclear. (Additionally, it appears his mother killed his father under murky circumstances.) He came to the United States at the age of three or four, received a BA and MA from Columbia University and then a second BA and MA from Britain's Oxford University in the mid-1930s. He married Ione Boulinger, a Belgian, in 1936. His first job in journalism was with the *Herald Tribune* in Paris in 1936, the same year he was hired by United Press (UP) as a correspondent. Based in Paris from 1936 to 1939, he subsequently moved to Copenhagen and Stockholm, from where he covered the German occupation of Norway and the Soviet annexation of the Baltic states. He returned to the United States in mid-

1940 via Moscow and Siberia and across the Pacific. Rhodes worked for UP in America until January 1941, then took a job as a fundraiser for United China Relief until August, when he joined the FBMS of the FCC and was sent to England to set up a system of foreign broadcast monitoring to cover Europe. He worked there until October 1942, then returned to Washington to assist in establishing radio monitoring aimed at French North Africa. In London he worked with OWI propaganda activities aimed at occupied Europe. He returned to the United States in November 1944 on another OWI assignment but then shifted to the State Department to assist in setting up radio broadcasts to the Balkans.

Rhodes's attachment to communism was long-standing. As a UP correspondent in the late 1930s, he wrote extensively about the Americans fighting with the International Brigades in Spain and became an ardent partisan of their cause, including serving as an American delegate to the International Coordinating Committee for Aid to Republican Spain. A German Communist who had been with the International Brigades entered the United States illegally using Rhodes's passport, apparently given to him by Rhodes. In 1939 and 1940 Rhodes also signed nominating petitions to put Communist Party candidates on the New York ballot (shortening his signature from Peter Christopher Rhodes to Christopher Rhodes). The Comintern archive contains a February 1940 coded cable from Rudy Baker, then chief of the CPUSA's covert arm, reporting that Rhodes had not gone to Bucharest, Rumania, as planned earlier and, consequently, was unable to make his scheduled contact there with Soviet agents. The FBI, while conducting surveillance of Jacob Golos, observed him meeting with Rhodes in 1941, prior to his FBMS assignment in London, and then again in 1942 after his return. When FBI agents interviewed Rhodes in 1947 and asked about his relationship with Golos, he denied ever meeting him.[78]

"Yun," another of the four journalist sources, was Stephen Laird. "Yun" appeared in a number of KGB cables deciphered by the Venona project, and the information in the cables allowed the FBI to identify "Yun" as Laird without difficulty. Born Laird Lichtenwalner to a Pennsylvania Dutch family, he attended Swarthmore College in the mid-1930s and then embarked on a career as a journalist. He first appeared in KGB files in 1941, when he worked for *Time* magazine, where he and Peter Rhodes were contacts of Jacob Golos. At this point Moscow Center told its New York station: "'We are becoming convinced that the Time publishing house is a well organized intelligence agency that sells its material to the FBI, the State Department's intelligence service, and military and naval intelligence.'" Laird, the magazine's London correspondent, was at this point already a KGB contact with the cover name "Yun." Later that year the KGB New York station sent Moscow Center a report from "Yun," described as a "probationer" (KGB term for its agents), with brief descriptions of American reporters in Germany, Switzerland, and the United States, and: "'In addition, "Yun" [Laird] gives quotations from comments by highly prominent members of American circles with whom he personally discussed U.S. foreign-policy issues. All of these individuals hold anti-Soviet positions and say that support for the USSR in its war with Germany lays the groundwork for the 'spread of Bolshevism throughout the world.'"" Moscow, however, was concerned about Laird's bona fides. In November 1941 it informed the KGB New York station that it continued to be concerned about the "'intelligence apparatus inside the Time complex'" that reported to American security agencies and had "'suspicions regarding the involvement of our sources 'Paul' [Rhodes] and 'Yun' [Laird] in it.'" Despite Moscow's queries, New York had not yet investigated further. Since both these sources were being used overseas, "'this aspect must be cleared up as soon as possible.'" In as much as both remained in good standing as sources, the matter was apparently resolved.[79]

When he returned to the United States, Laird, newly divorced and distraught, was supervised by Elizabeth Zarubin. There was some concern because Laird's wife "knows about everything and is also working for us. Her new husband knows everything, too." But Zarubin met with her and reported to Moscow that "she had a good impression" and there was nothing to worry about. By the middle of 1944 contact with Laird had been turned over to Konstantin Chugunov. A KGB message from August 1944 positively evaluated Laird.

[He] gives the impression of a politically well-developed person who wishes to help us. However, he considers his potentialities to be limited, for he deals only with technical work on the magazine. He can pass on correspondents' telegrams but we receive them from other sources. Using his connections among journalists and studying the magazine's materials, he could draw up political reports for us but he lacks perseverance for that. Besides, [undeciphered words] breakup with his wife. Yun [Laird] declares that he is used to reporters' work and would like to go abroad again, but the owner of the magazine will not send him because he disapproves of his radical views. The other day the film company RKO took him on as a film producer, which he succeeded in getting thanks to social connections in actor and producer circles. According to Yun's words, Vardo [Elizabeth Zarubin] in her time did not object to such a maneuver and afterwards it may give him an opportunity to make trips to Europe and do work useful to us. In the middle of September Yun is moving to Hollywood. We consider it expedient to continue liaison with him in Hollywood. Telegraph whether a new password should be agreed upon.

KGB cables confirm that Laird remained in contact with the KGB in Hollywood. One plaintive telegram from a KGB officer in September 1945 asked for an automobile to meet Laird in Los Angeles since otherwise "I should be simply walked off my feet." Laird remained a reliably pro-Soviet journalist, reporting the rigged 1947 Polish elections were free and fair. He spent most of the remainder of his life abroad, settling in Switzerland, before returning to Pennsylvania, where he died in 1990.[80]

While it is not certain, the remaining overseas journalist source, "Eagle," may have been Winston Burdett and his cover name a KGB play on the newspaper for which he worked, the *Brooklyn Eagle*. Deciphered KGB cables, Comintern records, FBI investigatory files, and Burdett's own testimony confirm that in 1940 Golos approached Burdett, a secret Communist. He asked him to obtain credentials as a foreign correspondent from the *Eagle* and to undertake Soviet intelligence tasks while traveling in Europe as a war correspondent. Burdett traveled first to Stockholm and later to Norway, Rumania, Yugoslavia, and Turkey, all the while meeting with Soviet agents to relay reports on what he had heard and seen. "Eagle," an unidentified cover name in the Venona decryptions, was deactivated in 1944, a pattern consistent with Burdett, who drifted away from Soviet intelligence after a few years. He testified to Congress regarding his involvement with Soviet espionage in 1955.[81]

Far Eastern Sources

Several KGB journalist contacts had connections to China or Far Eastern affairs. Although none of them were particularly productive sources, their stories illustrate the many lines Soviet intelligence threw out in order to reel in information.

Andrew J. Steiger was born near Pittsburgh in 1900. After attending the Union Theological Seminary for a few years in the early 1930s, he turned to journalism. He never admitted any links to the CPUSA, but Louis Budenz testified before a Senate investigating committee that Steiger had been a secret Communist in the 1930s and had written for the *Daily Worker*. At some point in the 1930s he traveled to the USSR, learned Russian (he later did some professional translation), married a Russian, and became a specialist on the Soviet Far East. He returned to the United States by 1941, but the Soviets refused to give his wife a visa and she remained in Moscow.

Steiger wrote for numerous magazines and worked for CBS Radio for a time. In 1942 he co-authored *Soviet Asia, Democracy's First Line of Defense* with another former Moscow correspondent. In mid-1944 Vice-President Henry Wallace toured China and Soviet Siberia on a wartime goodwill mission. In a remarkable act of deception, Soviet authorities showed Wallace a massive Gulag camp at Magadan, where they had temporarily taken down the guard towers, camouflaged the barbed wire fences, locked the prisoners into their barracks, offered the guards' barracks and recreational facilities as workers' quarters, dressed guards as workers, and had them perform dramatics for the visiting Americans. The vice-president accepted at face value Soviet claims that the slave labor camp was a combination industrial development community and TVA-like reclamation project. After his return to the United States, Wallace authored a book, *Soviet Asia Mission,* praising Soviet accomplishments in Siberia. In the book Wallace acknowledged that Steiger had written the text based on notes Wallace had kept during the trip. In 1949 Steiger became a Reuters stringer in Moscow and rejoined his Russian wife. She finally received a visa after Stalin's death and they returned to the United States, but he soon returned to Moscow as a stringer for several small newspapers and died there in the late 1960s.[82]

At some point, likely when in the USSR, Steiger was recruited by Soviet intelligence. In April 1941 Moscow reminded Gayk Ovakimyan, KGB New York station chief, of its desire that he contact Steiger using the passwords arranged while he was in the USSR:

"In our last two letters we wrote you about the necessity of finding out the particulars about agent 'Fakir,' Andrew Steiger, but to date we haven't had a reply from you regarding this matter. We learned from the magazine *Amerasia* for March, which we have received, that 'Fakir' is in New York and is contributing to many newspapers and magazines. The March issue of *Amerasia* magazine contains his article, 'How Strong Is Soviet Siberia?' The article is very good and one can sense that he is well versed in the international situation and the world economy. Find out the particulars about 'Fakir' through *Amerasia* magazine, make contact with him (we enclose the meeting instructions), and activate him, using him for econ. intelligence and the press. Report immediately when you have made contact with him.

Meeting instructions: The meeting must take place on the 8th or the 15th at 12 noon on the corner of West End Avenue and 85 Street. . . . The source will have a *Life* magazine in the right pocket of his overcoat, and if the weather is good, a hat in his left hand. You will say in English, 'Regards from Alice.' He will reply, 'Thanks. I would like to visit her.' You will say, 'She will be very glad to see you.' After that you can get down to business."

Ovakimyan, however, was arrested by the FBI shortly after receiving Moscow Center's instructions. It was not until November 1941 that the New York station reported that it had established contact with Steiger and learned that he worked at CBS, compiling summaries of international radio reports for broadcast and distribution to newspapers. Despite the delay, Steiger was willing to renew contact and reported that he "can obtain interesting information." "Fakir" appears in the Venona decryptions as an unidentified cover name (later redesignated "Arnold"), and the deciphered cables show that Steiger during 1943 and 1944 supplied the KGB with information of a foreign policy/diplomatic character that presumably came to his attention or from contacts he developed as a journalist.[83]

One journalist associated with Soviet intelligence spent only a few years in the United States, from 1945 to 1951, before returning to China, where he had first been recruited. Israel Epstein was born in Warsaw in 1915; he moved to Tianjin, China, at the age of two with his Marxist parents. A 1949 KGB report listing sources available for use suggested: ""Minayev"—Israel Epstein, a journalist. An agent since '37, recruited in China. Came to the USA in '45. Lives as a resident alien. Gained Soviet citizenship in '43, but his papers were not issued for oper. reasons."[84]

Moscow had first alerted the New York station about Epstein in 1943 during a critical review of its progress on developing sources on China. Moscow Center warned that the United States was increasing its engagement with China and the KGB needed to respond, explaining:

"While the elaboration of issues related to the course of the war in Europe and issues of postwar Europe is one of the leading areas of the office's everyday activities, the office is clearly not giving enough attention to coverage of issues related to the war in the Pacific and U.S. policy toward the countries of the Pacific. Meanwhile, our operatives in Chungking and in Sinkiang note an exceptional increase in the Americans' activities in China and their effort to penetrate into China's northwestern provinces, to the border with the USSR and the MPR [Mongolian People's Republic]. For example, in the winter of this year a group of American competitors toured all of northwestern China up to our border with Sinkiang. The group consisted of: Clabb, second secretary of the U.S. Embassy in Chungking; Lieutenant Roy, assistant military attaché; *Adler, a financial expert,* and others. We have information regarding the planned opening in a number of northwestern Chinese cities of American consulates and regarding the intention of the U.S. to finance the development of natural resources in northwestern China.

The Americans are taking every measure in order to seize the moment and maximize their influence in China: they are providing a great deal of financial assistance to Chinese higher educational institutions, they are creating and subsidizing 'young men's Christian associations, etc.' . . . In our cable of 9.11–1942 we gave you the task of cultivating through *"Girl Friend"* [Fairfax-Cholmeley] and other probationers of the office the activities of members of American organizations that deal with issues related to China and editorial staffers of magazines: *Asia, China Today, Amerasia, Pacific Affairs,* and others that publish articles on countries of the Pacific and on issues of U.S. Pacific policy. To date we have no materials from you that would indicate that the station is performing this task.

In connection with the forthcoming departure of "Girl Friend's" husband, "Minayev" [Epstein], we are giving you the task of intensifying the cultivation of the above-mentioned contingent. A large number of these individuals regularly visit China, and they could be extremely useful to us in cultivating the leading Chinese circles and the activities of foreign missions in China. We are interested in the structure of numerous organizations, institutes, associations, and various societies that manage the study of the Pacific problem, especially the Pacific Institute, whose regular session was held in December 1942 in Canada. To what extent is their work directed by the "Bank" [U.S. State Department] and competitor [American intelligence] organizations?"

Elsie Fairfax-Cholmeley, Epstein's wife, worked for United China Relief in New York. She was the daughter of Christian missionaries in China and also a Communist. "Girl Friend" was unidentified in the Venona decryptions but listed as an asset of the KGB New York station who was put into "cold storage" in 1944.[85]

Arriving in the United States in 1945, Epstein wrote for Allied Labor News; became active in the Committee for a Democratic Far Eastern Policy, which supported the Chinese Communists; and in 1947 published *The Unfinished Revolution in China,* an unabashedly partisan celebration of the Communist movement in China. In 1950 the plan of work for the KGB Washington station assigned "Minayev"/Epstein the duty of "covering the activities of Amer. left trade unions." He and Elsie, however, left for China in 1951, where he became editor of a PRC English-language journal, *China Reconstructs,* later renamed *China Today,* and served as a correspondent for the *National Guardian,* edited by another former KGB agent, Cedric Belfrage. Fanatically devoted to Chinese communism, he was part of a team charged with translating Mao's works into

English beginning in 1960. Other members included such one-time KGB sources as Frank Coe and Solomon Adler. When Anna Louise Strong, another ex-KGB agent, settled in the PRC, Epstein became close to her as well. Despite his long service to the Chinese Communist movement, he and his wife were arrested during the Cultural Revolution in 1967 and served five years in prison before being released with an apology. His faith unshaken, he claimed that his imprisonment had "helped improve him by shrinking his ego."[86]

Epstein was restored to his editorial position and became a member of the Standing Committee of the National Committee of the Chinese People's Political Consultative Conference. In 1982 he returned to the United States for a reunion conference of reporters who had served in China; he harbored no doubts or second thoughts about his life or causes. Elsie died in 1984. Israel Epstein died in May 2005.[87]

Other Journalists Who Cooperated with the KGB

The myriad of ways that journalists assisted the KGB—as sources of inside information, talent spotters, purveyors of disinformation and propaganda, couriers—is testimony to how valuable they were perceived as being. Those profiled above do not exhaust the list of journalists who cooperated with Soviet intelligence. *Samuel Krafsur* ("Ide"), CPUSA member and veteran of the International Brigades, an asset of the KGB New York station, worked as a journalist for TASS. The KGB used Krafsur to cultivate American journalists with particular attention to recruiting some as KGB sources.[88] *Cedric Belfrage* ("Charlie"), an Englishman who later edited the *National Guardian,* wrote angry books denouncing what he depicted as a paranoid America's anti-Communist "inquisition," which looked for non-existent spies. A concealed Communist, he worked for British Security Coordination, a branch of British intelligence, in the United States during World War II. He reported both British and American information to the New York office of the KGB.[89] *Richard Lauterbach* ("Pa"), a *Time* magazine Moscow correspondent, carried out discussions with Jack Soble (an illegal KGB officer) that led the New York station to ask Moscow Center for sanction for his formal recruitment, but it is unclear if this relationship was consummated.[90] *Johannes Steele* ("Dicky"), radio commentator and columnist, assisted the KGB with contacts with refugees and exiles.[91] *Ricardo Setaro* ("Express Messenger" and "Jean"), deputy chief of the Latin American department at CBS Radio, worked as a courier and communications link for KGB South

American operations.[92] *Helen Scott* ("Fir") was a journalist and KGB source who worked as a secretary to a French journalist, Geneviève Tabouis, and later for the Coordinator of Inter-American Affairs and the U.S. Chief of Counsel for Prosecution of Axis War Criminals.[93] *Peter MacLean* ("101st") was a reporter and photojournalist who did unspecified work for Soviet intelligence, likely for GRU, in the mid-1930s.[94] *David Carpenter* ("103rd"), one-time reporter for the *Baltimore Sun* and later for the *Daily Worker,* was part of Whittaker Chambers's GRU-linked 1930s espionage apparatus.[95] "Bough" was an unidentified journalist who provided information on senior American journalists in 1944–45.[96]

By the early 1950s nearly all of the KGB's sources, including the journalists, had dried up. A number had been exposed by defectors or tracked down by the FBI. Others had quietly dropped away or lost contact with Soviet intelligence. A handful had left the country. One of the last journalists to remain available for KGB use was a prominent and open member of the CPUSA. James Allen, born Solomon Auerbach, graduated from the University of Pennsylvania and later taught philosophy there. Fired for radical activities in 1928, he joined the CPUSA and wrote for the *Daily Worker* before editing the *Southern Worker* and serving as one of the party's leaders in the South. He also wrote major party tomes on the Negro question. In the late 1930s he served as the Comintern's representative in the Philippines. In addition to service as the *Daily Worker's* foreign editor, he later headed International Publishers.

Since virtually his entire adult life had been spent within the orbit of the CPUSA, Allen was unlikely to be a source of much significant intelligence in his own right. Yet in 1949 a plan of work for the KGB New York station noted that KGB co-optee Valentin Sorokin handled the connection with ""Jack"—James Allen, CPUSA member, no permanent place of employment, works at a progressive press agency. Puts together reports on econ. questions, Amer. political figures, and the CPUSA." From the point of view of operational utility, use of an openly identified Communist journalist whose entire career had been within the CPUSA's organizational environment and who was well known to American security agencies was not optimal tradecraft. A senior Moscow Center official referred to the Washington station's use of James Allen as following the "path of least resistance." Using him was a measure of the reduced circumstances of the KGB compared to the halcyon days of the 1930s and 1940s, when such established journalists as I. F. Stone, Robert S. Allen, Ludwig Lore, John Spivak, Frank Palmer, Winston Burdett, and others covertly worked with the KGB.[97]

That these journalists did less immediate damage to American interests than such government spies as Alger Hiss or scientists like Theodore Hall should not diminish their importance to the KGB or the harm they inflicted on American society. Unlike government employees or scientists who broke the law by turning over classified information to the KGB, most of the journalists profiled in this chapter violated no statute of that era. Few had any access to secret data. Members of a profession dedicated to openness, however, they covertly enlisted in an organization dedicated to deception. They used their access to information to deceive their employers, their colleagues, and their publics about their loyalties and veracity. They betrayed confidences and pursued political agendas while pretending to be professional journalists. In several cases, notably that of Stone, they later wrote prolifically about issues of subversion and espionage without ever acknowledging that they knew far more about how the KGB operated than they cared to express. Writing about the American intellectuals who knowingly accepted assistance from the CIA in the 1940s and 1950s to counter Communist influence, critics have charged that they had been untrue to their calling. How much more apt is the characterization directed at men who worked not for their own government, but for the intelligence service of a dictatorship?[98]

сообщил Юнб, к--му сказал сам Д. Компаньон Ю. уехал куда работа Д. и уехал по фашизм, Кинта и Юнб знал б лицо, не фашизм незнаеб.

10.09.34

с. 31 Джонни Дейвис — в делле, Изъять можно долго с помощью адвоката.
"Уинстон" сообщает что Дейвис помещен в сейф вместе с бумагами записи на русском языке.

На Николай: М-б — Центр, 22.09.34

с. 33 Было 2 встречи с Юнбом после смерти Дейвиса. Юнб рассказал об операх—й безграмотность Кинта при установлении связи с Дейвисом: сразу назначил ему 400 вол в мес, назвал наблюдающей линией и записал линией в дело, фирму. Но работает Кинт Юнеш. "Дейвиш держит Кинта в своих руках полностью" Следует до приезда настоящего руководителя никаких об людях дел не принимать, Дейвиша и Грабор об Кинта знают лично Юнгу.

с. 38 Письмо Юнба в Центр 7.10.34.

О сотрудница Дейвиса. "Кинт ее встречает и осторожно обрабатывает, понедая добиться ее, чтобы она хорошо могла выводить сейф у нас. Она обещала подумать и даст скоро ответ. Мы не уверены что она поведет. Она лично не выдвинется из этого города, имеет родственные связи. Кинт думает, что она не способна на плохие вещи. Будем держать ее под наблюдением, если она будет нужда временно будет подкармливать."

с. 38 "Сотрудница Дейвиса знает очень хорошо о фирму и ее если Кинт мы заметим что-нибудь плохое в ее настроения, добьемся от фирмы отказался и уничтожаем карбину, что Кинт делал дома. В случае прекращения нашей службы фирма не сможет существовать. Со стороны компаньона плохо используется, он нашим, желает стать к нам, пока с конторой связан Кинт. В будущем Кинт будешь компаньоном."

с. 39 Рапорт нач-ка 1-ого сектора ИНО ГУГБ Графпен зам.нач. ИНО ГУГБ г. Берману, от 27.11.34:

Существовали агенты Даниэля и Альберта дерзал нами под сомнение. Даниэль якобы завербован ??? уж три сведущими ваших. Связь держит Лео. Лурвенб и его помощники с агентом не встречались.

с. 40 Проверили по справочнику "гид". Подобов в делле, и б не был официально соприкасаться с Дан—ми, к-е наш переводчик.
Вороббева Альберта — Лео. Но все инф но, к-е получаем об Д. и А., имеет Вилли/нач-к отдела связи и архива нида/ (телеграфная переписка, шифры, хранение дел-дов).

с. 41 "...Допускаем, что Д. и А. неб в природе и что последние фиктивно созданы Лео с целью увеличения получаемого вознаграждения. Лео получает 250 долларов в месяц, Даниэль—500 и

CHAPTER 4

· ·

Infiltration of the
U.S. Government

I n the late 1940s Elizabeth Bentley and Whittaker Chambers publicly identified dozens of U.S. government officials as having knowingly assisted Soviet intelligence in the 1930s and early 1940s. Their
revelations and subsequent charges by Senator Joseph McCarthy
precipitated a bitter and long-standing debate about the extent of Soviet
subversion. Chambers and Bentley, however, only knew the half of it.
KGB sources of whom they were unaware honeycombed the federal government and its scientific laboratories. But Senator McCarthy's charges
were also wildly off the mark. Very few of the people he accused appeared
in KGB documents (or the Venona decryptions), and by the time he made
his charges, almost all Soviet agents had been forced out of the government and Soviet intelligence networks were largely defunct.

The documents transcribed or summarized in Vassiliev's notebooks
confirm that those named by Bentley and Chambers were Soviet sources.
One internal KGB list alone included forty-two people who had worked
for the federal government and were endangered by their revelations.

Identifies KGB source "Willy" as the 1934 chief of the State Department's Communications and Records
Division, a post held by the veteran civil servant David Salmon. Courtesy of Alexander Vassiliev.

Although most of these people were also identified in the Venona decryptions or other material that has emerged from previously closed archives, these newly available documents fill in previously puzzling gaps in some of their stories. They demonstrate, for example, that one of the figures named by Bentley, Harold Glasser, was one of the KGB's most productive spies in Washington. More important, they expose a number of other unlikely Soviet sources, some of whom came under varying levels of FBI suspicion or surveillance, and others of whom remained entirely under the counterintelligence radar, including a hitherto unsuspected Soviet source at the U.S. State Department.[1]

"Willy": The State Department Spy before Hiss

Soviet intelligence had a source in the State Department with access to all American diplomatic communications before Alger Hiss was recruited. A 1934 internal Moscow Center memo stated: "Willy (chief of the DOS's communication and archives division) . . . (all telegraph correspondence, ciphers, store of documents)." Another Moscow Center message said: "'Willy—gives copies of reports addressed to the State Department from ambassadors, consuls, and U.S. military attachés in Europe and the Far East. The materials are very valuable to the corresponding echelons [Soviet foreign ministry and relevant agencies]. Could give cabinet resolutions regarding the affairs of StateD and G-2 (war intelligence).'" Moscow Center believed that "Willy's" material was so valuable that it proposed doubling his KGB compensation: "'Willy gets 5,600 dollars a year at his Department. From us, he gets 6,000 dollars a year. We are suggesting setting his salary at 12,000–15,000 dollars a year in order to get the most he can give.'"[2]

Why was the KGB considering paying "Willy" $15,000 annually (the equivalent of $232,000 in 2008 dollars) for U.S. State Department information? In the 1930s the Soviet Union did not regard the United States as the "Main Adversary," as it did in the Cold War. America was distant from Soviet concerns about the German threat in the West and the Japanese threat in the East. Nonetheless, in early 1934 Moscow Center sent Valentin Markin, chief of the recently established illegal KGB station, a memo emphasizing the key role played by the United States in world affairs:

"In the system of states, the USA is the deciding factor in questions of world politics. There are no problems, not even 'purely' European ones, that America doesn't take part in resolving by virtue of its economic and financial might. It plays a special role in the resolution of Far Eastern problems. It follows that America must be well informed about European and Far Eastern affairs, and hence, in all likelihood—the active role of its intelligence. This situation necessitates from our intelligence in the USA (especially illegal intelligence) the following highly important tasks: It is essential that available agents and those intended for recruitment provide us with documents and agent-verified materials covering the USA's position with regard to what is mentioned above and, in particular, the USA's position on the Far Eastern problem."[3]

Who was "Willy"? KGB documents in Vassiliev's notebooks do not contain his real name, but details they provide are sufficient to identify him, and he was a most unexpected Soviet source. David A. Salmon was born in Connecticut in 1879 and joined the War Department in 1896 as a junior clerk. His efficient work attracted the attention of Secretary of War Elihu Root, and when Root became secretary of state in 1905, he brought Salmon with him to bring order to the State Department's handling of codes, ciphers, and diplomatic communications. Salmon became chief of the Bureau of Indexes and Archives in 1916 and its successor, the Division of Communications and Records, in 1931. Although the position lacked the prestige of the diplomatic offices and divisions headed by foreign service officers, with 150 employees it was the largest single office in the department. As its chief in 1934, Salmon's government salary was $5,600. He held that position until he retired in 1948. A 1939 *Washington Post* story noted: "In times of international stress, the nerve center of the department is the obscurely placed Division of Communications and Records where the staff of the genial 60-year-old David A. Salmon (in the department since the days of Elihu Root) receives, decodes, and transmits the messages that flood in from the scene of discord. During the Munich crisis from 45,000 to 50,000 words and code symbols were handled in the division daily, to say nothing of the transocean and domestic telephone calls."

In one of those stranger-than-fiction episodes, shortly after Salmon retired, the House Committee on Un-American Activities asked him to examine copies of 1938 State Department cables that Whittaker Chambers had produced to support his assertions that Alger Hiss had given him DOS documents in 1938. Salmon stated that the cables were authentic and would have been encoded using the department's highest cipher.[4]

There is something incongruous in looking back and seeing one hidden Soviet spy providing evidence that assisted in exposing another So-

viet spy, but the two had very different motivations. Alger Hiss was a secret Communist and regarded assisting Soviet intelligence as a moral
duty. There is no indication that Salmon had any sympathy for communism or the Soviet Union. His motive appears to have been entirely monetary, more than doubling his civil servant salary. Also, by the time of his
testimony, Salmon was an ex-Soviet source, the KGB having cut off contact with him in 1937.

The path that led the KGB to cease contact with such a valuable
source was an odd one, linked to the growing pains of the KGB's American station. Salmon was not recruited by a professional KGB officer, and,
indeed, it does not appear that a KGB officer ever met directly with him.
Instead, Ludwig Lore, an American agent of the KGB New York station,
recruited Salmon and handled all of the KGB's dealings with him.

The KGB conducted intelligence operations in the United States in
the 1920s and recruited a number of sources. But for reasons that are
not clear, it largely shut down its American operations at the end of the
decade, not reviving its New York station until 1933. At first, however,
neither the legal nor illegal station had enough officers with adequate
English-language skills or familiarity with American society to operate
efficiently. By 1934 Moscow Center began to realize that its American
stations were having teething difficulties, and in a letter (written in round-
about language in case of interception) it ordered illegal station chief
Valentin Markin to travel to Denmark to meet with senior Moscow Center officials to discuss in detail the work of his station. Moscow explained:

"Your company's operations have expanded too far, and we are concerned that
your small apparatus will be unable to serve your clients in accordance with
the principles and fundamentals of our profession. Not to mention the dissipa-
tion of forces and insufficient attention to your main clients. During your stay
in the USA, your work expanded very successfully, but so quickly that there
was no opportunity to process, consolidate, and organize it. It is this in particular that attests to the timeliness and necessity of reevaluating the principles behind your company's existence, its finances, and its circle of clients." . . . The
meeting place in Copenhagen—the Gorbaldsen Museum, room 32, at 2 P.M.
Holding the newspaper "Berliner Tagesblat." Password: You: "How do you get
to the exit." Reply: "I'm leaving myself; I can show you."[5]

One of the new station's problems was excessive reliance on American
agents who were sometimes inadequately supervised by professional officers, and Ludwig Lore was a prime example.

Lore (discussed in chapter 3) had readily accepted an offer from the newly established KGB New York station to become one of its American agents, with a monthly stipend of $350 (equivalent to $5,500 in 2008 dollars). A journalist, in 1934 he wrote a column, "Behind the Cables," for the *New York Post* that focused on foreign affairs, and it was likely Lore's search for diplomatic information that led him to David Salmon, through whose office passed every American diplomatic cable and letter. Lore recruited "Willy"/Salmon at a premium rate, $500 a month.[6]

It is not entirely clear if Lore told Salmon that his information was going to Moscow or if he allowed Salmon to believe that the *New York Post* paid so well that Lore could afford a $500-a-month bribe to get access to diplomatic cables to assist in writing his column. Salmon, however, could have had no illusions about where his information went after the following fall 1934 incident, relayed in a message to Moscow from Iskhak Akhmerov, an illegal officer who had just met with Lore:

"During Leo's [Lore's] meeting with Willy [Salmon] (about two weeks ago) in Center [Washington], Willy reported that B. [U.S. ambassador Bullitt] . . . had reported from your city [Moscow] to Center that the contents of his reports are known in your city. Willy was terribly dismayed and worried. He had a nervous breakdown for a couple of days. The Assistant Secretary of this company [State Department] personally questioned the directors and Willy as to whether these reports were being leaked here, in Center. The Assistant Secretary instructed Willy to run a check of his employees and to undertake an investigation of the division he oversees. Willy says (thinks) that a corresponding investigation of this affair is also being undertaken through companies of our sort [FBI]. Please use utmost caution when delivering B's reports to neighboring offices [Soviet foreign ministry and other agencies]. B's cunning, aptitude, gregariousness, and connections among prominent individuals in your city give him the opportunity to feel out a number of people. It is enough to drop an indirect hint during a conversation."[7]

As Akhmerov explained, Ambassador William Bullitt had complained to the State Department that some Soviet officials appeared to have knowledge of the contents of his secret reports to Washington. All of Bullitt's reports passed through Salmon's Division of Communications and Records. Consequently one of the assistant secretaries of state had instructed Salmon to review his staff to see if there was a leak, and Salmon also thought the FBI had been called in to investigate. Since the leaker was Salmon himself, he was distraught. Akhmerov also asked Moscow Center to be more careful with the distribution of the information Salmon was providing and to warn its recipients (principally Soviet foreign ministry officials) of the dangers of displaying too much knowledge of American diplomatic matters when meeting with the perceptive Bullitt. If Salmon had been under the illusion that Lore was just another journalist seeking inside information, that fantasy had surely been dispelled.

The relationship with Salmon fell apart because the KGB concluded that Lore had invented another State Department source, attributing some of Salmon's genuine material to him, to obtain additional money from the KGB by pocketing the subsidies for the nonexistent source. By February 1937 Boris Bazarov, new head of the illegal station, told Moscow Center that he had become convinced that Lore, possibly with Salmon's assistance, had "apparently been deceiving the station." Moscow Center judged Salmon's material authentic and highly valuable, but approaching Salmon directly was risky because no KGB officer had ever met him and the KGB did not understand the basis of Lore's relationship with him. An independent approach bypassing Lore might panic Salmon and cause him to go to security officials and initiate a diplomatic scandal. Additionally, the KGB suspected that Lore had developed links to the Trotskyists, a deadly ideological taint during the time of Stalin's Terror.[8]

There is no report about exactly how the KGB cut its ties with Lore, but there is no mention of him or "Willy"/Salmon after April 1937. While the KGB developed other State Department sources, some of senior rank, none would have the broad access to DOS communications that "Willy"/Salmon had had from 1934 to 1937.[9]

"Morris," the Mole in the Justice Department

An important Soviet espionage source in the Justice Department in the late 1930s was later exposed but avoided prosecution and was lauded by some academicians as an innocent victim of McCarthyism. In 1937 the KGB New York station chief, Peter Gutzeit, notified Moscow of a new source it was developing in Washington:

"In the local fellowcountryman [Communist] organization, there is a comrade who studied at Princeton University with Morris [Abraham Glasser]. He enlisted his help for the Communist movement. They contacted the party organizer in Washington. M. did not officially join the cell. He started procuring documents from his department. We instructed "Sound" [Jacob Golos] to go to Washington and arrange with the party organizer to have him handed over

to a different person, 'who is apparently a worker in the local fellowcountryman organization.' The party organizer spoke with M., and the latter agreed.
The person is new, but not the line. In order to be consistent throughout the
connection with M., this line required someone who would not arouse any suspicions on M.'s part (knowledge of the language, local conditions, etc.) for
being of foreign descent, and given these prerequisites, there was unfortunately no other candidate besides Brit [KGB officer Armand Feldman]. . . . I
ask that you look kindly on Brit's actual report on M., which could have been
much better both in content and style. Having become American enough to
pass for an American, he simultaneously lost his command of Russian. Dialec-
tics."

Real name—Abe Glasser. 22 year old bachelor, lives in W. Works in the
Anti-Trust Division of the Department of Justice. M. works in a separate office
studying various problems and receives materials from the Justice Department
archives. He said that he does not work for the money. Brit, however, gave him
$50 to treat some secretaries he knew.

Abraham Glasser, born in New Jersey in 1914, had compiled a distinguished academic record at Rutgers and Princeton Universities before
coming to Washington in December 1935 to join the Justice Department
as a "special attorney assigned to research." (Abraham Glasser had no relationship to Harold Glasser, discussed elsewhere.) Gutzeit's memo
makes clear that initially the KGB let Glasser believe he was reporting to
the American Communist Party and not to the agency of a foreign power.
A later KGB New York station report reinforced the point, commenting
that Glasser was "glad that he is not a spy and that he works to improve
America" and "gave materials on work being carried out against the
American Communist organizations and foreign spies."[10]

While Glasser worked on a number of research tasks, his principal
job was writing "The Use of Military Force by the Federal Government
in Domestic Disturbances, 1900–1938," a report that focused on government use of military force in labor strikes and race riots and against
subversives. His assignment gave him access not only to Justice Department files (including those of the FBI) but also to reports from the Military Intelligence Division of the War Department. He used his assignment to build a massive collection of documents. His research files,
designated the "Glasser Files," are part of the Justice Department records
at the National Archives, and the microfilm version fills nineteen reels.
From the point of view of the KGB, it was an ideal assignment for a
source. In January 1938 New York station officer Gayk Ovakimyan told
Moscow Center about Glasser's research assignment, noting, "In the mid-

dle of '37, in connection with work that had been assigned to him, he was granted special authorization to access the War Intelligence archive," and that using this access, ""Morris" [Glasser] obtained: a) materials of Amer. War Intelligence on the activities of Russian White Guard organizations in Manchuria and China (report from intelligence agent in China). b) top secret material on the so-called 'partisan movement in Siberia' (from an agent in Warsaw). c) [materials] on the internal economic and polit. situation in Germany. He obtained them at the end of Jan. '38. + Materials from the archive of the Justice Department, in particular, the FBI." Ovakimyan also reported delivery of

"The latest materials from Amer. mil. intelligence secured by us through source "Morris." . . . 1) P. I.—top-secret reports from the Amer. mil. attaché in Germany about issues of Hitler's for. policy, the tactics of German diplomacy, the tasks of the German fascists regarding the USSR, etc. The reports cover the period Nov. '35 through November '37. 2) P. II.—top-secret reports from the Amer. mil. attaché in Poland about the following issues: the separatist movement in the Ukraine, the Ukrainian mil. org. in Poland, Poland's assistance to the Ukraine during the revolution. The reports cover the period '30– '33. 3) P. III–IV.—Top-secret reports from the Amer. mil. attaché in Switzerland about the following issues: the international policies of certain Europ. countries, the work of the League of Nations, as well as about the issue of the Italo-German-Japanese alliance. Material covers '35–'37."

Given the foreign subject matter of the material Glasser delivered, he surely understood by that time that the destination of his material was not the American Communist Party headquarters in New York.[11]

Ovakimyan also reported that Glasser had been tasked to help expose a "provocateur" in the CPUSA. In Justice Department archives, he had discovered two reports, one on a conference of CPUSA cadres held in Chicago on 18 January 1938, and the other of party activists in Detroit from September 1937. Ovakimyan told Moscow:

"because in the process of investigating this affair, we studied the autobiographies of most of the members of the Central Committee and local fellowcountryman organization and, in particular, of the aforementioned participants in the conference, we automatically narrowed the candidacy down, by process of elimination, to William Weinstone." Sound [Golos] was instructed to obtain biographical information about him. 42 years old. From '29 to '30, he was the district organizer for NY. In '31–'32–delegate in the Amer. section of the Comintern in Moscow. Returned in '33. Serious disagreements with Browder. From '34 to the pres.—leader of the Michigan organization, which has its center in Detroit.[12]

Weinstone, a founding member of the American Communist Party and one of its leading figures in the 1920s, had challenged Earl Browder for supremacy in the CPUSA in the early 1930s. He had lost but still retained a significant post as district organizer for the influential Michigan party organization. By 1938 he was already in bad odor in the CPUSA because of his rocky stewardship of the Michigan organization and dissatisfaction with his relationship with Communist cadres in the United Auto Workers. When this report charging him with being an FBI informant (for which there is no independent evidence) reached Moscow and, presumably, Browder (via Golos), it further undermined Weinstone's standing. In mid-1938 Browder removed him from his position and demoted him to party educational work, ending his career in the party's executive leadership. Despite being shunted aside, Weinstone remained in the CPUSA and in his position supervising party education programs loyally promoted whatever was the ideological line of the day. In 1951 the government convicted him of sedition under the Smith Act, and he was sentenced to two years in prison, something that would not have happened if he had ever cooperated with the FBI as Ovakimyan believed.[13]

Glasser also alerted the KGB to the FBI's opening of an investigation of Jacob Golos and "World Tourists," his CPUSA-linked travel firm. He was, however, able to reassure the Soviets that the Bureau was mainly interested in Golos's role in the recruitment and transport to Europe of volunteers for the International Brigades and was unaware of Golos's links to the KGB.[14]

Glasser's work for the KGB was interrupted in mid-1938, when Armand Feldman, his Soviet contact, vanished (see chapter 6), and Gutzeit noted, "Brit [Feldman] disappeared with Morris's [Glasser's] materials: a report on the cultivation of an espionage ring in the U.S." Fearing Feldman had defected, the KGB New York station deactivated Glasser at the end of June 1938. However, as the USSR prepared to sign its non-aggression pact with Nazi Germany, Moscow pressed to reestablish contact with this valued source. In August 1939 Moscow Center told Ovakimyan, the new KGB New York station chief: "'We think that at present, it would be expedient to renew ties with Morris. Now in particular, the American intelligence documents he gave could be of great interest to us. Taking into account the fact that Morris might have been betrayed by Brit, it is essential to be very careful when renewing ties with him and to keep up the connection infrequently. One meeting per month is quite enough, and these infrequent meetings could be arranged in a way that would preclude failure. It is essential to send someone local to contact Morris, rather than contact him directly yourself.'"[15]

The New York station moved cautiously, but Glasser had no inhibitions. In November 1939 Moscow Center noted that Glasser had already delivered "1) An excerpt from a file of the Dies Committee (the Dept. of Justice requested these materials from the Committee, and Morris [Glasser] made a copy; 2) Excerpts from the files and correspondence of the Justice Dept. pertaining to various matters; 3) copies of reports by the West Coast Division of U.S. War Intelligence (San Francisco) for 1918–1920. ''Morris' obtained all the aforementioned materials on his own initiative and without our permission. We have not yet recommenced work with him and think it is essential to wait until the investigation by the Dies Committee is over.'"[16]

Moscow Center planned to reactivate Glasser in 1941 through the new illegal station chief it had dispatched to the United States, but the latter died when a U-boat sunk his ship in transit. In August 1941 the KGB reestablished direct contact with Glasser through one of its American couriers, Zalmond Franklin. Franklin brought back the bad news that Glasser "has come under suspicion and was dismissed from his job. He is charged with belonging to the fellowcountrymen [CPUSA] and passing secret documents to the Germans on the instructions of the fellowcountryman organization." (The FBI charged that Glasser was cooperating with the Soviet Union. The reference to Glasser passing documents "to the Germans" was either a misstatement by Franklin or "Glan," the KGB New York station officer who sent the report to Moscow, or a reflection of the FBI's assumption that in light of the Nazi-Soviet Pact, Soviet spies in the United States directly or indirectly assisted German intelligence.) A follow-up message stated:

"Morris [Glasser] was connected to our operative 'Brit' [Feldman], who suddenly and mysteriously disappeared. There is reason to believe that 'Brit' was taken by FBI agents. . . . To top it all off, the justice operative who was in charge of 'Morris's' case, by the name of McGuire, mentioned the name of 'the Soviet engineer Ovakimyan' and asked whether 'Morris' knows of him. 'Morris' didn't know Ovakimyan, but the mention of some Soviet engineer puzzled him. In short, this whole matter is so mixed up that we're not able to form a clear picture of the situation. We are convinced, however, that unless all of this was a set-up, Morris was given up by one of his numerous connections, and now it's extremely difficult to determine in what area the betrayal took place."[17]

The KGB's suspicion that Feldman had betrayed Glasser, was, in fact, correct. He had quietly moved to Canada hoping to avoid the attention of American security and the KGB. But in 1940 the Royal Canadian Mounted Police (RCMP) located him, and, facing deportation to the Soviet Union, he and his wife provided information about his intelligence work (including a network that procured false Canadian passports) in return for being allowed to stay. The RCMP informed the FBI, and while Feldman refused to return to the United States (and possibly be required to give public testimony), he gave a limited account of his American activity to FBI agents. Among the items he provided were the identification of Ovakimyan as a KGB officer operating under Amtorg cover and Abraham Glasser as a Soviet source in the Justice Department. Mrs. Feldman said her husband had received a gold watch as a reward for developing contact with a Justice Department official "through whom he was able to obtain information which exposed a traitor to the OGPU organization." While Feldman described Glasser as "a fanatical Communist sympathizer" with whom he had met several times, he told the FBI that the "only information he ever obtained from the individual pertained to Spanish loyalists and efforts to send them planes and munitions." In light of KGB documents, the last statement was inaccurate, and Feldman was seeking to minimize the extent of Glasser's espionage.[18]

With Feldman unwilling to return to the United States and testify, the FBI felt it did not have enough evidence to prosecute Glasser but that at least he could be discharged from federal service. In May 1941, Assistant Attorney General Thurman Arnold, Glasser's boss and friend in the Justice Department, told him that a loyalty issue dealing with communism had come up. Glasser immediately went on the offensive; in a letter to Arnold he denied any involvement with communism and claimed that three years earlier similar charges against him had been made by the stepfather of his then fiancée, now his wife, because that person hated Jews. Arnold accepted Glasser's statements at face value and gave him his wholehearted support. But the FBI was adamant that it had reliable information that Glasser had been delivering Justice Department documents to Soviet agents. In June Attorney General Robert Jackson suspended Glasser without pay and ordered the case reviewed by Assistant Attorney General Matthew McGuire.[19]

Meanwhile the FBI tapped Glasser's telephone and searched his apartment. A special departmental committee heard his case in October. Glasser disavowed any Communist sympathies and claimed he had been shocked by the Nazi-Soviet Pact and disliked the CPUSA. He refused to answer questions about Armand Feldman and claimed not to recognize his photograph. He denied turning over information about the Spanish Civil War to any unauthorized people but admitted to sympathies for the Spanish Republican cause and that he had examined Justice Department files on neutrality issues, munitions shipments, and enlistments of Americans in the International Brigades, all matters that had nothing to do with his assigned research projects. Assistant Attorney General Arnold continued to provide Glasser with unquestioning support. (Arnold had gotten Glasser restored to pay status in August although he remained suspended.)

The outcome was a compromise. The committee found that the charge of Communist sympathies had not been proved and held that Glasser's contacts with people outside the Justice Department were not inspired by disloyalty. On this basis Glasser would later repeatedly state that the Justice Department had "cleared" him in 1941, and his assertion was widely accepted, including by major journalists. But the departmental committee went on to find him guilty of having been "negligent in the manner in which he has treated the contents of the official files and papers of the Department of Justice" and "because of his careless and improper disclosure of official information" he was asked to resign.[20]

Glasser did resign, but once again Thurman Arnold intervened to soften the blow, accepting it "without prejudice," meaning that Glasser could later ask for reinstatement. Arnold also arranged for Glasser to get a new job with the Office of Price Administration (OPA). J. Edgar Hoover, incensed at a Soviet spy's soft landing, sent a futile protest to his new agency. In 1944 and 1946 the OPA asked that Glasser be given Justice Department status as a special assistant attorney general to assist it in handling some agency litigation. On both occasions the Justice Department reviewed the reasons for his earlier separation and denied the requests.[21]

Glasser left the OPA in 1946 and was appointed a lecturer at Rutgers Law School in May 1947, promoted to assistant professor in 1948, and became an associate professor with tenure in 1950. A series of newspaper stories in the early 1950s, while never directly naming him, linked Glasser with espionage. They were based on a 1951 congressional report, *The Shameful Years*, which mentioned an unnamed Justice Department employee, forced to resign, who then worked for the OPA and who was described as a spy on the same level as Alger Hiss or Judith Coplon. The House Committee on Un-American Activities finally subpoenaed Glasser on 18 March 1953. He was argumentative and frequently sparred with committee members, distributing a statement calling his subpoena an attempt to "terrorize college teachers." Invoking the Fifth Amendment, he declined to answer any questions regarding contact with Ovakimyan, Feldman, or any other Soviet agents. After his testimony, I. F. Stone denounced the persecution of a man of "liberal or progressive outlook who, to the best of my knowledge, has never been charged with being a Communist by any responsible person."[22]

The president of Rutgers, however, suspended Glasser for violating university policy by taking the Fifth Amendment and convened a faculty committee to investigate. Testifying under oath, Glasser falsely assured the committee that he had already answered all the questions asked him during prior investigations and therefore felt entitled to decline to answer those posed by Congress. He justified invoking the Fifth Amendment because he feared being indicted for perjury in the charged atmosphere of "hysteria." He claimed he was particularly concerned that the government might produce Armand Feldman—whom he insisted he had never met—to falsely testify that he had committed espionage. Finally, he proclaimed that his refusal to answer questions about contact with Soviet agents was based on a principled moral position. While once again denying party membership, he admitted to sympathy with "certain important objectives" of the CPUSA. Asked with what things he sympathized, he cited the CPUSA's effort to enlarge democracy to economic democracy and asserted that its objectives were parallel to those of Roosevelt's New Deal. He said he opposed the party's dogmatism and acceptance of intellectual guidance from Moscow.[23]

The committee found that Glasser had violated Rutgers's policy that faculty should not invoke the Fifth Amendment and recommended that he be permitted to resign from the school. He resigned. As a consequence, the American Association of University Professors in 1956 and the Association of American Law Schools in 1958 censured Rutgers for failure to observe standards of academic due process. Glasser found work as a lawyer doing research for other attorneys before retiring and moving to Massachusetts, where he died in 1976.[24]

David Wahl

In the course of its investigation of persons identified by Elizabeth Bentley as Soviet spies, the FBI heard from one informant that David Wahl was "a master spy." Those files were heavily redacted, few details about

what had led the informant to this conclusion have ever surfaced, and
Wahl has been little mentioned in books and articles about Soviet espi-
onage. Documents in Vassiliev's notebooks offer a glimpse of some of
Wahl's work for Soviet intelligence and hints of his importance.[25]

Wahl was born in Cleveland, Ohio, in 1909. He graduated from Ober-
lin College and earned a master's degree in librarianship from Western
Reserve University. After initial employment at the New York Public Library (NYPL), he worked at the Library of Congress from 1937 to 1942
and was then on the staff of the Board of Economic Warfare. In 1943
Representative Martin Dies identified Wahl as a hidden Communist and
demanded that he be fired. Testifying before Dies's Special Committee
on Un-American Activities in 1943, Wahl denied any link to the CPUSA,
insisted he was not associated with a CPUSA shop paper at the NYPL or
the Communist-aligned American Peace Mobilization, and disclaimed
any association with such Communist union officials as Eleanor Nelson.
He admitted, however, that he was chairman of the board of trustees of
the Washington Book Shop but denied that it had any Communist links.
(The Washington Book Shop was dominated by members of the CPUSA.)
A subcommittee of the House Appropriations Committee headed by
Representative John H. Kerr (D-NC) also investigated Wahl, and he
again adamantly denied any link to any Communist organization. He
brazened it out, and although the Kerr subcommittee recommended and
Congress agreed to deny funds for the salaries of three federal employees judged to be secret Communists, Wahl was not among them.[26]

Nonetheless, Wahl left the Foreign Economic Administration (into
which the BEW had merged) late in 1943 and found a position with the
Office of Strategic Services, although what he did there is unclear. The
OSS demobilized in late 1945, and he went to work for the American
Jewish Conference as secretary of its Washington office in 1946, dealing
with issues of displaced persons and immigration to Palestine. Wahl became the first executive director of Americans for Haganah the following
year. Created to raise money and political support for the self-defense
force that became the nucleus of the Israeli Army, it was largely funded
by a well-connected, self-made New York garment manufacturer, Abraham Feinberg. Feinberg had befriended Harry Truman in 1944, when
the latter was vice-president; raised the money to finance his highly successful whistle-stop railroad tour during the 1948 campaign; and played
a major role in soliciting Truman's support for the establishment of the
state of Israel.

As executive secretary of Americans for Haganah, Wahl was in frequent contact with American diplomats and politicians. He also traveled to Israel in both 1948 and 1949 and met with such figures as Teddy Kolleck and David Ben-Gurion. Americans for Haganah mounted campaigns against supporters of Menachem Begin's Irgun in the United States, with Wahl charging that Begin represented a "fascist" threat to the democratic Israeli government. Once the Haganah had been transformed into the Israeli Defense Force, the organization agreed to change its name to Americans United for Israel, but it became embroiled in intra-Zionist politics, with the Zionist Organization of America insisting that it should remain the premier support group for Israel in the United States and the Israeli government fretting that *Israel Speaks* (the group's newsletter, which had replaced *Haganah Speaks*) should not get involved in internal American or Israeli politics, and Wahl and Feinberg eventually allowed it to wither away.

Wahl had, in fact, been a Soviet intelligence agent from the mid-1930s until at least the late 1940s. A Moscow communication in 1948 suggested reestablishing connections with an agent code-named "Pink." Wahl's real name never appears, but the details fit Wahl and no one else. "Pink" was described as the "ex. secretary of the Jewish American organization 'Americans for Haganah.'" A Moscow Center memo went on to state:

Recruited in '36 by GRU agent handler Aronberg, who handled him until '45. In Apr. '45, having become displeased with Aronberg's conspicuous behavior and crude working methods, "P" ["Pink"/Wahl] refused to work with him and reported this to MGB [the KGB of that era] agent "Vendor" [Harry Kagan], whom he had known for a long time as a member of the CP USA. . . . With C's [Center's] approval, "Vadim" [Gorsky] contacted P. on 18.04.45. In November '45, he was deactivated. . . . He participated in party work until '37. The Americans suspected him of belonging to the CPUSA. In '41–'43, he twice found himself under investigation on suspicion of being affiliated with various Communists, but in '45, by a special resolution of Congress, these charges were dropped and he was rehabilitated.

Philip Aronberg, Wahl's recruiter, was a long-serving CPUSA cadre whom Nicholas Dozenberg (himself a former CPUSA official turned GRU agent) recruited into GRU service in the 1930s and who later appeared to have occasionally undertaken KGB assignments.[27]

Aside from his role in recruiting Philip and Mary Jane Keeney (see chapter 5), nothing is known of the substance of Wahl's work for GRU from 1936 to 1945. When he shifted to the KGB in 1945, he worked for only a brief time before he was deactivated, and what assistance he provided the KGB in this period is unknown. The earliest mention of him in KGB communications came in June 1945, when Moscow received from British diplomat (and KGB agent) Donald Maclean a lengthy evaluation of American "domestic and foreign policies and about Truman and his circle" that he had obtained from British ambassador Lord Halifax. The KGB knew little about Truman and welcomed the information, but it was also anxious to get a measure of how much it could rely on Halifax's judgment about the new American president and his advisers. Consequently it ordered the KGB New York station to assign some of its American sources, including "Pink"/Wahl, to provide background information on Truman to assist in verifying Halifax's conclusions. In October Anatoly Gorsky reported that the Foreign Economic Administration (a wartime agency) had been abolished and "Pink" had not been able to find a government job, so he had "decided for now to become a Washington representative of a conservative Jewish American conference," a reference to Wahl's new position at the American Jewish Conference. Gorsky suggested that the KGB ante up $10,000 to enable Wahl to join his brother in starting "a small company in Washington as a cover." Andrey Graur, a senior officer at Moscow Center, wrote on Gorsky's cable, "Clearly we are not going to give $10,000." Wahl was then deactivated.[28]

Nearly two years later, Grigory Dolbin, KGB Washington station chief, informed Moscow that one of the station's co-optees, Soviet diplomat Mikhail Vavilov, "ran into 'Pink,' who works at the 'American Jewish Conference.'" They were meeting frequently, and Vavilov "receives legal oral information"—that is, Vavilov was meeting Wahl in his official role as a Soviet diplomat listening to Wahl discuss Palestine and did not have a covert "agent" relationship with him. Moscow promptly replied that Wahl was one of "the neighbors' [GRU's] agents." Moreover, it warned: "'Pink' [Wahl] is actively being investigated by Amer. counterintelligence. The neighbors' [GRU's] work with "Pink" and his group was very careless. . . . Any contact between Soviets and "Pink" or anyone from his group 'is very dangerous.'" Moscow Center went on to instruct Dolbin (a new and unprepared station chief) that he "should not have tolerated 'Oleg's' [Vavilov's] anarch. [anarchic] activities" in meeting frequently with former GRU agents without supervision and to order Vavilov to cut all contact with Wahl because of the threat that it might trigger American counterintelligence interest.[29]

Dolbin took Moscow's warning to heart and ordered Vavilov to break the connection. Vavilov, a diplomat on temporary assignment to the KGB and not a professional officer, grumbled that he would lose access to information he needed for his diplomatic work but complied. Wahl, however, proved persistent. Ignoring hints that the encounters were undesirable, he visited Vavilov at the embassy, insisting that he was not under surveillance but finally agreeing not to meet personally but to mail Vavilov "official materials" from the American Jewish Conference.[30]

Wahl's shift from the American Jewish Conference to his new job as executive secretary of Americans for Haganah stimulated the KGB's interest. Moscow Center put aside its earlier concerns, and in May 1948 Sergey Striganov, the first secretary of the Soviet Embassy and also a KGB co-optee, reestablished agent contact with him. In August the station reported to Moscow that they were meeting every three weeks. Wahl, the KGB Washington station explained, "currently occupies a key position in work pertaining to Palestine. He has a chance to receive info. on the State Dep. line." The station also asked for information on whether he had ever been paid for his intelligence and whether he should be offered money "'as a stimulus for him to step up his work with us.'" He had also been asked "to select someone from the State Dept. or FBI for recruitment. Pink promised to do so."[31]

By the end of 1948, however, Aleksandr Panyushkin, the new ambassador and KGB station chief, became fearful about the growing assault on Soviet intelligence. Warning Moscow that news in the press suggested that mass arrests of people named by Bentley were in the offing, he thought continued use of old agents such as Wahl was risky and that, in any case, Wahl's information was "of no value." The last mention of Wahl appeared in 1950: ""Saushkin" [Striganov] has worked with P ["Pink"/Wahl] since '48. Since he started working, Pink recruited 5 people and gave a large amount of valuable doc. information. He never aroused suspicion. He went to Israel in '48, where he met with its leaders." The memo added: "Later transferred to the GRU." Exactly why Wahl had been returned to Soviet military intelligence is unclear. But his GRU connection, if it remained a live one, might have later given the USSR access to some very significant information.[32]

It is not known what Wahl did between 1950 and 1956. But in 1956 he became chief librarian at the Weizmann Institute in Israel, remaining in that position until 1963. One of its major financial benefactors was Abraham Feinberg, Truman's old friend and Wahl's former boss at Americans for Haganah. Feinberg remained committed to building up Israeli security. In the late 1950s Ben-Gurion's government used him to secretly finance construction of the Dimona nuclear reactor, where Israel built its nuclear weapons in a program carefully hidden from the United States.

Feinberg led a secret fund-raising campaign for the nuclear project, which garnered about $40 million ($250 million in 2008 dollars) from "some twenty-five millionaires." Many of the scientists working on the project had affiliations with the Weizmann Institute, Israel's preeminent technical research center. Was David Wahl still working for GRU while he lived in Israel? Did he ever break with Soviet intelligence? These questions are, for now, unanswered. Wahl came back to the United States in 1963 and died three years later.[33]

Henry Ware

Henry Ware's name never surfaced publicly during the investigations into Soviet espionage. Even though the FBI briefly investigated him, he escaped intense surveillance and personal or professional problems. He had been, however, a useful KGB source for a period. It was Ware's good luck that no defector had known him and he had managed to disengage from the KGB in time to avoid American counterintelligence.

Ware was born July 11, 1908, in New Jersey, the second son in a family steeped in the abolitionism and reformism of liberal Protestantism. His father, Edward, although born in Georgia, was not a native Southerner but the son of Edmund Asa Ware, a leading figure in the American Missionary Association and later the Freedman's Bureau, who was instrumental in the founding of Atlanta University (AU) as a center for Negro education after the Civil War. The elder Ware served as AU's first president from 1869 until his death in 1885. Edward, born in 1874, graduated from Yale and after serving in several positions at AU, including chaplain, became its third president in 1907. During his tenure he clashed with the school's most prominent faculty member, W. E. B. DuBois, whose increasingly radical writings threatened philanthropic support; DuBois resigned to join the National Association for the Advancement of Colored People in 1910. Edward remained president until 1919 when, suffering from tuberculosis, he moved for treatment to Colorado and then Claremont, California, dying in 1927. His widow, Alice, joined numerous Communist fronts in the 1930s and early 1940s, including the American Peace Mobilization, League of American Writers, and National Council of American-Soviet Friendship. The *Daily Worker* positively reviewed *Scorched Earth,* her play about Soviet partisan warfare behind German lines, and she also wrote *Mighty Wind A' Blowing* for the Communist-aligned New Theatre League in 1936 and *The Freedom Bell* for the National Negro Congress (also a Communist-controlled body) in 1944.

Henry Ware was raised on the Atlanta University campus. He moved to California with his parents and attended Pomona College, from which he graduated with honors in 1932. Shortly afterwards, he went to Moscow, where he taught at the Anglo-American School; studied at the Plekhanov Institute of National Economy; and wrote for the *Moscow Daily News,* an English-language newspaper controlled by the Soviet regime and edited by former Comintern operative Mikhail Borodin (father of KGB operative Norman Borodin). A 1948 KGB memo on Ware stated: "In '35, he was recruited by the OO NKVD USSR to cover the American colony in the Soviet Union." The OO NKVD was the "special department" of the NKVD (predecessor to the KGB) that conducted internal counterintelligence. In other words, Ware was an informant reporting on fellow Americans in Moscow. The KGB memo also noted that Ware's NKVD Moscow handler, Mulyarov, had been arrested in 1938 during the purge of the security services and confessed that Ware had recruited him to spy for American intelligence in 1935. The memo noted that this confession "'was not verified,'" a polite euphemism indicating that Mulyarov had been forced to confess to non-existent crimes.[34]

Ware returned to the United States in 1937 and obtained his master's and doctorate in economics from Columbia University. He moved to Washington in 1940, becoming acting chief in the Office of International Trade in the Commerce Department. He was not recontacted by Soviet intelligence until 1942, after the New York station "obtained a positive reference" about him from the CPUSA and, using Elizabeth Zarubin, it "independently decided to recruit him." From 1942 to 1944 Ware provided "information about his agency's [Commerce Department's] activities." In his summary report of his tenure as station chief, Zarubin noted: "With tips from fellowcountrymen [Communists] we recruited 'Vick' Henry . . . , assistant chief of the Russian desk at the Commerce Department." A letter from Moscow to Zarubin in March 1943 concluded: "'Judging by the information you have received from 'Vick' [Ware] to date, the section he works in possesses information not only on our country. Let us know what tasks in obtaining valuable information for us you have given him, considering his capabilities, and how he is carrying them out.'"[35]

Zarubin was ultimately disappointed in Ware, noting that he "'did not fulfill the hopes we pinned on'" him, mostly because he left the Commerce Department to join the Army "'and therefore could not be put to wider use by us.'" He did, however, provide leads for other KGB sources from among his former economist acquaintances at Columbia. Referring to the recruitment of Bela Gold, a government economist, Zarubin noted:

"'We first learned about him from Vick as someone who was close to fellowcountrymen [CPUSA] and was well disposed to us.'" After Golos vetted Gold, the KGB recruited both him and his wife Sonia. Likewise, Ware recommended William Remington (also an economist) "'as a very serious and devoted comrade.'"[36]

The KGB's greatest disappointment with Ware, however, came after he entered the U.S. Army. Ware's Russian-language skills landed him a position with the American Military Mission to Russia (headed by General John Deane), where he served as an interpreter. To have a Soviet source as Deane's interpreter would have been an intelligence coup, but the 1948 KGB report on Ware explained, "In Oct. '44, Vick was in Moscow, on the staff of Deane's mission. The 2nd Directorate of the MGB attempted to establish agent ties, but he refused." He went on to translate at Tehran, Yalta, and Potsdam and at Germany's surrender negotiations and served as a liaison officer in the Ukraine. Ware came back to the Commerce Department to work on Soviet economic issues after the war.[37]

Ware briefly attracted the FBI's attention in June 1946, when a wiretap on the home of William Remington picked up a telephone call from Mrs. Ware and the Bureau learned that he worked at the Commerce Department and was in frequent contact with Joseph Gregg and Remington, both identified by Elizabeth Bentley as Soviet sources. But after a cursory investigation the FBI turned its attention elsewhere. In the 1950s Henry Ware went into business with his wife and also worked for the National Education Association before establishing a bartering service in Fairfax County, Virginia, that was emulated around the world. A founder of the Fairfax Unitarian Universalist Church, president of the Friends of the Library, and an adviser to the Boy Scouts, he died in 1999.[38]

William Akets

The KGB had another, earlier, source in the Commerce Department, but frustratingly little is known about him. William Akets was a professional staff member of the Commerce Department's Bureau of Foreign and Domestic Commerce. A 1933 KGB memo described Akets as

"a lieutenant in the reserve corps of the Army Intelligence corps. Speaks, reads and writes Japanese fluently. Was on active service in Japan and China and the Philippines during and following the World War. Is kept in more than ordinary close touch with current operations of the intelligence corps work at present time, engages in special studies at the War College and is better posted on Japanese internal affairs than most reserve officers or regular officers for that matter, as he keeps in close touch with Far Eastern economic data through employment in the Bureau of Foreign and Domestic Commerce. His own specialty is Scandinavian Commerce."

The KGB reported Akets providing "military information, about mil. industry" with specific material on American intelligence reports on the Japanese military, the delivery of American military aircraft to China to assist it against Japan, increases in U.S. naval shipbuilding, and the American Army's attitudes toward diplomatic recognition of the USSR. But after a brief burst of productivity in 1933, Akets is not mentioned again.[39]

Gerald Graze

Gerald Graze was one-half of an unusual set of brother spies (Stanley, who worked for the OSS, is discussed in chapter 5). Although the FBI concluded that both were secret Communists and possibly involved in covert activities, it never had enough evidence to prosecute either one. Their uncooperative testimony before congressional committees attracted little press coverage. No defector identified them as sources. Their cover names, "Arena" and "Dan," appeared in deciphered KGB cables, but NSA/FBI analysts misidentified the former and were unable to identify the latter.

Their parents were Russian Jews living in Great Britain, where Gerald was born in 1914 along with another brother, Cyril. Several younger children were born in New York, including Stanley in 1918, where Alfred Graze owned a neon sign company. Gerald and Stanley both graduated from the City College of New York.

In 1936 Iskhak Akhmerov asked Josef Peters "'to find me one or two decent chaps among the Washington officials'" who were part of the CPUSA's underground organization in Washington that Peters supervised. Peters in turn asked Victor Perlo, leader of one of the larger Washington underground party units, for a recommendation, and he suggested Gerald Graze, who, with his wife Ruth, belonged to Perlo's CPUSA group. Peters told Perlo that Graze, who was quickly given the code name "Arena," was needed "'for special fraternal [Communist] work.'" Akhmerov met with Graze in July 1937 and told Moscow Center:

"I established a connection with an official of the Civil Service Commission and had two meetings with him. We will call this official by the cover name

"Arena." . . . "Arena" and his wife are members of the Comparty; moreover, he is in the Communist organization illegally. "Storm" [Peters] introduced me to "Arena" as a Comparty official and told "Arena" that he should help me any way he can. "Arena's" work consists of investigating claims by officials who are dissatisfied with their position or salary at work. "Arena" thus has the opportunity to find out every detail about the nature of the work of an official who submits a claim. During my meetings with "Arena," I asked him in depth about the sort of work he does and explained which materials were of interest to us. These materials were brought by "Arena" to the second meeting.

I asked that in the future, "Arena" write down the addresses of persons who were of interest to us, and try to determine, by means of discreet personal conversations, the political identity of various officials whose cases he will be investigating, along with their financial situations, and so forth. "Arena" promised to carry out my request. I hope that "Arena" could become useful to us as a talent-spotting agent. He could also find out what job openings are available and where. We could then attempt to plant someone close to us in some government department."

Akhmerov also noted that Graze at this early stage "'thinks that I am a local Communist who works for a Communist organization.'" By 1938 that illusion had vanished: "'I haven't told them [Gerald and Ruth Graze] explicitly that they work directly for Hammer [USSR], but from the nature of our conversations they understand that Arena's materials are sent to Hammer and that they benefit the fraternal movement and Hammer.'"[40]

Moscow was intrigued by Graze's potential but worried that his ties to the CPUSA posed security risks and that Peters knew about his "'special party assignments.'" It told Akhmerov that Graze "'must be completely isolated from the Comparty'" and "'be known to everyone around him as nothing more than an average joe.'" Dutifully, the KGB New York station reported that it had arranged to cut Gerald off from CPUSA activities while continuing to supply him with party literature and to collect party dues ($10 a month). Akhmerov also had to take on some ideological training, such as when Graze voiced misgivings about the charges that high-level Soviet leaders had become traitors. Akhmerov educated him "'about the roots of counterrevolutionary Trotskyism.'"[41]

Gerald Graze's position gave the KGB the opportunity to access U.S. government personnel records. On the KGB's instructions, Graze rented a small apartment for $25 a month that was used by Norman Borodin, his direct KGB liaison, to photograph materials Graze brought by. He did not receive a salary but "occasionally, he would be given a one-time payment." Whatever he was paid, Graze was worth it. A report written in 1940 noted: "'Arena [Graze] gave us lists with layouts and detailed work descriptions for employees of the American secret police, military and naval intelligence agencies, the secret service (intelligence agency of the Treasury Department), the State Department, and other important government agencies.'"[42]

The connection with Graze was broken in late 1939, when Akhmerov returned to Moscow and the illegal station ceased to operate. But in February 1941 Moscow instructed Gayk Ovakimyan, New York legal station chief, to make contact with him at the Civil Service Commission with an eye for opportunities to develop or insert sources in the FBI, the Dies Committee, and the Immigration and Naturalization Service (INS). The message advised: "'At one time 'Arena' [Graze] gave us very valuable materials.'" While "'we worked with him under the guise of providing assistance to a fraternal movement, he realized that his materials were being passed to us.'" But Ovakimyan was arrested in May, and the KGB New York station, already at a low ebb, did not follow up. Moscow dispatched a new station chief, Vasily Zarubin, and in November 1941 sent him suggestions on reviving old agents: "'"Arena,' [Graze] . . . , deactivated with Jung's [Akhmerov's] departure, must be brought back and used. . . . 'Arena,' if he continues to work in the civil service, is of interest for his very specific capability of obtaining interesting information.'" But it was not until April 1942 that Akhmerov, back in the United States, reestablished contact and found that Graze was no longer at the Civil Service Commission. He had moved first to the Office of Price Administration and, in 1943, fearing he would be drafted unless he had a military-related position, took a routine administrative job with the Navy Department, severely curtailing his access to useful information. In a report summarizing his work directing the New York station from 1942 to mid-1944, Vasily Zarubin noted that after his revival Graze "'has never had access to information that interests us, and 'Mer' [Akhmerov] uses him mostly for an apartment in which he can stay during his visits to Carthage [Washington]. In addition, 'Arena' can be used as a talent-spotter and courier.'" There are numerous references to "Arena"/Graze as a part of the KGB's agent network from 1942 to 1945 but, as Zarubin's summary suggests, few mentions of specific information that he supplied. In 1946 there is a reference to his having earlier supplied "materials on radar, sonar, and other naval equipment," likely from the period after Zarubin left in mid-1944.[43]

While less of a source than he had been earlier, Graze did become part of the KGB's support structure for its clandestine operations. Not just Akhmerov but also his wife, Helen Lowry, a courier for the KGB's illegal station, stayed at Graze's apartment when on missions to Washington (hotels and housing were in notoriously short supply during the war). The KGB also kept a camera there, and operatives photographed material furnished by a variety of sources. (The Grazes' apartment was not, however, used as a safe house for meetings between KGB officers and agents because it shared a thin wall (through which sound easily carried) with an apartment occupied by an American Army G-2 lieutenant colonel.) In November 1944 liaison with Gerald shifted from the illegal station under Akhmerov to the legal station run by Anatoly Gorsky. Joseph Katz became the Grazes' liaison and he trained Gerald in photography, but it was a difficult task. Gorsky reported:

"Materials for 'Raid' [Perlo] are photographed by 'Arena' [Graze]. We used to think that he was a good photographer. In practice, however, it turned out that 'Arena' has no idea how to take photographs. 'X' [Katz] led a thorough and detailed tutorial with him, but 'Arena' nevertheless ruined two batches of 'Tan's' [Magdoff's] and 'Raid's' materials. Now he is slowly getting the hang of it. 'Arena' himself was very eager to start photographing materials, but his wife opposed it for a long time because she did not want to be put at risk and only agreed 'grudgingly.' As we have already written, 'Arena's' wife works somewhere of interest to us, but 'X' has so far not been able to get any substantial or interesting material from her."

Ruth Graze worked in a section of Army G-2 that evaluated the state of Japanese radio and radar manufacturing. Katz was annoyed to learn that she had recently had access to a valuable report on Mitsubishi equipment, and he reported: "'It did not occur to her to take notes of any kind or to make a copy of it, even though she had had it in her house. I suggested that it wouldn't be a bad idea to photograph this report, seeing as he has a camera and is familiar with photography techniques. They were both horrified at the thought. I explained to her that in my opinion, her place of work was of enormous interest and assured her that we would take all possible precautions to ensure her own safety and the safety of the work itself.'" But there is no indication that Ruth's reluctance to become an active source was ever overcome.[44]

Gerald Graze also continued to function as a talent spotter. He had first been recommended to Soviet intelligence by Victor Perlo through Jacob Golos. Graze then brought Perlo to Akhmerov's attention in 1939, and the latter told Moscow Center:

Perlo works at the Brookings Institution in Washington. An old friend. At one time, Arena had been connected with Storm [Josef Peters] through Perlo. A. ["Arena"/Graze] and P. had belonged to the same fraternal group. When A. joined us for good, he withdrew from this group. They occasionally meet as friends. . . . "Arena considers him a loyal and very well-developed fraternal member [Communist]. During my last meeting with Storm, I asked him in passing about Perlo. At one time, he had spoken to me of him as a good worker. Storm affirmed the same thing, saying that he was a good, loyal, and developed Marxist. They are using him for the fraternal's [CPUSA's] purposes."

But nothing was done in 1939, in part because Moscow Center didn't want to work with Peters, who it feared had been exposed to American counterintelligence by Whittaker Chambers's defection. However, Akhmerov's reconnection with Graze in 1942 revived the Perlo matter. After numerous delays and false starts caused by the need to coordinate among the CPUSA, GRU, and KGB, Victor Perlo and his group of highly productive sources became KGB assets.[45]

Along with all the other agents put at risk by Bentley's defection, Gerald Graze was deactivated in November 1945. But Bentley never mentioned Graze to the FBI and likely had not heard of him from Perlo. He left the Navy Department and soon found a job with the U.S. government's Public Health Service, not an agency of much interest to Soviet intelligence. Joseph Katz was assigned to reestablish the KGB's connection with Graze in 1948, but he could not be located at the time, and the matter was dropped. Senator Joseph McCarthy in a speech to the Senate on 20 February 1950 listed eighty-one cases of what he called serious government security risks. Gerald Graze was number twenty-nine on the list, but McCarthy used only numbers in the speech, not real names. The names were later made available to a subcommittee of the Senate Foreign Relations Committee (referred to in the press as the "Tydings Committee" from its chairman, Senator Millard Tydings), and eventually the real names leaked to the press. Graze, however, had resigned from his government post, likely to avoid scrutiny. McCarthy never pursued his case, and Graze attracted almost no public or press attention. In later years he headed the grants management office at the Albert Einstein College of Medicine, became executive director of the research foundation of the City University of New York, and retired in the 1980s after returning to the National Institutes of Health as special assistant to the associate director for administration. He died in 1999; his obituary never mentioned his few moments of public notoriety when his name had been bandied about as a security risk, and nothing was written, because it was unknown, that he had been a Soviet agent from 1937 to 1945.[46]

Laurence Duggan

After being questioned by FBI agents about possible involvement with Soviet espionage, former State Department official Laurence Duggan jumped to his death in December 1948 from his sixteenth-floor office at the Institute of International Education in New York. A few days later a reporter asked Congressman Karl Mundt, a member of the House Committee on Un-American Activities, when the committee would name other Soviet spies, and he tactlessly responded, "We'll name them as they jump out of windows." Enraged, Duggan's prominent friends—including former undersecretary of state Sumner Welles, former first lady Eleanor Roosevelt, poet Archibald MacLeish, and prominent journalists Drew Pearson and Edward R. Murrow—all defended his reputation and integrity. Attorney General Thomas Clark announced that Duggan was "a loyal employee of the United States Government." Several generations of historians agreed. As late as 1995 historian Arthur Schlesinger, Jr., denounced Yale University Press for publishing a book that referred to Duggan as a Soviet source, angrily writing that it "should not have permitted this book to blacken the name of a man whom many knew as an able public servant." All of them were wrong. Duggan was a Soviet spy, albeit a nervous one requiring repeated reassurances and KGB handholding.[47]

Laurence Duggan was born in 1905, the son of Stephen Duggan, a professor of international relations at City College of New York and founder of the Institute of International Education (IIE), a pioneer in international student exchanges. He studied at Phillips Exeter Academy and Harvard University, graduating in 1927. With the assistance of Sumner Welles, a friend of his father, Duggan got a position at the State Department in 1930. With all the right elite credentials and the backing of Welles, he was on track to rise rapidly.

Once in Washington, Duggan gravitated to a circle of young, pro-Soviet left-wing enthusiasts. In 1934 a KGB informant, "S-17," met with Duggan at the suggestion of Alice Barrows, a secret member of the CPUSA who held a mid-level position in the U.S. Office of Education. Barrows recommended Duggan "as someone who could be useful to us" because of his strong Communist sympathies (he had voted for the CPUSA's William Foster for president in 1932) and closeness to Welles, then an assistant secretary of state. In October 1934 Peter Gutzeit, chief of the KGB legal station, reported: "'The meeting with Duggan took place. He made a decent impression, an educated, sensible, and seasoned man. With a positive reference for him and in view of his sentiments, we may turn directly to the question of recruitment after an appropriate check in two or three follow-up conversations.'"[48]

It was, however, a year before the KGB established a firm relationship with Duggan. The illegal New York station assigned Hede Massing (see chapter 1) as his primary contact. She quickly developed a close relationship with both Larry, who "declared that he is sympathetic toward the USSR," and his wife, Helen Boyd Duggan. Helen impressed her KGB contacts. Although a meeting was not documented, KGB officer Leonid Eitingon appeared to have met with Helen and described her in the following way:

"Helen Boyd—wife of the ch-f of the Lat. Amer. div. at the State Dep. Lives with her husband not far from Washington—half an hour's ride by car. Owns a house, garage, and yard outside the city. The house is tastefully decorated. The rooms are furnished in the antique Amer. style. The silver collections are interesting and attest to her good taste and wealth. Helen Boyd, roughly 28 years old, works on her own for the economic planning commission at the NRA [National Recovery Administration]. An extraordinarily beautiful woman: typically American, a tall blond, reserved, well-read, athletic, and independent. Disappointed after lack of success at the NRA and would like to 'do something real.' Her husband does not have much influence over her. She could be exceedingly useful, if we could succeed in recruiting her. She was very courteous to "Redhead" [Massing] and invited her to stay for a week to discuss 'Communism in America.'"

Massing herself wrote:

"During this time I met with Helen very frequently and saw Larry twice. On both occasions we held lengthy discussions about a future war and about the Brazilian situation, regarding which Larry openly declared that he stands 'on the other side,' implying us. . . . Larry also spoke rather candidly about the extremely negative role played by the U.S. official Hugh Gibson in the Prestes-Barron affair; he was deeply dismayed (and voiced his disapproval in the State Department) that an Amer-n diplomat was functioning as a provocateur. He asked my opinion and conveyed to me 'more information concerning the participation of the Germans (Berger) in this affair, in case it is of interest to me.' He spoke at length about Gibson's career as [Herbert] Hoover's right-hand man and of his recent activities in China."[49]

The "Prestes-Barron affair" that Massing and Duggan discussed referred to an abortive coup in 1935 against Brazil's Vargas regime led by

Luís Prestes with Communist International support. Brazilian authorities arrested Victor Barron, an American Communist sent to Brazil as the Comintern's radio operator; a man carrying an American passport in the name of Harry Berger; and Berger's wife, carrying an American passport as Machla Lencsyski. U.S. ambassador Hugh Gibson intervened, believing three Americans had been arrested. But checks with the U.S. passport office established that the Berger passport was false. The real Harry Berger had died as an infant. The CPUSA, which ran a false passport operation for the Soviets, had procured a copy of the dead infant's birth certificate and supplied perjuring witnesses to support the passport application in the name of Harry Berger. The fake Berger was Arthur Ewert, a German Comintern operative. Ewert's wife's false passport had been gained using the U.S. naturalization papers of Machla Lencsyski. The real Lencsyski claimed that her papers had been lost. However, her brother was one of the perjuring witnesses to the fake Berger passport. Once the Bergers' American citizenship was shown to be bogus, Gibson dropped interest in them. But Gibson continued to negotiate with Brazilian authorities about Barron, who was an American. Duggan, then chief of the State Department's Latin American Division, attempted to get Gibson to drop official interest in Barron. But Gibson urged Brazilian police to deport Barron to the United States in exchange for Barron's cooperation. This option ended in March 1935, when Barron died, having jumped (the Brazilian police version) or been pushed from a high prison window. The discussion shows that Duggan's attempt to short-circuit Ambassador Gibson was a spontaneous action of his own, not one ordered or requested by the Soviets. Sometimes the actions of concealed Communists such as Duggan within the U.S. government on policy matters are described as those of an "agent of influence" of Soviet intelligence, and there were such incidents. More often, however, as with Duggan and the Prestes-Barron matter, their actions were independent attempts to nudge American policy in a direction that they thought would assist the Communist cause.[50]

The KGB's plan to draw Duggan fully into its apparatus was delayed by the imbroglio over Alger Hiss's attempt to recruit Noel Field for his GRU-linked network and the subsequent fear that Hiss, Field, and Duggan had all been exposed to each other as Soviet sources (see chapter 1). Hiss had also made a direct approach to Duggan, urging him to meet with Frederick Field, (no relation to Noel), a secret member of the CPUSA's covert arm. Massing met with the Duggans in mid-May 1936, and Boris Bazarov, illegal station chief, reported: ""Jurist" [Hiss] called

19 [Duggan] and asked him to receive [Frederick] Field and speak with him. (Jurist knows "19" through the capital's circle of supporters of 'New Deal' policies.) 19 informed Redhead [Massing] that he had not given Field any sort of reply and was putting it aside until her arrival (of which 19 was informed ahead of time). . . . 19 then reported that he would favor not having a connection with Field, not because it would be more secure, but because he, by being linked directly with us (he identified our country by name), can be of greater value.'" In 1948 Whittaker Chambers testified to an executive session of the House Committee on Un-American Activities that he had asked Frederick Field to approach Duggan to explore a relationship with Chambers's GRU-linked apparatus, of which Hiss was a part. He said that Field reported: "Duggan was already connected with another apparatus." Inasmuch as Bazarov's 1936 report on the incident states that Hiss set up Frederick Field's meeting with Duggan, it appears that Chambers in 1948 had forgotten his use of Hiss to set up the meeting with Field.[51] Bazarov went on to say:

"19 [Duggan] further reported that overall his line of action is completely clear to him and that the only thing that induces him to stay in a job he despises in the department, having to wear a dinner jacket for 2 weeks at a time when attending a reception every evening (with nearly 20 countries in his division), is the notion of being useful to our cause. He reported that he is not quite firm in the saddle yet and does not yet have access to everything. Many envy his extraordinary career, a career highly unusual for one of his age (he is 32–33), but after several months he will consolidate his position. It is true that he is widely known as a liberal and a typical New Dealer and that his family is known for its liberalism. But this is not a problem. To be on the safe side, he asked that we meet with him once a month and would very much like our man to make shorthand notes of the meetings. He is unable to give us documents for now, but later, apparently, he will manage it."[52]

Massing left for Paris in July 1936 to join her husband after arranging for Duggan to meet with Norman Borodin, a young KGB officer. A report Borodin wrote in 1948 regarding his work with Duggan brings out the latter's nervousness and need for reassurance:

"Around the end of 1935 or the beginning of 1936 (I can't remember the exact date), agent "Redhead" [Massing] gave us a lead on her acquaintance, "19" [Duggan], telling us that he was sympathetic toward the Soviet Union and the American Comparty. She agreed with him that the Communist George Ryan . . . would come to Washington from NY to discuss, or rather, receive information about the situation in the State Dep., where he was working at the time as Chief of the Latin American Division. After some hesitation, 19 agreed to meet once. I left for Washington soon after, along with the station chief, 'Nord' [Bazarov].

I contacted 19 by phone at his apartment, calling myself Ryan, and we agreed to have dinner together at one of the hotels in Washington. At dinner, we began our conversation by discussing the international situation, and then I turned the conversation to State Dep. employees; I asked for descriptions of the senior staff, the functions of various divisions, etc. "19" readily answered my questions and then asked whether I represented the New York Comparty. I replied that I was a Communist, though not directly affiliated with the American Comparty, and that therefore he should not be afraid to meet with me from time to time for similar discussions.

At first, 19 categorically refused to have future meetings, saying that he couldn't bear the risk; his wife was pregnant and he had to think about his family's welfare. He believed that sooner or later, the authorities could record his meetings with me, and then he would be fired from the State Dep. and blacklisted. I reassured him by saying that no one in the USA knew that I was a Communist and that there was no possibility of his being exposed.

19 calmed down somewhat and almost agreed to have future meetings. Since his lunch break was coming to an end, we agreed to continue our conversation the following day, sort out the details of future meetings, and determine which questions were of interest to us. After that, our first meeting was over. When I arrived at the boarding house where 'Nord' was waiting for me, I told him the results of my conversation with 19. We carefully discussed all the details of the conversation in question (having taken my car to a park in Virginia for that purpose) and concluded that 19's misgivings were sincere, he was not a stooge, and further meetings with him could be arranged. The next day at our meeting, 19 again tried to back out of collaboration, saying that it was unlikely he could give us anything interesting. In the end, though, he yielded to my arguments, and we agreed to meet roughly once every 2 weeks. I regularly traveled to Washington from NY to meet with 19, either in his car (we drove outside the city), or in his home, since he was sick several times. . . .

When Tukhachevsky, Yagoda, and others were put on trial in Moscow, 19 became extremely anxious. By that time I had already made it clear to him that he was dealing with Soviet intelligence, and this thought appealed to him. With the commencement of the trials, however, 19 began flatly refusing to work with us, saying that if the head of Soviet intelligence had turned out to be a spy, then his own exposure was inevitable. . . . As I recall, it took an incredible amount of effort to convince 19 not to break with us. I brought all my eloquence to bear in order to prove to 19 that the Soviet intelligence service with which we were affiliated was not the intelligence service that had been headed by Yagoda, and that only three people knew of his cooperation with us, all of whom were still alive and well, working, etc."

Borodin assured Duggan that none of the KGB officers who knew of his assistance to Soviet intelligence had become traitors.[53]

KGB New York station reports in 1936 show that by September Duggan was providing copies of documents or originals to be filmed and returned. But Bazarov observed, "'Unfortunately, the materials provided by 19 [Duggan] are, I believe, of very little interest to us. And for all his good intentions, he is unable to obtain any others for now.'" However, Grigory Grafpen, a Moscow Center officer, looked through Duggan's material and told Abram Slutsky, chief of foreign intelligence: "'Nord [Bazarov] managed for the first time to receive authentic State Department materials from "19" [Duggan] regarding the following matters: Anglo-Argentine trade negotiations and a draft treaty on trade relations between America and Argentina, and so forth. Even though these doc-s do not cover matters of great urgency for the USSR, I nonetheless think it would be useful to process and publish them in a collected format.'" Slutsky accepted Grafpen's suggestion, and told the New York station: "'The materials sent from "19" [Duggan] have been put together as a compendium and sent to the directive echelon [Soviet high leadership]. You should continue to receive materials from him elucidating the politics of your country and oth. countries of Lat. America. Simultaneous with this, the task for developing "19" should be an expansion of his opportunities outside his division in the Surrogate [State Department] and giving a precise overview of the work of all points in the Surrogate, both inside the country and outside it.'"[54]

New State Department security measures complicated KGB hopes that Duggan would smuggle out copies of telegrams slated for destruction. (Duggan's reports indicated that William Bullitt, ardently anti-Soviet by this time, was the leading advocate of increased State Department security.) The new plan required that cables would not be disposed of in the division using them (thus allowing Duggan to steal them) but would be tracked and picked up once a week by the Division of Communications and Records and destroyed centrally. In December Duggan reported he had attempted to get around the new regulations about cables by transcribing a number of telegrams but became careless and left five of them inside a telephone book in his desk one day, only to find later that the book had been replaced with a new edition for 1937. He was unable to locate his copy in a big pile of discards, leading Moscow Center to urge suspension of contact with him until it became clear that he was not under suspicion.[55]

Unlike the KGB's first State Department source, David Salmon, Laurence Duggan was not a mercenary. In 1937 Bazarov, illegal station chief, told Moscow Center:

"You ask if it isn't time to start paying him. It is almost certain that he will refuse any money, and even likely that he will view the offer of money as an insult. A few months ago, Granite [Borodin] wanted to bring "19" [Duggan] a gift on his birthday. He bought a lovely crocodile skin handbag monogrammed with "19's" initials. The latter categorically refused to accept the gift, declaring that he is working for the common idea, and indicated that he is not helping us out of any material incentive. This incident is characteristic of "19." If at any point in the future "19" is in need of money, we'll use the moment and offer him friendly assistance. Granite characterizes "19" as a straightforward, candid, and brave man. "19" is interested in Marxist literature and the development of the USSR."[56]

Duggan himself, however, felt he was on shaky ground in the State Department in early 1937. The post of undersecretary of state, the department's second ranking position, fell vacant; Duggan feared that Sumner Welles would leave the department if he did not get the job, and without Welles's protection, Duggan's own position would become untenable. Welles, however, prevailed over other contenders and got the job. And Duggan was soon a beneficiary. The sizable Mexican Division was added to his Latin American Division, and in April he became chief of the enlarged "Division of the American Republics." Duggan's enhanced position increased his ability to provide material of interest to Moscow. He immediately delivered a memorandum from the State Department's Office of Arms and Munitions Control to the KGB. The office, headed by Joseph C. Green, regulated export of military goods from the United States. Moscow Center was pleased, telling the New York station: "'We can certify that the work with '19' [Duggan] has been successful. The materials that were sent regarding 'Hammer's' [the USSR's] military-naval supply orders in Angora [United States] are current. Is there hope of receiving them in the future? It is very important.'" Duggan's liaison, Norman Borodin, provided a detailed report on obtaining the material:

"'19' [Duggan] again asserts that receiving the folder (which you now have) from Green did not arouse suspicion of any kind from anyone. . . . According to him, everything went off without a hitch. He has for a long time and with some frequency been talking to Green, with whom he is quite close, about the policies of the USA vis-à-vis the export of weapons. '19' gets a lot of inquiries from South American countries about these issues, and naturally, he must be well-informed in these matters.

The approach to the folder began a while ago, when Green himself told 19 about Soviet military-naval supply orders amounting to 200,000,000 dollars. . . . The South American countries have also been trying to purchase military-naval weapons here, and as a result 19 maintained contact with Green, who from time to time informed him how licensing talks were progressing. . . . "19" thinks that attempting to receive other, similar folders today, with German, Japanese, and British or Italian supply orders, would be tantamount to 'playing with fire.' He will get a better sense in the future, but for now, in his opinion, Green should be left alone. We approved of his point of view completely but expressed hope that in the future, circumstances would allow for other folders to be received as well." (He provided a document about weapons purchases in Mexico for government forces in Spain and about preparations for a fascist uprising in Mexico. They requested materials about Trotsky.)[57]

By mid-August 1937, Duggan's earlier qualms appeared to have abated, and Iskhak Akhmerov confidently reported: "" 19" [Duggan] now receives every telegram coming to the SD [State Department]. He agreed to pass them on to us. 'At first we will receive them once every two weeks, and later we will try to intensify and make more frequent the reception of these telegrams.'" Several of the reports Duggan provided to the KGB are extracted or listed in Vassiliev's notebooks. Some dealt with interdepartmental gossip; others bore on U.S. government responses to military export requests and secret instructions given to President Roosevelt's special envoys to Europe. Duggan also reported on internal State Department discussions on shifting ambassadorial assignments and provided such memos as "Recent trends in German competition with United States export trade in the other American republics" (forwarded to Stalin, Molotov, and Kliment Voroshilov); Moscow Embassy chargé d'affaires Loy Henderson's report on Sam Carp, Molotov's brother-in-law and head of an export firm based in the United States (forwarded to Stalin and Molotov); and a "Memorandum on Italian fascist and German Nazi activity in the American Republics" prepared by Duggan's own division (passed on to Stalin, Molotov, and Voroshilov).[58]

No sooner had the KGB gotten Duggan into an increasingly productive mode than his earlier fears revived that traitors within the Soviet regime might expose him. He was particularly discombobulated when Stalin struck at the Red Army in the spring of 1937. Given that Duggan was then its only State Department source (Salmon having been lost when ties with Lore were cut), the illegal KGB station treated his concerns with great seriousness. Akhmerov met with Borodin to ensure he was prepared: "'Before the meeting with 19 [Duggan], we carefully walked Granite [Borodin] through the lead articles in 'Pravda' and materials from Central Committee plenums and local party conferences. Granite was equipped and prepared to discuss with 19 all the questions that 19 himself touched on.'" On 2 July 1937 Borodin reported at length:

"As soon as we met this time, '19' [Duggan] announced the following. He can't make sense of the events taking place in the USSR. He is very troubled by the exposure of nine former commanders of the RKKA [Red Army] and by the exposure of Trotskyite-Fascist spies in almost every industrial branch and government institution. People he learned to respect have turned out to be traitors to their homeland and to the socialist cause. He can't wrap his mind around it. How could such prominent people fall into such an abyss? He can't understand it at all, and the whole thing seems to him 'a distant, incomprehensible nightmare.' What would happen to him if there turned out to be a fascist spy in the institution where his information was being sent? It seems beyond the realm of possibility, yet two months ago the same thing could have been said about those nine soldiers. This begs the conclusion that the Soviet Union is not as solid as had been thought. Its army was not as invincible as others claimed if such scoundrels had been at its head. Again and again he repeats that he doesn't understand, that it troubles him and keeps him awake at night.

He admits that he can't be very useful with such an attitude, and he wants to sever ties with us and try to get involved with the American Comparty, to help it with its work here. He has an excellent understanding of the situation in America and could be useful to the party. He does not, however, wish to work for a country where he does not understand what is happening.

"19" ended this first declaration of his by saying that he can't even be 100% certain where his information ultimately ends up. He doesn't want to cast any aspersions on me as well, and yet—"19" asks—at this point how can one be sure that the materials don't ultimately end up in the enemies' hands?

I spoke with "19" for six hours straight. I told him the history of the struggle between the band of Trotskyites against the party and government. I explained to him the USSR's global position and the implications of the capitalist encirclement that sends thousands of spies into the Soviet Union, who, naturally, try to penetrate into the most sensitive areas. The state is obligated to expose these traitors and destroy them. There can be no question about that. The extermination of these traitors only goes to strengthen the nation and its army immeasurably, and as for weakness, all these events only demonstrate the weaknesses of fascist intelligence and not, by any means, of the Soviet Union.

The country is united as never before around the party and government, and it is precisely for this reason that the traitors' work was intercepted.

Gradually, "19" agreed with all of my arguments. I told him that his attitude toward working with us was hardly serious and that he in particular, and all American liberals in general, would have to decide once and for all whether they will stand for socialism and progress or cross over into the fascist and reactionary camp. This argument affected him more than all the others. He declared that of course he will remain in the first category and agreed that his proposal had been poorly thought out. 'Let's forget,' said '19,' 'about my temporary weakness and continue our work together; however, if there is another "purge" in the highest circles of government, I'm afraid I simply won't be able to continue our work.'

And so we were back at the beginning. I told him that unfortunately our fascist enemies are not good Christians, as many would think, and will doubtless send their spies and wrongdoers our way. Does that mean they should be left alone and not destroyed? Only an enemy of the Soviet Union could say that, not a serious, forward-thinking liberal like "19." 'Yes, of course,' he said, 'they must be caught and destroyed,' but if it touches government circles again, he can come to only one conclusion, namely that there is something rotten with the whole system if even its leaders become traitors. More arguments and attempts at persuasion followed. He agreed with everything, but the whole time I could feel a barely palpable ambivalence. As for his uncertainty as to where his information ultimately ends up, or will end up, I said that it all depends on establishing an absolute trust between us. At the moment there are no proofs I can give him. He doesn't want them anyway, he says, because he does not suspect me; but supposing even that I was from the other camp, a proof could be fabricated very easily. No, he does not suspect me; but mainly he is afraid that his materials, arriving home, will somehow pass through spies into the enemy's hands, along with the source's name. I assured him that his name does not appear anywhere, and so forth.

He wanted very much to have a rendezvous arranged between him and Hede [Massing] . . . , through whom he had been given our secret meeting place. He wants to discuss all of his doubts with her, b/c there is an absolute trust between them. Ultimately, we agreed that "19" would continue his cooperation and try to rethink his views on current events. I should stress that practically every newspaper, with the obvious exception of the party press, is engaged in a frenzied anti-Soviet campaign of lies and slander. In the front ranks of this pandemonium stands 'NYT' correspondent Harold Denny. I am singling out Denny because in all of '19's' arguments about the weakness of the Soviet Union and its army, he continually used facts from Denny's articles. If every day, every other newspaper prints several articles full of fiction and anti-

Soviet propaganda, naturally this will influence the thoughts of American liberals. '19' is undoubtedly a victim of this propaganda. Before now he had never expressed any doubts. The turning point was concurrent with the appearance of a new crop of anti-Soviet articles. '19' is in a fairly isolated position; that is to say, on our instructions he has distanced himself from every liberal and left circle."

A week later Akhmerov reported: "19 [Duggan] stated firmly that he has decided to continue working with us, having agreed with the arguments we set forth. . . . 19 gave a number of materials."[59]

Laurence Duggan's fears that he could be betrayed by a traitor were not, as it happens, that remote from reality. The traitor, however, was not one of the thousands of Soviet officials publicly or secretly tried and executed in the "Moscow trials" that had so upset him. In September 1939 Whittaker Chambers told Assistant Secretary of State Adolf Berle that Duggan was a secret Communist and likely involved in espionage. The path that led Chambers, a former American Communist and GRU agent, to Berle was a complex one, involving three earlier defectors, Juliet Poyntz (see chapter 9), Ignace Poretsky, and Walter Krivitsky. All three played roles in Chambers's decision to defect, but the latter two were also linked to Duggan.

In July 1937 Poretsky, a senior officer, deserted the KGB and wrote a letter to Stalin denouncing the Soviet leader as a "traitor to the cause of the working class and socialism" for having instigated the purges and announcing his own support for Stalin's enemy, the exiled Leon Trotsky. Poretsky (often known by his pseudonym, Ignace Reiss) had never served in the United States, and his knowledge of KGB operations was thought to deal mostly with Western Europe. But he had recruited Hede and Paul Massing and been in contact with them shortly before he deserted. They had introduced him to Noel Field, whom Hede had recruited as a KGB source when he worked at the U.S. State Department. Poretsky met Field while the latter worked at the League of Nations' headquarters in Switzerland.[60]

Hede and Paul Massing were back in the United States at the time of Poretsky's desertion, and Akhmerov checked with them to learn what Poretsky might know about KGB sources in the United States. In August he sent Moscow Center the bad news: "'Redhead and Vacek [Hede and Paul Massing] told me that Raymond [Poretsky] knew about 19 [Duggan] and his wife.'" Poretsky had also been contacting KGB sources and agents he knew in Western Europe and urging them to join him in rebelling against Stalin. Paul Massing offered the opinion that if Poretsky contacted Noel Field unawares, Field might panic. He urged Moscow Center to send someone to prepare Field. Akhmerov also reminded Moscow that Field was a close friend of Laurence Duggan, and the two were in frequent correspondence. He told Moscow: "'It is very important to keep E. ["Ernst"/Field] on our side. If E. is tarnished as a result of Raymond's [Poretsky's] exposure, then apparently 19 [Duggan] will become frightened and want to sever ties with us.'"[61]

Whether at Akhmerov's prompting or its own initiative, Moscow Center did as he suggested. In 1954 during a debriefing by Hungarian Communist security police Noel Field said that Walter Krivitsky, then his KGB contact, came to Geneva and told him

that Reiss had become a traitor and that preventive measures must be taken. . . . He required me to go with him to Paris in order to discuss my duties. I went with him that very night. He took me to a café—I don't remember the name or address—where he introduced me to a Soviet agent. Following the introduction Krivitsky left and I did not meet him again. I don't know the Soviet man's name. Later, when I went to Moscow, I learned that he was one of the NKVD's high officials. In fact, he wore the Order of Lenin. He told me that they had evidence concerning Reiss's betrayal. . . . This was very dangerous as Reiss knew many people, and this betrayal could put many people in danger. He advised me that he had been ordered to protect the connections known to Reiss from this danger, i.e. to silence him. . . . He also said that as far as he knew, Reiss was in Switzerland again, and he was expected to look me up. Thus I would be drawn into the operation. He asked me if I trusted my wife completely and whether she could also be involved in the operation. Having received my positive answer, he gave me the task to welcome Reiss amicably and detain him. In the meantime, my wife or I should inform a person he would introduce me to, and who would travel to Geneva with me, of Reiss's arrival. After our conversation he introduced me to a young Soviet man called Max, with whom I was to keep in touch in the future. That very night I went to Geneva with Max. Having arrived, I introduced him to my wife and informed her about the matter concerning Reiss and the task we had. We arranged with Max that when Reiss arrives, I would contact him at a certain telephone number using a certain name. We also settled on meeting personally every day. Reiss didn't show up.[62]

The reason Poretsky/Reiss didn't approach the Fields was that a KGB assassination team got to him first. Swiss police found Poretsky beside a road near Lausanne on 4 September, dead from multiple gunshot wounds. Moscow Center promptly informed Akhmerov of the outcome:

"Raymond [Poretsky] has been liquidated. His wife, so far, has not. She knows about 19 [Duggan] to some extent, and at the moment we are not aware what steps she will take in the future. For now the danger of 19 being exposed through Raymond's line is significantly diminished. However, this does not mean by any means that you should observe him and work him over any less strenuously. The political work with 19 needs to become systematic. You should answer all of 19's perplexing questions exhaustively. Do not leave anything unclear or unaddressed. Always make a note of the questions that interest 19 and report them to us.

Who could influence 19? First of all, Redhead and Vacek [Hede and Paul Massing]. Betty [Vasily Zarubin] will have to orient you regarding the extent to which they will take this step. Second of all, Ernst [Field]. The latter is well-mannered and impressed a comrade with whom he is connected as a sincere man, willing to report back about Raymond as soon as the latter turns to him. It is very likely that Ernst will write about this to Redhead and.Vacek, who connected him with Raymond in the past."[63]

Despite the ominous remarks about Elizabeth Poretsky, she was left unmolested and later wrote a detailed account of her tumultuous life. Swiss police caught one of the accomplices in the murder of Ignace Poretsky, but the chief assassin escaped, later to serve in the United States as a KGB officer working as a TASS correspondent using the name Vladimir Pravdin. In an autobiography written for the KGB in 1944 Pravdin boasted, "On my own, tracked down and liquidated 'Raymond' [Poretsky]." Moscow went on to tell Akhmerov the following:

"It is possible that Ernst [Field], who corresponds with 19 [Duggan], could somehow hint at certain facts. Certain caprices will possibly then come from 19's end, which you will have to overcome. At this point we cannot approach Ernst about influencing 19, because 19 is very frightened that Ernst will find out he works with us. For the time being Ernst has not been tarnished in connection with the business with Raymond [Poretsky], so everything is fine from that end—at least for the time being.

As for 19's value, it has gone up a great deal in connection with his new position and with the reorganization of internal relations between division chiefs, and we cannot under any circumstances lose him. It appears that the frequency of the rendezvous will have to be limited to once every two weeks at first, but for this he is only providing materials to be photographed. The rendezvous where he provides agent materials, on the other hand, should be made more frequent. In addition, send his agent reports by telegraph immediately, because all of that is exceedingly urgent material."[64]

Duggan's "new position" (head of the State Department's Division of the American Republics) also led the KGB to assign a more senior officer to work with him. Akhmerov, Bazarov's chief aide in the illegal station, replaced Borodin. Akhmerov informed Moscow that he had held his first meeting with Duggan in August 1937:

"From the very first meeting we were able to establish a candid and sincere rapport. He is a straightforward and sincere person. Meeting and working with him is a pleasure compared to what it was like with "10" [Ludwig Lore] or James [Thomas Schwartz]. At the same time, working with "19" [Duggan] invests me with a great deal of responsibility in terms of my ideological influence over him. His ideological closeness to us is the foundation of our work. In terms of ideology he is not yet firmly formed as our man. He lives and moves in a circle of Surrogate [State Department] bureaucrats who form a rather privileged and conservative caste in Washington. The newspapers, which he reads every day, are primarily of an anti-Soviet character. Because he is exceptionally busy, he is unable to read Marxist literature or our fraternal newspapers. Without a doubt, these factors play a significant part in his hesitations. These hesitations have yet to disappear. At the very first meeting he made somewhat venomous remarks about the ongoing arrests in Hammer [USSR]."

Despite Duggan's continued "hesitations," Akhmerov added:

"One week after my first meeting, i.e., on August 30, he gave me Surrogate [State Department] telegrams, numbering roughly 60 pages, for one hour. These documents were photographed and are included in this mailing. At the third meeting on September 13, he gave me a second batch of documents totaling about 100 pages—also for an hour. Managing to switch taxis and take photographs in under an hour requires exceptional speed. At present, I meet with him to receive documents approximately once every two weeks. I spoke with 19 [Duggan] about making these receiving meetings weekly. He has not given a firm promise yet, but I hope to achieve this in the future. I photographed the materials in Julia's [unidentified] apartment. Granite [Borodin] accompanies me to Washington. He waits for me in the apartment with a camera ready and goes home with the materials once they have been photographed."

(In particular, the materials *Naval Communications for the State Department*, which were sent to the State Dept. for information by the Naval Dept., have been received.) "It is difficult to meet with him more frequently to receive materials because he has a very heavy workload and cannot leave the Surrogate very often without being noticed. These materials are in his hands only during the workday. By the time office hours are over, they are sent back to the chief of archives' office. He is sent for quite often by the Secretary of

State or his assistant, and his workday schedule is also known to the secretary in 19's division."[65]

In October Moscow Center warned Akhmerov to be on the alert for signs that Duggan and Noel Field had been in communications: "'Ernst's [Field's] influence on 19 [Duggan] is still a pressing matter. The connection with Ernst has been disrupted again, and it is possible that one of the traitors will try to influence him. For this reason, take special care to learn about the correspondence between 19 and Ernst and about the attitudes both of the latter and of 19 himself.'" Moscow's comment that the "connection with Ernst [Field] has been disrupted again" was a circumspect allusion to another defection. Walter Krivitsky had been the KGB's chief liaison with Noel Field. He had also been Poretsky's friend. In the aftermath of his friend's murder, Krivitsky decided he was also a marked man, and when he was recalled to Moscow in early October, he defected.[66]

Anxious to create a channel that would enable Duggan to transmit urgent material between his regularly scheduled meetings, Akhmerov suggested using Kansas-born Helen Lowry, Earl Browder's niece, as a courier. (Lowry had earlier worked with Vasily Zarubin.) He described her as "very serious, quiet and thoughtful . . . devoted to us with all her heart." Akhmerov planned to relocate her from New York to Washington and enroll her in a secretarial school. Whenever Duggan had the time, he could stop at her apartment and "dictate important, urgent reports to her." This plan was never put into effect, but Akhmerov and Lowry fell in love and married; she later accompanied him back to the Soviet Union.[67]

The excitement generated by Duggan's burst of productivity for the KGB quickly subsided. After returning from vacation in December 1937, he asked not to meet more than once every two weeks. A month later, early in January 1938, he told Akhmerov that he wanted to sever his ties because of a new round of Soviet purges. Akhmerov reported: "'He says that he just can't wrap his mind around the events in the Soviet Union; he believes that something is fundamentally wrong and that there can't be so many oppositionists on the right and left who have become traitors.'" Akhmerov further told Moscow that Duggan was also worried that the Soviet state really was honeycombed with traitors: "'19 is very attached to his family—his wife and child, and he values his career. He has repeatedly asked me if there are any traitors in our department and if it weren't possible that he will be exposed.'"[68]

Given his confusion and fear about what was happening in the Soviet

Union, it is not surprising that Duggan was in a near panic when he met with Akhmerov on 3 March 1938. He explained that at the end of February he had been summoned to a meeting with one of Secretary of State Hull's assistants and warned about his ideological views, radical connections, and Marxist books in his home. He was convinced he was under investigation and that his house had been searched. Akhmerov also suspected that Duggan "'has been very frightened by the recent arrests of German spies in NY and fears that such traitors, like Yagoda and others, could expose his collaboration with us.'" (Yagoda was accused of cooperating with German intelligence.) Akhmerov had no choice but to accept what he said but also told Moscow that Duggan was so nervous about his safety that he might have made up the story in order to justify interrupting contact.[69]

Duggan was out of contact for three months, but in June he met with Akhmerov, who observed that he was "nervous and frightened" and reported:

"Our fairly agonizing conversation lasted more than three hours. At the beginning of the conversation, having expressed to him my happiness that our friendly connection had once more been restored, I explained to him how fascism was mobilizing reactionary forces against progressive humanity, how fascism and fascist imperialism [spills] the blood of hundreds of thousands of workers in Spain and China, and how fascism is brewing a world war. I explained to him the exceptional significance of his help precisely at this time and explained again how by helping Hammer [USSR], he was simultaneously helping the worldwide working class and progressive humanity in general. I explained the significance of Hammer as a historically important factor in the fight against fascist imperialism and the fascist reaction. On the basis of all this I asked him to renew our collaboration and to do everything in our power to benefit our mutual cause."

Akhmerov was convincing enough that Duggan continued meeting on an irregular basis and for the next year occasionally turned over State Department reports and summaries or copies of diplomatic telegrams, gave accounts of inside gossip about policy matters, and provided an assessment of Laurence Steinhardt, appointed ambassador to the USSR in 1939.[70]

But when Akhmerov met with Duggan on 2 October 1939, an anguished Duggan reported that he, as he had long feared, had been compromised by a "'traitor.'" Duggan's distress had been precipitated by the meeting a month earlier between Whittaker Chambers and Assistant Secretary of State Berle, at which Chambers had identified several dozen government officials as hidden Communists and hinted of their involvement in espionage. Seven of them were State Department employees, and Laurence Duggan was one of them. In his diary two days later Berle recorded the incident and wrote that it involved "Russian espionage" and that "it becomes necessary to take a few simple measures."[71]

Nothing in the records of the State Department indicates that Berle informed State's own personnel security office of the Chambers interview. He did not turn his notes of the meeting over to the FBI until 1943, after it contacted him, having heard of the meeting from Chambers. And until now it has never been clear what Berle actually did. But Berle did act, after a fashion, and that was why at the October 1939 meeting Akhmerov reported that Duggan was "sullen and broken-hearted." Akhmerov told Moscow Center:

"A week ago, mechanic's assistant [Berle], who had been very friendly with Nineteenth [Duggan] in the past, called him into his office and told him that the Surrogate [State Department] is in possession of intelligence confirming that he had collaborated with Hammer [USSR] and provided the latter with secret material and information. The assistant then said that it would be in his best interest to find another job. The assistant also said that his case would ultimately be decided upon the return of Mechanic's deputy [Welles], who is currently presiding over a conference in the South. Nineteenth's division is under the deputy's jurisdiction. Moreover, the deputy had previously taken Nineteenth under his wing and thought of him as his man. Nineteenth said that he is completely isolated in the Surrogate and subjected to intolerable conditions. He says he is already looking for another job. He said that this was a huge blow for him, that he has suffered terribly this whole time, and that all this puts him in a very difficult position.

I expressed deep sympathy and cheered him up with examples from the experience of the struggles of revolutionaries, who had sacrificed their lives for the victory of our ideas. . . . I explained to him that there was absolutely no evidence of any kind attesting to his collaboration with us. He says that apparently, someone in your chain turned out to be a traitor, and this traitor informed on him. I told him that nothing of the sort had happened and that he was known to a very limited and loyal inner circle made up of two or three workers, that his name had never been used for anything. . . . He repeatedly and earnestly asked to sever all ties with me. I tried my best to convince him to meet with me, if only 2 or 3 months from now, in order to find out how this matter had ended and, if necessary, to give him our advice. He practically begged me not to do this, telling me not to put him in the unpleasant position of forcing him to say that he can no longer meet with us. . . . I expressed to him our deep gratitude for all his services rendered to us.

He said that in time he would return to the fraternal movement [Communist Party], that he is not leaving the movement forever, and that ideologically, he stands on the fraternal side. He said that international events had not had a negative effect on his views. We parted ways like close friends. He spoke very convincingly and sincerely about everything mentioned above. I don't think he made the whole thing up. Of course, it's possible that he became very frightened as a result of the sensationalistic hunt for our kind of people and for the officials connected to the fraternal movement and chose to make up the entire aforementioned story as a valid reason for severing ties with us. If he remains at his current job, then this explanation will be closer to the truth."

Moscow Center recalled Akhmerov in November 1939, and the depleted KGB New York station had no one available to meet with Duggan. It briefly considered having Hede Massing renew ties to Duggan, but nothing appears to have come of that notion.[72]

Moscow inquired whether Duggan was still at the State Department in April 1940, pointing out: "'If he is still working there, then we must assume that he has not been completely exposed; otherwise, he would long since have been fired.'" It also reminded New York that Akhmerov had earlier given Duggan passwords and conditions for renewed contact. In December 1938 Akhmerov had reported to Moscow Center:

"Our worker should tell 19 [Duggan] over the phone that Hansen is speaking and that he would be very happy to have lunch with him. 19 will set the date without indicating the time. At 1:30 P.M. on the agreed-upon date, our worker will be waiting for 19 at Scholls Café, 1032 Connecticut Av., Wash-n D.C. There should be a book with a red binding on the table where our worker will be sitting. Our worker should sit at a table near the entrance. 19 will approach our worker and ask him whether he is Mr. Hansen. At this, our worker, having greeted him, hands him the enclosed envelope containing a green receipt, telling 19 that it is from Alexander. After opening the envelope, 19 will ask how his son is doing. 19 knows me under the name Alexander Hansen."[73]

Duggan was still at the State Department, but it wasn't until the fall of 1940 that the under-strength New York station could reach him. "Glan," a KGB New York officer, called Duggan on the phone on 21 October and identified himself as "Hansen." "Glan" reported that initially Duggan did not recognize the name; once he realized who was calling, he tried to put him off, claimed he was busy, and asked him to call back in a week. "Glan" did so, but a woman who answered the phone said Duggan wasn't home and was very busy. Meanwhile, Moscow Center spotted a story in the *New York Times* that caused it to make Duggan a high priority. An excited Moscow Center report read: "According to the 'NYT' from 3.11.40, our source in Circus [State Department], "19" [Duggan], has been appointed personal adviser to Hull. In this connection, he has access to absolutely all of the SD's [State Department's] information. . . . 1. Activate 19 immediately. 2. Send a special agent to Washington . . . for contact with 19." The report also noted that the need to use the KGB New York station was due to the fact that "there hasn't been an operative at the embassy in Washington since May 1940."[74]

While the *New York Times* story gave Moscow hope that its old source had not merely weathered his November 1939 difficulties but had risen to new heights, the reality was different, as it soon learned when "Glan" finally met with Duggan. Even sitting down with Duggan proved difficult. On the phone with "Glan," Duggan had suggested meeting at the Cosmos Club (which catered to senior government officials). "Glan" carefully showed up earlier at Scholl's Cafeteria (not café), as provided by Akhmerov's 1938 instructions, in case Duggan remembered them, and then walked over to the Cosmos. Duggan, however, didn't appear at the appointed time, and "Glan" called him at home. Duggan apologized, claimed he had been held up, but promised to come over. He finally arrived, and the two then had dinner at a nearby hotel and talked for several hours. "Glan" reported that Duggan "'thinks he is not trusted at work and his situation there is unstable.' (19 is no longer a division chief but an adviser on S. American affairs. He sees it as a diversion from more important work, without having to lose face: no one reports to him, and no one asks his advice. They had wanted to send him off to Paraguay as 1st secretary.) 'To my question as to why he had not been fired in the 'presence' of distrust toward him and had instead been promoted, Nineteenth [Duggan] replied that 'they' didn't have any evidence and were afraid of the scandal he could cause.'" What appeared to have happened was that Duggan's mentor, Sumner Welles, intervened and prevailed against Berle's attempt to force Duggan from the State Department. But Berle had succeeded in getting him removed as chief of the Division of the American Republics and kicked upstairs to the more prestigious but less operationally important post of adviser to the secretary of state. "Glan" went on to say:

"He insists that his attitude toward us has not changed and that in theory, he has no objection to working with us again; however, he firmly asserts that for now it doesn't make any sense, that he can't be of use to us and doesn't want to meet again, at the very least for the rest of 1941. He said he was disillusioned, because when he started working with us, he had been guaranteed complete secrecy, but the incident of his having to appear before the authorities convinced him that there was a leak somewhere in our line. . . .

Before we parted ways, Nineteenth [Duggan] asked me not to call him on the phone anymore, for any reason. He said that despite the fact that the FBI was still 'like children lost in the woods' in matters of counterintelligence, nevertheless he knows for a fact that all the phones in Washington are tapped. Naturally, I gave him my word. Speaking of tradecraft, it should be noted that he completely forgot the meeting place, password, and material evidence. Only at the end of the meeting did I say to him, with a smile: 'Here you talk about peace of mind and security, yet how could you forget all the arrangements? You didn't even make an attempt to verify who it was that was meeting with you or speaking to you.' He turned very red and admitted that he had made a mistake in that regard. I handed him the envelope with material evidence, which he looked over and tore up in front of me."

The purpose of "Glan's" visit had been to reestablish a full agent relationship with Duggan. Despite Duggan's reluctance, "Glan" concluded: "'I think it is entirely possible to resume work with Nineteenth, but I also think it will require an enormous amount of time, attention, and patience just to get him re-accustomed to meetings at first, and then to shorten the intervals between meetings and begin work, progressing very slowly and gradually from very minor, general concerns to individual, concrete problems and general political information.'"[75]

While nothing was done for a year, Moscow Center thought reviving Duggan worth the effort. In late 1941 it urged Vasily Zarubin, the new U.S. station chief, to use Duggan for information on German activities in South America and internal State Department organization and to exploit his relationship with Sumner Welles. With American entrance into the war in December, Moscow became even more optimistic about reviving Duggan. In January 1942 it told Zarubin that the establishment of a wartime Soviet-American alliance should assuage Duggan's "waverings." It urged that Iskhak Akhmerov, newly returned to the United States as chief of the revived illegal station, reestablish contact. Since he had worked with Duggan in 1939, he would be able to quickly restore "complete mutual trust." It also suggested Helen Lowry as the principal courier to Duggan. As an American, she would be better able to meet with him in Washington without attracting FBI attention.[76]

In February the KGB New York station reported that Akhmerov had succeeded in meeting with Duggan and that "he was willing to help us," "promised to tell us everything he knows," and agreed to monthly meetings. But Duggan had also cautioned that his opportunities were limited, as Akhmerov reported: "A month ago Berle, after drinking a good deal of wine, reminded 19 [Duggan] about his affinity for left elements. 19 says that as long as Berle is with the firm [State Department], 19 will not be able to get ahead." In a plan for diplomatic and political work written in April 1942, Moscow Center listed Duggan as its only source in the State Department, characterizing him as a "very valuable agent" but noting his full potential had never been realized because of his fearfulness. This continued to be the case. In July Akhmerov related:

"My relationship with him has improved significantly. He is not displaying his former nervousness and conveys the impression of a person who is sincerely sympathetic to us. . . . Unfortunately, "Frank" [Duggan] is not especially active in serving us needed information. True, events have confirmed some of his principal reports over the past few months. He still refuses to meet more than once every four or five weeks. He attributes the skimpiness of his information to the fact that he deals primarily with his own area and doesn't have any access to materials in other areas. He views himself as mistreated and oppressed in the office and doesn't seek out close contact with his colleagues. Just to be on the safe side, I tried to introduce him to "Nelly" [Lowry]. He politely declined this idea. I offered him a phone number and address here or in Washington where he could call or write a message to me; he gently turned this down, too. All this shows that he prizes his safety and doesn't want to become tightly connected to us."

By November Akhmerov reported to Moscow that Duggan's cooperation continued to be limited and that Duggan

"sympathizes with us and understands our role in this war, but at the same time, he is an American patriot through and through. His intellect is shaped by his continued, concrete work putting into practice America's influence on its neighbors. He is not a fellowcountryman [Communist Party member] or a paid probationer [agent], and he is absolutely determined not to risk his position. Having once been burned, he is prone to significantly exaggerating any danger. He used to bring me bundles of the most interesting materials from his office; now he does everything he can to avoid even citing his sources when he reports something to me."[77]

Such news was not to Moscow's liking. The Center deemed "'your [Akhmerov's] work with him unsatisfactory,'" pointing out that Duggan's position gave him "access to many materials that are of primary interest to us." It demanded that Akhmerov "'take a firmer stance,'" demand weekly meetings, and remind him, "'by agreeing to work with us in the past, he took upon himself a kind of moral obligation toward us.'" The message hastened to add, "'We are not, of course, suggesting that he should be blackmailed with the fact that he gave us documentary material in the past,'" but Duggan needed a stern talking-to. Moscow enclosed a handwritten letter to Duggan from Borodin, his liaison in the late 1930s, recalling old times, justifying the purge trials for eliminating a potential fifth column, and chiding him for "'hardly doing your utmost'" in these critical days. Akhmerov firmly replied that Moscow Center's suggestions were unwise and Borodin's letter would more likely sever the KGB's relationship with Duggan than encourage greater cooperation. Akhmerov explained:

"Shared ideology and personal friendship are the mainsprings of our connection with Frank [Duggan]. Because of his personal qualities—he is an exceptionally honorable man—he could never imagine that we might put pressure on him, exploiting the work he did for us in the past. If this thought had ever seriously occurred to him, he would have long since rid himself of us. Any hint on our part (regardless of how delicately or diplomatically we put it) about the fact that he is firmly connected with us and that, having agreed to work for us, he took upon himself a certain obligation, would make it clear to him which way the wind was blowing. I am absolutely convinced that he would become angry with us and, sooner or later, break with us for good. We could afford to try such an experiment if we had a few more people like Frank to spare. A paid probationer [agent] could understand being treated this way; Frank would never forgive us for it.

Suppose we did give him to understand more clearly his firm bond with us, his responsibility, and so forth. Would we be able to frighten him and compel him to work? Of course not. He knows we would never deliberately expose him. Moreover, he knows that we have nothing with which to compromise him. It doesn't say on the documents we received through him from his department that he gave them to us. And as for his separate notes? He could say they had been written as keepsakes for his personal use and that he can't imagine how anyone could have 'swiped' them off his desk. He could use our efforts to compromise him in order to restore his position. This, roughly, is the level on which his logic could operate. Pressure of this sort or any other can be applied if it guarantees some measure of success. In Frank's case, this method will lead to nothing. So far, I have only one method of working with him: serious politico-educational influence; instilling in him the thought that, in helping us, he is helping the very best of humanity; expressing our sincere gratitude; persistently appealing to his conscience to help us more actively; and developing our personal friendship."

Surprisingly, Moscow Center deferred to Akhmerov's judgment, simply urging him to meet Duggan more frequently and "devote more energy to 19's [Duggan's] ideological education."[78]

Duggan continued to provide the KGB with American diplomatic information, reporting on Anglo-American plans for the invasion of Italy, consideration of an invasion of Nazi-occupied Norway, U.S. diplomatic approaches to Argentina's military government, and secret discussions regarding a common Anglo-American policy toward Middle Eastern oil resources. But the volume was not as much as he had provided in the late 1930s and never as much as Moscow Center wanted. When he returned to Moscow in 1944, Vasily Zarubin, in a retrospective report on his tenure as New York station chief, judged that during the 1942–44 period Duggan "verbally provided a certain amount of occasionally interesting information, but not much, not complete enough and in most cases not on his own initiative, but by way of responses to questions that had been posed to him."[79]

Duggan resigned from the State Department in July 1944, following his mentor, Sumner Welles, who had left in August 1943. Akhmerov admitted to Moscow that although Duggan had told him that his posting had become "especially shaky" after Welles's departure, nonetheless his "resignation came as a surprise to me." Optimistically, the KGB New York station told Moscow, "Prospects for the future are being looked into." Duggan was able to get a position with the United Nations Relief and Rehabilitation Administration (UNRRA). More promising, in November the New York station reported rumors that President Roosevelt would shortly replace Secretary of State Hull with Henry Wallace as consolation for having dropped him as vice-president in the 1944 election. Duggan was close to Wallace, and the KGB New York station speculated he might be able to reenter the State Department "in a leading post." Even if Wallace did not get the appointment, the KGB cable went on to say, Duggan could still be useful by "using his friendship" with Wallace for "extracting . . . interesting information" that would inevitably come to someone of Wallace's political standing. Roosevelt did, in fact, replace Hull but installed Edward Stettinius as secretary of state. A KGB memo on Duggan simply stated that after he was at UNRRA "the connection was lost and was never renewed."[80]

The KGB set about reinvigorating its American operations in 1948. Reviving agents who had been put on an inactive status was a quick way to get operations up to speed once more, and Laurence Duggan was on the list. By that time he was president of the Institute of International Education in New York, the organization founded by his father. Borodin wrote a report pointing out that its work "'is undoubtedly of great interest with respect to our work in the USA, especially vis-à-vis the possibility of obtaining student entry visas into the USA for our European illegals and eventually having them legalized in the USA and other countries.'" He went over the history of Duggan's nervousness but offered this judgment: "'I do not think that 19 [Duggan] will be too fearful about resuming work with us, considering that he does not currently work in a government department and therefore will not be afraid of being labeled an 'unloyal' American, providing, of course, that someone has a sensible talk with him.'"[81]

In May 1948 Moscow ordered the New York station to arrange a meeting with Duggan on the pretext of official Soviet cooperation with his organization and suggested using Sergey Striganov, a Soviet diplomat who had been working as a KGB co-optee since 1941. Among his other diplomatic duties, Striganov was American representative for the All-Union Society for Cultural Relations (VOKS), the Soviet agency that oversaw international cultural contacts and exchanges, so an approach would appear entirely aboveboard. Moscow told the New York station:

"The purpose of this activity is to ascertain his current political views and attitudes, which will allow us to determine the usefulness of re-establishing contact with him as an agent and the likelihood of getting leads from him on people working in the State Dep., using him to legalize our workers, and obtaining information about American intelligence's use of the student exchange program in its work against us. When establishing official contact with "Prince" [Duggan], one should bear in mind his hesitation and persistent attempts to break off all relations with us in the past. Therefore, it is essential to take great care not to reveal our worker's identity to him or to antagonize him with our over-eager interest in him."[82]

As directed, Striganov arranged an appointment with Duggan at his New York office in July and reported: "'He received me cordially, was attentive, gave me a detailed account of the institute's work, showed me his office, and having done this, led me to the door. I detained him with a question, and we talked for another 10–15 minutes, but then I had to leave because Duggan, having led me to the elevator, let me know unequivocally that it was time for me to go. He had not wished to talk about anything other than the institute and had tried the whole time to take an official tone. I got the impression . . . that he was constantly on his guard, anticipating that I would ask some unexpected question.'" Striganov got Duggan's agreement to meet again to discuss Soviet cooperation with the IIE, but attempts to schedule the follow-up were turned aside, and Duggan did not attend an official Soviet diplomatic reception to which he was invited. Finally, on 15 December 1948, the Soviet diplomat phoned again, and when a secretary said Duggan was not available, Striganov asked her to take down his name and let Duggan know he had called. Five days later Laurence Duggan jumped from his sixteenth-floor office window and died.[83]

What the KGB didn't know at the time but soon learned was that it was not the only security agency calling on Duggan in the fall of 1948. As the Hiss-Chambers investigation heated up in 1948, the FBI interviewed Hede Massing. She and her husband had quietly dropped their connections to the KGB sometime toward the end of World War II. Deeply disillusioned with the Communist movement and increasingly anti-Soviet, she provided an account of her work as a KGB agent to the FBI when it interviewed her on 7–8 December 1948, including her role in recruiting Duggan as a Soviet source.[84]

FBI agents interviewed Duggan on 10 December, five days before Striganov's call and ten days prior to his suicide. Duggan admitted having known Hede Massing but denied that she had ever attempted to recruit him for espionage. However, he told the FBI that two other persons, Henry Collins and Frederick Vanderbilt Field, had approached him and argued that American diplomatic information should be shared with the Soviet Union. Duggan said he had brushed them off but had no explanation for why he had not reported the incidents to the State Department. Duggan then cut short the interview.[85]

The KGB reports demonstrate that from his earliest days as a contact Duggan had been nervous and frightened about exposure. He had only barely survived the fallout of Chambers's 1939 revelations to Adolf Berle. But Undersecretary of State Welles and the State Department establishment had carefully hushed up that incident without involving such outsiders as the FBI and the Justice Department. This time it was very different. Duggan was on his own without the patronage of a senior official. The Cold War had begun. And public discussion of Soviet espionage, sparked by Bentley and Chambers, had become heated. The FBI was ringing at his front door while the KGB was knocking at his back door. His way out was suicide.

Clueless that their friend had been a Soviet agent, Duggan's prominent defenders and much of the media blamed the FBI, the House Committee on Un-American Activities, and anti-Communist paranoia for his death. But Aleksandr Panyushkin, the Soviet ambassador and KGB station chief, in a cable to Moscow on Christmas Day ruefully admitted that Striganov's contacts with Duggan might have "to some degree influenced his decision to kill himself."[86]

Michael Straight

Despite all his vacillations Laurence Duggan was a more valuable source for the KGB inside the State Department than another recruit in whom it had placed high hopes. Michael Straight was both a more fervent Communist and even better connected within the rarefied air of the American establishment than Duggan, but his shifting political commitments came to limit what he was willing to do for the KGB.

The son of the millionaire owners of the *New Republic,* Michael Straight was educated in England and joined the Communist Party of Great Britain while a student at Cambridge University in 1935. Guy Burgess, a few years older, was already a Soviet agent by the time Straight arrived at Cambridge. Although Burgess left Cambridge in 1935, he kept in touch through visits and his ties to Anthony Blunt, a Cambridge don, secret Communist, and KGB talent spotter and recruiter. A January 1937 Burgess report praised Straight:

"Michael, whom I have known for several years now, worked with us for two years. He is one of the leaders (as a person, he is not an organizer) of the [Communist] Party in Cambridge. He is the Party's orator, as well as a first-rate economist. He is an extremely devoted member of the Party and completely dependable, although he has not quite let go of certain romantic notions. Considering his family connections, impending fortune, and abilities, it stands to reason that he has a bright future ahead of him. . . . He strikes one as being very young and full of enthusiasm, and he can be considered capable of secret work; he is devoted enough for it."

Burgess in February reported that Blunt had successfully carried out Straight's recruitment. Theodore Mally, the KGB illegal supervising Burgess, thought Straight showed promise and "he could be used either here or in America."[87]

Straight's prominence among Cambridge's Communists was a liability for intelligence work, so Burgess took advantage of the death of his close friend, John Cornford, fighting with the International Brigades in Spain, to have Straight pretend to break his left-wing ties. Burgess reported to Moscow Center that through Blunt he had informed Straight

"that it was necessary to use America and his family as a means to disappear. He could show how John C's death has crushed him, could spend the rest of the semester sitting alone in his room . . . behave like someone who has been physically crushed. With regard to politics, to go no further than to say: 'did any good come of John's death?' Then, when the university term is over, to go to the USA and show that Roosevelt's experiment made a great impression on him. Leave the Party under the pretext that it 'proved to be inevitable because of his family and his family's connections.' He could write letters to A. B. [Anthony Blunt] about his impression of Roosevelt's activities and his growing enthusiasm about him, and A. B. could show these letters to his friends at Cambridge.

A. B. proposed this plan, which to all appearances has the greatest likelihood of success and would bring the least harm to Nigel [Straight]. N. agreed and proposed that he leave with the Int'l Student Society expedition, which is going to the USA on 17 March to learn about the Tennessee Valley Experiment [TVA]."[88]

After his visit to the United States in March 1937, Straight prepared a report for the KGB on his prospects. He noted that he "'spoke with Roosevelt and his wife'" and discussed several options he had and their usefulness for Soviet needs, ranging from the TVA and the Farm Credit Association to the Federal Reserve Board or as a secretary to FDR himself. President Roosevelt had recommended the National Resources Board as the best choice. Straight casually mentioned the top New Dealers whom he and his parents knew—Secretary of the Treasury Henry Morgenthau, Works Progress administrator Harry Hopkins, Secretary of Agriculture Henry Wallace—"'this means I could easily find any position.'" His reputation as a radical still clung to him, and he flippantly told the KGB that in order to free himself of it "'I use brilliantine and keep my nails clean . . . in some cases, passionate speeches against the Reds.'" He also told the KGB that his personal income from his family fortune was $75,000 a year, the equivalent of more than $1 million in 2008 dollars.[89]

Arnold Deutsch, a KGB officer, met with Straight several times before his final departure for America in August 1937. He assessed him as "'a typical American. Someone who thinks big. He thinks he can do everything himself.'" Straight struck Deutsch "'as being a dilettante, a young fellow who has everything he wants, more money than he can spend, which is why, in part, he has an uneasy conscience and strives to do something.'" In another report written the day before Straight's departure, Deutsch emphasized that Straight was "'very inexperienced and sometimes behaves like a child in the sense that he has romantic ideals. He thinks he works for the Comintern, and it is necessary to keep him in this illusion for the time being.'" Deutsch forwarded to Moscow Center both a handwritten note that would function as a material password for establishing contact with Straight in New York and the rendezvous protocol: "'During that week (the best thing would be to write him the letter on Friday or Saturday), he will be at this apartment every day until 10 o'clock in the morning (it is his mother's apartment). When our friend calls on him, he should say the following: 'I am here from Anthony. He says hello.' Nigel [Straight] will reply: 'Is he still at Cambridge?' At this time, our friend will pass him the handwritten note enclosed here.'"[90]

In September Moscow instructed Iskhak Akhmerov to contact Straight, explaining that "'proper development of work with him and capable guidance will lead us to sources of exceptional importance and value.'" A subsequent Moscow Center communication warned that it had learned that Straight was "'actively being cultivated by the Trotskyites'" and instructed Akhmerov to "'use all your skill to keep him from leaving us.'" The relationship, however, got off to a somewhat rocky start. Moscow Center had forgotten to send the proper contact information, and Straight was constantly asking about it. More seriously, he had concluded that his future lay in industry and decided that he should take a job with General Motors in Detroit rather than join the State Department and risk being sent to some "backwater." Moscow scotched that idea, telling Akhmerov that his agreement to the plan was "ludicrous," and by the end of 1937 Straight was working at the State Department.[91]

Akhmerov also reported to Moscow Center about his relationship with Straight and attempts to guide his political orientation:

"He and I have cemented our friendship. He is eager to listen and take my advice. I am exerting as much ideological influence as I can on him. We discuss polit. topics at length. I pick out the appropriate literature and give it to him. His milieu in the circles of the 'New Republic' does not have a particularly healthy effect on him. Such liberals as Roger Baldwin, a friend of the USSR on the surface but who in his heart is its enemy and who sympathizes a great deal with Trotsky, and people like him, whom N. ["Nigel"/Straight] sees, can only have a negative influence on him. N. is not as firm and established a Party member as you write about him. Apparently, Baldwin is trying to get his hands on him. He sends N. invitation cards for liberal meetings, invites him to lunch, etc. N. told me that Baldwin is OK. I explained to him, and continue to explain at every meeting, that Baldwin and certain people like him look OK on the surface but are in fact our enemies. I asked N. not to make any donations without first consulting me. During one conversation, N. said that he has 10–12,000 Am. dollars he doesn't need, and he doesn't know what to do with it; he asked if I needed money, he could give it to me. This is his spare pocket money. I said that I didn't need money personally and that he should keep it or put it in the bank. As for his former regular dues, I will take them and pass them on to the appropriate person. At another meeting, he gave me $2,000 as his quarterly Party dues and said that in the future he would give more. I am sending this money."

With an eye to the account books, Moscow Center ordered Akhmerov: "'Go back with N ["Nigel"/Straight] to the subject of his pocket money (12,000). Get this money from him and send it to us.'" An entry in Vassiliev's notebooks records that Moscow Center forwarded the $2,000 Akhmerov sent to the Comintern for crediting to the British Communist Party.[92]

In his 1983 autobiography Michael Straight admitted periodic meetings beginning in 1938 with a Soviet agent he knew as Michael Green, who was clearly Akhmerov, at which he handed over what he claimed were unimportant government memoranda and reports he had written. Straight insisted that these contacts were inconsequential and his contacts with Soviet intelligence were youthful indiscretions that had no practical import. Some portions of that story are confirmed by KGB documents, but others suggest he was a more active and productive source than he admitted.[93]

Almost immediately after he started work at the State Department, the KGB faced the problem of keeping Straight isolated from other Soviet agents. Friends urged him to meet Laurence Duggan as someone with similar ideological views, but Akhmerov steered him away with the warning that it could damage his career. Another danger arose in June 1938 after Straight met Alger Hiss and quickly identified him as sharing his own ideological sympathies. Not wanting a repeat of the Hiss—Noel Field mess, Akhmerov urged Moscow Center to see that GRU ordered Hiss not to approach Straight.[94]

Akhmerov reported in January 1938 that Straight worked on international economic problems and was happy with his position and expected to be able to advance. He had just been assigned to write a report on in-

ternational armaments and "'promised to give us a copy.'" He was mem-
orizing portions of various ambassadors' reports on armament questions
and giving them to Akhmerov. Moscow was not overly impressed with
what he was supplying, asking Akhmerov to "'teach him how to pick out
material that will be of interest to us'" and provide more detail about the
documents about which he was reporting, since "'in the absence of this
information, his agent reports are losing their value.'" Moreover, the data
were outdated: "'Does he have nothing but last year's material on his
desk?'" Moscow pushed Akhmerov to make Straight "'more active at
once,'" "'to increase the amount of information'" he obtained, and to
"'send any information by telegraph as soon as possible.'" In response,
Akhmerov encouraged Straight to transfer into the European Division,
where he would have access to material more directly of interest to the
USSR and to provide the names of potential recruits; the first two names
that Straight suggested were Laurence Duggan and Alger Hiss. He, of
course, was unaware that they were already recruited (by the KGB and
GRU respectively).[95]

At the end of May 1938, nonetheless, Akhmerov had to report to
Moscow that overall results had been meager. He met with Straight every
week but had received little. The promised armaments report had not
been completed, and Straight was no longer receiving current ambassadorial reports. Straight's attempt to get close to Charles Yost, assistant
chief of the Division of Arms and Munitions Control, came to nothing.
Still, when White House domestic adviser Thomas Corcoran asked
Straight to become his secretary, both Akhmerov and Moscow advised
him to remain at the State Department until and unless he could gain an
appointment to Roosevelt's personal staff. Similarly, Akhmerov dissuaded
him from accepting a post with New Deal administrator Harry Hopkins
(then working on domestic issues). Straight did hand over some routine
DOS reports during the remainder of the year and in early 1939, as well
as a few more significant items, including a lengthy analysis by an American diplomat in Great Britain on British reserves of munitions industry
raw materials and one top-secret report "on the premises and outcomes
of the Munich Conference," but Moscow Center was not upset or fazed.
Putting aside its earlier impatience, it considered the long-term prospects
and warned Akhmerov in late March 1939 not to allow Straight to take
any risks: "'Nigel [Straight] has the potential to be a major agent, and it
is not our intention to squander him on minor intelligence. It would be
better to receive one or two fewer outdated materials or to pass on a

rough idea of their content than to subject our work and our countries' relations to unwarranted risk.'"96

The Nazi-Soviet Pact abruptly shook Straight's willingness to cooperate. He was critical of Soviet policy and the response of the CPUSA. In a three-hour conversation, Akhmerov was unable to sway him and reported that Straight took the view that the "'non-aggression pact was tantamount to collaboration, that instead of fighting against Fascism and Fascist aggression, the USSR had chosen to collaborate with Germany.'" Straight did not come to meetings for a month, but by late October Akhmerov reported that he told him "'everything is now clear to him and that my [Akhmerov's] analysis of the int'l situation had been correct.'" He once again began to contribute money to the CPUSA but produced little or nothing for the KGB in the next month or so. When Akhmerov prepared to leave the United States at the end of 1939, Moscow Center concluded that "'to prevent him from being lost altogether,'" Straight should not be deactivated but turned over to Konstantin Kukin, another KGB operative. But with Moscow Center recalling most of its officers from American stations, contact was soon lost. One report noted in regard to Straight that the station "stopped receiving materials. At the end of 1940, there were no workers at all in Wash., and there was no one from NY suitable for contact with N. ["Nigel"/Straight]." It wasn't until the American stations were being rebuilt in 1941 that a KGB agent recontacted Michael Straight. When Zalmond Franklin met with him in July, he learned that Straight had resigned from the State Department because he thought that the work was boring and had taken a job at the family-owned *New Republic*.97

Ever hopeful, Moscow thought something could be salvaged. In late November 1941 it sent a message to Vasily Zarubin urging attention to Straight: "'He is a very valuable source who has vast connections in U.S. industrial-financial and political circles. His relatives are owners of large aircraft plants. He also has access to the White House, enjoys the favor of Ickes, and is close to the State Department. The principal area of "Nigel's" activities is to cultivate these connections, obtain information about military orders and deliveries and about various kinds of deals, and to obtain information from the White House and the State Department. The most expedient use of him at present can proceed on the line of cultivating current connections who are relatives.'" Moscow Center followed with another ambitious directive to Zarubin in January 1942 variously suggesting that the KGB New York station persuade Straight to join one of the government war information agencies or the new Office of Strategic Services, take control of the *New Republic,* or become politically active in the Democratic Party.[98]

Straight's former liaison, Iskhak Akhmerov, back in the United States, had reestablished contact and was much less sanguine. In July he warned:

""Nigel's" [Straight's] behavior is progressively deteriorating. I wrote you in detail about him in the last memorandum. He has begun quite often not to show up for meetings, even though he is well aware of the difficulties that our trips to Washington to meet with him involve. His behavior indicates that he is trying to get rid of us. His letter and sarcasm toward the fraternal movement [CPUSA] show that ideologically he has turned into a bourgeois apologist with liberal-progressive phraseology. Nevertheless, we are trying to keep him as our probationer [agent] in the hope of deriving some benefit from him. Working with him has become much more difficult."

It didn't get any better. Akhmerov reported that after missing some meetings, Straight finally showed up:

"As usual, he apologized and made up a story that he had come at a different time. Of course he's lying. I emphasized in a friendly manner that his failure to come to meetings puts us in an unpleasant position, and I asked him to mend his ways. This is not the first time. All this has to be put forth in a 'nice' form. Criticisms or pushiness will not lead to success. As I wrote you a few months ago, we are attempting to straighten him out with the proper amount of attention, feelings of love and solicitude, and an educational influence. He has an excellent understanding of all this. I hope we still have a chance to make him into a person who is more useful to us."

Despite his reservations, Straight was occasionally useful or conciliatory. In 1942 he pointed the KGB at a friend from his college days, William Sherwood, being sent to London on a war-related assignment. Akhmerov reported that Straight "'believes he can be very useful to us. 'Nigel' says he could send Sherwood to one or two of his old buddies in London who, according to his information, are still involved with the fraternal movement [Communist Party]. These guys could educate Sherwood.'" There is no indication whether this lead was followed up.[99]

Straight was drafted into the Army in 1943, and the KGB deactivated him, convinced, at long last, that he would no longer be even minimally useful. In a summary report on his tenure in the United States, Zarubin absolved Akhmerov of responsibility for the lack of results with Straight. By the time he had been recontacted in 1941, his ideological convictions had altered and he avoided meetings. He openly expressed disdain for the CPUSA. Thinking that Earl Browder, chief of the CPUSA, might be able to straighten him out, the station had considered arranging a meeting, but then Straight himself showed up in Browder's company and later "'gave a devastating assessment of him [Browder] and his political principles'" to Akhmerov. Zarubin sadly confessed, "'We were never able to turn 'Nigel' [Straight] around.'"[100]

While Straight severed his connections with Soviet intelligence, he retained enough loyalty to his old comrades in Great Britain that he was unwilling to expose them or risk his own security. On a trip to England in May 1946, he met Guy Burgess and Anthony Blunt. While he admitted that his views had changed, he reassured them that he would not betray them. When Moscow considered how to rebuild its devastated American networks in 1948–50, it included Straight, by now publisher of the *New Republic,* on the list of agents with whom the Washington station was asked to renew ties, but nothing happened. A 1948 memo, likely based on information from Martha Dodd Stern, disparaged Straight as "'a prominent millionaire, who in the past was a member of the American Young Communist League, then broke off his connection with it and is now hostile toward Communists.'"[101]

Straight's political path after World War II was complex. When President Truman fired Henry Wallace as secretary of commerce for opposing a tougher stance against the Soviet Union, Straight made Wallace editor of the *New Republic,* from which position he advocated an accommodation with Joseph Stalin. Yet when Wallace became the Progressive Party candidate for president in 1948, Straight, who replaced him as editor, supported Truman and the Democrats and slowly moved toward anti-Communist liberalism. Nevertheless, when the issue of Soviet espionage became a heated public issue in 1948 and 1949, Straight, who knew from his personal experience that their stories were credible, published numerous articles harshly disparaging Elizabeth Bentley and Whittaker Chambers.[102]

Straight continued to hide his past until 1963, when President John F. Kennedy nominated him to be chairman of the National Endowment for the Arts. Concerned that a mandatory security check would expose him, he went to the FBI and provided a partial account of his ties to Soviet intelligence. The FBI forwarded his statements about Anthony Blunt's role in recruiting him for Soviet intelligence to the British Security Service, enabling it to force a partial confession out of Blunt in 1964. Straight's own role in Soviet espionage did not become public until publication of his carefully parsed memoir in 1983.[103]

Robert Miller, Jack Fahy, and Joseph Gregg

In addition to Duggan, the KGB also had a number of sources in the Office of the Coordinator of Inter-American Affairs, headed by Nelson Rockefeller. (President Roosevelt had created the Rockefeller Commission, as it was often called, with a vague mandate and uncertain authority to coordinate the activities of government agencies in Central and South America.)

Three Soviet sources in the Rockefeller Commission came from the Hemispheric News Service, a press agency that concentrated on Latin American affairs. Robert Miller served as president, Jack Fahy as vice-president, and Joseph Gregg as manager. All three were secret Communists and all three shared experience in the Spanish Civil War: Miller as an employee of a Spanish Republican government information agency, Fahy and Gregg as soldiers in the Comintern's International Brigades. All three also became Soviet intelligence sources during World War II.

In the spring of 1940, the KGB New York station informed Moscow that in response to its request to the CPUSA to recommend two secret Communist journalists for its use, "'The head master [Browder] of the local fellowcountrymen [Communist Party] recommended . . . through Sound [Golos]: Robert Miller and George Seldes. The former has only just applied for membership in the organization (meaning a secret enrollment). . . . They both run independent newspaper agencies (financially well-off and independent), which we could put to successful use. We could carry on work with them through Sound.'"[104]

Robert T. Miller, III, new recruit to the CPUSA, soon became a new recruit to the KGB. Miller was born 5 April 1910 in Pittsburgh, where his father was a prominent wealthy surgeon. He attended Princeton and received a master's in English in 1932. Through family connections he traveled to Russia in September 1934 for a company trying to develop U.S.-Soviet trade. The business floundered, and in 1935 Miller began to file reports for American and British newspapers, including Reuters and the *Baltimore Sun*. While in Moscow, he met and married Jennifer Levy, a New Yorker of Russian descent who had arrived there in 1932 and worked for the *Moscow Daily News*. Miller and his wife left Russia in 1937. He was employed by the Spanish Republican government news agency for a year before returning to the United States in 1939. That summer he met Jack Fahy, and they agreed to set up Hemispheric News Service, financed from Miller's family inheritance. It concentrated on Latin American affairs, and Miller served as president, Fahy as vice-president, and Jennifer Levy Miller as secretary.[105]

The firm moved to Washington in 1941, and Joseph Gregg joined as its manager. Renamed the Export Information Bureau and devoted exclusively to research for the Coordinator of Inter-American Affairs with a yearly contract of $18,000, it was eventually absorbed by the CIAA, and Miller, Fahy, and Gregg became staff officers. All three also became Soviet intelligence assets, although apparently (and in accordance with good espionage tradecraft) unknown to each other.[106]

In the spring of 1941 Golos introduced Miller to his assistant, Elizabeth Bentley, and he began passing her material on Latin America, continuing to do so until 1944, including typewritten summaries of reports from the Office of Naval Intelligence, Army G-2 and the FBI that came to the CIAA. Miller transferred to a State Department position handling U.S.-USSR relations in June 1944 and later became assistant chief of the Division of Research and Publication before resigning in December 1946. Bentley told the FBI that Miller became increasingly nervous over his activities and stopped providing information after he entered the State Department. Miller acknowledged to the FBI in 1947 that he had met Bentley in New York and Washington, denied ever giving her government documents, but "did admit that he may have discussed confidential matters with the informant generally and in a casual way." He told the FBI agents that he could not remember ever meeting Golos and denied being a member of the CPUSA, although he conceded he had been pro-Soviet ever since his sojourn in the USSR. His wording of his denial to the FBI that he did not "remember" meeting Golos rather than a flat denial possibly saved him from a perjury indictment inasmuch as FBI agents had observed and documented their encounter in April 1941.[107]

Anatoly Gorsky's 1948 memo on the exposure of Soviet assets in the United States listed Miller as a source endangered by Bentley's defection. Miller was identified as "Mirage." "Mirage" appears in the Venona decryptions as the cover name of an unidentified source turning over information on South American issues and details of German machinations south of the border. Additionally, one cable reported that "Mirage's wife" (Jennifer Levy Miller) had also provided information of assistance to the KGB. A November 1941 Moscow Center message noted, "Sound [Golos] receives information from "Mirage" [Miller], who works on the Rockefeller Committee in processing all the material that comes in from South America. Enclosure: "Sound's" three-page report." Miller is listed as among Bentley's sources in a 1944 KGB report but designated as having become "inactive" in a report Bentley gave to the KGB in January 1945, corroborating Bentley's FBI statement that he developed cold feet after he transferred to the Department of State.[108]

Like Miller, Jack Fahy had moved from a life of privilege into the hothouse of radical politics in the 1930s. Born in Washington, D.C., in 1908, he grew up in New York, where his father was senior partner of Walter J. Fahy and Co., a stock exchange firm. After working for Senator George Moses (R-NH) and campaigning for Herbert Hoover's election in 1928, Fahy joined the family firm. The stock market crash of 1929 jolted him out of Republicanism, and he joined the Socialist Party. Fahy was both adventurous and peripatetic; at various times he attended New York University, the Institute of International Affairs in Geneva, San Marcus University in Peru, Black Mountain College in North Carolina, and Montana State University, where he took courses in animal husbandry. He established several small companies, including a food business in Peru in 1933. He went to Spain in 1937 to fight in the International Brigades but under the auspices of the Socialist Party.[109]

Fahy was wounded in Spain and returned to the United States. He quickly quarreled with Norman Thomas over Socialist Party policy toward the Spanish Civil War and publicly resigned, with a letter published in the Communist *Daily Worker.* In the summer of 1939 Fahy met Miller, and they set up the Hemispheric News Service. After a brief stint at the CIAA, Fahy moved on to the Board of Economic Warfare where he held a position as "Principal Intelligence Officer." In 1943, just as he was about to move to the Department of the Interior to become chairman of the Territorial Affairs Bureau, Congressman Martin Dies included him on a list of government employees suspected of communism. He testified before Congress's Kerr Commission and claimed that his resignation letter from the Socialist Party was "silly and foolish" and described his past association with Communists as a youthful misadventure. The commission agreed, concluding that after 1938 he "returned to his affairs, has joined no organizations, written no articles and made no speeches" and noted that many persons had testified to his good character. It praised his "loyal service" and concluded that he "has not been guilty of any subversive activity." Deciphered Soviet cables show that the Kerr Commission could not have been more mistaken. Almost precisely when he was denying before a congressional committee any Communist involvement and proclaiming his divorce from political activity, Fahy was transmitting government documents to Georgy Pasko, secretary to the Soviet naval attaché in Washington and a Naval GRU officer. In January 1943 Naval

GRU in Moscow approved a special cash payment to Fahy as recognition of his service.[110]

Unlike his two partners in the Hemispheric News Service, Joseph Gregg was not wealthy. The son of Russian immigrants, he was born in Columbus, Ohio, in 1909 as Joseph Greenstein. He attended Ohio State University and held several jobs in the Midwest before moving to New York to work for the Department of Public Welfare. In 1936 he snared a position as a writer with the WPA. He met Fahy while both served as truck drivers with the International Brigades in Spain. He joined Hemispheric News Service when it moved to Washington in 1941 and followed it into the Rockefeller Commission.[111]

In November 1945 Elizabeth Bentley told the FBI that Jacob Golos recruited Gregg shortly after he began work for the CIAA and that she began liaison work with him in 1942 and continued to be in contact with him until well into 1944. She said he turned over enough ONI, Army G-2, and FBI information on South America that came to his office that in 1943 Golos gave him a Leica camera to photograph his material. Golos liked to reassure his sources that their information went to the CPUSA. In Gregg's case, she noted, she had once taken him to a private meeting in New York to discuss Latin American affairs with Communist chief Earl Browder. Bentley said that early in 1945 Joseph Katz told her that Gregg "had become somewhat alarmed in passing on this information and felt that, if this information was going directly to the Russians, he, as an American, was doing something he should not be doing. However, his Russian contact was able to convince Gregg that as a good Communist he was performing a service that any other good Communist would perform and succeeded in convincing Gregg to continue with his activities. Jack subsequently told me that they were considering using Gregg as a courier or liaison man in Washington, D.C., on behalf of the Russians."[112]

KGB documents largely corroborate Bentley's account. An April 1944 report stated: "On "Maxim's" [Zarubin's] instructions "Mer" [Akhmerov] attempted several times to turn "Dir" [Mary Price], "Koch" [Duncan Lee] "Mirage," [Robert Miller], "Hare" [Maurice Halperin], and "Gor" [Joseph Gregg] over to "Maxim's" operatives. But each time there have been obstacles: Helmsman's [Browder's] personal approval is needed, a probationer is too squeamish and fearful, equipment is needed for communications and so forth." Akhmerov indicated that it was Bentley who was putting up the obstacles, and "it's imperative to insist to Helmsman [Browder] that the probationers be turned over." And they were, including Gregg. By January 1945 a report by Gorsky, Washington station chief, listed Gregg as one of the agents being managed by Joseph Katz and noted that Gregg was being groomed to be a "group leader" of other sources. A late 1944 retrospective report by Vasily Zarubin, station chief before Gorsky, summarized Gregg's role: ""Gor" is Joseph . . . , a fellowcountryman [Communist], who was with the Lincoln Brigade in Spain and was described by "Sound" [Golos] as a reliable and tested comrade. He works in the Information Section of the Rockefeller Committee on South American Affairs. He provided a lot of interesting documented polit. information. He worked hard and was glad to do so. He photographed documents himself with a camera that we passed to him.'" Zarubin also noted that Golos had told him that Gregg "'didn't know that he was working specifically for us [KGB],'" a situation with which Katz had to deal when he took over direct liaison from Bentley.[113]

Nathan Gregory Silvermaster

Gregory Silvermaster, in partnership with his wife, Helen, and their close friend Ludwig Ullmann, led a World War II espionage network drawn from the CPUSA's underground in Washington with more than a dozen government sources. Initially a CPUSA enterprise that reported to the KGB via Jacob Golos and Elizabeth Bentley, starting in late 1944 it came under direct KGB supervision.

The broad outline of the Silvermaster network has been known ever since Bentley's defection. The Venona decryptions also contain dozens of KGB cables dealing with its activities and members. KGB documents in Vassiliev's notebooks bring out matters that postdated Bentley's involvement and fill in details about Silvermaster himself that were only imperfectly understood. Iskhak Akhmerov, chief of the KGB's illegal station, first met Silvermaster in mid-1944, and in August 1945 he sent Moscow Center a biographical sketch:

He is 46 years old. Born near Odessa. Father—owned a stone quarry; previously—a plain worker. In 1905, during the Odessa pogrom, his family moved to Harbin, Manchuria. At the age of 12, he enrolled at the English school in Shanghai, and after graduating at the age of 15, he moved to the USA. From 1915 to 1920 he studied at the University of California and later at the University of Washington in Seattle; he worked as a laborer, as a farm-hand, in shipyards, canneries, etc. In 1917, he took part in various student and Russian immigrant organizations and held Bolshevik views. He joined the Comparty [Communist Party] in Seattle immediately upon its foundation in 1919. He took part in the University movement and oth. groups during the general strike in Seattle, as well as in demonstrations by Russian immigrants. He wrote articles for the Russian newspaper, which was financed by the "International Workers Organization."

In 1920, Robert [Gregory Silvermaster] left Seattle because of his asthma and went back to California, where he worked on farms and in oth. places. From 1924 to 1931, he taught at a Catholic college in Oakland, California. At the time, he did not maintain systematic ties with the Comparty. In 1932, he got his PhD from the University of California, where he was teaching at the time. That same year, he renewed ties with the CP under an assumed name. He worked with George Harrison, who published one Chinese and two Japanese trade union newspapers. In 1933–35, he worked for various government agencies of the state of California and worked for George on certain confidential matters. He met "Helmsman" [Browder] in 1934, and during the general strike in San Francisco, he gave him cover and acted as his courier during his stay in San Francisco. He performed the same functions concurrently for the secretary of the Japanese CP—Okano.

In 1935, he relocated to Washington to work in government agencies: the Resettlement Administration . . . , the Maritime Labor Board . . . , the Farm Security Administration, and the Board of Economic Warfare. In 1935–39, on Helmsman's advice, he neither made contacts in Washington nor in NY (that is, contacts with the CP). On "Helmsman's" advice, "Robert" took part in the liberal movement. Before going to prison, "Helmsman" gave Sound [Golos] permission to approach Robert with the aim of expanding our work in Washington. Robert soon became the handler of a group consisting of Peak [Frank Coe] and Sachs [Solomon Adler], with the subsequent addition of Aileron [George Silverman] and Richard [Harry White]. The latter two were in contact with anoth. group, which conducted analogous work.[114]

Harry Dexter White

The most important member of the Silvermaster network and the most highly placed asset the Soviets possessed in the American government was Harry Dexter White, assistant secretary of the treasury. More than two dozen KGB documents, spanning 1941 to 1948, spell out his assistance to Soviet intelligence.[115]

White was born in 1892 to a family of Lithuanian Jewish immigrants, his father a successful entrepreneur who built a small chain of four hardware stores. He served in World War I as an Army officer, graduated from Stanford University, and received a PhD from Harvard. White joined the Treasury in 1934 and rose swiftly, becoming director of the Division of Monetary Research in 1938, assistant to the secretary of the treasury in

1941, and assistant secretary of the treasury in 1945. Secretary of the Treasury Henry Morgenthau's extensive diary shows that no individual had greater influence on him in the late 1930s and during World War II than White. He and John Maynard Keynes were also the chief financial/technical architects in 1944 of the historic Bretton Woods monetary agreement, which structured international monetary policy for decades to come. President Truman appointed White the first American director of the International Monetary Fund (IMF) in 1946. Vice-President Henry Wallace regarded White as a trusted adviser and confidant and stated that had he become president, White would have been his secretary of the treasury.[116]

New KGB materials fill in the gaps in the existing body of evidence regarding White's participation in espionage. Whittaker Chambers stated that in the mid-1930s White had been a source for his GRU-CPUSA network. He had provided information both in oral briefings and in handwritten summaries, one of which Chambers hid in 1938 and produced in 1948, along with State Department documents provided by Alger Hiss. Chambers described White as more of a Soviet sympathizer than a disciplined CPUSA member, someone who cooperated with the party underground to the extent he wished but didn't take orders, an attitude that occasionally irritated Chambers's GRU superior. White's independence continued when he came into the KGB's orbit in the early 1940s. In 1944, Vasily Zarubin, in the report on his tenure as New York KGB station chief, wrote: "'"Jurist" [White] is rough around the edges and a lot of work has to be done on him before he will make a valuable informant. To date he has reported only what he deemed necessary himself.'" Earlier Moscow Center had told the KGB New York station: "'According to information we have received, "Jurist" [White] at one time was a probationer [agent] for the neighbors [GRU]. We will communicate detailed information about him separately. He should, at last, be properly recruited for work and taken on for direct communications. In view of "Jurist's" value and the necessity of adhering to the rules of covert work, we consider it advisable to assign a special illegal to work with him.'"[117]

Moscow Center assigned a high priority to establishing direct access to White and wanted to remove Silvermaster as an intermediary, but this goal was difficult. First, as Elizabeth Bentley told the FBI in 1945 and as Venona decryptions confirmed, Silvermaster fiercely resisted being removed from the loop, jealous that it diminished his importance. Second, given White's high standing in Washington, direct meetings with a Soviet contact required great care. The KGB was not, however, concerned that

White himself was under an illusion that his information only went to the Communist Party. Akhmerov reported: "'When asked what 'Jurist' [White] knew about 'Pal's' [Silvermaster's] work, the latter replied that 'J' knows where his info. goes, which is precisely why he transmits it in the first place.'" A Soviet operative held the first direct covert KGB contact with White in July 1944. White answered a series of questions about American foreign policy, and the report on the meeting went on to say: "As regards the technique of further work with us Jurist [White] said that his wife was ready for any self-sacrifice; he himself did not think about his personal security, but a compromise would lead to a political scandal and the discredit of all supporters of the new course, therefore he would have to be very cautious. . . . Jurist has no suitable apartment for a permanent meeting place; all his friends are family people. Meetings could be held at their houses in such a way that one meeting devolved on each every 4–5 months. He proposes infrequent conversations lasting up to half an hour while driving in his automobile." Silvermaster, however, was angered by the meeting, and his hostile reaction to having been bypassed appeared to have caused the KGB New York station to defer additional direct contacts for a time.[118]

But when Moscow Center learned that White would be a senior adviser to the U.S. delegation at the founding conference of the United Nations in San Francisco, it ordered Akhmerov to arrange contact protocols through Silvermaster so that a KGB officer could meet with him. White met KGB officer Vladimir Pravdin in San Francisco, gave him information on the American negotiating strategy, assured him that "Truman and Stettinius want to achieve the success of the conference at any price," and advised that if Soviet diplomats held firmly to their demand that the USSR get a veto of UN actions, the Americans "will agree." He offered other tactical advice on how the Soviets might defeat or water down positions advanced by his own government and answered a long series of questions on a variety of issues about which Soviet diplomats wanted to know American positions. Moscow Center told the KGB New York station that the results demonstrated what "'skillful guidance'" could get from White. Moscow also appointed Pravdin as the new KGB station chief in New York.[119]

Throughout 1945 White kept Moscow fully informed about the internal discussions within the government about Soviet requests for financial aid and a massive dollar loan. Despite his tendency to turn over material that he thought of importance rather than following Moscow's priorities, the KGB regarded him as an exceedingly valuable source. After

President Truman replaced Morgenthau with Frederick Vinson in July 1945, White's influence diminished, and he considered leaving the Treasury for a private Washington consulting business. Pravdin met with White in October 1945 and urged him to hang on: "'It was pointed out to Reed [White] how important it was to us for him to keep his post and so forth. Reed replied, however, that we wouldn't lose anything from his departure, since Peak [Frank Coe] would replace him perfectly well. Besides, according to Reed, if he succeeded in establishing the planned office in Carthage [Washington], he would not only retain his capabilities for informing us, but would even be able to expand his connections.'" (Frank Coe, who replaced White as director of the Treasury's Division of Monetary Research, was a secret Communist and an active KGB source.)[120]

White did not stay at Treasury, but neither did he open a private consulting firm. He assumed his position as director of the IMF in May 1946. His contact with the KGB by this point, however, was over. In November 1945 Moscow had learned of Bentley's defection and assumed, rightly, that she had briefed the FBI on White's cooperation with Soviet intelligence. It ordered the New York station and Pravdin to "break off contact" with White. There is nothing indicating a renewal of contact prior to his death in August 1948.[121]

Increasingly at odds with American policy and suffering from heart problems, White resigned from the IMF in March 1947. He supported Henry Wallace's decision to launch the Progressive Party in 1948, but his health prevented him from taking an active role. On 31 July Elizabeth Bentley described White in testimony to the House Committee on Un-American Activities as one of the government officials who had assisted Soviet intelligence through the Silvermaster apparatus in 1943 and 1944. Whittaker Chambers testified on 3 August that White had assisted the CPUSA's underground organization in Washington in the mid-1930s. White demanded an opportunity to respond and testified on 13 August 1948. He vehemently denied giving any assistance to the Communist Party or Soviet intelligence and insisted that he had no knowledge that any of his close associates had been Communists. He cited more than a decade of public service, and in ringing tones declared: "I believe in freedom of religion, freedom of speech, freedom of thought, freedom of the press, freedom of criticism, and freedom of movement. I believe in the goal of equality of opportunity, and the right of each individual to follow the calling of his or her own choice, and the right of every individual to an opportunity to develop his or her capacity to the fullest. I consider these principles sacred. I regard them as the basic fabric of our American way of life, and I believe in them as living realities, and not mere words on paper. That is my creed." It was a powerful statement, the audience applauded, and the press treated it as a convincing repudiation of Bentley's and Chambers's charges. White dramatically died of a heart attack three days later, passing into mythology as a martyr to liberalism. But the evidence is overwhelming. Harry Dexter White assisted Soviet military intelligence in the mid-1930s and the KGB from 1943 to 1945 and perjured himself in his congressional testimony.[122]

Lauchlin Currie

Lauchlin Currie was another high-ranking government official who steadfastly denied ever working with Soviet intelligence but who passed information to the Soviets through the Silvermaster network. When Whittaker Chambers met with Adolf Berle in 1939, he identified Currie as a "'Fellow Traveler'—helped various Communists—never went the whole way." Bentley's deposition to the FBI in 1945 stated that Currie had helped Silvermaster get a job at the Board of Economic Warfare and:

Lauchlin Currie was friendly with the Silvermasters and was particularly friendly with George Silverman. To the best of my recollection, Currie did not supply Silverman or the Silvermasters with any documents, but used to inform Silverman orally on various matters. As an example of the information orally furnished Silverman, I recall one occasion when Currie informed him that the United States was on the verge of breaking the Soviet code. I recall that Currie was a social guest on occasion at the Silvermaster home, although never when I was present as I have never met him, and the only significant information concerning him I presently recall is that after Golos' death there was a discussion between Silvermaster and 'Bill' [Iskhak Akhmerov] as to the advisability of introducing Currie and Harry White directly to the Russian contact. . . . Currie himself was actively assisting in passing on information coming to him in the course of his duties.[123]

Born in Nova Scotia in 1902 and educated at the London School of Economics, Lauchlin Currie went to Harvard for a doctorate in economics. In 1934 he became an American citizen and got a job with Harry White in the U.S. Treasury and then moved to the Federal Reserve Board. Currie joined the White House staff in 1939 as a senior administrative assistant to President Roosevelt, who sent him to China in 1941 and 1942 on special missions as his personal representative. The White House detailed Currie to serve as deputy administrator and day-to-day head of the Foreign Economic Administration in 1943, an indication of his key role in wartime Washington. After FDR's death in April 1945, however, President Truman accepted his resignation and Currie left government service.

The FBI interviewed Currie in 1947, and he denied that he had assisted Soviet intelligence, although he admitted a close relationship with Gregory Silvermaster and George Silverman (he insisted he had no reason to suspect either of Communist sympathies). He hedged on one of the few specifics that Bentley had remembered. In response to a question about American efforts to decipher Soviet codes, Currie said he did not remember discussing the matter with Silverman but said he might have done so since his friend was a government employee (an economist at the Railroad Retirement Board). When Currie testified to Congress in 1948, likely realizing that Bentley had only indirect knowledge of his activities through Silvermaster and Silverman, neither of whom was cooperating with the FBI, he flatly denied any indiscretion and also denied any suspicions that any of his friends had Communist sympathies.[124]

While the press paid relatively little attention to Currie during the 1948 hearings, the FBI, which believed Currie had lied repeatedly, continued its investigation. It interviewed William Y. Elliott, a senior official with the National Security Council, who recalled that sometime in 1944, when he was an administrator at the War Production Board, Currie had told him that American cryptanalysts had broken the Soviet diplomatic code. Elliott reported that Currie claimed to have "tipped off" the Soviets because he was attempting to prevent "the sowing of seeds of distrust between allies." Meanwhile, Lauchlin Currie took a permanent job in Colombia in 1950 and later married a Colombian citizen. In 1955 he lost his naturalized American citizenship and later became a Colombian national.[125]

Nine deciphered KGB cables discussed Currie. While Bentley had been under the impression that Currie provided only verbal briefings, an August 1943 KGB New York cable reported to Moscow that Currie gave Silverman a memorandum on an unspecified political subject that was either from or for the State Department. More significant, in June 1944 the KGB New York reported that Currie provided information on President Roosevelt's reasons for keeping Charles de Gaulle at arm's length. Currie also told the Soviets that contrary to his publicly stated position, Roosevelt was willing to accept Stalin's demand that the USSR keep the half of Poland that it had received under the Nazi-Soviet Pact of 1939 and that FDR would put pressure on the Polish government-in-exile to make concessions to the Soviets.[126]

Up to 1944 Currie dealt with Soviet intelligence at a distance through Silverman and Silvermaster. Vasily Zarubin, reflecting on his time as a KGB station chief, said: "'Page' [Currie] cannot be considered organizationally connected to 'Pal's' [Silvermaster's] group. He is merely a good acquaintance of 'Aileron' [Silverman] and sometimes meets with 'Pal' himself. The latter pair draw some information on polit. issues from him.'" Zarubin noted that he wanted to meet with Currie directly, but he had come under FBI surveillance (due to the "anonymous letter"; see chapter 9), and: "'I personally made an attempt to establish a personal relationship with 'Page.' However, the circumstances under which I was in 'Carthage' [Washington] made it impossible for me to have contact with him. His status was too high for mine, and in addition this already occurred during the period I was under surveillance. It was impossible to create a situation for meetings with him, let alone explain these meetings, without drawing suspicion to him.'"[127]

Deciphered KGB cables confirm Bentley's statement that the KGB sought direct contact with Currie but had not achieved it during her tenure as the group's liaison up to the early fall of 1944 because of objections from Silvermaster. An October 1944 cable refers to Akhmerov meeting with Currie, along with Silvermaster and Silverman. Akhmerov, however, usually presented himself to his sources as an American Communist who assisted Soviet intelligence and not as what he was, a KGB officer and chief of the illegal station. A February 1945 Moscow Center to New York station message directed: "Find out from Albert [Akhmerov] and Robert [Silvermaster] whether it would be possible for us to approach Page [Currie] direct." A March 1945 message from Moscow noted, "Page [Currie] trusts Robert [Silvermaster], informs him not only orally, but also by handing over documents." But Fitin, head of KGB foreign intelligence, told his New York station that he wanted more out of Currie: "Up to now Page's [Currie's] relations with Robert [Silvermaster] were expressed, from our point of view, only in common feelings and personal sympathies. [Unrecovered code groups] question of more profound relations and an understanding by Page of Robert's role. If Robert does not get Page's transfer to our worker, then he [unrecovered code groups] raising with Page the question of Page's closer complicity with Robert." The March 1945 message was the last one concerning Currie that the National Security Agency deciphered, so the Venona decryptions do not establish that the KGB succeeded in removing Silvermaster and Silverman as intermediaries and establishing direct contact with Currie. A reasonable interpretation of all the evidence leads to the conclusion that

Currie was well aware that the documents and information he gave Silverman and Silvermaster went to Moscow. Nonetheless, his defenders have clung to the view that Currie simply was indiscreet, naively briefing and handing over documents about sensitive policy matters to friends who turned out to be Soviet spies.[128]

More than two dozen KGB documents in Vassiliev's notebooks, the earliest from 1941 and the latest from 1948, settle the matter. They show that Currie actively assisted Soviet intelligence via Silvermaster and Silverman from 1941 until 1945. They also show that after Zarubin's departure in mid-1944, Moscow Center continually pressed its American stations to bring Currie into a more direct agent relationship, which Silvermaster resisted but to which he eventually acceded. In late 1945 the KGB Washington station reported: "In Oct. 1945 a recruitment conversation was held with L. C. [Lauchlin Currie]. After some hesitation, he agreed to cooperate and gave several informational materials." There is no indication which KGB officer held the "recruitment conversation" with Currie, but in 1947 Currie admitted to the FBI that in 1945 he met several times with the first secretary of the Soviet Embassy, Anatoly Gromov; he described the meetings as harmless discussions on cultural subjects. Gromov was the pseudonym used by Anatoly Gorsky, chief of the KGB Washington station, who had replaced Zarubin as the senior KGB officer in the United States. Gorsky's report of his expenses for meetings with persons of "oper. [operational] interest" includes $15 for dinner with Currie in January 1945. (This was an expensive dinner, the equivalent of a restaurant bill of $175 in 2008.)[129]

The first KGB document dealing with Currie was from April 1941, noting that Silvermaster had sent in a summary of Currie's report on his first trip to China. He followed this with a summary of Currie's briefings on American Far Eastern policy. Moscow Center recognized Currie's importance and directed that Silvermaster should make recruiting his friend as a regular source a high priority. By January 1942 Moscow Center treated Currie as part of Silvermaster's group and assigned him the cover name "Page" but recognized that he did not yet have a regular agent relationship and was "being used without his knowledge," meaning without being explicitly told his information went to Moscow via the KGB. (One may doubt that Currie, a man of political sophistication, really thought that Silvermaster, then a mid-level economist with the Farm Security Administration, needed to be told the details of America's China policy and that the information went no further.)[130]

In 1942 Silvermaster won a transfer from the Farm Security Administration (a place of no interest to the KGB) to the Board of Economic Warfare. But no sooner had Silvermaster arrived than Army security officers objected, citing evidence that he was a secret Communist. Silvermaster submitted a lengthy rebuttal to the allegations in which he denied any participation in Communist activity and passed a copy of his statement to the KGB New York station. Additionally, his new boss at the BEW met with General George Strong, chief of Army G-2, and attempted to placate him, but Strong adamantly demanded that Silvermaster be removed from any position with access to sensitive information. Silvermaster then appealed to Robert Patterson, assistant secretary of war. Jacob Golos sent a report to Moscow about what happened next:

"A large number of people was dismayed by 'Pal's' [Silvermaster's] dismissal. The head of the Farm Security Administration, Baldwin—'P's' former superior—was very angry. Currie called Assistant Secretary of War Patterson to protest. He told Patterson that 'P' did not follow the 'Party line,' that 'P.' had supported general military efforts long before the attack on the Sov. Union, and that his position had not abruptly changed after 22 June 1941. Patterson replied that this changed things to a considerable degree and asked him to produce documentary evidence. Currie said that he did not have any written evidence but that he had spoken to 'P.' on numerous occasions and is confident about his views. Currie subsequently spoke with Baldwin, and the latter agreed with him in this matter, saying that he might be able to find some memoranda corroborating Currie's point of view. A Treasury Department official, White, called Patterson to protest the actions being taken against 'P.'"

Calvin "Beanie" Baldwin, Silvermaster's former superior at the Farm Security Administration, was a secret Communist. Harry White, like Currie, was a KGB source delivering information via the Silvermaster network. Patterson deferred to the highly placed Currie and White, overruled Army G-2, and thus enabled Silvermaster to expand his espionage activities, becoming a source in his own right as well as managing a network of sources.[131]

Silvermaster's problems, however, were not over. In 1943 the FBI opened an independent investigation. Again Currie rushed to the rescue. Two FBI agents interviewed him, and again Currie assured the investigators that suspicions about Silvermaster were misplaced. The KGB New York station followed the matter closely; Vasily Zarubin, station chief, reported to Moscow: "'At the demand of Attorney General Biddle, the "Hut" [FBI] has resumed his investigation. "Page" [Currie] was recently visited by two "Hut" agents: they wanted to find out whether "Pal" [Silvermaster] was a fellowcountryman [Communist]. "Page" supposedly replied that he had known "Pal" for a long time and that the latter did not belong to a fellowcountryman organization. We are following the progress of this matter and will report on the results.'" A few weeks later Zarubin reported that Currie's work was paying off: "'One of our telegrams reported to you that the investigation of "Pal's" [Silvermaster's] case had been resumed on the demand of Attorney General Biddle. Recently a message came in from "Pal" saying that "Page" [Currie] had made every effort to close his case: when "Pal's" case was submitted for consideration by the committee of five under "Captain" [Roosevelt], he managed to sway most of the committee members in favor of dropping the investigation. He doesn't know the committee's final decision, but "Page" believes that the investigation will be terminated.'" Currie was right. With an influential presidential aide vouching for Silvermaster, the FBI decided to drop the matter.[132]

In her 1945 FBI deposition Bentley explained that her removal as liaison with the Silvermaster group by the fall of 1944 was the KGB's first step in its intentions to take direct control, split the group into more manageable units, and establish direct agent ties with such valuable sources as Lauchlin Currie. KGB cables confirm her story and carry it into 1945 as Silvermaster fought to retain control of the extraordinarily large network he had created. In regard to Currie in particular, a Moscow Center report in January 1945 noted Silvermaster's attempt to stave off direct KGB contact: "'Robert [Silvermaster] doesn't consider the recruitment of "Page" [Currie] feasible ("Robert" bases his view on the fact that "Page" isn't ready to become a fellowcountryman [Communist]).'" Moscow Center, however, told the KGB New York station it wasn't buying that argument, insisting: "'We believe that it is inadvisable to give up on him [Currie], because even sporadic contact with him is highly useful to us.'" Roosevelt's death and Currie's discharge from the White House delayed the matter, but in October 1945 that "recruitment conversation" with Currie took place, and "after some hesitation, he agreed to cooperate and gave several informational materials."[133]

The KGB had finally achieved direct contact and formally recruited Lauchlin Currie. While he was no longer a White House aide and did not have direct access to sensitive government information, he knew a great deal and might once again become a key figure in Washington. But no sooner had he been recruited than Elizabeth Bentley defected. A Moscow Center cable on 23 November 1945 ordered the KGB New York station to "break off contact" with thirteen high-value agents known to her; one was "Page"/Currie. There is no indication that the KGB ever reestablished contact.[134]

Bela and Sonia Gold

Another member of the Silvermaster network was steered to it on the recommendation of Henry Ware. While Bela Gold was not quite as lucky in avoiding public scrutiny as Ware, he did manage to outlive a brief spate of notoriety. Illustrating the adage that American life provides for improbable second acts, Gold found remarkable academic success as an expert on technology transfer. His first career in covertly transferring information from the United States to the Soviet Union, like that of so many others, began in Communist student groups in New York.

Bela Gold was born in 1915 in Kolozsvár, Hungary, and came to the United States with his parents when he was four years old. He graduated from New York University with a degree in industrial engineering and then went to study economics at Columbia University, where he encountered Ware. Along with his wife, Sonia Steinman Gold, whom he married in 1938, Gold, who sometimes anglicized his name as Bill or William, moved to Washington in the early 1940s to work for the Senate Subcommittee on War Mobilization and then for the Agriculture Department and the Foreign Economic Administration. Sonia also held government research positions and served for a time as Harry Dexter White's assistant.

The Golds established ties with an underground CPUSA unit led by Henry Collins, whose members included Edward Fitzgerald. Later Fitzgerald became a leading figure in the Perlo espionage group. Evaluating Bela Gold, whom he had known as a member of Collins's CPUSA cell, Fitzgerald told the KGB:

"When he and his wife worked in my group, he struck me as an excellent worker. He is extremely engaging and gives the impression of being exceptionally educated. His political views are for the most part correct, though in my opinion they are a little bit formalist. He is not as good at judging people. . . . Gold always expressed willingness to receive assignments. However, after some time it became obvious that he could not manage the work. He would usually look for various excuses. These incidents became more and more frequent. . . .

He left my group to work on a senate committee. I contacted him, and he told me that he had established a connection with another group. . . . I explained to him that I did not have any directives about his leaving for another group and pointed out to him that another group could not, in that case, have recruited him for work. He told me that this matter had been settled by a higher authority. . . . It was easy to see that he was talking about a group that was higher up than the Central Committee; he also alluded to this group's international connections. . . . When I turned to NY for advice, I was told not to bring this matter up and to avoid it."[135]

Gold's new group did indeed have international connections. Following Henry Ware's recommendation, the KGB had assigned Jacob Golos to evaluate the Golds and gave them cover names: Bela was "Acorn" and Sonia was "Zhenya." Vasily Zarubin noted that Silvermaster "'got in touch with him [Gold] and his wife'" and obtained "'good information from them and considers them to be valuable people.'" Another KGB report indicates that Silvermaster first recruited Sonia in 1943 and then Bela.[136]

Cables in 1944 and 1945 describe the Golds as "conscientious and disciplined," and in special recognition of Sonia's productivity, the KGB gave her a $500 bonus in late 1945. (She had obtained reports on American loans to China and negotiations with French leader Charles de Gaulle.) When the KGB got direct control of the Silvermaster network, one of its priorities was to get direct access to the Golds and separate them from Silvermaster. But the KGB New York station noted: "It costs Robert [Silvermaster] great pains to keep the couple and other probationers [agents] in check and to get good work out of them. Being their leader in the fellowcountrymanly [CPUSA] line Robert has the opportunity to give them orders. In Albert's [Akhmerov] opinion our workers would hardly manage to work with the same success under the fellowcountrymanly flag." By the fall of 1945 the Golds' productivity had declined. Sonia went on maternity leave, and with the war over, the Foreign Economic Administration, where Bela worked, was slated for abolition. An attempt to find him a position at the State Department came to nothing. George Silverman offered his KGB contact the opinion in October 1945 that Bela Gold no longer had "'any major opportunities and will not be able to provide us with important information.'"[137]

It was all over, in any event. While Elizabeth Bentley had not dealt with the Golds directly, Silvermaster had discussed them and delivered their espionage product to her. Moscow cut ties with both Golds. The FBI interviewed them, but they both denied passing along information. Both testified to the House Committee on Un-American Activities in 1948 and denied Communist Party membership and any cooperation with Soviet intelligence. The evidence from KGB documents in Vassiliev's notebooks, as well as deciphered KGB cables of the Venona project, shows that both provided perjured testimony.[138]

Possibly because they denied Bentley's charges and did not invoke the Fifth Amendment, unlike most of their comrades, Bela and Sonia Gold were able to escape relatively unscathed from the 1948 House Committee on Un-American Activities hearings. After leaving government service, Bela secured a teaching position at the University of Pittsburgh business school and embarked on a career as a professor, and memories of Bentley's charges and his testimony faded away. By 1981 he was director of research in industrial economics at Case Western Reserve and a member of the Committee on Computer-Aided Manufacturing of the National Research Council. He authored several books and numerous scholarly articles, lectured around the world, and received grants from the Ford Foundation. His career ended as the Fletcher Jones Professor of Technology and Management at Claremont Graduate School.

Other Bentley Sources

All of the other members of the Silvermaster network who worked for the federal government and were identified by Bentley appear in documents in Vassiliev's notebooks, ranging from Silvermaster's chief assistant, Ludwig Ullmann, to such figures as Solomon Adler, David Weintraub, George Perazich, Frank Coe, Norman Bursler, and Irving Kaplan. Additionally, virtually all of the singleton agents whom Bentley named also make at least cameo appearances, including William Remington and Willard Park. One of the main challenges to Bentley's veracity came from William Taylor, a Treasury Department official working on international financial questions who sued the *Washington Daily News* in 1954 for libel for reporting Bentley's statement that he was part of an espionage ring. Not wanting the expense of a trial, the newspaper settled out of court and withdrew its statements about Taylor. Bentley never retracted her charges. Taylor's lawyers prepared a wide-ranging study that assailed Bentley as a fraud and circulated it to the press. Despite the FBI's preparing a memo that replied point-by-point to Taylor's claims and that supported Bentley's credibility, numerous historians have accepted Taylor's claims and his legal victory as demonstrating that Bentley's charges were false. Taylor, however, was identified in KGB documents as a source codenamed "Odysseus," reporting to the KGB through Silvermaster's apparatus, just as Bentley said. Likewise, William Remington, an economist with the War Production Board and Commerce Department, convicted of perjury in 1953 for denying Bentley's charges and later murdered in prison, was depicted by some historians as innocent of espionage. Zarubin identified him in a report as a source who "'provided information on war-production matters'" with the cover name "Fedya."[139]

Zarubin's September 1944 report evaluated other members of the Silvermaster group as well. Ludwig Ullmann, who worked for the Army Air Force and held officer's rank, "'obtains information himself, maintains communication with 'Peak' [Frank Coe] and 'Aileron' [George Silverman] and, in addition, photographs materials . . . and he is privy to all of the group's business.'" Zarubin noted that while some were aware of the group's relationship to the KGB, others were not as clear about for whom they were stealing information. Coe, Harry White's assistant, had "'provided many valuable materials,'" but, according to Silvermaster, "'believes he is working for the Helmsman [Browder].'" George Silverman, "'a tested and reliable fellowcountryman [Communist],'" likewise "'doesn't know that he is working for us.'" By 1945, after the group was broken into smaller units reporting directly to Iskhak Akhmerov, Vladimir Pravdin, and Joseph Katz, that illusion, to the extent it still existed, ended.[140]

Victor Perlo

While the Silvermaster network was the largest espionage apparatus reporting to the KGB, that headed by Victor Perlo was a close second. Although it didn't have sources as highly placed as Harry White and Lauchlin Currie, in Harold Glasser, Charles Kramer, and Donald Wheeler (see chapter 5) it possessed well-connected and highly productive agents. Like Silvermaster, Perlo, a long-time leader of the Communist underground in Washington, drew his sources from mid-level government officials who were veteran members of the party's secret organization and ran his apparatus like a party unit.[141]

Perlo prepared an autobiography for the KGB, and in December 1944 Anatoly Gorsky, KGB station chief, sent a summary to Moscow Center:

Victor Perlo, born in Queens, New York, in 1912 to a family of Jews who had come to the USA from Tsarist Russia as children. Father—Samuel—is a lawyer; mother—Rachel—is a teacher.
Graduated from Columbia U. in 1933.
Worked: Summer 1932—waiter and gardener at a children's camp in Great Barrington.
Middle of 1933–June 1935—statistical analyst, assistant to a division chief at the National Recovery Administration. June 1935–Oct. 1937—assistant sta-

tistical analyst at the Federal Home Loan Bank Board. Oct. 1937–November 1939—researcher at the "Brookings Institution." November 1939–November 1940—secretary to the economic adviser at the Department of Commerce. November 1940–March 1943—head of the economic statistics division at the Office of Price Administration. March 1943–Sep. 1944—head of the Aviation Division of the Bureau of Programs and Statistics at the WPB [War Production Board]. September 1944–to present time—special assistant to the director of the Programs and Statistics Bureau of the WPB. Salary—$6,500 a year. . . .

Raid [Perlo] himself describes his present job as a sinecure, where he is tolerated only because there is no one to replace him. Through his job, "Raid" has access to the minutes of the WPB and of its various committees, to interdepartmental econ. summaries (about which "Gor" [Joseph Gregg] had previously informed us), and to various documents on military industry.

R. joined the Columbia University cell of the Comparty at the end of 1932 or the beginning of 1933, and during that time, he took part in propagandistic work among cafe workers. In 1933, he moved to Washington, where he did some kind of work individually with the unemployed. . . . In 1935, Raid belonged to the Washington Communist organization under the leadership of "Steve" [Josef Peters]. During this time, he met once or twice on "Steve's" instructions with V. J. Jerome, Gene Dennis, Roy Hudson, and a certain "Eugene" [unidentified]. "Vadim" [Gorsky] is not yet aware of the nature of the connection or the position of these people. R. repeatedly wrote various econ. articles for various Comm. newspapers and magazines, signing with various pseudonyms, and transmitted them through his Party leaders. In 1942–43, R. secretly helped "Pancake" [I. F. Stone] compile materials for various exposés by the latter.[142]

In the wake of Bentley's defection Perlo left the Treasury Department. The House Committee on Un-American Activities asked him to testify in 1948. He initially presented himself as a liberal and told the committee that he had only been "helping in my humble way to carry out the great New Deal program under the leadership of Franklin D. Roosevelt" but then invoked the Fifth Amendment to refuse to answer questions on his Communist and espionage links. In later years the theoretical journal of the American Communist Party announced that Perlo was "chairman of the Economic Commission of the CPUSA."[143]

Harold Glasser

Ample evidence has existed since 1948 that Harold Glasser had assisted Soviet intelligence. Whittaker Chambers identified him as a member of the Communist underground in Washington in the mid-1930s who assisted his GRU-linked apparatus. Elizabeth Bentley identified him as a source of the Perlo network in World War II. Eleven KGB cables deciphered by the Venona project discussed his work for the KGB under the cover name "Ruble." The documents in Vassiliev's notebooks not only add considerable depth and detail to what was known of Glasser's cooperation with the KGB, but also show that in 1945 the KGB Washington station, with very good reason, regarded Glasser as its most valuable source. The volume of high-level U.S. government documents he turned over to Moscow was astounding and unexpected. (Harold Glasser was not related to Abraham Glasser, discussed above.)[144]

Glasser and his wife both prepared short autobiographies for the KGB. His parents were Lithuanian Jews who settled in Chicago, where he was born in 1905. His father, a garment worker, died in 1909, and Harold, youngest of seven children, grew up in poverty. Nonetheless, he was able to graduate from the University of Chicago and pursue advanced studies at Harvard University. He secretly joined the Communist Party in 1933 while teaching at the People's Junior College in Chicago and became an active member of the CPUSA's clandestine party organization in Washington when he obtained a post as an economist at the Treasury Department in 1936.[145]

Glasser briefly discussed his work with Chambers's GRU network in his KGB autobiography (see chapter 1). After a cooling-off period to see if Chambers's defection resulted in FBI interest, GRU attempted to revive contact with his sources and did succeed in reestablishing contact with Alger Hiss. But it was unsuccessful in Glasser's case because Maxim Lieber, its agent, contacted Glasser just as he was about to depart on a two-year Treasury Department assignment to Ecuador. In his autobiography Glasser also noted that while on assignment in Ecuador "'the FBI's secret police were conducting an investigation. I was unable to get any information about the nature of this investigation, except for a suspicion that it was my membership in the Comparty [Communist Party] that was under investigation.'" He wrote that he was supported by the U.S. ambassador, Boaz Long, and nothing happened, but later, "'when I applied to the embassy for a passport, [Assistant Secretary of State] Berle . . . refused to issue me one, b/c I was supposedly still under investigation. Under pressure and attack from Harry White, Berle gave up and issued me a dip. [diplomatic] passport. Since then, I have not had any more problems getting a passport.'" Glasser had been protected in these security probes by the hidden network of Communists within the Treasury

Department. At various times in his Treasury career, fellow Communists and Soviet agents Frank Coe and Ludwig Ullmann determined his promotions and job ratings and Harry White reviewed and endorsed his civil service ratings. The FBI report on its suspicions about Glasser's party links went to White and nothing happened. And, as Glasser noted, White intervened with the State Department to see that the investigation didn't prevent him from getting an American diplomatic passport.[146]

The KGB attempted to enlist Glasser in early 1943 but aborted the recruitment when he left for Algeria on a Treasury Department assignment with American forces in North Africa. Following his return further delays developed over concern that he was still connected to GRU and the recall of Vasily Zarubin in mid-1944. A November 1944 memo by Elizabeth Zarubin discussed this first attempt and touched on the KGB's reliance on the CPUSA, personal rivalries among American Communists over assisting Soviet intelligence, and muddled lines of communications with Soviet military intelligence:

"In his time, 'Maxim' [Zarubin] arranged for the recruitment of 'Ruble' [Glasser] as our agent with Gene Dennis, who had received a corresponding directive from 'Helmsman' [Browder]. At the time, 'Ruble' was leaving on a business trip on behalf of the Treasury Department—to North Africa, where he was supposed to create a separate investigative branch of the Treasury Department. . . . Already there was no chance of our person setting up a personal meeting with 'Ruble,' b/c 'Ruble' departed without warning for his destination. Through Dennis, a password was specified with 'R.,' by which someone on behalf of Dennis was supposed to have contacted him in North Africa; furthermore, 'R.' was warned about the fact that this person might be Russian. Home [Moscow] was informed of this password, but no one contacted 'R.' in North Africa. When 'R.' came back from N. Africa, 'Maxim' asked Home for permission to have 'R' handed over to 'Pal' [Silvermaster] for a connection. When 'Mer' [Akhmerov] was informed of this, he said that 'Pal' told him that in a conversation with him, 'R.' had wanted information. 'Pal,' who has known 'R.' a long time, did not like being spoken to like this by 'R.,' and on the basis of his conversation with 'Pal,' 'Mer' got the impression that the personal relationship between 'Pal' and 'Ruble' was strained somehow. . . . 'Maxim' and 'Mer' stopped insisting to 'Pal' that he take 'Ruble' as a contact.

During her last conversation with 'Helmsman,' 'Vardo' [Elizabeth Zarubin] told him that we wanted to make 'Ruble' a direct contact of ours. 'Helmsman' agreed and said that he would give a corresponding order to Gene Dennis, who maintained contact with 'Ruble' on the Party line after his return from North Africa. Because our stations were under surveillance and 'Maxim' left, 'Ruble' failed to have been handed over to our worker.

'Ruble' should be familiar to 'Storm' ('Steve') [Josef Peters] as a member of the CPUSA, b/c he belongs to that group of Communist officials in Washington, with whom 'Storm' was affiliated several years ago. 'Ruble' is also known as a member of the CP to John Abt, whom 'Storm' used as a liaison with this group—for receiving party dues and information from them for 'Helmsman.' 'Reyna' [Marion Bachrach] had described 'Ruble' to Maxim and 'Vardo' as a secret member of the Party and a very loyal and reliable Communist of many years. 'Reyna' and her brother, John Abt, keep up a personal friendship with 'Ruble' and his wife.

'Pal' knows about John Abt and about the fact that he had a group of Communist workers from various government departments in Washington. It is possible that 'Pal' knows individual people from this group as well—besides 'Ruble.' There has always existed a kind of rivalry between 'Pal' and John Abt when it came to working with secret Communists in Washington, judging from our old files (see, for example, 'Pal's' file) and from certain remarks made by 'Sound' [Golos] in conversation with 'Vardo' and in the latter's conversation with Abt. Maybe Bayer, one of the editors of 'Soviet Russia Today' in Washington, was using Abt for the neighbors [GRU]. With regard to Bayer, we had certain pieces of information about the fact that he was the neighbors' worker. Soviet Russia Today is published by Jessica Smith, who is John Abt's wife. 'Ruble' could be adopted as a contact for our worker with the help of 'Helmsman's' brother, who could contact Dennis and arrange with him on 'Helmsman's' behalf to hand 'Ruble' over to someone by means of a password, or at a personal meeting."

(Dennis ran the CPUSA while Earl Browder served a prison sentence for use of a false passport. GRU cables deciphered by the Venona project confirm that Theodore Bayer was a GRU agent. Abt managed a group of government officials who were secret CPUSA members. On Browder's orders, in 1944 Abt turned over his group to Elizabeth Bentley, who referred to it as the "Perlo group" from its most influential figure and group manager, Victor Perlo. Bentley in her FBI deposition treated Glasser as a Perlo group source.)[147]

Moscow Center told Anatoly Gorsky in December 1944, "'Considering that 'Ruble' [Glasser] might become one of our most valuable probationers [sources] . . . it would be expedient to contact him directly,'" bypassing Perlo. Gorsky reported on Christmas Eve that he had made direct contact and another meeting would take place shortly. On New Year's Eve he forwarded to Moscow Glasser's description of what sort of information he could obtain, details of his public and private life, and how his role in the Communist underground might affect cooperation with the KGB. Gorsky noted: ""R." ["Ruble"/Glasser] undoubtedly knows which country and organization he works for, by name. According to him, no one has told him about this explicitly, but 'he is not such a child that he doesn't realize where and to whom exactly his materials have been going all these years.'" There was, however, considerable disentangling to do in regard to Glasser's dual role in the party underground and Soviet espionage. So loose had security been under Golos and Bentley that everyone in their Washington networks appeared to know what many of the others were doing. One can only imagine professionals at Moscow Center shaking their heads as they read Gorsky's report explaining that Glasser and his close friend Allan Rosenberg, an economist with the Foreign Economic Administration "discuss information that they send through "Raid" [Perlo] with each other, show it to each other, and essentially work together." Or the discomfort they felt when they learned that in Rome in early 1944 on a Treasury Department mission, Glasser had revealed to Italian Communist leader Palmiro Togliatti that he was a secret Communist and had given Togliatti information and American documents that would assist the Italian Communist Party.[148]

Also exasperating to Moscow would have been Gorsky's news that Silvermaster, apparently jealous that Perlo's group had in Glasser a source in the Treasury Department nearly as good as his own group's Harry White, was lobbying the KGB New York station to get Glasser handed over to his apparatus (already grossly too large in the KGB's view). Moscow Center told Gorsky: "Try to isolate "R." ["Ruble"/Glasser] from "Raid's" [Perlo's] group. Tactfully teach him the skills of konspiratsia [espionage tradecraft]. Tell him that a repeat of the Italian incident would be unacceptable." It also approved use of Faye Glasser as a courier between the KGB station and her husband Harold. Gorsky brushed away Silvermaster's attempt to get control of Glasser and also extracted him from the Perlo group. When Glasser proved inept with the Leica camera the KGB gave him, Gorsky decided to take advantage of his close friendship with Allan Rosenberg, an amateur photographer with a dark room at his home, by using him for that job.[149]

Eventually everything did get sorted out, and Glasser proved to be enormously productive. The summary inventory of government documents and memoranda that Glasser turned over to the KGB in 1945 takes up *five pages* of Vassiliev's notebooks, while the complete inventory in the KGB file from which Vassiliev made his summary takes up *twenty-one pages.* The inventory for January alone included the following:

5.1.45—Contents of a draft by Morgenthau's department [Treasury] with Allied policies with regard to neutral countries.

6.1.45—Draft instruction from the Commander-in-Chief of the armed forces of the USA, / England / (USSR)—control of German foodstuffs and agriculture.

8.1.45—On a conversation between Taylor and the Legal Counsel of the Polish government in London, Kulsky, about Poland's attitude to postwar Germany and about Sov.-Polish relations.

17.1.45—On a session of the Committee on Liberated Regions under the State Department, at which questions pertaining to civilian deliveries for liberated regions were discussed.

15.1.45—On the discussion in London of the draft instruction, "On the dismissal of German personnel from the German financial system."

9.1.45—On Eisenhower's telegram to the SSAS regarding forced evacuees to Germany.

18.1.45—Contents of a memorandum from the Subcommittee on Private Monopolies and Cartels dated 21 November '44–regarding the views of the Allied Military Occupation Board on German participation in int'l cartels.

20.1.45—Contents of a draft instruction to the Amer. Commander-in-Chief dated 22.11.44—Control of Germany's finances.

. . . —Draft instruction on the dissolution of the Nazi Party and the purging of Nazi personnel, dated 13 Oct. '44.

5.1.45—Memorandum regarding a meeting of the Amer. members of the Joint Committee on Civil Affairs to discuss: the dissolution of the Allied Commission in Italy, the unauthorized dispatch of rations from Allied storehouses by the English to Greece, and of Eng. assistance to the Norwegians.

25.1.45—Int. memorandum from "Ruble" [Glasser] to "Richard" [Harry White] regarding the state of negotiations with the English on changes to armistice terms with Italy.

29.1.45—Internal memorandum from Morgenthau's department regarding a conversation between "R-le" ["Ruble"/Glasser] and Emile Despres (from the State Dept) about the stance of the State Dep. and White House on Germany.

30.1.45—Int. memorandum from Morgenthau's representatives in London, L. A. Aarons and Gardner Patterson, dated 20.11.44, regarding their stay in Belgium and Belgian reactions to the treatment of Germany in the postwar period.

27.1.45—On negotiations by the Italian financial committee in the USA regarding the settlement of Italian-American financial relations.

30.1.45—On Taylor and Aarons' meeting with Kulsky and Freyd—Poles from the Armistice Committee—and the conversation between them about exacting reparations from Germany.

The KGB forwarded a number of Glasser's high-value documents to Stalin, Molotov, and Beria for their review. Moscow Center told Gorsky: "'Ruble' [Glasser] is one of the primary sources of information in your station. Of 'R's' materials that were forwarded to us by telegraph at the beginning of this year alone, 74 special reports were released to the echelon [Soviet leadership]. Your having established direct contact with 'Ruble' and the work that has been done to cultivate in him the necessary probationer [agent] qualities have served to improve his work.'" Under these circumstances, it is not surprising that Moscow Center recommended that Glasser receive the "Order of the Red Star." But it all came to an end with Bentley's defection. On 23 November 1945 the KGB New York station received the order: "Break off contact with: 'Ruble.'"[150]

Harold Glasser had many influential friends in Washington, and the FBI took its time moving against him. Meanwhile, he continued to work in senior-level positions. He became assistant director of the Office of International Finance, served as economic adviser to the American delegation at the Allied powers' Council of Foreign Ministers meeting in Moscow in 1947, and was economic adviser to the secretary of the treasury at the board of governors meeting of the World Bank. But in April and May 1947 the FBI finally interviewed him about Bentley's allegations. While admitting a social acquaintance with many members of the Perlo and Silvermaster networks, he denied knowing any of them were Communists. He described his own politics as "liberal" and not "radical," disclaimed Communist Party membership at any time, and denied ever passing any government documents or information to any unauthorized person, but he refused to sign a statement attesting to these claims. He resigned his Treasury position in December, taking a job as an economist with the New York City Council of Jewish Federations and Welfare Funds.[151]

Glasser was not called to testify to the House Committee on Un-American Activities in 1948, and the press largely ignored him. But in 1953 he had to testify twice: before the Senate Internal Security Subcommittee and the Permanent Subcommittee on Investigations of the Committee on Government Operations (Joseph McCarthy's committee). In both cases he invoked the Fifth Amendment. By 1954 he was working for Liberty Brush Company. Thereafter one of the KGB's most productive spies in Washington faded from public sight.[152]

Charles Kramer

Charles Kramer, another valuable Perlo group source, was born Charles Krivitsky in New York in 1906, attended New York University, and received BA and MA degrees in economics. He was hired as an economist by the Agricultural Adjustment Administration in 1933 and went on to join other federal agencies, including the National Youth Administration, National Labor Relations Board (NLRB), and Civil Liberties Subcommittee of the Senate Education and Labor Committee. He also worked for the CIO in 1937–38. During World War II Kramer worked for the Office of Price Administration, the Senate Subcommittee on War Mobilization (chaired by Senator Harley Kilgore), and the Senate Subcommittee on Wartime Health and Education (chaired by Senator Claude Pepper). In 1944 he temporarily left government service to work as a speech writer for the Democratic National Committee and two years later wrote speeches for the reelection campaign of Ellis Patterson (D-CA).[153]

When Kramer went to work for the AAA in 1933, he quickly became a member of the "Ware group," a secret caucus of young Communist professionals. Nathaniel Weyl, an original member of the group, wrote that Kramer was not one of the founding members but joined shortly thereafter. He soon became an active and influential figure in the Communist Party's Washington underground. A 1945 memo on Kramer that Victor Perlo, a founding member of the Ware group, prepared for the KGB stated that "Mole [Kramer] has actively participated in Party work since 1933." Hope Hale Davis remembered her branch of the party underground meeting at the Kramer residence. Fellow members of the CPUSA underground assisted him in obtaining his various jobs. John Abt hired Kramer for the Civil Liberties Subcommittee, Nathan Witt helped him get the job with the NLRB, and Victor Perlo signed his job performance rating at the OPA and provided an employment reference.[154]

Whittaker Chambers identified Kramer as an underground Communist and hinted of his involvement in espionage when he met with Adolf Berle in 1939, and Elizabeth Bentley identified him as a participant in the Perlo group in 1945. The FBI confronted Kramer in August 1947, but he refused to cooperate and claimed the Justice Department had "smeared" him. In the summer of 1948, while Kramer was working for the Progressive Party, Bentley publicly identified him as a hidden Communist and espionage source in congressional testimony. (A dozen KGB cables deciphered by the Venona project confirmed that Kramer had been a Soviet spy with the cover names "Mole" and "Plumb.") The House Committee on Un-American Activities subpoenaed him in 1948, but he refused to answer questions about his Communist links.[155]

With Earl Browder's endorsement, Bentley took over liaison with the Perlo group, including Kramer, in March 1944, and began to collect material from its members. Bentley told the FBI that she remembered Kramer mostly providing "Capitol Hill gossip." But she also reported on the composition of the group to the KGB, and in June Moscow Center told the New York station: "'Plumb' [Kramer] is of great interest to us." By the fall of 1944 the KGB had taken over direct liaison with the Perlo group and set about reorganizing it for maximum utility. At its request Kramer was asked to write an autobiography in which he discussed his family background, education, and employment history in detail. Of his political activity, he wrote:

"I officially joined the CP in 1933, although I had participated in CP work for two years beforehand. I was there for all the organizational changes in the Washington group of the CP that have taken place since I joined, with the exception of the three years I spent in the NY Party organization, of which I am currently a member. . . . In NY, my wife worked as a courier at first, and subsequently in various oth. positions, and worked for center [CPUSA headquarters] under "Peter's" [Josef Peters's] leadership. I am not familiar with the nature of the work. My wife joined the CP officially in 1934 after several years of active work, which she carried out in the Party group at the University of California, Berkeley. Three sisters and two out of three brothers are also CP members; they joined in 1930."

Kramer assured the KGB, however, that although known as left-wing, he was not publicly identified as a Communist, the Civil Service Commission had never investigated him for Communist ties, and he had not been the subject of congressional inquiry.[156]

The KGB Washington station also discovered that personal relations between Perlo and Kramer had become strained and might be affecting the latter's productivity. In April 1945 Moscow Center reminded Gorsky, "'Mole' [Kramer] is the only source in his station who has begun to systematically hand us info. about the U.S. Congress, the policies, views, and personalities of its individual members,'" and it ordered that the KGB Washington station establish direct contact with Kramer, bypassing Perlo.[157]

It did so in May, using Joseph Katz, who reported that Kramer was potentially a productive source being held back by poor leadership from Perlo and the structural difficulty of Perlo's group being simultaneously a KGB intelligence unit and a functioning part of the CPUSA underground arm and the consequent overburdening of Kramer with requests from two different masters:

""Mole" [Kramer] has no doubts about where his materials are sent. One of the main problems he brought up was how he was experiencing difficulties simultaneously meeting the requirements of the Comparty and 'our organization.' In light of this, I did not try to conceal from him the true state of affairs and spoke with him frankly. "Mole" said that he has been doing this work for many years and is quite aware of the differences between the two organizations. "Mole" had been a personal friend of "Steve's" [J. Peters's], who used to oversee this group, and they had discussed all matters pertaining to work. "Mole" raised the following issue relating to his work: Someone named Blumberg, who lives in Baltimore and oversees the Washington Party group, is in constant contact with "Mole," receives various materials from him, discusses every possible issue, and gives instructions through him to other friends who work with him."

(Albert Blumberg headed the Maryland-Washington CPUSA district.) Katz also discussed Kramer's relationship with his employer, Senator Harley Kilgore (D-WV):

"The relationship between Mole [Kramer] and Kilgore is very close, and he has significant influence over him. Whenever a decision has to be made, Kilgore discusses it with "Mole"; "Mole" writes memoranda for Kilgore, which Kilgore makes use of when working on the corresponding issues. According to "Mole," Kilgore is very weak-willed and indecisive, but at the same time he is very amenable and gives in easily to influence. "Mole" thinks that Kilgore has an excellent chance of becoming Secretary of Labor, whereupon "Mole" could go with him as his assistant, providing he wants to.

I asked Mole about the matter that had been raised by Raid [Perlo], namely, that in "Mole's" opinion, his contribution to our work should be directed toward influencing gov't policy, and that therefore he should not be used to gather info. Mole assured me that this was not the case and that he understands full well that it was possible to do both things at once."

Katz and Kramer discussed disentangling him from Blumberg and Perlo, and Katz concluded: "'I explained to M. ["Mole"/Kramer] the type of info. we would like to receive from him, and he said that from now on, he would organize his work in accordance with our instructions.'" Kramer's access to information further increased when he later left Kilgore to become chief of staff (with budget and hiring powers) for Senator Claude Pepper (D-FL), chairman of the Senate Subcommittee on Wartime Health and Education.[158]

Kramer handed over documents dealing with American policy toward Germany that came to Kilgore's committee and briefed KGB officers about Truman's choices for secretary of state (James Byrnes) and secretary of the treasury (Frederick Vinson), former senators with whom he had worked; discontent with Truman by some labor unions and their prodding Pepper to lead a liberal anti-Truman bloc in the Senate; and the political evolution of Truman's policies. A number of KGB reports based on Kramer's material were of sufficient interest to be forwarded to Stalin, Molotov, and Beria. The KGB awarded him a $500 bonus (nearly $6,000 in 2008 dollars) in October 1945. But the next month Bentley's defection ended contact. Because Bentley had met with Kramer personally, Moscow instructed Gorsky to have an agent tell him what had happened and that he should be prepared for FBI questions on their relationship.[159]

Democrats lost their congressional majority in both houses in the 1946 elections, resulting in Pepper's loss of his subcommittee chairmanship and with it Kramer's Senate job, although he remained a close friend and adviser of Pepper. In late 1946 Mikhail Vavilov, first secretary of the USSR's embassy, attended a dinner at the home of Lee Pressman, then chief counsel of the CIO; met Kramer; and cultivated a friendship. Vavilov was a diplomat rather than a professional intelligence officer, but he was also a KGB co-optee who carried out tasks for the then seriously undermanned KGB station. In July 1947 he sent Moscow Center a detailed report on his conversations with Kramer. From their contents, Vavilov does not appear to have known that Kramer was a former KGB source, and Kramer did not enlighten him. However, he did give Vavilov a detailed briefing on Senator Pepper's stance at the time. Vavilov reported:

K. [Kramer] works as an adviser to Senator Pepper, who is known for his liberal views. The senator's polit. views are close to ours. . . . "According to K., Pepper now behaves very cautiously. He fears that reactionary Dems. who manage the Dem. Party apparatus will influence his voters in Florida, which could lead to his defeat in 1950 when his term as senator runs out." (Truman hates Pepper.) "As an example of the serious blows that have been dealt to P's career by the combined efforts of reactionary Dems. K. considers the machinations of Dem. Party leaders in Congress that resulted in P.'s being unable to become a member of a Senate Committee on Foreign Affairs at the start of this year, despite the fact that he was technically more eligible than the other candidate."

Kramer went on to note that Pepper was "'troubled'" by the increase in hostile letters from citizens accusing him of "'pro-Soviet views.'" He also related that Pepper's nervousness had led him to a "'hasty'" rejection of the idea of a left-liberal third party and it had been difficult to get Pepper to agree to introduce Henry Wallace at a speech in June 1947. Kramer then related to Vavilov

one more example of excessive caution on P's [Pepper's] part. In the middle of last year, P. decided to write a book about the USA's foreign policy. It was his intention that the book present a development of the ideas which he expounded in his very good speech of 20 March 1946 before the Senate, where P. spoke out against the outcry about a new war, in favor of cooperation between the Great Powers, in favor of the need to strengthen Sov-Amer. relations, and against the anti-Sov. campaign. After dictating part of the book, P. instructed K. [Kramer] to look over the shorthand and pick out materials for subsequent parts. K. said that he had begun working more intensively on it, given how important it was to publish a book like that. However, P. worried that developing the ideas of the aforementioned speech would come off sounding so at odds with the U.S. gov't's increasingly reactionary politics and the unrelenting anti-Sov. press campaign that it might damage his career. K. said that P. is practically too busy now to write the book. K. said that he is tactfully trying to convince P. that this book needs to be published before the 1948 presidential election campaign.

Kramer went on to discuss Pepper's ambitions to become the Democratic vice-presidential candidate in 1948, as well as noting that the CPUSA was attempting to nudge Henry Wallace in the direction of a third party.[160]

While Vavilov didn't know that Charles Kramer was a compromised former agent, Moscow Center did. After receiving his report, it promptly sent a cable to Washington: "Because M. ["Mole"/Kramer] was betrayed by Myrna [Bentley], Oleg's [Vavilov's] connection with him must be terminated at once." There are no additional reports of Soviet intelligence contact with Kramer. In 1948 Bentley's allegations against Kramer became public. Senator Pepper publicly stood by him, stating Kramer had provided "able and faithful service" to his Subcommittee on Wartime Health and Education. Pepper's book on foreign policy, ghostwritten by Kramer, never appeared. Kramer worked as a researcher and speech writer for Henry Wallace in 1948 and then for the Progressive Party until it collapsed in the early 1950s. Thereafter he moved to Oregon and faded from public sight.[161]

Other Perlo Group Members

Every other person identified by Bentley as a member of the Perlo group appears in documents in Vassiliev's notebooks, including Solomon Lischinsky, Allan Rosenberg, Charles Flato, and Joel Gordon. Harry Magdoff boasted in an autobiography written for the KGB that he had joined the CPUSA's youth group, the Young Pioneers, at eleven and remained active in party-aligned groups thereafter. Beginning government service in 1936 as a researcher with the WPA's National Research Project, he later worked for the Council of National Defense, the Office of Production Management, the War Production Board, and the Department of Commerce. When the KGB took over direct supervision of the Perlo group, Joseph Katz reported: "'Raid [Perlo] told him some time ago that he no longer gives materials to "Helmsman" [Browder], but gives them to us [KGB] instead. . . . Tan [Magdoff] felt very proud of himself thanks to this circumstance.'" The KGB cut contact with Magdoff after Bentley's defection, and he resigned from his government job a year later. In the late 1940s the KGB contacted Magdoff to check on the status of some of its deactivated agents. He later became the editor of the Marxist theoretical journal *Monthly Review*. Up until his death in 2006 he refused requests by friends, unable to credit deciphered KGB cables implicating him in espionage, to give his version of events.[162]

Another economist and secret Communist, Edward Fitzgerald, worked at the War Production Board from 1941 until 1945 before transferring to the Foreign Economic Administration and the Commerce Department. Documents from 1944 and 1945 list Fitzgerald as a source, initially through Victor Perlo, but later in direct contact with the KGB. In a brief autobiography he gave to the KGB in 1945 he wrote that his wife, sister, and all of his first cousins were members of the CPUSA and that he had been a member in "'closed groups'" (underground party units) supervised by Josef Peters for ten years. The only specific details have him delivering information on American food aid to Europe in 1945, American occupation policy toward German economic matters, and Swiss resistance to providing information on hidden German assets.[163]

The FBI interviewed Fitzgerald several times about Bentley's allegations, but he denied any participation in Soviet espionage or links to the CPUSA. However, in 1950 the KGB noted that he was having difficulty with psychological pressure: "There were fears that he would prove weak. He was under special supervision by "Tan" [Magdoff]. In March of 1949, he was placed in a psychiatric hospital. At center [KGB Moscow], they were considering whether to provide him with monetary aid." Fitzgerald, however, regained his composure sufficiently to invoke the Fifth Amendment during congressional testimony in 1953. Perhaps sensing that his morale was brittle, the Justice Department had one last go at him. A federal grand jury questioned him in 1955, and once again he refused to testify. The government then gave him immunity from prosecution, thereby removing his grounds for invoking the Fifth Amendment, but he continued to refuse to answer questions. He received a six-month contempt of court sentence and went to prison in 1956.[164]

Samuel Dickstein

While Charles Kramer was a Soviet spy who was a senior congressional aide, Samuel Dickstein was an actual congressman (D-NY). First revealed in *The Haunted Wood,* his work for the KGB was one of the unexpected revelations of Alexander Vassiliev's access to the KGB's archives.

The House of Representatives created the "Special Committee on Un-American Activities," known as the McCormack-Dickstein Committee, in 1934. Dickstein spearheaded its probe of the pro-Nazi German-American Bund and other domestic fascist groups. The McCormack-Dickstein Committee focused public attention on the growth of quasi-fascist groups and helped to develop a popular anti-fascist movement. There was, however, a price. Dickstein exaggerated the extremist threat far beyond its small size (claiming that the Bund had two hundred thousand armed men ready to don their brown uniforms and overthrow the government); greatly exaggerated the links between domestic fascists and Berlin; and vastly overstated the threat of espionage, sabotage, and violence. Dickstein coerced witnesses to explain their political beliefs and then condemned those answers that did not conform to his idea of American patriotism. He verbally abused uncooperative witnesses and lectured them about their moral shortcomings. When Chairman John McCormack (D-MA) insisted that names and accusatory testimony not be published because they were unverified, Dickstein, the committee's second-ranking member, simply picked out the most sensational parts and inserted them in the *Congressional Record* on his own authority, labeling various individuals as Nazi spies or fascists.[165]

Dickstein was also corrupt. He ran a lucrative immigration-fixing service out of his law office in New York. As chairman of the House Committee on Immigration and Naturalization, he sold his influence to individuals who wanted assistance in getting visas to enter the United States or gaining permanent residence status once here. The KGB first noticed Representative Dickstein in 1937, when Leo Helfgott, an Austrian KGB operative, paid him a $1,000 bribe (more than $14,000 in 2008 dollars) to obtain a permanent residence visa.[166]

Dickstein had first approached Soviet ambassador Aleksandr Troyanovsky in December 1936 and suggested that for $5,000–$6,000 he could provide the USSR with the investigatory files the Special Committee on Un-American Activities had gathered on Anastase Vonsiatsky, an anti-Bolshevik Russian exile who headed the elaborately named Russian National Revolutionary Labor and Workers Peasant Party of Fascists. The New York station was dubious, regarding Dickstein as chiefly interested in a large bribe, but Ambassador Troyanovsky and Moscow Center were impressed with the notion of renting an American congressman. Abram Slutsky, chief of KGB foreign intelligence, wrote, "'The people's commissar [Nikolay Yezhov] has accepted Dickstein's offer.'" After a series of meetings, on 18 May 1937 the Soviets agreed to pay Dickstein a secret monthly stipend of $1,250, and he agreed to sign receipts and pursue investigations of White Russian immigrant organizations, Trotskyists, and other anti-Bolshevik groups.[167]

No sooner had this agreement been reached, however, than the KGB began to realize that Dickstein was promising much more than he could deliver. While his use of the Special Committee on Un-American Activities to attack domestic fascists had garnered him enormous publicity and was extremely popular on the left, he was not personally popular with his congressional colleagues. Dickstein wanted the temporary McCormack-Dickstein Committee continued, but the House Democratic leadership was uninterested in backing such a resolution with him as the chief author, since under congressional custom he would become chairman. Dickstein enlisted Representative Martin Dies, a conservative Texas Democrat, to sponsor the resolution. Dickstein assumed that even with Dies as chairman, he could dominate the committee as he had when McCormack had chaired it. But after Dies's resolution passed, the House leadership excluded Dickstein from membership on the committee.

While he assured the KGB that he would continue to operate as before from behind the scenes, the New York station was skeptical. It had given Dickstein the cover name "Crook" and told Moscow: "'We are perfectly aware of whom we are dealing with. C. ["Crook"/Dickstein] fully justifies his cover name; he is an unscrupulous character, greedy for money, who has agreed to work because of the money, a very clever snake, etc. So it is hard for us to guarantee fulfillment of the program that has been planned, even the part of it that he presented to us himself. We will make every effort, however, to see to it that the program is fulfilled.'" Moscow Center continued to hope that something useful would come from having an American congressman on its payroll. Dickstein did partially carry out one helpful task. The KGB wanted Walter Krivitsky, a KGB defector who had embarrassed the USSR by his denunciations of Stalin, to be deported. Dickstein used his influence with the immigration authorities to deny him any visa extensions and did his best to discredit Krivitsky. Although Dickstein's efforts caused Krivitsky great anxiety, he was not deported, in part because Congressman Dies wanted him to testify to his committee and pressured the INS to allow Krivitsky to stay. The quality of material Dickstein produced—old files from the McCormack-Dickstein Committee and a few items he picked up from friendly staffers at the new Dies Committee—disappointed the KGB. Several times it cut off his monthly bribe, Dickstein promised to do more, and partial payments resumed, but in the end Moscow decided it was not getting much for its generous stipend (in excess of $200,000 a year in 2008 dollars) and cut contact in early 1940. A notation in the KGB archive attempted to blame the lack of return on this investment on Slutsky, the foreign intelligence chief who had supported Dickstein's recruitment and who had subsequently been murdered during the purges and denounced as an enemy of the people. There are references to occasional later contacts with Dickstein in Vassiliev's notebooks, but nothing appeared to have resulted. Samuel Dickstein continued to serve in Congress until 1946. He then became a judge of the New York Supreme Court and served until his death in 1954, his corrupt relationship with Soviet intelligence never suspected.[168]

Judith Coplon

Abraham Glasser had used his position at the Justice Department to provide the KGB with information on American counterintelligence operations, and his exposure in 1941 had been a painful loss. Within a few years, it recruited an even more productive replacement.

In 1949 FBI agents arrested Judith Coplon, a U.S. Justice Department analyst, in the act of turning over Justice Department documents to Valentin Gubichev, a Soviet intelligence operative working under the cover of employment by the United Nations. Two different federal courts convicted her of espionage-related charges in 1949 and 1950. However, with one of the appeals court judges commenting that her "guilt was plain," in both cases her convictions were overturned on legal technical-ities.[169]

Coplon attended Barnard College, where she participated in student groups aligned with the Communist Party. After graduation in 1943 she got a job with the New York office of the Economic Warfare section of the U.S. Justice Department. Among her Barnard college friends was an-other young Communist, Flora Wovschin, already a KGB source, re-porting to the Soviets on her work at the Office of War Information. Wovschin was also an energetic talent spotter for the KGB, drawing a number of young Communists into Soviet espionage. One of her recruits was her friend Judith Coplon.

It was not until January 1945 that Vladimir Pravdin of the KGB New York station met with Coplon and formally recruited her. To the KGB's delight, she had already obtained a highly desirable post in the Foreign Agents Registration section of the Justice Department in Washington. Anyone acting on behalf of a foreign government had to register with the Justice Department. Those legitimately hired by foreign governments as lobbyists or publicists routinely registered, but for obvious reasons, those engaged in espionage did not. While other laws also criminalized espi-onage, this one provided a simple statutory basis for federal investigation and prosecution of covert agents working for foreign powers. Conse-quently, Coplon's section of the Justice Department worked closely with the FBI, which furnished it with reports of counterintelligence investi-gations so that its staff could determine when the evidence would support arrest and prosecution. Coplon was in a position to give the KGB notice when one of its operatives was under investigation and allow it to warn its agents to cease activity and destroy evidence.[170]

Pravdin reported to Moscow Center that he had been impressed by his recruitment meeting with Coplon:

"She gives the impression of a very serious, modest, thoughtful young woman who is ideologically close to us. . . . There is no question about the sincerity of her desire to work with us. In the process of the conversation S. ["Sima"/ Coplon] stressed how much she appreciates the trust placed in her and that, knowing whom she is working for, from now on she will redouble her efforts. In the very first phase of her work with Zora [Wovschin], S. assumed that she was assisting the local fellowcountrymen [CPUSA]. Subsequently, from her conversations with Z. and based on the nature of the materials that were re-quested from her, she figured out that this work was related to our country. When Sergey [Pravdin] asked how she had arrived at this conclusion, S. replied that she knew about Zora's past connections with the [Soviet] consulate; besides that, she thought that the materials she was obtaining couldn't be of interest to the fellowcountrymen but could be of interest to an organization like the Comintern or another institution linked to us. At the same time she added that she had hoped that she was working specifically for us, since she considered it the greatest honor to receive an opportunity to give us her modest assistance."

Although initially concerned that she was moving too aggressively to steal documents before her position was secure, the KGB was well pleased with Coplon. In August 1945 the New York station told Moscow Center: "'She treats our assignments very seriously and conscientiously and considers our work the main job in her life. This serious attitude is borne out by her decision to back out of marrying her former fiancé because otherwise she wouldn't have been able to continue working with us.'" Perhaps as partial compensation for this sacrifice, the KGB New York station noted it had given Coplon a cash bonus to help buy furniture for her new apartment in Washington.[171]

From 1945 until her arrest in 1949 Coplon copied and turned over to the KGB numerous FBI and counterintelligence documents. The Venona project, however, ended her career as a Soviet spy. In late 1948 several deciphered KGB cables indicated that the KGB in 1945 had a source, cover-named "Sima," working in the Foreign Agents Registration section at the Justice Department in Washington and that "Sima" had been in New York in 1944 working for the Economic Warfare section of the Department of Justice. The FBI quickly established that only one person fit those criteria: Judith Coplon.

Hoping to catch her in the act, the FBI had her superiors at the Justice Department show her a fake FBI report about a source inside Amtorg reporting on Soviet activities. She took the bait and traveled to New York, where she was arrested after meeting Gubichev in March 1949. In her purse she had not only a portion of the FBI "bait" material, but also thirty pages of notes, reports, and copies of government documents, including extracts from Foreign Agents Registration section "data slips" that summarized FBI reports on thirty-four specific espionage investigations.

Coplon turned over a considerable volume of documents on FBI counterintelligence operations to the KGB. One of the earliest reports, from March 1945, alerted the KGB that the FBI and the Justice Department, after earlier emphasizing German, Japanese, and domestic fascists, had shifted priorities: "The Club's [Foreign Agents Registration section of the Justice Department's] main focus, according to Sima [Coplon], is on Sov. institutions and fellowcountrymen [Communists]. . . . The Club has abundant archives and a card catalog, compiled from the information of the Club, the Hut [FBI], the Cabin [OSS], and the milit. and nav. intelligence agencies. She has been instructed to closely study the review procedure." An October KGB report stated:

Sima removed from the Club's card catalog duplicates of Hut memoranda containing agent materials on the investigation of Sov. institutions, the fraternal [CPUSA], progress. orgs, polecats [Trotskyists], White monarchists [anti-Bolshevik Russians], etc. A portion are outdated. . . . "It's obvious from the materials what a meticulous record is made of the tiniest facts from discussions, correspondence, and phone conversations conducted by our organizations, individual representatives, and operatives in the country. What is notable is large numbers of Hut personnel who are engaged in the above investigations."

Coplon also furnished the KGB information about a contact of Gregory Silvermaster who was under FBI surveillance; its first confirmation that it had been Armand Feldman whose information had led the FBI to arrest Gayk Ovakimyan in 1941; news that the FBI continued to investigate people associated with Jacob Golos, even though he had died in 1943; reports on FBI wiretapping of San Francisco Bay Area Communists; and a list of the people identified to the FBI as hidden Communists in Washington by Catherine Perlo, the estranged ex-wife of Victor Perlo.[172]

After legal technicalities overturned Coplon's two convictions, the Justice Department kept her indictments alive for some years, hoping it could find a way around the rulings that had precluded its use of its best evidence (the stolen Justice Department material found on Coplon at the time of her arrest). But in 1967 the Justice Department dropped the indictments. Coplon married one of her defense attorneys and later opened a restaurant in New York.

Soviet Intelligence Infiltration of the U.S. Government

The dozens of Soviet sources who supplied information that came to them as part of their duties as employees of the U.S. government gave the Soviet Union a unique insight into all aspects of Washington affairs. Not every source occupied a sensitive post or had access to valuable material. Nor were all of them productive; some handed over materials grudgingly or only occasionally. But others were able to inform the KGB of high-level policy deliberations and decisions; supply highly classified data on diplomatic, political, or military capabilities or plans; or identify and sometimes recruit other sources. Some were able to deflect investigations of friends or prevent their dismissals. And, as insurance, the KGB also recruited sources with access to American counterintelligence investigations to monitor the danger its agents faced and to warn them when they were in jeopardy.

While a handful of the spies in the American government were mercenaries—notably David Salmon and Samuel Dickstein—the vast majority were Communists or Communist sympathizers who took little profit for their activities but willingly supplied information out of devotion to the Soviet Union and the Communist cause.

Д. в устной форме сообщил, что для названия "Интелли-дженс Сервис" (английской) были применяются два коду-рочных слова: "Бродвей" и иногда "Хоум" (Ноит). Это часто применяется в телефонных разговорах.

<u>с. 34</u>   Справка о встрече 29.9.45.

Помимо прилагаемого при сем мат-ла, содержание к-го переваем телеграммой, Д. сообщил, что в распоряжении ОСС имеется мат-л — опрос бывших советских военноплен-ных, к-е находились в германской армии. Большинство этих военнопленных — солдаты армии предателя генерала Власова, среди к-х есть также и офицера.

Источнику дано задание просмотреть этот материал еще раз и отобрать лиц из офицерского состава, особенно имеющих высшее образование. Постараться записать содержание их по-казаний.

Кроме того, в распоряжении ОСС имеются специальные папки на каждое предприятие как военного, так и граж-данского хар-ра в СССР. Папки содержат материал 30-х годов с указанием дислокации заводов, хар-ра выпускаемой продукции, производственной мощности, личного состава, в особенности руков-ве заводов с характеристиками на директоров, партийных руководителей и инженерный состав. Все эти мат-лы получены от британской разведки, поскольку между ОСС и британ. Интеллидженс Сервис существует соглашение об обмене информацией. Д. заявил, что этот материал слишком старый давности и уже не представляет интереса, однако, если он нужен, он постарается что-нибудь сделать для его получения. После подробного обсуждения хар-ра этого мат-ла я
<u>с. 35</u>   пришел к заключению, что риск, связанный с получением этого мат-ла, не стоит самого мат-ла."

<u>с. 36</u>   На встрече 23.9. Д. сообщил, что указом Трумэна об 20.9.45 УСС с 1.10 ликвидируется. Работавшая против СССР Восточно-Европ. секция перейдет в ГД под названи-ем исследовательская и информац-я служба. Контрраз-я секция Х2 и разв-я Е1 перейдут в G2 (анти-2) (разведка воен. мин-ва). Аппарат УСС в Австрии и Гер-мании перейдет в подчинение воен. мин-ва.

<u>с. 38</u>   Встреча 3.10.45.

Д. заявил, что за это время ничего интересного не про-изошло. Уже почти не работаю → нет инф-ции. Принес копии опроса сов. военнопленных.

<u>с. 40</u>   Встреча 8.10.45.

Получил телеграмму об откомандировании в США. Говорили о сотр-ках ОСС в Лондоне, о продвижении у Дена с/р ОСС (лейтенант Леонард Хоукин, с ф... активен, много информации с. 156).
"Д." сообщил, что ОСС в Вене располагается в какой-то гостинице. Название гост-цы ему неизвестно. Практика работы ОСС в Вене примерно такова: сотрудники ОСС

CHAPTER 5

Infiltration of the Office of Strategic Services

T he KGB regarded the Office of Strategic Services, America's World War II intelligence agency, as a prime target and developed an astounding number of sources within it. Documents in Vassiliev's notebooks contain details about twelve of them. This success was due in part to the vulnerability to infiltration provided by the speed and organizational chaos that attended OSS's development. Remarkably, the United States did not possess a foreign intelligence service until 1942. Various government agencies carried out foreign intelligence, but their activities were uncoordinated, episodic, and frequently amateurish. The War Department's Military Intelligence Division focused on battlefield intelligence and security (counterintelligence). Military attachés at American embassies occasionally recruited sources and conducted espionage operations, but such efforts were usually the product of an aggressive individual officer and evaporated on his routine reassignment. Other than purely military "order-of-battle" appraisals of the

---

Report on a 1945 meeting between a KGB officer in London and Stanley Graze, a Soviet source inside America's World War II intelligence agency, the Office of Strategic Services. Graze provides information about OSS operations in Vienna. Courtesy of Alexander Vassiliev.

size and capabilities of foreign forces, there was little institutional support by the Army or Navy for strategic, diplomatic, and political intelligence, while the State Department regarded espionage as incompatible with its diplomatic mission. Famously, Secretary of State Henry Stimson, learning in 1929 that the State Department was funding a small code-breaking operation to read diplomatic ciphers, had it shut down, indignantly observing, "Gentlemen don't read each other's mail."[1]

After war began in Europe in 1939, President Roosevelt realized the woeful inadequacy of American intelligence capability. He appointed William Donovan, a Wall Street lawyer and World War I military hero, as "Coordinator of Information" in July 1941, with a mandate to systematically compile information of strategic value. When the United States entered the war, Donovan's office split, with its propaganda arm becoming the Office of War Information and its intelligence arm becoming the Office of Strategic Services, with Donovan in command. The OSS reported to the Joint Chiefs of Staff, and many of its personnel held military rank, including General Donovan. The OSS was America's first foreign intelligence agency. It systematically collected and analyzed military, strategic, diplomatic, and technical intelligence. OSS operatives recruited and ran agent networks in foreign nations and also set up special operation units that assisted underground resistance forces and engaged in sabotage and behind-the-lines combat operations.

In addition to OSS's newness, explosive growth (by 1944 it included fourteen thousand personnel), and lack of institutional structure, General Donovan's immediate focus—defeating Nazism—assisted Soviet infiltration. He once remarked to an aide, "I'd put Stalin on the OSS payroll if I thought it would help us defeat Hitler." Researchers have identified Communists in the Russian, Spanish, Balkan, Hungarian, and Latin American divisions of the OSS's Research and Analysis Branch and its operational Japanese, Korean, Italian, Spanish, Hungarian, Indonesian, and German divisions. In the midst of World War II, with Hitler the main enemy, General Donovan's attitude was a sensible one, but it was also fraught with risk. While the arrangement allowed the OSS to make use of Communists, it also allowed Communists to make use of the OSS.[2]

Elizabeth Bentley publicly identified several Soviet sources in the OSS in 1948, and the Venona decryptions confirmed her testimony. In addition to adding considerable detail to those revelations, KGB documents in Vassiliev's notebooks identify four previously unknown sources.

Alfred Tanz and Irving Goff

Two previously unidentified Soviet sources came to the OSS via the International Brigades of the Spanish Civil War and the American Communist Party. In the fall of 1941 Donovan, then just organizing the OSS, asked Milton Wolff, last commander of the Abraham Lincoln battalion and head of its veterans' organization, to recommend some of his comrades. Donovan wanted to use these men as OSS operatives with the anti-Nazi resistance in Europe. While Communists had held aloof from the anti-Nazi resistance in German-occupied nations during the Nazi-Soviet Pact, once Germany attacked the USSR in June 1941, they quickly joined the resistance, and Donovan believed that the Lincoln battalion veterans would be able to work well with Communists in the anti-Nazi underground. After receiving permission from the CPUSA, Wolff recommended a number of International Brigades veterans who became OSS officers, including Irving Goff, William Aalto, Milton Felsen, Michael Jiminez, Vincent Lossowski, and Alfred Tanz. Later Wolff joined the OSS as well.[3]

In a 1944 report KGB station chief Vasily Zarubin referred to the OSS's obtaining men through the Communist Party and noted that the KGB had recruited several of Wolff's choices for Soviet intelligence work inside the OSS: "Our agent "Tyazh" departed for the "shore" [North Africa] with communications instructions, a call sign, and a cipher. He arrived on the "shore," but contact was not established with him. . . . "Amigo" was recruited, but his special assignment was canceled at the last minute. Later he left with Amer. troops and had a password and communications instructions."[4]

In addition to Zarubin's comment, "Tyazh" and "Amigo" appeared only once more in the notebooks. In neither instance was a real name given, but in "Amigo's" case, the information provided is sufficient to make a positive identification. In a lengthy November 1944 report on his tenure as an officer of the KGB New York station Semen Semenov wrote: "'On instructions from the station I carried out the recruitment of "Amigo." At the time, on the "Cabin" [OSS] line, he was supposed to leave to perform special work in Africa and then in Italy. The work was general training of an agent, teaching him ciphers, establishing passwords for contact, and so forth. In 1943 he transferred from the U.S. to Britain, where people were supposed to establish contact with him. By education "Amigo" is a lawyer, and he was in Spain.'"[5]

These details fit Alfred Tanz, who joined the CPUSA in 1935 and served with the Lincoln battalion in the Spanish Civil War. International Brigades records contain a 1937 memo written in Russian and labeled "top secret" that identifies Tanz as a "reliable" comrade and a candidate for undefined "organizational-technical work." After Wolff's recommendation, Tanz joined the OSS, which sent him to Great Britain, and he was among the OSS troops dropped into France in preparation for the June 1944 Normandy invasion. Tanz was also the *only* lawyer among the Lincoln battalion veterans recruited for the OSS. In addition, in February 1943, shortly after he joined the OSS, the Comintern received a vetting inquiry from the KGB asking for a report on Tanz's background. The Comintern replied that he had been an active Communist since 1935 and served in the International Brigades.[6]

Although it is not as positive, the one additional mention of "Tyazh" very strongly suggests he was Irving Goff. A KGB evaluation of the work of Duncan Lee, a senior OSS officer and KGB source, noted: "'In September 1944 he gave Myrna [Bentley] a list of employees which supposedly the OSS security division has and who, according to the division's information, hand info. over to us. 'Izra' and 'Tyazh' are listed among them.'" "Izra" was Donald Wheeler, who was among the twenty-six OSS personnel on the list that Lee handed over to Bentley (also in Vassiliev's notebooks). The list included only three veterans of the Lincoln battalion: Irving Goff, Manuel T. Jiminez, and Michael A. Jiminez. Of the three, only Goff is known to have served in North Africa with the OSS. "Tyazh," who Zarubin had said had "departed for the "shore" [North Africa]," is most likely Irving Goff.[7]

Later in the war senior OSS officers suspected that Goff, then running an OSS radio network assisting anti-Nazi resistance forces in Italy, had allowed Italian Communists to use it for political work in preparation for the postwar struggle for political dominance. After World War II Goff became a full-time organizer for the CPUSA, heading the party in Louisiana and serving as a senior officer of its New York organization.[8]

Stanley Graze

Akhmerov cabled Moscow in March 1939 that Gerald Graze (discussed in chapter 4) had nominated both his older brother Cyril and his younger brother Stanley for recruitment. Both were members of the CPUSA; Cyril, a junior high school teacher, was "'a highly developed Marxist—is completely devoted to Communism.'" Stanley, born in 1918 and a recent graduate of CCNY, was "'devoted to our cause, but for now he is a little bit young to handle responsible assignments.'" There is no indication that the KGB ever approached Cyril, who, nonetheless, achieved some notoriety in the 1950s. A long-time chairman of the Academic Freedom Committee of the Communist-dominated Teachers Union in New York, he was fired by the school board in 1953 for refusing to answer questions about whether he was a Communist.[9]

In an odd bit of timing, on the same day that Cyril appeared before a Senate subcommittee investigating Communist activity in the schools, his younger brother Stanley, whom he had tutored in communism, testified before another Senate subcommittee looking into Communist connections of American employees of the United Nations. Both showed up at the same federal building in New York, and both took the Fifth Amendment. While Cyril refused to discuss his Communist affiliations, however, the key question Stanley refused to answer was far more serious. When asked "Have you ever in the past engaged in espionage against the United States," he invoked his right to silence on the grounds of self-incrimination. Stanley had never been publicly accused of espionage by anyone, nor had the Justice Department undertaken any prosecution. But, as he told a KGB officer three years later, since "certain people from Myrna's [Bentley's] group knew about him and could testify against him," he decided that denying espionage under oath risked a perjury indictment, and it was less hazardous to invoke the Fifth Amendment and refuse to answer. Stanley Graze's prudence was understandable, but, in fact, there was no usable evidence against him. Elizabeth Bentley had not identified him to the FBI, nor had others in the Perlo network cooperated with authorities. Neither had he been identified in the Venona decryptions. All the government had were suspicions. They were well-founded.[10]

Stanley Graze had been active in the Communist movement as a college student at CCNY. He did graduate work in economics at Columbia and held several research positions before moving to Washington in 1943 to take a job as an economist in the Tool Division of the War Production Board. Both he and his wife were members of the underground CPUSA group run by Victor Perlo and, by Perlo's accounting, provided government documents to the party unit. His brother Gerald was already working in Washington and was a KGB agent of some years' standing. Gerald also told Akhmerov that Stanley handed material to Victor Perlo. On Akhmerov's initiative, Gerald questioned Stanley about rumors of "sabotage" of Soviet Lend-Lease equipment orders by WPB officials.[11]

Stanley Graze was drafted in 1943 and served overseas as an Army officer and was, consequently, out of reach of the KGB until mid-1945, when he obtained a post in the Russian Division of the OSS. He immediately became an active espionage source via Victor Perlo. (Stanley Graze's relationship as a source with Victor Perlo thus was in 1943, before Perlo was in liaison with Elizabeth Bentley, and in 1945, after the KGB had replaced Bentley with one of its own agents. Consequently Bentley had not heard of him and did not identify him as a member of the Perlo apparatus when she went to the FBI in 1945.) In August 1945 the KGB New York station informed Moscow that the OSS was sending him to London, where, among other assignments, he would be monitoring the activities of Arcos (the USSR's trading agency in London) and Amtorg, gaining information about Soviet transport; the USSR's machine-building, metallurgy, chemical, and rubber industries; and Soviet foreign policy, as well as collecting information on Vlasov's Army, an anti-Soviet force of Russians and Ukrainians backed by the Nazis. Even before he left for London, the KGB New York station reported that Stanley (referred to by his CPUSA party name, "Stan," and his new KGB cover name, "Dan") had provided several valuable items:

"While looking through 'Cabin's' [OSS's] files on Soviet railway transport, 'Stan' found a detailed report on the Baikal-Amur mainline, dated October 1943, and issued by the commander of the Amur naval flotilla, Junior Captain Brakhtman. It is impossible to determine how the report got there, but judging from its contents, Captain Brakhtman had been used unwittingly. In the same file, 'Stan' saw a photo of a tunnel under the Amur river that was taken by a certain Major Nelson, who had supposedly been assigned to the R.A. [Red Army] as an expert on tanks." . . . Stan gave a description of the work of the Russian division of "Cabin," along with descriptions of the people working there.[12]

Once in London, Graze would be out of touch with Perlo and would need another contact to deliver his material. Several memos about establishing contact with him in London detail KGB tradecraft and illustrate the practical difficulties of establishing liaison. The KGB New York station reported the arrangement made at the U.S. end: "In the middle of August, Dan [Graze] left for London. He and "Raid" [Perlo] agreed on secret meeting conditions. Every Sunday, beginning on September 2nd, D. will arrive for the meeting at 20.00 and wait 10–15 min. by the exit of the metro station 'Regent Park.' He will be holding the magazine 'John Bull.' Our man: 'Didn't I meet you at Vick's restaurant at Connecticut Avenue?'—'Yes, Vick himself introduced you.' Afterwards, the operational officer should produce the price tag that was sent to C. [Center], and Dan should show his exact duplicate." In addition, the New York station sent a photograph to Moscow to be forwarded to the London officer who would make the contact.[13]

It wasn't until the third Sunday in September that a KGB officer, Michael Korneev, was able to attempt the rendezvous. His report read:

"When I arrived at the agreed-upon time at the exit of the 'Regent's Park' Tube station, I noticed an American officer in uniform standing by the exit who looked the same age as 'Dan' [Graze]; however, he did not have the afore-mentioned magazine 'John Bull.' Walking past him as the clock struck 8, I also noticed that the officer looked at his watch. When I got to the corner, I turned back and walked down the opposite side of the street. Meanwhile, the officer had taken from his pocket some kind of book or magazine. I crossed the street and walked up to the Tube station. It turned out that he was holding some kind of book. It was seven minutes past eight, and there was nothing left for me to do but to try to talk to this officer. I started my conversation as follows:

ME: Do you have a light?
HIM: Yes, please.
ME: Thank you. . . . Women, they're never on time, are they. . . . I take it you're also waiting for your girlfriend?
HIM: No, I'm waiting for a friend.
ME: Been out of the States long?
HIM: No, not too long . . . .
ME: I've been to the USA, too. It made quite an impression on me.
HIM: Were you there a long time ago?
ME: Oh, it was relatively long ago, in 1939.
HIM: Where did you go when you were there?
ME: NY. It's quite different from London. I liked NY, with its big buildings and restaurants. It's a lively, cheerful city. I spent a lot of time in restaurants there. I especially liked this one restaurant there called "Vick's."
HIM: The one on Connecticut Avenue.
ME: Oh yes. Come to think of it, you look sort of familiar. Didn't we meet there?
HIM: That's right—Vick himself introduced us.

When he had spoken his password, I became confident that he was indeed "Dan." We shook hands and continued talking, and "Dan" invited me to go back to his apartment. Just then, a policeman walked by us, and so for the sake of appearances, I gladly took him up on his offer. When we had gone a bit fur-ther from the station, D. said that I had given him the password incorrectly. I explained to him why this had happened and repeated my password as it was stipulated, adding that I had a small card for him. (The cards were identical. They are enclosed.)

When I said that I had expected him to be holding 'John Bull,' and that this was the only sign I had to go by, "Dan" replied that he had already gone to the meeting place three times with 'John Bull' but had practically lost hope of contacting us, become upset, and forgotten it today. He wanted to know why it had taken us so long to show up for the meeting. With regard to the sign, he was sure that we ought to have a photo of him, because he had provided two of his cards expressly for that purpose before leaving. During the conversation, "Dan" remarked that, in essence, he had agreed to come here in order to help us here. 'If I hadn't met up with you, there wouldn't have been any point in coming here at all,' he said."[14]

Korneev held five meetings with Stanley Graze during his tenure at the OSS's London office. Graze provided the KGB with copies of the interrogation of former Soviet prisoners-of-war who had been serving with the German Army (Moscow Center had a high interest in this material) and related what he had learned about OSS operations in Vienna, a city under joint Allied occupation, from an OSS officer who had recently returned from there. He also described material on the USSR that the OSS had received from British intelligence, but the London station decided it was too risky for Graze to attempt to steal copies. Graze also noted that while British intelligence had provided the OSS with information on the USSR during the war, it was declining to continue to do so with the war over. With the OSS in the process of dissolution and its London office closing down, Graze returned to the United States in October 1945. He immediately reestablished contact with the KGB via Victor Perlo, but it coincided with Bentley's defection, and the entire network, including Graze, was deactivated.[15]

Attempting to revive the crippled American station, in 1948 the KGB decided to renew connections with old agents, including Graze, who had successfully transferred from the OSS to the State Department. It assigned Joseph Katz to the task, but for unknown reasons he never reached Graze. The KGB did not return its attention to Stanley Graze until 1951, at which time he was working at the United Nations. A Russian UN employee (and KGB co-optee) arranged to meet him for dinner at the White Horse Restaurant. After introducing Graze to "Jour," a KGB officer, the co-worker left, while "Jour" used the old 1945 London passwords to establish his bona fides. He met with Graze again and learned he had come under investigation in the State Department in the fall of 1947 for suspected Communist ties. Although Secretary of State George Marshall rejected the security office's recommendation to discharge him, Graze thought it prudent to leave. He resigned in May 1948 and invested his savings in a small advertising business. After it failed, he taught part time and took a job at the United Nations. He told "Jour" he regretted that he had not been in contact with anyone from Soviet intelligence in late 1950 because he had had the opportunity to join Radio Free Europe and might have been useful as a source there. "Jour" continued to meet with Graze over the next several months. Moscow cabled New York in June 1951, however, that Graze's current position (executive secretary of the railways operations study unit of the UN Technical Assistance Administration) was of limited interest and urged the station to "determine the most practical way to utilize his potential," "'bearing in mind that D. ["Dan"/Graze] is loyal to us and is the only American agent who even now has opportunities at his disposal for our work.'" That remark was more of a comment on the depleted resources of the KGB's American stations in 1951 than an indication of Graze's access to information of significant intelligence value. He did, however, hand over a 1947 intelligence report he had saved from his State Department days exposing a Soviet engineer working in the USSR who was furnishing information to American intelligence.[16]

The KGB and Graze discussed various possibilities about using him, but nothing came to fruition before the Congress called him to testify in October 1952. After he invoked the Fifth Amendment, UN secretary general Trygve Lie discharged him. The KGB immediately provided $2,000 to assist him to establish a business but concluded: "'On 23 Oct. 1952, D. ["Dan"/Graze] was fired from the UN Secretariat in connection with the loyalty checks of Americans working there. D. was subsequently called before the U.S. Senate by the Internal Security Commission, and there followed the publication of materials against him in the American press, where it was reported that D. is suspected of espionage activities and that the FBI has an extensive file on him. In connection with this, the station was issued a directive to terminate its connection with D. until further notice. At present, D. is out of commission.'"[17]

In January 1955 the KGB considered reactivating Graze. Moscow told the New York station that it was considering him "as a possible candidate for work in illegal conditions" and ordered that he be contacted to see if he was willing and able to consider changing his identity and moving to the West Coast or Europe. The New York station called upon Michael Korneev, who had met with Stanley in London in 1945, to make the contact. Wanting to intercept Graze on the street, Korneev made five visits to his neighborhood. He discovered on his first trip that few people walked or spent much time outdoors in Stanley's suburban neighborhood. The next time no one was home. On the third visit he managed to speak to his wife and learned Stanley was still at work. As the conversation went on, Mrs. Graze began to get an inkling of her visitor's business. She agreed to tell Stanley he would return a few days later. On Korneev's fourth visit, no one was home, leading him to suspect that Stanley was deliberately avoiding him. Finally, on 22 June his persistence paid off. Stanley Graze, it turned out, was still loyal to the Communist cause, but he was very cautious. The KGB report explained:

"'Dan' [Graze] did not recognize A. ["Alan"/Korneev], and, as he is very sensitive to provocation, he gave Alan the third degree. When he had stepped outside his house, he again insisted that he had never met A. and that he does not know of any "Robert" from London. A. began to recount the circumstances of their meeting in London; the meeting place, subsequent meeting places, the number of meetings, the fact that D. had once brought him chewing gum and cigarettes. Little by little, D. began to acknowledge A. and answer his questions to the point. For the duration of the meeting, he kept bringing up the subject of working with A. in London. In particular, he asked A. to name the person whose photograph A. had shown D. in London. At first, A. could not remember, but after D. said that he greatly admired this person, A. remembered that it had been a personal photograph of Maurice Thorez. Later, A. also remembered that D. had known him as "Michael" in London. D. also asked A. to give him the password he had used to contact him in London. A. remembered part of the password but was unable to recall the whole thing. It was especially important for D. that A. name the restaurant that was included in the password. A. remembered the material recognition signal.

After all this, when he was almost sure of A., D. apologized for all the questioning, noting that the times weren't what they used to be, and he had to be very careful. D. wanted to tell A. about the lapses that had been allowed on our part during our work with him recently, but he put this matter aside until the next meeting. It was apparent that he was hurt by the manner in which the meeting with him [the connection with him] . . . had been broken off."

Stanley, Korneev reported, was currently working at a stock trading company but indicated his willingness "'to continue working with us, because in our work he sees the purpose of his life.'"[18]

Over a period of several months the KGB met with Graze and discussed various schemes for using him in France, England, or Mexico, but in November 1955 Moscow Center concluded that "for now, D. ["Dan"/Graze] cannot be used on N's line [illegal line], neither in the USA nor any other capitalist country. Considering that he might be under FBI surveillance, we cannot attach him to any of the illegal stations. Dan should find a lower profile cover in NY, consolidate his position, and refuse any incriminating contacts, so as to fall off the FBI's radar. Deactivate."[19]

In 1958 the KGB once more attempted to reestablish contact, but the operatives who went to Graze's house thought they saw surveillance and abandoned the project. In 1959 Moscow Center considered bringing in "foreign specialists" to assist the Soviet understanding of American society, and a draft proposal recommended

"relocating to the USSR Victor Perlo, Stanley Graze, and Lauchlin Currie, who could be used, according to their knowledge and professional experience, by the Ministry of Foreign Affairs, the State Security Committee under the Council of Ministers of the USSR, and the Committee on Cultural Liaisons with Foreign Countries as consultants in our work against the USA.

It would be expedient to provide the relocated American specialists and their families with apartments in Moscow and furnish them with jobs at our institutes or magazine editorial offices, as well as to secure them a state subsidy."

The KGB leadership, however, rejected the idea. The KGB attempted yet another contact with Graze late in 1961, but he ignored the prearranged signals given over the telephone. In June 1962 a KGB officer showed up at his house. He did not recognize Stanley: "'He had gotten older, gained weight, and gone almost completely bald.'" After expressing some suspicion, Graze told the agent that the FBI checked on him only sporadically and his life was less worrisome. While "'in principle he is ready to help us as before, he does not see any realistic opportunities to do so.'" They agreed on another contact in August but again nothing developed.[20]

Stanley Graze then took a different direction in life. After decades of devotion to an ideology that saw capitalists as criminals, he turned into a criminal capitalist. He became vice-president of Love, Douglas and Company, a Wall Street brokerage firm, and then BWA, Inc., a West Coast broker. There, in April 1968, he wrote a glowing report on International Controls Corporation, a highly leveraged New Jersey firm that owned a few dozen small manufacturing companies. His praise of its management caught the eye of its chief executive officer (CEO), Robert Vesco, just beginning a meteoric career based on fraud and deceit. Four years later, after seizing control of troubled Investors Overseas Services (IOS), the world's largest offshore mutual fund family, Vesco installed Graze as the IOS fund manager.[21]

During the next year, with the assistance of a group of associates, including Stanley Graze, Vesco looted IOS accounts of more than $200 million, using a bewildering array of shell companies, money transfers, fake arms-length sales, stock swaps with dummy corporations, and other swindles. As funds manager, Stanley Graze participated in these activities; in one transaction in April 1972, he authorized the sale of $224 million invested in U.S. blue chip securities and transferred the proceeds to a bank in the Bahamas controlled by Vesco's aides. Another investment went into a company chartered in the Bahamas that Graze ran from London and in which he held a 4 percent ownership interest.[22]

In November 1972 the Securities and Exchange Commission (SEC) filed a civil fraud complaint against Vesco and forty-one other individuals and corporations, including Stanley Graze. The largest fraud charge in the SEC's history to that time, it triggered years of litigation, and Vesco fled the United States, successfully fighting extradition for years in the Bahamas and Costa Rica and, ultimately, seeking sanctuary in Castro's Cuba. Graze refused to testify in an SEC hearing in 1973, citing the Fifth Amendment (making him perhaps the only person ever to use the Fifth Amendment in response to questions about both espionage and financial swindles). He also settled in Costa Rica, where he received resident status and a passport. In 1976 the Justice Department indicted him and five other Vesco associates, charging them with misappropriating more than $100 million. He was also cited for contempt for refusing to appear before a grand jury. Because he never returned to the United States, the case was never prosecuted. Likewise, in the civil case, a default judgment amounting to $224 million and yet another contempt conviction ensured that he would never come home.[23]

Fourteen years after his last contact with the KGB, in October 1976, Stanley Graze reappeared on Moscow Center's radar screen. In San Jose, Costa Rica, a KGB agent attending a wedding reported falling into intimate conversation with another guest, Stanley Graze, and informed Moscow:

"According to him, he had helped us a great deal politically; however, during the McCarthy period, he had been fired from his job and persecuted. He said that because the people who worked with him 'were not always competent,' there had been a failure (in connection with the . . . Gouzenko affair, Graze fell into the sights of the FBI). For a long time, he did not have the means to support himself, and as a result he had agreed to work for Vesco. Graze said that while he was working with us (it appears that his wife cooperated as well), he had been told that in our country he held the rank of Lieutenant Colonel. 'Maybe now I'm ranked as a General in your country, or there's a pension waiting for me over there,' said Graze. Graze feels burdened by his work for Vesco and thinks he's scum. . . . In his opinion, our policies with regard to Israel and the events in Czechoslovakia had a negative influence on his views.

Having started a conversation with me on this subject, Graze said: 'I just want you to know that I'm not trying to impose on you or entrap you, I'm not a CIA agent.' When I approached Graze on my own initiative before leaving the party and we continued our conversation, he said: 'I have said all this because

I have met a Russian after all these years, and I've had a bit too much to drink, and my heart aches. But talking to you has made me feel better.'"[24]

Moscow checked its records and instructed its officer to find out what he could about Graze, including his present situation and his political views. A week later they met again. Graze indicated he no longer worked for Vesco and the American authorities were pressing him to testify, but he had refused. He was working as a consultant for an American company with a branch in Costa Rica; his sons were now a doctor and a lawyer in the United States. He mentioned his old friend and fellow KGB asset, Frank Coe, now a financial expert working for the People's Republic of China. During another conversation a few days later, Graze admitted that some of his views had changed over the years ("'the exposure of Stalin's cult of personality affected him negatively'"). Still, he described himself as Marxist, and the KGB officer judged:

"He is seeking validation that his convictions are right, and that his help for us in the past had really served the cause of victory over fascism and the foundation of world peace, rather than having been used only 'to destroy the families of 20 Russian traitors.' To this day, D. ["Dan"/Graze] lives in his past work and apparently thinks of that period of his life as having caused much personal misfortune, but at the same time as having been the most interesting, fruitful, and beneficial to the cause of world peace. It seems that under certain conditions, he would not object to doing what he could to help."

(Graze's reference to "having been used only 'to destroy the families of 20 Russian traitors'" was likely a reference to his having given the KGB information on Russians who served with Vlasov's Army and the Soviet practice of punishing family members.) There were additional meetings into early 1977, but nothing resulted. Stanley Graze died in Costa Rica in June 1987, a one-time Communist and Soviet spy turned international business swindler.[25]

Donald Wheeler

The KGB's most productive source in the OSS was probably Donald Wheeler, who grew up in an environment very far removed from the New York Russian Jewish immigrant world of Stanley Graze. An autobiography he prepared for the KGB in January 1945 explained that he was descended from a Puritan family that had arrived in Massachusetts in the 1630s. At the time of the American Revolution his ancestors lived in upstate New York. His father grew up in Wisconsin and became a bricklayer. A Bellamyite Populist who welcomed the Russian Revolution without ever joining the Communist Party, his father "'consistently defended the Soviet regime from the beginning. He has never been disturbed by purges, by pacts, or by any of the aspects of Soviet policy which have upset so many middle-class liberals.'"[26]

Wheeler himself was born on an isolated farm in White Bluffs, Washington, in 1913 and grew up with five siblings in a poor economic backwater in the eastern part of the state: "'We lived in a tenthouse: there was neither electricity, nor running water, nor telephone, and it was a hard struggle to provide even the least heat in winter. Drifting wood from [the] Columbia furnished all our fuel, and much of our timber.'" He attended Reed College, joined the Communist-dominated National Student League, and won a Rhodes Scholarship to Oxford in 1935. He explained his political development in this fashion:

"My childhood political development was a curious mixture of agrarian radicalism, utopian socialism (from books mainly) and faith in militant trade unionism. I was taught to admire Eugene Debs along with John Brown, Lincoln, and Lenin; but on the issues of the day I was naturally rather confused. I supported La Follette in 1924 (at the age of 11) and the Socialist candidates in 1923 and 1932. . . . Beginning about 1934 I began to lose some illusions and acquire a better understanding of politics. I met Elizabeth Gurley Flynn and was much influenced by her. . . . When I arrived in Oxford in the fall of 1935 I joined the October Club, the left-wing political organization, which very soon thereafter was amalgamated with the Labour Club, in accordance with the People's Front policy. In a few weeks, on my own initiative, I approached some of the student Party leaders and asked to be admitted to the Party. After being examined by the secretariat, I was admitted to the CPGB [Communist Party of Great Britain] I believe in December 1935."

Wheeler spent the third year of his Rhodes award at the University of Paris and worked on behalf of the International Brigades in his spare time. Returning to the United States in 1938, he taught briefly at Yale and then joined the Treasury Department, working under Harry White, before moving to the staff of the Senate Banking and Currency Committee. In October 1941, he transferred to the Office of the Coordinator of Information, forerunner of the OSS.[27]

When he first arrived in Washington, Wheeler told the KGB, he was isolated from party contacts and made the mistake of approaching Martin Chancey, an open CPUSA leader. He believed that this action led to a Civil Service Commission investigation that threatened his OSS career, but his boss, Emile Despres, vouched for his loyalty and saved his job. (Despres had the distinction of intervening on behalf of two hidden Communists. Later working at the State Department, he also defended Carl Marzani, unsuccessfully in his case.)[28]

Wheeler worked on issues of German manpower for the OSS. Franz Neumann, a co-worker, recommended him to the KGB in 1943 "as someone who was talented and progressive." The New York station checked the recommendation with Duncan Lee, a senior OSS officer and KGB source. Lee and Wheeler had both been Rhodes scholars and had met on the boat on the way to Oxford. They had also been at Yale together in the late 1930s, Wheeler as a political science instructor and Lee as a law student. In Washington the Lees and the Wheelers socialized. The New York station reported, "We intend to recruit Wheeler through Sound [Golos]."[29]

Golos managed the approach through Victor Perlo. In a report to the KGB Perlo recalled that Wheeler had been part of a secret but otherwise ordinary CPUSA political unit of government employees but had dropped out of that group by 1943. Perlo had a member of his apparatus, Edward Fitzgerald, approach and connect Wheeler with Perlo's unit, but Wheeler had produced little until the end of 1943, when Perlo himself "'established contact with him for a special assignment.'" Earl Browder first put the Perlo group in touch with Golos in November 1943, and Elizabeth Bentley had her first meeting with several of its members in March 1944. The KGB moved swiftly, however, to take direct control of the Perlo group, and by the fall of 1944 Joseph Katz, a veteran KGB agent, had replaced Bentley as the group's chief liaison.[30]

Regarding Wheeler's contribution, Victor Perlo in a report to the KGB, likely prepared in 1945, wrote:

"He has access to excellent material, and once given explanation of what was wanted, worked hard and bravely to get it. He had planned to leave the OSS because of boredom with work, but when explained why it was important for us, he wholeheartedly accepted the idea of staying indefinitely, so long as it would be useful in our judgment. His expressed attitude to the dangers involved is that our work is the only important thing he can do, and that there is no point in maintaining his personal security if he doesn't do the work. His actions bear out this expression. He has not been reckless, but has gotten materials regularly under security conditions more difficult than those faced by most others."

Late in May 1944 Akhmerov, chief of the KGB's illegal station, sent a cable to General Fitin about Wheeler's position and availability that was quickly answered with the news that he was "especially" of great interest. Wheeler was soon justifying that evaluation. An internal KGB memo from mid-1944 said of ten documents that he had provided, "all the materials are of interest and all are valuable" and were "'a rich source of material'" on Germany's economic position, and some had been forwarded to GRU, which had made use of them in evaluating the military-political situation there. In September a telegram from Moscow Center praised the "very valuable materials" Wheeler had sent about both the Soviet Union and Germany. The Center also wrote that it was interested in another report on "'Russia's external economic relations and its interest in monetary stabilization,'" referenced in Wheeler's material and "'located in 'Izra's [Wheeler's] department.'" Moscow instructed: "'Try to get it.'"[31]

Up until August 1944 the KGB's only contact with Wheeler had been indirect, via Perlo. At that time Akhmerov reported: "'Izra [Wheeler] has given us a larger amount of interesting material than anyone else in that group. Three weeks ago, Myrna [Bentley] met with him for the first time. He made a very good impression on her. I asked Myrna to tell him to be very careful and to do everything possible to consolidate his position in the department. He is very brave, it seems, and unconcerned about his position. He says it doesn't make sense to be afraid—after all, a person only dies once. He is very critical of his colleagues and considers them all to be feather-brained.'" Akhmerov also observed, "'I think he understands full well that he is helping us. He is undoubtedly the most active one in the group.'"[32]

Perlo detailed several potential threats to Wheeler's position in his 1945 report. In addition to the Civil Service Commission investigation that he had survived, his brother George, also a secret Communist, worked for the Foreign Economic Administration and had come under Civil Service Commission suspicion. Donald's wife was also publicly active in various Communist-linked causes in Washington. (Incredibly, despite these issues, the OSS assigned *Donald* to investigate security suspects in his division of the OSS!) Donald's wife also worked, and with three children, Perlo thought the time Wheeler spent on household duties was cutting into his espionage productivity, and he had suggested her "'quitting her job, and helping him with typing etc.'"[33]

In September 1944 the KGB suddenly feared a more serious peril. Akhmerov passed along from Bentley that Duncan Lee "'told us some very unpleasant news about 'Izra's' [Wheeler's] official situation in his department. The news is that he was included on a list of several employees who allegedly provide us with information from their department.'" Bentley noted that Lee might be forced to fire his old friend Wheeler. (Lee did not know that Wheeler was a fellow KGB source.) Follow-up messages based on information from Lee showed that not only was Donald Wheeler on the list, but so also were two other KGB sources: Maurice Halperin and Irving Goff. But subsequent messages indicated that the problem was not quite as bad as the initial report. The OSS security list identified Wheeler as a suspected Communist and Halperin as a sympathizer, but the only persons suspected of passing information to the Soviets were two OSS officers who had served with the International Brigades, Manuel T. and Michael A. Jiminez, and David Zablodowsky, a hidden Communist with links to Whittaker Chambers's mid-1930s GRU network. Further, OSS officials, reflecting General Donovan's policy of tolerating Communists, had decided to take measures against these individuals only "if they side with the USSR against the USA in the future." Nonetheless, as a security measure, Moscow Center ordered a temporary cessation of contact with both Wheeler and Halperin and insisted that it had to approve any recontact.[34]

Anatoly Gorsky, Washington KGB station chief, met with Harold Glasser in December 1944 and noted that Glasser knew Wheeler and referred to him as "'temporarily in quarantine.'" Glasser was also a member of the Perlo group, and, typical of the relaxed security and lack of compartmentalization of the CPUSA-based networks, evidently Glasser and other members knew contact with Wheeler had been temporarily suspended. By March 1945 Wheeler was being cautiously reintroduced to espionage work. Explaining that his group needed better facilities for photographing their material, Perlo told the KGB that Wheeler had "'a well equipped shop, and is skillful in handling it.'" He proposed that Wheeler become his group's "'technical specialist, and be given responsibility for jobs of this sort.'" He also suggested that the KGB pay Mrs. Wheeler to assist the group's work "'if and when'" she quit her regular job, a suggestion echoed by Joseph Katz, who proposed paying her $75 a month. Gorsky, however, was unenthusiastic about overburdening Wheeler, a prime source of OSS documents, with additional duties as a covert photographer. Instead, in April 1945 he told Moscow Center that another KGB agent in Washington, Gerald Graze, was photographing the material produced by Wheeler, Perlo, and Edward Fitzgerald (then a KGB source at the War Production Board).[35]

By the end of 1944 the KGB had pushed Bentley to the side and in 1945 began taking direct control of the Perlo and Silvermaster groups. Moscow Center wanted the networks restructured, instructing Gorsky: "Take note of how the probationer [agent] network is formed so as to guarantee security. The most prudent thing—to form small probationer groups of 2–3 people . . . 1) the most guidance for each worker, 2) maximum secrecy in work." In the process of reorganization Moscow Center emphasized Wheeler's importance. Vassiliev's notes show that Moscow told Gorsky to put Wheeler in a three-person subgroup: "Probationers [sources] in "Cabin" OSS "Cautious" [Julius Joseph]—in the Japanese Section: U.S. policies in the Far East, in China and Korea, leads on individuals. "Izra" [Wheeler] gives valuable materials. The main thing—secrecy. "Muse" [Helen Tenney]—Russian Section of "Cabin." Erratic behavior in day-to-day life . . . could get noticed by counterintelligence. C. [Center] proposes giving "Izra" and "Muse" to "Cautious"—a reliable and experienced probationer who will impart secrecy skills to them." Another Moscow Center message repeated the point: ""Cautious's' subgroup. Handles 'Izra' and 'Muse.' Use the utmost caution when working with this subgroup and especially with 'Izra.' 'Vadim' [Gorsky] should meet with 'Izra' personally once every two or three months.'"[36]

Once reactivated, Wheeler again demonstrated his worth. One June 1945 report noted, "In accordance with instructions, 'Izra' is constantly working to uncover specific OSS agents." Wheeler exposed a number of OSS agents working covertly in Soviet-controlled territory. A spring 1945 report from Gorsky stated:

"'Izra' [Wheeler] spoke with Lieutenant of airborne troops Bookbinder . . . who works in 'Cabin's' [OSS's] secret intelligence division. From the conversation, he found out that Bookbinder had just returned from a secret mission across Russian lines in Germany. He and his group (a major and a captain) stayed in Berlin, visited a calculating machine factory, contacted the wife of the factory director, and supposedly set up an informing network to report on any movement of equipment by Sov. agencies.

The factory is located in the city of Spandau—a center of heavy industry. According to B., the director has been working for an Am. company for many years. This trip took place around May 22nd. B. said that he also set up an informing network in Plosht, where he had gone the day before the Russians arrived. He made a similar illegal trip to Transylvania accompanied by Robert Wolff, who works in the balance division of Cabin's research and analysis department. B. speaks fluent Russian, knows a little German, and speaks English well, though with a Jewish accent." (Detailed description of Bookbinder's distinguishing marks, including a large ring on the middle finger of his left hand. The ring is made of gold with a blue semi-transparent stone.)

In June Wheeler exposed another clandestine American agent to the KGB: ""Izra' discovered that Wayne Voosling, a correspondent for 'Life' magazine, is an OSS agent. 'Izra' got a look at a cover letter addressed to the OSS from Voosling, which was attached.'" In addition to outing American intelligence officers and foreign sources, Wheeler also reported on internal disagreements within the government about policies in the military government occupational administration for Germany.[37]

Responding to President Truman's decision to abolish the OSS in the fall of 1945, Gorsky cabled Moscow that he had

instructed the agents to stay in Cabin [OSS] for now and to transfer onto the staff of the org. that is being created in its place. Such a directive was given to Izra [Wheeler] in particular. I. ["Izra"] was in complete agreement with it but said that any vetting prior to his joining the new intel. org. could uncover his past. At pres., all the functions and affairs of the division where I. and "Akr" [unidentified] work are being taken over by Bank [State Department], and its employees are being individually selected to work in Bank. Akr hopes he will be admitted to Bank. Izra can't say anything for certain yet but hopes that in October his position will become clear.[38]

Wheeler successfully made the transition, and by November he was installed at the State Department as part of the Interim Research and Intelligence Service (IRIS). He provided the KGB with his assessment of the new organization's prospects, noting that it was in a difficult administrative and bureaucratic position, having lost its military personnel and facing hostility from State Department veterans who resented the new organization injected into their midst. Despite these problems Wheeler continued to supply documents, sending the OSS's final reports on events in the USSR, correspondence between OSS officers in Germany and Washington, and State Department evaluations of the Middle East situation.[39]

Wheeler also stole reports from the Joint Technical Intelligence Subcommittee, which coordinated Army, Navy, and Air Force technical intelligence efforts. Leonid Kvasnikov offered his colleagues a positive evaluation of Wheeler's material:

"I am sending you an assessment of the following materials: 1. Report of the Joint Technical Intelligence Subcommittee of Amer. Military Intelligence, 'German guided missiles.' Source "Izra" [Wheeler], mailing No. 17 of 1945. Material is of interest. 2. Report of the Joint Technical Intelligence Subcommittee of Amer. Mil. Intelligence, 'Description of the German X-4 rocket.' Source "Izra," mailing No. 17 of 1945. Material is of interest. 3. Report of the Joint Tech. Intelligence Subcommittee of Amer. Mil. Intelligence, 'On sound-absorbent submarine hulls.' Source "Izra," mailing No. 16 from 1945. Material is valuable. 4. Report of the Joint Technical Intelligence Subcommittee of Amer. Mil. Intelligence 'On trends in the design of German tanks.' Source "Izra," mailing No. 16 from 1945. Material is of info. interest."[40]

But the good times came to an end. Reacting to Igor Gouzenko's de-fection, General Fitin ordered the American station in October 1945 to "safeguard from failure" five of its most valuable sources—Donald Maclean, Harold Glasser, Victor Perlo, Charles Kramer, and Donald Wheeler—by reducing "meetings with them to once or twice a month." Then the KGB learned in November that Elizabeth Bentley had defected and named Wheeler to the FBI. His days as a Soviet source and govern-ment employee were over. He left the State Department in June 1946. In the face of several subpoenas from federal grand juries and the House Committee on Un-American Activities, Wheeler refused to answer ques-tions, invoking his Fifth Amendment rights. He settled his family on a dairy farm in Sequim, Washington, and became a leader in the local Communist Party. He later earned a doctorate at Oxford, taught at Canadian and Amer-ican universities, and remained a devoted Communist until his death in 2002. He never spoke candidly of his work for Soviet intelligence.[41]

Maurice Halperin

In the 1930s Maurice Halperin was a Latin American specialist at the University of Oklahoma and at some point secretly joined the Commu-nist Party. Although he kept his party membership secret, Halperin was a highly visible champion of far left political causes. With Communists coming under public opprobrium over the Nazi-Soviet Pact, he got into trouble in 1940. Although he vigorously denied CPUSA membership, the Oklahoma legislature pushed for his dismissal. The university's president, however, believed Halperin and arranged a paid year-long sabbatical, after which Halperin resigned and joined the Office of the Coordinator of Information's research department. After the United States entered the war, the agency divided, and Halperin became head of the Latin American division of the OSS's Research and Analysis Branch.[42]

Halperin first made contact with the Washington party underground through Bruce Minton, who worked as a talent spotter and agent han-dler for Jacob Golos. Golos agreed that Halperin was a promising new source and sent Elizabeth Bentley to contact him and eventually receive material he passed along. Moscow Center, however, was disappointed with the limited quantity of information Halperin supplied during 1942: "'Hare [Halperin] promised to compile for "Sound" [Golos] weekly sum-mary reports of materials accessible to him. Since then, however, we have received only two brief reports of little value, whereas you emphasized that he has access to all the materials coming in to the "Cabin" [OSS]. Have you given him any specific assignments? Why didn't "Hare" indicate from which sources he obtained the information about the German offensive that is being prepared against Vologda?'" By early 1943, Moscow Center allowed that Halperin was finally providing "'some interesting information'" but continued to think the volume "'stingy and sporadic'" and urged the New York station to "'show the appropriate persistence'" in pushing Halperin to deliver more.[43]

Whether it was the station's persistence or some other factor, Halperin's productivity accelerated. Twenty-two KGB cables, spanning June 1943 to September 1944, show him delivering OSS reports and American diplomatic cables that ranged far beyond his area of responsibility at the agency. Halperin handed over U.S. diplomatic cables regarding Turkey's policies toward Rumania, State Department instructions to the American ambassador in Spain, U.S. embassy reports about Morocco, dispatches from Ambassador John Winant in London about the stance of the Polish exile government toward negotiations with Stalin, reports on the U.S. relationship with various exile French groups, accounts of peace feelers from dissident Germans being passed on by the Vatican, U.S. perceptions of Tito's activities in Yugoslavia, and discussions between the Greek government and the United States regarding Soviet ambitions in the Balkans.[44]

As the KGB began to professionalize Golos's operations after his death, Halperin was one of the first of his sources removed from Bentley's control. By 1944 Joseph Katz had become his supervisor. When he wrote an account of his years as station chief in America, Zarubin characterized Halperin positively as having "'provided interesting, sometimes documented information.'"[45]

Moscow Center ordered contact cut with Halperin as soon as it heard that Bentley had defected. By that time the OSS had dissolved, but Halperin had managed to transfer into the State Department. He resigned in 1946 and emphatically denied to the FBI that he was a Communist, had ever met Bentley, or had any contact with Soviet intelligence. Halperin was able to ride out the initial storm after Bentley's public testimony in 1948, but in 1953, while he was serving as head of Boston University's Latin American studies program, the Senate Internal Security Subcommittee called him to testify. He took the Fifth Amendment and, at first, refused to answer questions put to him by a university committee. After agreeing to a compromise in which he assured Boston University that he was not a Communist, Halperin abruptly left for Mexico when the Justice Department released an FBI report that described him as a Soviet spy. When he refused to return, he was fired. Initially Halperin remained in Mexico, but by 1956 he became nervous that the United States government might extradite him. A KGB memo stated: "'He gave us valuable information, which he personally dictated to "Myrna" [Bentley] at their meetings. After M.'s betrayal he fled to Mexico. On 20.03.56 Halperin officially applied to our emb. in Mexico for citizenship and permanent residence in the USSR. Department 1 of the PGU [First Chief Directorate, the KGB's foreign intelligence arm] gave instructions to handle the matter officially through the MID [Ministry of Foreign Affairs]. There was no supervision on our part. We need to find out . . . what the Halperins' situation is and make an offer for the H's to move to the USSR.'" Halperin moved to Moscow in 1958 and was given an academic post. But he did not find Soviet life to his taste and decamped to Communist Cuba in 1962. By 1967, disillusioned with Castro-style communism as well, he accepted a teaching job in Canada, where he remained until his death. Later in his life Halperin became critical of communism but never admitted to his cooperation with Soviet intelligence.[46]

Duncan Lee

Duncan Lee was descended from the Lees of Virginia. His father was an Episcopalian priest, former missionary to China, and rector at Chatham Hall, an elite girl's school in Virginia. Duncan attended the prestigious St. Alban's preparatory school in Washington, went to Yale, played football, and graduated first in his class in 1935. He then went to Oxford as a Rhodes scholar, returned to Yale to get a law degree, and in 1939 joined the Wall Street firm of Donovan, Leisure, Newton and Lumbard. In 1942 he joined the Office of Strategic Services, headed by William Donovan, the senior partner of his law firm. Elizabeth Bentley described Lee's cooperation with Soviet intelligence in detail in her 1945 FBI deposition and testified publicly about it in 1948. Lee also testified, did not resort to the Fifth Amendment, and firmly denied the charges, stating emphatically that he was not and had never been a Communist and had known Bentley only as a social acquaintance he had met through his friend Mary Price.[47]

The FBI, however, did not credit the story Lee had earlier told when it interviewed him in 1947. Lee admitted meeting with Bentley and Golos privately on a number of occasions over a period of two years, both in Washington and during trips to New York. But, he insisted, he had known Bentley only as "Helen," had never known her last name, and knew nothing of her activities. Lee also said he had known Golos only as Helen's friend "John." Nor did the FBI believe that an OSS lieutenant colonel engaged in intelligence work in wartime would meet someone privately over two years without learning her full name or occupation. (When Lee testified to the House Committee on Un-American Activities a year later, he did not advance the claim that he had never known Bentley's name.) Lee also told the FBI he was a New Deal liberal and had no links to the Communist Party. The FBI agents conducting the interview noted: "At the outset of the interview Lee appeared to be visibly shaken and extremely nervous. After talking for approximately an hour, he became calm and stopped trembling. His shaking was so noticeable at the outset of the interview that it was noted he had difficulty in lighting a cigarette." FBI investigations also turned up his active role in various Communist-led organizations, including service on the executive board of the China Aid Council, a group supporting the Chinese Communist Party and headed by Mildred Price, Mary Price's sister and a secret Communist. The question of Lee's cooperation with Soviet intelligence ended in the mid-1990s with the release of the Venona decryptions; nine of the deciphered KGB cables confirmed Lee's cooperation with Soviet intelligence.[48]

New KGB documents fill in missing parts and provide more detail of Lee's role in Soviet espionage. The FBI was convinced that Lee was a Communist but unsure if he had joined when at Oxford in the mid-1930s or in 1939 while attending Yale Law School. A 1942 memo on Lee prepared by Jacob Golos stated, "He joined the party in 1939, while he was at Yale University. His wife joined the party around the same time." Bentley told the FBI that during her period of contact Lee had provided verbal briefings and avoided delivering documents and that his production was episodic and the information sometimes vague. Although she recalled few details, she stated that from time to time his information was of value. During the period when Bentley was his primary liaison, KGB documents confirm, Lee generally avoided providing documents; although he did so on a few occasions, his delivery was irregular, and the quality varied from useful to materials that were often, in the view of Moscow Center analysts, "'not specific enough and have no value.'" He passed along reports on the OSS's relationship with Polish intelligence, discussions between the American and Chinese ambassadors in Moscow, discussions between the American ambassador in London and Polish leader Władyslaw Sikorski, and OSS reports on internal Bulgarian politics. Reviewing the first quarter of 1944, a KGB Moscow officer commented on Lee's productivity:

"The source submitted info. on five occasions. The scope of information collected by the source is extremely varied (Bulgarian emigration, Papen's group in Germany, Hungary's peace intrigues, revolutionary movement in Europe, Donovan's trip to Europe, the opening of an Amer. intelligence branch in India, etc.), but mostly it deals with the situation in Europe. The information is for the most part too vague. Of all the source's info. for this quarter, only two reports have been used: one on contact between Amer. intelligence and the

Bulgarian underground group 'Link' (reported to the NKID [People's Commissariat of Foreign Affairs]), and one on Donovan's upcoming trip to Europe (reported to the GRU)."[49]

Bentley told the FBI that Lee never lived up to the KGB's expectation, was very apprehensive about possible FBI investigations, and at times appeared to regret his decision to cooperate and "to be troubled with a severe conflict of ideas." KGB reports reinforce her judgment. One noted:

"Characteristic of K's ["Koch"/Lee's] work is the fact that he only wants to give info. to fellowcountrymen [CPUSA], under no circumstances to us. The least hint about the fact that his info. ends up in our hands displeases him. For instance, in March 1944, he told Myrna [Bentley] the following: 'The OSS received a report from Moscow that one of Donovan's representatives had spoken with Cde. Molotov about "Link" group and was surprised to learn that the latter already knew about this and even mentioned Kuyumzhitsky's name.' Based on this, K. concluded that the information he had reported earlier on this matter had fallen into the hands of the Soviet gov't, which he does not want because it 'puts him in danger.' With this attitude of K's in mind, Myrna tried to convince him that the info. he provides is meant exclusively for the fellowcountryman leadership. But even this did not have the desired effect. 'Myrna' claims that the only reason for K's limited activity is his cowardice."

The KGB had hopes that once it had direct contact, its professional operatives could get more out of him than Bentley had. The chief of the Washington station reported in March 1945 on a meeting between Lee and Joseph Katz:

"'X' [Katz] held two rendezvous with K ["Koch"/Lee], and detailed reports on them were sent home by mail on March 6th. K. came to both meetings so frightened that he couldn't hold a cup of coffee in his hands b/c they were shaking. K. said that gathering info. for fellowcountrymen [CPUSA], and possibly for us as well, filled him with terror. Every night he has nightmares. He cannot for a minute believe that the FBI doesn't know about all fellowcountrymen's work gathering info. in the USA. He thinks the FBI knows who all the Amer. fellow countrymen informants are, but because overall conditions do not favor taking harsh measures, they are not taking any measures for the time being. . . .

K. also said that Myrna's [Bentley's] big mouth and indiscretion did not inspire confidence that the latter had not told some outsider something about him. According to K., Myrna once told him a number of details about Sound [Golos], although Koch refused to tell X what these details were. It should be noted that K. could have found something out from Dir [Mary Price], whom he still sees and sleeps with. As a result, K. asked that he be left alone and accompanied this with various excuses (he realizes what a coward he is, how ashamed he is of himself, how wrongly he is acting, etc). According to Myrna, in one of his most recent conversations with Dir, K. spoke highly of X (Koch knows X by an assumed name) and explained his decision to stop working with us by the fact that he could not lead a 'double life,' that he had a 'guilty' conscience for 'deceiving the USA,' that he was constantly having a crisis of conscience, and so forth."

Moscow Center briefly considered maintaining some contact with Lee, but in April suggested that Gorsky deactivate him, a suggestion that became an order in November 1945, after Bentley's defection. There is no indication that Lee provided information to the KGB after his March 1945 meeting with Katz. Bentley, echoing Golos, had argued that many of the sources they had developed needed the illusion that they were dealing with the CPUSA and not directly with Soviet intelligence officers. The KGB believed that concern overblown, convinced that most of the sources were aware where their information went and welcomed direct Soviet contact. In most cases the KGB was right, but Bentley and Golos had been on target about Lee. Putting him in direct contact with a KGB agent had thoroughly spooked him and destroyed his usefulness.[50]

Franz Neumann

Deciphered KGB cables released in the mid-1990s contained an intriguing cover name, "Ruff," a Soviet source in the OSS, but the four messages that mentioned him had too little information to allow identification. He is unambiguously named in a KGB report in Vassiliev's notebooks:

"Ruff"—Franz Neumann, b. 1900 in Germany, U.S. citizen. Lived in Germany till 1933, was a left social dem., and worked as a lawyer for trade unions. In 1933, he emigrated to England, where he graduated from an econ. inst. (The London School of Economics . . .). He came to the USA in 1936. Prior to Feb. 1942, Ruff worked as a teacher, engaged in scientific work, and, in addition, worked as a consultant for the German division of the Board of Economic Warfare. He simultaneously wrote a book on Germany's econ. questions, which was published in the USA. In Feb. 1942, R. was transferred to Cabin [OSS], where he began work as a consultant in the foreign division.

Ruff—Mary's [Massing's] lead; he is a good friend of his. Mary, Noah [unidentified], and Git [unidentified] give Ruff a positive reference, describing him as pro-Soviet, with left views, and unaffiliated with any emigrant organizations. In 1942, R. was contracted with Mary's help. At the initial meeting, R. promised to pass us all the information that came his way. According to him, numerous copies of telegrams from Amer. ambassadors to Bank are sent to him; in addition, he has access to materials on Germany in Cabin.

An August 1942 report from "Mary"/Massing stated:

Neumann said that he has seen three reports devoted to the Caucasus: from the Board of Econ. Warfare, the Euro. Division of the Board of Military Info., and the OSS. The first two are not of interest. The report from the OSS contains a lot of valuable material and is excellently written. The author—Robinson, is Chief of the Russian Division at the OSS. The report is 124 pages long and contains very detailed facts and figures about the Caucasus: railroads, stations, warehouses, workshops, the number of trains passing through in a particular year, etc. Neumann says that Robinson has an unfriendly attitude toward the USSR but is highly competent in matters pertaining to the USSR.

Neumann and Paul Massing were both participants in the exiled neo-Marxist "Frankfurt School of Social Research," which had relocated from Germany to Columbia University after the Nazis took power. Neumann was best known for his impressive 1942 analysis of Nazi totalitarianism, *Behemoth: The Structure and Practice of National Socialism.* In addition to the Massings, Elizabeth Zarubin also met with Neumann.[51]

Neumann's position in the Research and Analysis Branch of the OSS gave him wide access to OSS documents, and initially he was a productive source. An early report stated:

"The info. received this time from R. ["Ruff"/Neumann] amounts to the following:

   1. The Amer. ambassador to Spain, [Carlton] Hayes, informed "Bank" [State Department] that he spoke with the Duke of Alba, who recently returned from Germany and Italy. In both these countries, Alba—as he himself put it—met with generals and industrialists who said they were willing to overthrow Hitler and Mussolini and make a deal with the Allies. R. says that Hayes is a sworn enemy of the Sov. Union.

   2. [Archbishop Francis] Spellman traveled to the Vatican with the intention of recruiting the Pope on the Allied side. The latter declared that the Allies must stop bombing civilian populations. The USA does not object to this, but England turned down the Pope's suggestion, which Sp-n seconded as well. Based on all the information that was obtained by R., it can be concluded that Sp-n's trip did not meet its goal.

   3. "Bank" received a report from [Ambassador William] Standley stating

that he had informed Comrade Molotov about the upcoming meeting of Allied countries to discuss issuing provisions and proposed that the Sov. gov't send a delegate to this meeting. In response, Comrade Molotov supposedly expressed a wish that in the future, questions of conducting this or that meeting be discussed with the Soviet gov't as well. According to Standley's report, the Poles had told him that the Soviet gov't was not addressing their complaints about the supposedly compulsory adoption of Soviet citizenship for Poles living in the USSR, on pain of expulsion. According to R., not one of the reports by Standley he had read betray any hint of anti-Soviet prejudice.

4. For now, Americans are not hiring any German immigrants. At the same time, however, Cabin [OSS] has been asked to thoroughly study who could be hired. Thus, a certain Walter Dorn, Chief of the Division of Foreign Nationalities Groups at Cabin, was sent to Mexico to study the question of German emigrants (including CP members).

5. According to the Polish ambassador to the USA, [Jan] Ciechanowski, the politics and claims of the Polish people are not supported by "Radio Station" [Office of War Information] supposedly because the people working there are for the most part Jews (both local and immigrant). C. intends to conduct a campaign against "Radio Station" if it does not rethink its line of conduct. R. explained that Radio Station has instructions not to respond to the 'Poles' complaints' in its propaganda work."[52]

But Neumann's productivity did not continue. A KGB report from late 1943 complained, "R. ["Ruff'/Neumann] does practically nothing." One of the Massings met with him and asked if he had reconsidered assisting the KGB and reported: "'R. answered the following: 'I have not changed my mind. If anything truly important comes up, I will tell you without hesitation.' He then gave the usual explanation that he did not have anything worth telling us about.'" The KGB wasn't happy with this explanation, but it took what it could get, and occasionally Neumann handed over material of interest:

On 10 June 1944, R. ["Ruff'/Neumann] informed Mary [Massing] that a Cabin [OSS] representative at the Amer. embassy in Bern (Switzerland), Dulles, whom we know, telegraphed the following info. to Bank [State Department]: Supposedly, General [Walther] von Brauchitsch came to him personally from Germany and said that on behalf of a group of servicemen, he was offering peace on the following terms:

1. This group of military men would overthrow Hitler.
2. A military gov't would be established, which would agree to unconditional surrender.
3. Sov. forces should not take part in occupying any German territory.

To this message, the director of Bank replied to Dulles that without the involvement of its allies, the Americans would not conduct any peace negotiations with Germany.

Around the 25th–26th of May, R. reported the following to Mary: Dulles informed Bank that he had been approached by a representative of a German group. This group is made up of prominent military men, including Zeitzler, industrialists, and right-wing socialist democrats who had remained in Ger. The group offered to conduct peace negotiations on terms that occupied territories in W. Europe would be cleared of German forces and they would have freedom to operate in the East in order to continue the war against the USSR.

The dir. of Bank supposedly informed Gromyko of this offer. The bureau is checking this information through oth. sources. The bureau adds that in spite of the fact that R. gives little information, all of his previous reports have been corroborated by reports from oth. probationers [sources] at "Cabin."[53]

But in July 1944 a Moscow Center analyst called Neumann's recent material "'superficial'" and suspected disinformation in his report on Allen Dulles's contact with anti-Hitler Germans. However, in the spring of 1945 a Moscow Center evaluation reconsidered: "'R's ["Ruff"/Neumann's] report on Dulles' negotiations in Bern is of great interest. . . . At one time, this info. was labeled disinformation by the operational department. However, subsequent agent materials have confirmed that Amer. intelligence had conducted negotiations with representatives from the German opposition in Bern at that time.'" The report went on to note that Elizabeth Zarubin's sudden recall to Moscow in July 1944 cut off contact with Neumann but that liaison could be reestablished via the Massings. There is, however, nothing indicating that contact was reestablished.[54]

Neumann went on to serve on Justice Robert Jackson's prosecutorial staff at the Nuremberg War Crimes trials. He also plunged into German politics and supported a merger of the German Social Democratic Party with the Communists. But heavy-handed Soviet repression in East Germany soon disillusioned him about cooperation with Communists. He helped found the Free University of Berlin and in 1948 accepted a professorship at Columbia University before he died in an auto accident in 1954. He never publicly disclosed his clandestine wartime cooperation with the KGB, and no congressional investigating committee called him to testify. His name, however, was included among State Department security risks by Senator McCarthy in 1950.

Helen Tenney

Helen Tenney, cover name "Muse," appears in numerous KGB documents. Tenney had excellent language skills and in late 1942 got a job in the OSS's Spanish section but later shifted to its Russian section. Bentley identified her as a useful and productive source recruited by Golos on the recommendation of CPUSA contacts. "Muse" appears in the Venona decryptions as a KGB source in the OSS, but NSA/FBI analysts were unable to attach a real name to the cover name. The deciphered cables and Bentley, who met with Tenney to pick up her material, showed that she provided copies of State Department diplomatic messages on topics of interest and monitored the extent of OSS knowledge of Soviet matters from her post in the OSS's Russian section.[55]

The KGB Washington station attempted to contact Tenney to inform her of Bentley's defection and to arrange future meetings because she had a chance to transfer to the State Department. Tenney had a scheduled meeting with Eva Getzov, a KGB courier, in early December 1945. But the station feared that she might be under surveillance or had even been turned by the FBI. As a security measure Joseph Katz shadowed Tenney on her way to the meeting with Getzov. Station chief Gorsky reported: ""Muse" [Tenney] was supposed to have a meeting with "Adam" [Getzov]. "Muse" was tailed by X [Katz]. When she exited from her building, Muse walked up to one of the cars parked in front of her building and said something to the person sitting in it. At the meeting place X spotted the same car with the same person in it. The car was parked so that the entire meeting site could be surveyed from it. This place had never been used before. X used a prearranged signal to warn Adam not to come to the meeting. In the past Muse was very close to Myrna [Bentley]."[56] Fearing that Tenney was under surveillance and might be cooperating with the FBI, the KGB abandoned further efforts to contact her. In fact, she had not been turned, and there is no record in FBI files that it had established surveillance on Tenney at that time.

But this abortive December meeting contributed to Tenney's later partial collapse by leaving her feeling abandoned. After the OSS dissolved, she succeeded in transferring to the State Department and worked in its Russian analytic section, but she was without any Soviet contact. In any case, her tenure there was short. With Bentley's statements in hand, the FBI informed State Department security of Tenney's Soviet ties, and she was quietly forced out in mid-1946. The State Department also revoked her passport. Realizing that she was under suspicion but feeling abandoned by the Soviets, Tenney suffered a nervous breakdown. Friends had her hospitalized briefly in January 1947, when she started babbling about Soviet spies and being under FBI surveillance. Noting her condition, the FBI thought that she might break if Bentley approached her. Unaware that Bentley had defected, Tenney told her in early February 1947 that she had been out of touch with the Soviets for some time, felt completely isolated, and hoped that Bentley was reestablishing contact. Tenney did not, however, show any sign she was disillusioned about the Soviet cause, and the FBI dropped any expectation she might cooperate. Soon afterwards, in a formal interview with the Bureau, Tenney denied any role in espionage. She admitted knowing Bentley but under another name and only during 1942 and 1943, unaware that their meeting just a few months earlier had been set up by and observed by FBI agents. Tenney eventually recovered from her breakdown and invoked the Fifth Amendment when questioned by the Senate Internal Security Subcommittee in 1953. She then faded from public notice.[57]

Julius and Bella Joseph

KGB archives detail several husband-and-wife espionage teams. Occasionally, a wife like Ethel Rosenberg knew about her husband's activities and provided assistance. Sometimes both spouses were fully operational agents. But Julius and Bella Joseph were unusual in that both were sources at the same agency, the OSS. A KGB New York station report in 1941 stated: "Sound [Golos] reported on Julius J. Joseph. . . . As 'Sound's' report makes clear, Joseph and his wife have long shown interest in the local fellowcountryman [Communist] movement and have been connected with the leading comrades and secret fellowcountryman organizations. . . . Henceforth "Cautious," and his wife is "Colleague.""[58]

At that point, Julius was an economist working for the Social Security Board, not a high priority target. But in 1943 Zarubin reported: "A few weeks ago "Colleague" [Bella Joseph] got a job with the "cabin" [OSS] in the photo department as a stenographer. Photographs of localities, mil. installations, inventions, weaponry. Sound [Golos] considers her a reliable and able "fellowcountryman" [Communist]. "Cautious" [Julius Joseph] will soon be called up into the army. "Sound" suggested to him that "Colleague" arrange at the "cabin" for him to be taken in there." Initially, Zarubin noted that Bella's effort to find a position for Julius at the OSS was unsuccessful: "It didn't work out." But they kept at it. After Julius was drafted, he was able to obtain a commission as an Army lieutenant, and in December Zarubin reported that Julius "hasn't gotten a job with the "Cabin" yet, but on assignment from the "Cabin" he is working at the library on questions pertaining to Japan's manpower reserves and has promised to give us a copy of his report."[59]

There were, however, complications. The KGB New York station chief noted in August 1943 that not only were his Communist ties an obstacle to Julius's getting a position at the OSS, but also "'the issue of "Colleague" [Bella Joseph] is even worse. She has gotten involved with another man and is asking "Cautious" [Julius Joseph] for a divorce. No attempts at dissuasion by "Sound" [Golos] have helped. "Colleague" plans to move to California with her lover and, as a result, to quit her job in the "Cabin's" [OSS's] film department.'" Bella Joseph was still among Elizabeth Bentley's contacts on a list she turned over to the KGB Washington station chief in October 1944, so presumably the Joseph marriage got past this difficulty.[60]

In any event, Julius was able to convert his temporary detail to the OSS into a permanent posting, and he spent the rest of the war there. By 1945 he was deputy chief of his division, which dealt with Japanese intelligence; he turned over material to the KGB and managed a small unit of KGB sources at the OSS that included Helen Tenney and Donald Wheeler. Bentley discussed the Josephs at length in her 1945 FBI deposition, and Julius appears in three Venona decryptions with the cover name "Cautious." "Colleague" [Bella Joseph] also appears in one cable deciphered by Venona, but NSA/FBI analysts were unable to identify the cover name.[61]

After the OSS dissolved, Julius Joseph went to work for UNRRA and then directed the New York Committee for the Arts, Sciences, and Professions, a Popular Front group aligned with the CPUSA. Called to testify about Bentley's allegations by the Senate Internal Security Subcommittee in 1953, he used the Fifth Amendment and accused the committee of questioning him in order to "create unemployment and a blacklist for loyal Americans."[62]

Philip and Mary Jane Keeney

Documents in Vassiliev's notebooks provide additional details about the espionage careers of two librarians, one of whom worked for the OSS. Philip and Mary Jane Keeney first came into prominence in 1937, when Philip's firing by the president of the University of Montana in a case involving library censorship, union organizing, and radical activity elicited widespread protests. The Keeneys publicly denied Communist Party membership, but while awaiting resolution of their court challenge to the dismissal, they moved to California and joined a local Communist Party club. Mary Jane's diary, later obtained by the FBI, had such entries as this for 17 June 1939: "Get to Mill Valley at 2:00. C.P. Marin County branch membership meeting from 2:00 to 6:00 P.M." Philip eventually won reinstatement at the University of Montana but faced a hostile university president and a renewed effort to fire him. Through the efforts of David Wahl (discussed in chapter 4), another concealed Communist librarian, the Library of Congress hired Philip in 1940. When President Roosevelt created the Office of the Coordinator of Information (OCI), much of its initial research staff was drawn from and housed at the Library of Congress; Philip moved from the OCI into the OSS. He shifted to the Foreign Economic Administration in 1943 and then the Office of the Secretary of War in December 1945 for an assignment with the U.S. Army occupation authority in Japan as a librarian managing classified documents. Mary Jane, also a librarian, worked for the Board of Economic Warfare and its successor, the FEA, during World War II; in 1946 she transferred to the Department of State for assignments dealing with the occupation of Germany and reparations but resigned in the same year.

A partially deciphered May 1942 KGB cable from Fitin in Moscow to New York station chief Zarubin discussed infiltration of the OSS and noted that Jacob Golos had met Philip Keeney, then an OSS librarian. In response Zarubin noted that Keeney "is being entrusted to our agentura," an indication that his recruitment would be undertaken. The KGB, however, did not recruit Keeney in 1942. He and his wife, it turned out, were already working for GRU. Sergey Kurnakov, a KGB agent, noted in a report in August 1944, "Keeney and his wife were signed on apparently by the Neighbors [GRU] for work in 1940." David Wahl, the man who had gotten Philip his position at the Library of Congress in 1940, was then also a GRU agent and likely had recruited his friend.[63]

Through "a highly confidential source"—an FBI euphemism for a surreptitious break-in—the Bureau obtained a copy of Mary Jane Keeney's diaries from 1938 to 1945 and intercepted correspondence between Mary Jane and Philip. Written in a crude code, the material chronicled their transition from GRU to the KGB. One month before Kurnakov's August 1944 report about their GRU affiliations, the Keeneys had dinner with someone identified in the diaries as Colonel Thomas. Thomas "takes us to dinner and then discovers he came on a wild goose chase," in Mary Jane's words. Thomas was, the FBI determined, Mary Jane's cover name in her diary for Kurnakov. The "wild goose chase" was

Thomas's discovery that the Keeneys were already working for another branch of Soviet intelligence.[64]

But it turned out that Thomas/Kurnakov was not wasting his time. At some point in late 1944 the Keeneys lost touch with GRU. In a deciphered January 1945 cable the KGB New York station reported that "Cerberus," a GRU agent, contacted Gregory Silvermaster, seeking to reconnect with Soviet intelligence. Venona analysts could never identify "Cerberus," but combining the information in the Venona decryptions with additional information in KGB documents in Vassiliev's notebooks is sufficient to identify him as Philip Keeney. The cable said "Cerberus" worked in "'Peak's' department." At the time, Frank Coe, "Peak," was assistant administrator of the FEA, where Keeney worked. The cable went on to state that since Fitin had recently "advised . . . that Cerberus was a probationer of the Neighbors [GRU]," Apresyan wanted permission to let the GRU station chief know. Much of the remainder of the message was not broken, but a fragment implies that if GRU had "lost contact with him," the KGB might consider recruiting him, which is what happened.[65]

Undeterred by the GRU connection, Kurnakov had persisted in the fall of 1944. In November Philip was in New York, preparing to leave for Japan for his job with the occupation government. He wrote Mary Jane several letters that made his intentions and loyalties clear. On 22 November he noted, "Our friends, including Thomas, have made it clear there is a job to do and it falls to my lot to do it." On 24 November he indicated that while in New York, he intended to see Kurnakov. On 29 November he proudly wrote that he had spent several hours "with Col. Thomas which is a pass word to use in the higher circles." On 1 December: "Last night I had a long session with Col Thomas and I left with a terrible sense of responsibility."[66]

Philip Keeney had been recruited by the KGB but had not yet provided intelligence information when he went to Japan. Several letters to his wife suggested that his work for Soviet Military Intelligence had not been very productive. On 2 February 1946 he wrote to Mary Jane from Tokyo: "I presume word from Col. Thomas will be reaching us both in due course. I am certain we will be reached when something turns up for us to do. I have the feeling, at any rate, that we are both on call now which is more that I have felt for months past." And, two months later, he reflected: "Probably, I might not have come to Japan, had it not been for my serious confabs with Col. Thomas. Now that I am here it seems as if I were repeating the long dry spell that twice occurred when we were part of Joe B's [Joseph Bernstein's] plans. I should have followed Greg's [Gregory Silvermaster's] advice and relaxed."[67]

The Keeneys' equanimity, however, did not survive the escalating investigations into Soviet espionage prompted by Bentley's and Gouzenko's defections. Mary Jane sent a letter to Philip in Japan via a friend in March 1946 warning him to be careful what he wrote to such old acquaintances as the Silvermasters. Their friends were afraid they were being wiretapped and their mail examined. She concluded: "Joe [Bernstein] told me to be on the lookout as well as several others in New York. There is no reason for alarm on your part or mine only it is well to remember that it's better to be safe than sorry." Two months later she wrote that their old GRU contact, Joseph Bernstein, was temporarily on ice: "Joe B. doesn't expect to be back in the swim for a long long time. He says that the Canadian affair [Gouzenko] will have a very lingering effect."[68]

The Keeneys' security problems began in 1947. The Army dismissed Philip from his position in Japan on security grounds in June. Just a month later, the KGB received a report from Washington that Mikhail Vavilov, a Soviet diplomat and KGB co-optee, occasionally "meets with other former agents of ours. ("Akra" [unidentified], "Cerberus" [Philip Keeney] spouses)," indicating that Vavilov met both Keeneys as well as the unidentified "Akra" and his or her spouse. But tainted by his firing, Philip Keeney was in no position to help the KGB. There remained, however, Mary Jane. She had begun work as an editor in the Documents Control Division of the United Nations in June 1948. An August 1948 KGB document said, "Cerberus's wife got a job in the UNO Secretariat. She is of interest; her husband is not."[69]

The interest was short-lived. Philip Keeney, feeling the heat, decided to leave the United States, but the State Department refused to issue him a passport. Nonetheless, in 1949 he attempted to board a Polish ship, stating he had been offered a job by a Czechoslovak university. Immigration officials, however, stopped him. Both Keeneys testified to the U.S. House Committee on Un-American Activities in 1949. Philip answered some questions but invoked the Fifth Amendment to avoid discussing his Communist ties. Mary Jane did not refuse to answer and denied Communist Party membership. At the same time, an FBI data slip that Judith Coplon had stolen from the Justice Department reporting a source telling the FBI that Mary Jane was "well known on the East Coast for her Communist espionage activities" was entered into evidence in her trial. Given this indication of FBI interest, the KGB dropped any thought of using the Keeneys.[70]

Mary Jane continued as a UN employee until 1951, when she and several others were dismissed by Secretary General Trygve Lie. She claimed it was political, while the United Nations attributed her dismissal to administrative reorganization. A UN employee panel ordered her reinstated, but Lie refused. Another panel then awarded her $6,500 in compensation. In 1952 she refused to answer questions from the Senate Internal Security Subcommittee about how she had obtained her UN position and about Communist links. In 1953 the government indicted, tried, and convicted her for contempt of Congress. An appeals court ordered a retrial, and in 1955 she won acquittal. The Keeneys eventually opened an art film club.[71]

Jane Foster

Jane Foster, daughter of a wealthy businessman, graduated from exclusive Mills College in 1935. She toured Europe, married a Dutch government official in 1936, and moved with him to the Dutch East Indies. On a visit to her parents in California in 1938, she joined the American Communist Party and soon after divorced her husband. Shortly after she moved to New York in 1941, friends introduced her to George Zlatowski, a fellow Communist and veteran of the International Brigades. They married but George was soon drafted and sent overseas. With her Indonesian experience and Malay language skills Foster found work with the Netherlands Study Unit, a wartime agency set up to coordinate intelligence on the Dutch East Indies (and later absorbed by the Board of Economic Warfare). She transferred to the Office of Strategic Services in the fall of 1943 and early in 1944 was sent to Ceylon.

Vasily Zarubin listed "'Slang,' Jane . . . of the Far Eastern Department of the 'cabin' [OSS]" as one of the sources recruited during his tenure (1942–44) as chief of KGB operations in the United States. A 1957 retrospective KGB memo noted: "On a lead from "Liza" [Martha Dodd] the agent "Slang" [Jane Foster] was recruited, followed by "Slang's" husband, the agent "Rector" [George Zlatowski], who once worked for Amer. counterintelligence in Austria." (At the end of the war Zlatowski was serving as a U.S. Army counterintelligence officer in Austria.) After the OSS dissolved, Jane Foster Zlatowski and her husband continued to work for a KGB apparatus in Europe run by Jack Soble.[72]

The Soble network, however, included an FBI double agent, Boris Morros (see chapter 8). In 1957 the Justice Department indicted members of the Soble ring. Jane and George Zlatowski were then in Paris and refused to return to the United States. It appears that they may have cooperated with French security in exchange for avoiding deportation to face trial in the United States. Jane later published a memoir in which she admitted to having been a secret Communist but denied any cooperation with Soviet intelligence.[73]

KGB Infiltration of the OSS

The dozen identified sources discussed in this chapter do not exhaust the KGB's assets in the OSS; others mentioned in various documents have unidentified code names. A 1945 document, for example, refers to a KGB source in the OSS with the cover name "Akra" (variant "Akr"). Vasily Zarubin's retrospective 1944 memo refers to several OSS sources sent to Yugoslavia but gives no names or details. Venona decryptions of KGB cables identify two other OSS sources, Linn Farish and John Scott. Farish, cover name "Attila," was an OSS officer who served as liaison with Tito's Partisan forces in Yugoslavia. He died in an aircraft crash in the Balkans in September 1944 and may have been one of those alluded to by Zarubin. In a deciphered cable discussing the Russian section of the OSS sent in May 1942, Vasily Zarubin noted that Scott, an OSS analyst on Soviet industry, was "our source Ivanov." David Wahl (discussed in chapter 4) was a longtime GRU agent but shifted to the KGB in early 1945, and he was employed by the OSS late in World War II.[74]

Some of these sources, notably Donald Wheeler and Maurice Halperin, were highly productive. Duncan Lee and Franz Neumann provided excellent material, but Moscow Center felt both fell far short of their potential. Philip Keeney was, properly speaking, a GRU source while at the OSS rather than a KGB source, and what he provided GRU is unknown. Nonetheless, by any measure, the KGB's development of more than a dozen sources in the OSS in just three years was a remarkable achievement. (In contrast, the OSS never recruited, and as a matter of policy never even attempted to recruit, a source within the KGB.)

None of these sources served a day in prison for espionage, although Halperin became a refugee and Foster a fugitive. Stanley Graze was indicted but for purely commercial criminal behavior. Several others were pilloried before congressional committees and lost their government jobs, but only Duncan Lee and Helen Tenney appeared to pay an emotional price for their activities.

Eleven of the sources were secret Communists and came to the KGB via the American Communist Party; in most cases Jacob Golos handled the initial recruitment. The exception was Franz Neumann, who had been a left-wing Social Democrat in Germany who supported an alliance with the Communists. Although the eleven Americans were secret Communists, their prior party links were not so hidden that they would have survived an investigation had the OSS had a firm anti-Communist policy. But General Donovan made a decision that he would allow Communists to participate in the OSS as long as they were not blatant in their Communist partisanship. (Several Communists in the OSS displayed their loyalties so brazenly that Donovan's tolerance ran out and he fired them.) Donovan's policy was an informal one, and in perjured testimony to Congress he flatly denied that he had ever knowingly recruited or tolerated Communists in the OSS. Donovan's decision that the United States benefited by making use of Communist talent at the risk (and the reality) of facilitating Soviet espionage may have been defensible at the time, but in retrospect it was a problematic policy. Donovan also fervently sought to establish a formal institutional relationship between the OSS and KGB, a plan ultimately dropped due to the FBI's objections that an official KGB presence in the United States would pose serious security problems. Vassiliev's notebooks quote or summarize a number of KGB documents on this issue.[75]

President Truman's decision to dissolve the Office of Strategic Services in the fall of 1945 had, in the long run, a silver lining. The government demobilized the majority of OSS personnel, closed its offices, and shut down most of its agent networks. It dispersed OSS remnants to the State Department and to the Joint Chiefs of Staff, where they were treated as unwanted guests. The result was a dearth of knowledge and information as American policymakers confronted one crisis after another in the chaotic aftermath of World War II, while Communists, anti-Communists, and non-Communists of various sorts squared off for control of Europe and East Asia. By 1947 Truman realized the United States needed a robust foreign intelligence agency, and at his urging Congress passed the National Security Act of 1947, which created the Central Intelligence Agency. The new CIA brought together the remnants of the OSS and recruited a number of veteran OSS officers and staff, but this time security was much more thorough. Created to fight the Cold War, the new agency subjected all of its personnel to background checks to remove those with Communist ties. None of the persons now known to have been KGB or GRU sources within the OSS or to have had Communist ties made the transition into the CIA. It would be many years before the KGB developed any sources within the CIA, and its later successes, to the extent they are known, never came close to its impressively thorough infiltration of the OSS.

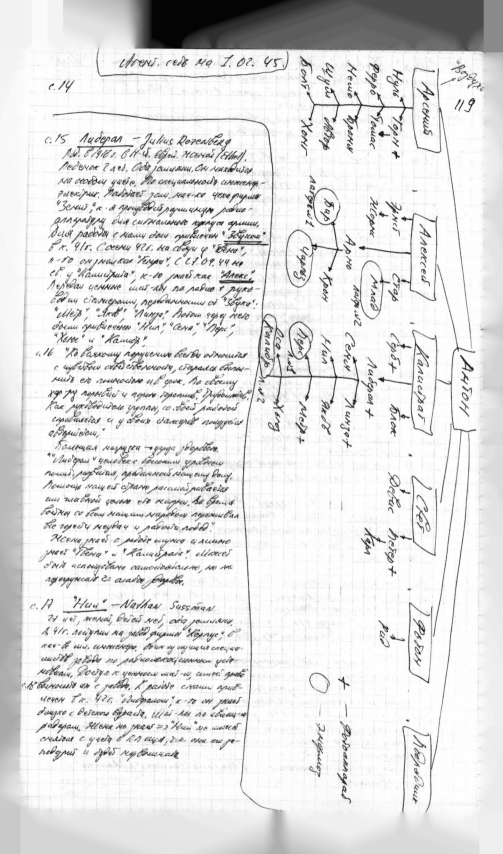

«Ворон»

Арсений
Алексей
Калистрат
Серб
Рубин
«Антон»
«Либерал»

с.15 Либерал — Julius Rosenberg
...

с.16 ...

с.17 «Нил» — Nathan Sussman
...

с.18 ...

CHAPTER 6

· ·

The XY Line

Technical, Scientific, and Industrial Espionage

Technical, scientific, and industrial espionage lacks the glamour of diplomatic and political intelligence (atomic espionage excepted). Nonetheless, technical intelligence, called the "XY line" in KGB jargon, was the "meat and potatoes" of KGB work in America. In 1934 Moscow Center reminded its American officers: "'Nowhere is technology as advanced in every sphere of industry as in A. [America]. The most important thing with regard to the procurement of tech. materials for our industry is that the scale of production in A. has the closest correspondence to our scale of production. This makes tech. intelligence in the USA the main focus of work.'" To fulfill that priority, the KGB actively sought out and recruited dozens of technical sources. A 1941 KGB report broke down the occupations of its American agents in the prior decade; forty-nine were engineers—more than half of all the agency's sources. A 1943 report on the XY line in America listed twenty-eight active American sources being handled by five KGB officers. This report further described the sources as including eleven chemists and

---

KGB scientific and technical agent network in 1945 and description of the members of Julius Rosenberg's espionage apparatus. Courtesy of Alexander Vassiliev.

bacteriologists, six radio and communications specialists (mostly engineers), five aviation sources (again chiefly engineers), four who worked on various types of high-tech "devices," one naval technology specialist, and one nuclear specialist. Aside from those involved in atomic espionage (discussed in chapter 2) few of the KGB's technical sources ever became prominent or the subjects of newspaper headlines; nonetheless, they provided the Soviet Union with vital industrial, military, and technological secrets. They included a few long-serving agents and more than a few eccentrics. A number of long-standing controversies about Soviet sources can also be answered by the newly available documentation.[1]

Unknown Members of the Rosenberg Ring

Documents in Vassiliev's notebooks significantly deepen what is known of the most successful KGB technical intelligence network, the group of Communist engineers organized by Julius Rosenberg. The material identifies two additional members of Rosenberg's apparatus and confirms and expands what was known from trial testimony, FBI investigations, and Venona decryptions about other members of his ring. The most surprising revelation is that Julius Rosenberg recruited *two* sources on the Manhattan atomic project, not just his long-known brother-in-law, David Greenglass. (The story of Rosenberg's second atomic spy recruit, Russell McNutt, is in chapter 2.)

The other previously unknown Rosenberg source was listed in KGB cables first by a cover name only partially deciphered by the Venona project, "Tu . . . ," changed after September 1944 to "Nil." The FBI, however, was unable to discover the real name behind the two cover names. KGB documents show that the first cover name was "Tuk," and a 1945 memo identified him as Nathan Sussman, a Communist colleague of Rosenberg's and an engineer at the Western Electric company who specialized in aviation radar. With the identification of the hitherto unknown McNutt and Sussman, the first complete account of the remarkable size and effectiveness of the Rosenberg network is now possible.[2]

One persistent claim of innocence by a convicted member of Rosenberg's network was not finally put to rest until 2008. Morton Sobell, a Communist engineer, was convicted along with Julius and Ethel Rosenberg in 1951 on charges of conspiring to commit espionage. Sobell was not charged with atomic espionage, and the chief evidence at the trial linking him to stealing secrets was the testimony of Max Elitcher, a Communist engineer who worked on technical questions regarding heavy naval guns for the U.S. Bureau of Standards and who had known Rosen-

berg at CCNY. Elitcher swore that Sobell and Rosenberg had both tried
to recruit him, and the former had once taken him along when he went
to deliver some material to Julius. Sobell and his family had fled to Mexico as the FBI closed in on the Rosenbergs and used pseudonyms in an
effort to book passage to Eastern Europe. Mexican authorities seized Sobell and delivered him to the United States to face trial with the Rosenbergs. Convicted, he was sentenced to thirty years in prison and served
nineteen. Throughout his trial and imprisonment Sobell continued to
maintain his innocence, and after his release he spent decades lecturing
to civic groups and college audiences that he had been the victim of a
government frame-up and published an updated edition of his autobiography in 2001 reiterating that he and the Rosenbergs were innocent.[3]

While Rosenberg, Greenglass, and most of their associates had appeared in the Venona decryptions, Sobell had not, leading some skeptics
and Sobell himself to suggest that the lack of confirmation of his guilt in
Venona was evidence of his innocence. Such a claim was not logical. The
Venona project decoded about three thousand messages out of hundreds
of thousands the Soviets sent, and the absence of a deciphered message
dealing with a specific person was an absence of positive corroboration,
not negative evidence. In any event, the same KGB report that listed
Sussman also listed ""Senya,"—Morton Sobell" as another member of
Rosenberg's apparatus. Numerous other documents in the KGB archives
confirm his assistance to the KGB. And finally in September 2008, after
fifty-seven years of lying, Sobell admitted to the *New York Times* that he
had engaged in espionage, and so had Julius Rosenberg.[4]

Origins of the Rosenberg Apparatus

Sobell's and Sussman's recruiter, Julius Rosenberg, had been a leading
member of the Young Communist League when he attended engineering school at CCNY. After graduation he got a job in 1940 as an inspector reviewing production of electronic equipment for the Army Signal
Corps. A number of his comrades from the YCL club at CCNY's engineering school also quickly found jobs in the New York area facilities of
Western Electric, Reeves Electronics, Zenith, Bell Laboratories, and
other plants expanding rapidly to meet the demand created by the American military mobilization that began in 1940. Rosenberg quickly realized
that their positions offered them access to America's advanced radio,
radar, sonar, and other military electronics technology and decided to
seek out Soviet intelligence to deliver these secrets to the USSR.

Finding a contact with Soviet intelligence, however, was not easy even for a fervent young Communist like Rosenberg. Stalin's purge of his security services had left the American stations with only a few experienced officers, and in 1941 the KGB had just begun to rebuild what Stalin's paranoia had destroyed. Ruth Greenglass, Julius's sister-in-law, testified at his trial that he had told her he had tried for two years to make contact with the Soviets before he succeeded. Some time in the first half of 1941 he asked Abraham Osheroff, a veteran of the International Brigades and an open Communist, for a lead to Soviet intelligence, but Osheroff offered no assistance. After the Nazi invasion of the Soviet Union in June 1941 Rosenberg's repeated inquiries in Communist circles came to the attention of Bernard Schuster, a key figure in the CPUSA's underground apparatus. He, in turn, put Rosenberg in touch with Jacob Golos, and a September 1942 letter from Moscow Center to its New York station noted that Golos recommended Rosenberg "'for use on the technical line.'" By late 1942, Rosenberg had acquired a cover name, "Antenna" (later changed to "Liberal"), and had begun to build his espionage apparatus of young engineers, chiefly friends like Sussman, who shared his Communist loyalties. When Rosenberg had accumulated sufficient material, he arranged a meeting with Golos by phoning Elizabeth Bentley. She knew him only as a voice on the phone who identified himself as "Julius" and never learned his family name.[5]

Given the lapse in Soviet intelligence coverage caused by the purges and the Soviet leadership's demands after June 1941 for greatly expanded intelligence, the KGB was grateful to Golos for filling in the gap with his party-based networks. Nonetheless, from the point of view of KGB professionals Golos's arrangements also had liabilities. He allowed and even encouraged his sources to continue Communist Party activity. Rosenberg, for example, continued to subscribe to Communist publications, and he and his engineer friends were still members, albeit discreet ones, of local CPUSA clubs. The KGB, however, regarded continued links to the CPUSA as a serious security risk because it feared FBI penetration of the party. In January 1942 Vasily Zarubin arrived to take over as station chief. He spent much of 1942 rebuilding the American stations and restoring and expanding networks run by professional officers and longtime KGB American agents. One of his goals was to end Golos's independence and the amateurish way his sources worked. He ordered Golos, who had no background in technical matters, to focus on developing political and government sources in Washington and hand over his technical sources to the KGB.

Golos's chief KGB contact in early 1942 was Aleksey Prokhorov, a junior officer who had come to admire him. Zarubin replaced Prokhorov with his own wife Elizabeth, a veteran KGB officer who had accompanied her husband on his American assignment. When Prokhorov's American tour ended, he was debriefed at Moscow Center and expressed the view that Golos's contributions had not been sufficiently appreciated by the senior officers of the KGB New York station. He described his role in the transfer of Rosenberg's network, explaining that he took Elizabeth Zarubin to meet Golos and informed him that she would be his contact. He said that at the very first meeting

"Vardo [Elizabeth Zarubin] brought up the possibility of transferring "Antenna's" [Rosenberg's] technical group from Sound [Golos] to other workers. "Sound" reacted very badly to this, became nervous, and didn't want to hand this group over, and in response to "Vardo's" observations and arguments, he said: 'I know it myself. I can manage it myself,' etc.

Q: Did you warn Sound in advance that he would be transferred to someone different?
A: Yes, I warned him about this. In response, he asked me, what's the matter? Aren't I leaving? Why did all this need to be done? And when I informed him that henceforth he would be working with a woman, he openly expressed his displeasure.

Q: How did you explain why he was being transferred to a diff. person?
A: I explained to him that our bosses were doing this in the interests of our work. Sound replied, 'I don't see any need for it.' And when I accompanied "Vardo" to meetings with "Sound," I would notice that in conversation with V., Sound would speak reluctantly and various pieces of material had to be 'dragged' out of him. During conversations, he would more often than not address me, would look only at me, and would pretend not to notice "Vardo.""

Zarubin was insistent, however; Golos gave in, and the transfer was made. In a 1944 retrospective report on his tour in the United States Zarubin wrote:

"During the initial period of our work with Sound [Golos] we did not raise the issue of organizational changes in his group. We first encountered the difficulties of breaking up "Sound" into smaller units when we expressed our views regarding the need for him, in order to deepen his group's work in obtaining political and economic information, to get rid of several people who didn't work on these matters. The first issue in this regard was "Antenna's" [Rosenberg's] group. "Sound" got this group, consisting of three young fellowcountryman engineers working in war production, from "Echo" [Schuster] but was unable to give enough attention to working with it. We convinced him that it was advisable to transfer these people to our man, for whom it would be easier to manage the group and utilize it more properly. The group was transferred to our regular operative on the "XY" line, "Twain" [Semenov].

The experiment of transferring "Antenna's" group to direct communication with us proved completely worthwhile. The group began to work in a more organized and single-minded fashion and provided us with a number of valuable materials. "Antenna" was pleased with the switch to direct communications with us. He said that only after that did he start getting guidance and direction in his work."[6]

The officer Zarubin assigned to manage Rosenberg, Semen Semenov, was well qualified to assume direct liaison. He had arrived in the United States in 1938, an inexperienced junior officer. But he was not used at that time for operational duties. He enrolled in an engineering course at the Massachusetts Institute of Technology and spent two years improving his technical education, his English skills, and his understanding of American society. By 1942 he was the lead XY line officer at the rebuilt KGB New York station. When he returned from his tour in the United States in 1944, Semenov prepared a lengthy report on his activities, including his contact with Julius Rosenberg:

"In 1942 I learned that "Sound" [Golos] was working with a group of local fellowcountrymen [Communists] in the field of technical intelligence. One could infer from the center's letters that nothing was known about this group, that fragmentary materials came in from them that were given low marks. While I had fragmentary data about this group, I still determined that it had great potential in the field of radio engineering and aviation. Based on this, I proposed to the station chiefs that "Antenna" [Rosenberg] and his group be turned over to me for communications, which was done despite some resistance from "Sound."

I found in "Antenna" a young party member who wanted to use the channels of the fraternal organization to provide our country with tech. assistance. On matters of agent work, our requirements for the nature of the materials to be obtained, and elementary rules of covert work, he was completely green. The group worked along the lines of a party group and "Antenna" controlled it like a party organizer. Besides handling the group with regard to obtaining materials of interest to us, I started working regularly on educating "Antenna," and through him the group members, to be agents working in the complex field of tech. intelligence. As a result, "Antenna," "Tuk" [Sussman], "Scout" [Barr], and "Gnome" [Perl] undoubtedly matured and obtained a number of highly valuable materials. In addition, starting from when "Antenna" transferred to me for communications he recruited valuable agents: "Senya" [Sobell] for radio and "Fogel" [McNutt] for "Enormous."

"Antenna" is a group leader. Radio engineer. Recruited for work by "Sound" through the fellowcountrymen. A skilled agent, commands authority with the group, which he is successfully handling. He is enthusiastic about his work and wants to do as much as possible. Therefore he sometimes rushes and doesn't think through certain aspects well enough. Our operative must carefully check and monitor his work and give him detailed instructions. His wife is devoted to us, and she knows about "Antenna's" work with us. To improve the work of "Antenna" and his group and ensure greater security, he must be supplied with a safe-house apartment and photographic equipment."

With Semenov's encouragement and tutelage Rosenberg expanded his network and gradually shifted his management style toward one more in line with professional KGB tradecraft. He dropped out of CPUSA activity, although he continued to pay dues secretly through Bernard Schuster.[7]

Semenov supervised the Rosenberg apparatus for about a year and a half. But increased FBI surveillance sparked by his identification as a KGB officer in an anonymous letter received by the Bureau (see chapter 9) forced him to turn over most of his agents to other officers. In April 1944 Alexander Feklisov took over liaison and managed Rosenberg until he returned to Moscow in 1946. Feklisov greatly appreciated Rosenberg's dedication to the Soviet cause and later wrote a memoir, *The Man Behind the Rosenbergs*, that contained an affectionate and admiring portrait of him.[8]

Feklisov implemented several of Semenov's recommendations. The latter had noted that the practice of having KGB officers pick up documents from Rosenberg, photograph them, and then return them was time consuming and insecure due to the volume of material produced by Rosenberg's apparatus. By the fall of 1944 Feklisov ended that procedure. Initially he gave Rosenberg a Leica (the KGB's preferred camera for photographing documents) and supplied him with film. This, however, simply transferred the heavy photographic workload from KGB officers to Rosenberg, already overburdened with managing his network. Consequently, Feklisov arranged for a second photographer for the Rosenberg network. The KGB New York station told Moscow: "Liberal [Rosenberg] had safely carried through the contracting of Hughes [Alfred Sarant]. Hughes is a good pal of Meter [Barr]. We propose to pair them off and get them to photograph having given a camera for that purpose. Hughes is a good photographer and has a large darkroom and all the equipment but he does not have a Leica. Liberal will receive the films through Meter for passing on. Direction for the probationers [agents] will be continued through Liberal, this will ease the load on him." By early 1945, the New York station reported that Barr and Sarant, the most productive of Rosenberg's sources, were photographing their own material while Rosenberg filmed the material produced by Sussman, Sobell, and Perl.[9]

The Rosenberg Network at Its Peak

By early 1945 Rosenberg and his network were at the top of their productivity. A KGB report on the status of the New York station networks demonstrates its size and importance:

Liberal—Julius Rosenberg. B. in 1918 in NY. A Jew. Married (Ethel). 2 year-old child. Both are fellowcountrymen [Communists]. He is on a special register [secret CPUSA membership roll]. He is an electrical engineer by training. He works as an assistant workshop chief at the "Zenith" company, which manufactures radio devices for the army signal corps. He was recruited to work with us through "*Sound*" [Golos] in late '41. Starting in the fall of '42, he was handled by "Twain" [Semenov], whom he knew as "Henry." Since 27.04.44, he has been handled by "Callistratus" [Feklisov], whom he knows as "*Alex.*" He gave valuable materials on radio + oversaw probationers [sources] who had been handed over from "Sound": "Meter" [Barr], "Yakov" [Perl], "Lens" [Sidorovich]. "Nil" [Sussman], "Senya" [Sobell], "Persian" [McNutt], "Hughes" [Sarant], and "Caliber" [Greenglass] were later recruited through him. "He always regards any assignment with a sense of responsibility and makes an effort to carry it out fully and on time. He is impetuous by nature and occasionally hasty. He is diligent. As a group handler, he is equal to the task and enjoys a certain degree of authority among his probationers [agents]." Large workload → dangerous to his health. "'Liberal' is highly politically developed and devoted to our cause. He considers helping our country to be the principal aim of his life. During the war, he experienced all the sorrows of defeat and the joys of victory alongside all our people." His wife knows about her husband's work and personally knows "Twain" and "Callistratus." She could be used independently, but she should not be overworked → poor health.

    "*Nil*"—Nathan Sussman 27 years old, married, no children, both are fellowcountrymen. In '41 he got a job as a jr. engineer at a factory of the "Corpus" [Western Electric] company. He is one of the factory's top specialists on radar installations. He has access to valuable materials, and has the right to take them out of the factory. He was recruited for work with us at the end of '42 by "Liberal," whom he has known well since they were children. Materials on aviation radars. His wife does not know → "Nil" cannot be taken off the CPUSA register, b/c she would become suspicious of him and worry.

    "*Meter*"—Joel Barr. B. in 1916. Fellowcountryman. Included on a special secret register. A bachelor. Radio engineer. Recruited through "*Sound.*" One of the most productive probationers in "Liberal's" group. Currently lives with "Hughes," a personal friend. "The probationer is politically developed and conscientious. He is devoted to our cause."

"Hughes"—Alfred Sarant. B. in 1919 in the USA. A radar engineer at one of "Corpus's" factories. His parents are Greek, they own a house. He joined the CPUSA in 1940. He cut down on his activities in the Workers party [New York's American Labor Party] after we established contact with him in '44. Recruited through "Liberal". . . .

"Senya,"—Morton Sobell. Fellowcountryman, a bachelor. B. in 1915 in the USA. An electrical engineer. Recruited at the end of '43 by "Liberal." Friends since they were children. Wanted to leave his job, where he won't be promoted b/c he is a Jew ("Hydro" [RCA]). He stayed at our request.

"Persian"—Russell McNutt. B. in 1916 in the USA. A civil engineer at the "Kellex" company. Married, 1 child. A fellowcountryman; his father—a longtime fellowcountryman, a close friend of "Helmsman's" [Browder's]. He is well-to-do. Gave materials on equipment used for "Enormous" [Manhattan Project]. + A floor-plan of camp No.1 [Oak Ridge].

"Yakov"—William Mutterperl. B. in '18 in NY to a family of Jewish emigrants from Poland. A specialist on aerodynamics. Recruited by "*Sound*" on the basis of a lead by "Liberal" in Apr. '42. Subsequently met with "Twain," whom he knew as "Henry." A fellowcountryman since '41. His wife doesn't know. . . .

"Caliber" [David Greenglass]—"Liberal's" brother-in-law. A sergeant, works as a mechanic in camp No.2 [Los Alamos]. Gives general information about work in the camp. He doesn't know the details, however.

"Wasp" [Ruth Greenglass]—"Caliber's" wife, lives in Albuquerque.[10]

By any standard, Rosenberg's network was a remarkable technical intelligence apparatus. It included five engineers (Rosenberg, Sussman, Barr, Sarant, and Sobell) working at leading electronic firms producing advanced military radio, radar, sonar, and cutting-edge avionics; one leading military aviation scientist (Perl) who worked on the development of America's first jet fighter; a civil design engineer (McNutt) working for Kellex, the contractor building the Manhattan Project's uranium separation plant at Oak Ridge; and a skilled machinist (Greenglass) working at Los Alamos and assisting in machining the trigger mechanism for the first plutonium bomb. In a report to Moscow Center, Feklisov wrote of Rosenberg and his network:

"During the war a great many valuable materials for our national industry were received personally from "Liberal" [Rosenberg]. Since March 1945 alone detailed, complete sets of materials were received on the radars AN/APS-2,

AN/APS-12, SM, AN-CRT-4, AN/APS-1, AN/APN-12; on infrared communications equipment; and so forth. We should take special note of the materials given us by the agent on the AN/CPQ-1 bomb fuse and a model of the fuse itself, which were given the highest marks by the Council on Radar. "Liberal's" successful work in handling agents and in supplying us with valuable secret materials was repeatedly cited by the center, and it was rewarded with large monetary payments. "Liberal" is definitely a person who is completely devoted to us and accumulated significant experience during the war years in illegal work. He views working with us as the main purpose of his life."[11]

William Perl was the single most valuable agent in the Rosenberg apparatus. He provided documents on a long-distance fighter under development by Vultee aircraft; technical reports on the jet engine under development by Westinghouse; other technical reports of the National Advisory Committee for Aeronautics (predecessor to the National Aeronautics and Space Administration); and, amazingly, blueprints of the Lockheed P-80 (America's first operational jet fighter). Feklisov wrote that Perl provided ninety-eight technical studies totaling five thousand pages and that Moscow Center judged half the material "very valuable" and most of the rest "valuable." In September 1944 the KGB New York station told Moscow that Perl thus far had received reimbursement only for the extra expenses incurred by his espionage work but that it felt his productivity had already earned him a bonus of $500, similar to that of other veteran sources of Rosenberg's network. Moscow agreed and also judged Perl's aviation intelligence as so important that when he moved to the Lewis Flight Propulsion Laboratory near Cleveland, Ohio, to work on advanced military aircraft, the KGB authorized Rosenberg to set up Michael Sidorovich and his wife Ann as hosts of a safe house in Cleveland devoted solely to receiving Perl's intelligence and transmitting it to the KGB.[12]

Protecting the Rosenberg Network

In late 1944 the FBI furnished the Army with information that Julius Rosenberg, then employed as an engineer-inspector by the Army Signal Corps, was a Communist. Given his access to sensitive military electronic equipment, the Army discharged him in February 1945. The news alarmed Moscow Center, and it ordered defensive measures:

"The most recent events with L ["Liberal"/Rosenberg] are extremely serious and require us, first of all, to properly evaluate what happened, and secondly, to make a decision about L's role in the future. In deciding the latter, we should proceed from the fact that in him, we have a loyal man whom we can trust completely, a man who in his practical work over the course of several years has shown how strong his desire is to help our country. Besides this, in L. we have a talented agent who knows how to work with people and has considerable experience recruiting new agents.

We can assume that, besides the reason that was put forward when L was fired about his belonging to the fellowcountrymen [CPUSA], the competitors [American security] could have in their possession oth. incriminating information about him, including something about his affiliation with us. On the basis of this argument in particular, we believe that L. should not take any legal action to be reinstated at his job and should leave this matter to the trade union, which should do whatever is done for other union members in similar cases. There should not be any pressure in this regard coming from L's end.

Although we do not have any documentary information indicating that the competitors are to any degree aware of his connection with us, . . . nevertheless, taking into account the circumstances that preceded L's dismissal, his exceedingly energetic activity, especially when he had initially begun working with us, as well as the occasional rashness he showed in his work, we believe it is necessary to take immediate action in order to ensure the safety of L. himself, as well as the agents with whom he had been connected. In order to accomplish this, we proposed in our telegram from 16.II, No. 966, to relieve L. of his duties as a group handler, reassign his agents to oth. operatives, and sever the direct connection between our operative and Liberal, reinstating it with the help of a courier. For this to happen, we think it is necessary to enact the following measures:

1. Reassign "Hughes" [Sarant] and "Nil" [Sussman] to "Meter" [Barr], thereby creating a new group headed by "Meter." Neither "Hughes" nor "Nil" should know about each other's work. "Meter" should meet with each of them separately, while observing the strictest caution and secrecy. "Callistratus" [Feklisov] should meet with "Meter" to oversee his work and process materials.
2. "Senya" [Sobell] should be reassigned to our operative "Light" [Aleksandr Raev]. It is essential to have a serious talk with the latter, b/c from his previous work with agents who had been transferred to him (Peter [Thomas Black], Karl [William Stapler]), it is obvious that he has not yet become accustomed to his work and does not treat it with the seriousness it demands. It is essential that you personally check his work with agents, demand that he regularly submit reports on meetings he has conducted, and give him instructions for work and demand that they be carried out.
3. Connect "Lens" [Sidorovich] with either "Light" or "Photon" [Ivan Kamenev], as you see fit. . . .
4. Manage the connection between "Callistratus" and "Liberal" through a

courier, for which position we recommend that you use "Leslie" [Lona
Cohen]—"Volunteer's" [Morris Cohen's] wife. In response to your query, we
have already approved the renewal of ties with her. It should be noted that
she does not have experience in our work, but she has already run small errands for the station in the past, for instance: contact with "Link's" [William
Weisband's] brother, etc. You should have a series of instructional talks with
"Leslie" regarding caution and secrecy in our work, and also teach her a
number of practical methods for checking oneself when going to a meeting,
leaving a meeting, etc.

5. Reassign "Wasp" [Ruth Greenglass] and "Persian" [Russell McNutt] to
"Arno" [Harry Gold].

Before severing the direct connection with L, it is essential to explain to
him why it is necessary to suspend personal contact and to instruct him about
the need to observe caution and to keep an eye on himself. You should continue to pay him his wages. Warn him not to make any important decisions
about his work in the future without our knowledge and consent. When addressing him at pres., we should make it clear to him that we are far from indifferent about his fate, that we value him as a worker, and that he absolutely
can and should count on us for help."[13]

Moscow Center's instructions were carried out, Rosenberg was deactivated, and his large network was broken into smaller units. In March
the KGB New York station reported:

"Liberal's [Rosenberg's] group was one of the largest groups, but after Liberal
was fired from his new job—as an inspecting officer of the AAF signal corps,
on account of Hut [FBI] allegedly knowing that he was a member of the fellowcountrymen [CPUSA], we were forced to suspend L's activities and completely discharge him of all his connections in order to avoid failure. Liberal
had handled: Lens [Sidorovich], Yakov [Perl], Senya [Sobell], Nil [Sussman],
Meter [Barr], Persian [McNutt], Hughes [Sarant], Wasp [Ruth Greenglass],
and Caliber [David Greenglass].
    In accordance with Center's instructions and our proposals, the group has
been broken down as follows: Yakov, along with Lens's/Objective's [Michael
and Ann Sidorovich's] s/h [safe house] was given to Callistratus [Feklisov] for
debriefing. Yakov's materials will be transmitted via Objective to Squirrel
[unidentified courier]; the latter will also be connected with Callistratus.
Hughes [Sarant] works with Meter. Nil is also being reassigned to Meter.
Meter is in his turn connected with Callistratus. Persian is connected with
Aleksey [Anatoly Yatskov]. Senya—with Light [Raev]. This leaves only Wasp
and Caliber, who are currently in the Preserve [Los Alamos], and they can be
contacted through any of our new people using our password."

The KGB New York station in June also reported: "'Liberal [Rosenberg] is rather upset about the fact that he was left without any people, but he fully realizes the correctness of our plans to break his group up into smaller units. The main thing with which he currently has the hardest time reconciling is his relative inactivity. At every meeting, he asks to be allowed to take material out of the factory [Emerson Radio] himself and thus make himself useful to us.'"[14]

While prudent, the KGB's actions were, in retrospect, unnecessary. The FBI had identified Rosenberg as a Communist and security risk but had no indication that he was actually engaged in espionage and no suspicion that he headed a large KGB-linked network. Aside from providing the Signal Corps with the basis for his firing, the FBI did not initiate an espionage investigation of Rosenberg or his contacts. It was an example of the lax nature of American security at the time that Rosenberg quickly found work as an electrical engineer for Emerson Radio, a major defense contractor from whom, in his role as a Signal Corps inspector, he had earlier stolen and given to the KGB a working artillery proximity fuse, one of America's most effective military technological innovations.

But in the fall of 1945 another threat appeared to the security of the Rosenberg network. Elizabeth Bentley defected and told the FBI of her work as a courier and agent handler for several dozen sources that had been recruited for Soviet intelligence by Jacob Golos, and Rosenberg had come to the KGB via Golos. Among the sources she identified to the FBI, the KGB feared, was Julius Rosenberg.

Moscow Center informed its Washington and New York stations of Bentley's defection on 22 November and ordered immediate defensive measures. Because Rosenberg had been deactivated in the spring, the KGB no longer had direct contact with him. Consequently Feklisov used a previously scheduled 12 December meeting with Joel Barr, a personal friend of Rosenberg and leader of one of the groups broken from the larger Rosenberg network, to set up a meeting with him. Feklisov reported to Moscow that his meeting had originally been scheduled to deliver film to Barr for use in photographing documents, but in response to Moscow's cable about Bentley

He did not give the film to "Meter" [Barr], saying that he wanted to see "Liberal" [Rosenberg]. "Meter" should pass on the rendezvous terms: if things are calm at L's house, at 23:00 on 15.12, he should send his wife to the drug-store at the end of the street. The wife should not approach him; she should just buy something and go home. → 5 minutes later, "C." ["Callistratus"/Feklisov] arrives at "L's." house.

C. left his house to go to the meeting with L. at 18:00. From 19:00 to 19:30, he was in the Brooklyn maternity ward, where his wife was staying. From there—to the Turkish baths on 46th Street, where he stayed until 21:40. After that, he checked out in a taxi, on the subway, and in courtyards on 24th Street. At 23:00, he went into the drug-store and saw L's wife. She was buying cotton balls. When she saw C, she went outside. C. drank a cup of coffee and went out as well. In order to make it seem like he lived at L's house, he bought bread and 2 bottles of milk. He didn't run into anybody and went into L's house unnoticed. "We went into the kitchen and immediately got to talking. I asked the probationer [agent] whether he knew any of Sound's [Golos's] friends. He replied that he only knew Sound and Echo [Schuster]. When I asked whether he knew any women, he at first replied in the negative, but then added that he had an agreement with Sound: any time he urgently needed to see Sound, L. was supposed to call him from a pay phone and tell his secretary that he wanted to see him. He only gave his first name—Julius— to this secretary. He never met her face to face. He did say, however, that he had given Sound identifying data for himself, Yakov [Perl], Meter [Barr], and Nil [Sussman]. This data was typed up, and therefore it is possible that it never fell into 'Myrna's' [Bentley's] hands. It is essential that you locate this data in the correspondence from 1941–42 and compare the font of their typewriter with the typewriter used by Myrna. The probationer assured me that Sound was unaware of Senya [Sobell], Persian [McNutt], Hughes [Sarant], Lens [Sidorovich], and Caliber's [Greenglass's] work with us.

At the end of the conversation, I informed L. that Sound's secretary (I didn't give her name) had betrayed us and that we were very worried about him as a result. I instructed him on how it is necessary to behave in the event that he is summoned before Hut [FBI]. We decided that he should deny that he is a member of the fellowcountrymen [CPUSA], because he had already done so in 1941 and again in 1945. If he doesn't deny this now, as it says in your telegram—then it would be illogical. He will also deny that he has ties with Sound and Echo. If he is asked to give the names of his friends, he will name Meter and Nil, who are old friends of his. He will also repudiate any photographs and similar documents in which he appears with me, Sound, or Echo. I gave him very strict orders to burn any notes containing the addresses of probationers and materials that could be used as evidence of his affiliation with fellowcountrymen.

Liberal and I agreed that the connection with him will be suspended for 3 1/2 months. The next meeting is scheduled for the third Sunday in March, 1946, at 8 o'clock P.M., next to the 'Colony' theater, 79th Street and 2nd Avenue. I warned him that someone else might come to this meeting instead of me. Therefore, I asked him to come to the meeting holding the magazine

'Post.' Our person should be holding 'Reader's Scope' in his left hand. Our person should approach Liberal and ask him: 'Aren't you waiting for Al?' Liberal will answer: 'No, I am waiting for Helen.' Our person should say: 'I am Helene's brother. She asked me to tell you something.'"[15]

Once again, the KGB's prudent defensive measures were unnecessary, but only barely so. Bentley told the FBI in 1945 that in 1942 she had received calls from a "Julius" setting up meetings with Golos, but while indicating Julius was a valued espionage source, Golos never told her his family name; nor did he ever tell her the identity of any members of Julius's network. She told the FBI, however, that once she had been with Golos when he drove to meet Julius near the Knickerbocker Village apartments. She had stayed in the car while he left to meet with Julius and had seen him only at a distance. The FBI's investigation of Bentley's allegations was a thorough one, and the resulting file contained thousands of pages of investigatory reports. Dozens of Golos's sources and contacts that Bentley had remembered only with a family name or only with a first name or only phonetically with the exact spelling unclear were tracked down with the clues to their real identity that she remembered. But Julius remained unidentified. In this instance, FBI field agents overlooked an elementary step. No agent ever checked with the Knickerbocker Village rental management office, where he would have quickly learned that a *Julius* Rosenberg had been renting an apartment there in 1942 (and was still resident); that his physical description was compatible with Bentley's memory; and that he had been fired from the Signal Corps for Communist affiliation at the recommendation of the FBI.[16]

The Rosenberg Network: Deactivation, Revival, and Collapse

While Rosenberg and his network dodged the bullet of Bentley's defection in late 1945, their espionage, nonetheless, came to a temporary end. Rosenberg himself had already been deactivated, and all of his former network sources were soon "put on ice," in KGB speak. Moscow recalled most of the experienced officers it had in the United States. XY line officers Feklisov and Yatskov, illegal station chief Iskhak Akhmerov, legal station chief Anatoly Gorsky, and others left the United States. Before departing, KGB officers attempted to notify their sources that contact was being cut, advised them to cease all espionage and destroy any evidence of intelligence work, and gave guidance on how they should respond if the FBI questioned them. They also arranged passwords so that the KGB could revive contact in the future. One sign of Rosenberg's importance to Soviet intelligence was that Lavrenty Beria himself ordered the American stations to cut contact with Rosenberg as a security measure to protect him.[17]

The KGB began to revive its networks in 1948, and in March Moscow Center ordered the KGB New York station to contact Rosenberg and see if Perl, Sobell, and Barr were still willing to assist the Soviet Union. It turned out to be easier said than done. KGB officer Gavriil Panchenko first phoned Rosenberg, but he refused to meet and indicated that he expected an authentic approach to come via his old CPUSA contact, Bernard Schuster. But Panchenko succeeded in reestablishing contact in May. In June 1948 a KGB report spoke of the revived ""Liberal's" [Rosenberg's] group: . . . Yakov [Perl], Lens [Michael Sidorovich], Objective [Ann Sidorovich], Nil [Sussman], Hughes [Sarant], Senya [Sobell], Persian [McNutt], Zenith [unidentified], Caliber [David Greenglass], Wasp [Ruth Greenglass]." A July KGB report expanded on the renewal: "From August's [Panchenko's] meetings with L. ["Liberal"/Rosenberg], it is obvious that while the connection was deactivated, his group had, for the most part, stayed unchanged and ready to carry out assignments and that it has good info. resources. 'In view of this, it is essential to take note of the way L. himself behaves; despite the fact that his connection with us was interrupted for over 2 years, he continued to conscientiously and faithfully fulfill his obligations as a group handler, to stay in touch with the athletes [agents], lending them vital moral and material support, and to continue gathering the most valuable tech. information.'"[18]

Despite Rosenberg's continued enthusiasm, it is not clear that his revived network or other KGB initiatives of the period were able to gain traction in the more hostile environment of the Cold War, with public opinion increasingly anti-Communist, and enhanced internal security regulations. An October 1948 Moscow Center cable pointed to Rosenberg as an asset to exploit. But the New York station only reported Rosenberg's difficulties keeping his machine shop financially afloat and the inadvisability of his seeking an engineering job with a defense contractor in view of heightened security regulations. It did report that Rosenberg was cultivating two new contacts, "Plumb" and "List." "List" was not otherwise identified, while "Plumb" was described only as a student who led a small group of college Communists, someone with future prospects but no current access to information of interest. ("Plumb" was likely Maxwell Finestone, a leader of the YCL at Cornell and a Rosenberg contact at the time.)[19]

There is no indication whether Rosenberg's revived network produced any significant volume of intelligence in 1948 and 1949. In 1950, following the arrests of Fuchs, Gold, and David Greenglass (discussed in chapter 2), the latter confessed and identified Rosenberg as his recruiter and handler. Julius Rosenberg and his wife, along with Morton Sobell, were tried in 1951. Convicted, the Rosenbergs, who refused offers of clemency in return for cooperation, were executed in 1953; as noted above, Sobell went to prison for nineteen years while Greenglass served ten years.

Other members of the Rosenberg network were more fortunate. Joel Barr was in Paris studying music when Rosenberg was arrested. He disappeared. Alfred Sarant, employed at Cornell University, was questioned by the FBI but escaped surveillance and fled to Mexico, where he disappeared. He abandoned his wife and children, taking with him his neighbor's wife, who herself abandoned her husband and children. The KGB resettled Barr and Sarant under false identities in Czechoslovakia. Later they were both moved to the Soviet Union, where they headed a secret electronics laboratory that developed cutting-edge Soviet military technology. The KGB attempted to get William Perl to leave the United States, sending a courier to him with $2,000 in cash. But he declined, hoping to ride out the storm. While he escaped prosecution for espionage, he was convicted of perjury and sentenced to five years in prison. Perl's couriers, the Sidorovichs, avoided prosecution, as did atomic spy Russell McNutt. "Zenith," "Plumb," and "List," part of Rosenberg's post-1948 network, were never identified by the FBI.[20]

The fate of "Nil," Nathan Sussman, was curious. As noted, Sussman had been a friend of Julius Rosenberg since childhood and had been one of the most active Communists among the young engineering students at CCNY. Born in 1918, he had received both a BA and master's in engineering at CCNY and had done course work for his PhD at Brooklyn Polytechnical Institute. During his first interview with the FBI in December 1950, he lied, denying that he knew Julius very well or that either Rosenberg or Sobell had tried to recruit him into the CPUSA. Just a month later, reinterviewed, he was more forthcoming, admitting that he had been a member of the YCL from 1935 to 1940, even serving as president of the CCNY chapter, and had joined the CPUSA in 1942. He had belonged to the same party industrial branch as the Rosenbergs; when it was dissolved in late 1943, he moved to a residential branch along with his wife. Sussman worked for Western Electric and was transferred to Winston-Salem, North Carolina, in 1944, not returning to New York until

1947, when he took a job with Fairchild Aviation, working on classified research. During his initial interview Sussman appeared to the FBI to be "very nervous, gave cryptic answers to the questions." During a reinterview he tried to avoid naming specific CPUSA members he had known but swore that he no longer held any sympathy for communism or had ever been asked for or given information about his work to unauthorized persons. He admitted that he had been a party member prior to signing an affidavit for Western Electric denying such membership. With the threat of an indictment for perjury, he named other engineers who had belonged to a CPUSA industrial branch and agreed to testify, if needed, at the Rosenberg trial regarding his knowledge of Julius's party membership. If Julius took the stand and denied being a member of the CPUSA, the government could call Nathan Sussman to rebut his testimony. However, at the trial the Rosenberg defense chose not to have Julius testify on the question of party membership, and the prosecution never called Sussman as a witness.[21]

In 1953 the Senate Committee on Government Operations, chaired by Senator Joseph McCarthy, held hearings on Communist infiltration of Army Signal Corps facilities and called Sussman to testify. The committee counsel, Roy Cohn, a McCarthy aide, questioned him. Cohn had been one of the government prosecutors in the Rosenberg trial and would have been fully cognizant of Sussman's statements to the FBI. He also had a well-deserved reputation as a ruthless, demanding, and often rude interrogator.

Sussman appeared first in executive session, where he was the model of a cooperative witness. Instead of taking the Fifth Amendment, a tactic adopted by almost every other witness still linked to the Communist Party, he willingly admitted being a member of the YCL at CCNY and named a host of others, including not only Rosenberg, Sobell, Barr, and Elitcher, but also several others who had denied being Communists. He admitted that he and Julius were two of the most active participants in Communist activities at CCNY and acknowledged his continued membership in CPUSA branches until his resignation in 1945. Cohn's questioning was polite, and he never asked about espionage, even though other witnesses who had known Rosenberg far less intimately or less long were badgered about whether they had ever mishandled confidential documents or assisted Julius in his activities. Sussman then appeared in public session, where he again admitted to having belonged to the YCL from 1935 to 1938 and to the CPUSA from 1938 to 1940 and from 1942 to 1945. The break coincided with the two years he worked for the govern-

ment as a Signal Corps inspector. He also admitted that while at Western
Electric from 1942 to 1947, he worked on classified contracts. Directly
contradicting the sworn testimony of another engineer, Aaron Coleman,
he insisted that Coleman had been a fellow Communist. Roy Cohn asked
if Sussman had given the FBI information about the Communist connections of Rosenberg, Sobell, and others shortly before their trial, and
he acknowledged that he had done so. The proceedings were altogether
polite and calm.[22]

Sussman had pursued a high-risk strategy. He had never admitted espionage to the FBI but had admitted concealing his Communist Party
membership, named numerous others who were secret members, and
agreed to testify about Rosenberg's party membership if needed. The
FBI had no direct evidence of his participation in espionage, although
under questioning David Greenglass had speculated that Sussman had
been a source for Julius. Possibly the Bureau and federal prosecutors, including Roy Cohn, may have decided not to pursue the matter of espionage in view of Sussman's willingness to testify on the matter of Rosenberg's CPUSA membership. And Sussman must have believed that none
of his old comrades who knew about his activities would confess. Whatever the explanation, Nathan Sussman, one of the earliest and longest
serving of Julius Rosenberg's spies, successfully maneuvered through
these difficulties and disappeared from public view.

"Block" and "Serb": Feklisov's Other Agents

The Rosenberg network at its peak in early 1945 had nine agents, all reporting to the KGB via Julius Rosenberg. He, in turn, was under the supervision of KGB officer Alexander Feklisov. Managing the KGB's most
productive XY network was a top priority. But Feklisov also supervised
two independent XY line sources, "Block" and "Serb." A 1945 KGB report stated: ""Block"—Stephen Urewich. B. in '13 in the USA. In '40
he got a job at "Corpus's" [Western Electric's] radio valve factory. Not a
fellowcountryman. Sympathetic toward the USSR. Married, 1 child.
"Block's" parents are from Belarus. Recruited by "Aleksey" [Yatskov] in
November '42. Since November '43, he has been handled by "Callistratus" [Feklisov]. Only gives radio valves; no oth. opportunities. $75 a
month."[23]

American "radio valves"—that is, electronic vacuum tubes—were the
world's most advanced, but Feklisov's other agent, "Serb," was higher on
the espionage food chain. Formerly cover-named "Relay," he had been

assigned in July 1944 as an agent handler for both Urewich and an unidentified "Nina." The 1945 KGB memo identified him as

"Serb"—Joseph Chmilevski. 26 years old, b. in the USA. Mother is Polish, father is Ukrainian. Married (Helene). 1 child. A fellowcountryman [Communist] since '37. He was in Spain from Jan. to Oct. '37. He was wounded, and his right leg was amputated. Prosthesis. Recruited in Aug. '42 by "Volunteer" [Morris Cohen]. A radio operator and a jr. engineer at a sonar laboratory in Camden ("Hydro" [RCA]). Until July '44, "Serb" worked with "Twain" [Semenov], whom he knew as "Norman." Now—handled by "Callistratus" [Feklisov], whom he knows as "Alex." Hot-tempered personality, shattered nerves. His wife used to know "Twain."

Despite his "shattered nerves," Semenov told Moscow Center, Chmilevski provided "valuable materials on radio, especially radar technology."[24]

"Solid"

An agent cover-named "Solid" appeared in three decoded KGB cables in 1943 and 1944, but the broken messages had no information that pointed to "Solid's" identity, and the FBI made no progress on uncovering him. However, "Solid," whose cover name shifted to "Reed" in late 1944, appears in Vassiliev's notebooks in numerous KGB reports dated from the mid-1930s to the mid-1940s. His real name is nowhere given, but ample details about the KGB's contact with him make his identification easy. The most telling entries: a 1943 report describing "Solid" as "the chief of the Chem. Division of the U.S. Tariff Commission" and a 1945 report on XY line sources that stated: "Sources: 1. Reed ("Solid")— chief of the Chem. Division of the country's Tariff Commission, PhD in chemistry. With us since '35. Materials were paid on delivery." In 1943 and 1945 the chief of the Tariff Commission's Chemical Division was James Hibben.[25]

James Herbert Hibben was born in Indianapolis on 14 May 1897. He graduated from the University of Illinois in 1920, after serving in the Army in World War I, and received a PhD from the University of Paris in 1924. From 1925 to 1927 he was a National Research Fellow at Princeton, consulted for the Bureau of Standards, and then served on the research staff of the geophysical laboratory of the Carnegie Institution from 1928 to 1939. He had a distinguished scientific career; his best-known work, *The Raman Effect and Its Chemical Application* (1939), dealt with a new form of secondary radiation. As chief of the Chemical Division of the U.S. Tariff Commission from 1939 until his death in 1959, his job was to provide information to government agencies, industry, and Congress on foreign trade issues pertaining to chemicals and chemical products. During World War II, he served on numerous interdepartmental committees dealing with military-industrial mobilization.[26]

Hibben's older and more famous brother, Paxton, may have first stimulated James's sympathy for the Soviet cause. During a brief and controversy-filled seven years with the State Department early in the twentieth century, Paxton Hibben served in St. Petersburg and learned Russian. He next turned to journalism and declared his sympathy for socialism. After World War I, he became involved in humanitarian relief efforts in Armenia and Russia, praising the Bolsheviks and criticizing Herbert Hoover's refusal to work through the Russian Red Cross, an organization Hoover castigated as a political tool of the Soviet regime. In one speech Paxton Hibben compared "Lenin's vision for Russia with that of Christ on the Mount of Olives." As an officer in the Army Reserves, he was tried in 1923 on grounds that his defense of the USSR constituted disloyalty, but he was acquitted after testifying that he was not a member of the Communist Party. A prominent defender of Italian anarchists Nicola Sacco and Bartolomeo Vanzetti, he was arrested numerous times in Boston protesting their convictions for murder. He wrote for the Communist-aligned cultural journal *New Masses* and produced popular biographies of Henry Ward Beecher and William Jennings Bryan before dying of pneumonia in December 1928. The high regard with which the Soviet Union held Paxton was attested to by its decision to bury his ashes in Moscow's Novodevichy Cemetery, the favored burial grounds of the Soviet elite.[27]

The 1945 XY line report stated that James Hibben began working for Soviet intelligence in 1935, and under his cover names of "Solid" and "Reed" he was noted as an XY line agent in 1937, 1938, 1942, 1943, and 1945. The entries offer few specifics about the information he provided, although presumably it was in his area of expertise, chemistry. But his work was clearly valued. A 1943 memo noted that he had been paid a regular monthly stipend of $350 in the 1930s (in excess of $5,000 a month in 2008 dollars), with bonuses for especially valuable materials. In addition, Hibben gave a lead on a new source, a secretary on the staff of Senator Robert Wagner (D-New York) who was given the cover name "Riddle" after she was recruited by a KGB officer. A KGB report said: "'Solid' [Hibben] described 'Riddle' [unidentified] as a young woman from a working class family, a true friend of the Soviet Union, and an honest and potentially useful person.' Frank [unidentified KGB officer] met with her several times, and the facts were confirmed. She agreed to work with us. Her connections in government agencies are of interest." (The latter remark suggests that "Riddle" worked for the Senate Labor Committee, which Wagner chaired.)[28]

One of the KGB officers who worked with Hibben was Gayk Ovakimyan, chief of the legal station. As the KGB American stations began to shrink in the late 1930s, Ovakimyan prudently warned Hibben that there might be an interruption in contact and received from him a material password of some sort that the KGB could use to establish the bona fides of an officer reestablishing contact. And in 1939 contact was suspended.

In late 1942 the KGB began to reactivate old agents. The New York station sent Semenov, its senior XY line officer, to Washington to renew contact with James Hibben. The disruption in operations, however, included everyone forgetting the arrangements Ovakimyan had made in 1938; the material password Hibben had given him had been lost or misplaced. Ovakimyan himself had been arrested by the FBI in 1941 and deported. Semenov's attempt to reestablish contact, consequently, had a somewhat farcical quality. The KGB New York station reported to Moscow:

"Twain" [Semenov] went to Wash. to restore the connection with "Solid" [Hibben], which had been interrupted in '39. We know very little about him or his work with us. We only know that he had been connected with Gennady [Ovakimyan], whom "Solid" and his wife knew as "Victor," and that he had signed his name on receipts as "George Jackson."

"Solid" lives in Chevy Chase. "Twain" arrived by taxi at the same time as another car with a man and a woman in it (the woman was driving). He stepped out and went to open the garage. At that point, "Twain" asked the woman if "S" lived in that house. Then—the conversation was as follows:

T—Hello, are you Dr. N's friend?

S—Yes. What can I do for you?

T—A good friend of mine, who is also a friend of yours, asked me to stop by and say hello. . . .

S—(interrupting) Who are you talking about?

T—Your friend Victor. He told me that you were very kind to him, helped him with his work, advised him on a number of issues, etc.

S—I have no idea who or what you're talking about. I also don't understand why you wanted to meet me.

T—Victor spoke very highly of you, as someone who could be trusted. I'd like you to help me the same way you helped him.

S—I'm very flattered to hear such a high opinion of me, but I still don't know who or what you're talking about.

T—To convince you that I'm not here by accident, I can remind you that you did some work for him for which you were rewarded. At the time, you used the name "George Jackson." Does this convince you that I really am a friend of Victor's and that you can trust me completely?

S—I've used a lot of names in my lifetime. Incidentally, what does this Victor you keep talking about look like and where is he now?

T. described Gennady, but S. did not admit to knowing him. It was obvious that he was frightened of provocation and knew full well what T. was talking about.

T. was unable to convince S. He promised to ask for oth. information and relate it to S. at their next meeting. S. made it clear that he was prepared to meet again.

It was a frustrating result. But early in 1943 the KGB New York station reported: "After receiving additional information from C. [Center] about "S's" ["Solid's"/Hibben's] work with "Gennady" [Ovakimyan], a 2nd meeting was held, where we managed to win his trust." But the problems of reestablishing a working relationship with Hibben were not entirely over. The New York station continued:

At the 3rd meeting, "S" was even more friendly to "Twain." According to a cipher telegram from C. he used to get $350 a month + valuable materials were paid for extra. "You indicate that this system is currently unsuitable and even think that we can work with him without compensation, on an ideological basis, by carrying out educational work, etc. We will take this directive of yours into account in future work with the probationer, but at the same time, we will be unable to begin work with him solely on ideological grounds. Prior to 1939, we worked with him on the basis of paying him well for his services. Therefore, it isn't entirely clear to us why you think that now, in time of war, when the risk is significantly greater, he would have a more conscientious attitude toward his work than before and agree to work solely on an ideological basis."

And in April 1943 the New York station added:

"S." harbors mistrust, even though he talks about his past work. "He maintains that about a year before the connection with him was broken off, he and his wife came to NY, where they met with 'Gennady.' During this meeting, 'Gennady' suggested that they might have to discontinue meetings for a while. 'Solid' says that in connection with this, he had given 'Gennady' some object

or other, which was supposed to have served as a material recognition signal
for any comrade of ours approaching him with the aim of re-establishing a
connection. All of our arguments about the fact that this object might have
long since been destroyed have come to nothing. At the last meeting, he said
that it was enough for him if 'Twain' were to name the object he had given to
'Gennady.' We reported this by telegraph and hope to receive a description of
this object in the coming days."

Perhaps the object was found or Ovakimyan back in Moscow remembered what it was. In any event, later documents show that Hibben became once more a valued XY line source.[29]

Moscow Center accepted that it would have to continue to pay Hibben to elicit information. In a report on technical intelligence for 1944,
the Center suggested: "'After the war, "Reed" [Hibben] should be stirred
to greater activity, in part on a mater. [material—that is, cash] basis. For
now, we propose to use him to cover the Bureau of Standards, which
works on questions pertaining to "E." ["Enormous"/Manhattan Project].'"
Other reports on Hibben's activities during the war show that the KGB
considered using him to contact a Washington acquaintance of his, the
prominent atomic physicist George Gamow, and that in 1943 he was
"'used to cover the military medical school, the Franklin Institute of Research, etc.'" After he returned to the Soviet Union, Semenov offered
this evaluation of Hibben: "'"Solid" [Hibben]. Contact was re-established
with him in 1943 after a 4-year interruption. For a long time he was extremely reticent, demanding that the material password be produced that
had been arranged at the time communications with him were terminated. We managed, however, to obtain from him valuable materials regarding the location of the Japanese chem. industry, the production of
mil. chemicals in Germany and occupied Europe, etc.'"[30]

The FBI became interested in Hibben in December 1945, when he
tried to contact Mary Price, already under investigation and surveillance
because Elizabeth Bentley had named her as a Soviet source. The investigation noted his close relationship with people at Amtorg and the Soviet
Embassy and reports that he had used his position to attempt to obtain
classified information on explosives for which he had no clear professional
need. But nothing turned up to cause the FBI to focus on Hibben. Neither the FBI nor any congressional committee seemed to have questioned him. Presumably deactivated with other sources after Bentley's
defection, Hibben remained undisturbed as chief of the Tariff Commission Chemical Division until his death in 1959.[31]

"Talent"

One of the KGB's longest-serving, although occasionally vexing, technical sources was William Malisoff. Born in Russia in 1895, he immigrated to the United States as a child and became a citizen when his father was naturalized. He got his BS from Columbia University in 1916 and received a doctorate from New York University in 1925 in chemistry. Described by former professors as either brilliant or a cheater who faked laboratory results, from his college days onward Malisoff was a committed Communist, a prolific writer on science and society, and a political activist. He worked for several chemical companies before becoming a director, executive vice-president, and technical consultant to Consumers Union, an organization founded by consumer activists with CPUSA ties (see chapter 3). In the early 1940s, he created and ran his own company, United Laboratories, which undertook a variety of technical tasks on contract. He used United Laboratories as a vehicle to obtain proprietary industrial information from several American firms for the KGB. In a sense, the KGB was a hidden contractor to whom Malisoff furnished stolen copies of the technical work he did for American companies on a confidential, commercial basis.

Malisoff's relationship with the KGB New York station went back to 1933, when he was listed as a contact of Ovakimyan, then a KGB officer under Amtorg cover who specialized in industrial espionage. Through the rest of the 1930s his cover name, "Talent," continued to appear among agents on the XY line. Not all industrial espionage involved high-tech processes or secret material bearing on armaments. In 1937 the New York station sent documents Malisoff obtained to Moscow Center for delivery to Polina Zhemchuzhina, head of the "Chief Administration of the Perfume, Cosmetics, Synthetics, and Soap-Making Industry" (and wife of Stalin confidant Vyacheslav Molotov). The New York station explained: "'During Cde. Zhemchuzhina's stay in the USA, she received from us various samples of perfume and cosmetic products from the American company Alco which were obtained by the source Talent [Malisoff]. Now the source has also received formulas for these 23 products from the "Alco" Company, which we are sending you. The recipes were obtained free of charge. We request that as soon as you receive the package, you give these recipes to Cde. Zhemchuzhina.'"[32]

When Moscow withdrew many of its field officers in the late 1930s, it also drastically cut the KGB New York station budget, and in January 1939 Malisoff's monthly stipend was suspended. But the chief of the New York station protested to Moscow:

"As of Jan. 1st, I have stopped paying the source 'Talent' [Malisoff]. The source took this very badly, for the most part because it makes it look like we are only interested in the tech. materials he can get for us, rather than him personally. Not to mention the fact that the source happens just now to be going through a difficult financial period, I think that it would be absolutely correct if, putting a new principle into effect, we should consider, in this particular case, the following circumstance:

The source 'Talent' has been affiliated with us for many years. After 'Sound' [Golos], he is the foremost of all our other Amer. sources who work with us for ideological reasons. He is one of the few chemistry professors with a grounding in Marxism to be found among all our friends, who is willing to do anything for us, and for whom the interests of our homeland and the worldwide revolution are the principal ideals of his life."

He urged headquarters to make an exception and continue Malisoff's $250 monthly subsidy (equivalent to $3,700+ in 2008 dollars). Moscow agreed.[33]

"Tal-1"

Not only did Malisoff provide information, but he also recruited and supervised other sources. One of his sub-sources was Paul Williams, a pioneering black airman and aircraft component designer. Born in Youngstown, Ohio, in 1907, Williams attended the Ohio Institute of Aeronautics and became a pilot. The federal Works Progress Administration employed him as an aeronautics instructor from 1934 to 1937. After being turned down for a job by Douglas Aircraft (he thought because of his color), Williams heard that the Spanish Republican government was paying foreign pilots $1,000 a month. He told the FBI in 1955 that he arrived in Spain in August 1937 and flew one mission but was told that the Spanish Republican air force had enough volunteers that it no longer needed foreign mercenaries. He returned to the United States in December 1937 and discovered that he was a useful symbol for the Communist-aligned Veterans of the Abraham Lincoln Brigade (VALB). (The VALB and the CPUSA's *Daily Worker* promoted stories that he had been a combat pilot in Spain.) The VALB found him jobs teaching aviation courses for the Federation of Architects, Engineers, Chemists and Technicians (FAECT, a small Communist-aligned CIO union) and for the International Workers Order (a Communist-aligned fraternal insurance company). Among his FAECT students were Julius Rosenberg and Michael Sidorovich. In 1939 he started his own aircraft components design business, Williams

Aeronautical Research Corporation, and hired them as his staff, along with Ethel Rosenberg as company secretary.

Although Williams willingly admitted to the FBI that he had been in the CPUSA's orbit, participated in its activities, gave speeches and attended meetings, and even had a Communist Party card with his name on it, he denied actually being a Communist since he never paid any dues. He explained that he was simply grateful to the party for its assistance and had thought well of its stand against racism. But, he claimed, by 1940 he had become disillusioned and felt the party was just using him as a Negro symbol. Around the same time the Rosenbergs, who had worked nights at his company and rarely been paid, hoping to make money if one of Williams's patents proved commercially successful, left his firm. With his company unsuccessful, Williams then went to work at the U.S. government aeronautical research facility at Wright Field (later Wright-Patterson Air Force Base) in Ohio. He was fired in 1947 for having falsified application materials about his education and background and concealing an arrest. By the time the FBI interviewed him in 1955, he was working as a draftsman in Washington, D.C., living with his fourth wife, and was a practicing Jehovah's Witness. Williams denied ever participating in espionage but did admit that in 1940, while he was running Williams Aeronautical, someone at Amtorg had offered him a commission if he would buy a new type of propeller manufactured by Curtis Aircraft, ostensibly for his company, and transfer it to the Soviet Union. He did try to make the purchase, but Curtis refused to sell.[34]

While not a very productive technological source, Williams had a longer and more intimate relationship with the KGB than he was willing to admit to the FBI. With the cover name "Tal-1," he appears as a Malisoff sub-source in 1939. The relationship continued to 1942, but by that point Moscow Center had received reports that caused it to become upset with Williams's tendency to drop names. Williams's company had been organized with Malisoff's help, and Moscow Center sternly told the New York station: "'A report on 'Tal-1's' [Williams's] company by an outsider—Julius Rosenberg—which was obtained through 'Sound' [Golos] states that 'Tal-1' introduced 'Talent' [Malisoff] as one of the people working behind the scenes who was in contact with Mikhail Kaganovich [Soviet aviation official]. Thus, with the founding of his first company, 'Talent' has become known to persons unaffiliated with us as an agent of the Sov. Union.' Stop doing business with "Tal-1" and his company. The company has done nothing for us but use up resources and expose "Talent's" identity." No additional documents link Paul Williams to the KGB.[35]

"Outpost"

Malisoff also had a role in recruiting one of his friends, Earl Flosdorf, in the mid-1930s. Flosdorf, who had the code name "Outpost," was a chemist who taught at the University of Pennsylvania in the Department of Biochemistry. He was credited with inventing a method to freeze-dry blood plasma (an advance of immense value to military medicine that saved many wounded soldiers in World War II) and a skin test to measure susceptibility for whooping cough. He also served as a consultant to the War Department on issues relating to bacteriological warfare. As a hobby, he collected antique cars and even acquired an 1895 Hurtu-Benz roadster, reportedly the oldest-running gas powered automobile in America.[36]

Flosdorf's specialization in biochemistry interested the KGB. In the mid-1930s Moscow Center put emphasis on bacteriological warfare as a priority for technical intelligence. A 1937 directive to the KGB New York station stated: "'It is absolutely essential that we receive a culture of parrot disease, 'Psittacosis' . . . as it's called. This microbe was found in sick parrots in Europe (in Germany) and America. Interest in the microbe came about in connection with the enormous death rate among owners of sick parrots, since many petty bourgeois families owned parrots. Germany is putting especially strong efforts into studying this microbe; having chosen it as one of its weapons in the coming war. The mortality rate among those infected by this disease—100%.'"[37]

Collecting antique automobiles was an expensive hobby, and Flosdorf worked for the KGB on a paid basis. Initially he assisted the KGB in 1936–38, and Thomas Black, who served as a courier to him in 1942, told the FBI in 1950 that his KGB superior had mentioned that it had earlier paid Flosdorf $25,000—an enormous sum at the time—for one of his apparatuses and its biochemical process. A retrospective KGB appraisal stated: "'Outpost' [Flosdorf]—significant resources through the University of Pennsylvania, gave valuable materials from '36 to '38, including means of biological attack. Created a device that dries out materials for germ warfare. Relations with him—on a material basis." The KGB deactivated Flosdorf at the end of 1938, along with many other agents as part of its purge-induced reduction in force.[38]

As part of rebuilding the American networks, in November 1941 Moscow Center ordered the New York station to contact Flosdorf and attempt reactivation: "'Outpost'—Flosdorf, a chemistry PhD at the University of Pennsylvania in Philadelphia and chair of the bacteriology department. A good friend of "Talent's" [Malisoff's], through whom he was recruited. He worked on assignments from the War Department. He knew about the latest research in the field of biological warfare. He worked on a mater. [material/cash] basis, although he was sympathetic toward the USSR. He was deactivated in November of '38. He should be reactivated. We are sending "Outpost's" signature as proof that the person coming to him was sent by us." The New York station sent Black, one of its veteran American couriers, to see Flosdorf; the date is not clear but appears to be in mid-1942 or later. In addition to Flosdorf's signature, likely on a receipt, Black carried with him a letter from Dr. Grigory Rabinovich, a Soviet contact of Flosdorf's in the 1930s. It read:

"My Dear Dr. Flosdorff: It is of particular pleasure to me to hear from my friends in the United States that you are in good health and progressing in your research work. I remember our short meetings in the Benjamin Franklin Hotel, and I shall never forget your very kind assistance you rendered to me and my country at those peaceful times when I was in the USA as a representative of the Soviet Red Cross. I am now working in the same organization and trying to do my best in taking care of our wounded Red Army men. I am absolutely sure that you will not refuse to continue to be helpful to us in case of need as you did it before. My best regards and sincere gratitude. Very truly yours, /s/ Dr. G. L. Rabinovitch 5/7/42."

Grigory Rabinovich was a medical doctor and had been in the United States in the 1930s as a representative of the Russian Red Cross. He was also, however, a professional KGB officer and had worked chiefly on anti-Trotsky matters but also on technical intelligence, particularly related to medical and biological matters, where his medical degree gave him the necessary background and his Red Cross cover provided access. Black, who discussed this episode with the FBI in 1950, reported that Flosdorf indicated he was willing to reestablish his prior relationship. Black also said that while he had nominally presented himself as representing the Russian Red Cross, both he and Flosdorf understood that they were discussing his previous KGB connection, not Red Cross work.[39]

Black also told the FBI that this 1942 meeting was his sole contact with Flosdorf and that another Soviet agent would have followed up on the contact if it had been pursued. But in October 1943 Moscow Center sent guidance to the KGB New York station on the organization of XY line work. It suggested that Black be assigned to work directly for Leonid Kvasnikov, chief of technical intelligence at the New York station, and that he be assigned two sub-sources, one of whom was Flosdorf. It is possible that this was a suggestion never implemented, but it is also possible that in 1950

Black was seeking to minimize the extent of his espionage in his admissions to the FBI. As for Flosdorf, after World War II he worked for the F. J. Stokes Machine Company, a manufacturer of pharmaceutical equipment, as research director, and he lived in an elegant home in the Philadelphia suburbs, where he housed his outstanding collection of antique cars. In April 1958, following a series of arguments with his wife, he killed her with a shotgun in front of their horrified son and then turned the weapon on himself.[40]

Malisoff during World War II

When the FBI arrested Ovakimyan on 5 May 1941, the KGB New York station temporarily suspended contact with all of its active XY line sources as a security measure. By July 1941 it had reestablished contact with Malisoff. But the intense publicity about the arrest, increased industrial security triggered by the outbreak of war in Europe, and rapid flaring of public anti-Communist sentiment after the Nazi-Soviet Pact chilled XY line activities for a time. Even after the Nazi attack on the USSR and the U.S. entrance into the war as a Soviet ally in December 1941, some of the XY line sources of the 1930s, who often had been motivated by money, hesitated in the face of greatly increased wartime security. Two of Malisoff's sub-sources refused to continue to work and a third reported FBI surveillance. In part as a way around security problems, in January 1942 the KGB New York station suggested agreeing with Malisoff's proposal that he expand his business with the help of KGB funding. Moscow Center, however, was not interested and told New York: "We do not agree to the idea of starting companies with "Talent's" [Malisoff's] help. This method—tens of thousands of dollars. Initially, "Talent" listed 8 processes, and he proposes to start a company on the basis of each one. If we finance Talent, it could lead to his identity being exposed."[41]

William Malisoff continued to be an XY line source for the rest of World War II, but the relationship became quarrelsome as he felt increasingly underappreciated and Moscow Center (more than the New York station) began to think the KGB wasn't getting its money's worth and that "Talent" was a bit of a blunderer. In 1942 the New York station, under pressure to produce atomic intelligence, reported: "In the past, "Talent" [Malisoff] had been acquainted with Grosse, Urey, Wittenberg, and Gamow. At pres., however, he has no means of approach. He met with Wittenberg and tried to draw him into a conversation about nuclear fission but was unsuccessful." Moscow Center, however, was not pleased with how Malisoff conducted himself:

The practice of discussing "Enormous" [atomic bomb project] directly with individuals who were working on it should be ruled out in advance. Such discussions can only arouse suspicion on the part of these individuals. This work requires the application of truly agent methods of cultivation. It is obvious from "Talent's" report, received in mailing No. 2–42, that these methods of direct discussions are just the kind he uses when he secures meetings with individuals working on E. In view of this, we propose giving up working with "Talent" in this cultivation. Discontinue the meetings to discuss this matter between "Talent" and Urey, Grosse, and Wittenberg. He can be told that this problem no longer interests us and that we think it is unrealistic in practice.[42]

(Other KGB attempts to approach atomic scientists Harold Urey, Aristide Grosse, George Gamow, and Davrun Wittenberg are discussed in chapter 2.)

But if Moscow Center was unhappy with Malisoff, Malisoff was unhappy with Moscow. In 1943 Malisoff's KGB contact reported:

At the meeting on 26.03.43, "Talent" [Malisoff] said that several years ago he discovered that some of the personal processes he had developed and given to us had been used by some of our chemists and published in Sov. publications as their discoveries. As for him, he had never received a reply regarding how his material was being used. He had spoken about this with "Gennady" [Ovakimyan]. If it had been someone else in his place, we would have turned a friend into an enemy. "Gennady" supposedly assured him that this would not happen again in the future. The list of winners of the Stalin Prize for research in the field of chemistry and oth. branches of industry was recently published. He found a topic on which he had given us his work a year and a half ago. He isn't asking for money, only that his work be referenced.

But public recognition was the last thing the KGB could, or would, give its American espionage sources.[43]

Until the end of 1944 Malisoff continued to supply information but was increasingly discontented. In May 1944 Kvasnikov, the New York station technical intelligence chief, met with him. The station reported:

Anton [Kvasnikov] has informed Talent [Malisoff] of the impossibility of large-scale one-time aid. Just as we expected, Talent took this announcement exceptionally morbidly. Talent considers that his request has not been conveyed to the leadership of the House [Moscow Center]. He declared that the refusal to help him set up a laboratory or manufacturing business has been repeated several times. . . . With irritation he states that the materials handed over by him on one question alone—oil, by his estimate had yielded the Union [USSR] a saving of millions during past years, and the aid requested by him was trifling.

In a lengthy talk he said that his help to us was the result of his views on the Union and that he would meet us. However he emphasized that in future he will be unable to have extensive dealings with people and firms and consequently it is impossible to expect much help from him. There can be no responsible conversations about the prospect of work with him at present. One cannot put him into cold storage in this condition, it will look like an attempt to get rid of him altogether. We shall continue meeting.[44]

And meet they did. In December 1944 Kvasnikov noted in a cable to Moscow Center that he had met with Malisoff twenty times since his arrival in the United States in 1943. But by this point Moscow Center had decided to cut the connection, in part due to concern that the FBI had begun surveillance of Malisoff. Kvasnikov suggested that it would be wise to meet one last time with Malisoff to explain the decision; otherwise he might attempt to contact someone at Amtorg, where he was seeking a consulting contract, and attempt to reestablish contact himself. It isn't clear if there was a final meeting, but in January 1945 Moscow Center declared it wanted a total break: "'As you have already been told, there is documentary evidence confirming that both 'Henry' [Malisoff's new cover name] and our workers [KGB officers] who were connected with him were the objects of an active investigation by the competitors [American security]. . . . In light of this, we suggest intercepting any attempts by 'Henry' to renew ties with you, efforts to meet with our people, visits to our agencies, and under no circumstances should you allow 'Henry' to realize his intention of getting a job at 'Amtorg.'''" Malisoff's business soon collapsed; United Laboratories closed in 1945, and he died 16 May 1947.[45]

Good Vibrations

One of the most exotic Soviet spies in America was Leon Theremin, a Soviet citizen who came to the United States to promote his cutting-edge musical instrument and other inventions but also worked as an industrial spy on the side.

Descended from a wealthy Huguenot family (possibly the inspiration for his KGB cover name, "Frenchman") that had settled in Russia, Theremin was born in 1896 in St. Petersburg. A child scientific prodigy, he became a protégé of famed physicist Abraham Joffe after serving in the Russian Army during World War I and also embraced Bolshevism. While working on high-frequency oscillations in 1920, he invented a new musical instrument, the "Theremin." Without touching the instrument, the musician's hands moving between two antennas modify the pitch and volume of surreal and eerie-sounding electronic music coming from the instrument's electronic speakers. Theremin's performances across Russia, including one for Lenin, gained him fame. He followed this discovery with the invention of a "radio watchman," a motion detector that emitted a signal when someone approached, and did early work on television. His inventions interested the KGB, anxious to develop means of border surveillance, and he was recruited as an agent by Soviet military intelligence (GRU) just before a trip to Germany in 1925, where he applied for patents for his work and attempted to gain access to Western technology.

Hailed as "the Russian Edison," Theremin arrived in the United States in December 1927. He performed several concerts under the auspices of the CPUSA but focused his efforts on producing Theremins; by 1929 he had made arrangements with RCA to manufacture the instrument. While this venture proved unprofitable (the onset of the Great Depression didn't help), he worked on a variety of technical problems in his personal laboratory, including altimeters, remote-control devices, and autopilots, all the while using his research contacts with American electronic firms and other scientists as an opportunity to ferret out American industrial secrets. Later in his life, he told a biographer, "I did a lot of spying work for the military department in connection with secret information on airplanes. I had my tactics for these things. To find out something new, and foreign, I wouldn't ask about it, I would suggest something new of my own. When you show something of your own it's easier to find out what the other people are working at." While initially working for GRU, at some point he became an agent of the KGB New York station.[46]

Theremin had a messy personal life. His Russian-born wife, Katerina Konstantinova, had followed him to New York, but they soon separated and divorced in 1934, and she became an ardent anti-Bolshevik. Theremin had numerous affairs; in 1938 he married Lavinia Williams, a black dancer with the American Negro Ballet. The first mention of him in Vassiliev's notebooks actually dealt with his ex-wife. In 1935 one of the KGB New York station sources, Thomas Schwartz, a former German diplomat, reported that a German national, Count Alfred Sauerman, had come to the United States and had been promoting the story that the Reichstag fire trial in Germany, blamed on Communists by Nazi authorities, was a fraud and that Marinus Van der Lubbe, the man arrested and guillotined by Nazi authorities for the affair, had actually been secretly sent to the United States under an assumed name and someone else executed in his place. The sensationalistic report noted: "Sauerman has disappeared. His wife has not filed a report about S.'s abduction, but she looks despondent. 'Sauerman's wife is the daughter of a German colonel or general. Sauerman himself had been castrated, and his wife—according to Schwartz—is a hermaphrodite. Sauerman's abduction had something to do with a Russian woman named Konstantinova, a Nazi agent-provocateur. She is the former wife of Prof. Theremin, who in his day invented an extraordinary musical instrument.'" Peter Gutzeit, head of the KGB New York station, explained to Moscow: "'We tried to find out about Konstantinova's activities through Frenchman [Theremin], but all our efforts came to naught. Frenchman says that he and K. have nothing in common and that he has known nothing about her way of life or her activities for a number of years. A year ago, Frenchman filed for divorce from Konstantinova at the consulate.'"[47]

Oddly, the KGB New York station took upon itself the task of selling (taking a very generous seller's commission for itself) several of Theremin's prototype inventions to *Soviet* industrial representatives in the United States who were there purchasing advanced American technology on the commercial market:

"We received a $6,000 order from Siniavsky [Soviet purchasing agent] and sent $4,000 to Frenchman [Theremin] for the manufacture for them of two two-way radio stations that will transmit and receive dispatches by printing them on typewriters. The devices will be finished in January and sent to your address. You will receive Siniavsky's money in Moscow."

Regarding the designs for the theatrical television: "For the designs, we are receiving $2,000 from the clients, which they have agreed to pay. We ourselves are paying Frenchman almost 500 dollars, which is consistent with the actual value of draft work. Bear in mind that we quoted the clients a price of $30,000 for the television. We will have to pay Frenchman around $9,000. . . . For the airplane television, we quoted Bordovsky [Soviet purchasing agent] (also works in NY) a price of $15,000. It will cost us 6 or 7 thousand."[48]

As innovative as Theremin's devices were, the New York station noted his limitations: "'Frenchman's [Theremin's] work is entirely satisfactory, but it is worth bearing in mind that he is an inventor who runs a makeshift workshop. He can manufacture one or two devices at a time, and of course as far as construction goes, his installations cannot be streamlined to the same degree as would be done in factories with standard mass production.'" With that in mind, it told Moscow Center: "The major American corporation Bendix ordered a capacity altimeter (for aircraft) from

Frenchman + Bendix offered Frenchman a job at his [Bendix's] company and promised to pay him $1,000 a week. 'We instructed Frenchman to accept this offer and keep us informed at all times about negotiations. If this can be accomplished, we will gain access to work of Bendix's that is extremely important for our . . . industry . . . , including his [Bendix's] work on blind flight and blind landings. Frenchman's altimeter is important to Bendix precisely as part of that work.'"[49]

For some reason the arrangement with Bendix did not get implemented, and by 1938 Theremin's business pursuits floundered, creditors secured judgments against him, and American officials became more reluctant to continue extending his temporary visa. He decided to return to the Soviet Union, confident that his work for Soviet intelligence and knowledge of American industrial secrets would ensure a welcoming reception. Smuggled abroad a Soviet ship (to avoid creditors), Theremin returned home, but what he found was not a warm welcome but a nation in the grip of Stalin's Terror. In the United States he had cooperated with the KGB's external foreign intelligence arm. Back in the USSR, the KGB internal security arm arrested him, and in March 1939 he confessed to being a member of a fascist organization and a Western spy and was sentenced to eight years in the Gulag. Although initially sent to a hard labor camp in Kolyma (among the worse in the Gulag system), he was recalled in December 1939 to a *sharashka,* a special Gulag prison/laboratory where imprisoned scientists, engineers, and academics worked on scientific and technological problems for the Soviet state. Living conditions, while very austere, were nonetheless much better than in a regular Gulag labor camp. (Sharashkas are best known in the West as the setting of Aleksandr Solzhenitsyn's novel *The First Circle.*) During the war he worked on military radio beacons and also made special devices for the Soviet security services. In 1945, Soviet schoolchildren presented a two-foot wooden replica of the Great Seal of the United States to American ambassador Averell Harriman as a symbol of American-Soviet friendship, and Harriman hung the seal in his office at the U.S. Embassy. In 1952 a routine security check discovered that it contained a sophisticated radio broadcasting microphone and a cleverly designed resonant cavity that could be stimulated from an outside radio signal. Leon Theremin had designed the system.[50]

Released from the Gulag at the end of World War II, Theremin received the Stalin Prize in 1947 for his technological contributions to the Soviet state. He remarried (Lavinia had not been allowed to accompany him to the USSR) and continued to work on technological devices for the Soviet security services and, consequently, to have restrictions on his residence and outside contacts. In 1962 one of his former American music students met him in Moscow. Word that he was still alive gradually trickled back to the West. In 1987, during the freer Gorbachev period, the English-language *Moscow News* published a series about him and his secret work. He was allowed to travel and received accolades on visits to Paris and the United States, where his electronic musical instrument, the Theremin, continued to have a cult following and even influence on popular music via the Beach Boys' ground-breaking album, *Good Vibrations*. Still devoted to communism, he joined the Communist Party of Russia in 1991 just as the Soviet system imploded. He died in November 1993.[51]

"Blerio's" Aviation Spies

Stanislav Shumovsky, a KGB New York station XY line officer, specialized in seeking aviation sources. In KGB messages he had the cover name "Blerio," after the pioneering French aviation engineer who first flew across the English Channel in 1909. Shumovsky, trained as an engineer, held a cover job in the United States as a purchasing agent for the People's Commissariat of Heavy Industry. He used his visits to American aircraft and aviation components plants, ostensibly to examine products for possible Soviet purchase, as opportunities to recruit industrial spies. He traveled to California in 1935 and developed contacts that led to the eventual recruitment of three aviation sources: "Gapon," an engineer at Douglas aircraft; "Tikhon," a specialist involved in high-altitude flight; and "Falcon," a draftsman at Douglas. (All three remain unidentified.) The most productive part of Shumovsky's West Coast swing, however, was "the work with the inventor from Northrop with the cover name Needle. He resisted but was ultimately convinced. A mechanism for dropping bombs and a reloading mechanism for machine guns."[52]

"Needle" was Jones Orin York, born in Germany in 1890 but a naturalized American citizen. A KGB report explained Shumovsky's approach. At a dinner for Northrop employees and the visiting Russians, "He met "Needle." Last name—York. They don't pay him enough, and he wants to start his own business. He showed Blerio [Shumovsky] a design for a motor. Blerio suggested sending it to Moscow to get the opinion of people who work on similar things." With that as the opening, Shumovsky proceeded with recruitment, and by January 1936 the KGB New York station reported, ""Needle" has been transferred over completely to agent relations. Blerio received from him the general shape and dimensions of the newest fighter from the Northrop company." (An annotation on the report noted that York's material was sent to the Tupolev aircraft design bureau.) Three months later he took a job at Lockheed to design the armaments for a new high-speed, long-range fighter. The KGB was delighted with his productivity and attitude. A report enthused: "'Needle has a wonderful attitude toward his work. He carries out all of our assignments with precision and care. He is extremely happy with the work and has repeatedly expressed his warm feelings with regard to the Soviet Union. He recently came to Eduard [unidentified KGB officer] with a request to allow him a two-week vacation, which the latter did. This is characteristic of Needle and underscores his discipline and seriousness.'" York's material was also of such value that in October 1937 Moscow Center told its KGB New York station that a special technical committee was being formed just to evaluate it. However, this proved to be overly optimistic. A second Moscow Center message noted that "in light of the most recent changes in the aviation industry" the committee was not formed. The "recent changes" most likely referred to a new phase of the Terror that led to the arrest of Andrey Tupolev and other leading Soviet aircraft designers.[53]

In June 1938 Shumovsky returned to Moscow but left contact protocols with other officers for keeping in touch with York. This coincided, however, with the disruption of KGB operations in America, and it was a year before the station dispatched one of its American couriers, Zalmond Franklin, to the West Coast to renew contact. As the New York station explained to Moscow, he returned with disappointing news about its prime aviation source: "We sent "Chap" [Franklin] to "Needle" [York] in Los Angeles, but Needle had vanished, as his ex-wife told us. She said that he had had other women and spent his money on them. She thinks "Needle" has left the country." York, however, had only left California, not the United States, and the KGB was able to restore contact on his return. He continued to work as a productive aviation source until late 1943, receiving a $200 monthly stipend (equivalent to about $2,400 in 2008 dollars). In his espionage career from 1935 to 1943 he was in contact not only with Shumovsky but also Grigory Kheifets, chief of the KGB station in San Francisco, as well as three of the KGB's veteran American couriers, Franklin, William Weisband, and Amadeo Sabatini. Included among the materials he turned over to the KGB were extensive technical documents on Northrop's P-61 Black Widow, the Army Air Force's very advanced and highly successful radar-equipped night fighter, and the XP-58, an experimental longer-range and more heavily armed version of Lockheed's P-38 Lightning.[54]

A 1947 retrospective KGB report summarized York's agent career and explained his temporary disappearance in 1939:

Background on "Needle" Jo York—J. York, a U.S. cit., German, born c. 1890. Airplane design engineer. Until '36–Northrop; '36–'37—Lockheed—'37–'38—Douglas. Later returned to Lockheed. Recruited by Blerio [Shumovsky] in 1935 and actively worked up to Oct. 1943. Cooperated on a fin. [financial] basis and knew that it was for the USSR.

"In Jan. 1939 "Needle" suddenly abandoned his family, quit his job at the plant, and left Los Angeles. It was later learned that he had arrived in NY and attempted to meet with "Blerio" at the representative office of Narkomtyazhprom [People's Commisariate of Heavy Industry]. The meeting didn't take place and "Needle," after leaving a letter for "Blerio," left for the New England region, the states of Vermont and New Hampshire. "Needle" returned to Los Angeles in Jan. 1940 and soon thereafter appeared at the Soviet consulate, where he left his address and name, declaring that he was a friend of the Soviet Union. Chap [Franklin] was sent to contact Needle, and Needle explained the reason for his sudden departure to him. It turned out that shortly before his departure the FBI began to show intense interest in him; in particular, an FBI agent visited his wife and questioned her about him. While Needle was in New England the FBI also took an interest in him, and Needle explained to one of its agents that he was in New England out of a desire to escape from the numerous relatives who were burdening him and out of a need to strengthen his health."

. . . N. returned to LA and reported his whereabouts to the FBI. The next day an FBI agent inquired about his contacts with Rus. engineers, with Blerio in particular. He replied that they were purely professional acquaintances related to his line of work at the plant. Why did he take materials out? Overtime work at home with mgt.'s permission. After that he wasn't bothered. In late Aug. '41 Link [Weisband] renewed contact with Needle, in November '42 Link was drafted into the army → turned over to "Nick" [Sabatini]. The materials on airplanes were given high marks. The last meeting with Nick was in late 1943. Needle gave Nick a package and said that it contained two reports. There turned out to be only one. Soon afterward, in late Oct. '43, Nick detected a tail → contact with Needle was broken off (Hypothesis: Needle's tail → Nick).[55]

Other documents fill in additional details. A message about Franklin's reconnection with York in June 1940 noted York's report of FBI interest in him and Moscow Center's concern, a likely explanation why his agent relationship was not renewed until August 1941. The intervening year without contact would have been sufficient to alleviate FBI suspicions. (It was also a period when the KGB's American stations were seriously undermanned.) The final passages of the 1947 summary indicated that Amadeo Sabatini/"Nick" thought he had come under surveillance after a rendezvous with York in October 1943. Fearing this indicated a renewal of the FBI's interest in York, the KGB cut contact as a security measure. It was, however, Sabatini who exposed York to the FBI in 1949, when he provided the FBI a partial account of his work for Soviet intelligence (see chapter 7).[56]

Shumovsky received his engineering education at the Massachusetts Institute of Technology (MIT). He was, however, already a KGB officer when he arrived at MIT, and his education was a KGB assignment to spot potential sources. He found one. A 1944 retrospective KGB report highlighted one of his recruits:

Benjamin Smilg is "Lever," a US citizen, Jewish, born in Boston in 1913. Parents emigrated from Russia in 1905 with the assistance of the Jewish committee. Father is a cutter at a shoe factory. Brother works at the National cash-register factory. Family has a very friendly attitude toward the USSR. Upon graduating from high school, thanks to exceptional abilities he was accepted at the Massachusetts Inst. of Technology for a free education, where he was always one of the most brilliant students. . . . "Lever" was a student in the same group with "Blerio" [Shumovsky] beginning in 1931 and had a friendship with him. He was recruited by Blerio in July 1934.[57]

After MIT, Smilg worked for the Budd Company (best known as a manufacturer of automotive and railroad equipment but in the 1930s attempting to break into aircraft manufacturing), then Glenn Martin (a major manufacturer of naval aircraft), and finally—and best of all from the KGB point of view—at the aeronautical laboratories at Wright Field outside of Dayton, Ohio, where the U.S. military sponsored cutting-edge research on aviation and tested new aircraft and airplane components. The KGB New York station listed Smilg as an XY line source in 1935, 1936, and 1937, and the 1944 report noted: "He provided materials on a dirigible, calculations on the vibration of bomber tail assemblies, NACA materials." (NACA was the National Advisory Committee for Aeronautics, predecessor to the National Aeronautics and Space Administration, and supervised much of the work at Wright Field.) Smilg boded well to become a prime aviation source.[58]

But no sooner had Smilg arrived at Wright Field than he began to raise difficulties. In January 1937 the KGB New York station told Moscow:

"Before the new year, Blerio [Shumovsky] . . . met with Lever [Smilg] in Chicago. He currently works in the research division of Wright Field. . . . All Wright Field employees are supplied with plenty of information regarding developments in aviation in the USA and other countries. Numerous reports from the military attachés in Europe, with descriptions of the characteristics of individual airplanes fighting in Spain.

Lever also said that, because W.F. is a repository of secrets from various aviation companies and there is a fear that W.F. employees might give one company's secrets to another, all employees—especially civilians—are kept under constant surveillance. They are categorically forbidden to meet with representatives from other companies, especially outside the walls of the establishment. Surveillance is set up so well that, no sooner has someone dined with a company representative, than the next day he is summoned by the boss for questioning and disciplining. Both for this reason and because, as a new employee and a Jew, he would be shadowed even more closely, Lever asks that we not meet with him for the next 3 months, at the end of which he will go to Boston on vacation and then give us materials he will have accumulated and agree on the future of the connection. . . . Despite Blerio's best efforts to convince him that it would be preferable to meet earlier and set up the connection, Lever held his ground, asserting that it would be better to lose 3 months and afterwards begin regular work, than to get exposed from the start. Considering the complexity of the situation and the fact that we agree with some of Lever's arguments, we will not meet with him until April. By that time, we will have developed a system for contacting Lever that would allow us to receive materials from him with ease, while minimizing the risk. Because Blerio is a Soviet engineer, he will not meet with Lever after April to avoid compromising the latter."

Even so, Smilg had not declined to provide information, only insisted on providing it on his terms and with more delay than the KGB wished.[59]

However, this was just the beginning of Smilg's increasing resistance. In August 1938 the KGB New York station reported:

"Between the 20th and 30th of Sept. '38, Lever [Smilg] informed Blerio [Shumovsky] that in view of the discovery of a German spy ring working, in part, at Mitchell Field (the eastern base of the U.S. AAC [Army Air Corps]) and at Seversky's factory, which filled orders for fighters, the U.S. War Department is taking special precautions to check up on its staff and increase vigilance. At Wright Field, all the locks on doors, closets, desks, etc. have been changed. Tables are searched more frequently. We have information that all workers are being shadowed by detectives. Lever asked Blerio not to meet with him for the next 2 months."

In view of increased security at Wright Field, Smilg's meetings with a Soviet official would be difficult to explain if noticed by American authorities. The KGB New York station responded quickly, telling Moscow: "'Goose' [Gold] was brought to Cincinnati specifically for a connection with 'Lever.' He is a student at the University in the chem. department. He is a good student, gets 'excellent' grades, and is happy to have been given the opportunity to get an education." Harry Gold ("Goose") was then in transition. Thomas Black had recruited Gold originally as an industrial source stealing chemical secrets from his employer, the Philadelphia Sugar Company. Impressed by his reliability, however, the KGB groomed him for work as a courier and agent handler for other industrial spies. By sending him to Xavier University for graduate work in chemistry, the KGB improved Gold's utility as an XY line agent while also providing Smilg with a nearby American contact to whom he could deliver material without the risk of being observed meeting with a Soviet official.[60]

It was a sensible plan, but Smilg didn't cooperate. Gold met with Smilg in November 1938 and on a number of occasions thereafter, but the latter found excuses not to deliver material and grew increasingly hostile. In March 1940 the New York station had to tell Moscow center: "Lever [Smilg] made it clear to Goose [Gold] that he doesn't want to work. He said that he had wanted to denounce Goose in November of '38, but decided not to, b/c Goose was a Jew, and that would have been detrimental to the entire race." Nor was Smilg the only technical source going sour on the KGB. Stalin's purges had left the American stations undermanned, the Nazi-Soviet Pact of August 1939 had seriously undermined the anti-Fascist appeal of the Soviet Union and heightened public anti-communism, and the start of war in Europe had greatly enhanced American internal security activities. The New York station told Moscow: "The conditions of work on the XY line have worsened. The 'Defense Boom,' the increase in the operations of Amer. intelligence and counterintelligence organizations, the spy-mania campaign, the spread of Amer. patriotism, and the persecution of liber. and left organizations. It has become more difficult to work. Some sources—'Lever,' 'Gifted,' 'Ural,' and 'Shrewd'—have been trying to stop working with us." Not much is known of the other three recalcitrant technical sources. "Shrewd" was completely unidentified. "Gifted" was also unidentified, but a 1943 message indicated that he was back in good standing as an active XY line source. "Ural" was identified as Frank Ullman and described as an "Austrian Jew" and employee of Westinghouse who received a monthly KGB stipend and had provided material on U.S. Army tanks. Ullman spent time overseas, presumably on assignments for Westinghouse, and the New York station reported in 1942 that he had been in the Philippines at the time of the Japanese invasion and interned.[61]

Benjamin Smilg had access to too much highly valuable aviation information for the KGB to drop the matter, and the New York station tried blackmail, but to no avail: "Meeting with "Goose" [Gold] at "Lever's" [Smilg's] apartment (the city of Dayton). "Goose" showed documents and receipts, but "Lever" flatly refused to work." When both were students at MIT, Shumovsky had paid Smilg for tutoring him in some subjects. Possibly the tutoring did assist Shumovsky's studies, but it was also part of his cultivation of Smilg, and he kept the receipts he asked Smilg to sign at the time. The KGB had Gold show them to Smilg with the implied threat that the receipts might be construed as evidence of espionage if turned over to American security officials. Smilg, however, refused to be bullied, and the KGB did not carry out the threat. Instead, the New York station tried another tack, first sending Semenov to attempt to reestablish contact, but Smilg "categorically refused to meet" him. It then reported: "Blerio [Shumovsky] is meeting with Lever in an attempt to restore the friendly relations that had once existed between them. It is difficult to meet, however, b/c Lever was drafted into the Armed Forces and walks around in an officer's uniform." This didn't work either. The KGB gave up, and its 1944 summary of the Smilg case concluded that after being a productive source in 1935, 1936, and into 1937, "In 1937 the materials stopped coming in. In the fall of '38 he was turned over to "Goose," but it proved impossible to set up a working relationship with him." This was not, however, the end of the matter.[62]

In 1950 Harry Gold confessed to his long career as a Soviet industrial source, courier, and agent handler. During the course of his statements he discussed his contacts with Benjamin Smilg, then working as a research aeronautical engineer at a government laboratory at Wright-Patterson Air Force Base. Smilg was called before government loyalty board hearings and asked about their relationship. He acknowledged meeting with Gold but denied knowing that Gold was engaged in espionage and strenuously disclaimed any spying on his part. Smilg maintained that Gold had tried to blackmail him with the threat of using the signed receipts, but he had refused. He was suspended from his job, and in 1952 a U.S. grand jury indicted Smilg for perjury for denying knowledge of Gold's status as a spy. Gold was the chief witness against Smilg at a subsequent trial in November held in Dayton, Ohio. He testified that Smilg had refused to provide espionage data but certainly knew that he was a KGB agent. Smilg testified that he had thought Gold was some sort of a radical "screwball" rather than a spy. Smilg's lawyer convinced the jury that Smilg could not have been sure that Gold was a spy and that, at any rate, he should get credit for refusing to provide espionage information, and he was acquitted. Smilg did tell the truth about rebuffing requests to spy after 1937 and being threatened with blackmail. However, from 1934 until late 1937 he was a KGB source, something he never admitted to American authorities.[63]

"Arseny's" Aviation Spies

Stanislav Shumovsky was not the only KGB officer who concentrated on aviation intelligence. So did Andrey Shevchenko, cover name "Arseny." While Shumovsky's aviation heyday was in the mid-1930s, Shevchenko operated in the early 1940s, during America's wartime alliance with the USSR. Shevchenko had a cover job as an aviation engineer with the Soviet Government Purchasing Commission, and his trips to American aviation plants to inspect aircraft being supplied to the USSR under Lend-Lease provided the opportunity to recruit aviation sources for the KGB. The chief aircraft supplied the Soviets (nearly five thousand) was the P-39 Airacobra and its successor, P-63 Kingcobra, single-seat fighters produced at Bell Aircraft plants in upstate New York, and many of Shevchenko's sources came from aviation plants in that region. A February 1945 report had a chart of agent assignments on the XY line that listed Shevchenko with ten sources, all devoted to aviation intelligence. Their cover names were "Zero," "Bugle," "Ferro," "Thomas," "Nemo," "Armor," "Noise," "Author," "Bolt," and "Hong." It further elaborated:

"Zero"—Mrs. Leona Oliver Franey 32 years old. Works in the secretariat of the head of the design office at factory No. 2 of the "Bell" Company. Has access to secret work. Gives "Arseny" [Shevchenko] materials in return for money.
"Ferro"—Alex N. Petroff. 46 years old, Russian. Living in the USA since '22. Kolchak veteran. Did his doctoral work at MIT. A professor of aerodynamics. Married to a very religious American woman from Kansas City. Two daughters. With Arseny—2 years ago when they were working together at the Curtis factory. Good personal relationship. "Arseny"—occasional rewards, gifts. His wife does not know. A fanatic. Does not believe in science or medicine. Her daughter cut off one of her fingers, and she forbade calling a doctor and called a nun instead. Family strife. His wife berates him for working at a factory and making so little money, even though he is a professor.

"Noise"—Michael K. Cham. 27 years old, b. in Canada, Ukrainian, a U.S. citizen. Works at the "Douglas" airplane factory in Chicago. From '42 to '43, he worked at the Curtis factory in Buffalo, where he was recruited by "Arseny."
"Armor"—Harold Smeltzer, 31 years old, a U.S. citizen. Graduated from Massachusetts ins-t. From '39 to '43, he was a division chief at factory No. 1 of the "Bell" Company in Buffalo. Moved to NY, but the connection was lost.
"Nemo"—William Pinsly. 31 years old. Aeronautical engineer. "Curtis" factory, Buffalo. Married. Only gives materials to "Arseny" at the factory. Occasionally —gifts. Thinks of himself as unlucky in his personal life. On 1.1.45, he bought a child in Chicago for $4,000; he spent all his savings and took out a loan at the bank.
"Author"—Vladimir Borisovich Morkovin. 29 years old, Czech. PhD in technical sciences, an aerodynamics engineer. With "Arseny"—a year and a half. Tech. info. orally.
"Bolt"—Inoke N. Varie (Innokenty Nikol. Vorozheyka). 44 y.o. Russian. Living in the USA since '20. Recruited by "Arseny" in '44. Told us about a radio-controlled bomb.
"Hong"—Loren Haas. 37 years old. Motor-mechanical engineer at the Bell factory.

"Bugle" and "Thomas" were not identified.[64]

An anonymous letter sent to the FBI in August 1943 (see chapter 9) identified Shevchenko and other Soviet officials in the United States as KGB officers. Initially unsure of what to make of the bizarre letter, the Bureau eventually decided that it should be taken seriously and put Shevchenko under periodic surveillance. Agents observed him meeting with Leona and Joseph Franey on 26 July 1944. Leona/"Zero" was chief librarian at Bell Aircraft, while Joseph worked in the rubber section of nearby Hooker Electro-Chemical. Bureau agents observed a second meeting on 30 July, during which Shevchenko met the Franeys on a parkway near the Niagara Falls and took them to a leisurely dinner.

FBI agents contacted the Franeys in August 1944, and they agreed to assist the government. They reported that Shevchenko, whom Leona had met the previous November, when he first began using the Bell Aircraft library, gave them theater tickets and small gifts; took them out to dinner; and related how social conditions in the USSR were superior to those in the United States. Leona told the FBI, and later publicly testified, that she had not actually given Shevchenko any Bell Aircraft documents at that point. (Deciphered KGB cables and these new documents suggest that she had actually begun to supply him with material prior to the FBI approach.) The Franeys continued their relationship with Shevchenko, and Leona supplied him with Bell Aircraft material that had FBI approval. In 1949 they testified to a congressional committee about their work as double agents. They stated that the KGB officer gave them cash bonuses and provided a camera to photograph secret documents to which Leona had access in the secure section of Bell Aircraft's library. Leona testified that Shevchenko was particularly interested in material on Bell's development of the prototype American jet aircraft, the P-59; technical questions about jet engine design; and design problems with the innovative swept-back wing.[65]

Bureau agents also observed Shevchenko's cultivation of Loren Haas/"Hong," a Bell engineer who assisted in the technical training of Soviet personnel in maintaining the P-39 and P-63. Haas also agreed to assist the FBI. As with the Franeys, Shevchenko provided Haas with a camera to assist his espionage. One late 1944 deciphered KGB cable noted that Haas had given Shevchenko detailed drawings of a jet engine under development. Haas left Bell in 1945 to take a position with Westinghouse, soon to become a major producer of jet aircraft engines. Shevchenko renewed contact with Haas, and he continued to function as a double agent for the FBI. KGB contact with Shevchenko's aviation sources likely was cut by early 1946 in the wake of the Bentley, Budenz, and Gouzenko defections.[66]

"Black"

One of the longest serving and most eccentric Soviet XY line agents was Tasso (Thomas) Lessing Black, born 5 July 1907 in Bloomsburg, Pennsylvania, where his father taught Shakespeare at Bloomsburg State Teachers College. He attended Pennsylvania State University, studying chemistry, but left in 1929 without a degree. Old friends interviewed by the FBI recalled that he was constantly in trouble. In one incident he poured benzene on the floor of the dormitory and set it on fire. He took morphine and talked constantly about the coming American revolution.[67]

Black moved to the New York area in 1931, found a job at a chemical company, and joined the CPUSA. But he found party activities boring and decided he wanted to emigrate to the Soviet Union. He dropped out of the CPUSA in part because he had heard that the party might refuse him permission to go on the grounds that Communists were needed to build the movement in the United States. He began to take lessons in Russian and visited Amtorg with his friend Fred Heller to explore whether there were jobs for chemists in the Soviet Union. At Amtorg he was directed to Gayk Ovakimyan. In 1950 Black explained to the FBI that he told Ovakimyan that from his work he was well informed about key areas of industrial chemistry and thought that in the Soviet Union he could put that knowledge to work. He then recounted what happened next: "So Ovakimian wanted to know what I knew and what information was available. I told him well I could get him probably a lot of information on the manufacture of sulphinated oils, textile specialties, leather specialties, industrial chemicals generally. He said that would be of very great interest to the Soviet Union. He said that perhaps it could be arranged that we could go to the Soviet Union to work, but first he would like to have samples of the sort of information that was available and also, before he could recommend that we be sent to the Soviet Union to work, he wanted to know how good a chemist we were." Black stole some proprietary chemical processes from his employer and brought them in, and Ovakimyan asked for more. Ovakimyan, however, was a KGB officer, not the Amtorg official that he pretended to be, and was not really interested in finding Black a job in the USSR. Gradually, Ovakimyan converted Black from a job seeker stealing information from his old employer and offering it to a possible new employer into a full-fledged industrial spy. He first appears as a KGB source in 1935 with the cover name in Russian of "Cherny," which is simply Russian for "Black." While initially a source of technical intelligence, Black later undertook a variety of tasks for the KGB, working as a courier, agent handler, and recruiter.[68]

Deactivated in 1946 along with many other agents, Black likely would have faded into obscurity except that one of his recruits was Harry Gold. Like Black, Gold had gone from being an industrial intelligence source to a KGB courier and agent handler. Klaus Fuchs identified Gold as his courier in 1950, and Gold implicated Black as the man who had first recruited him into espionage.

The FBI first interviewed Black on 15 May 1950, at which time he denied almost everything. Agents were convinced he was not telling the truth; he also bemused them with his odd lifestyle and habits. Acquaintances described Black as "very shabby in appearance and dress, carefree, and good-hearted but very eccentric." He kept mice, rats, and snakes in his home, as well as a pet crow, and sometimes carried out smelly chemical experiments in his residence. Occasionally he brought what were described as "downtrodden individuals" to his apartment to live with him for a time. Within a month, however, he had become more forthcoming and eventually the transcripts of his interviews with FBI agents were many hundreds of pages in length.

Black also gave the FBI access to material he had stored at a warehouse. Black appears to have been one of those individuals who couldn't bring himself to throw anything away. In addition to piles of old laboratory equipment, chemicals, and a variety of household items, FBI agents were surprised and pleased to find that Black had ignored elementary rules of intelligence tradecraft (and common sense) and had saved memorabilia from his espionage career. Included in his stored papers was the contact information the KGB had given him in 1942, when he went to revive its relationship with biochemist Earl Flosdorf, as well as the original signed letter from Grigory Rabinovich that he had shown to Flosdorf. Also in the papers was a mid-1930s autobiography he had prepared for his KGB contact with the following incriminating statement: "Joined FSU [Friends of the Soviet Union] and later CP [Communist Party], Fall 1931; started to work for National Oil Products Company, Spring 1933, as Analytical Chemist; made Research Chemist, Fall 1933; dropped out of all radical activity (CP, FSU) because opportunity was present for obtaining technical information of value to the Soviet Union."[69]

Black admitted involvement in industrial espionage from the early 1930s through the mid-1940s and also to having infiltrated the American Trotskyist movement on KGB orders. He confirmed that he had recruited Harry Gold. Industrial espionage was not clearly a federal crime until passage of the Economic Espionage Act of 1996, nor was spying on a private political movement such as the Trotskyists. In view of his cooperation and because there was no evidence that he had transmitted military or government secrets, he was never prosecuted. The government, however, did force him to register under the Foreign Agents Registration Act.

Black had a checkered career as a chemist. Under pressure from the KGB and distressed and nervous about a marriage proposal from one of the Trotskyists on whom he was spying, he inadvertently caused an ether explosion at his laboratory in 1938 and was severely burned, spending twenty weeks in the hospital. In November 1954 an explosion at a chemical storage tank at the Berg plant in Philadelphia, where Black worked, killed ten firemen and injured twenty-three. The district attorney and police questioned Black, the consulting chemist for the company, and discovered that he did not have a college degree. He had begun work there in 1946 and was never asked to show any credentials. For a while, local authorities considered arresting him for negligence. Called before the Senate Internal Security Subcommittee in 1956, he told a sanitized version of his activities and then disappeared from public view. While generally accurate, his statements to the FBI tended to minimize the extent of his long service for the KGB, during which he supervised several other minor agents about whom he kept silent.[70]

Richard Briggs and Alfred Slack

In addition to Black, Harry Gold led the FBI to another technical spy, Alfred Slack, whose confession enabled the Bureau to unearth still another ring of agents, most of them minor sources. The ringleader of the group, a brilliant but twisted alcoholic named Richard Briggs, was already dead by the time his circle was discovered. To the FBI's surprise, it learned that he had come into its sights years before, although not for espionage.

Richard Briggs, born in 1902, attended McGill University and the University of Rochester and then went to work in 1924 at Eastman Kodak in Rochester, New York, as a chemist. A frequent candidate for pubic office on the Socialist Party ticket, he was recalled by fellow employees as a "screwball" and drunkard. In 1936, while inebriated, he set fire to a laundry at a Catholic seminary. Fired from his job, he approached Amtorg about obtaining a position in the Soviet Union and met Ovakimyan. Just like with Thomas Black, Ovakimyan soon converted the job seeker into an industrial spy.[71]

For the next three years Briggs recruited a small stable of sources while he worked for short periods at various chemical companies. In 1938 a KGB New York station message stated: "The source "Film" [Briggs] works at the 'Eastman Kodak Co.' and obtained the following through his sub-source, "El" [variant of "Ell"/Slack]: 1. the company's secret materials on the production of motion picture film. 2. minutes of technical production conferences. "El's" father—a qualified chemical engineer, who worked for over 30 years at the 'Allied Chemical Co.'" Briggs's initial recruits were also usually family or friends. Although not married, he lived with a woman named Sara Weber, whose sister was married to Alfred Slack, a chemist. At first Slack thought Briggs was using the information he furnished to further his own career, but when he discovered that it was going to the Soviets, he rationalized that he was helping a struggling country.[72]

In addition to his drinking, Briggs was also an inveterate womanizer. Before taking up with Sara Weber, he had an affair with her niece, fifteen-year-old Libby Volpi. Family objections canceled their engagement, but Briggs provided the money to enable her to attend college in West Virginia. There she met and married a left-wing laborer with little formal education named Stanley Glass. During family visits to New York, Briggs befriended Stanley and introduced him to Ovakimyan. In West Virginia Glass worked at the Belle plant of DuPont, which produced nylon. Although he denied taking part in any espionage, he did admit to the FBI that he might have obtained weekly internal DuPont reports and sent them to Briggs. He also introduced Briggs to one of his contacts at the plant, a young chemist's assistant named Howard Gochenour. Gochenour, a German-Irish medical school dropout anxious to earn extra money to finance his dental school education, began supplying Briggs information on the manufacture of nylon.

Even before Briggs's death in 1939, brought on by acute alcoholism —he was downing two to five quarts of whiskey a day—Ovakimyan had met with Slack to solidify their relationship, and after Briggs died, Slack began to supply him directly with material he stole from his employer. A 1942 evaluation stated: "Work with "El" [Slack] was running smoothly. "Goose" [Harry Gold] met with him once every 3–4 weeks, and "Twain" [Semenov] met with him during his trips to NY. He is conscientious toward work and takes it seriously and gives materials at almost every meeting." Slack not only became a reliable industrial source, but he also took over Briggs's role as agent handler and recruiter. Slack arranged to have Glass introduce him to Gochenour, and Briggs's arrangement with the latter continued, with Slack paying him several hundred dollars for his reports. Later, when Gochenour decided to attend dental school, Slack offered him $100 a month to remain at DuPont, but Gochenour was by now suspicious about what he was involved in and declined.[73]

Interviewed by the FBI many years later, both Glass and Gochenour denied being aware they were involved in Soviet espionage. Even though by 1950 Glass was a union leader in the fervently anti-Communist International Union of Electrical Workers, the FBI suspected that he might have been more knowledgeable than he let on, and his former wife described him as an opportunist. Gochenour insisted that he thought Briggs and Slack were stealing industrial secrets for other American companies.[74]

According to KGB documents Slack did mislead Gochenour and used what in intelligence jargon is known as a "false-flag" recruitment. These are approaches where the source thinks he has been recruited to provide material to "X" country, but he has been misled by his recruiter and the material actually goes to "Y" country (thus the "false flag"). The variation in KGB technical intelligence work was to recruit American sources working for private companies who thought they were selling their employer's secrets to a commercial rival, when actually the information went to the USSR. A 1942 KGB report noted Slack's use of a false-flag deception with Gochenour:

"Ell [Slack] willingly accepted the assignment to reestablish contact with Yang [Gochenour] and got down to work at once. At the first meeting, Yang acted very cautious and El had to work hard to gain his trust. After several meetings, Yang agreed to carry out the assignment on nylon. He asked for $1,500 for this work. 'Ell' notes that Yang is a big coward who only works because of the compensation. Yang's cowardliness became especially obvious after the start of the war with Japan. Ell's explanation for this is that Yang is of German descent. According to the cover story, these materials go to South America. Although in conversation the probationer [source] did not reveal hostility toward us, considering his heritage, we thought it would be a good idea to make the 'buyer' a neutral country. 'Ell' thinks that Yang is a fine expert who currently works in the nylon industry and will be able to give us very valuable material. We explained to Ell the importance of these mater-als and assigned him to check Y's work and submit his conclusions about the value of the mater-als."[75]

Slack used a false-flag recruitment with another chemical source as well. Medes Grineff was a neighbor and also a chemist at Eastman Kodak. Born in Russia, he was anti-Soviet, an adherent of an anti-Bolshevik émigré group. Grineff denied to the FBI that he had ever given Slack any material and Slack insisted that he had been rebuffed the only time he asked, but the KGB reported in 1942 that Grineff had fallen for another Slack false-flag approach: ""El" [Slack] receives materials from "Grineff" (hereinafter "Em"), supposedly for South America." Harry Gold, who was Slack's courier for a time, recalled writing up a report on Grineff for his KGB superiors but remembered nothing of the nature of Slack's relationship with him. Grineff continued to be cited as a XY line source until October 1943 and disappeared thereafter, likely because Slack had moved, and the KGB lost its contact with Grineff.[76]

Slack had one brush with the FBI during World War II. While living in Florida in 1938, Briggs had been arrested and charged with child molestation by his landlady. He later told Slack that he had only been responding to her daughter's questions about "the birds and the bees," but considering his relationship with the fifteen-year-old niece, that is suspect. A few years later the FBI became interested in him because his address book, seized during his earlier arrest, had contained the name "Levine," coincidentally the name of a child victim of a highly publicized 1938 kidnapping-murder that had taken place not far from Briggs's home town of Rochester. Briggs was dead, but in 1943, attempting to close the still unsolved Peter Levine case, Bureau agents tracked down Al Slack, then living in Cincinnati, who assured the agents that Briggs had been too gentle to have been involved in such violence and drank too heavily to have been capable of carrying out a carefully planned kidnapping. Years later, when the FBI learned that Briggs had been a KGB agent, it tried assiduously to locate the address book (possibly containing the names of Briggs's espionage contacts), but it had long since vanished. In a remarkable coincidence, one of the FBI officers who followed up on Briggs in 1943 was Robert Lamphere, later one of the bureau's lead counterespionage investigators, who was part of the FBI team that investigated Slack's espionage and from him heard of Briggs's involvement in industrial spying.[77]

When Slack got a job at the Oak Ridge atomic facility in the fall of 1944, he ceased to cooperate with the KGB for reasons that remain unclear. After Gold was arrested in 1950, he identified Slack as one of his sources. FBI agents confronted him, and he quickly confessed that he had provided Gold with technical information from 1940 to 1944, receiving payments of $200 per report, but denied supplying anything atomic-related. He was tried and convicted in September 1950 and sentenced to fifteen years in prison.[78]

Spying for Revenge

Ideological sympathy for the Soviet Union and simple greed were the major motives for espionage for most XY agents. But occasionally bitterness and revenge played a role as well. For example, a 1945 entry describes one source with such motives: "Karl ("Ray")—a chemical engineer at the Hercules Powder Company. With us since '34. Recruited "Electric Pole," from the DuPont Company, to work with us, which he did until '41. However, "Electric Pole" was exposed to Hut [FBI]. The connection with Karl was interrupted. Resumed in Oct. '42."[79]

"Electric Pole," the source at DuPont, received only one other mention, a note that he became too frightened to continue assisting the KGB, and he was not identified. The real name of "Ray" (later "Karl") was also not provided, but the details supplied about him make it easy to identify him as William Stapler. Thomas Black also dealt with Stapler when working as an XY line courier and in the 1950s provided the FBI with considerable information about him. Black didn't know Stapler's cover name, but the details he provided match the description of "Ray"/"Karl" in KGB documents. Stapler received his BS in Chemical Engineering at the University of Illinois in 1915 and immediately went to work for DuPont. Laid off in 1920 during the recession following World War I, he was unable to obtain a good job until 1933, when Hercules Powder Company, a DuPont subsidiary, hired him. He had no discernible interest in or concern with communism, but he had become embittered by his economic travails in the 1920s and blamed DuPont. He contacted the Soviets in 1934 and began supplying Hercules Powder and DuPont technical secrets for money and revenge. He appears as an active XY line source through the rest of the 1930s until May 1941, when the KGB cut contact in the aftermath of Ovakimyan's arrest.

It was a sensible decision because Ovakimyan's arrest was sparked by information from Armand Labis Feldman, who knew that Ovakimyan had a source at DuPont. Born Iosif Volodarsky in the Ukraine in 1903, Feldman was educated as an engineer and in the 1920s went to work for Soyuzneft, the All-Union Association of the Oil and Gas Industry, which managed the Soviet petroleum industry. London was then a world center for the oil market, and Soyuzneft sent him there in 1930. The KGB London station, however, co-opted him for various technical intelligence tasks. Scotland Yard arrested Volodarsky for industrial espionage in 1932; he was fined and forced to return to the USSR. He then entered the KGB ranks as a professional officer and was sent to the United States as an illegal in 1933, using a fraudulent Canadian passport in the name of Armand Labis Feldman. A 1934 memo, "On the tasks of the USA station," indicated, "Brit [Feldman] was supposed to have worked on economic espionage. His task had been to establish a network to shed light on oil concerns." As it worked out, Feldman's work in the United States expanded beyond oil to include other industries and also overseeing a source, Abraham Glasser, in the U.S. Justice Department (discussed in chapter 4).[80]

In 1938 Feldman faced twin threats. In January British counterintelligence broke up a Soviet espionage ring seeking information from the Woolwich Arsenal. One of the Soviet operatives involved in the attempted infiltration had a Canadian passport as Willy Brandes. His real name was Mikhail Borovoy, and British and Canadian investigation of the false Brandes passport pointed toward Feldman, who had helped procure the fake document, and the FBI began a search for Feldman. The KGB considered recalling Feldman, but he prudently thought it unwise to return to Moscow at the height of the Terror. The KGB New York station chief told Moscow what happened next: "On 22 Apr. Nikolay [Gutzeit] informed Brit [Feldman] that he was heading for Mexico to arrange the tapping of Old Man's [Leon Trotsky's] phones. Brit didn't come to the next meeting on 26 Apr." A later KGB memo noted: "On 25 Apr. 1938 Brit disappeared after cashing checks from his business at the bank. A search yielded no positive results." The KGB didn't know it, but Feldman had moved secretly to a home in New Jersey and later quietly moved to Canada.[81]

But after World War II began, the Royal Canadian Mounted Police located him, and Feldman faced internment and possible deportation to the USSR. He began to cooperate with the RCMP, who informed American authorities. FBI agents interviewed him, and although he held back a good deal, he revealed some of his activities in the United States. The most important item Feldman provided was the identification of Ovakimyan as a senior KGB officer, and one particular he added was that Ovakimyan had recruited an industrial spy at DuPont. FBI inquiries at DuPont resulted in company executives disclosing that in 1938 Paul Lawrence, an employee, had come to them with a story of being approached to spy by someone he would not identify. When the FBI interviewed Lawrence, he admitted that in 1938 William Stapler had contacted him about a job in Russia. Stapler's contact was a man named "George" at the Rockefeller Institute in New York. (At that time Ovakimyan held a fellowship at Rockefeller, arranged for him by Phoebus Theodore Levene, a prominent biochemist born in Russia.) Stapler told Lawrence that he had been selling information for years to "George," who was a Soviet agent, because of his long-standing grudge about being fired in 1920. Although he thought Stapler was spinning a tall tale, Lawrence informed his superiors but declined to name Stapler, and nothing happened.[82]

Even though the FBI received this information about Stapler in 1941, it failed to pursue the matter at the time. Consequently, the KGB reestablished its relationship with him in late 1942. An October 1942 KGB New York station letter noted: ""Ray" [Stapler] was worried because we hadn't met with him. He hadn't received money in over a year. When he was told that now we would be actively working, he was very happy." Stapler continued to work as an industrial spy until 1945. Thomas Black, who served as his courier for a while, recalled to the FBI that Stapler was a demanding source who complained when his $125–150 payment per report he had furnished was reduced to $100 and refused to supply material until he was compensated for previous handovers. After one blowup, KGB agent Joseph Katz, Black's superior, took out a wad of cash and gave it to him to transmit to Stapler, complaining that the KGB was paying too much.[83]

"Ray" and "Karl," Stapler's cover names, also appeared in the Venona decryptions, and NSA/FBI analysis identified the real name but redacted it. However, a 1951 FBI memo noted that nine persons exposed by Venona had already died. Stapler, who had died in 1947, was on the list. Along with Black's evidence, that indicates that the blacked-out name in the Venona decryptions for "Ray"/"Karl" was William Stapler.[84]

Feldman's Other Technical and Industrial Spies

A retrospective KGB "Memorandum on the Feldman case" mentions eleven American agents whom the defecting KGB agent had known in the mid-1930s: "S-1," "S-2," "S-3," "S-7," "Morris," "Sound," "Vit," "Yankee," "Frost," "Zvezda," and "Gadfly." Three of these—"Morris"/Abraham Glasser, "Sound"/Jacob Golos, and "Frost"/Boris Morros—are discussed elsewhere. As for the others, Feldman identified the real names of only a very few of his American and Canadian sources to either the RCMP or the FBI. Nonetheless, the FBI uncovered several of the sources he did not speak about after it came across a check written by Simon Rosenberg while investigating Feldman's business dealings. When agents showed up at his Yonkers home, Rosenberg immediately confessed to working for Feldman from 1934 to 1938. Born in Poland, he came to the United States in 1924 and six years later went to work for Amtorg. During a sojourn in Russia in 1932, he was, according to his account, coerced to spy for the KGB by threats against his Russian sister. Rosenberg most likely appears in Vassiliev's notebooks as: "S-7—engineer, American citizen, recruited in the Soviet Union. Verified at work. We are making him a group handler." Simon Rosenberg told the FBI that among his sub-sources were Stanley Bruno, a designer at Youngstown Sheet and Tube; Patrick Keenan, an engineer working as a rolling mill foreman at Carnegie Illinois Steel Company in Chicago; and John Berger, an engineer for United Engineering in Pittsburgh.[85]

At Ovakimyan's direction Feldman created a business front, Round the World Trading Company, in New York. Feldman's partner in business was Herman Jacobson. Born in Latvia on 22 December 1898, Jacobson arrived in America in 1906. Involved with the Communist Party from its inception, he was a leader of the Young Communists in Philadelphia in 1922. After moving to New York in 1930, he worked as an accountant for Amtorg. Jacobson organized Round the World in 1935 and disbanded it in 1938 after Feldman's disappearance. The KGB used the company's bank accounts to transfer money to Soviet agents throughout the world. Rosenberg recalled sending checks to someone later arrested as a Soviet spy in Greece and others in Europe and China. In 1937 Moscow sent instructions about using Round the World Trading Company:

"We are developing a plan to provide a connection between our organizations and center in the event of war. We therefore need the following information: 1. All information and regulations regarding the organization of a steamship society in America, so that this society's steamships can sail under American flags in European waters. 2. All information about small steamship companies (2–4 steamships of average tonnage built in the last 10–15 years) in Norway, Sweden, and Denmark, with an established name, which can be acquired at an inexpensive price. It would be desirable to get this information in Brit's [Feldman's] company's name, or in the name of some other American organization. 3. Report whether Brit's company can obtain several freight ships of average tonnage (3,000–4,000 tons) and guarantee that they can be utilized without loss in European waters under an American flag."

A 1933 memo on agents in the American station identified Jacobson as KGB agent S-1: "S-1. An American citizen by the name of Jacobson. Currently unemployed. S-II was recruited through him. Robert wanted to make him a bookkeeper in the accounting office. In Robert's opinion, S-1 is a recruiter with prospects. S-II. A secretary in the U.S. Department of Aviation. Gave blueprints. Recruited through S-1." ("Robert" was an officer at the KGB New York station named Rosenstein.)[86]

As for Jacobson's recruit, "S-II" (more often rendered "S-2" and "S/2" in KGB documents), her real name was not given in any documents and has not been identified. She did, however, provide information of value to the Soviets. The 1933 report referred to her working at the "U.S. Department of Aviation," but there was no such agency at the time. A 1934 KGB report more precisely described where she worked: "S-2— secretary in the Aviation Division of the Department of the Navy. Gives valuable materials." A 1944 KGB cable detailed a meeting among Semenov, a KGB technical-scientific specialist, Jacobson, and "S-2." The only detail about "S-2" in the cable was that she was then forty-five years old. But the NSA/FBI footnote to the Venona decryption was redacted, indicating that a real name had been attached to "S-2." In 1950 during a follow-up interview, Feldman admitted that Jacobson had given him information he had received from a relative who worked at the Navy Bureau of Aeronautics in Washington. Feldman remembered that she was a typist or stenographer and the only Jewish woman in the office. This

information apparently enabled the FBI to identify her, and it is probable that she cooperated with the Bureau, resulting in the redaction.[87]

In 1936 the U.S. Navy arrested Lieutenant Commander John
Farnsworth for selling naval secrets to Japan. (He was convicted and imprisoned in 1937.) Farnsworth's arrest prompted a tightening of security
at "S-2's" office, and the KGB New York station reported:

"Upon her return from vacation, the source was shown, 'for her information
and guidance,' an order to the agency regarding the 'vigilance' of all its employees (in light of exposed espionage cases. (This pertains to a group of
Japanese intelligence agents who were arrested in Los Angeles and to the
naval officer Farnsworth (a Japanese spy), who was arrested in Washington.)
In accordance with this order, it is forbidden for typists and secretaries not
named in the order to type up top-secret documents in their divisions.

The order names only three typists who can be used by division leaders to
type top-secret documents. We regret to inform you that our source was not
among those three. But departmental bureaucracy is not an easy thing to overcome, and for now—order or no order—the division leaders continue to use
their own secretaries (whom they have at hand) to type things up.

The source thinks that everything will remain as it was. Much talk in the
division about the espionage cases, but our source is calm enough. We also
gave the source corresponding directives regarding vigilance. Meetings are to
be scaled back to once a month."

A supplementary report from "S-2" the next month indicated that the security tightening had blown over: "S/2 reported that documents are still
typed up in every division, including hers." In 1940, with Europe at war,
things got more serious. The New York station told Moscow Center that
her courier, Jacobson, had reported: "S-2 works in the Department of the
Navy. S-1 [Jacobson] said that because of the Spy-mania campaign and
the activities of the Dies Committee [House Special Committee on Un-
American Activities], she is temporarily refusing to bring out documents.
She isn't breaking off with us and will start working again at the first opportunity." The report added, "She is willing to have us stop paying her
allowance," indicating she did not expect to receive her usual monthly
stipend during a period of non-performance. She continued to be in
touch with the KGB into 1944, but it is not clear if she returned to her
earlier status as a productive source.[88]

The most valuable material "S-2" stole from the Navy involved Robert
Goddard's rocket experiments (the Navy funded part of Goddard's pioneering work on liquid-fueled rockets). In 1935 Abram Slutsky, chief of

KGB foreign intelligence, prepared a special report on the material, stating that his officers had

"obtained through agents in the U.S. a report by the well-known Amer. scientist Dr. Goddard, who has been working for a number of years on a liquid-fuel rocket. The report is addressed to the U.S. Navy Department and sums up the results of Goddard's 10 years of work on a liquid-fuel rocket. In addition to covering certain phases of the work that has been done, the report contains a whole host of specific data on the rockets that the author has developed (dimensions, thrust, fuel consumption, etc.) and test results. The final section of the report comments on the prospects for the practical use of liquid-fuel rockets: 1) as an engine for super-speed planes; 2) as an engine for apparatuses sent to explore the upper reaches of the stratosphere (up to 160 km); 3) as an engine for aerial torpedoes (so-called "gunless" artillery). It is clear from the subsequent correspondence that Goddard's work was funded by private individuals. Now, however, liquid-fuel rockets have come under the Navy Department's authority and have been classified as secret defensive weapons.

Soviet organizations that work in the same field are highly interested in G.'s work, but so far they have not been able to obtain reliable information about his work. According to a preliminary expert examination, this material is very valuable. The material is being sent to Cde. Pavlunovsky, the head of the chief mil.-mobilization administration of the NKTP [People's Commissariat of Heavy Industry], which has jurisdiction over the jet-propulsion institute, for his use."[89]

Another scientific source exposed by Ovakimyan's arrest was one of the KGB's more mercurial recruits. While under FBI surveillance in December 1940, Ovakimyan met with Dr. Maurice Bacon Cooke. Shortly afterwards, Cooke showed up at an FBI office in New York, said he knew the Russian, and gave agents a list of questions on national defense that Ovakimyan had given him to answer, including queries on high-grade gasoline and camouflage at oil plants. Cooke explained that he had first met Ovakimyan in 1934 through contacts at Amtorg and eventually became an industrial spy. Over the years he had given him information from the TVA on phosphoric acid and, in 1940, on "catalytic cracking," a then groundbreaking oil-refining process, in return for more than $14,000. He also admitted turning over details about gasoline-refining plants that he had stolen from M. W. Kellogg Company.

Cooke was an accomplished, if controversial, chemical engineer, born in New Jersey in 1893. After graduating from Bucknell, he had worked at DuPont, the U.S. Bureau of Mines, Kellogg, and Alco Products Company (as director of research). He had first contacted Amtorg in 1933 and visited the Soviet Union that year and in 1936. One FBI memo reported that he had obtained a $12 million contract with Amtorg to build four aviation gasoline plants. The FBI memo summarizing his visit noted that he seemed unstable. Two months later the president of Kellogg reported that Cooke had come into his office crying and that he'd "practically confessed to stealing processes" and giving films to someone in February. Cooke talked to the FBI again and "fainted several times" during the interview. He admitted giving several rolls of Leica film to Ovakimyan on 17 February 1941, despite denying it earlier, and accepting money. He also spoke of suicide. In 1942 J. Edgar Hoover informed Assistant Attorney General Thurman Arnold that Cooke was working for the East Texas Petroleum Company, which had been barred from access to certain patents because it employed him. Later that year he somehow got a job with the War Production Board as a consultant, claiming to be a sworn counterespionage agent of the FBI. As soon as Hoover found out, Cooke was fired; one report on the incident called him "psychopathic."[90]

Cooke appeared in KGB reports in 1938 as a technical intelligence source of the KGB New York station with the cover name "Octane." ("Octane" also appeared in deciphered Venona cables, but analysts were never able to identify his real name.) It took some time before the KGB realized that he had talked to the FBI. In April 1941 a report on intelligence in the United States still listed him among the most valuable sources in the New York station. It was not until August 1941 that the KGB New York station told Moscow: ""Octane"—Dr. Cooke, according to "Sound" [Golos], was turned by the FBI. 'We lost him.' In connection with the case with "Gennady"[Ovakimyan]."[91]

The KGB cut contact with Cooke after learning he had cooperated with the FBI. Seemingly not realizing that he had burned his bridges, however, Cooke attempted to get in touch with Semenov at Amtorg in May 1943. And in mid-1945 the KGB New York station reported: ""Octane" [Cooke] went into the "Factory" [Amtorg] building twice and asked about Gennady [Ovakimyan]. He was told that they did not know of such a person. Apparently, he had wanted to get a consulting position, b/c he is currently unemployed." After that, Cooke dropped out of sight.[92]

"Vendor's" Group

The KGB also sought to use the American Communist Party's networks for its technical intelligence operations. Anatoly Gorsky, the Washington station chief, informed Moscow in 1945:

"In the process of working with "Vendor," the latter reported that for a number of years, he had been "Sound's" [Golos's] group leader and had handled a group of people for us on his behalf. In particular, "Vendor" indicated that his next meeting with "Sound" was to have taken place on the day of the latter's death." "Vendor's" contacts:

"1. Leon Josephson, 47 year-old lawyer, NY, owns a cafe, member of the CPUSA. Assistant group leader, handled "Sound's" people. Went to Europe several times, supposedly on our business. He failed in Copenhagen in '36 along with George Mink; he was convicted and extradited to the USA.
2. Hyman Colodny, 50–52 years old, pharmacy in Washington, a fellowcountryman. "Sound" used him for a rendezvous apartment. In '34–'36, he was in Shanghai on our business.
3. Rinis. A talent spotter.
4. Louis Tuchman, 55 years old, CP member, small-time building contractor. Rinis's partner. A talent spotter. He was secretary for an illegal group of Communists working in gov't agencies in Washington.
5. Marcel Scherer, 43–44 years old, CP member, an organizer for a trade union of chemistry workers. A talent spotter.
6. Paul Scherer (Marcel's brother). 46–47 years old, CP member, a chemist, a New York native, a trade union worker. In '30–'32 he and Marcel were handled by Josephson. Their handler on our line was a certain "Harry." In '35–'36, Paul was connected with G. Mink, collecting tech. information and obtaining books. Prior to "Sound's" death, both Scherer brothers were handled by Josephson."[93]

A strong candidate for "Vendor" is Harry Kagan, who worked for the Soviet Government Purchasing Commission and whom Elizabeth Bentley identified as one of Jacob Golos's agents. The reference to Leon Josephson having "failed in Copenhagen" (that is, been exposed to hostile security services) was to a 1935 incident in which Danish police charged a traveling party of three Americans with espionage. The three were George Mink (a former trade union organizer for the CPUSA then working for the Comintern), Leon Josephson (a CPUSA lawyer), and Nicholas Sherman. In Josephson's case, after four months in jail a Danish court decided there was insufficient evidence to proceed to a trial, and he was released. Mink and Sherman, however, were convicted of espionage, spent eighteen months in prison, and were then deported to the Soviet Union. Despite carrying an American passport, Sherman was not an American. He was Alexander Petrovich Ulanovsky, a GRU officer. Danish police found in his possession correspondence with Harry Kagan, and among the *four* passports Mink had in his possession one was that of

Harry Kagan. The American Communist Party ran a false passport operation (the "books" referred to in Gorsky's cable were passports), and GRU was a major recipient of its work. Likely the four passports carried by Mink were for delivery to GRU. (Kagan claimed his passport had been stolen. The real Nicholas Sherman had died in 1926. The CPUSA's false passport apparatus had used the dead man's naturalization papers along with a false witness to allow Ulanovsky to obtain an American passport as Nicholas Sherman.)[94]

"Rinis" was Joseph Rinis, a graduate of the Comintern's International Lenin School and a CPUSA activist in the FAECT. Marcel Scherer, who had been the founder of FAECT, was, like Rinis, described as "a talent spotter"—that is, someone who identifies likely sources to be recruited by Soviet intelligence. He had been born in Rumania in 1899 and was a founding member of the American Communist movement. Known as "the Bolshevik chemist" while a student at CCNY, he studied at the Lenin School in 1930–31, before returning to be the leader of the FAECT chapter in New York. He spent more time in the mid-1930s working in the Anglo-American Secretariat of the Comintern. As the president of FAECT, he was instrumental in its organizing efforts in the late 1930s and early 1940s, personally overseeing the attempt to organize a chapter at the Radiation Laboratory at Berkeley in 1942, the site of much atomic bomb research. FAECT halted its campaign after President Roosevelt personally appealed to Philip Murray, chief of the CIO, to end the effort on grounds of national security. Many of the scientists and engineers implicated in Soviet espionage were FAECT members, including Julius Rosenberg, Russell McNutt, and Joseph Weinberg. With easy access to thousands of radically inclined scientific and technical personnel and knowledge of the projects on which they were working, Marcel Scherer was in an ideal position to assist Soviet intelligence and steal American secrets, but there is no further mention of him or his activities in the notebooks. He remained a steadfast member of the CPUSA until his death.[95]

XY

Scores of other technical sources, many identified with real names and others with only cover names, appear in KGB reports. Some are described in detail, while most have only walk-on appearances. Some had previously appeared in FBI investigations or congressional investigations, but others, even when identified by their real names, are obscure and will require additional research to determine their contribution to Soviet technical and scientific intelligence. What is clear is that the KGB invested a substantial amount of resources and personnel in its efforts to steal American scientific, technological, and industrial secrets and harvested a rich return.

1. "Щора" – рейсбанд Вильям, амер. гр-н, сотр-к дешифровальной службой мин-ва обороны США. Наш агент с 34 г. С 45 г. по 48 г. был законсервирован. В февр. 48 г. восстановлена связь.

"За один год от "Щоры" получено большое кол-во весьма ценных вещ-й, мат-лов о работе амер-в над расшифров-кой советских шифров по перехвату и анализу открытой радиопередачи сов. ведомств. Из полученных от "Щоры" мат-лов нам стало известно, что в результате этой работы амер. руководству удалось получить важные сведения о дислокации вооруж. сил СССР, производст-ве отдельных различных отраслей пром-ти и работах, проведённых в СССР в области атомной энергии."

До авг. 48 г. – докум. мат-лы на личных встречах. С авг. 48 г. – новая система. "Павел" встреч-ся раз в полтора-два месяца только для проведения инструктажа после каждой проверки. Передача док-тов – через тайники.

с. 26

с. 27   "На основании полученных от "Щоры" материалов наши органы госбезопасности провели ряд защитных меро-приятий, в результате чего эффективность работы амер. дешифровальной службы значительно снизилась. Это привело к тому, что в н/вр объём работы дешифр. и аналит. службы амер-цев значительно сократился."

Увеличение агент. обстановки => консервация. Обусловлены контр. встречи в ресторане за горбин. 16.07, 19.08, 16.09, 16.10 а затем каждые 3 месяца – 16.01.50, 16.04.50 Имеется догов-ть об условных средств. опознания, паролях, взаимных сиг-налах для вызова на жстр. встречу.

с. 28.   Особо ценный агент. (Связь в безопасности поддерживать через 4-е упр-е КИ (нелегал.?)

2. "Язб" – Кравсор, Самуил, гр. США, член КП США, сотр-к башенного отделения ТАСС.

с. 29   У "Крока":

"Снеддон" – Соколов Борис Романов, ?-й секр. пв. части Йоллнеботочной комиссии, с 43 г.

У "Лери"
Сотр-ки румынского пос-ва: "Оццуи", "Жана"
Шифровальщик котор. пос-ва "Хде". Владеет только перваденни языком => трудности у "Лери".

CHAPTER 7

American Couriers and Support Personnel

oviet espionage networks in the United States would not have
been able to function without the assistance of a number of dedicated support personnel whose role was as essential as that of
the sources who actually took documents from the government
offices in which they worked or communicated secrets to which they were
privy. Once the latter had obtained their information, they had to transmit it to the Soviets. Few of those who obtained government or technical secrets could easily meet with someone readily identified as a Soviet
national without exciting suspicion or triggering surveillance. In order to
avoid alerting American counterintelligence, a chain of clandestine contacts had to get the material from the original source and transmit it to either a "legal" KGB officer working in an official capacity in a consulate or
embassy with a cover job or an "illegal" officer living in the United States
under a false name and pretending to be an American or an immigrant.
Such illegals, once they obtained material from their sources, still had to

---

A 1950 KGB report on William Weisband, a one-time KGB courier who became a Soviet spy within the
super-secret National Security Agency and revealed to the USSR that the United States had broken its military codes. Courtesy of Alexander Vassiliev.

covertly transmit it to a legal officer for final passage to the USSR by protected diplomatic pouch. These networks required couriers who could meet the sources without arousing suspicion, pick up the material, and then hand it on to the next person in the chain. Jacob Golos, for example, used Elizabeth Bentley as his courier to the Silvermaster group because he himself was in poor health and unable to travel frequently to Washington and because he believed himself under FBI surveillance. The KGB needed a corps of such discreet, dedicated Americans willing to undertake unglamorous jobs that required regular travel and a low profile.

These courier chains, moreover, were sometimes intricate and complex. While this protected both the original source and the KGB officer ultimately receiving the material by insulating them from each other, it could cause delays in the Soviets' receipt of information, delays in the passage of instructions from the Soviets to the source, and an inability to control the source's behavior. For example, George Silverman, one of the sources of the Silvermaster network, was civilian chief of analysis and plans of the Army Air Force, a position of obvious interest for Soviet intelligence. But Moscow Center felt it wasn't receiving what it should from him and in 1943 complained to its New York station: "'You communicate with him through a highly elaborate system: "Aileron" [Silverman]—"Pal" [Silvermaster]—"Clever Girl" [Bentley]—"Sound" [Golos]—"Vardo" [Elizabeth Zarubin]. Clearly, with this kind of communication it is inconceivable to exert any kind of serious influence on a probationer's [source's] work, not to mention his education. . . . Think over the question of improving the line of communications with "Aileron" (primarily by, so to speak, 'shortening' it).'" Moscow had a point. Silverman, the original source, was a hidden Communist, but he was an economist, not a trained intelligence operative. He turned his material over to and got his guidance from Gregory Silvermaster, another economist with no more training in espionage than Silverman. He, in turn, handed the material over to Elizabeth Bentley, Golos's assistant and lover. While she had experience in covert party work, Bentley was not an intelligence professional either. Such instruction as Bentley got was from Golos, a senior CPUSA official whose techniques came from the Communist *political* underground, not the world of intelligence. It was not until the material reached the fifth person in the chain, Elizabeth Zarubin, that it got to a KGB professional. Moscow's complaint that Silverman lacked proper guidance about what it needed or appropriate conspiratorial techniques when there were three intermediaries was not misplaced.[1]

In some cases, American couriers also provided a psychological cover for the source. Since the person to whom he or she gave information was not a Russian but an American, the source could pretend or rationalize that he or she was not turning over material to a foreign power but to the CPUSA. Bentley used that argument to resist turning members of the Silvermaster network over to the direct supervision of the Soviets. On the other hand, some sources thrilled to direct contact with Soviets. Silvermaster believed that Iskhak Akhmerov, an illegal officer with whom he met frequently, was an American Communist; when he finally met with Vladimir Pravdin, a legal officer operating under TASS cover, in September 1945, he gushed that he "'was sincerely pleased to meet with a Soviet representative'" at last, saying "'that he had long hoped that they would meet him, since all these years he had been connected 'only to local fellowcountrymen' [American Communists].'"[2]

It was crucial to have the right courier for a source. Jacob Golos agreed to surrender control of Julius Rosenberg and his circle of engineers at least in part in response to Soviet arguments that without a technical specialist to guide them, their value would be wasted. In 1942 Martha Dodd Stern, a socialite, writer, and KGB agent, complained that her courier was an American and politically unsophisticated. The KGB New York station chief reported: "'"Liza" [Stern] was unhappy over the fact that the person who was connected to her ("Chap" [Zalmond Franklin]) was, first of all, not a Soviet operative, and second, not adequately developed politically and unqualified in her tasks and topics. "Liza" was offended by the fact that we downgraded her work with us to such a level.'"[3]

The KGB also experienced problems finding enough couriers. Not only did the job require discretion and reliability, but it also meant that the would-be couriers needed to break their overt ties to the Communist movement. Finding a regular job that allowed them the flexibility to travel at irregular intervals was not easy. KGB officers periodically considered setting up Harry Gold with his own laboratory business to allow him more time to visit sources to get their material and grumbled when his work obligations as a corporate chemist caused him to miss appointments. In contrast, Elizabeth Bentley ran U.S. Service and Shipping Corporation, a cover business that arranged shipping of packages to the USSR. As its supervisor, Bentley could take off time for her courier work as needed, but its connections to the Soviet Union proved worrisome.

Sometimes couriers needed to relocate. Ann and Michael Sidorovich moved from New York to Cleveland, giving up their friends and jobs, to set up a safe house to service William Perl, a valued KGB technical aviation source working at nearby Wright Field. The KGB gave them $500 to finance the move. Amadeo Sabatini moved from Pennsylvania to the West Coast and then back to the East Coast at the behest of the KGB. Years earlier Whittaker Chambers had walked away from the editorship of the *New Masses* to plunge anonymously into the underground and shuttle documents and money among Washington, New York, and points in between.[4]

Ideally, couriers needed to be inconspicuous. Gold was an undistinguished and bland-looking man. Moscow considered Victor Perlo's wife as a potential courier in 1945 but concluded that because she suffered from Basedow's disease (a form of hyperthyroidism characterized by bulging eyeballs), she was too conspicuous to be suitable. During World War II able-bodied men not in the military invited suspicion. All these caveats meant there was a chronic shortage of couriers. Searching for one for Donald Maclean, the KGB's valuable British diplomatic source serving in Washington in 1945, Anatoly Gorsky notified Moscow: "'We undoubtedly need to find a good courier for 'Homer' [Maclean]; however, this has so far been exceptionally difficult for us.'" He indicated that the station was considering Helen Scott, then secretary for a French journalist. If she proved unsuitable "'and we don't find another candidate, we will consider maintaining contact through 'Homer's' wife'" [Melinda Maclean], who would transmit the materials to a Soviet operative.[5]

Maclean's history as a Soviet source also illustrated yet another potential problem with couriers. Canadian Communist Kitty Harris had a long career as a KGB operative. She became Maclean's courier in early 1938 while he was still stationed in London. He made frequent visits to her apartment, where she photographed the documents he brought along, and they eventually became lovers. While such relationships were regarded as poor tradecraft, the KGB accepted their liaison and transferred her to Paris when Maclean was posted there in the fall of 1938. Their affair lasted for eighteen months before ending in 1940, when Maclean met and later married Melinda. While their affair may have given him a logical reason to visit Kitty, it also added a volatile emotional mixture to his espionage that made Moscow Center uneasy.[6]

Such complications likely contributed to Moscow Center's reaction when Joseph Katz, one of its most devoted and effective American agent handlers, became overwhelmed with contacts and meetings. The Washington station told Moscow in early 1945 that Katz met with five of the station's sources: Maurice Halperin, Julius Joseph, Harry Magdoff, Victor Perlo, and Joseph Gregg. Moreover, three of them were themselves group leaders, with Perlo passing on Donald Wheeler's material, Gregg acting as the channel for Helen Tenney, and Magdoff handling Edward Fitzgerald. In addition, Katz also met occasionally with Elizabeth Bentley and "Zero," an unidentified agent in Washington. Katz wanted help, and Gorsky agreed, telling Moscow:

"'X's' [Katz's] requests about the need to have a courier between him, the probationers [sources], and the group leaders are undoubtedly justified. Unfortunately, we do not have suitable candidates. Our intentions of using "Zero" [unidentified] could not be realized, as we reported elsewhere. None of the wives is suitable for this work. At every meeting, "X" asks us to give him "Adam" [Eva Getzov]—with whom you are familiar—for this purpose. Considering our critical situation in this regard, we earnestly ask you to consider once more the possibility of handing us "Adam." In the first place, a courier like that should be used for contact between "X" and his group leaders: "Raid" [Perlo], "Tan" [Magdoff], "Gor" [Gregg]."

The need was clear and Moscow gave its consent, but reluctantly, telling Gorsky: "'We agree with the proposal to use 'Adam' as a courier. However, it is essential to note that 'X' [Katz] lives with her, and therefore there could be potential complications with his [Katz's] wife. You should discuss this in earnest with 'X,' noting that such behavior on his part could have disastrous consequences for our work.'"[7]

As for "Zero," she had first worked with the KGB via the CPUSA underground in the 1930s, when she was on the staff of the Nye Committee investigating munitions manufacturers. She continued as a source, working for various congressional committees, until 1942, when "'she left her job for family reasons'" and the KGB New York station deactivated her. When the KGB reestablished contact with her in 1945, hoping that she would work as a liaison agent, Gorsky reported, "'Incidentally, 'Zero' told 'X' [Katz] flat out that she knows exactly which country 'X' has ties to,'" and "'she would be happy to help.'" But, "'as it turns out, 'Zero' has a husband who does not share her polit. beliefs at all and who watches his wife's every move out of jealousy.'" Given spousal suspicion, Gorsky abandoned the notion of using "Zero."[8]

Even after Bentley's defection had closed down most of the KGB's American networks, there still weren't enough couriers to service the much smaller number of sources. By 1948 some of them had also been exposed or had defected. In 1948, for example, a KGB Washington station letter to Moscow explained that meetings with David Wahl took place every three weeks. This was a longer interval than desired, but intensified FBI surveillance of its legal officers had forced it to reduce the frequency of meetings. The station wanted "to switch to a courier, but there isn't anyone."[9]

Other KGB documents provide detailed evidence of the importance of the couriers' work. For a number of them, the notes also enable us to reconstruct a good deal about their history and the trajectory that led them to their key roles within the espionage networks. A handful, like Harry Gold and Elizabeth Bentley, became household names, but most remained in the shadows, even when the FBI succeeded in uncovering their activities.

William Weisband

Not all couriers remained just couriers. Some became active sources in their own right and some sources morphed into couriers. Thomas Black, for example, transmitted industrial secrets from laboratories at which he worked before the KGB assigned him to infiltrate the Trotskyist movement. He later became an active courier handling several technical spies. Harry Gold provided low-level industrial secrets before becoming one of the KGB's busiest technical intelligence couriers and agent handlers. (Black is discussed in chapter 6, Gold in chapter 2). The most remarkable transition was engineered by William Weisband, who began his espionage career as a courier servicing KGB technical/scientific sources and after World War II became the KGB's most valuable source, one who did incalculable damage to American interests and likely changed the course of the early Cold War.

Much about William Weisband's early life remains shrouded in mystery. Although he claimed to have been born in Alexandria, Egypt, it appears more likely that he was a native of Odessa, Russia, born in 1908; moved to Egypt with his parents; and then came with them to the United States in 1925. He worked at the Waldorf Astoria Hotel in New York in the early 1930s, but what he did after that is unclear. On the basis of evidence that is not public, American counterintelligence officers believed that he went to the Soviet Union sometime in the early 1930s, perhaps to study at the Comintern's Lenin School. While he was in Moscow, Soviet intelligence recruited him in 1934, and he worked in the USSR to get some practical experience before it sent him back to the United States. (Weisband once told Jones York, for whom he served as a courier, that he had been a KGB operative in Soviet Central Asia.) What is clear is that by 1936 he was working as a courier for the KGB New York station. Vassiliev's notebooks record that in 1936 "Link," Weisband's cover name at the time, handled "Zero," the female KGB source working for the Senate Nye Committee. Expense reports for the New York station in the latter half of the 1930s list him as a regularly subsidized agent. Later FBI investigations indicated that by 1938 his financial situation had improved dramatically, even though he appeared to work only at low-paying jobs.[10]

Moscow Center transferred Weisband to California in mid-1941 to reestablish contact with Jones York (see chapter 6), an aeronautical engineer. At their first meeting Weisband handed over half of a Shirley Temple picture, a contact protocol that York's previous liaison had arranged, to establish his bona fides. York agreed to revive his espionage relationship but said he needed a camera; "Bill," as York knew Weisband, provided $250 to purchase one. Over the next year, Bill met with York about ten times, delivering lists of specific aviation technical questions the Soviets wanted addressed. York later told the FBI that Bill paid him about $1,500 for the material he delivered. The two became very friendly, meeting at York's home as well as nearby bars and restaurants. York showed him a poem, entitled "The Vandal's Doom," that he had written about the Nazi invasion of the USSR, and Bill, stating he was impressed, typed out a copy to show his superiors. At one meeting, York learned that Bill spoke and wrote Arabic, and, in a serious breach of intelligence tradecraft, Bill once mentioned his family name, which years later, when talking to the FBI, York remembered as "Villesbend." A KGB memo on York noted that Weisband was drafted into the American Army and in November 1942 turned liaison with York over to another courier, Amadeo Sabatini.[11]

Weisband had a talent for languages. Russian was his native tongue, but he spoke English virtually without accent and had picked up some Arabic from his childhood in Egypt. The Army recognized his skills and sent him to a language school to study Italian and to Officer Candidate School; he received a commission and, at his request, assignment to the U.S. Army Signal Security Agency (predecessor of the National Security Agency). He left for Great Britain in July 1943 and later served in North Africa and Italy. When one of its couriers or low-level sources entered the military in World War II, the KGB usually simply deactivated him for the duration because it was too difficult to maintain contact with peripatetic military personnel. And most servicemen in typical military jobs were of little intelligence interest anyway. Weisband, however, was an exception, possibly because of his assignment with the code breakers of the Signal Security Agency. A KGB New York station cable in June alerted

Moscow that Weisband had finished his Italian course and suggested a password for approaching him in Britain, stating that Weisband would await contact each Sunday at the entrance to the Leicester Galleries in London. While Weisband was overseas, he also kept in touch with the KGB by writing to Lona Cohen, another KGB courier, via his brother. A February 1945 KGB cable only partially deciphered by the Venona project suggested that Weisband had some contact with Soviet naval intelligence; this likely related to his Army assignment in Italy as liaison with several Soviet naval officers.[12]

In late 1944 Semen Semenov returned to Moscow and wrote a summary report on his American tour. He had worked with Weisband and offered this assessment: "'"Link" [Weisband]. Helped me in receiving materials from "Emulsion" [unidentified technical source] and "Brother" [unidentified technical source]. Was connected to agents "Smart" [oil industry source Elliot Goldberg] and "Needle" [Jones York]. Has a great desire to work with us. Shows composure and calm at work. Considering his nice work in the West and indisputable growth during his time in the army (Africa, Italy, Britain, France), he should be utilized upon his return as an illegal in technology and assigned as the handler of a group.'" Weisband, however, had a brighter espionage future than a return to courier and agent-handling work. After his discharge at the end of the war, the Army Signal Security Agency promptly rehired him as a civilian linguist assigned to Arlington Hall, the military's super-secret code-breaking facility then in the process of shifting from breaking German and Japanese codes to deciphering Soviet codes. With his native Russian, Weisband became a lead translator for decrypted Soviet messages. With the exception of atomic espionage, one could hardly imagine a post of greater interest to Soviet intelligence. In October 1945, following Igor Gouzenko's defection, Moscow issued a warning to safeguard six valuable American agents, including Weisband, by now code-named "Zhora": "Surveillance has been increased. Safeguard from failure: Homer [Donald Maclean], Ruble [Harold Glasser], Raid [Victor Perlo], Mole [Charles Kramer], Zhora [Weisband], and Izra [Donald Wheeler]. Reduce meetings with them to once or twice a month. Minor agents should be deactivated. Carefully check out against surveillance when going to meetings, and if anything seems suspicious, do not go through with them." But with news of Bentley's defection in November, Moscow Center ordered more drastic measures, and the KGB cut contact with scores of American sources, including William Weisband.[13]

Every nation's intelligence and security services have strengths and weaknesses. In the jargon of the intelligence world, while the Soviet Union excelled in "humint" (human intelligence, the recruiting of sources who steal documents and provide information), the United States excelled in "sigint" (signals intelligence, the interception and deciphering of electronic communications). During World War II the Army and Navy paired America's highly advanced radio and early computer technology with thousands of cryptanalysts, linguists, mathematicians, and other specialists and created the most powerful and advanced cryptologic capacity in the world. The Army's Signal Security facility at Arlington Hall was the largest, and eventually the Navy's and Air Force's counterparts merged into it to form the Armed Forces Security Agency. A later reorganization transformed it into the National Security Agency. Once so secret that the inside joke was that "NSA" stood for "No Such Agency," it now has a more public profile, but its significance in the public mind is still much less than the better known Central Intelligence Agency, even though the NSA's budget easily exceeds that of the CIA.

Winston Churchill observed in March 1946, "From Stettin in the Baltic to Trieste in the Adriatic, an iron curtain has descended across the Continent." During the early years of the Cold War, America had little ability to peer behind the curtain. President Truman had dissolved the Office of Strategic Services in the fall of 1945, leaving the nation without a comprehensive foreign intelligence service, while bits and pieces left over from the OSS were parceled out to different agencies. Realizing the need for coordinated foreign intelligence, in 1947 Congress with Truman's support created the CIA, but it would be years before it reconstituted the capability achieved by the OSS by the end of World War II.

The one bright light in America's intelligence capacity in the early postwar period was Arlington Hall and signals intelligence. The NSA's Venona project allowed the FBI to build on the information provided by such defectors as Bentley to neutralize most of the KGB's impressive Communist Party–based espionage networks of World War II origin. Of even greater immediate importance to the Cold War, in 1946 the NSA broke into the radio codes used by the Soviet armed forces. Two years later the NSA was reading Soviet military logistics traffic almost as soon as the messages were sent. By tracking the movement of Soviet military equipment and supplies, American military commanders and the president could confidently judge Soviet military capabilities, separate Stalin's diplomatic bluffs from serious threats, and spot preparations for invasions or attacks that needed serious diplomatic or militarily attention.

But in 1948, over a period of a few months, every one of the Soviet military cipher systems the United States had broken "went dark," in code-breaker terminology, when the Soviet military implemented new and much more secure cipher systems. The consequences were extremely grave. Stalin approved Communist North Korea's plans for an invasion of South Korea in 1950. The North Korean military depended entirely on the Soviet Union for the logistics of war, and starting in the spring of 1950 a massive transfer of weapons, aircraft, artillery, tanks, trucks, ammunition, fuel, and supplies from the USSR to North Korea allowed the invasion to proceed in June. Had the NSA retained the ability to read Soviet military logistics communications, the United States might have been forewarned of the threat of invasion and possibly been able to use diplomatic or military action to block it. As it was, the massive North Korea attack surprised and overwhelmed the unprepared South Korean and American forces. The war cost more than thirty-five thousand American lives and several million Koreans and Chinese.

In 1950 the FBI identified Weisband as having been a Soviet spy in the early 1940s. He never admitted anything, and no independent evidence appeared, but given his position assisting in translating deciphered Russian messages, the NSA concluded that Weisband had most likely alerted the Soviets of the NSA's break into their military communications and enabled the USSR to change its cipher systems and protect its messages from American cryptanalysts. An NSA report obtained by the *Baltimore Sun* in 2000 surmised that due to Weisband's betrayal, "In rapid succession, every one of [the] cipher systems went dark," and "this dreary situation continued up to the Korean War, denying American policy makers access to vital decrypts in this critical period." There was, however, one puzzle. Weisband had been at Arlington Hall from late 1945 onward. Why had it taken the Soviets until 1948 to realize that the United States was reading its military radio traffic?[14]

Documents in Vassiliev's notebooks establish that it was indeed William Weisband who betrayed the NSA's success against the Soviet military codes. They also explain why it was not until 1948 that the Soviets took remedial action: ""Zhora"—William Weisband, Amer. citizen, employed by the decryption service of the U.S. Dept. of Defense. Our agent since '34. From '45 to '48, he was inactive. In Feb. '48, the connection was restored." Thus, it was not until February 1948 that the KGB reestablished liaison with Weisband, deactivated in late 1945 in the wake of Bentley's defection. Until the KGB spoke with Weisband in early 1948, Soviet authorities had no idea that the United States was reading Soviet Army communications.[15]

A 1949 KGB report explained in detail what happened after the KGB restored contact with Weisband:

"In a single year, we received from "Zhora" [Weisband] a large quantity of highly valuable doc. materials on the efforts of Americans to decipher Soviet ciphers and on the interception and analysis of the open radio correspondence of Sov. agencies. From materials received from "Zhora," we learned that as a result of this work, Amer. intelligence was able to obtain important information about the disposition of Soviet armed forces, the production capacity of various branches of industry, and the work being done in the USSR in the field of atomic energy. . . . On the basis of materials received from "Zhora," our state security agencies implemented a set of defensive measures, which resulted in a significant decrease in the effectiveness of the efforts of the Amer. decryption service. As a result, at pres. the volume of the American decryption and analysis service's work has decreased significantly."

Here is confirmation that Weisband's material triggered the Soviet military's implementation of new ciphers that left American intelligence and American policymakers in the dark in the run-up to the Korean War.[16]

Having delivered this material to the KGB in 1948, Weisband wanted out, not just from espionage but out of the United States. The KGB Washington station chief told Moscow in August 1948, "'Zhora' [Weisband] is asking to be granted asylum in the USSR." Moscow, however, didn't want to lose a highly valuable source unless there was a clear danger, and at the time there was no indication that American security had any suspicions about Weisband; his request was put off. The KGB, however, did seek to make his life easier. He received subsidies—$600 in December 1948 plus an additional $400 to assist him with a recent automobile accident. He received another one-time payment of $1,694 in 1950. (Always careful, the KGB insisted Weisband sign his real name to receipts.) The KGB noted that Weisband had "'big expenses.'" It also kept his goal of fleeing to the Soviet Union alive; in 1950 Moscow Center agreed to his becoming a secret Soviet citizen, psychologically assuring him of an eventual safe haven.[17]

Weisband met with KGB officer Nikolay Statskevich in July 1949, and he brought back a worrisome report: "'Zhora' [Weisband] reported that his agency was all of a sudden no longer able to read our cipher telegrams. The leaders are worried, and it was suggested that there is an agent at work. "Zhora" asked us not to be overly hasty in introducing reforms on the basis of his reports, b/c failure [exposure] is possible." In as much as Weisband was the "agent" involved, he had reason for concern.[18]

Moscow Center did not take Weisband's security lightly. The KGB Washington station used a variety of methods to pick up his stolen material. Dead drops were preferred for picking up documents, with face-to-face meetings every two to three months in 1948 at a restaurant outside Washington so that his KGB contact could "provide instruction." To increase security the Washington station had the restaurant under surveillance prior to the meetings to watch for FBI interest. In September 1949 documents were handed over in an automobile "brush pass," where one party was in a parked car and the other pulled up next to it, documents were passed through the windows, and the second car then departed. A KGB memo noted: "On days that he meets with operatives [KGB officers], Zhora [Weisband] removes documents from his agency twice: once during lunch, and the 2nd time—after work. On his person, under his shirt. He hides the materials taken the 1st time around in the trunk of his car. He had been instructed not to keep them in his car. To choose only the most valuable ones. He asked for a camera, but he shouldn't be given one. Careless storage or use could lead to failure [exposure]." Twice in 1950 Moscow Center indicated a desire to shift liaison with Weisband from the legal officers of the Washington station to an illegal officer in order to increase security, but it is a measure of the KGB's difficulties in the late 1940s and early 1950s that it didn't have one available for the task.[19]

The KGB was careful with Weisband because he was easily the most valuable agent it possessed in this era. Moscow Center delivered a highly critical review of the work of its American stations in 1948, finding it "extremely weak and ineffective," complaining that the information delivered was "questionable" and that less than a fifth was even thought worthy of reporting to the Soviet leadership. However, it carefully exempted Weisband's material from its condemnation. And in 1950 it sent an angry message to the Washington station chief when it received a report that Statskevich had gone to a meeting with Weisband even though he suspected he was under surveillance: "'Such an attitude toward meetings with 'Zhora' [Weisband] is completely at odds with our repeated instructions about the need to observe all precautions during work with this valuable agent.'"[20]

Weisband's undoing, however, did not come from tradecraft errors by the KGB Washington station. Appropriately, it was the NSA's own Venona project (a project on which he had assisted in translating the messages) that led to his exposure. "Link," Weisband's cover name during World War II, appeared in three Venona decryptions. But the details about "Link" were insufficient to identify him. There was, however, ample detail to identify "Nick," the cover name of Amadeo Sabatini. Confronted by the FBI in 1949, Sabatini made a partial confession, admitted to working as a courier, and identified one of the technical sources he had managed in 1943 as Jones York. The FBI confronted York, and he admitted providing military aviation technical material to Sabatini and to an earlier KGB liaison whom York had known as "Bill," who had let slip his family name, remembered as "Villesbend." The trail led to Weisband, whom York visually identified as his former courier. Interviewed by the FBI, Weisband initially denied any involvement in espionage; later he said he would neither confirm nor deny it. In 1953 Weisband admitted that he knew York but refused to answer any other questions about him. He refused to answer a federal grand jury subpoena and spent a year in prison for contempt of court. Both he and his wife lost their jobs with the NSA. (Barring a confession, the NSA argued vociferously against any prosecution of Weisband, fearing that his defense lawyers would resort to "graymail" and expose in open court information about the NSA's code-breaking operations that would do even more damage to American security than Weisband had already done.) William Weisband, whose betrayal of American code breaking caused incalculable damage to American security, died in 1967.[21]

Alexander and Helen Koral

Two of the KGB's long-serving couriers were the Korals, Alexander and his wife Helen. Their devotion also included steering their oldest son, Richard, into the family business. Even after American counterintelligence uncovered them, the Korals successfully avoided revealing the full extent of their espionage careers or their contacts, lying to the FBI and evading prosecution.

Alexander was born in London in 1897, the child of East European Jews, and was brought to the United States as a child. He studied at Cooper Union and Brooklyn Polytechnical Institute and began working for the New York Board of Education in 1922, in school maintenance as a plumbing and drainage engineer. After taking a leave of absence in 1928, he returned in 1932 on a part-time basis and three years later became a permanent mechanical engineer. Helen was born in New York in 1904; they were married in 1923 and had two sons, Richard, born in 1924, and Gilbert, born in 1926.[22]

An ordinary-looking couple, the Korals were members of the Communist Party and at some point in the late 1920s or early 1930s assisted a CPUSA-based network led by Dr. Philip Rosenbliett and linked to Soviet military intelligence. An autobiography that Alexander Koral wrote for the KGB in the late 1930s related what happened next: "In Oct. 1932, Dr. Philip Rosenbliett . . . introduced me to Irving Steppin." Steppin was a pseudonym used by Valentin Markin, then in the process of setting up the illegal KGB station in the United States operating out of New York. Koral went to work for Markin and summarized his duties: "Taught English to Irving [Markin] and his wife for about 6 months. In 1932, I helped Irving get his passport extended for 6 months or so. At Irving's request, I bribed an official in the immigration service. . . . From 1933 until (roughly) 1936, I worked on photography. At Will's [Akhmerov] suggestion, I went to Windsor, Canada, to receive luggage. Delivered mail abroad—Jan. 2, 1937. At pres., I work with Will; safeguard documents, etc." Helen Koral also wrote an autobiography, in which she described her work as a courier in New York for Akhmerov, as well as carrying mail to Europe and back for the illegal station. Akhmerov sent Moscow his own evaluation of their work in late 1936:

"Don [Alexander Koral]. He was recruited for work under Davis [Markin]. Don in turn was recommended to Davis through circles that were apparently connected with the neighbors' [GRU's] station. Under Davis, Don had been used not only as the tenant of the clandestine apartment, but also as a photographer. All materials and cash funds were kept at Don's apartment. I photographed materials myself at Don's apartment. . . . Don's wife, Carmen [Helen Koral], is used by the station as a courier to Europe. In the future, we intend to use Don himself for this purpose as well. In terms of politics, Don and Carmen are completely loyal to us. . . . Before the connection with Davis, Don and Carmen participated in party work. When he agreed with them about their cooperation with us, Davis unconditionally ordered them to sever all ties with the party circles. They carry out all instructions irreproachably. Don and Carmen understand full well that they are working for our agency. His name is Alexander Koral; Carmen's name is Helen Koral."

In a 1937 communication to Moscow Center, Akhmerov noted that the illegal station was then using Helen to ferry material to the legal KGB station operating out of the Soviet consulate in New York.[23]

Moscow Center briefly expressed concern in 1937 that the Korals had been recommended by Ludwig Lore (see chapter 3), once an important agent handler but by then regarded as a "renegade" and Trotskyist. Akhmerov, however, told Moscow that he didn't think that Lore knew the Korals, and the matter was not pursued. While Moscow didn't raise the matter with New York in 1937, the KGB file on the Korals also contained a 1947 report on what had happened to Philip Rosenbliett, the GRU agent who had introduced the Korals to the KGB in 1932.[24]

In the 1920s Rosenbliett assisted the Comintern in channeling secret subsidies to the American Communist movement. By the early 1930s he ran an extensive apparatus for GRU, and Whittaker Chambers had dealings with him at the time. Tired of his clandestine work and anxious to live in the Communist society he had served covertly for more than a decade, Rosenbliett immigrated to Moscow in 1936 and opened a dental clinic. His fate after that has been unclear. One of his sisters was married to James Cannon, one of the founders of the American Communist Party. But Cannon in 1928 sided with Leon Trotsky against Stalin, was expelled from the CPUSA, and went on to become the leading Trotskyist in the United States, and a relationship by marriage to a leading Trotskyist was a position fraught with peril for anyone who came within the Soviet orbit in the 1930s. Chambers thought Rosenbliett had faced difficulties but had survived the Terror. Others supposed he had been either secretly executed or sent to the Gulag. A nephew who had grown up in his household in New York, however, recently wrote that family correspondence with Rosenbliett's wife in the USSR indicated that while possibly he was arrested or investigated, he was not sent to the Gulag, and his shift of residence to Siberia resulted from the evacuation of Moscow in 1941 under the German invasion threat. The 1947 KGB report gives the first clear account of his fate up to 1945:

Rosenbliett P-p Sam-ch [Philip Samoilovich], YOB 1888, native of the city of Mogilev, a Jew, former American citizen, a dentist. When he was in the USA, Rosenbliett worked for the RU RKKA [Intelligence Directorate of the Workers and Peasants Red Army—that is, GRU] USSR starting in 1925 on the technological line, but in 1935, supposedly, in connection with the threat of failure [exposure], he was deactivated, and that same year, he was sent to the USSR. According to the reports of the RU RKKA, Rosenbliett had proven himself at his job. He was connected by blood to a well-known American Trotskyite but was never a Trotskyite himself. In 1936, on assignment from the RU RKKA, Ros. [Rosenbliett] went to NY, returning to Moscow that same year.

In 1937, the 7th department of the GUGB [Chief Administration of State Security] NKVD USSR began an active investigation of Ros., suspecting him of Trotskyite activities. On 31.12.37, P. S. Ros. was arrested by the NKVD USSR in the city of Moscow for espionage on behalf of Germany and involvement in a counterrevolutionary organization. At the preliminary hearing, Ros.

pleaded guilty and testified to his intelligence activities on behalf of Germany and his Trotskyite activities. He had been recruited for this work in 1925 in NY by a regular officer of the RU RKKA—a Trotskyite and German spy—Wolf. With the help of the former director of the RU RKKA, the Trotskyite Berzin, Ros. and his wife were given Soviet citizenship. At the trial, however, Ros. retracted the testimony he had given at the preliminary hearing, and his case was returned to the NKVD USSR. On the basis of testimonies by the Trotskyites and German spies, former regular officers of the RU RKKA Murzin, Ikal . . . , and Herman, Ros. was convicted and sentenced on 17.9.39 to 8 years in a corrective labor camp by the Special Board of the NKVD USSR. On 15.11.45, Ros. still committed to Karlag.

Karlag, Rosenbliett's prison in 1945, was one of the Gulag's largest and most infamous camps, in northern Kazakhstan. General Yan Berzin headed the GRU, while Felix Wolf, Dick Murzin, and Arnold Ikal were GRU officers who operated in the United States in the late 1920s and 1930s (Herman is unknown). Soviet authorities executed Berzin and Wolf during Stalin's purge of GRU in the late 1930s and sent Ikal to the Gulag, where he died. Murzin's fate is unclear.[25]

With Moscow reassured in 1937 that the Korals were not connected to Lore and no sign that their ties to Rosenbliett had stained them, they went on to undertake a number of sensitive courier assignments for several of the KGB's most valuable agents. The New York station planned to put Laurence Duggan "in touch with Art [Helen Koral] and will thus create, as it were, a reserve line of communication with Albert [Akhmerov]" in November 1944. The Korals also provided a telephone and mail drop for communications with Michael Straight. Alexander served as the courier between the KGB technical intelligence officers operating out of the Soviet Consulate in New York and Byron Darling, a Detroit-based physicist trying to recruit atomic spies. In addition, in 1950 a KGB memo noted that Alexander had known Weisband in the 1930s, when Weisband also worked as a KGB courier. Helen also served as a courier between Gregory Silvermaster and the KGB.[26]

Helen Koral was also in contact with Iosif Grigulevich, one of the KGB's most important illegal officers operating in Latin America. The KGB grew concerned in 1944 when it learned that American and British counterintelligence had intercepted and deciphered some of Grigulevich's correspondence and identified some of his contacts and feared Helen might come under surveillance. Akhmerov, however, reassured Moscow that she had gone to Florida for several months with her younger son, who suffered from tuberculosis. The Center approved a

$500 expenditure for his treatment, in addition to the regular monthly stipend it had been paying the couple for many years ($150 a month in 1937, upped to $200 by 1945). Nor were these regular payments the only remuneration the Korals received. Akhmerov explained in a message to Moscow in late 1944 that years before, on his advice and with money he lent them, they had bought a small, isolated farm in Connecticut, seventy-five miles from New York, which they used for several weeks every summer. Since it was "'an ideal place to meet with someone, where one can spend the weekend in a peaceful environment and discuss everything in absolute safety,'" he now proposed to see if it could be upgraded for use during winter for meetings with Silvermaster, "'where we can discuss matters under normal and pleasant conditions.'" Moscow threw cold water on his proposal, responding that it was "expedient to meet with Robert [Silvermaster] in A and B's ["Art"/Helen and "Berg"/Alexander Koral's] apartment, if possible. At the dacha it could arouse suspicion, especially during the winter when no one lives there."[27]

Akhmerov also decided to recruit Richard, the Korals' older son, whom he had known back in the early 1930s, when he had used their apartment to photograph documents. Richard, he told Moscow in November 1945,

"served some time in the army a year and a half ago but was demobilized because of some minor physical defect. Until last fall, he attended the City College of NY, majoring in sociology. In college, Richard participated quite actively in the youth movement and belonged to the fellowcountryman [Communist] society. About 6 months ago, he decided to go to the University of North Carolina, where, in his opinion, he could become better acquainted with the life of the American south. When he was already attending the City College here, I told 'Berg' [Alexander Koral] that Richard should not participate too actively in political and public activities. For a long time, I have intended to use him for our work in the future. Before he left for North Carolina last fall, I advised Berg to have a serious talk with Richard and force him to leave off political activities associated with the fraternal [Communist Party].

About 2 months ago, 'Sergey' [Vladimir Pravdin] told me that he had instructions from you to select talented young men who could be useful for our work in the future. 'Sergey' said that it would be great if we could arrange with Richard for his future cooperation with us. Pursuant to your approval of my meeting and speaking with Richard, we invited him to come to NY for a few days at the end of the academic semester. I hadn't seen him since 1939. I knew him and his younger brother Gilbert very well when they were children. Two weeks ago, I met with Richard and had a lengthy conversation with him. Before I met with Richard, Art [Helen Koral] and Berg spoke with him about our intention to invite him to take part in our work. At the meeting, I explained to him the social and political importance and necessity of helping our cause. I also explained to him how crucial it would be for him to distance himself from fellowcountryman activities if he decided to accept our invitation. I told Richard about our decision to provide him with material assistance until he finishes his education. He said that he believes in open political activity and that it is a part of his life and the joy of it; that he belongs to this country [USA] and has always intended to struggle for its future; that he was very displeased by the fact that Berg and Art didn't take part in public and political activities.

Richard also wanted to know why we decided to go to him specifically with a request to help in our work, how he could be of use, and whether we couldn't find a better man for the job. At the same time, he acknowledged the importance of our work, its political significance.

After our detailed conversation, he expressed a desire to accept our offer. I explained to him that he would have far more opportunities in his future career if he switched from the department of economics to law. Richard agreed with this. I advised him to focus all of his attention on his studies and promised to send him to Harvard University for his last year to complete his education. A degree from the law school of Harvard University would undoubtedly help him a great deal in the future in his career. We'll see if he gets into Harvard (they have a very strict quota for Jewish students, for whom it isn't very easy to get in).

If he is not accepted to Harvard University, I think it would be a very good idea to let him join the law school of Columbia University for his last year or year-and-a-half. Columbia University also has a lot of prestige. It will take a couple of years for him to finish his college education. As for his expenses, in accordance with the law, he can study for 8 more months at the government's expense. During this time, I will send him only 50 dollars a month and will give certain sums to 'Art' for the purchase of his clothes. After 8 months, we will pay all of his expenses, which will amount to roughly 2,000 dollars a year. Richard is a tall, attractive young man, very intelligent, well-developed politically, devoted to the fraternal cause, sincere, and all in all a very likable fellow. I hope that in the future, he will become a very useful member of our family."

Akhmerov's high hopes, however, came to nothing. By the time Richard Koral went to Chapel Hill, Bentley had defected. There are no indications that Richard was ever again contacted.[28]

Iskhak Akhmerov noted that while Helen Koral was "more cautious and thoughtful," Alexander sometimes failed to observe the rules of "konspiratsia," the term for espionage tradecraft. In mid-1945 Akhmerov met with him in Washington to transfer materials he had picked up from Silvermaster. Alexander, in turn, would hand them over to O. V. Shimmel, a legal KGB officer who worked in the Soviet Consulate in New York. But just after Akhmerov made the handover, they ran across several Soviet sailors on the street. Akhmerov reported, "'Berg [Alexander Koral] with Robert's [Silvermaster's] materials bundled under his arm and, holding out his hand,'" congratulated the Soviet captain on the victory over Germany. But his exuberance was not what cost Koral his anonymity. It was a New York station blunder.[29]

The KGB was normally quite cautious about its couriers. Late in 1944, for example, Moscow Center instructed Shimmel not to meet with either of the Korals more than three times a month and that the Korals and Helen Lowry should take turns making trips to Washington to pick up Silvermaster's material. After Bentley's defection a note in the files indicated that on 23 November the KGB New York station decided to deactivate the Korals, and Shimmel met with Helen Koral two days later to give her $1,200 (their allowance through April 1946) and $300 more to subsidize their son's education and to provide details for a clandestine meeting place and password for the future.[30]

The KGB, however, assigned Alexander Koral one more mission, and it proved his undoing. The New York station asked him to return to Washington and visit the Silvermasters one final time. But by the time he went to Washington on 1 December 1945, the FBI had the Silvermasters under surveillance. Agents observed a man meeting with Gregory and Helen Silvermaster for several hours. Followed on his trip back to New York, he "executed a number of diversionary maneuvers which appeared to the surveilling Agents to be calculated to ascertain the presence of a surveillance." The FBI identified the man as Alexander Koral. When the Bureau checked its files, it discovered that its agents had observed Koral meeting Gayk Ovakimyan, the KGB station chief in New York, in 1939. A later check on the Korals' address indicated that during the 1941 investigation of Ovakimyan FBI agents had tracked an unidentified woman who appeared to be a courier, wearing a leopard skin coat, to the Korals' apartment house. Helen Koral owned a leopard skin coat. (At the time the FBI did not follow up these leads, however.)[31]

The FBI began interviewing members of the Silvermaster espionage ring in January and February 1947, hoping to get confessions that would enable it to bring charges against some of the suspects. For more than a year, it had wiretapped those Bentley had named, investigated their activities, followed them, and otherwise sought to obtain direct evidence of participation in espionage that would provide a basis for prosecution. All the efforts had failed. Warned that she had gone to the FBI, those who knew her or might have been known by her had destroyed any incriminating correspondence, ceased removing documents, and pretended to be ordinary, if left-wing, liberals.

Thus prepared, when confronted by the FBI, most did not panic and either refused to answer questions or gave misleading or untruthful accounts. But when the Bureau questioned the Korals, Alexander made some damaging admissions. At his first interview, he felt he had to account for being seen at the Silvermaster home. He claimed that he had indeed acted as a courier for a mysterious individual named Frank, whom he had met in 1939 and for whom he had made twelve contacts with individuals in New York and Washington. Because of his younger son's illness, he was in dire need of money; "he would give his own life's blood for the health of his boy." Frank approached him, saying he knew from a friend that Koral needed money to care for his son. Koral's task was to meet someone, using a magazine as a signal, identify himself as Al, obtain material, and deliver it to Frank the next day. For these services Frank had paid him $2,000 in cash.[32]

Questioned about what he thought this activity was, Koral explained that Frank said he was in the woolens business, and he assumed it involved illegal procurement of government contracts. In another interview he did express some misgivings that arose after he read about the Gouzenko spy case in Canada: "This matter bothered him considerably and he realizes that what he did is not legal." Returning home from the second of his two visits to Silvermaster, he told Frank, who came to his house, that he was being watched, and that was their last contact. He denied being a Communist but admitted his wife received Communist literature. Helen Koral professed ignorance. She claimed not to know Frank but was aware about his financial arrangement with her husband. She denied being a Communist or ever participating in clandestine meetings. Both Korals refused to name people who knew about their son's illness in 1939 or their current friends. Richard Koral, also questioned, admitted being a member of the American Youth for Democracy, a Communist youth group, and knowing Anatole Volkov, a graduate student at the University of North Carolina and Helen Silvermaster's son and Gregory's stepson. (Bentley had identified Volkov as assisting in his parents' espionage network.) The FBI didn't believe the Korals' mix of partial admissions combined with a cock-and-bull story, but neither did it have sufficient evidence to bring a criminal charge. They were never prosecuted.[33]

The KGB had had no contact with the Korals since the end of 1945 and was unaware of their contact with the FBI in 1947, the year it attempted to revive some of its old American networks. Andrey Graur, a senior KGB officer, wrote a memo in September asking permission to contact Gregory Silvermaster and proposing that "'Art [Helen Koral], a former courier between our division and 'Robert' [Silvermaster], before he was deactivated in connection with 'Myrna's' [Bentley's] betrayal,'" be assigned to the task. Graur also set out the recontact protocol that had been set up in 1945. But in October, before Helen could be contacted, Moscow Center heard from its American station that Alexander Koral had been summoned to a "trial," likely a U.S. grand jury or possibly a congressional committee hearing, and with that it ended attempts to recontact them. The House Committee on Un-American Activities called Alexander to testify in mid-1948, but he invoked the Fifth Amendment and also refused to confirm that he had admitted to the FBI that he had carried out courier missions to those accused of having been Soviet sources. The KGB concluded that the Korals had cooperated with the FBI and wrote them down as "traitors."[34]

Anatoly Gorsky, former Washington KGB station chief, in late 1948 prepared a list of Soviet officers, agents, and sources who might have been exposed by betrayals by six former agents. For each defector Gorsky listed those whom he or she might have identified to American authorities, along with their cover names. Four were well known—Chambers, Bentley, Hede Massing, and Budenz; the fifth and sixth were the Korals:

"Berg" and "Art's" group

1. "Berg"—Alexander Koral, f. [former] engineer of the municipality of NY
2. "Art"—Helen Koral, "Berg's" wife. Housewife.
3. "San"—Richard Koral, son. Student.
4. "Long"—Norman Hait, engineer for the "Sperry Gyroscope Company" in New Jersey.
5. "Smart"—Elliot Goldberg, engineer for an oil equipment manufacturing company in NY.
6. "Huron"—Byron T. Darling, engineer for the "Rubber" Company
7. "Teacher"—Melamed, teacher at a music school in NY
8. "Cora"—Emma Phillips, housewife

9. "Lok"—Sylvia Koral, former employee of the Code Section of the Office of War Information.
10. "Siskin"—Eduardo Pequeño, businessman in Caracas (Venezuela)
11. "Express Messenger"—Richard Setaro, journalist/writer, f. employee of the "Columbia Broadcasting System." Currently in Buenos Aires.
12. "Artem"—A. Slavyagin, our cadre employee. Currently in the USSR.
13. "Twain"—S. M. Semenov, station chief of KI [Committee of Information] tech. intelligence in Paris. At pres.—on leave in Moscow.
14. "Aleksey"—A. A. Yatskov, our cadre employee, currently in the USSR.
15. "Julia"—O. V. Shimmel, our cadre employee, currently in the USSR.
16. "Shah"—K. A. Chugunov, our cadre employee, currently in the USSR.[35]

Aside from Alexander, Helen, and Richard Koral, four of the other thirteen listed in "Berg" and "Art's" group were KGB officers who had served at the KGB New York or Washington stations ("Artem"/Slavyagin, "Twain"/Semenov, "Aleksey"/Yatskov, and "Julia"/Shimmel). The other eight were KGB sources and agents, seven American and one South American. "Huron"/Darling appeared in the Venona decryptions, but the FBI had never been able to identify him (see chapter 2). Richard (Ricardo) Setaro, deputy chief of the Latin American department of CBS Radio (see chapter 3), had been identified in the decryptions as a Soviet agent who "was used by us [KGB] earlier for the most part on liaison with Artur [Grigulevich], as a meeting point for couriers," and to do background checks on Central and South Americans of interest to the KGB. Eduardo Pequeño's cover name, "Siskin," appeared in the decryptions as a South American KGB contact, but the FBI could not attach a real name to it. Leah Melamed and her father ran a safe house in New York and did other tasks for the KGB New York station. She was, for example, a mail drop used by Boris Morros (see chapter 8) for communications with the KGB. The Korals recruited Sylvia Koral (Alexander's cousin) as a Soviet source shortly before she left for London to work in the code section of the Office of War Information, where the KGB London station took over her management. Nothing is known of Norman Hait, and even the English spelling of the name is uncertain. Nor is anything known of Elliot Goldberg other than what Gorsky wrote of him. Emma Phillips's cover name, "Cora," appeared in a deciphered 1944 KGB cable as an American Communist recruited by Akhmerov, but nothing was said of her activities. The FBI attached a real name, presumably Phillips, to "Cora," but the NSA redacted the name when it opened Venona in the mid-1990s, possibly indicating that she had co-operated with the FBI.[36]

Despite the KGB's conviction that the Korals had betrayed it, their cooperation with the FBI appears to have been limited to the fantasy they invented about doing courier work for the unknown "Frank." Neither admitted any knowledge of espionage or awareness of the materials they were picking up or delivering, and both lied about their Communist attachments. Apart from Silvermaster, whom the FBI had observed meeting Alexander, and Semen Semenov, who Alexander told the FBI resembled one of the men he had met, they implicated no one else. Certainly Alexander said nothing of Byron Darling, who was the real person behind the "Huron" in the Venona decryptions whom the FBI was intent on tracking down because of hints in the deciphered messages that the unknown "Huron" was involved in atomic espionage. In his congressional testimony Alexander took the Fifth Amendment on all substantive questions. He lost his job with the New York school system and sued to get it back; a court upheld the dismissal in 1950. He died in July 1968. Helen Koral died in April 1979.

Richard Koral's future career may not have included working for Soviet intelligence, but it certainly was not commonplace. He finished law school at Chapel Hill, where he and his wife "were the most radical people in the left in North Carolina," and received his degree but was never admitted to the bar. After returning to New York, Richard became an organizer for the United Furniture Workers union. Police arrested him in October 1951 with two other men in a Westchester factory with "acid and knives, burglars' tools, stench bombs and several vials of chemicals that could be used in starting fires." Before being caught, they had destroyed furniture worth $1,700 with acid and knives. "The acid was so strong that it had eaten into the trousers of two defendants, and when they were arraigned the men wore cell blankets around their legs." Koral, still dressed, was charged with burglary and malicious mischief and held on $40,000 bail. Police linked the case to the destruction of $9,000 worth of furniture in another factory, where two locals of the United Furniture Workers were engaged in a jurisdictional dispute.[37]

Richard Koral went to jail for five years. Someone sent him a magazine on cooling large buildings, and he began to correspond with the editor. After his release, he joined the magazine and eventually became managing editor and an acknowledged expert on air-conditioning machinery for large buildings. He was founder and director of the Apartment House Institute, which trained building superintendents—like his father. The author of a book, *Foundation for the Solar Future,* as late as 2000 he served as director of the Division of Continuing Education at the New York City College of Technology.

Amadeo Sabatini

The KGB picked several of its couriers from Communists who had proven their reliability and acquired experience abroad, often on Comintern assignments. One was Amadeo Sabatini, born in Italy in 1909, who came to the United States as a child. A Young Communist League member since 1923, Sabatini joined the CPUSA in 1930 in Pennsylvania. He had dropped out of grade school and gone to work in the mines, where he was a stalwart in the small Communist-aligned National Miners Union. He rose swiftly in the party, and in 1933 the CPUSA sent Sabatini to the International Lenin School (the Communist International's elite training academy), but he attended classes for only a few months before being recruited to work for the next two years as a Comintern courier throughout Europe.[38]

Sabatini fought in the Spanish Civil War with the Abraham Lincoln battalion. Records in Moscow show that he served with the Communist Party's "Control Commission," which exercised political discipline over Americans serving with the International Brigades. He held the rank of company political commissar, and one history of the Americans in the brigades noted his uncompromising speech calling for the execution of deserters. At some point, possibly in Spain, the KGB recruited him as an agent. In 1938 it dispatched him to France for a surveillance mission on KGB defector Walter Krivitsky. Sabatini returned to the United States in November 1938.[39]

From 1939 to 1943 Sabatini worked for the KGB on various support tasks, generally under the direction of Joseph Katz. At first he and another agent, Irving Schuman, continued surveillance of Krivitsky, then living in New York. Sabatini even rented an apartment across the street from Krivitsky's residence. Katz gave Sabatini and Schuman $400 to purchase peanut-vending machines, and they operated a business as a cover for a few months. Sabatini also ran a parking lot that adjoined one run by Katz. After Krivitsky's suicide in 1940, Sabatini worked regularly as a courier. One KGB report evaluating operations in the United States between 1939 and 1941 noted: "'There is, in addition, a group of valuable agents who are used for the station's operational activities (surveillance, background checks, removals, eavesdropping, etc)—'Informer,' 'Nick,' 'Veil,' 'Adam,' and 'Carmen' as a safe-house.'" These American agents were "Informer"/Katz, "Nick"/Sabatini, "Veil" (unidentified but possibly Irving Schuman), "Adam"/Eva Getzov, and "Carmen"/Helen Koral.[40]

Beginning in 1943, Sabatini lived in Los Angeles, employed by the Bohn Aluminum and Brass Company, which made shaped metal parts for aircraft plants, and worked under Gregory Kheifets, chief of the KGB San Francisco station. His most important contact was Jones York, a long-serving and valued KGB source in the aircraft industry. One year later, however, Sabatini reported that he was under surveillance and his telephone was tapped, so he stopped coming to meetings and warned his contacts that there should be no more communications. Although Sabatini thought that York might have betrayed him (or that York had come under suspicion and he had been observed visiting him), the explanation was different. In August 1943 J. Edgar Hoover received an anonymous letter identifying a number of Soviet diplomats as KGB officers. One of those named was Kheifets, officially a Soviet diplomat at the USSR's San Francisco consulate. The FBI put him under surveillance and in October watched as he "exchanged envelopes and packages on the streets of Los Angeles" with Sabatini. The FBI then installed wiretaps on Sabatini's phone and in January 1944 picked up a telephone call from someone who knew Sabatini and was trying to arrange a meeting. Sabatini told the caller he didn't know him and made other statements that indicated an effort to warn off the caller and break contact, a sign that he suspected his phone was tapped.[41]

Sabatini did nothing else to interest the FBI, and the surveillance ceased by the summer of 1944. Joseph Katz traveled to Los Angeles and met with Sabatini. He reported that he was ready to resume work, but Katz felt it unwise to continue to use him on the West Coast. In September Katz summoned him to New York. Several partially decrypted messages suggest that the KGB gave him a new assignment and worked out a cover story justifying his travels as part of his familial duties to care for his aged father. Other messages report that the KGB reimbursed him for expenses, and his wife received a $50 monthly stipend.[42]

The KGB deactivated Sabatini early in 1945, when he was inducted into the Army. Discharged in September 1946, he moved back to the Pittsburgh area. As discussed in chapter 2, in 1948 Moscow Center ordered him reactivated "to create a group on 'Enormous'"—that is, on atomic intelligence. But nothing came of this. Even as the KGB recontacted him, the FBI also showed up. He denied any covert work for the Soviets, and for the moment the FBI put him aside. But in 1949 the

Venona project decrypted a message that enabled the FBI to identify Sabatini as "Nick," and the Bureau's interest revived. It discovered that he had moved to California and was undergoing treatment for cancer. Questioned again, Sabatini offered limited cooperation. One internal FBI memo noted that he had provided information, "but only what he thinks we know." He discussed Katz, his surveillance of Krivitsky, and a few other details of his covert career. Of particular importance, however, he identified Jones York, which enabled the FBI eventually to expose William Weisband. Sabatini, suffering from throat cancer, died in 1952.[43]

Zalmond Franklin

Like Sabatini, Zalmond David Franklin was a veteran of the Spanish Civil War. He was born in 1909 in Milwaukee and studied bacteriology at the University of Wisconsin. His parents were immigrants from Russia, and his father was a physician active in Communist causes in Wisconsin. He and his father both went to Spain in 1937; his father worked as a doctor, and Franklin later told FBI agents that he worked as a bacteriologist at a Spanish Republican hospital. However, he was a member of the Veterans of the Abraham Lincoln Brigade and may have minimized the extent of his International Brigades connection. He also reported his American passport lost in Spain in 1938. The International Brigades had a policy (not always enforced) of confiscating the passports of its soldiers, and many of the Americans who fought with the International Brigades reported their passports "lost" when they returned from Spain.[44]

Franklin returned to the United States in 1938 (although the timing is not clear). A 1944 KGB report stated: "'Chap' [Franklin] was recruited for our work in 1938; for the most part he performs the function of a courier." It is likely that the KGB spotted and recruited Franklin while he was in Spain. Louis Budenz, a senior CPUSA official who departed from the Communist movement in a blaze of publicity in 1945, later testified that he had been told that Franklin had done "secret work" in Spain and after his return had been sent on clandestine missions to Canada on behalf of Soviet intelligence. Budenz explained that in 1937 the party sent him to Chicago to edit a new Communist newspaper, the *Midwest Daily Record.* He said that a KGB officer, Gregory Rabinowitz (a pseudonym used by Grigory Rabinovich) asked him to find someone in the Chicago area Communist Party who could infiltrate the Trotskyist movement, with a goal of moving to New York and obtaining a position at the Socialist Workers Party (SWP) headquarters. Jack Kling, head of the Young Communist League in Chicago, introduced Budenz to Sylvia Callen, a young Communist social worker who was anxious to help. Her married name was Sylvia Franklin, and Budenz learned that her husband, Zalmond Franklin, already worked for the KGB. Budenz recommended her; she successfully infiltrated the SWP, moved to New York, eventually became secretary to James Cannon, the SWP's leader, and fed the KGB information on its foe. The KGB provided an apartment for Zalmond in New York where he and his wife could rendezvous.[45]

Over the next few years, Franklin carried out a variety of courier jobs for the KGB. He served as a liaison for Martha Dodd Stern, her brother William Dodd, Abraham Glasser, and Michael Straight. Not all of these contacts went smoothly. From his first meeting with Franklin, Glasser "'began to show nervousness and distrust of 'Chap' [Franklin].'" The KGB did not blame Franklin because Glasser had been spooked by the defection of his previous contact, Armand Feldman, and he was being questioned by his superiors regarding his contacts with Russians. Martha Stern and William Dodd were also dissatisfied with him. The New York station noted: "'It is clear from the reports that the reason 'Chap' [Franklin] is not doing a good job of guiding these probationers is not that he is a poor group leader or is very underdeveloped politically or . . . his attitude toward his work, but that these sources require a more mature and authoritative figure.'" But, the station told Moscow, it didn't have anyone else available for the job. And despite his flaws, Franklin also had connections that the KGB New York station valued highly, such as his personal relationship with Clarence Hiskey, a scientist working on the Manhattan Project (discussed in chapter 2).[46]

However, Franklin's relationship with Sylvia Callen deteriorated, and the KGB was forced into marriage counseling. In February 1943 the KGB New York station told Moscow:

"We have noticed that in the past few months "Chap" [Franklin] has been upset, nervous about something. In late December, in a conversation with "Informer" [Katz], "Chap" declared that while he had still been in Spain he had been planning to divorce "Satyr" [Callen] when he arrived in the U.S., but after she was recruited for our work, "Chap" was dissuaded from divorcing "Satyr," that he didn't love "Satyr" and had married her by accident. He hadn't lived with her for about a year already, attributing this to illness. . . .

When "Informer" asked whether he was living with another woman, "Chap" replied 'no,' but admitted at the following meeting that he was in fact living with another woman. After two or three weeks "Chap" declared that he was, after all, still attached to "Satyr" and thought that he was wrong in saying that he didn't love her. This whole confusion of "Chap's" regarding his personal issues is no surprise to us, since he yields easily to influences. We gave an assignment to "Informer" to have a thorough discussion with "Chap" and to explain that he made a mistake by not telling us promptly about his acquaintance with another woman and trying to conceal that fact for several months."[47]

Franklin divorced Sylvia in 1943 and married Rose Richter in January 1944. His new marriage also got him in trouble with the KGB, this time when he boasted to his wife's relatives that he was working for Soviet intelligence. His brother-in-law, Nathan Einhorn, was executive secretary of the Newspaper Guild in New York, a Communist, and a KGB contact with the cover name "Egorn." Stepan Apresyan, KGB New York station chief, informed Moscow in May 1944 that Einhorn had told Bernard Schuster, the KGB's CPUSA liaison, that Franklin said "he worked for us and has a special task." Einhorn didn't believe him but thought such loose talk could cause problems and reported it to Schuster. This incident confirmed Apresyan's earlier judgment that Franklin was unsuited to intelligence work and should be put "into cold storage." Franklin would be instructed "to put an end to his criminal chatter about liaison with us." But the KGB New York station had a chronic need for couriers, and Franklin was not entirely put aside.[48]

When Jones York began cooperating with the FBI in the late 1940s, he identified Franklin as one of his couriers, and the FBI placed him under investigation. Louis Budenz also identified him as a KGB agent, although Budenz knew him only through Sylvia Callen and had no knowledge of the details of his work for Soviet intelligence. Years later, Michael Straight also told the FBI that Franklin had been one of his couriers. Franklin, who then worked for an optical instrument company, did not cooperate with the FBI. The Justice Department decided that there was not sufficient evidence it could use in court to warrant a prosecution. Franklin died in 1958.

Morris and Lona Cohen

By all odds among the longest-serving Soviet couriers were Morris and Lona Cohen. Morris Cohen had joined the American Communist Party in 1935, at age twenty-five. Two years later he was among the more than two thousand young American Communists who traveled to Spain to fight with the Communist-led International Brigades. He served with the Mackenzie-Papineau battalion, a nominally Canadian but largely American unit. Always an ideological militant, he quickly became one of the battalion's Communist political commissars. During fighting at Fuentes del Ebro in October 1937, Cohen was wounded and hospitalized. When he recovered, International Brigades officials sent him to a training course in covert radio operations at a secret Soviet-run school in Spain, where the KGB recruited him. A report written sometime in 1940 for the KGB indicated: "The greater part of those sent to Spain was chosen by the Comparty [Communist Party] leadership. The Party's confidence was borne out by many." Soviet authorities hired ten of these veterans "to work in the Soviet pavilion at the World's Fair in NY (as security guards, restaurant and movie theater employees, etc). Two of them still work in Amtorg: one as a chauffeur, the other in the restaurant (*the source Volunteer*)." *"The source Volunteer"* was Morris Cohen. He also worked as a substitute teacher in the New York schools. These, however, were his "day" jobs. His real work was for KGB officer Semen Semenov as a courier and talent spotter for new sources. In 1941 he married Lona Petka, a fellow Communist, and she soon became a full partner in his espionage.[49]

Drafted in mid-1942, Morris Cohen served in the Army until 1945. Before this involuntary leave from the KGB, however, he recruited one of his International Brigades comrades from Spain, Joseph Chmilevski, as a technical intelligence source (see chapter 6). While her husband was overseas, Lona Cohen was used by the KGB as a courier, even as she worked in two different defense plants. One note in the files indicates that the KGB formally recruited her in 1942. Semenov used her to pick up blueprints smuggled out of defense factories by agents; to contact Communist seamen to deliver and receive messages; and to communicate with William Weisband, then with the Army Signal Security Agency, through his brother. But in September 1944 Moscow Center recalled Semenov to the USSR after intense FBI surveillance had destroyed his usefulness, and Lona Cohen was "put on ice."[50]

Back in Moscow Semenov wrote a long report on his work in America for General Fitin. He was particularly effusive in his appraisal of the Cohens:

""Volunteer" [Morris Cohen].—Before going into the army he was used to receive materials from me at meetings with "Emulsion" [unidentified technical source] and as a talent-spotter, as well as for covering the activities and studying former members of the Lincoln Brigade in Spain. A lead was received from him and the highly valuable agent "Relay" [Chmilevski] was recruited with his help. He is fully aware of whom he's working with, he is sincerely devoted to us, ready to carry out any assignment for us. Exceptionally honest, mature, politically well versed. Ready to dedicate his whole life to our work. Upon returning from the army he should be used as our full-time illegal. He can be used along the following lines: a) as a courier; b) to select illegal operatives from among former veterans; c) to arrange safe houses and covers. He knows the restaurant business well; he could open a small snack bar that would serve as a meeting place to pass materials, letters, etc. "Volunteer" should be given full trust.

"Leslie" [Lona Cohen] ("Volunteer's" wife). Was recruited for contact with us by "Volunteer." Devoted to us. No special independent work should be assigned to her for now. She could work as a courier and take care of a safe house. Later she should work as "Volunteer's" assistant. Was used for contact with "Link" [Weisband] through the latter's brother."[51]

In January 1945 Leonid Kvasnikov, chief of technical intelligence at the KGB New York station, cabled Moscow asking for permission to reactivate Lona. In February Fitin approved "'the renewal of ties with her'" but cautioned: "'She does not have experience in our work, but she has already run small errands for the station in the past, for instance: contact with "Link's" [Weisband's] brother, etc. You should have a series of instructional talks with "Leslie" [Lona Cohen] regarding caution and secrecy in our work and also teach her a number of practical methods for checking oneself when going to a meeting, leaving a meeting, etc.'"[52] Lona was listed as a regular agent of the New York station in 1945, usually working under the direction of Alexander Feklisov. The KGB New York station used her on "Enormous," including one courier run to Los Alamos to pick up Theodore Hall's material. Along with many other agents, the KGB deactivated the Cohens in the late fall of 1945.

Moscow Center attempted to revive its American operations in 1948 and in April ordered the New York station to "renew ties with "Volunteer" and "Leslie" [Morris and Lona Cohen]. Volunteer—group handler, extensive connections among veterans, gave leads, recruited "Serb" [Chmilevski]. He was in the army from '42 to '45. "Leslie"—courier, "Volunteer's" wife. She was used to stay in touch with "Mlad" [Theodore Hall]." A week later Moscow followed up with an order to recontact Hall, who was finishing his PhD at the University of Chicago, via "Volunteer's group." Moscow wanted Hall to attempt to return to atomic bomb work at Los Alamos. The Cohens periodically met with Hall for the next few years.[53]

As the pace of the FBI's investigation of atomic espionage picked up in 1950, the Cohens remained under the FBI's radar. The KGB, however, didn't know that and took no chances. In March 1950 they were warned to prepare to flee the country, and in the summer they quietly left New York, making their way to the Soviet Union via Mexico. The FBI remained unaware of them until an informant in 1953 mentioned having known Morris Cohen as an ardent Communist. A routine check found that in mid-1950 Morris had abruptly resigned as a New York City school-teacher, and the couple had also abandoned their furniture in the apart-ment they hastily vacated. They had told their family that they were mov-ing to the West Coast, but correspondence from them had been brief, had not provided a new address, and then ceased. Although suspicious, the FBI had no leads until 1957, when it arrested Rudolf Abel (real name William Fischer), a KGB illegal officer operating under a false identity in the United States. In his safe deposit box the FBI discovered photographs of the Cohens, with recognition phrases used to establish contact between agents who have not met previously. Not surprisingly, that spurred a major FBI effort that generated information on their backgrounds but no real clues as to what had happened after they disappeared in 1950.

In 1961 the British Security Service rolled up a Soviet espionage ring that ran a source at the Portland Underwater Weapons Establishment, which carried out British nuclear submarine work. Among those arrested was a New Zealand couple, Helen and Peter Kroger, antiquarian book dealers who ran the ring's safe house and shortwave radio. A fingerprint check showed that the Krogers were the long lost Cohens. Defiant, the Cohens denied all, including refusing to admit their true identity. They received twenty-year sentences but were exchanged in 1969 for several Britons being held by the Soviet Union. After the exchange, the Cohens lived in Moscow on KGB pensions, lionized in their final years as heroes of Soviet espionage. Lona died in 1992, Morris in 1995.[54]

Kenneth Richardson

A handful of Americans did technical work for the KGB, serving as radio operators. By and large, Soviet intelligence used its own officers as radio operators. Most often, particularly in the 1930s and 1940s, it used ci-phered commercial telegrams and radiograms to and from Moscow as its primary means of quick communication. Lengthier reports and docu-ments were shipped in diplomatic pouches. The Soviet Embassy and con-sulates also had radio transmitters and used them as well—or, rather, tried to use them. Moscow Center sent Alexander Feklisov to the United States in February 1941 with orders to set up and run the station's shortwave radio transmitter. But Feklisov noted in a report: "We were unable to obtain radio transmitters for all of '41. We attempted to in late '41, but the transmitter sent by the Home [Moscow] didn't work well. We built a new one in the summer of 1942 with the help of agent "Condenser." "[55]

"Condenser" was Kenneth Richardson, who was born in Baltimore in 1884. By the early 1920s he was a wealthy man, owner of a factory that produced radio parts. He went bankrupt, however, and worked thereafter as a ship's radio operator. A longtime Communist, he married a woman who concealed her own Communist ties behind membership in the Daughters of the American Revolution. Richardson had been friends with Earl Browder since the 1920s. Jack Childs, a high-level CPUSA official who became a secret FBI informant in the 1950s, told the Bureau that Browder had selected Richardson to attend a Comintern training school around 1934 or 1935. He returned to New York in late 1936 and began work as a radio operator for a Comintern network.[56]

In 1939 Browder turned Richardson over to the KGB. A report states that the KGB sent him "to the USSR with his wife to study techniques of conducting illegal intel. work." He returned later that year but "was not actively used by us until 1942," when Feklisov needed assistance making the shortwave radio link work. He helped Feklisov by building "several radio transmitters for us for the needs of our stations in the West," for which he was paid $150 a month.

American law, however, required that long-range radio transmitters be licensed by the Federal Communications Commission. The Soviets had ignored the requirement, and in 1943 the government leaked to the press that the USSR was operating unlicensed radio transmitters from its embassy and consulates. In the Soviet view American regulations did not apply to their diplomatic facilities, but rather than argue about it, Moscow Center ordered the transmitters shut down, and the relationship with Richardson ended. The KGB revived contact in 1945, but in 1947 Feklisov offered a cautionary note:

"Condenser [Richardson] has great respect for and is devoted to "Helmsman" [Browder], whom he considers the most educated and experienced Marxist in the U.S. So it was a heavy blow to him when "Helmsman" was expelled from the party in early 1945 for pursuing a policy of conciliation with capitalism, which resulted in the weakening of the class struggle in the U.S. and a pullback by the Communist Party from leadership of this struggle. Although the split that had occurred in the party had apparently not affected "Condenser's" attitude toward our country and our work, it was still not hard to notice traces of a certain personal dissatisfaction with us, over our leaders' supposed indifference toward the affairs and fate of the local CP." . . . In the future he should be recruited for work only on condition that the relationship between us and "Helmsman" is good. He will work only after he gets consent from Helmsman.

Nothing more was written of Richardson in KGB documents in Vassiliev's notebooks. Given that relations between the Soviets and Browder only got worse, at some point Richardson and the KGB probably went separate ways.[57]

Lee Pressman

In 1950 Moscow Center criticized its Washington station for producing only limited intelligence. In an indignant reply, Washington placed the major blame for its problems on Bentley's defection, as well as on the large number of agents who had been exposed. But it also mentioned that "'Vig has chosen to betray us.'" On inspection, the defensive Washington station had exaggerated the extent of "Vig's" betrayal.[58]

"Vig" was Lee Pressman, a prominent figure in American labor history. Born in 1906, Pressman attended Cornell; was a classmate of Alger Hiss at the Harvard Law School, where he graduated second in his class; and worked with Hiss at the Agricultural Adjustment Administration of the Department of Agriculture, where they together attended meetings of its secret Communist unit, the Ware group. He later held staff positions with the Works Progress Administration and the Resettlement Administration and briefly practiced law in New York before he went to work for the labor movement in 1936, serving as general counsel for the newly organized CIO, working closely with its leader, John L. Lewis, and his successor, Philip Murray. Neither Lewis nor Murray had any Communist sympathies, but they were willing to work with Communist trade unionists as long as they were in charge. One of Pressman's unofficial roles in the CIO was liaison between the CIO's Communist faction and its predominately non-Communist leadership.[59]

Pressman's position in the CIO became more and more untenable as Murray slowly separated himself from his former Communist allies after World War II. When the CIO signaled that it would not tolerate its constituent unions supporting Henry Wallace's Communist-backed candidacy for president in 1948, Pressman resigned and went to work for the Progressive Party, running on its ticket for Congress. The House Committee on Un-American Activities subpoenaed Pressman during its investigation of Alger Hiss, but he invoked the Fifth Amendment to avoid answering questions. In 1950, however, after the outbreak of the Korean War, he resigned from the American Labor Party (the New York affiliate of Wallace's Progressive Party), charging that it had fallen under Communist sway. Subpoenaed again by Congress, this time he testified grudgingly. It was this testimony that provoked the KGB Washington station to tell Moscow in October, "'Vig has chosen to betray us,'" as well as the earlier comment to Moscow that "'Vig,'" apparently, has chosen the path of provocation."[60]

But Pressman had only partially betrayed the Communist cause. Like Alexander Koral and engineer spy Nathan Sussman (discussed in chapter 6), "Vig" found himself pressed by the FBI and potentially facing espionage-related charges, so he sought to make partial disclosures and offer partial cooperation to stave off prosecution while providing only a fraction of what he really knew. He admitted that he had been a CPUSA member from 1934 to 1936, naming John Abt, Charles Kramer, and Nathan Witt as fellow members of the Ware group, but he exonerated Hiss and, in any case, described the group as a harmless Marxist study group. And he acknowledged that despite not carrying a party card, he had considered himself to be a covert ally of the Communist Party until the late 1940s. Beyond that, however, he deceived, misled, and lied.[61]

In the late 1940s Pressman functioned as part of the KGB's support network. With many of its former sources exposed and facing grand juries, congressional investigations, and possible indictments, the KGB needed to assure its exposed agents of financial and legal assistance. Pressman, then in a private legal practice in New York, assisted in that task. In September 1949, acting through him, the KGB paid Victor Perlo $250 for an analysis of the American economic situation and, more generously, simply delivered $1,000 in October to relieve his economic distress (these sums are the equivalent of approximately $11,000 in 2008 dollars). The plan of work for the Washington station in 1950 summarized Pressman's task: "Vig—covering the activities of the Progressive Party. Receiving general information about the status of our exposed agents." A 1951 KGB report noted that Pressman had been its conduit for funds to pay for lawyers for Harold Glasser, Victor Perlo, and other members of the Perlo apparatus when they were subpoenaed by the House Committee on Un-American Activities, but no details or the extent of financial aid were specified.[62]

A KGB 1951 report also said, "'Vig' turned traitor; however, we do not know whether he betrayed "Ruble" [Glasser] to the Amer. authorities.'" But, in fact, Pressman had not betrayed Glasser or the other Soviet agents he had assisted earlier. Instead, when interviewed by the FBI, Pressman said that in the fall of 1949 Yury Novikov, a Soviet diplomat, had hired him to handle legal work for estates left by Americans to Soviet beneficiaries and consulted with him on other issues, including which lawyer to hire to defend Valentin Gubichev, a Soviet citizen arrested along with Judith Coplon and charged with espionage. Pressman said that he became increasingly uneasy about the relationship and feared he was being slowly drawn into murky waters. The legal relationship he admitted with the Soviet Embassy provided a plausible pretext to pass money to Pressman that he could then pass along to members of the Perlo group, and his story appears to have been crafted to explain meetings with a Soviet official that he feared he would have to explain. In fact, Novikov was a KGB officer; he appears in KGB files under the code name "Krok." (In 1953 the government declared Novikov *persona non grata* for his role in Soviet espionage.)[63]

Pressman also had assisted Soviet intelligence in the mid-1930s. In December 1948 Anatoly Gorsky prepared a report on Soviet sources who might have been exposed by defectors. Among those Gorsky listed as potentially compromised by Whittaker Chambers was "'Vig'—Lee Pressman, former legal adviser of the Congress of Industrial Organizations."[64]

Chambers told Assistant Secretary of State Berle in 1939 that Pressman had been a member of the Ware group and publicly repeated the assertion in 1948. At that time Pressman indignantly denounced Chambers's statement as "the stale and lurid mouthings of a Republican exhibitionist," only to reverse himself in 1950 and admit his participation in the Ware group. But Gorsky was writing about more than Chambers's revelation that Pressman had been a secret Communist in the mid-1930s. Chambers had also told Berle (and elaborated in the late 1940s) that in late 1936 or early 1937 GRU agent Philip Rosenbliett had asked him to find a lawyer willing to help with the purchase of arms for the Soviet-backed Spanish Republican government (illegal under American neutrality laws). Berle's notes indicated that Chambers had introduced Mack Moren (pseudonym of an unidentified GRU agent) to Pressman, then in private law practice in New York. Chambers stated that Pressman had accompanied Moren on a trip to Mexico to obtain American aircraft for use in Spain. During his 1950 testimony Pressman admitted meeting Whittaker Chambers in 1936 and stated that Chambers brought him a client, a J. Eckhart, who had credentials from the Spanish Republican government and wanted Pressman to accompany him to Mexico to assist in purchasing munitions. According to Pressman, they made the trip, but the mission did not succeed. But Pressman insisted that the affair had been a routine legal matter with no connection to espionage.[65]

Eckhart also appears in KGB documents. In the autobiography she wrote for the KGB in 1944 Elizabeth Bentley stated that in November 1936 one of her Communist contacts "'introduced me to one of the "neighbors'" [GRU's] operatives, who was involved in obtaining planes for Spain. Two meetings, then he left until the late spring of 1937. He was interested in getting into an Amer. aircraft plant, but his plan failed. He continued to keep in contact with me, but in the fall of 1937 he said that the work was finished and he was going home. He was called "Joe." He left in Jan. '38 after turning me over to his assistant, "Marcel."'" A note in Bentley's KGB file recorded that Moscow Center "sent an inquiry to the Red Army Intelligence Directorate in Dec. 1944." It responded, "'Joe' is an old GRU probationer who is living in NY and is in the active network. Marcel, too." In her 1945 FBI deposition Bentley elaborated that "Joe" was Joseph Eckhart and "Marcel" was Michael Endelman. The FBI located Endelman in 1947, then a UN employee. He admitted knowing Eckhart and Bentley in the mid-1930s and that he might have used the name "Marcel" with Bentley. He insisted that no espionage was involved but had no clear explanation for what had been going on aside from his having a sexual relationship with Bentley. The FBI did not locate Eckhart but determined that he had entered the United States in 1921 and become a citizen in 1935.[66]

While the KGB labeled Pressman a "traitor," his carefully limited testimony before the House Committee on Un-American Activities in 1950 and his interviews with the FBI sidestepped most of his knowledge of the early days of the Communist underground in Washington and his own involvement with Soviet intelligence, first with Chambers's GRU network in the 1930s and later with the KGB. He had never been the classic "spy" who stole documents. Neither his work in domestically oriented New Deal agencies in the early 1930s nor his later role as a labor lawyer gave him access to information of Soviet interest. Instead, he functioned as part of the KGB espionage support network, assisting and facilitating its officers and agents. He gambled that there would not be anyone to contradict his evasions and that government investigators would not be able to charge him with perjury. He won his bet, continued to practice labor law, faded from the limelight, and died in 1969.

The Espionage Enterprise

As the stories of these KGB couriers illustrate, espionage is more than the source who steals a document and the professional intelligence officer who recruits the spy and takes his material. There is an array of supporting personnel who make the espionage enterprise function: talent spotters, background checkers, radio operators, photographers, and couriers. Without the work of these mostly American agents, Soviet intelligence in America could have functioned at only a fraction of the effectiveness that it actually did.

of the German air force, Louis Ferdinand, grandson of
the Kaiser, and some guy in the French Embassy in Berlin.
(a real internationalist.)

The information about Udet, Martha offered herself.
Louis Ferdinand I had to press her on. (Noticed his name
mentioned several times in "The Diary.") She hated to admit
having had slept with Louis Ferdinand. She was most emba-
rassed — her face flushed red and she smiled in a most silly
manner. But immediately she added — this coyly — "I had a
contact in the French Embassy too." (Perhaps it was the guy
I was drinking for at this moment I felt slightly overwhelmed.
I considered for a moment to excuse myself and retire to the
washroom, stick my head in a basin of water — cold — and in
general overhaul myself. But realizing seriously, that I
must show poise to Martha, I called over the waiter and
ordered another drink — for Martha, I was under control).

(Perhaps I should look over the Diary for other "contacts."
Surely there must be other countries represented in this International Brigade — including the Scandinavian.)

I asked her why she slept with Udet. Her answer: Boris
(Winogradov) had told her to get next to every important
Nazi. Udet she considered important — so she slept with him.
And, so she says, she learned much from him. Winogradov had
not been in Berlin while she was having this affair with
Udet. When she told him (Winogradov) about it he did not object.
(He sure must have loved her.) I did not ask her why she had
slept with Louis Ferdinand or the "French contact." The girl
seemed to be suffering under my direct questions. I actually
felt sorry for her. (She is honest to say the least — she didn't
have to admit to these promiscuous relationships.)

I somewhat exposed myself to this very intelligent and
alert girl. In her mind she put two and two together and came
to the conclusion (this aloud) that this was the reason for the
delay. (Она члена Бюро ССССР — и.л.) She asked me if it was now a
rule that people in our work were not to have a sexual life.
Of course not, no such rule I answered. We are interested
in personal morals only when they reach the political plane.
They followed a discussion of when and when not were morals
morals to be considered political. Martha's attitude was not
belligerent or defiant but rather one of a student listening
to a Professor lecture. A most difficult situation to find
one's self in — lecturing on a subject never studied. But I
was in it and I had to see it through in a manner befitting
my position. Externally presenting a cool and confident
appearance, I lectured on middle class morals, proletarian
morals, when sex is permissible in our kind of work, when
not, discussion of hormones and sheep ovarian extract
influence on humans, etc. I lectured on more than I knew.

The above may sound most silly but it had a good effect on
Martha. She became very sober. And she remarked: "I should have
been told these things in Berlin. Nobody taught me anything

· ·

CHAPTER 8

Celebrities and Obsessions

The KGB, like any organization, had to make choices about where its assets would be deployed. From time to time it pruned its stable of agents, deactivating those who ceased providing information or whose security became endangered. At times a shortage of KGB officers necessitated breaking contact even with productive sources. But the KGB was also sometimes obsessed with the social status and celebrity connections of some of the agents it recruited and continued to remain in contact with them while nurturing the futile hope that they would produce useful intelligence. Meanwhile, it pursued ideological enemies with a fervor so intense and out of proportion to their threat that it sometimes interfered with efforts to obtain real secrets.

Martha Dodd and Alfred Stern

Franklin Roosevelt's appointment of William Dodd as ambassador to Germany in 1933 placed a well-known anti-Nazi academic in a crucial

---

A 1941 report written in English by an American agent of the KGB on his meeting with Martha Dodd, daughter of the American ambassador to Germany and a KGB source. Dodd discussed her use of sex to elicit information when she was at the American Embassy in Berlin in the mid-1930s. Courtesy of Alexander Vassiliev.

position dealing with the new Hitler regime. Martha, his daughter, cut a wide swath through Berlin, conducting affairs with a variety of diplomats and some leading figures in the Nazi regime, and began a relationship with the KGB that continued for decades. Martha Dodd had met Boris Vinogradov (a Soviet diplomat and KGB co-optee) at a social event at the Russian Embassy and offered to provide him with information, and "'he soon became her lover.'"[1]

By March 1934 Moscow Center had decided to formalize Dodd's heretofore ad hoc collaboration with Vinogradov, sending instructions: "'Tell Boris Vinogradov that we want to use him to carry out a project that interests us. It has to do with the fact that, according to our information, the sentiments of his acquaintance (Martha Dodd) have fully ripened for her to be recruited once and for all to work for us. So we request that V. write her a warm, comradely letter summoning her to a meeting in Paris, where an operative of ours whom V. knows personally will come. In Paris they will take the necessary actions to recruit Martha for our work.'" The recruitment was completed, and she was soon providing a steady stream of information to Vinogradov. When he was transferred back to Moscow, an *Izvestia* correspondent, Bukhartsev, replaced him, although not in her affections. At meetings in 1936 she described Moscow ambassador William Bullitt's views and behavior; conversations between steel magnate Krupp (unclear if this refers to Gustav Krupp or his son Alfred) and an American consul; and progress reports about her intensive study of Lenin under the tutelage of Mildred Fish Harnack, an American Communist married to a German. (During World War II both Mildred and her husband Arvid became leading figures in a GRU network known as the "Red Orchestra." Both were arrested. Arvid was hung and Mildred guillotined.) One KGB memo, apparently written sometime in 1936, included Martha's claim that she helped her father in his diplomatic work and was "up to date regarding everything he is doing." A KGB officer reported that "'Martha says the main interest in her life is secret assistance to the cause of revolution.'"[2]

While she professed her loyalty to the USSR, Martha's personal life complicated it. Her romance with Vinogradov, begun in 1934, did not diminish over time. She wanted to marry him; wrote him passionate letters that the KGB monitored; and, on a visit to Moscow in 1937, officially requested permission for them to wed. Vinogradov told Moscow Center:

"Everything went well with Juliet No. 2 [Martha Dodd], and I think you did a good thing by approving her visit to Moscow. But I don't quite understand why you have taken such an approving stance regarding our wedding? I asked you to tell her that this is completely impossible and in any case will not work out in the next few years. Yet you, according to her, spoke highly optimistically on this subject and decided on a postponement of only 6 months or a year. . . . I assured her in Warsaw before her trip to Moscow that if they tell her 'yes' there, then that's the way it will be, since she is dealing with highly authoritative people ('Manuilsky'). If no, then it's no. Six months will fly by quickly and who knows—she could present a bill of exchange, which neither you nor I intend to pay. Wouldn't it be better to make your promises somewhat less categorical if you indeed made them."

(Dmitry Manuilsky was a senior Comintern official and leading Stalinist. Dodd, however, had been confused or misled. The man in Moscow with whom she discussed marrying Vinogradov had been a senior Moscow Center officer, not Manuilsky. In her early years of contact, the KGB allowed her to think she was working for the Comintern. Later she would realize the truth.) In November 1937 the couple met in Warsaw (it would be the last time), and Vinogradov reported:

"The meeting with "Liza" [Dodd] was successful. She was in a good mood. She is leaving on 15 December for NY, where a meeting has been arranged with her. . . . "Liza" continues to be occupied with marriage plans and is waiting for me to carry out our promise, despite the fact that her parents have warned that nothing will come of it. The journalist Louis Fischer, who is not unknown to you, has proposed to "Liza." She is not giving her consent, since she hopes to marry me. But if we tell her that under no circumstances will I ever marry her, then she will not be averse to accepting Fischer's proposal. I don't think she can be left in the dark regarding the real state of affairs, because if we mislead her, she could become embittered and lose faith in us. At present she consents to work for us, even if it becomes clear that I won't marry her."

Unrequited love, however, turned out to be the least of Vinogradov's problems. The KGB arrested him and Bukhartsev as traitors and later shot them. The executions were secret, and it would be years before Martha realized that Vinogradov was dead.[3]

In early 1937, Abram Slutsky, chief of KGB foreign intelligence, forwarded to Nikolay Yezhov, people's commissar for internal affairs, a report Dodd wrote and noted the KGB's high hopes for her utility:

Some time ago we recruited Martha Dodd, the daughter of the Amer. ambassador in Germany. We made use of her brief trip to the USSR for detailed talks with her and determined that she has highly valuable capabilities and can be actively used by us on a broad scale. At our request, she has set forth herself her position in society, her father's position, and the prospects for her future work for us:

"Needless to say, my services, of any nature and at any time, are available to the party for it to use at its discretion. At present I have access mainly to the personal confidential correspondence of my father and the State Department, as well as the President of the US. The source of information on military and naval matters, as well as aviation, is solely personal contact with the personnel of our embassy. I have lost almost all contact with Germans, except perhaps for chance encounters and meetings in society, which yields almost nothing.

I still have contact with the diplomatic corps, but on the whole this doesn't produce much. I have established very close contact with journalists. The Germans, foreign diplomats and our own personnel are suspicious, hostile and (with regard to the Germans) insulting toward us. Is the information that I get from my father, who is hated in Germany and who is isolated among foreign diplomats, and therefore access for him to any secret information is closed, important enough for me to stay in Germany? Couldn't I do more valuable work in America or for some European organization like the International Peace Conference, or the Spanish Agency, which have a bourgeois cover and use bourgeois contacts? In America I'm not suspected of anything, except for the Germans, and I have countless valuable contacts in all circles. In other words, is my potential work valuable enough to stay in Germany, even for the time that my father is here?

I've done everything possible to make my father stay in Germany—I'm still going to continue doing everything I can in this direction—I'm afraid, however, that he will retire in the summer or fall. He has been of great use in turning the opinion of the Amer. govt. against the Nazis. At any rate that applies to Hull and Roosevelt—most of the State Dept. staffers are working with the Nazis."

Impressed that his foreign intelligence arm had recruited the daughter of an American ambassador, Yezhov sent the report, marked "Top Secret. Eyes Only" to Stalin, requesting "instructions regarding the use of Martha Dodd."[4]

After Martha decided to return to the United States, Moscow informed illegal station chief Iskhak Akhmerov in January 1938 that she was now in New York and provided contact information. But a monkey wrench soon intervened. Legal station chief Ovakimyan told Moscow in April that Dodd had been trying to find out Vinogradov's fate. Although one handwritten comment on the message advised that the New York station could accept a letter she wrote to him, the more important consideration was whether she was "'a deliberate accomplice'" of her now disgraced lover. Moscow Center advised the New York station: "'Entrust contact with Luisa [Dodd] to a worker whose failure [exposure] would not be very damaging to us; if L. is not giving valuable materials—leave her alone.'" A KGB officer in Moscow questioned Vinogradov, imprisoned and awaiting his fate, and he refused to implicate Dodd in his "crimes." Reassured, the KGB New York station put her in contact with Konstantin Kukin, personal secretary to the Soviet ambassador and a KGB operative.[5]

At their first meeting in June 1938 Dodd's first question was whether her paramour had been arrested. Reassured that he was alive and working in Moscow, she complained that she had not heard from him in more than a year and was anxious to learn whether their marriage was still a possibility or if she should go ahead and marry her American fiancé, Alfred Stern. Even if they did tie the knot, "'she does not think her marriage would get in the way of her work with us, although she is not altogether sure what she should do.'" A letter from Vinogradov duly arrived; he had not yet been executed, and the letter was dictated by the KGB. Martha happily wrote back, lamenting their sidetracked love and informing him that she had finally gotten married; she and her new husband hoped to travel to the USSR in the late summer and meet him, the man who "'meant more to me in my life than anybody else.'" Her persistent requests to Soviet diplomat Konstantin Umansky for assistance in getting a visa produced some concern and a decision to deny her permission to enter the USSR, but she eventually was talked out of her planned visit.[6]

With all these distractions out of the way, the New York station anticipated using Dodd to get contacts within the State Department. One potential target was the former American ambassador to Spain, Claude Bowers, an old friend of Martha's father. But it quickly became apparent to the KGB that Martha was not always very realistic about her opportunities. In December 1938 the New York station sent a letter to Moscow that her circumstances had dramatically changed: "Since becoming the wife of a millionaire, Liza [Martha Dodd] has experienced significant changes in her lifestyle; she lives in a luxurious apartment on 57th Street in New York, has two servants, a chauffeur, and a personal secretary." (Alfred Stern, born in 1897, was educated at Phillips Exeter Academy and Harvard. In 1921 he married Marion Rosenwald, daughter of the head of the Sears Roebuck mail order firm, and directed the Rosenwald Foundation for a decade. After divorcing his wife in 1936, he obtained a $1 million settlement.) Martha's ambitions, moreover, had expanded: "'She is very excited about her plan to travel to Moscow as the wife of the American ambassador. According to her, her husband is ready to give 50 thousand dollars to the Democratic Party fund if that post is promised to him. He hasn't heard anything concrete yet. He is currently seeking a means of getting to President Roosevelt through Wall Street. We already wrote to you that so far, his chances are very low.'"[7]

Most of Martha's energies went into editing her father's diaries, about his tenure as ambassador, for publication and writing her own account of her Berlin years, *Through Embassy Eyes*. Although there are few references to her in KGB documents recorded in Vassiliev's notebooks from 1938 to 1941, she impressed the KGB with her prowess; one memo evaluating "'agents working on diplomatic and political intelligence'" complained that as of 1 January 1939, most agents "'were of low value. Only two agents were very valuable'"—namely, Martha Dodd and Abraham Glasser. That September, Moscow instructed Ovakimyan that one of its priorities was ensuring the election of a New Deal supporter. To that end, it told him "'to gather compromising materials'" on FDR's opponents to discredit them. Martha was one of three agents suggested for this task, along with her brother and Congressman Samuel Dickstein.[8]

Notwithstanding Moscow's appraisal of her value, Martha was deactivated late in 1939 as part of the reduction-in-force occasioned by the withdrawal of many KGB officers from the United States. By August 1941, however, the KGB had resumed contact with her through Zalmond Franklin, one of the New York station's American couriers. It was undoubtedly a surreal experience for the former Lincoln Brigade soldier, who wrote one lengthy report about a meeting with Martha on 24 September. Under instructions to determine her attitude toward her previous handlers, several of whom had been shot as traitors, he heard a detailed account of her trysts with Vinogradov and her appeals to Stalin to allow them to marry, which he concluded might have been part of a plot by Vinogradov to flee the Soviet Union. Franklin gave a detailed account of Martha's musings about her attraction to Russians:

"MARTHA: I don't know. There's something about them (with glowing eyes). Maybe it's because I have such a hot-blooded nature. I react easily.

ME: Sometimes we must discipline ourselves. It's undesirable for people who have our kind of relationship to allow emotions to interfere in the relationship.

MARTHA: Why? What's wrong with that?

ME: It can be demoralizing. The work can suffer. The relationship will suffer because it becomes too intimate. People in love talk too much, especially in bed.

MARTHA: Yes, I suppose so.

Martha mentioned again that if we didn't permit Alfred to join the party, there would be a divorce. It seems to me that M. is ready to divorce him as it is. Her apparent excessive preoccupation with sex may reflect a stormy sex life. (If the reader is more than 40 years old, he should skip the following section.) Alfred is more than 40 years old. He isn't old, but he isn't young, either—a middle-aged man. A middle-aged man 'isn't what he was.' It may be that Alfred can't satisfy Martha. I firmly believe that if she is unable to go to the USSR, she will be disappointed, if for no other than sexual reasons."[9]

One week later Franklin and Dodd met again, and he "'bluntly and frankly'" inquired "'if her sexual relationship with her husband was satisfactory,'" given her previous comments about the possibility of divorce. Although she did not feel "'the wild love she felt for Boris Vinogradov,'" she assured Franklin that she "'loved her husband very much.'" That launched her on a disquisition about her life in Berlin that left Franklin agape:

"Seemingly, she spent most [of] her time in bed. In addition to the Russian or Russians, she slept with a full blown fascist—General Ernest Udet, second in command (next to Goering) of the German air force; Louis Ferdinand, grandson of the Kaiser; and some guy in the French Embassy in Berlin. (A real internationalist.) . . . She was most embarrassed—her face flushed red and she smiled in a most silly manner. But immediately she added—this coyly—'I had a contact in the French Embassy too.' (Perhaps it was the gin I was drinking but at this moment I felt slightly overwhelmed. I considered for a moment to excuse myself and retire to the washroom, stick my head in a basin of water—cold—and in general overhaul myself. But realizing, seriously, that I must show poise to Martha, I called over to the waiter and ordered another drink—for Martha. I was under control.) (. . . Surely there must be other countries represented in this International Brigade—including the Scandinavian.)

I asked her why she slept with Udet. Her answer: Boris (Vinogradov) had told her to get next to every important Nazi. Udet she considered important—so she slept with him. And, so she says, she learned much from him. Vinogradov had not been in Berlin while she was having this affair with Udet. When she told him (Vinogradov) about it he did not object. (He sure must have loved her.) I did not ask her why she had slept with Louis Ferdinand or the 'French contact.' The girl seemed to be suffering under my direct questions. I actually felt sorry for her. (She is honest to say the least—she didn't have to admit to these promiscuous relationships.) . . .

She asked me if it was now a rule that people in our work were not to have a sexual life. Of course not, no such rule, I answered. We are interested in personal morals only when they reach the political plane. . . . Martha's attitude was not belligerent or defiant but rather one of a student listening to a Professor lecture. A most difficult situation to find one's self in—lecturing on a subject never studied. But I was in it and I had to see it through in a manner befitting my position. Externally presenting a cool and confident appearance, I lectured on middle class morals, proletarian morals, when sex is permissible in our kind of work, when not, discussion of hormones and sheep ovarian extract influence on humans, etc. I lectured on more than I knew. The above may sound most silly but it had a good effect on Martha. She became very sober. And she remarked: 'I should have been told these things in Berlin. Nobody taught me anything there. I see your point.' And then later: 'I don't want to seem to be trying to impress you but I don't want you to have the wrong impression of me. I am not weak on these matters. If you tell me not to have a sexual affair in the S.U. I won't.'

Sometime during our conversation—I don't recall exactly when—Martha made the remark that all men were vulnerable . . . somewhere. Does this mean, I asked her, that you feel that you could sleep with most any man if you so chose? 'Yes.' she said. And then: 'It might be advantageous at times.' (This she meant in terms of political work.)"

Franklin was impressed: "'This is a worldly wise girl. . . . I believe her to be sincere.'" Moscow Center, however, was less so, seeing no intelligence value in her suggestion that she and her brother come to the Soviet Union as journalists, preferring that she work either in the Middle East or the United States. An undated memorandum that likely was written in this period noted that although "'she considers herself a Communist and states that she recognizes the party's program and statutes,'" Martha was "'a typical representative of American Bohemia, a woman who has become sexually depraved, ready to sleep with any handsome man.'"[10]

However scandalized by her sexual mores, the KGB gratefully accepted her intelligence assistance. She delivered a report of a meeting that she and her brother had held with Secretary or State Cordell Hull, and in late December 1941 Martha discussed her contacts with various exiled German writers, indicating that Leon Feuchtwanger was "'very reliable'" and "'must have at his fingertips many many French names useful for us. I am sure he would not hesitate to cooperate fully if he knew the source asking for it.'" She also recommended Jurgen Kuczynski (an exiled German Communist; see chapter 2), whom she knew "'to be perfectly reliable from the Harnacks and from my own observation and experience with him. He worked for the Freedom station at one time and as far as I know has never deviated an inch on any matter whatsoever.'" He "'would be more valuable and trustworthy for us than anyone I know besides the Harnacks in Berlin.'"[11]

Moscow Center was pleased but informed Zarubin in January 1942 that Dodd required "'constant supervision of her behavior. It is essential to give her firm guidance, get her interested in our work, and direct her energy toward benefiting our cause.'" She needed to be "'oriented toward getting close and getting introduced to the president's wife, Eleanor, on the line of various public organizations, committees, societies, etc. Here we should make use of the special interest that the Roosevelts show in China and everything related to it.'" Moscow insisted she sever her social ties to staff at the Soviet Embassy. Finally, Martha had to not only "'refrain from recruiting her husband for our work and letting him know about it, but must also not recruit him into the party, which, judging by your last letter, she is stubbornly trying to do.'"[12]

These strictures, however, had little effect on the headstrong Dodd. In early February she reported that Alfred had seen Loy Henderson at the State Department and renewed his campaign for a diplomatic position. She insisted that "'it would be a great mistake if he were not obtained for our work.'" Because of his earlier marriage to a member of the Rosenwald family, he had wide connections with wealthy Americans. Martha was "'sure he could recapture many of his past friends over a period of time,'" although "'if he were forced constantly to meet useless, worthless high society people, the dregs of the capitalist system, he would be thrown back into the frustrated miserable state he was in when he was married to the Rosenwald family.'" He needed a productive job. She also reported that he had recently joined the CPUSA, but Martha felt "'that he is not being used to his fullest capacity by the Party and is at the same time being exposed by them. Therefore again I urge, after full discussion of all the above points, that he be accepted for work with us.'"[13]

No reply to that report is in Vassiliev's notebooks, but Moscow must have relented because in March, Martha wrote that she had discussed her underground work with Alfred, without specifying exactly for whom she worked: "'He was enthusiastic about the work and wanted to do something immediately'" but "'stated that he could not work for any organization that did not include Communists and that did not follow the policy of the Soviet Union.'" They had discussed his forming some kind of business or going into government work. While reluctant to do the former, he was willing to consider it

"if I [Martha] could suggest how it could be done without arousing suspicion and adverse criticism, and without jeopardizing his funds. He argued that if he lost his money he could be of comparatively little use to the progressive movement and would not be able to maintain a covered social and moneyed posi-

tion to attract other contacts. . . . I asked him to get the names of as many
business firms as possible who still traded with neutral countries or had men
who traveled to Europe who in any way could be considered reliable. I told
him this was to establish a means of getting money and messages to people in
occupied countries. He fully understood this. . . . He recognizes the secrecy of
the work, is anxious and enthusiastic to help."

Martha suggested he meet with Elizabeth Zarubin and added that Alfred
"'also asked if he would have to discontinue his class in Marxist theory. I
told him I thought so but that somehow or other we might arrange for
him to have a two hour conference once a week discussing what he has
read with one of the underground workers. He agreed to this, urging only
that he continue his studies, otherwise he would be a less effective person in every way if he did not master the theory of Marxism which he has
been practicing for so long.'" She repeated her demand that he "'be taken
in to our work. If he is not seen I must resign, as he is exposing both of
us,'" since his activities in the American Labor Party required him to associate closely with Communists.[14]

Martha Dodd followed this demand with another letter in which she
explained that she had gone a bit further, telling Alfred Stern that the organization with which she was connected was not dealing with refugees
but illegally plotting "'the overthrow of Hitler in occupied countries'"
and that its activities were directed from the USSR. As she "'knew he
would be, he was extremely enthusiastic and extremely thankful that the
work was in such reliable hands.'"[15]

Zarubin discussed Martha's letters in a message to Moscow in April,
explaining that the increasing ties between the Sterns and various Communists had been hurting Martha's ability to develop "'interesting connections'" and her proposal to recruit Alfred had been her solution. He
was scornful of their amateurish effort to buy an ambassadorship for Alfred, noting that he lacked "'any attributes that would support seeking
such a career.'" Nevertheless, the station had recruited him, and "Louis,"
as he was dubbed, "'knows who he is working for, and he is gradually assimilating the rules and interests of our work.'" Zarubin was not overly
impressed by his potential. While Martha thought that Alfred was "'a
brilliant man with the qualities of a leader,'" he actually "'conveys the
impression of a man of average abilities, not very smart, but energetic
and with quite a bit of initiative. He seems to be an honest and modest
man. He has a very good attitude toward us.'"[16]

Moscow was even less impressed. A message sent to Zarubin in June
complained that Martha's reports "'are of no practical value.'" Her old

connections in Europe had become useless, and her assessments devoted "'more attention to describing their appearance ('a blond man,' 'pretty eyes,' and so forth) than to information about how these people could be useful to us in our work.'" (She did, however, spot and recommend Jane Foster for recruitment. Foster worked as a KGB agent while on the staff of the OSS and after World War II in Europe until the mid-1950s; see chapter 5.) In late 1943 Moscow ordered New York to "'deactivate agents without future prospects,'" including Martha Dodd.[17]

Vasily Zarubin had, however, figured out a way to use Alfred Stern. In 1936 Zarubin had first contacted a Russian émigré working as a musical producer for Paramount Pictures, Boris Morros, and in return for assistance to his relatives, still living in Russia, Morros obtained a cover job for Zarubin as a Paramount talent scout in Germany. Morros also agreed in 1943 to join with a wealthy investor in a sheet music company that would serve as a cover for Soviet espionage. In December Zarubin and Morros visited the Sterns at their Connecticut home, and Alfred invested $130,000 (over $1.5 million in 2008 dollars) in the Boris Morros Music Company. In the fall of 1944 Zarubin handed supervision of Morros and Stern to Jack Soble. But by early 1945 Morros had frittered away the initial capital. During one trip to Hollywood, Stern and Morros got into a heated argument. Jack Soble explained to Moscow that instead of publishing sheet music, as had been planned, Morros had decided to manufacture records, a decision that complicated future plans to use the business to provide cover for hiring agents in foreign countries. All of Stern's initial investment of $130,000 was gone; so were virtually all of Morros's funds, and he wanted Moscow to invest another $150,000. Soble was skeptical, warning that the business was unlikely to succeed with Morros in charge and that Zarubin "'made a big mistake'" in trusting him with so much money and guaranteeing Stern that his investment would be protected without his having any responsibility for the business or risk. Moscow issued instructions to liquidate the company, pay Stern $100,000, and assure him that it would give him an opportunity "to conduct a commercial operation with Amtorg so that he can recoup his losses." Anatoly Gorsky, Washington station chief, assured Moscow in June 1945 that the incident had not soured Alfred on working with the KGB: he remained ready and willing "to invest up to 250,000 Am. dollars into any solid business of our choosing." The Sterns' usefulness, however, never very impressive, was coming to an end. A memo records that they were both deactivated in 1945.[18]

By 1948, however, a new set of KGB officers manned the station, and they had very few sources, making eager, if dilettantish, old agents like the Sterns more attractive. Valentin Sorokin, a KGB co-optee and staff member of the Soviet Information Bureau, met them at a January party attended by Communist writers like Howard Fast, James Allen, and A. B. Magil. Martha asked to meet with one of the Soviet operatives whom she had known in Berlin. The Center suggested Sorokin probe how she felt about the USSR, "what capabilities she has for work as a talent-spotter," and whether the KGB should resume meeting with her. At other meetings she chastised the Soviets for maintaining ties with Earl Browder, began demanding more secretive ways to arrange future meetings, revealed that she had contacted a Soviet consular official to check on Sorokin's bona fides ("'After all, we don't know whether you're a good Sov. cit. or some Kravchenko [Soviet defector], maybe after the meeting with us you'll go to the FBI and tell them everything'"), and boasted of the Sterns' close ties to Henry Wallace. Martha explained that they could influence him, "'but we need to receive direction.'" Sorokin asked her to provide information about Michael Straight and the *New Republic* and to compile a memorandum on American writers and Alfred to do an analysis of the Progressive Party. That concerned Alfred, who said, "'As long as it was a matter of talk and discussion, that was one thing, but writing for you is something else. In the first case everything remains words. Nobody can prove that we were the ones who said this. A document is different.'" While he was willing to write the analysis, he wanted clarification of Sorokin's status. The Sterns were convinced that American security was watching them and that their phones were tapped.[19]

These meetings produced little besides political gossip from Progressive Party circles and claims about the Sterns' influence. Martha maintained that Wallace had asked her to write campaign speeches, and she wanted the Soviets to give her themes; that elicited a warning from Moscow that using her for such work was "inadvisable." Alfred asked Sorokin to tell Soviet authorities that it could assist the Wallace campaign by having a senior official, such as Andrey Vyshinsky, deliver a speech recalling "'the joint struggle by the USSR and the U.S. against fascist Germany and precisely what the USSR did, what casualties it suffered in order to save the world and in particular the U.S. from German fascism.'" Alfred claimed such a speech "'would make an impression. We need this right now.'" The Washington station wrote to Moscow that in its view Martha was "'talkative, not completely serious, and not secretive enough. Keeps trying to impose herself for establishment of an agent contact.'" It recommended against reestablishing an agent relationship.[20]

When Olga Kasenkina, a teacher at the Russian Consulate in New York, decided to defect in 1948, the consul, Yakov Lomakin, led a raid on the upstate farm where she had sought refuge, forcibly brought her to the consulate, and refused to allow her to leave, at one point displaying a visibly drugged woman who, he claimed, now wanted to go home. When state Supreme Court justice Samuel Dickstein (himself a one-time Soviet agent) ordered her appearance in court, Lomakin refused to comply. The next day, Kasenkina jumped out of a window. Severely injured, she was rescued over the furious protests of consular officials, taken to a New York hospital, where she recovered, and was granted political asylum. The Sterns complained about the inept way the affair had been handled, and Martha insisted that it had convinced her of the need to reactivate "'our group'" to give advice to such Soviet leaders as Molotov and Vyshinsky.[21]

The Sterns' behavior only became more bizarre. In mid-1949 Martha gave Sorokin a list of fifty-three people who were potential contacts. It was in the form of a movie script, with thumbnail sketches of such people as Howard Fast, Herbert Biberman, John Abt, and Charles Kramer. The undermanned station thought the information she provided was insufficient and was unable to check the names out. The Sterns were transferred to another KGB officer a month later and, while attending a reception at the Soviet Embassy drank too much and "behaved indiscreetly," introducing the two officers to each other. The KGB dropped contact with them.[22]

But the KGB was not yet through with this odd couple. In March 1955, still in dire need of leads for agents and sources, it decided to reactivate them but discovered they lived most of the year in Mexico. Moscow Center asked the Mexico City station to investigate and determine if Martha was a suitable and willing candidate for "'re-establishing a confidential relationship.'" But in the midst of this renewal, the Sterns came under increasing pressure from congressional subpoenas and possible indictment for espionage. After Jack Soble's spy ring was exposed, they asked for assistance in leaving Mexico. Their Mexican attorney paid $10,000 to a Paraguayan diplomat who arranged for them to become naturalized citizens and given Paraguayan passports. They went into exile in Czechoslovakia and promised to "continue cooperating" with the KGB. Once there, they pondered moving to Moscow or China, offered to donate artwork and a Mexican villa to the Soviets, and demanded that the KGB help extract a friend, Maurice Halperin (discussed in chapter 5), from Mexico since he was known to American authorities as a Soviet agent. Moscow Center was not anxious to have them settle in the Soviet Union, rejected the villa for fear it could cause diplomatic problems, didn't want the paintings ("otherwise we will find ourselves indebted to the Sterns"), and explained that Halperin had already applied to come to the USSR and his case would be moved ahead.[23]

The Sterns were upset they were refused permission to live in the USSR and also complained that Jack Soble had bilked them out of money. The KGB reversed course and arranged their visit to Moscow in September 1957, but they eventually decided to seek permanent residence in Czechoslovakia. In a letter delivered to the Czechoslovak Embassy in Moscow, Alfred explained:

"After careful thought and experience we believe that Czechoslovakia is the country in which we can best adjust for the following reasons: 1. We are more familiar with the customs, habits and way of life in Czechoslovakia. 2. Until we can acquire a working knowledge of the Czech language we are able to communicate more freely with most of the people with our limited knowledge of German. 3. We are attracted to the quieter way of life and to the more western living conditions. Quite simply, we immediately loved the country and its sturdy spirited people. Czechoslovakia is a beautiful and extremely important country, a model in the heart of Europe of socialism in the making. We want to contribute to its future in whatever way we are qualified. My wife thinks she could be an editor and reader for a publishing house which translates and publishes books in the English language, or help in any other place where the understanding and writing of English is very important. She also wants to continue her own creative writing. I feel I can fit into and contribute most to some aspect of the export-import field and perhaps advise in other lines such as housing."

Before departing for Prague in January 1958, Alfred, who had been involved in public housing construction in the 1930s, sent Soviet leader Nikita Khrushchev a letter offering to discuss housing and delivered a detailed critique of Soviet apartment construction to authorities.[24]

The Sterns soon grew bored with Czechoslovakia. (Earlier they had also sought permission to move to Communist China, but the government had refused to admit them.) Enamored by the glamour of Fidel Castro, they moved to Cuba in 1963, but that adventure paled and they returned to Prague in 1970. Wanting the option of returning to the United States, where they remained under indictment for espionage, beginning in 1975 they offered to meet FBI agents in a Communist country to try to get the charges against them dismissed, but they would not agree to government demands for an interview in a Western nation. The KGB was not inclined to interfere, and Moscow Center told its Prague station:

"If the Sterns manage to reach an agreement with the Amer. authorities to drop the past charges filed against them, we will scarcely be able to block their effort to move to the U.S. for permanent residence. In that case it cannot be ruled out that their return may be used by the adversary for propaganda purposes to whip up spy mania, even though those events occurred a long time ago and were widely publicized in connection with the trial of "Czech" [Soble] and "John" [Morros]. The information that the Sterns may possess about the activities of Sov. intelligence is outdated and mostly known to the adversary from the testimony of the traitor "John." Based on the foregoing, if we receive an official inquiry from the relevant agencies of the CSSR [Czechoslovak Socialist Republic] regarding the Sterns, we deem it possible to respond that there are no objections on our part to their moving to the West."

The final chapter in their saga came during the Carter administration, when the Sterns enlisted the assistance of Congressman Don Edwards (D-CA). Insisting that the indictment had little basis, he persuaded the Justice Department to drop the charges. The FBI objected unless the Sterns agreed to provide a candid statement of their activities, but the charges were dropped in 1979 with no requirement of any cooperation from the Sterns. (Alfred arranged campaign contributions for Edwards both before and after this episode.) The Sterns, nonetheless, decided not to return to the United States after all. Alfred died in 1986, and Martha Dodd Stern died in Prague in 1990.[25]

Boris Morros

The Sterns performed some useful tasks for the KGB but never came close to living up to the potential Moscow saw in them. But if they were a disappointment, the assistance provided to the KGB by Boris Morros, their one-time business partner, was eventually dwarfed by the damage he inflicted.

A Soviet diplomat working with the KGB first met Morros in 1934, when he came to the New York consulate to arrange for his father's return to the USSR. He had five brothers in the USSR, and several were Communist Party members, and his father was going back because of his avowed disgust with living in a capitalist country. Boris, who was born in Russia in 1895, had made his way to the United States in the early 1920s and worked for Paramount Studios chiefly on projects arranging music for films. The report on his visit to the consulate noted that he might be amenable to providing cover jobs at Paramount for "'our workers.'" In subsequent conversations, Morros was assured that he was trusted and his brothers respected, and he agreed to obtain a job for someone in Paramount's Berlin office, provided the person was knowledgeable about the industry, spoke German, and was not Jewish. Morros understood "'that this is not an ordinary favor he is doing for a Soviet official.'" The man to whom he eventually provided Paramount credentials, known to him as Edward Herbert, was Vasily Zarubin, an experienced Soviet intelligence officer and later station chief in the United States.[26]

Moscow Center stated that "'having an opportunity to get our illegals jobs at capitalist companies appeals to us,'" calling Morros "'a valuable acquisition, one worth holding onto,'" and envisaged placing its agents in Paramount offices around the world, particularly in the Far East, but agreed that it would be a mistake to put too much pressure on Morros too quickly, lest he be scared off. In addition to using Morros to give its agents cover jobs abroad, Moscow wanted to use him to get people visas to enter the United States. Meanwhile, Morros reported that he had been promoted to a Paramount Studios executive office post in Hollywood, and the KGB anticipated having him admit its agents to Paramount's training programs as "'a wonderful way to create cadres for underground work abroad.'"[27]

When Morros returned to Russia in August 1935 to visit his dying mother, the KGB arranged to meet him in Moscow "'to agree with him on a plan for use.'" But, when he returned to the United States, the New York station began to worry about his commitment and veracity. A KGB officer traveled to Los Angeles in December to contact Morros but was first rebuffed by a secretary, had to use a ruse to reach him on the telephone, and even then sensed coldness. When they finally met, Morros pleaded that the press of business had prevented him from carrying out a KGB assignment. Operative "Archimedes" also concluded that Morros was not as highly placed at Paramount as he had led the KGB to believe, a fact confirmed at a later meeting, when Morros admitted that "'his functions are minor and administrative'" and that he had no authority to hire anyone. Assimilating this information, station chief Peter Gutzeit concluded that Morros wanted to break his ties to the KGB and, in any case, lacked the opportunities to help that he had promised. His location in far-away Los Angeles limited the ability to pressure him (at that time the KGB had little presence on the West Coast), but Gutzeit promised to meet him again in a few months and try to persuade him to help.[28]

Even though Morros was not to be the magical source of cover jobs for KGB agents envisioned earlier, he did give concrete assistance to Zarubin, who attested to his usefulness in a 1938 report, noting that Morros had provided papers that had enabled him to function effectively in Germany for three and a half years and had regularly sent him money. Since Morros was so busy, all of these arrangements had been handled by his secretary, giving the relationship a protective veneer of ordinary business dealing. Zarubin noted that Morros's potential had not been realized: his large number of contacts in both the United States and abroad had never been cultivated properly, and he had been neglected. But now he "'can and should be used primarily as someone who can arrange for our people to be legalized.'" Zarubin concluded by noting that "'everything this man says or promises, he does.'"[29]

Despite this endorsement, contact with Morros remained sporadic for the next several years. Moscow Center requested that he be contacted in late 1940, and Ovakimyan met him in New York in November. He reported that even after a two-year hiatus, Morros, code-named "Frost," was willing to help and was "well-disposed toward us." (Boris's original Russian name, "Moroz," is also the Russian term for frost.) Although he was not immediately given an assignment, in February 1941 Ovakimyan conveyed a request that he help obtain visas for three people to enter the United States. That request was apparently not fulfilled because some time later a query from Moscow asked about the status of that project and whether Morros would consider going to Japan, using the pretext of studying Japanese music to renew his claimed ties with the brother of the prime minister.[30]

Morros's relationship with the KGB moved to a new level at the end of 1941. Vasily Zarubin arrived on the West Coast from the USSR en route to his new posting in New York as KGB station chief. Before traveling east, he met with Morros in Los Angeles; in April he wrote a report for Moscow that his old friend had "made a very good impression." He was, however, worried about his family in Russia, who faced a variety of difficulties. Zarubin asked that they receive assistance and that news of their situation be sent every month to help cement Morros's loyalty. Morros had agreed to create business cover jobs for two people in Switzerland; one, "West," would be tasked to lift the Swiss ban on one of Morros's movies, *The Flying Deuces*. The KGB fulfilled its part of the bargain, at least in part. It not only provided money and better living conditions for some of Morros's family in Russia, but it also allowed his father to immigrate to the United States in 1942 "as a special case."[31]

But while the KGB's foreign intelligence arm arranged for assistance to Morros's family, its internal security arm had wreaked havoc on it. In October 1946 the KGB prepared a memo on the fate of Boris's brothers and sisters who remained in the Soviet Union. In bureaucratic prose it laid out the tragedy of a family in the Stalin era. While two sisters and one brother escaped the attention of the Soviet security services, four other brothers did not:

"A brother, Yuly Mikhailovich Moroz, b. 1906 in Zaporozhie, UkrSSR, [Ukrainian SSR] higher education, non-Party man; worked as an economist on the Volkhovsky Front Directorate until 1943. In December 1943, the Volkhovsky Front Military Tribunal sentenced Y. M. Moroz to 10 years' imprisonment, with 5 years' subsequent disenfranchisement with confiscation of personal property, pursuant to article 58–10, part 2 and 193–17 'a' of the UK RSFSR [Criminal Code of the Russian Socialist Federal Soviet Republic]. Following a petition by the NKGB [People's Commissariat of State Security] USSR in July 1944, Moroz was released early by decree of the Presidium of the Supreme Soviet of the USSR and sent to the front. While at the front, M. was awarded the Order of the 'Red Star' and medals: 'For the capture of Warsaw' and 'For victory against Germany.' M. currently lives in Leningrad. . . . He works at the Trade Institute.

A brother, Savely Mikhailovich Moroz, b. 1912 in the city of Zaporozhie, USSR, incomplete higher education, worked as an engineer on engine maintenance and repair for the 'Artiksnab' organization. In January 1944, the Irkutsk Region Court sentenced S. M. Moroz to 10 years' imprisonment, with confiscation of all his personal property and with 5 years' subsequent disenfranchisement, pursuant to statute p. 'a' p. 31 of the UK RSFSR from 7 August 1932. Following a petition by the NKGB USSR in October 1944, S. M. Moroz was released early by decree of the Presidium of the Supr. Soviet of the USSR and sent to the front. In 1945, following demobilization from the army, S. M. Moroz went to live in the city of Zaporozhie, where he continues to live at pres. . . .

A brother—Aleksandr Mikh. M., b. 1900 in the city of Bobruysk, worked as chairman of Starobelsky city council of the Donetsk Region until 1937. In Dec. 1937, A. M. M. was sentenced to VMN [Supreme Penalty: execution] by the Military Board of the Supr. Soviet of the USSR for participation in a counterrevolutionary Trotskyite terrorist org. His wife, Lyubov Grigorievna M., was sentenced to 8 years' imprisonment by the Special Board in Dec. 1937, as a family member of a traitor to the Homeland.

A brother, Zaromsky—Isaak Mikh. Moroz, b. 1898 in the city of Bobruysk, has an incomplete higher education in law. Worked until 1938 as chairman of the Region Planning Commission in the city of Yoshkar-Ola in Mariysk ASSR [Autonomous Soviet Socialist Republic]. In 1938, he was arrested by the organs [units] of the Mariysk ASSR NKVD [People's Commissariat of Internal Affairs]. I. M. M.'s current whereabouts are unknown. According to documents in his file, in 1942–43 he was living in the city of Tulun in the Irkutsk Reg.; according to the same files, I. M. M. died in a prison hospital in 1938."

How much of the fate of his brothers Boris Morros knew is difficult to say. His father would surely have told him something about the 1937 and 1938 arrests of two of his brothers, but not necessarily their fate. Boris's brother Aleksandr had been shot in 1937, but most executions during the Terror were secret, and family members were often told that the prisoner had been sentenced to the Gulag without the right of communication. Years later they might get a notice that the prisoner had died of an illness.[32]

Through 1943 the KGB toyed with ways to use Morros more productively. Zarubin hit upon the scheme to create a new business, the Boris Morros Music Company (discussed above), which would provide cover jobs for KGB agents, and he persuaded Alfred Stern to finance it. In a report he wrote for Moscow in September 1944, Zarubin boasted about the company's great promise and pledged it would be ready for "'us to use as a cover'" by the winter. "'We can trust F . . . t ["Frost"/Morros]; he won't take off with the money.'" Pleased by his role in midwifing a potentially valuable KGB asset, Zarubin handed Morros off to Jack Soble upon his recall to Moscow in mid-1944.[33]

It soon became apparent that Morros was not as reliable as Zarubin had thought. The business collapsed and hopes that the Morros Music Company would provide a cover for KGB operations came to nothing. Soble's 1945 report on the investment fiasco soured the KGB on Morros for a time. In addition to his commercial incompetence, he had also boasted that he knew Beria personally and that Zarubin had introduced him to Molotov during one of his New York visits. Just as worrisome as his garrulousness was his inability to observe elementary security precautions. In June 1945 he called Soble at the latter's apartment in New York, demonstrating not only that he knew his real name, but also possibly exposing him to the FBI. Anatoly Gorsky, the new American station chief, reported that Morros "knows which organization he works for; he is not averse to boasting about it, and sometimes, completely out of place, he will bring up his acquaintance with Cde. Pavel [Beria]." Notwithstanding his wide circle of acquaintances, he was also a scamster; he had

recently summoned Soble to Chicago to give him urgent information he
had obtained from Archbishop Francis Spellman, widely considered the
most powerful Catholic prelate in America, but as soon as he relayed it,
Soble realized it was a warmed-over report from a recent *New York Times*
article. Gorsky also warned that Soble thought Morros viewed the KGB
"as a goldmine from which he can extract money."[34]

Moscow took the warning signs to heart and on 14 June ordered that
Morros be deactivated and that Soble stay away from him because of the
danger. "'Under no circumstances'" should he meet Morros. Yet in De-
cember Soble reported that on Morros's invitation, he had visited him in
New York to hear that the record business stock had been largely sold,
Morros was back making movies, and he was willing to partner with the
KGB to create a distribution company to release them if it would ante up
$200,000.[35]

While it appears that the KGB decided to pass on this opportunity,
Jack Soble, like Zarubin before him, had joined the Boris Morros fan
club. In a report he wrote in August 1947 Soble praised Morros as "'talented, energetic and enterprising.'" His problem was that living in Hollywood, "'he does not understand the value of money. Thousands of dollars are thrown right and left.'" But he was honest; when informed he
had to return money to Stern, he had agreed and kept his word, transmitting $100,000 to partially reimburse Stern. Soble reconsidered the
Morros Music Company failure, blaming Stern, not Morros, and commenting: "'One must be a man of steel to put up with Alfred Stern when
doing business, especially in America, where risk, enterprise, and speed
are the main elements of any commercial undertaking.'" Soble was much
taken with the critical and financial success of Morros's latest film release,
Carnegie Hall, and even more by the close friendship it had revealed between the Hollywood operator and recently named Cardinal Spellman.
And perhaps he was dazzled by Morros's reiterating a desire for a KGB-
financed business in which he, Soble, would play a key role.[36]

In a series of reports about his meetings with Morros in New York
and Paris in mid-1948 Soble argued, much as KGB officers had done
more than a decade before, that Morros "'could undoubtedly do a lot of
good for our cause in every respect, namely: major connections, getting
people jobs, getting entry visas through various channels, transferring
funds to various countries, legalizing people through film divisions in the
USA and in Europe, and setting up courier links between the USA and
Europe.'" As Morros dropped the names of his friends and exaggerated
his relationships with them, Soble practically salivated at the possibili-

ties. Not only was he a confidant of Cardinal Spellman, but he also claimed to be a drinking buddy of Eisenhower's brother, to have given Republican presidential candidate Thomas Dewey elocution lessons, and to have trolled for women with General Bedell Smith's aide, who had also introduced him to the wife of General Lucius Clay (U.S. Army commander in Germany), who was, according to Morros, cheating on her husband "'with gusto.'" At one gala charity event at the Louvre, which Soble attended, Morros skillfully orchestrated the crowd, including ambassadors, generals, and ministers, leaving the KGB agent agape at the "'extent to which "John" [Morros] can pull the wool over this entire distinguished public's eyes.'" It never occurred to him that the Hollywood charm, celebrity dazzle, and gift of gab that Morros used to confound the crowd in Paris were also employed to confound the KGB. Morros told Soble that he wanted to work with the KGB but insisted that he could not be supervised by amateurs, denigrating his previous handlers for lacking the élan and imagination to take advantage of his prodigious talents. Soble occasionally qualified his star-struck dispatches, warning that Morros could be immensely valuable, "'but only on one firm condition: supervision, strict supervision on our part.'" He concluded one report with a gushing: "'That's all in a nutshell. I am sure that this amounts to 1/20th of the info. John [Morros] has. . . . And so, my dear comrades, the word is with you! Act!'"[37]

In one of these missives, Soble confidently asserted that Morros was not under suspicion by the FBI, despite the highly publicized search for Hollywood Communists drawing newspaper headlines. Soble had ignored a number of warning signals. While the KGB didn't know it, an "anonymous" letter (discussed in chapter 9) received by the FBI in 1943 had specifically named Boris Morros as a Soviet agent, the only American singled out, and the FBI followed up. In 1944 Morros had even missed a scheduled meeting with Soble because, he said, he had noticed surveillance. Soble himself had complained in 1945 that Morros's indiscretions had probably alerted the FBI to his own role. In his autobiography Morros explained that in 1947 he had been approached by Bureau agents, confessed his involvement with the KGB, and agreed to be an FBI double agent. Consequently, Morros's 1947 proposal to Soble to have the Soviets finance a new company was an FBI sting operation, and every contact he had with the KGB after that point was under FBI supervision and review.[38]

Moscow was sufficiently intrigued by Soble's glowing reports to arrange for Morros to meet Aleksandr Korotkov, head of the KGB illegals department, in Switzerland in August 1948. Morros continued to inflate his own past history, boasting that his teacher at the Petrograd Conservatory had been Nikolay Rimsky-Korsakov and that he had been close friends with Sergei Prokofiev. His most implausible and startling assertion was that he had attended the First Congress of Eastern Peoples in Baku just after the Bolshevik Revolution, where he had met Beria and was ordered to go abroad and wait to be contacted. Morros told Soble, "'I wasn't brought over from Soviet Russia 30 years ago for this. I was sent by Lavrenty Pavlovich [Beria], and I finally want to speak with the leaders of the Sov. power.'" Since Beria was still alive, it is unlikely that the Bureau had put Morros up to this tall tale; he had a congenital impulse to magnify his importance. This Hollywood self-promoter couldn't and wouldn't turn it off even when dealing with the KGB and the FBI, two exceedingly non-frivolous organizations. He demanded to be used for something important or else "discharged and sent to Russia together with his wife." Korotkov was not impressed, discerning that this was a "'theatrical gesture.'" He also was skeptical of many of the biographical claims about Morros's youth in Russia and suggested a more detailed investigation to determine their truth. He deflected Morros's desire for $300,000 to start a new company to produce television shows and merely suggested they meet again. Despite these reservations, Korotkov's conclusions were far off the mark. Morros, he decided, was a businessman with a fondness for Russia, anxious to obtain money and fame. He saw no sign he was working for the FBI. Even if he was exaggerating, the opportunities he suggested were intriguing. Korotkov recommended against putting up the money but not ruling out some contributions in the future. In the meantime, he wanted to test Morros's loyalty with assignments for getting information on his high-level contacts. Moscow Center concurred.[39]

Soble was present at some of Korotkov's meetings with Morros, and the Russian noticed that he supported the impresario "'albeit rather timidly.'" That led Korotkov to suspect that his proposed role in the new business as Morros's partner and the KGB's representative might not be disinterested and that Soble "'hoped to play a lucrative part in it.'" When Korotkov asked at a second meeting if a refusal to fund the business meant a parting of ways with Morros, the latter insisted that he was still committed to working with the KGB. He agreed to cultivate Thomas Dewey but said he would need to make a $10,000 contribution to his political campaign. Korotkov did not respond to that overture but said Moscow would not want him to use his personal funds for its purposes and would decide on a case-by-case basis about what it would support. He concluded that Boris Morros hoped to obtain future Soviet investments, was hedging his bets so as to profit if American-Soviet relations got better, and "'is to some degree bound to us through his past work.'"[40]

Morros tantalized the KGB over the next year, offering a detailed account of his meeting with Pope Pius XII and their conversation at the Vatican in September 1948 and an account of his visit to the White House at the invitation of President Truman's daughter Margaret in February 1949, adding that he had also met with Vice-President Alben Barkley, Ambassador Averell Harriman, and Treasury Secretary John Snyder. Morros did meet with the people he named. Social interchanges between Hollywood and the American governmental elite had a long history. But Morros attributed to these meetings an exaggerated personal intensity and intimacy. Once again, Moscow asked Soble to have Morros gather information on all his famous acquaintances and agreed to consider his business proposal to distribute Soviet music in the United States, eventually arranging negotiations with the Ministry of Film in Moscow in 1950.[41]

While in Moscow in January 1950, Morros met with Korotkov once again. Chastised for "'coming empty-handed,'" he claimed to have provided some information earlier to Soble. When Korotkov disparaged the value of that material, Morros agreed it was inadequate and blamed the press of business, his extended stay in Europe, and the need to develop further his film activities, which would give him additional entree "'to the circles that interest us in the USA.'" Pleading that he lacked skill at "'our work,'" he asked for someone to be assigned to direct contact with him and "'that he be given absolutely concrete assignments.'" He blustered that he could arrange for someone to get employment in Cardinal Spellman's office, could influence Margaret Truman, and could even be elected to Congress. The KGB was not terribly bothered by his tendency to brag and boast; it concluded, for example, that he had never been given any assignments by Beria but had spun that story "'to raise his prestige in our eyes.'" He was given instructions again to obtain details about prominent Americans with whom he had ties.[42]

In addition to the lure of his high-level contacts, Morros was of use to the KGB because of his close ties to its longtime illegal operative Jack Soble. A memo summarized his history:

"In the interest of conducting anti-U.S. intellig-nce work in France in 1948, we set up an illegal station led by the illegal agent Cz. ["Czech"/Soble] As a cover, Cz. opened a bristle company in Paris with our financial assistance. For this purpose, Center allotted him $57,000 on the condition that he return it. 'Czech'—*Jack Soble,* born 1903 in the USSR, Jewish. Citizen and CPSU member since 1933. Married with a son. He has no close relatives in the USSR. . . . He has two brothers, as well as oth. relatives, in the USA and Canada. We recruited Cz. for intelligence work in 1931. From 1933 to 1940, he lived in the USSR and carried out individual intellig-nce assignments. In 1940, he left the USSR on our orders with a group of his rel-tives and went to the USA, where he was successfully legalized and where he conducted intellig-nce work until 1945. In 1946, he became an Amer. citizen. Starting in 1948, he and his family lived in Paris, where he would oversee the work of the company he had organized and simultaneously carry out our assignments."[43]

Meeting with Soble in Austria in late 1950, Morros concluded that two people with him, Jane Foster Zlatowski and her husband George, were KGB agents. Agents were supposed to be kept isolated and unknown to each other, and although Soble insisted that "'I, for one, did not say anything to him about this, and I am sure they didn't say anything to him about it either,'" the KGB concluded that the blunder probably lay with Soble. And Morros claimed that Soble had dropped hints about the Zlatowskis. (And it was a blunder: Morros told the FBI about the Zlatowskis.) Morros was also one of the KGB's few communications links with Soble. At his last meeting with a regular KGB contact in January 1951, Soble had warned that he was under investigation by authorities and direct contacts should be suspended. (Given that Morros had long ago told the FBI about Soble, likely he was under surveillance.) By late 1951 Moscow had approved a plan to liquidate Soble's station because it had produced little of value. Unable to locate Soble and hearing that he had sold his business in Paris, wired the money to the United States, and opened a similar bristle factory with the funds, the KGB decided to use Morros to meet with him and persuade him to come to a meeting in either Paris or Vienna. Although Soble met several times with Morros, he resisted suggestions that he travel to Europe, insisted he had not sold the bristle factory, and would eventually repay the money. Exasperated yet again by Soble's evasions and Morros's convoluted stories, a senior Moscow Center officer fumed: "'We need to make a concerted effort to drag out both of them, take their money, and arrest them.'"[44]

In November 1952 the KGB concluded:

"Although in the last year and a half, none of our operatives has met with Cz., ["Czech"/Soble] we have no doubt that he has guessed about our intentions to bring him back to the USSR and has decided to sever ties with us once and for all, not to return the money we gave him, and to remain in the USA permanently. Given that it is highly undesirable for us to leave Cz. abroad, our primary task at present with regard to him is to return Cz. to the USSR by any means, and then to collect the money that was invested in his cover (in full or in part). Since it will be difficult to accomplish this now, as Cz. is currently on his guard, we will give the impression that we believe the allegedly 'serious' reasons that prompted him to move to the USA and intend to continue intell. work with him in that country. We then intend to pick a more suitable time and invite Cz. allegedly for 'negotiations' in Europe, where we will abduct him and bring him back to the USSR."

Although using Morros to attempt to persuade Soble to travel abroad, the report noted that "'we have begun to have certain suspicions about him as well,'" because of his inability to complete tasks assigned to him and his constant requests for the names of Soviet contacts in the United States.[45]

In addition to recovering its money, the KGB was anxious to salvage whatever intelligence could be gleaned from Soble's ring. Morros reported to his KGB contact that at one of their meetings Soble had told him that his nephew, Ilya Wolston, had been transferred from the State Department to the Defense Department and had important material to give to the Soviets. (Recruited by his uncle, Wolston had worked for the KGB during World War II, when he entered the U.S. Army and became a military intelligence officer. After the war he worked for the State Department as a Russian translator.) In July 1953 Morros passed along another message from Soble that he was trying to get a foreign passport, promising to eventually repay the money, and wanted to transmit some important material. Morros asked for permission to pick it up, also relaying news in December that Soble was worried that he would be exposed by ongoing investigations into Martha Dodd Stern. Aleksandr Korotkov ordered: "'Get to the bottom of these letters. Same objective—how are we going to get our hands on these bastards?'"[46]

In May 1954 Soble informed Moscow through Morros that he had an investment opportunity with a hospital and needed $25,000. Morros offered to give him $10,000 and have the Center put up the rest, but nothing happened. Repeated efforts to arrange a meeting with Wolston in Paris or Vienna to obtain his supposedly valuable information all fell through. At a March 1955 meeting in Vienna Morros said that Soble had claimed he gave $25,000 and some diamonds to Jacob Albam (a KGB operative and Soble's assistant) and had lost the rest of the KGB's money in business, but when Morros met with Albam, he denied receiving anything. Morros had also determined that Wolston was mentally ill and was not the potential rich source Soble had held him out to be. He also offered to take over all of Soble's contacts and suggested that he might be able to induce Robert Oppenheimer to defect to the USSR, given Oppenheimer's loss of his security clearance and public attacks on him by anti-Communists. Moscow Center took these suggestions seriously. It rejected, however, his attempt to get the KGB to intervene with Soviet authorities in a dispute Morros was having with them about television rights to Prokofiev's opera *War and Peace*.[47]

Soon afterwards, the KGB lost contact with Morros. But it hadn't heard the last of him. The FBI had decided that running Morros as a double agent had reached the limit of its usefulness. In early 1957 the Justice Department indicted Jack Soble and his wife Myra, Jacob Albam, Alfred and Martha Stern, and George and Jane Zlatowski on espionage-related charges, and Morros surfaced as a double agent in a blaze of publicity. Jack Soble initially claimed complete innocence and prepared a vigorous legal defense. But he soon realized that with Morros's evidence and a decade of FBI surveillance, along with a government threat to seek the death penalty, his options were limited. Soble pled guilty, made a detailed statement of his activities, and agreed to testify against his sources. His wife also pleaded guilty, as did Albam. Jack Soble received a seven-year prison sentence, Myra got four years, while Albam was sentenced to five years. The Sterns were in Mexico at the time and soon departed for exile in Czechoslovakia. The Zlatowskis were in France and appeared to have provided information to French security about KGB operations there to avoid extradition to the United States. Jack also testified against his brother, Robert Soblen, another long-term KGB illegal operative. Soblen refused to cooperate and received a life sentence when convicted in 1961. He then jumped bail and fled to Israel, hoping to claim citizenship there. But Israel deported him, and he died of a self-administered overdose of barbiturates (whether intentional or accidental is unclear) while being returned to the United States.[48]

The Hammers

One of the oddest family odysseys in American history, involving communism, Soviet espionage, Russian art, and high finance, was that of the Hammers. Julius Hammer, born in Odessa, had immigrated to the United States in 1890, when he was sixteen. Quickly converted to socialism, he married and fathered two sons, Armand, born in 1898, and Victor, in 1901, just a year before Julius graduated from medical school. One other child, Harry, was a product of his wife Rose's first marriage. Julius had a history of shaky finances, filing for bankruptcy in 1906 and then being charged by the special master with fraud for trying to hide assets from his creditors. The business failures were caused by his purchase of a number of drugstores, financed by personal promissory notes. He used the money from the stores to finance his real passion, the Socialist Labor Party (SLP), instead of repaying the loans. As youngsters, the Hammer children were sent away to live with family friends, Victor with Daniel DeLeon, leader of the SLP.[49]

Julius Hammer had attended an international Socialist congress in Stuttgart in 1907, at which he met Lenin. Among those he recruited into the SLP was Armand, who joined while an undergraduate at Columbia. In 1918 Julius left the SLP and the following year became a stalwart of the revolutionary left wing of the Socialist Party and a financial supporter —using smuggled Russian jewels—of Ludwig Martens, head of the Bolsheviks' unofficial diplomatic mission in the United States. One of his motives for this venture was to provide an entree into Russia for the Allied Drug and Chemical Corporation, which he had formed, but there is little doubt that his fervent support for Bolshevism was the primary factor. He also used Allied Drug to smuggle spare parts and equipment into Russia via Latvia to evade American restrictions on trade with the Bolshevik regime. When the Communist Labor Party (later the CPUSA) formed in 1919, Julius held party card number 1.[50]

Busily involved in politics, Julius recruited Armand, still a medical student, to work in his medical practice in the afternoons. In August 1919 a Russian woman died a few days after procuring an abortion at Hammer's medical office, and Julius was indicted by a grand jury and convicted of manslaughter the following June. Armand later confessed to a mistress that he had actually performed the operation and his father shouldered the blame. While Julius went to prison, Armand assumed leadership of the pharmaceutical company and quickly demonstrated a talent for exploiting opportunities.

Julius's trial and conviction were not the only disasters the Hammer family faced at this time. In the summer of 1919 a New York state legislative investigating committee (the Lusk Committee) raided the offices of Martens's organization, seizing documents. Martens was later deported. Allied Drug was stuck with large amounts of goods destined for Russia that could not be shipped and faced severe financial difficulties. Now back in the USSR, Martens asked for someone to come to Moscow to work out a deal that could save the company. Shortly after graduating from medical school, Armand traveled to the USSR in 1921, where he struck deals to import American grain in exchange for Russian fur, lumber, and other commodities. His plans drew the attention of Lenin, who asked to meet him and offered him the first American concession in the new socialist society, an asbestos mine in the Urals. It came with a noncommercial price. Felix Dzerzhinsky, head of the Cheka (predecessor of the KGB), decided to use Allied Drug and Chemical, whose business relationship with the USSR gave it a plausible reason to transfer money, as a front to finance intelligence operations abroad. Allied Drug set up a banking operation in the United States that had exclusive rights to send money orders to the USSR. The American dollars shipped by Russian immigrants in the United States would be paid in far less valuable rubles to relatives in Russia. Armand, in turn, was given money to take back to America to be distributed to Comintern agents. Armand's brothers and father joined him in Moscow. Victor studied acting and "Armand doted on him." While they entertained royally and lavishly at the Brown House, their elegant residence, the Hammers kept their distance from old American Communist comrades who passed through. Jay Lovestone, a leading American party official, assumed it was because of the Hammers' ties to Soviet intelligence.[51]

Following Lenin's death, the Hammers faced increasing difficulties in their dealings with Soviet authorities. The concessions given to selected Western capitalists were scaled back and gradually eliminated. Armand, meanwhile, traveled throughout Europe in 1924–25, tending to family business and surreptitiously transferring money to the CPUSA and Soviet organs. The laundered money paid for the American party's newspaper, the *Daily Worker*, Soviet covert operations in the United States and England, and regular party activities in the United States, according to cables located in Russian archives.[52]

In 1925 Soviet officials gave the Hammers a new concession to manufacture pencils. Three years later Soviet investigators began to scrutinize the books, concerned that too much money was being expatriated, and *Pravda* criticized working conditions in the factory. Late in 1929 the concession was terminated. Victor Hammer, meanwhile, married Varvara Sumski, an aspiring young Russian actress, in mid-1925. Their son, named Armand in honor of his uncle, was born in 1927. The marriage soon foundered; Varvara's mother caught her committing adultery and told Victor. Varvara and Victor separated. When Victor left the USSR in 1929, he wanted to take young Armand, who had an American passport, but he was not allowed to do so.[53]

Through all the Hammers' complicated business affairs British and

American intelligence agencies harbored suspicions that they were serving covert Soviet interests; regarded Julius, Armand, and Victor as Soviet
agents; and uncovered bits and pieces of the money laundering. The
Hammer family had obviously been an integral part of an extensive Comintern operation involving illegal transfers of money and material aid to
illegal agents shuffling between Europe and the United States. Documents in Vassiliev's notebooks add to the Hammer saga, however, with evidence that four of the Hammers were recruited by the KGB. Surprisingly, Armand was not among them.

The first Hammer recruited by the KGB was the patriarch of the
family, Julius. Despite his sacrifices for the Communist cause, Julius
came under suspicion of Trotskyism in the late 1920s. He had known
Trotsky during the latter's sojourn in the United States and had not only
had personal contact with him after his arrival in the USSR, but had also
given him presents. In one letter Julius had asked Trotsky to keep Julius's
role in providing the Soviet state with an airplane "'secret so as not to
spoil my future usefulness to the cause,'" which the KGB interpreted as
a plea to conceal his usefulness for the *Trotskyist* cause. Additional
damnation came from a 1932 report received from someone close to
writer Max Eastman who claimed that the funding for his translation of
Trotsky's book on the Russian Revolution had been provided by Julius
Hammer.[54]

The economic losses suffered by the Hammer concessions due to the
siphoning off of money for Comintern operations also led to allegations
that they were "'engaged in extorting money from the Soviet govt.'" The
KGB's counterintelligence division in 1930 concluded that despite his
long-standing ties to the Communist movement, "'capitalist tendencies
are not alien to H. [Hammer], such as amassing personal funds not only
by working as a concessionaire but also in other indirect, peripheral ways,
for example, by buying valuable items in the USSR and exporting them
abroad and other profiteering methods.'" He was also accused of "'making money even by means of fraud and fictitious invoices.'" As a result, in
1930 the KGB's economic directorate (not its foreign intelligence arm) ordered him to leave the Soviet Union.[55]

Shocked by this decision, Julius Hammer wrote an impassioned statement defending his service to the Soviet cause:

"This is not only a blow to my fondest wishes and plans to remain to work in
the USSR, and once the settlements with Glavkontsesskom [Chief Concession
Committee] on the concession turned over to the government are completed,

to find a job in some state institution or a scientific institution, besides many years of general practice as a physician, as well as broad experience as a chemist and pharmacologist, I could also, thanks to long experience as an organizer and administrator, work as a manager—in the best sense of this word —and thereby take a direct part in building socialism in the USSR. But besides this, I take this denial as an undeserved punishment, since throughout the nearly 8 years I have been in the USSR I have always been devoted to Soviet power and an avid friend of Soviet-Amer. communications and trade. . . . I am compelled not only to inform you about my active work in the socialist movement in the NAUS [North American United States] for decades, but also to disclose to you regarding my real polit. position what, for technical and business reasons and so that I could be more helpful to the interests of the USSR, I had to keep secret from the broad public, especially from Amer. commercial circles and the govt., with the consent of the Amer. Com. Party [American Communist Party]. For more than 20 years I worked actively with Cde. Reinstein (from the Comintern) in the then-left Socialist Labor Party in the NAUS, sometimes in the position of a candidate member of the CC [Central Committee] of the party. In 1919, when the Com. Party was established in the NAUS, I was a delegate to the clandestine congress of the Com. Party. In 1919–1920 I supported, with active work and money totaling about 50,000 dollars, the work of Cde. L. K. Martens, who was representing the RSFSR [Russian Socialist Federal Soviet Republic] govt. in the NAUS on a mandate from the NKID [People's Commissariat of Foreign Affairs]. (Cde. Martens is now in Moscow at Lubyansky proyezd, 3, Apt. 53, Phone 5–78–79.) He can corroborate this. Besides the aforementioned 50,000 dollars, even before my son arrived in the USSR I loaned the Soviet govt. at the time, without any guarantee, another 110,000 dollars (oil equipment), and the Soviet govt. repaid the 160,000 dollars to my son in 1922.

During the raids on the 'Reds' in the NAUS I paid several thousand dollars in order to put up bail for them and give them a chance to flee to the USSR. Two such comrades—Fedotov and Volodin—are now here. When my son A. Hammer arrived here in 1921, he followed my advice and, with Cde. Lenin's support, took from the govt. the first concession (in the Urals) in the history of concessions in the USSR and was the first to start trade between the USSR and the NAUS by sending on credit two ships with grain for the starving workers in the Urals, for which he also received recognition from Cde. Lenin. During my time in the USSR I continuously provided the Amer. Com. Party and the international communist movement with a number of clandestine services, which need not be mentioned here (Cde. B. Reinstein of the Comintern knows all the details and can report to you personally about this in detail). . . .

All these years I have been a full-fledged member of the Amer. Com. Party of the late Cde. Ruthenberg and am a member of the Amer. Com. Party to this day, for which I have a certificate in 1930 from the Cde. Randolph, the Amer. Com. Party's representative in the Comintern. . . . I hope that when you review the facts I have presented, you will find it possible to permit me to remain in the USSR."[56]

Likely not coincidentally, the following year Julius Hammer agreed to add clandestine work for Soviet intelligence to his previous confidential work for the Comintern. He was "'in 1931 recruited by the OGPU to work among foreigners living in Moscow'" and "'signed a statement regarding voluntary cooperation with the Sov. security organs.'" Given the code name "Physician," he proved to be of little value as an agent, laying out "'various plans for cultivating foreigners'" but doing nothing to carry them out. An assessment noted that he "'yielded little benefit as an agent.'" Julius, however, "'raised the question with us of recruiting his elder son [Armand], who supposedly had extensive contacts in U.S. business, political and military circles and could be a valuable agent for us.'" There is no indication that the OGPU, as the KGB was then known, recruited Armand, but Julius had another suggestion: "'that our organs recruit "S." ["Sonny"/Victor Hammer] and promised to provide any assistance he could.'"[57]

The KGB recruited Victor Hammer in 1931. He "'gave his consent to work with us and provided us with a signed statement to that effect.'" He was expected to help "'legalize'" Soviet agents in the United States and obtain American documents they could use. A 1931 report included his signed statement in Russian pledging to "'keep my conversation with the OGPU representative in the strictest secrecy,'" establishing a mail drop in Berlin, and setting out the password for meeting him in New York: "'I have a letter and regards from Mrs. Perelman,'" with a response of "'Thank you, how is she and how is her daughter Doly?'" After Victor made several trips to the Soviet Union in the early 1930s to purchase or obtain art objects to be resold in the United States and to see his son, Soviet officials denied him further permission to enter the country, and there is no evidence of contact in the late 1930s. A later memo indicated that Victor Hammer's "personal file contains no information on how he was used."[58]

The KGB once again became interested in Victor Hammer and his Russian son and ex-wife in 1940. Victor had been trying for several years to bring his family to the United States. He had asked the American Embassy in Moscow to assist his son, familiarly called Armasha, and former wife Varvara. Varvara visited the American Embassy in August 1941. Soon afterwards she was questioned by the KGB and explained that starting in 1934 Victor had been urging her to move abroad with Armasha but she had resisted, fearing that the Hammer family would seize him once they were out of the USSR. As far back as 1930 Julius had offered her money in exchange for Armasha, and in 1934 Victor had suggested she could move to Paris and Armasha to the United States. Now Victor and his mother had offered to bring both Varvara and her son to the United States.[59]

Victor telegrammed Varvara in October 1942 that he had again requested the embassy to do everything possible to assist her and Armasha. In response, Gaik Ovakimyan asked the Visa and Registration Office to defer a decision and send Varvara's file to his office. After reading that Victor had once promised to work for the KGB but had not done so, Ovakimyan asked Vasily Zarubin in New York to "'Locate 'Screw' [Victor Hammer], find out his capabilities for our work and the advisability of reestablishing contact.'" That generated an April 1943 report that set out details about the businesses and backgrounds of the Hammers, which in turn revived the rumors of the Hammers' links to Trotskyism. An August 1943 Moscow Center directive to the KGB New York station read: "'According to our information, "Screw" [Victor Hammer] or his father financed and raised money for the publication of "The Old Man's" [Trotsky's] book 'The History of the Revolution,' which was prepared by the well-known "polecat" [Trotskyite] Eastman. Certainly the "polecats" know the father and "Screw" himself, both of whom took part in this publication. It is therefore advisable to re-establish contact with "Screw" on the condition that he has no direct connection to the "polecats," for infiltration of a WP [Workers Party] group.'"[60]

Ovakimyan also ordered a report with "'all the compromising information you have regarding Varvara Dmitrievna Hammer.'" A memorandum written in December 1942 described her "'as a modest woman, leads a normal lifestyle, literate, politically well versed, takes an active part in communal work of the building,'" but "'unsociable with neighbors.'" Still another report disclosed that the divorce from Victor had been precipitated by "'the frivolous lifestyle of Varvara Hammer, who had intimate liaisons with performers from the circle surrounding the Hammer family'" and hostility toward her from Julius. Despite their breakup Victor had continued to send her "'money and packages,'" and she, "'to all intents and purposes, is being supported by him.'" In March

1940 Varvara "'was recruited by Department 1 of the 3rd Directorate of the NKVD USSR to cultivate'" Julius's Russian contacts, likely suspected of Trotskyism. (One memo claimed, "'There is reason to believe that the Amer. Trotskyites, on Trotsky's instructions, are in contact with the Trotskyite underground in the USSR through Hammer.'") While she had initially agreed, she later "'refused to cooperate further with NKVD organs'" and was not actively used.[61]

The most serious information uncovered, however, dealt with Victor's son Armasha. He became enmeshed in a shocking crime in the summer of 1943 involving families of the Moscow elite. A classmate and friend, Vladimir Shakhurin, son of the aviation industry minister, was in love with Nina Umanskaya, daughter of Konstantin Umansky, just appointed ambassador to Mexico. Distressed that she was about to leave the country with her father, he shot and killed her on the stairs of the Bolshoy Kamenny Bridge, then turned the gun on himself, dying the next day. In the fallout, a number of Shakhurin's student friends were arrested, including two sons of Stalin's confidant Anastas Mikoyan and Armasha. He was jailed for one and a half years. He returned to Moscow and his schooling in January 1945, undoubtedly chastened, since he "'now behaves very modestly, spends all his free time in his apartment, preparing his lessons for the next day, and reading literature.'"[62]

Armasha's arrest put an end to Victor's 1943 effort to get him out of Russia, and the KGB put aside the notion of reactivating him. But in 1945 his son was out of prison, and Moscow asked the New York station to do a background check on Victor Hammer and to "clarify his capabilities for our work." But there is no indication it made any effort to activate him. The New York station had to contend with defections and the collapse of its networks. As it shut down agents, it had little incentive to try to recruit someone whose familial ties to the Soviet Union would surely excite suspicion and who, in any case, as an art dealer—Victor was running the Hammer Galleries—was unlikely to be of significant intelligence value.[63]

After World War II Victor was able to reestablish contact with Armasha and regularly send money and clothing to him and his mother. Because of his background, Armasha clearly enjoyed certain privileges. In 1947 an informant reported that Varvara, angered when Armasha received a Soviet draft notice, demanded that he visit U.S. ambassador Bedell Smith "'and tell him everything so that he sends you to your father in the U.S. or keeps you out of the army. I'm sick and tired of taking abuse from this damn country.'" Nor was that the only sign the KGB detected that the Russian Hammers harbored anti-Soviet ideas. One informant reported that at a Moscow restaurant in 1946 Armasha had complained: "'Here in the Sov. Union I live only with my mind, but my soul is absent, since it's impossible to live in this country with one's soul. There is nothing but oppression and enslavement here. Every serf in Russia's past was happier than today's engineer, professor, or prize winner. Our entire people are enslaved and pinned to the wall.'"[64]

By mid-1950 the KGB once again began to take an interest in the Hammers. In August Moscow Center ordered monitoring of all correspondence among Victor, Varvara, and Armasha and a full record check of previous investigations and contacts with the three. The mail check showed many pleas for money from Varvara and Armasha; one KGB memo in October noted that Hammer was "'very attached to his son Armand, every month sends him 100–200 dollars and packages and also is taking measures to arrange for him to move to the U.S.'" At the end of December a diplomatic co-optee with the cover name "Levin" reported that he had met Hammer at a reception at the Indian Embassy in New York. Slightly drunk, Victor, speaking in Russian, expressed his desire to bring his son to America but complained that he had been continually rebuffed. He brandished a picture of a grown-up Armasha and eagerly accepted "Levin's" offer to look him up when he returned to the USSR. When "Levin" stopped by Hammer Galleries, Victor asked him to tell Armasha "about his papa." A Moscow Center report concluded: "'Considering "Sonny's" [Victor Hammer's] extensive capabilities for working on our line, his past connection with our organs, and his desire to secure his son's emigration from the Sov. Union, we deem it advisable to re-establish contact with him through our station in New York.'"[65]

Armasha, who still lived with his mother while attending the Institute of Foreign Languages, was described around this time as "a mature, energetic person, courteous to his elders." Once anxious to move to the United States, he had changed his mind, explaining to his mother "that no matter where he lived, he would be in a bad situation; here in the Sov. Union people regard him as the son of the factory owner Hammer, and if he moves to America people there will regard him as a Communist." Questioned by the KGB after he had visited the American Embassy to receive gifts sent by his father, he got into another scrape in 1949 when he and some friends, riding in a car owned by a professor, tried to steal a tire from a parked ambulance. After being detained in prison, Armasha was found not guilty. Sometime in 1951, according to a memo from Anatoly Gorsky, the KGB recruited him for unspecified work, likely as an informant on fellow students. Although an evaluation noted that he "'dis-

tinguished himself as a smart, capable agent,'" it concluded that he had
failed to complete assignments, regularly detected and lost tails in ways
that suggested he had experience in covert work, and peppered his private correspondence with anti-Soviet remarks.[66]

In June 1951 Anatoly Gorsky wrote a memo that Victor Hammer had
"'extensive contacts in business circles, among diplomats, and attends
diplomatic receptions.'" At one of the latter "Miron," a KGB operative,
approached him and promised to arrange delivery of a letter to Armasha.
"Miron" met Victor at his office at the Hammer Galleries in late January
1952 and gave him Armasha's response. After reading the response Victor told "Miron" that his son "'had apparently inherited linguistic skills
from his grandfather'" and asked for assistance in remaining in correspondence with Armasha, to which "Miron" agreed. This conversation
inaugurated a dance between the American art dealer and the Soviet intelligence services with Armasha as the bait. During a subsequent breakfast, Victor complained about Armasha's continual need for money and
asked "'several times whether it was possible for 'Gherman' [Armasha] to
visit the U.S. when he finished his education.'" "Miron" deflected the inquiry with the comment that this was years away. Hammer dropped comments about his connections with Eleanor Roosevelt and Harry Hopkins
(although he had been dead for five years). The New York station concluded that Victor wanted "'an opportunity to set up a permanent line
of communications with his son'" and considered bringing him into covert contact with the agency. After another lunch meeting, Victor took
"Miron" on a tour of some of his valuable art and bragged about brother
Armand's connections with President Truman and General Eisenhower,
"'to both of whom he has rendered some valuable services,'" and the
KGB agent was duly impressed by inscribed photographs to Armand
from both men, "'from which one can infer that they know Armand
well.'" ("Miron" apparently was unaware that prominent American political figures handed out signed photographs to casual visitors.) Victor
also offered political gossip and his analysis of U.S.-Soviet relations.[67]

Moscow initially approved of a cautious approach, recognizing that it
was "still too early to re-establish an agent relationship" since a premature
request might spook Victor. It recommended using his affection for Armasha "'by giving him individual minor assignments in order to draw him
into cooperating.'" Nevertheless, by May 1952 it was scolding the New
York station for the slow pace of Victor's cultivation. Despite his "'operational value and high potential,'" "Miron" was "'listless and slow in conducting this interesting cultivation.'" Moscow demanded a plan that pro-

vided "'for a transition to an agent relationship with him'" by October 1952. Two weeks later "Miron" met with Hammer. After reading Armasha's letter, Victor again asked if he could be allowed to come to the United States. "Miron" was evasive, but commented that it would be difficult for Armasha "'to adapt to the empty life of young people in the U.S.'" or to leave his mother or Soviet girlfriend, whom he planned to marry. Victor agreed but repeated his desire for a reunion with his son. Two subsequent meetings yielded only Hammer's giving "Miron" his direct phone number.[68]

By the end of September Moscow Center was growing impatient and complained that "Miron" was unnecessarily dragging out the recruitment. It considered arranging a meeting with Victor on a trip to Europe, where he would meet "'an experienced operative.'" "Miron" was instructed to sound out Hammer to find a suitable location, but they could not meet until late October, at which time the Soviet operative boldly stated that "'an American who loves his country and values the preservation of peace between peoples should contribute to the success of Soviet diplomacy, which is aimed at preserving peace between people'" and noted that Victor, as a businessman interested in peace and trade, "'could not stand on the sidelines as a spectator but must help Soviet diplomats in every way he could with his numerous contacts, information, etc.'" Victor evaded, replying that while "'glad to provide such assistance,'" he doubted he could be effective and faulted Soviet diplomats for isolating themselves and failing to build relationships with prominent Americans. "Miron" concluded that Victor "'did not reject the proposal for cooperation'" and planned to return to it later, particularly mentioning "'exactly what issues he would like to get information on from him, in particular through his brother, who is close to the next president of the U.S.'"[69]

When "Miron" next raised the issue in late November 1952, Victor danced away again, explaining that he did not have high-level contacts in the diplomatic world; most people he knew were related to his business. None of this seemed to faze the KGB, in whom hope continued to spring eternal in regard to Hammer. After the October meeting, where Victor had evaded making a commitment, the station chief had written Moscow that he and "Miron" nonetheless saw Victor's not directly rejecting cooperation "'as a bit of a step forward.'" The station chief said a direct approach would not likely work, and it was necessary to continue "gradually" drawing him into a relationship. While Moscow agreed, it worried that continuing what had already been done would "'delay the prospect of actively using'" Hammer "'to a remote and indefinite time.'" It suggested

giving him assignments "'to gather data about some company, background information.'" If that worked, "'these assignments can be made
closer in nature to agent-information assignments'" except he would be
paid.[70]

In January 1953 "Miron" nudged Hammer yet again, explaining that
he was "'a diplomat who needs the help of people like 'S' ["Sonny"/Ham-
mer] with his intelligence and contacts and that he was patiently waiting
for 'S' to realize that actions speak louder than words.'" Victor reiterated
that his well-connected friends only spoke of art with him and did not
discuss sensitive matters. The New York station suggested putting "'some
psychological pressure on him'" by initiating an investigation of Armasha,
who would appeal to his father for help. "Miron," it was suggested, would
promise to look into the matter, report back that inappropriate friends
were the cause of the trouble, but that if Hammer resumed his aid to the
KGB "'this case involving G. ["Gherman"/Armasha] could be dropped.'"
Even if Hammer refused, he would probably not expose "Miron." This
option, however, was not pursued.[71]

On 3 April 1953 "Miron" peppered Hammer with questions about
Bedell Smith; the KGB's old source, Judge Samuel Dickstein; and others.
As they finished their conversation "Miron" asked if these meetings made
Victor nervous and whether they should meet more covertly. Victor, however, rejected the overture. While he did not discuss his meetings with
"Miron" with anyone, including his brothers, he saw no reason to try to
hide them. If asked, he would explain that he wanted to maintain good
relations with Soviet diplomats out of concern for his son and that as a
businessman who had once made a fortune in the USSR, he had an interest in resuming commercial ties. And he knew no secrets. By April
1953 Anatoly Gorsky again recommended having "'a recruitment talk
with him in the immediate future so as to change the current relationship
to an agent relationship'"[72]

At the end of April "Miron" again "'expressed dissatisfaction with
the information he was getting and said that to date he [Victor] hadn't
done anything.'" Victor again minimized his capabilities and promised to
learn about American views of the USSR. "Miron" responded that he was
"'following the line of least resistance'" and said, given Victor's views, he
"'expects more from him.'" The relationship paused once more after
stepped-up American surveillance of Soviet officials in May. October
1953 found Victor again deflecting "Miron's" complaints; now his business
trips to buy cattle for a Hammer family livestock-breeding business were
interfering with giving the diplomat any help. Overwork and a lack of

contacts prevented him from being as useful as he would like to be. Moscow was almost convinced. An analysis at the Center "'persuades us more and more that his cultivation offers no prospects.'" He didn't have the contacts the Center had assumed, lacked a close relationship with people like Bedell Smith, and didn't have sustained contact with people of interest. The cultivation had been far too slow. His refusal to establish a more covert relationship was a sign he would not work out. The New York station was ordered to abandon its efforts: "'He should be retained only as a neutral contact.'"[73]

Nonetheless, despite a decade of failure, Moscow Center was not yet ready to give up. In 1955 it mused: "'At present it is advisable to continue keeping in contact with "S." ["Sonny"/Hammer] in order to secure acquaintances through him in business circles, among cultural figures, in the theater world, where he has access through his second wife, an actress. He could be used to infiltrate our people into various clubs, societies, and associations in which representatives of business circles are members and to acquire through him literature and equipment that we cannot acquire by legal means.'"[74]

Victor visited Moscow in July 1956 and saw his son for the first time in a quarter century (Armasha was now married and had a child). In a message to the New York station in mid-August Moscow explained that he had visited the American ambassador, Charles Bohlen, twice and raised the possibility of registering Armasha as an American by birth but had not discussed his moving to the United States and had made no effort to meet "Miron" (then back in Moscow). A KGB informant, "Negro," assigned to watch Armasha and his mother (he also became Varvara's lover), reported that Armasha was thrilled with the warmth of his reception by his father, stepmother, and grandmother.[75]

While Victor's sudden departure after only a week had prevented the KGB from meeting him in Moscow, it continued to monitor him in New York. KGB operative "Ivan" introduced himself in January 1957 as a friend of "Miron" and they had five meetings, but "Ivan" concluded that Victor wanted to use their relationship only as a conduit to send Armasha letters and packages. As a "'shrewd person,'" Victor might also see his willingness to chat with KGB agents as a help to Armasha. The New York station chief reported that he had instructed "Ivan" to gather information on Hammer's acquaintances and what information they could provide if Victor was used "'in the dark'"—that is, without a conscious relationship to the KGB.[76]

"Ivan" also met Rose Hammer, Victor's mother, who made it clear that the family's goal to bring Armasha to the United States was compli-cated by his wife and child. Victor had believed that if Armasha could ob-tain an American passport, the American ambassador could get permis-sion for him to emigrate, but his marriage to an unsuitable woman had scotched that plan. Rose nurtured the hope that he still might come by himself; to "Ivan's" comment that he probably loved his wife and such pressure might be counterproductive, the grandmother reiterated that they could not allow "their boy to get lost in Russia." It began to dawn on "Ivan" that the family's pose of support for the USSR was a sham, and the "'conclusion suggests itself that he [Victor] is using the connection with us for his own personal motives.'" In retaliation, he began to refuse Victor's pleas to help him send special items to Armasha without going through parcel agencies. In Moscow Alexander Feklisov, anticipating a trip Victor planned to Moscow, thought a meeting necessary because "'the question of his cultivation must be settled.'" The New York station recommended a more overtly threatening approach:

"If "S." ["Sonny"/Victor Hammer] does go to Moscow, it might be advisable to try to put some pressure on him by making use of the consent to work with us that he gave before the war. (The file obviously contains his signature.) Per-haps the threat of exposure will induce him to cooperate with us in terms of gathering polit. and econom. information through his numerous acquain-tances. The current motivations for "S." to work with us (G.'s ["Gherman"/Ar-masha Hammer's] presence in the USSR) apparently aren't strong enough. If you deem such a discussion with "S." inadvisable, then, considering his pro-longed uselessness, further contact with him, in our view, should be termi-nated."

Victor, however, canceled his trip, and in mid-August 1957, Moscow re-sponded to New York that it agreed to end its relationship to Victor. A Moscow Center evaluation observed that Victor Hammer had

"used the contact with our operative in his own personal interests: to transmit letters and packages to his son, who lives in the Sov. Union, and to find out about the opportunities for making money from the sale and purchase of paintings in the Sov. Union. Moreover, the contacts with high-level people in the U.S. that "S." ["Sonny"/Victor Hammer] described to Miron proved to be patently exaggerated. . . . It became clear that "S." only wants to have a social relationship with our operative, using it for his own purposes, and isn't inter-ested in establishing a confidential or agent relationship. "S." doesn't have the necessary agent capabilities and cannot serve as a source of information, and at the same time he doesn't want to assist our operative in establishing interesting contacts through him. In light of the foregoing, it has been decided to terminate the contact with "S.," since he is not of interest to Department 1 of the PGU."[77]

Despite that decision, the KGB could not totally give up on Victor Hammer. When it learned of a possible visit in 1965, it devised a plan to put listening devices in his car and hotel room, then meet and try to recruit him. If he refused, it would haul out his signed 1931 agreement to cooperate and pressure him. If he agreed, the KGB wanted his insights on internal Democratic politics and his willingness "'to covert meetings with our rep.'" The trip, however, was canceled. That fall, a Soviet diplomat and KGB officer met four times with Victor in New York. Once again, he wanted assistance for his son, who wanted to switch his career from translator to teacher. Victor noted "'with tears in his eyes that this is his only child.'" In May 1966 another operative wrote another memo concluding that Victor was friendly to the USSR, had fond memories of his years there, opposed the Vietnam War, was skeptical of American culture, and no longer wanted American citizenship for his son, recognizing that he wouldn't be happy in America.[78]

When Victor did visit in 1966, Moscow Center prepared yet another plan to recruit him, "'conducted on an ideological basis,'" while also employing his old agreement and his affection for his son. He would be told that he was needed to infiltrate "'our comrade'" into the United States in some job connected to the fine arts. The report included the protocol for an operative to contact Hammer back in New York. It also recognized that as a quid pro quo, Victor would probably "'request assistance in getting his son a job'" as a teacher at a foreign language institute and that "'assistance will be promised him in a positive resolution of this matter.'" But there is no indication that this approach was either made or accepted or that the KGB made any more efforts to reenroll Victor.[79]

Victor Hammer died in 1985 after a decade of illness. His will left everything in trust to his wife, Irene, who was living in a nursing home. After her death, her daughter and Armasha would inherit the estate, which had liquid assets of about $700,000, in addition to a $400,000 house. His brother Armand was by this time a wealthy businessman, heading Occidental Petroleum and having interests in a variety of other businesses. But as executor of his brother's estate, he filed a claim for $667,000 he said was owed him for loans he had earlier made to Victor. To pressure Victor's stepdaughter, he refused to pay nursing home bills and took steps to sell the house, in which she lived. Irene died before the legal fight was resolved, and Armand settled, giving her daughter the house and providing Armasha with $200,000. As he lay mortally ill in November 1990, Armand arranged for Armasha to fly to Los Angeles and asked him to try to sanitize records in Moscow to make sure that bribes he had paid to Soviet leaders were not exposed after his death.[80]

Armand himself came under renewed suspicion as a Soviet agent by the CIA in the early 1960s. Anatoly Golytsin, a KGB officer, defected in December 1961; during his lengthy debriefing, he recalled someone dubbed "Capitalist Prince," whom the KGB had recruited in the 1920s and reactivated in the late 1950s. Golytsin did not know his real name but provided four clues: he was the son of an American millionaire, had come to Russia during the 1920s, had gone back to the United States in the 1930s, and had left a son behind in Russia, whom the KGB had used as leverage. James Angleton, chief of counterintelligence, concluded that Armand Hammer fit the bill of particulars. There is, however, nothing in the documents recorded in Vassiliev's notebooks suggesting that the KGB recruited Armand. For example, a KGB memo stated of Armand:

"In early 1961 he visited the Sov. Union as a tourist. On instructions from the secretary of commerce in the Kennedy admn. he conducted unofficial talks about expanding trade between the U.S. and the USSR. He was received by the leaders of the Sov. Govt. He made positive comments about his meeting with the Sov. leaders. While he was in M. [Moscow] did sightseeing around the city with his spouse and visited the Sacco and Vanzetti factory, where he met with workers who had started working under him. He was astonished by the growth in labor productivity. He repeatedly commented that the trip to the USSR made a big impression on him, and the achievements by Soviet people are enormous. While he engages in big business, he didn't shrink from carrying out small-scale operations. For example, when returning from the USSR in 1961 he took 18 tins of black caviar with him, saying that he would be able to profit with them."

As for Golytsin's "Capitalist Prince," it is more probable that Golytsin had heard a partial account of the KGB's 1930s enlistment of Victor and the futile efforts to reactivate him, and Angleton confused Victor with Armand. (Possibly contributing to Angleton's confusion, Armand, as part of the family's effort to extract Armasha from the USSR in 1942, had listed him as his son on some documents.)[81]

Whatever benefits it got from its business dealings with Armand Hammer or its covert connections with the Hammers in the 1920s, Soviet intelligence failed in its efforts to persuade or coerce Victor Hammer into providing it with information. He, on the other hand, managed to cajole the KGB into facilitating his communications and assistance to his son and former wife, while artfully avoiding its entreaties to be of assistance.

Corliss Lamont

Not every celebrity recruit became a KGB obsession. The KGB's illegal station in the United States ceased to exist at the end of 1939, when its chief (and last officer), Iskhak Akhmerov, returned to Moscow. In both 1940 and 1941 Moscow Center planned for a revived illegal station to take on a recruited but as yet unexploited agent with the cover name "Author." The 1940 plan described "Author" as a source who "has given his consent to work with us" but added that the new station needed to study him to determine his "practical use." A 1941 review of the status of KGB operations in the United States described "Author" as "a millionaire. Chairman of the Society of Friends of the Sov. Union. Recruited in Moscow. He was not passed over to the station. Could be a talent-spotting agent."[82]

While documents in Vassiliev's notebooks do not provide a real name for "Author," the description fits only one man: Corliss Lamont. Lamont had a lengthy and controversial career as an advocate for radicalism and sympathy for the USSR. Born in 1902 in New Jersey, he grew up in privilege as the son of Wall Street titan Thomas Lamont, a partner and later chairman of J. P. Morgan. Educated at Phillips Exeter and Harvard, he attended graduate school at Columbia University, earning his PhD under philosopher John Dewey. He visited the Soviet Union in 1932 and was impressed and enthralled. In 1934, however, he told Max Eastman that he was a "Truth Communist," in contrast to those members of Communist parties who accepted Stalin's official pronouncements.[83]

Within a few years, however, Lamont had changed his mind, publicly defending the purge trials, denouncing Trotsky and his defenders, and calling on liberals to support Stalin and his foreign policy. It was after this shift in Lamont's views that he was recruited as a KGB agent, likely on a visit to Moscow in the late 1930s. But there is no evidence that the recruitment led to an active relationship in the United States. The 1941 note about "Author"/Lamont, which states he was "not passed over to the station," indicated that Moscow Center had never authorized the New York legal station to establish liaison with him, and the 1940 and 1941 plans to have a revived illegal station establish contact had been aborted.

There is no reference to "Author"/Lamont after 1941. When the cover name appeared again in KGB documents and cables in 1944 and 1945, it designated Vladimir Morkovin, an engineer working for Bell Aircraft (see chapter 6).

Lamont, however, continued to serve the Soviet cause. He chaired the Friends of the Soviet Union, later renamed the National Council of American-Soviet Friendship. During the 1950s he was one of the most prominent defenders of American Communists facing political restrictions and investigations. He founded and chaired the National Emergency Civil Liberties Committee, was cited for contempt of Congress (later overturned on appeal), served as plaintiff in landmark Supreme Court cases that overturned inspection of foreign mail, and challenged denials of passports by the State Department. While he denounced any restriction on Communists in America, he justified and defended Stalin's Terror, the Nazi-Soviet Pact, the imposition of totalitarian regimes on Eastern Europe by the USSR, and the suppression of all dissent in the People's Republic of China and the People's Republic of Korea as necessary steps to bring about socialism. The author of numerous books on the philosophy of humanism, Lamont always insisted that he was not himself a member of the CPUSA, although Louis Budenz testified that he knew him to be a secret party member. He endowed the Corliss Lamont Chair of Civil Liberties at Columbia University. He died in 1995, lauded as a principled fighter for civil liberties and peace and apparently never called upon to fulfill his late 1930s pledge to work for the KGB.[84]

"Polecats"

The KGB devoted enormous resources to surveilling, infiltrating, and disrupting the American Trotskyist movement, the "Polecats" in KGB communications. James Cannon, a leader of the CPUSA, had attended the Sixth World Congress of the Communist International in Moscow in 1928 and been converted to Trotskyism. The CPUSA quickly expelled him and a small group of his supporters, who wandered in the political wilderness first as the Communist League of America (Left Opposition) and later as the Workers Party and then the Socialist Workers Party.

The American Trotskyist movement had only a few hundred active members in 1932 and no institutional base or financial resources, but the KGB already had at least three sources reporting on its activities, two unidentified, and one, John Spivak, a journalist. By 1935, it had added another journalist, Frank Palmer, and a woman named Shifra Tarr, who

attended Trotskyist meetings and was tapped to infiltrate the organization. (Spivak and Palmer are discussed in chapter 3.) For the rest of the
decade, as the purges gathered steam in Russia, work against American
Trotskyists intensified. In 1936 the KGB assigned Floyd Cleveland Miller
to listen to a wiretap on James Cannon's home, a task that lasted one year.
He then joined the Socialist Workers Party as Mike Cort, and from his
perch in the Sailors Union of the Pacific reported to the KGB on the
movements of Trotskyist seamen during World War II and spied on Trotsky's widow in Mexico.[85]

The KGB recruited Robert Owen Menaker, a scion of a radical family and a traveling salesman for a company whose owner worked for the
KGB, for anti-Trotsky work in 1937. At the time, he was still a nominal
member of the Socialist Party. Ironically, leading Trotskyist activists, including Max Shachtman, approached Menaker and another secret KGB
asset, "Actor," and recruited them as "permanent informants there and to
conduct work on demoralization" of the Socialists. Recruited to spy on the
Socialists by the Trotskyists, Menaker and "Actor" actually spied on the
Trotskyists for the Communists. The station explained: "'Our idea boils
down to continuing to watch the Trotskyites through the Socialist Party,
since we don't yet have any seasoned agents within the Trotskyite organization.'" Moscow was pleased: "'Your latest recruits ('Actor' [unidenti-
fied], 'Bob' [Menaker]) and the transfer of a number of other sources to
shedding light on the Trotskyites have significantly advanced our cultivation of the Trotskyites. Continue cultivating at the same rate, taking into
account preparations for the upcoming trial.'" (The "trial" likely referred
to a forthcoming investigation of Stalin's charges against Trotsky chaired
by John Dewey, an effort given significant support by American Trotskyists.) KGB documents in Vassiliev's notebooks indicate that Menaker
worked for the Soviets for nearly a decade, although they are largely silent
about his exact activities. "Actor" played a more sinister role. He had extensive connections with the Trotskyists and managed to travel to Trotsky's house in Mexico City, enabling him to give the KGB details about
Trotsky's surroundings and contacts. The KGB worried, however, that he
was "arousing the Trotskyites' suspicion with his curiosity."[86]

Originally recruited by the KGB as an industrial spy, Thomas Black
joined the Socialist Party (SP) in 1937 and became secretary of its Newark
branch. Assigned to spy on its Trotskyist faction, he supplied detailed personal information on Jack and Sara Weber, in whom the KGB was particularly interested. (Sara Weber had earlier been Leon Trotsky's secre-

tary and is a different person from the Sara Weber mentioned in chapter 6.) Black later testified that he was slated to travel to Mexico to infiltrate Trotsky's household in late 1938 but avoided the assignment.[87]

In the latter half of the 1930s Dr. Grigory Rabinovich, head of the American office of the Soviet Red Cross, oversaw the KGB's anti-Trotsky work, using Louis Budenz, who provided the KGB with its most successful spy within the American ranks of the Socialist Workers Party. Budenz recruited Sylvia Callen, a young Communist social worker. Sylvia joined the SWP in Chicago as Sylvia Caldwell, moved to New York, and eventually succeeded in becoming James Cannon's personal secretary. For years, she turned over copies of SWP leaders' correspondence, information about the finances of Trotskyist groups, and details about the Trotsky household in Mexico. She continued her assignment until 1947. Named as an unindicted co-conspirator in the Soble espionage case, she cooperated with a federal grand jury in 1958.[88]

Nor was infiltration of the Trotskyists the only route used by the KGB to gather information or harass Stalin's political rivals. The KGB New York station instructed Congressman Samuel Dickstein to get "'materials on the activities of Trotskyite organizations here. These materials could serve as a basis for dealing a powerful polit. blow to the Trotskyites, compromising them on the line of their ties with German and Japanese fascist organizations.'" Convinced that the Trotskyists were flirting with Ukrainian and Japanese "'counterrevolutionaries,'" the KGB planned to use Dickstein and the House Special Committee on Un-American Activities "'to prove that the isolationist position of the Amer. Trotskyites is no accident, that the Trotskyites' propaganda about removing America from Europ. and Asian problems, etc., is an outright betrayal by the Trotskyites, who are carrying out the orders of Japanese and German imperialism. The congressional committee can find the relevant documents in the CC [Central Committee] of the Trotskyites during a search. We have keys to all the entrances to the offices of the Trotskyite CC.'" Dickstein provided the KGB with shorthand copies of Dies Committee hearings that it hoped to use to identify individual Trotskyists, as well as copies of the correspondence between the Dies Committee and Trotsky about the possibility of Trotsky testifying. The KGB also hoped that it could use Dickstein's influence as chairman of the House Committee on Immigration and Naturalization to induce the U.S. government to hand over émigrés in whom it was interested: "'We intend through C. ["Crook"/Dickstein] to sound out the possibilities of arranging, with his participation, the deportation to our country on our instructions of White Guard and Trotskyite elements who are living in this country and could be of operational interest to us.'" Akhmerov pressed Laurence Duggan for State Department information about Trotsky's situation in Mexico, but Duggan responded that the State Department took little interest in Trotsky. Ovakimyan, however, obtained four pages of U.S. Justice Department material on Trotsky's activities in Mexico from Abraham Glasser, the KGB agent in the Justice Department (see chapter 4). Moscow Center directed that John Spivak, who covered the activities of pro-Nazi groups in the United States, "'should look for their connection to Trotskyites, both in America and against the USSR.'"[89]

A report records that as of January 1939, the KGB counted fifteen agents as the valuable sources in its American station. Three had infiltrated the Trotskyists: Sylvia Callen, Robert Menaker, and Floyd Miller. But having one-fifth of its most valuable sources reporting on a few thousand Trotskyists (of whom only a few hundred were activists) was not enough since the three were judged not suitable "for active struggle," rather than simply informing on Trotskyist activities. So at a time when it was deactivating technical and governmental sources, "'the station has been asked to acquire agents through whom we could wage an active battle to defeat the Trotskyites.'" In his memoirs, Pavel Sudoplatov recounts that he was summoned to meet with Stalin and Beria in March 1939; appointed deputy director of KGB foreign intelligence and head of the "fifth department"; and ordered to assassinate Trotsky, then in exile in Mexico. A report to Beria probably prepared sometime in 1939 identified the American branch of the Trotskyist movement as the linchpin of its worldwide efforts: "'In number of people and in financial capabilities, the American Trotskyite organization is the most powerful of all the Trotskyite groups that exist in European countries. In his counterrevolutionary work managing the 4th International and individual Trotskyite groups in China and European and South American countries, Trotsky relies first and foremost on his American cadres.'" The report went on to explain: "'Our intelligence operations in the fight against American Trotskyites have until now been only informational. All the conditions are in place to destroy the American Trotskyite organization; all that we lack are workers in the station who specialize in that line and who would organize this operation.'" The memo proposed sending employees of the fifth department to carry out the operation.[90]

Sudoplatov recounted how he had enlisted Leonid Eitingon, who had served an earlier tour in the United States, to supervise the murder. Eitingon in turn recruited two separate groups of potential assassins and arrived illegally in New York in October 1939 to oversee both projects. The first—unsuccessful—attempt to kill Trotsky took place on 24 May 1940, when, led by painter David Siqueiros and KGB officer Iosif Grigulevich, a group of Spanish and Mexican Communists (many veterans of the Spanish Civil War) stormed Trotsky's villa. Two of the gunmen were Leopolo and Luis Arenal, both of whom had connections to Jacob Golos. Luis's wife, Rose Arenal, an American Communist, later told the FBI she had acted as a mail drop for the brothers; her messages were picked up by Elizabeth Bentley.[91]

One of the minor mysteries of the affair was the precise role played by Robert Sheldon Harte, a twenty-five-year-old American Trotskyist who served as a guard at Trotsky's villa. He had joined the SWP in 1939 and in early 1940 volunteered to go to Mexico. Harte had opened the gate to the assault team, which raked Trotsky's residence and bedroom with gunfire and threw incendiary bombs, wounding the former Soviet leader's fourteen-year-old grandson. When the would-be assassins withdrew, they took Harte with them. He was found dead a few weeks later. Trotsky believed that he had been tricked into opening the gate, kidnapped, and murdered. He commissioned a plaque and had it placed next to the house with the text: "In Memory of Robert Sheldon Harte, 1915–1940, Murdered by Stalin." But others suspected that Harte might have been a plant. His father was surprised that his son had gone to guard Trotsky because he had a picture of Stalin in his room.[92]

KGB archival material brought to the West by Vasili Mitrokhin confirmed that Harte had collaborated with the attackers. A history of the KGB published in Russia in 1997 noted that Harte willingly opened the gate and left with the assailants, asserting that he had been recruited by the New York station and given the cover name "Cupid." The overall organizer of the Trotsky operation, Eitingon, later testified during an internal KGB probe that Harte had turned out to be a "traitor." After the assault, upset that Trotsky's grandson had been wounded, he had told the raiding party that "had he known all this, as an American he never would have agreed to participate in this raid. Such behavior served as the basis for deciding on the spot to liquidate him. He was killed by Mexicans." There is one mention of "Cupid" in a document in Vassiliev's notebooks. Moscow Center directed in November 1939 that in light of the recall of Rabinovich, who had handled anti-Trotsky work, several of his agents should be temporarily deactivated; one of them was "Cupid." Grigule-vich appears to have met Harte, perhaps in New York, reactivated him, and sent him to Mexico late in March 1940.[93]

The KGB finally succeeded in killing Trotsky through the help of an undercover American Communist, Ruby Weil. Weil worked for the CPUSA's secret apparatus and had been cultivating an ardent young Trotskyist, Sylvia Ageloff. Budenz transferred Weil to Grigory Rabinovich and the KGB in 1938. On a trip to Paris to attend a Trotskyist meeting Weil introduced Ageloff to Jacques Mornard, the alias of Ramon Mercader, the son of a prominent Spanish Communist, who worked for Eitingon. Mercader established a romantic relationship with her. Later Ageloff volunteered to work at Trotsky's residence in Mexico, enabling Mercader through her to gain access to Trotsky's house, arrange a private meeting with Trotsky in August 1940, and smash his skull with a small axe.[94]

Trotsky's murder did little to slow down the KGB's efforts to destroy his organization. Moscow instructed Ovakimyan in January 1941 "to intensify the struggle against the Trotskyites by making use of the disarray among the Trotskyites since the death of the "Old Man" [Trotsky], the departure of many of them, and the uncertainty and disillusionment among them." It was "essential that we acquire agents who are capable of vigorous actions to demoralize their ranks." A later message from Moscow suggested three candidates for recruitment and included specific tactics to use with them. Sara Weber, one of Thomas Black's targets several years before, remained of interest: "'The strategy toward Sara Weber should be designed on the basis that her relatives are in our territory. We have found out the particulars about her mother and sister here and begun actively cultivating them. Get started on the most meticulous study of Sara, her attitudes, connections, acquaintances and personal life, her feelings about her relatives, her financial situation, and so forth. It is imperative to ascertain whether she will agree to be recruited under threat of repression of her relatives or will 'consent' to work for us at her mother's 'request,' etc.'" The KGB also targeted Rose Karsner, wife of SWP leader James Cannon: "'She has a sister here [in the USSR] (who has been repressed [imprisoned]), and maybe in order to 'ransom' her freedom she will agree to cooperate with us. Can we get her on her 'love' for her husband, who is currently in a 'mental depression,' etc. Cannon himself could be cultivated for the same purpose.'" The third target was Harry Frankel, the SWP party name of Harry Braverman, whom KGB agents had been cultivating: "'Now that the work with him has started, it needs to be taken to a definite conclusion—either recruit him or compromise him. According to the latest reports, he is suffering a 'disaster' both psychologically and financially. Take note of this.'" Finally, Moscow was intrigued by reports from Sylvia Callen that items incriminating Soviet citizens might be found among Trotsky's papers, located in a bank vault, and suggested that "'if the opportunity presents itself, we need to obtain these archives.'" It also wanted Trotsky's papers at Harvard photographed.[95]

Still another Soviet operative targeted at the Trotskyists arrived in New York in 1942. Mark Zborowski had done major damage to the Trotskyists in France in the late 1930s. A message to Zarubin from Moscow explained that he had moved to Poland from the Soviet Union with his parents in 1921 at the age of thirteen. He had joined the Communist Party, been arrested, and fled to France to escape a prison sentence. While working for the Polish Communist Party in Paris,

"he was recruited in 1934 in France to cultivate Trotskyites. After that, on our instructions, T. ["Tulip"/Zborowski] left party work and broke off communications with the Polish Communists. In the summer of 1936 he began actively to cover Trotskyite activities. He established contact with French Trotskyites (Rousse, Nabal, and others), leaders of the international Trotskyite secretariat, and with the Russian section, headed by Sedov [Trotsky's son], then became Sedov's first assistant in the International Secretariat's work to publish 'Bulletin of the Opposition.' With his active participation we removed all of the secret archives of the International Secretariat, all of Sedov's archives, and a substantial portion of the "Old Man's" [Trotsky's] archives."

Moscow described Zborowski as "'a dedicated and tested operative; in terms of his personality he is not energetic enough and shows little initiative. He must be systematically guided in his future work. . . . Since 'Tulip' [Zborowski] is of great interest regarding use of him to cultivate Trotskyites in the U.S., try to find out his particulars through the agents in the circles of the Menshevik Nikolayevsky, Sara Weber and Estrina.'" Zborowski received instructions to insinuate himself with Trotskyists working on international affairs and particularly to "get very close to" Jean Van Heijenoort, Trotsky's former secretary, who had access to his archives at Harvard. A later message applauded that "'the opportunities for processing the "polecats" [Trotskyists] in the majority group have significantly increased,'" with the reestablishment of communications with Zborowski, but lamented that there were still no sources among the minority faction in the Trotskyist movement, likely a reference to Max Shachtman's tiny Workers Party, which had broken from the SWP.[96]

Zborowski's KGB liaison was yet another veteran of oppositional work among the Trotskyists, Jack Soble. A native of Lithuania, he had joined the German Communist Party in 1921. Married in the Soviet Union in 1927, he infiltrated the Trotskyist movement in 1929. Known as Abraham Senin, Soble and his brother, Robert Soblen, were leading figures in the German branch of the Trotskyists until they were expelled in 1932. The KGB dispatched both brothers and their families to Canada and then the United States in 1940, where Jack initially supervised infiltration of Trotskyists and other Russian émigré groups. As already discussed, he later worked with Martha Dodd, Alfred Stern, and Boris Morros.

By 1943 the American Trotskyist movement, never a significant force, was in dire straights. Leon Trotsky was dead. Its one toehold in the American trade union movement, leadership of Teamster Local 544, which controlled intracity trucking throughout much of the Midwest, had ended after the International Brotherhood of Teamsters expelled the Trotskyists from the union. Finally, the U.S. government tried and imprisoned SWP leaders under the sedition sections of the Smith Act in 1942. Nonetheless, in 1943 the New York station had Joseph Katz meet with one of its CPUSA liaisons, Bernard Schuster, to seek assistance for additional anti-Trotskyist work:

"On our instructions "Informer" [Katz] met with "Echo" [Schuster] to ascertain the latter's capabilities in cultivating the polecats [Trotskyists] "Dak" and "Gay" [likely James Cannon and Max Shachtman]. E. gladly expressed a desire to provide assistance to us in this matter. He can place at our disposal one person from "Dak's" group and one from "Gay's" group. Recommend two or three people from among the covert fellowcountrymen [Communists], whom we need to get close to the polecats. Arrange, if necessary, for a well-known local fellowcountryman to quit the fellowcountryman organization under the guise of dissenting on some issue, for the purpose of getting close to the polecats and gradually gaining the trust of their headquarters. E. will pass along autobiographical information on these people to us very shortly.

At the same time E. said that he had helped us for many years but had never received assistance from us in his fellowcountryman work. So he has made a request for assistance, if possible, in covering the following questions about the polecats, which are essential for orienting the fellowcountryman leadership: 1. Number of members in the organization. 2. Number of groups and number of members in them. 3. The first and last names of polecats in the "country" [USA]. 4. An analysis of their activities and their plans.

After that E. said that he has interesting connections in Cairo and Brazzaville (French Equatorial Africa) and capabilities for infiltrating agents into the "cabin" [OSS] on the line of its work for Bulgaria, Yugoslavia, and other countries. After discussing all these facts, we concluded that we should utilize "Echo's" capabilities and assign communications with him to "Informer" alone, while gradually pulling "Sound" [Golos] and the neighbors [GRU] away from him. In our view, we must help E. in supplying the information of interest to him about the polecats, since this will bolster his position in the leadership of the fellowcountryman organization of the "country" and will make it easier to work with him, which we can already begin now."[97]

The tiny Trotskyist movement in the United States never amounted to more than a few thousand members, had minimal financial resources, and had only a minor role in the trade union movement. Yet even when the KGB lacked enough officers to service valuable political and technical spies, it dispatched additional personnel to America to recruit and supervise sources and agents aimed at this weak threat. It devoted considerable resources to neutralizing and destroying it, sending in infiltrators to report on its activities, steal its documents, coerce its members, and harass its activists. It was an obsession that achieved its objective.

"Николаб" Дело 9995

с.1 Губцайт Петр Давидович, 1900 г.р. Днепропетровская обл.,
с. Бородаевка. член ВКП(б) с 1920 г.
в дом Охранка — шпионаж, принадлежность к
контр-рев. организации. в Н-б — вице-консул

с.4 Др. фамилия - Гусев П.Я. (под ней он был в Н-б.)
Жена - Губцайт Таиса Михайловна.

с.11 Из разных источников поступает сообщения об отриц.
отношении Николаб к ... работе (см. его письмо ранее)
от одного из тов. пред-б ?ОГПУ

с.12 Письмо, видимо, консулу, от 25.10.34.
Николаб часто общается с работы => иностранцы зава-
тотах в-сои, чем же он занимается. Не ходит на партсоб-
рания

с.13 Уклоняется от работы в кружках.
с.14 Николай должен вести себя так, чтобы не вызывать подозрения.

с.37 Губцайт Петр Давидович, род. 25 сент. 1910, село
Бородаевка Днепропет. обл., евреи.

с.40 ЦК ВКП(б) тов. Васильеву.

"...Гусев в течение двух с лишним лет игнорировал
партоганизацию, никогда не присутствовал на партсобраниях,
не участвовал в марксистско-ленинских кружках, он
не присутствовал и на собрании, где стоял негучие
вопрос и где выявилось лицо коммуниста в
осуждении контр-революционеров троцкистов."
[Гусева окружала группа троцкистов из числа сов. команди-
рованных] в д. с. "Шумовский, командированной
советским студент в Массачусетский Институт в Бостон.
...было обнаружено, что он в 1934 году получал троц-
кистскую литературу на свое имя и имел связь с
русской колонией в Бостоне."

с.43   Шапиро (подпер в силе)
Гусев расстрелян.

с.48 Арестован в к. 1938 г.

CHAPTER 9

The KGB in America

Strengths, Weaknesses, and Structural Problems

persistent popular and media myth holds that the KGB was a near superhuman organization, staffed by skilled officers carrying out sophisticated schemes designed by clever Moscow overlords who had a long-standing plan on how to subvert the West. (Historians have been less awed.) In this tabloid version of espionage history, the KGB effortlessly ran rings around American counterintelligence and deftly manipulated its resources to drain American secrets. Its operatives were carefully organized, followed strict guidelines, and carried out their assigned tasks according to a calibrated regimen of sophisticated intelligence tradecraft. Fed by alarmed Westerners eager to emphasize the mortal dangers the USSR posed to open and democratic societies, as well as by Soviet propagandists and their sympathizers anxious to buttress the reputation of Soviet power, this legend grew during the Cold War. And after it ended, the release of intelligence-related material from Russian and American archives magnified the all-powerful

In 1933 Peter Gutzeit organized and was the first chief of the KGB legal station in the United States. He was recalled in 1938, and KGB memos on this page note that he was executed during Stalin's purges on charges of Trotskyism. Courtesy of Alexander Vassiliev.

KGB story line. Influenced by the documentation of the extensive and even breathtaking number of Americans who had aided the KGB, many commentators emphasized the proficiency of Soviet intelligence. These revelations should not be minimized or avoided. The KGB's reach extended in many directions and touched many more Americans than historians once believed. Nevertheless, it is also important to understand that along with its strengths, there were also limitations and failings.

Another reason to keep its success in perspective is that for many years the KGB faced little serious or sustained opposition to its work. American counterintelligence was woefully inadequate and inattentive. While the KGB wasn't a ten-foot superman, until the mid-1940s its opposition could have been described as a four-foot dwarf. With Washington policymakers indifferent, for years the FBI devoted scant resources to counterintelligence, and once it began to pay attention in the late 1930s, its initial emphasis was on German and Japanese espionage. It took several years to develop counterintelligence expertise, and not until the end of World War II did the Bureau focus significant resources on the Soviet challenge. Soviet success, in other words, was not due solely to KGB skill, but also benefited from American incompetence and indifference. The KGB's problems were a combination of difficulties endemic to any espionage service, blunders and policies peculiar to a Stalinist bureaucracy, and the double-edged sword of its reliance on so many CPUSA resources.

Station Chiefs

KGB station chiefs faced daunting problems. The legal station chief, first of all, was a very busy man. He had to have an official cover job with a Soviet institution that gave him his official reason for being in the United States. To avoid suspicion on the part of American counterintelligence and to prevent internal gossip among Soviet personnel, he had to spend some time fulfilling the demands of that position, meaning that his real job supervising Soviet espionage required long hours.

There were also, particularly in the 1930s, political niceties to observe. The Soviet Union had finally managed to secure diplomatic recognition from the United States in 1933 after more than a decade of isolation. As part of the terms it had officially agreed to refrain from supporting Communist propaganda within the United States. Nevertheless, Communist International support for the CPUSA continued without any noticeable change. Irritated, the U.S. government delivered a diplomatic note to the Soviets in August 1935 with a "most emphatic protest against this flagrant

violation of the pledge given by the Government of the Union of Soviet Social Republics on Nov. 16, 1933, with respect to non-interference in the internal affairs of the United States." Despite its response that the Comintern
was a private body over which it had no control, the Soviet government worried that an espionage scandal linked to Soviet diplomats might ignite a
brouhaha that could get out of hand. Moscow Center warned its stations;
"'In the context of Washington, it is completely inadmissible to conduct recruitment in official agencies through our official division, as this will inevitably lead to the aforementioned complications.'" Consequently, the legal
station chiefs and their officers had to tread carefully for a time. (Nothing
came of the protest: President Roosevelt decided to ignore Moscow's failure to live up to its agreement.)[1]

Illegal station chiefs had their own problems. They also had to have
a cover job since people with no visible job might occasion notice or questions. But working for someone else involved risks, to say nothing of how
to explain or get permission for the frequent absences and irregular hours
that an espionage job necessitated. Lacking diplomatic protection, they
could not call on the Soviet Embassy for support if arrested. Living illegally in the United States required blending in with ordinary Americans
while avoiding official scrutiny. They socialized with people who might
become suspicious, and they had no entirely safe and secure place to
stash the tools of their trade. When things went wrong, the consequences
could be dangerous and unpredictable. The first illegal station chief in
New York, Valentin Markin, provided an object lesson when he died in
1934 under unclear circumstances, either murdered in a street robbery
or bar brawl or killed in a car accident. Moscow Center immediately ordered the illegal station to deactivate work on all lines and destroy letters
and telegrams. There were, however, complications. One of Markin's assistants, Iskhak Akhmerov, reported that Markin's partner in his cover
business knew his real name and had met other illegal officers. Even
more worrisome, Markin kept a safe deposit box that contained not only
money to finance his operation, but also notes he had written. Further, an
American lawyer would be needed to get access to this material. Nor did
the potential damage stop there. His American paramour knew what
Markin did and could expose not only his cover company but also Alexander and Helen Koral, KGB couriers, since "once, when 'Davis' [Markin]
was drunk, he brought her to their apartment." The KGB attempted to
persuade her to move to the Soviet Union, but Akhmerov reported:
"'King [unidentified KGB officer] meets with her and carefully cajoles
her, trying to persuade her to do what is best both for herself and us. She

promised to think it over and give us an answer soon. We are not sure if she will go. She has never left this city and has relatives here. King thinks that she is incapable of doing wrong. We will keep her under surveillance and offer her temporary assistance if she is in need.'" There is no indication that she moved to Moscow, but she also fulfilled the New York station's judgment that she would keep quiet.[2]

Even the best illegal station chiefs ran into problems. By most measures, Akhmerov, who served two tours as chief of the American illegal station (late 1930s and early 1940s), was one of the best. A Tatar born in 1901, Akhmerov joined the Communist Party in 1919 and was quickly singled out as a talented "minority" and marked for special schooling. He became a KGB officer in 1930 and served an initial tour in China, where he attended the American College in Peking posing as a Turk. Recalled to Moscow in 1934, he was tapped for the illegal station in the United States. He obtained false identity papers and enrolled at Columbia University to study English. He explained to young KGB officers how he turned himself into an "American":

"The transition from being a foreign student to being an American in such a large city as NY, with its population of millions, was not particularly difficult, as it turned out. At Columbia U., I was known well only to the English language instructor and nine or ten students—most of them foreigners—almost all of whom intended to return to their countries after graduation. It was also unlikely that I would be remembered from university registration, which was typically done by thousands of people. Therefore, the only people who could have known me well were one of the instructors and the landlord at whose apartment I was then living, a Jew by nationality. Thus, there was no particular risk involved. If I had subsequently run into these people by chance, we could have done little more than say 'hello' and 'goodbye' to each other. I therefore thought that I was not risking much by switching to new identity papers.

Because I knew that I would have to switch to new identity papers, I had made a point of not expanding my circle of acquaintants, and when I began living under American identity papers, I did not restrict myself when establishing connections. After adopting local identity papers, I kept my previous cover for a period of time: I attended classes, where lectures were given on economic, cultural, and sociopolitical sciences. I was not involved in any other work and therefore had free time at my disposal to learn the language well, study up on sociopolitical sciences, read magazines, go to libraries, etc."[3]

Akhmerov proved to be an effective illegal operative and became chief of the illegal station after Moscow recalled Boris Bazarov in late 1937 and executed him as an "enemy of the people." He further blended into American society by marrying a girl from Kansas, Helen Lowry, a niece of CPUSA chief Earl Browder, who was working as a courier for the KGB New York station. When Moscow Center recalled Akhmerov to the Soviet Union in 1939, it allowed him to take her with him.

Moscow Center sent Akhmerov back to the United States in December 1941 to once again run the illegal station, which had been shut down after his recall. Helen Lowry returned with him, and they resided at an apartment at 115 Cabrini Boulevard in New York. Akhmerov assumed the identity of Michael Adamec and claimed to have been born in Chicago in 1904. (An FBI investigation later determined that Michael Adamec's birth certificate was fraudulent, inserted into Cook County birth registration records by a crooked staff member of the registrar of births.) Vasily Zarubin, chief of the legal station and overall supervisor of KGB activities in America, wrote a lengthy report to Moscow explaining the difficulties that ensued from Akhmerov's assumption of the identity of a native-born American in wartime:

Laws related to mobilization were immediately enacted. M's ["Mer"/Akhmerov's] age made him subject to military service, and he had to go through military registration . . . the need to find a cover and legalize himself immediately. Even before I arrived, M. had gotten in touch with 'Boss' [Henry Bookman] . . . and joined his business as a partner. Through him he prepared the documents that were required for registration. M. was definitely going to be drafted, but then a law was enacted that required the call-up only of persons under 38 years of age for the army. M. was a little older, but there was still mobilization for military plants. This was no less dangerous, since it involved fingerprinting. He could not afford this, since he had entered the 'country' [USA] using documents from the 'Territory' [Canada] and had been fingerprinted when he received the 'country's' transit visa.

Despite the uncertainty regarding military service, M. contacted the agents and started working. His cover initially didn't seem solid to us. A shop selling women's hats. The prewar crisis . . . a decline in revenue, they could barely sustain themselves. I suggested that M. use 'Frost's [Boris Morros's] business as a cover and act as its representative in Tyre [New York]. M. didn't want to do that, since he had already specified 'Boss's' business everywhere . . . didn't want to get involved with a person whose relative had been repressed in the USSR.

We decided to move in the direction of expanding 'Boss's' business. We increased the firm's volume and the business grew stronger, although it didn't yield any profit. M. wanted to use Boss's facilities to open his own fur business, but he wanted to buy furs from our trading orgs. I felt that he couldn't do this, since all firms that work with the USSR are registered. M. has been with B. ["Boss"] for three years already, and the cover fits him. He works as a bookkeeper and furrier. He has complete control of his time.

The KGB invested $5,000 in Henry Bookman, Inc., at 19 West 57th Street in New York. There were, however, complications. Akhmerov wrote a letter Zarubin sent along to Moscow in 1942 in which he noted that Bookman had rented a room to a relative of Walter Krivitsky but thought it was not a problem: "I'm sure he and Krivitsky have not met here. We can't ask them because it would cause suspicion."[4]

Anxious to develop a more secure cover, Akhmerov proposed a variety of capitalist schemes. The first was to become a stock market speculator:

"Hundreds of thousands of people live primarily by clipping coupons. . . . Even with a small amount of capital you can get into this business, set up relations with a reputable Wall Street banking firm, and establish a certain business position for yourself. In the U.S., the more you engage in all kinds of commercial and financial business, the more respect you command and the better your social position. Here any semiliterate businessman looks down on a professor.

As another option establishing the following business: opening our own shop of fur products. This is a fashionable and reputable business. There are a great many small, stylish fur shops here. I understand a little bit in the fur business: at one time my grandfather had a fur shop. When I was a boy, I helped him in the business. Now I could start studying the business. "Nelly" [Helen Lowry] could also take an active part in it. She could be the shop manager and a saleslady. Meanwhile she could take fashion courses and train herself in a short time as a specialist.

The business could look like this: A nice shop selling fur products on Madison Avenue or in the 50s between Fifth and Madison avenues. "Nelly" and I are incorporated owners. "Nelly" is constantly at the shop as a saleslady and generally runs the business. I also take an active part as an owner: I buy furs from wholesalers, attend auctions, and so forth. It's not essential for me to be continuously at the shop myself. What will be for sale will be silver foxes, Persian lamb, and sealskin coats and jackets and other fur products. Besides selling ready-made items, custom orders will be accepted."

But neither Zarubin nor Moscow bought these grandiose entrepreneurial plans, and Akhmerov remained at Bookman's shop until his final departure from the United States in 1945.[5]

When the KGB sent Peter Gutzeit to the United States in 1933 to set up its first legal station, he did not have to concoct plans for a cover job, but he did have difficulty balancing the time required to carry out his official duties as a Soviet diplomat and his "real" job as station chief. One of the problems was that his KGB position was secret not only from

Americans, but for security reasons was also unknown to most of the Soviet diplomats and support personnel with whom he worked. Moscow Center received a number of complaints that he frequently absented himself from his cover job and that some of the Americans employed by the consulate wondered what he was doing. Additionally, due to the demands on his time, he rarely participated in mandatory Communist Party activities among Soviet nationals, occasioning more grumbling.[6]

Gutzeit knew he was being criticized but could not figure out how to do his KGB job and keep the consulate and the party happy. By mid-1938, after nearly five years on the job, he had had enough and asked to be recalled. He told Moscow Center: "'I don't attend meetings or clubs; nor did I enter into an agreement on socialist competition. All this, of course, could only have resulted in the fact that the Party community is in some form or other blackening my name. . . . My own situation in terms of time constraints and high levels of stress has also increased many times over. I have already received an invitation from the [party] secretary to visit him for a discussion. It's obvious what this discussion will be about, and it's also obvious to me that I cannot change a thing. The only way out I can think of is to leave this place.'" He also requested a recall due to his "'severe exhaustion and anxiety'"; he and his wife were anxious to get back to Moscow, where their son was being raised by elderly grandparents. Gutzeit got his wish. He was recalled late in 1938 but not to recuperate. Accused of being an enemy of the people, he was shot.[7]

Self-Destruction

Gutzeit's fate illustrated the consequences of Stalin's decision to purge his own security services. Under Gutzeit and Boris Bazarov, chief of the illegal station after Markin's death, the KGB had developed several well-placed sources at the U.S. State Department (David Salmon, Laurence Duggan, and Noel Field); an important source at the Justice Department (Abraham Glasser); and a scattering of lower-level but useful sources at other federal agencies and on congressional staffs, even putting one congressman, Samuel Dickstein, on Moscow's payroll. Gayk Ovakimyan had recruited an impressive array of technical and industrial informants in the chemical industry, while Stanislav Shumovsky had done the same for aviation. The American stations had also built an infrastructure of American couriers, talent spotters, and suppliers of false passports, safe houses, and the like. Yet beginning in 1938 and continuing into 1940, part of what had been built was destroyed entirely and much of the rest deactivated or left in disarray. This crippling attack came not at the hands of American counterintelligence but from Moscow.

The terror Stalin unleashed in the USSR beginning in 1934 consumed much of the leadership and large portions of the rank-and-file of the Soviet Communist Party. The KGB was both its chief instrument and one of its major victims. Most of the senior officers who had supervised the early years of the purges and hundreds of their subordinates were arrested as enemies of the people. The KGB's foreign intelligence arm was not exempt; most of its overseers were executed. Scores of GRU and KGB officers serving abroad were recalled, declared traitors, and shot or sent to the Gulag. Boris Bazarov and Peter Gutzeit were killed. Among the bill of particulars justifying Gutzeit's execution was the following: "'For more than two years Gusev [Gutzeit] ignored the party organization, never attended party meetings, didn't participate in Marxist-Leninist groups; he also didn't attend the meeting where burning issues were on the agenda and where the face of a Communist was unmasked in condemnation of counterrevolutionaries, Trotskyites.' (Gusev was surrounded by a group of Trotskyites from among Soviet people sent on assignment.)"[8]

Officers in the American stations joined in the hunt for imaginary traitors and Trotskyists in their ranks. Before Gutzeit's recall, KGB illegal officer Iosif Grigulevich met with "Kurt," one of the legal station's officers. Grigulevich told "Kurt" that he was convinced that letters to Moscow Center about treason and Trotskyism among the American station's operatives "'that he sent through "Nikolay" [Gutzeit] were being opened by him and possibly destroyed.'" "Kurt" went on to report that Grigulevich claimed "'while he knew an enormous number of documented facts, he wasn't able to bring this to the center's attention,'" and then he "'immediately added that if I could inconspicuously put his letter in the mail, he would consider that his party duty as a Chekist [KGB officer] had been fulfilled. At the same time he instructed me how to perform this operation with the maximum guarantee that the letter would not be opened by the station chief at the last moment before the mail was sent out.'" Grigulevich charged that the head of Amtorg in America was a secret Trotskyist, that Gutzeit was "'the protector of this gang,'" and that Ovakimyan (deputy station chief) had "'begun to turn corrupt'" as well. "Kurt" bypassed his station chief and sent a report to Moscow but took care to close his report by casting aspersions on Grigulevich: "'On the one hand, the exceedingly serious charge against the station and the deputy chief, as well as the chmn. of Amtorg, but on the other, the extremely strange method of communicating with Moscow suggested by

"Yuz" [Grigulevich] compels me to raise this question with the center in a fundamental way—either Nikolay [Gutzeit] indeed is a protector of enemies, or "Yuz" himself is no less our enemy.'"9

Shortly after "Kurt" sent his back-channel report, Moscow recalled, arrested, and later executed Gutzeit. Aware of which way the wind was blowing, "Kurt" became more aggressive. In January 1939, Ovakimyan, who had taken over as station chief, sent a letter to Zelman Passov, whom he mistakenly believed was still chief of foreign intelligence (he had been arrested and was later shot). Ovakimyan wrote:

""Kurt" began to conduct subversive work among the station's operatives under the guise of criticism of glaring shortcomings and supposed exposure of Nikolay's [Gutzeit's] activities. As a result he went so far as to begin having outrageous conversations with "Grimm" [station cipher officer], demanding that he show him cipher cables and demanding that he (Grimm) automatically refrain from carrying out the chief's orders. Finally a few days later, without any grounds whatsoever, "Kurt" called "Grimm" a provocateur, suspecting the latter of having told me everything. "Grimm" took all this very hard, and it took me great pains to temporarily settle this. On his own initiative "Grimm" wrote me a report on what had happened, which I am sending for your review."10

By April 1939 New York station officer Andrey Graur was back in Moscow, where he denounced the head of Amtorg and Gutzeit as Trotskyists and added that Ovakimyan was likely complicit in some way. He had encouraged another officer, Vasily Mironov, to bypass Ovakimyan, the new station chief, and report directly to Moscow Center. As for himself, Graur wrote: "'Sought in my work to find the origin of the criminal work that had been done in our representative offices in America and at the same time not dig so deep as to create a risk that certain employees of Amtorg, the representative offices, and the station won't return home [to Moscow].'" (At least two KGB officers did refuse to return. Armand Feldman quietly disappeared in mid-1938 and fled to Canada. An officer named Chivin, chief of a small special operations unit, also disappeared.) Graur went on to state that Moscow Center had been receiving tainted intelligence: "'I can safely say that our agents are plants intended to divert attention to a false path.'" Grigulevich joined him in discrediting the agents, reporting to Moscow, "'More than 40% of the Am. station's sources were obvious Trotskyites.'" Graur also told Moscow Center what should be done: "'1. Immediately summon Gennady [Ovakimyan] to Moscow, first without his family, while temporarily turning things over to his associate [Grigory] Rabinovich in order to disorient Gennady. 2. Then recall and replace our entire station staff. 3. Immediately cease working with agents and carefully review the list of agents, who in my view are almost all plants.'"[11]

In the nightmare atmosphere of the Terror, Moscow Center took Graur's paranoid fantasy seriously. At the end of September 1939, Pavel Fitin, the new head of KGB foreign intelligence, sent a memo to Lavrenty Beria, People's Commissar for Internal Affairs, outlining changes in the American station. (Fitin was only thirty-two when he became chief of foreign intelligence, and his rapid promotion after a short career in the KGB was due to the arrest and execution of most of its senior officers.) He did not adopt the more extreme recommendations of his subordinates but proposed a severe alteration in the station's operations. Due to the "'changed international situation in Europe and the existence of contamination both in the staff of the station itself and among agents in the USA, which could lead to undesirable consequences for us, I think it necessary to conduct all work of the American station with utmost caution and to minimize meetings with agents.'" He suggested a severe cutback in contacts with those working on the technical intelligence line; "'to meet only with those agents who are carrying out your special assignment'"; and advocated recalling seven of the station's officers. He noted that Akhmerov, then head of the illegal station, "'is unknown to any workers in the department.'" Similarly Grigulevich and "Martinez" (an unidentified illegal officer) "'are unknown to anyone in the department.'" So devastated was headquarters that none of the current staff knew these three long-serving illegal officers. And as an additional reason for recall, Fitin added that Grigulevich and "Martinez" had been sent "'abroad by the enemies Passov and Shpigelglaz,'" two former heads of KGB foreign intelligence recently executed as traitors. As for the agent networks developed by the American stations, Fitin recommended drastic reductions: "'1. In tech. intelligence, keep 10 of the 36 agents with whom we are connected. Break off ties with the rest for the time being. 2. On the polit. line, keep 13 of the 59 agents with whom we are connected, and keep 10 conditionally; altogether—23 agents. Break off ties with the rest.'"[12]

Fitin's plan included the recall of Gayk Ovakimyan, the station chief, who was scheduled to share Gutzeit's fate. Born in the Transcaucasus to an Armenian family in 1898, Ovakimyan had been a Bolshevik since 1918 and had been imprisoned in Armenia before it was incorporated into the USSR. After assisting in the Sovietization of Armenia in the early 1920s, he moved to Moscow to study chemistry, and the KGB recruited him for foreign intelligence work in 1931 while he was in graduate school. After an assignment in Germany, the KGB sent him to the United States to serve as Gutzeit's deputy, with primary responsibilities for technical intelligence. Formally, he worked at Amtorg and had a fellowship at the Rockefeller Institute. Under his guidance, the KGB recruited a slew of technical sources supplying information on topics ranging from oil refining to bacteriological research and occupying jobs in both private laboratories and government institutions.

As the Terror gathered momentum, however, Ovakimyan's successes in recruiting sources counted for little. Graur and a Moscow Center officer, Senior Lieutenant Butkov, prepared a damning report in September 1939 on his personal history and KGB career. It ominously noted that when he was studying chemistry at the Moscow Higher Technical School in 1928, the institution's dean was a "'now-exposed enemy of the people'" and that his station chief during his first assignment in Berlin had been KGB officer Abram Slutsky, since exposed as an enemy of the people. And, of course, it noted:

"[He] began working in the Amer. station in 1933 as Nikolay's [Gutzeit's] deputy, and Gennady [Ovakimyan] couldn't help but know about the wrecking activity that Nikolay was conducting in the station. . . . As the permanent deputy of the ex-station chief and enemy of the people Nikolay, Gennady must bear responsibility for the failure to provide Chekist service to Soviet people and to the work of Soviet institutions in the U.S. . . . As asst. to the station chief in the U.S. since Sept. 1933, Gennady not only failed to help expose the station's wrecking work but, on the contrary, took every measure, it seems to us, either to conceal a whole host of facts from the home [Moscow] or to confuse it."

Just as dangerous for Ovakimyan's survival was concern that he had relied too heavily on the CPUSA's Jacob Golos: "'"Gennady" allowed "Sound" [Golos] . . . to delve deeply into the station's work and made him the principal operative, his work adviser. Gennady doesn't decide the principal matters of station work without "Sound." All new recruits are checked by "Sound." "Sound" knows almost every agent. "Sound," meanwhile, turns up in the testimony of Durmashkin (sentenced to the supreme penalty), as a secret Trotskyite personally connected to Cannon, and that he and Cannon jointly infiltrated Mensheviks and Trotskyites into the Soviet Union from 1920 until recently for counterrev. work.'" (Ilya Durmashkin, a Russian immigrant to the United States, had joined the American Communist Party in the 1920s and worked for Amtorg. He returned to the Soviet Union in the early 1930s and worked in the Soviet printing industry. The KGB's internal arm arrested and executed him in 1938. Durmashkin's admissions recorded in KGB files were one of the typically absurd confessions of the Terror. He stated that he had been an agent of the

Tsarist secret police who had infiltrated the Russian Marxist movement; then a Menshevik who had infiltrated the Bolsheviks; then a Trotskyist; and, finally, a German spy.)[13]

Earlier Moscow Center had thought well of the technical information flowing in from Ovakimyan's sources. But Butkov and Graur decided retroactively that the material was of little value:

"a) Gennady [Ovakimyan] personally recruited all sources in chemistry without taking into account interest in defense matters. These agents were and are the principal supplier of worthless material and the principal absorber of the enormous amounts of money that the station has been spending.

According to American law, inventions in technology are a state secret for 2 years from the time they go into service in the U.S. Army, and upon expiration of the 2-year period they become merely a company secret. The materials received from Gennady were, as a rule, 2, 3, or 4 years old, i.e. materials that were easier and safer to obtain. Gennady was an ardent defender of the interests of the 'army of scoundrels' that 'nourished itself' around our station in the U.S. b) Gennady took the most active part in the wrecking work method that the station selected, namely: 'Fake it.'"

Graur and Butkov also argued that given how many sources Ovakimyan had recruited and flaws in his espionage tradecraft, the FBI must have known he was a Soviet operative, and the very fact that it had not moved against him was more evidence that he was actually under American control. They ended their report, "'On the basis of all of the foregoing, one conclusion can be drawn—recall Gennady home as soon as possible.'"[14]

Fitin formally recommended Ovakimyan's recall in October 1939, Beria approved, and Fitin then secretly contacted Pavel Pastelnyak, then an officer of the KGB New York station:

"Pavel [Beria] has decided to leave you working in the U.S. as assistant station chief so that, very soon, after Gennady [Ovakimyan] is recalled home and you get acquainted with the conditions of working abroad, you can take over things from him and head up all of the work of the Amer. station. Gennady will be recalled home in the near future. We will notify Gennady by special letter about your appointment as assistant station chief. Try to make maximum use of this segment of time to get acquainted with the work of the entire station. You should have the very best relationship with Gennady. Don't give him any indication that you are preparing to replace him. In order to correspond with you independently of Gennady, we are sending you a special cipher, and in the next few days we will send a reliable cipher clerk who will contact you upon arriving. All cables from us and to us must go only through this person. Absolutely no one, including Gennady, must know about our correspondence with you. Please keep this in mind."

The KGB's chief of foreign intelligence had contacted an officer of the KGB New York station by a back channel to prepare him to take over when his station chief was lured back to Moscow to face what was likely to be a grim fate. Moscow Center was even sending a new cipher officer to assist with the plot against its senior officer in the United States. It had convinced itself that Ovakimyan, like station chiefs Gutzeit and Bazarov, five former chiefs of KGB foreign intelligence itself, and thousands of other KGB officers, was an enemy of the people and might defect unless he was decoyed back to Moscow. As for Pastelnyak, he had only limited experience in foreign intelligence and spoke poor English. He came from the Soviet border guards (also run by the KGB) and had originally been sent to New York to oversee security at the Soviet exhibit at the 1939 New York World Fair. When that task ended and with most New York station officers recalled, the KGB shifted Pastelnyak over to foreign intelligence and made him Ovakimyan's assistant station chief.[15]

Ovakimyan received orders to leave New York in March 1940 and return to Moscow via Naples, Rome, and Berlin. He did not go and remained the KGB New York station chief. Did he realize that something was wrong and find plausible excuses to stay in New York? Did Moscow Center change its mind? Or had it only decided to postpone matters? Exactly what happened is not set out in the documents in Vassiliev's notebooks or elsewhere. Pastelnyak, however, continued back-channel communications with Moscow Center at least through April 1940.[16]

Ovakimyan was once again scheduled to return to Moscow in May 1941, although whether restored to good odor or still facing a dark future is unknown. In any event, the FBI intervened to end any doubts about his *bona fides*. Based on information from Armand Feldman, the FBI arrested him as an agent of a foreign government who had failed to register as required by law. As the panicked New York station posted additional guards and prepared to burn documents in case the FBI attempted to storm the consulate, the commissar for state security, Merkulov, instructed Pastelnyak, temporarily in command in New York: "Let Gennady [Ovakimyan] know: We will take all necessary measures in your case. Hold tight, deny everything. . . . Don't worry about your wife and daughter. We will take care of them. We are confident about a favorable outcome of the case and that you will conduct yourself in a worthy manner." The Nazi attack on the USSR in June brought a warming in

Soviet-American relations, and the State Department turned aside the FBI's desire for prosecution. Deported in exchange for the emigration of several Russian-born wives of Americans, Ovakimyan returned to Moscow as a respected senior officer, supervised Anglo-American operations, and rose to the post of deputy head of foreign intelligence.[17]

Graur and Butkov had treated Ovakimyan's reliance on Jacob Golos as damning evidence of his treasonable Trotskyist links in their 1939 indictment. Yet no relationship brought the KGB more benefit than its contact with Golos, and none ultimately caused it as much difficulty. Born in 1890 in Ekaterinoslav, Ukraine, Yakov Naumovich Tasin was first arrested in 1907 while managing an illegal Bolshevik printing press and sent to Siberia. He escaped and made his way to America via Japan and China. Active in the Socialist Party's Russian-language affiliate, he became a charter member of the American Communist Party in 1919 and adopted "Jacob Golos" as his public/party name. He lived and worked in the Soviet Union in the early 1920s and became a member of the Soviet party. He returned to the United States in 1923, after American party leader Jay Lovestone appealed to the Central Committee of the Soviet party to send him back, citing "his significant influence among the Russian working masses in the United States. . . . It was a mistake by our party to have allowed him to leave America to work in the Soviet Union." Golos held several mid-level CPUSA positions in the 1920s, including party organizer in Detroit; head of the Society for Technical Aid to Soviet Russia; and business manager of *Novy Mir*, a party-aligned Russian-language newspaper. He returned to the USSR a few years later for work at the CPUSA-backed American industrial colony in the Kuzbas region in Siberia and was again accepted into the Soviet Communist party. But with Soviet party permission, he once again came back to the United States in 1929 for new CPUSA assignments.[18]

Golos became president of World Tourists, a CPUSA-financed travel and shipping agency in 1932 and held that position until his death in 1943. Trafficking in false passports and facilitating the clandestine movement of both CPUSA and Comintern activists around the globe, the business enabled him to serve both American Communist and Soviet interests. A close friend of party leader Earl Browder, he also served on the powerful Central Control Commission, which oversaw party discipline and kept track of secret party members. The KGB first recruited him in 1930 "for work on the passport line." Through his connections with a clerk in the Brooklyn passport office who had a gambling problem, Golos procured genuine passports by having sham applicants provided by the CPUSA present birth certificates of people who had died young or naturalization papers provided by cooperating party members. The KGB tried to establish direct ties with the clerk, but he "categorically refused and wants to work only with Sound [Golos]." (The KGB's cover name for Golos, "Sound," was a play on words. "Golos" in Russian means "voice.")[19]

While his relationship with the KGB started with passports, over time Golos became its chief liaison with the CPUSA. With his personal relationship with Browder and position on the party's Control Commission, Golos could call on party resources to perform a multitude of tasks for the New York station. His Russian origins and status as an old Bolshevik also contributed to his easy working relationship with Soviet intelligence. Grigory Rabinovich, a KGB officer who had two tours in the United States, wrote in late 1939 that he had had "a total of 500–600 meetings with Sound [Golos] in two years." Describing him as the American "station's principal agent for 10 years," he listed the areas where he had provided assistance: "Trotskyites, the selection and checking of people for intel. work, passports, the establishment of covers, the settlement of problems with the leadership of the CPUSA, individual complex assignments." Rabinovich recalled that the press of the station's business with Golos required "sometimes 3–4 meetings a day." In a 1938 report Gutzeit observed that because of security concerns, the station's reliance on "party contacts" was "'of course, undesirable and dangerous,'" but given the demands on the station and its resources, "We have no choice but to work through Sound."[20]

Moscow Center first paid serious attention to Golos in 1937, when one of the New York station's officers, Liveit-Levit, suggested that he was not candid about where he was getting some of the information he gave the KGB. Golos, in fact, habitually protected his party-based sources and wanted the KGB to work through him and not directly with them. He may have wanted to enhance his importance, but he also feared that once the KGB found a source useful, for reasons of security it would isolate him or her from the party. Golos, a long-serving CPUSA official, saw no need to lose party assets. When Moscow asked about Liveit-Levit's comment, Gutzeit responded angrily:

"Re Sound [Golos]. Again some kind of nonsense. Sound has been known to our department for 7 years. Many people knew this source before Ten's [Liveit-Levit's] arrival, and no one had any doubts about his exceptional devotion to us. (After all, it's no secret that Sound is an old fellowcountryman [Communist] with the local organization.) But now Ten appears, starts some kind of review of people and work (neither one has anything to do with him), writes you about this, and you, instead of putting him in his place, also start to 'doubt' and ask questions: 'Who is Sound?' This would be funny if it didn't simultaneously show that you really don't know the people, even those who have a long record of contact with us."

Moscow was not chastised, demanding "'your opinion about Sound as of today'" and warning, "'The very fact that an agent has worked with us for many years, along with his fellowcountryman work, doesn't give us a guarantee against betrayal and under no circumstances provide grounds for complacency.'" Still, for the moment, Moscow Center was satisfied. Golos and Gutzeit visited Moscow in November 1937 and met with Abram Slutsky, chief of KGB foreign intelligence, to discuss the KGB's needs, particularly for arranging American passports and travel documents for its personnel. Golos also sent his Russian-born wife and American-born son to the USSR in the mid-1930s to live there permanently.[21]

But as the paranoia in Moscow deepened, KGB headquarters began to see its station's "principal American agent" in a sinister light. In April 1938 Golos's KGB file ominously recorded that he had known at least six officers arrested for treason, including Gutzeit. But when interrogated, Gutzeit, who does not appear to have confessed, praised Golos's assistance to the KGB New York station. In any event, officers at Moscow Center began to debate Golos's status. One memo took a favorable view, noting the many positive remarks in the file about his assistance to the KGB, Liveit-Levit's own status as an enemy of the people (undermining his criticism of Golos), and Golos's sending his family to the USSR as indications of his loyalty. But the file also noted Ilya Durmashkin's confession that Golos had sent Mensheviks and Trotskyists to the USSR.[22]

In September 1939 a Moscow Center officer, P. Pshenichny, wrote an unqualified condemnation of Golos:

"The defense of "Sound" [Golos] by the enemy Gutzeit, I think, also entitles one to think that "Sound" is not our man. During "Sound's" time in Moscow Slutsky received him in Gutzeit's presence. I think he probably received an assignment of a counterrevolutionary nature. "Sound" was an object of interest for the enemies Slutsky, especially Passov, Shpigelglaz, Grafpen, Kamensky, Sobol, Gutzeit. . . . An investigation conducted in early September 1939 revealed that Sound joined the Communist Party as a Menshevik in order to subvert the party from within, that he has been associated until recently with Cannon (one of the leaders of the Amer. Trotskyites, who is personally connected to Trotsky), Chertova (her real name is Sara Weber, who was Trotsky's secretary), managed through I. L. Durmashkin (sentenced to the supreme penalty in 1938) the Trotskyite organization at Amtorg and sent Trotskyites and SRs [Social Revolutionaries] to the Sov. Union for counterrevolutionary work (from I. L. Durmashkin's testimony).

In December 1937 Slutsky summoned "Sound" for a discussion, which was attended by the now-convicted Gutzeit. They also sent his wife Silvya Solomonovna Golos to the Union and she was accepted for Sov. citizenship. She is currently being investigated by Department 2 of the GUGB [Chief Administration of State Security] for an association with the Trotskyite Gladkov, who during the period 1928–1932 was in the Trotskyite organization of Amtorg. Based on the foregoing, "Sound" must not be left in the rosters of U.S. agents under any circumstances. Since "Sound" knows a great deal about the station's work, I would deem it advisable to bring him to the Soviet Union and arrest him."[23]

But then, just as its later arrest of Ovakimyan had put an end to doubts of his loyalty, the FBI intervened to complicate Pshenichny's damning portrait of Golos. In October 1939 five FBI agents appeared at World Tourists with a search warrant and a grand jury subpoena. The Nazi-Soviet Pact had temporarily ended the Justice Department's indifference to covert Soviet activities in the United States, and it charged that World Tourists had failed to register with the Justice Department as an agent of the Soviet Union. Ovakimyan, unaware that Golos was under suspicion in the USSR, wanted him to flee to Moscow to avoid testifying to the grand jury and possible prosecution. Ovakimyan worried that federal investigators would figure out from World Tourists' accounts that from May 1937 to July 1938 Moscow had transferred more than $54,000 through the company (the equivalent of nearly $800,000 in 2008 dollars), money laundering being one of the services Golos provided for the KGB and the Comintern. Golos, however, didn't want to go, citing a CPUSA policy of "'not running away,'" and Ovakimyan allowed that his "'disappearance will cause harm to the fellowcountrymen (CPUSA).'"[24]

If Moscow wanted Golos back to arrest him as a Trotskyist, it had a pretext. But the U.S. government's prosecution argued against his being a traitor. Initially, Moscow instructed Ovakimyan not to take any actions but observe how the situation played out. In early January 1940 he reported that he continued to feel it was essential for Golos to leave but Browder objected, and Moscow told him to defer to the latter's wishes. In the meantime the Comintern had provided a favorable biography on Golos, and a positive appraisal came from his former contact Grigory Rabinovich. The World Tourists matter ended with a plea bargain whereby Golos pled guilty and received a slap on the wrist: a fine and a suspended sentence.[25]

But at Moscow Center Pavel Fitin had decided that Ovakimyan was a traitor and his relationship with Golos was part of the problem. Pastelnyak, Ovakimyan's deputy, warned Moscow that Golos endangered the New York station's operations and recommended deactivating him. Pastelnyak secretly reported to Moscow Center that Ovakimyan had ordered him to meet Golos but he had refused: "'I was sure he had tails relentlessly dogging his heels,'" adding suspiciously, "'provided he himself was really honest in our work.'" Pastelnyak regarded Golos's role in KGB operations with contempt: "'There is a view among certain operatives . . . that Sound [Golos] is the de facto station chief in the U.S. He supplies people for all sorts of services and assignments in every area of work'" and "'if anything were to happen to them [Golos and American agent Joseph Katz], much of what has been created would fall apart.'"[26]

A KGB memorandum written in July 1940 asserted that further investigation had confirmed Durmashkin's 1938 confession that Golos was a Menshevik and Trotskyist who had "'at various times sent a number of persons to the USSR to conduct subversive work'" and concluded: "'It is urgently imperative to isolate "So." ["Sound"/Golos] from all of the station's affairs and to recall him immediately to the Union. For "So." to stay any longer in the U.S. jeopardizes all of our work just because of the absolutely impermissible situation that he knows in effect more than the station chief.'" At this time Golos also heard that his wife, residing in Moscow, might be seriously ill, and the KGB arranged for his son to cable him to return. Although the unsuspecting Golos was now ready to leave the United States, the CPUSA leadership was still reluctant and, in any case, the State Department refused two requests for a passport. Since he was under a two-year suspended sentence from his plea agreement and it was assumed that the FBI kept an eye on him, any attempt to leave illegally would risk arrest and serious legal consequences. He stayed in the United States, and after Ovakimyan's vindication and the Nazi attack in June 1941, Soviet intelligence priorities changed and concerns about Golos's loyalty vanished.[27]

The Cost

Not surprisingly, the recall, arrest, and execution of so many officers and the focus on hunting fantasy Trotskyists and traitors from 1938 into early 1941 gravely crippled the American KGB station's activities. When calm started to return, an April 1941 memo evaluating intelligence operations in the United States made clear the consequences of the turmoil. It noted that the American station had fifteen KGB officers, but only two, Ovakimyan and his deputy Pastelnyak, had been in the country prior to 1939.

The others were young officers, all commissioned since 1938, who "'do not have operational-Chekist [KGB] experience, especially in work abroad.'" Only four of the station's officers had good English skills, seven more were "'satisfactory,'" and the others were fair or poor. By the end of the 1930s the station had developed some ninety-two agents, an impressive number, but most had subsequently been deactivated. Twenty of those deactivated sources had been rated as valuable. Not only had it cut off relations with useful sources, but also those that remained were being serviced by inexperienced KGB officers whose grasp of English left a great deal to be desired.[28]

A later Moscow Center plan for expanding intelligence operations in the United States noted the ground that had to be made up:

"Everything depended on the existence of cadres—operatives who could oversee the activities of the aforementioned agents, but unfortunately, over the last several years, the Amer. station endured a sharp crisis with regard to operatives. Of those who were available, individual workers were systematically sent back home, both in 1939 and 1940. Thus, with breaches in the most important areas of our intelligence work, we were forced to de-activate a significant number of agents and, with whatever forces were available, to conduct our work on the smallest possible scale. This situation was also complicated by the fact that a significant portion of the remaining American station workers were young and newly arrived . . . who shouldn't have been used at all for independent, serious work, and because of this, our most qualified agents in the field of polit. and dip. work were left temporarily without guidance."[29]

As for the KGB's American illegal station, in April 1941 a Moscow Center memo bluntly stated that by 1939 "'the station comprised a single employee—Station Chief Jung [Akhmerov]. When Jung was recalled in December 1939 to the Sov. Union, the station ceased to exist.'" Fitin and his staff prepared, and Beria approved, a detailed plan in April 1940 to reestablish the illegal station with a new chief and officers sent from Moscow. But for unknown reasons Moscow Center never implemented the plan. Nine months later Fitin proposed and Beria approved a second attempt to reestablish the illegal station, providing a generous budget and designating Arnold Deutsch, a talented veteran illegal field officer as its new chief. Moscow Center prepared a detailed and elaborate plan to move Deutsch and his family to the United States in 1941 and to establish them with false identities:

"To arrange for 'Stephan' [Deutsch] and his family to be sent over to the USA, we are using his Austrian passport, which was issued under the name Alfred

Deutsch in Austria and expired in December 1937. For the purposes of using the passport to travel to the USA, we are preparing a copy of the document with 'Stephan's' wife written in, providing a 5-year extension (with a stamp from the Austrian consulate in Paris), and filling in a route from France to Latvia and all marks of Stephan's residence in Latvia until the present time.

Concurrently, we are assigning our station chief in New York the task of finding someone who could submit a petition to U.S. authorities for the issue of an immigration visa to the family, whom we plan to send from Latvia to the USA. This could, for example, be done by 'Frost' [Boris Morros] or 'Boss' [Henry Bookman]. Having been informed by the station that such a person has been found, Stephan will write him a warm, 'family letter,' in which he will inform him of his desire to come to live in the USA with his family and ask for help in this matter. As a courtesy for his relative, he will send in the 2nd or 1st letter several photographs of his family in a domestic setting.

We will receive the return address for this letter from the NKGB of the Latvian SSR [Soviet Socialist Republic], where Stephan 'lives,' according to the cover story. This address will be reported to the address department in Riga, and all the necessary information will be indicated on an address card. When he is informed by the station that the matter has turned out favorably, Stephan will submit a petition by mail to the Amer. embassy in Moscow about issuing him a visa to settle in the USA. Later, when he is requested to visit the embassy personally, Stephan will 'arrive from Riga' and speak with an embassy official in accordance with the cover story that we developed. In the course of the maneuvers, it is possible for Stephan to reside for a brief time in Riga at 'his' address. Old Latvian identity papers and a Soviet foreign residence permit will be prepared for Stephan and his family. These documents will be necessary for brief residency in Latvia and presentation at the American embassy. Stephan's mother will use her old passport, in which the necessary marks will be made, which will extend her trip from Austria to Latvia."

All this planning was for naught, however. In transit to the United States, Deutsch died when a German U-boat sunk his ship.[30]

Rebuilding the American Station

The Nazi attack on the USSR in June 1941 forced Moscow to put aside its obsessions about imagined traitors and concentrate on intelligence needed for the Soviet war effort and its future ambitions. The American environment also changed. The Nazi-Soviet Pact of August 1939 had heightened public and American government suspicion of the Soviet Union and led to an increasing political isolation of the American Communist Party and the breakdown of its Popular Front alliance with liberals. But with the Nazi attack all that vanished. President Roosevelt offered Lend-Lease aid to the USSR, and after Pearl Harbor, the United States and the Soviet Union became allies in the war against Germany. American Communists regained much of the influence they had lost in the broad New Deal coalition.

American industrial, military, and technological resources were vital to defeating Germany, and the Kremlin demanded covert intelligence in addition to the information supplied to the USSR through diplomatic channels and by massive American Lend-Lease aid. But because of the damage done by the Terror, the KGB's American station was ill-prepared to respond. Following Ovakimyan's arrest in May 1941, it was at it lowest point since it had been established in 1933. After Ovakimyan was deported, the New York station had only one senior officer remaining with field experience in the United States—Pastelnyak—to manage a group of inexperienced officers, most with inadequate English-language skills. And Pastelnyak himself had only limited foreign intelligence expertise and a poor command of English. As for the illegal station, as noted, it had been nonexistent since late 1939.

Moscow quickly dispatched several veteran senior officers. After Deutsch's death, Fitin ordered Iskhak Akhmerov and his wife, Helen Lowry, back to the United States in December 1941 to revive the illegal station. Fitin chose Vasily Zarubin as legal station chief and overall supervisor of KGB operations in the United States. The vicissitudes of wartime travel meant that he did not reach the West Coast until December 1941 and only got to the East Coast in January 1942. Zarubin had served as both a legal and illegal officer and also as a station chief in several European countries and China and, moreover, had carried out several short-term missions in the United States in the mid-1930s and spoke English well. (Zarubin's appointment also began a shift in KGB organization in America. In the 1930s the handful of KGB officers stationed at the Soviet Embassy in Washington was an appendage of the legal station operating out of the Soviet Consulate in New York. While Zarubin served as New York station chief, his cover job was as a diplomat in Washington. He gradually shifted more of the KGB's personnel to the capital, whose explosive growth during the war required more KGB attention. By 1945 the KGB Washington station was an independent entity, and its chief, Anatoly Gorsky, oversaw all KGB operations in America, including the New York station, headed by Vladimir Pravdin.)

With Zarubin came an influx of new officers and continued improvement in the professionalism of younger operatives already in the United States significantly upgraded the station's capabilities. But none of this happened overnight, and when Zarubin took up his post in January 1942, he had only an inadequate cadre of KGB professionals available at the legal station while Akhmerov had nothing at all in place for the illegal station. It would not be until 1944 that the KGB's American stations (legal stations in New York, Washington, and San Francisco plus the illegal station) were up to adequate strength with an appropriate mix of experienced and junior field officers and support staff. Meanwhile, the Soviet Union was fighting for its life against a massive German invasion, and Stalin's demands for intelligence and information from America could not wait for a methodical rebuilding of an intelligence apparatus that had been wrecked between 1938 and 1941.

Jacob Golos and the Party-Based Networks to the Rescue

Fortunately for the Soviet Union, Jacob Golos and the American Communist Party stepped forward to fill the vast gap between the KGB's limited capacity and its enormous needs for intelligence. From 1941 until 1945, Golos and the CPUSA provided the KGB with its most valuable political, diplomatic, military, and technical intelligence sources. The relationship was fraught with difficulties and tensions, and the KGB was always aware that its reliance on party-based networks might result in catastrophe. In the short run, the risk paid off, and the years from 1942 to 1945 were a golden age for the KGB. But later there was a price to be paid.

Ovakimyan had handled liaison with Golos directly, but for security reasons in April 1941 he transferred that responsibility to Aleksey Prokhorov, a junior officer who was impressed by his new contact. In June he noted that Golos "'has contacts with tons of people. He knows everything. He is informed about all our work. Everything at the station has been boiled down to 'Sound' [Golos], on all lines. Several agents who are connected to 'Sound' and provide reports are unknown to us other than by their cover names. He has been given the task of providing information on the entire network connected to him.'" Later that month the station asked Golos to arrange to send ethnic European-Americans into Germany disguised as journalists and relief workers, and Prokhorov also asked that "'he inform us in detail on the activities of the U.S. government regarding current events, as well as on the work of opposition groups in the government.'" A handwritten Moscow Center note on that report asked, "'What, is Sound a wizard?'" and another Moscow Center annotation directed that New York station officers be reminded that they "'should behave in a more purposeful manner and not try to turn him [Golos] into a department store. . . . Only give assignments that are really needed, and not whatever comes into somebody's head.'"[31]

But the KGB New York station had little else to rely on in late 1941 other than Jacob Golos and the party-based sources that he jealously guarded. Nor was the relationship helped by the fact that Pastelnyak, the acting station chief until Zarubin arrived, viewed Golos as "'an idiot and regarded him with distrust.'" Pastelnyak's limited foreign intelligence experience was also largely with the "White" line that dealt with Russian exiles, monarchists, and other anti-Bolshevik Russians and wasn't attuned to Moscow Center's shift to technical, diplomatic, and political intelligence of more immediate concern to the war effort. Zarubin, on the other hand, realized he needed Golos and his party networks precisely for those targets. His goal was to curb Golos's independence and ultimately gain control over his sources.[32]

Zarubin wrote a detailed account of his tenure as station chief for KGB chief Merkulov after being recalled to Moscow in 1944. He explained that his initial efforts to gain political intelligence led him to utilize contacts with the CPUSA: "'As a result of the war a number of new government institutions were established that were definitely of interest to us. Certain fellowcountrymen [Communists] and progressive people they knew went to work at these institutions. It seemed to me that by acquiring connections among them we would be able to obtain the information that interests us more quickly.'" Zarubin contacted Gene Dennis, number two man in the CPUSA (Earl Browder was then in prison on a false passport conviction). He was cooperative, and using Earl's brother Bill, Earl's Russian-born wife Irena, and other CPUSA contacts, the station recruited a number of sources who, while helpful, "'did not fulfill the hope we pinned on them.'"[33]

In contrast to the meager returns from these recruits, Zarubin reported, Golos's sources had been a gold mine, and he devoted nearly half of his report to the agents who had come to the KGB New York station from Golos. From the very beginning, however, Zarubin had instructions from Moscow to bring those sources under control: "'to study all the people in the group and to determine the possibilities of making them more active while they were in the system of 'Sound's' [Golos's] organization and to orient the group's work above all toward obtaining polit. and econ. information; to study the organizational system of S.'s work and on this basis to work out the problem of breaking up his group into smaller units and relieving him of all connections that he doesn't need to carry out the main tasks.'" This effort met resistance:

"'Sound's' behavior was extremely unfriendly, especially in the early going. 'Sound' regarded the interest we were displaying in the group's work, in the people and the methods and techniques of obtaining information, as completely extraordinary, unjustified interference by us in his affairs that had never taken place before. 'Sound' insisted that the question of sources for material and the techniques for obtaining it should play no role for us. We had no reason to know all the details about the people, since he didn't always know them himself and wasn't interested in this. 'Sound' believed that fellowcountrymen [CPUSA members] must not be made into agents. His people must remain fellowcountrymen, and teaching them the skills of intelligence work was wrong and harmful. Despite this position held by 'Sound' regarding our role in his work, we did gradually manage to familiarize ourselves in part with his people and to convince him of the need to keep us informed about all matters involving the group. Subsequently 'Sound' began to inform us in more detail about the operational and organizational aspect of the work. The material became less depersonalized and began to meet our needs better."[34]

Under pressure, Golos gradually surrendered some of his sources. The first group of agents he turned over was the network of engineers organized by Julius Rosenberg, after the KGB convinced him that their technical work was better suited to be overseen by Semen Semenov, a technical intelligence specialist. Zarubin also successfully detached Sergey Kurnakov and Michael Tkach, journalists he wanted for courier and talent-spotting duties. With Moscow's consent, Zarubin next proposed that Golos transfer the large apparatus run by Gregory Silvermaster to Iskhak Akhmerov and that he allow Joseph Katz access to his other Washington sources. At first, Golos categorically refused, insisting that neither Silvermaster nor any of his people would agree, saying that "he had gotten his people from the "Helmsman" [Browder], that any organizational changes whatsoever would require the latter's approval, that he would uphold his viewpoint in communicating with "Helmsman," and he even threatened to stop working with us." Zarubin placated him, and at their next meeting Golos was more accommodating. After being reassured that "'he would still retain a very big and important segment of the work, that he was very highly thought of in the C. [Center] and his work would very soon receive recognition,'" he "'grudgingly agreed to the transfer of several people,'" but not before traveling to Washington to argue personally with Zarubin.[35]

"Clever Girl"

Golos's death on 26 November 1943 slowed the reorganization. The KGB also quickly learned that "Clever Girl" (Elizabeth Bentley), the woman whom it assumed had been simply Golos's courier, was more than that. Bentley made it clear, according to Zarubin: "'She was privy to all of "Sound's" [Golos's] work and after his death began to consider herself the boss of his entire group. Regarding our role in the work of "Sound's" group, she expressed precisely the same views as he had.'" Immediately after Golos's death Akhmerov met with Bentley. She described in detail the circumstances of his death and the measures she had taken to destroy or safeguard any documents in his apartment that might compromise his networks. She also let him know for the first time that she and Golos had been lovers, that rather than just a message carrier, she had been Golos's agent handler and shared his opposition to a direct KGB takeover of his party-based sources. Although Akhmerov was annoyed by her resistance, he reported, "'She made a good impression on me. She's an intelligent, sensible and well-mannered woman. She gives the impression of a sincere person.'"[36]

Elizabeth Zarubin met with Browder on 12 December, and he vouched for Bentley, who was "'up to date on absolutely everything 'So.' ["Sound"/Golos] was doing, since he trusted her completely.'" But the KGB was not about to allow her the same freedom that Golos had exercised or be as patient with her as it had been with him. Golos had been a Russian, an old Bolshevik, and had a record of cooperation with the KGB going back to 1930. She was a young American Communist with no ethnic ties to Russia, and the KGB had barely heard of her before Golos's death. Zarubin sent a telegram to Moscow in mid-December 1943 that he would shortly begin taking over sources from her, beginning with Duncan Lee and Maurice Halperin. Eventually, he wanted all of her agents split into small groups handled by illegal station chief Iskhak Akhmerov or veteran American agent Joseph Katz. By the end of April 1944 Akhmerov reported that although he had finally met with Silvermaster in March, Bentley continued to throw up obstacles to arranging more direct meetings and that efforts to assume supervision of Lee, Halperin, Mary Price, Robert Miller, and Joseph Gregg were met with excuses from Bentley: "Helmsman's [Browder's] personal approval is needed, a probationer [source] is too squeamish and fearful, equipment is needed for communications, and so forth."[37]

Akhmerov explained to Moscow that Bentley insisted Browder had selected her to replace Golos and "that she was working for H. ["Helms-man"/Browder] and not for us." She presented herself as Browder's proxy and stated that she and her party-based networks fully accepted that their "'task is to provide information. But no one has the right to interfere in the organizational aspects of our [the CPUSA's] work except the leaders of the fraternal [CPUSA].'" Even when Akhmerov met Silvermaster, the latter had not been told with sufficient clarity that he now had to take orders from the KGB. His "'antagonism toward all of our activities reflects a petit-bourgeois, proprietorial ideology, which, combined with a purely American anarchism, is one of the most typical traits of a very large number of local fellowcountrymen [Communists].'" To clear up the confusion, Moscow ordered Zarubin to arrange for his wife to meet with Browder, tell him that Bentley was being recalcitrant, instruct Browder to order her to obey, and also immediately turn over one of Bentley's networks, the Perlo group, to direct KGB control. The meeting took place in late May 1944. Browder complied, agreed to give up control of the Golos-Bentley networks, and indicated the blame for the feuding rested with Bentley's stubbornness. But seeking to keep his hand in, Browder "requested that organizational matters be discussed with him in advance; any change in the procedure of contacting probationers [agents], or turning them over to other individuals."[38]

Although he had initially evaluated her as a serious, stable person, Akhmerov began to have second thoughts the more he worked with Bentley. On 15 June 1944 he noted:

"She has a rather complicated and contradictory personality. In her work and conversations she usually behaves like our operative, in her comments she says 'we,' implying our organization [KGB] and including herself in this concept. . . . Her behavior changes, however, when I ask her to arrange a meeting for me with 'Pal' [Silvermaster] or to get any of the probationers [sources] in contact with our operative. She becomes a completely different person and, apparently restraining herself, declares that she isn't our operative, that she works for 'Helmsman' [Browder]. . . . Sometimes I sense from the criticisms that are made that deep down she dislikes us. . . . She says that we all care little about Americans, that the USSR is the only country we love and for which we work. I tried to explain to her that she is wrong."

Akhmerov assured Bentley "'that by helping the USSR, we are working out of deeply held ideological motives and we don't stop being Americans. . . . She told me in response that 'Pal' isn't an American and that his wife isn't an American . . . that 'Raid' [Perlo] isn't an American, that he's a Russian. . . . [Still] I believe that she is indisputably 100 percent our person. I believe that with a tactful attitude, friendly treatment, and a firm, businesslike arrangement of a working relationship, her behavior can be corrected.'" Fitin was not persuaded; he worried about her "unbalanced and erratic personality."[39]

It took a while, but by the end of 1944 Bentley had handed over most of her agents to the KGB, although the KGB documents indicate there was a protracted transition that lasted into early 1945, longer than had been thought from earlier material available.

The Party-Based Networks

The KGB had long been aware that the party-based networks practiced poor "konspiratsia" and were ill-disciplined by KGB standards. But until it took them over, it did not realize just how serious the problem was.

First, the KGB came to appreciate that the issue was deeper than just Golos and Bentley. Although it finally convinced Bentley to allow direct contact with Gregory Silvermaster, which the latter welcomed, it soon discovered that he, in turn, was reluctant to allow the KGB to have direct contact with *his* sources, fearing a weakening of his authority as a party leader. At one contentious meeting in New York with Helen Silvermaster (Gregory's wife) and Ludwig Ullmann (Silvermaster's assistant and housemate) Akhmerov heard their objections to his plan for a direct connection with George Silverman, who Helen insisted could not be trusted, was mentally ill, and could "'be kept under control only if he is subordinate to Robert [Gregory Silvermaster].'" Silvermaster himself bitterly complained that because of Harry White's direct contact with a KGB officer he "'had started putting on airs and acting independently of them.'" Although irritated by Silvermaster's resistance and wounded *amour-propre,* Akhmerov backed away from demanding further access to other sources, justifying the coddling of Silvermaster on the grounds that it produced information:

"I had planned for quite some time to establish a direct connection with Zhenya [Sonia Gold] and Milton [Bela Gold]. I did not insist on it, because I knew how Robert would react to this, and I also took into account the consideration that they should not in fact be singled out. *Neither I nor any other of our people could achieve such effective results from working with them as Robert, Donald [Ullmann], and Dora [Helen Silvermaster]* during these important years of the war. I thought that it was much more important to maintain a regular flow of important documentary materials, than to engage in a feud with him with regard to establishing direct contact with these people."[40]

But when KGB officers finally got direct access to Silverman, they got an earful. Vladimir Pravdin met with Silverman in October 1945, and he let loose on Silvermaster, denouncing him as "'a petty tyrant'" who had alienated everyone else in the group except for Ullmann. He "'treats the members of his group as his dependents, rudely coercing them and refusing to tolerate objections of any kind.'" If his "'orders are not carried out unquestioningly, he yells, curses, issues threats of punishment, and then tells everyone that the 'guilty party' is a scoundrel, a bourgeois, and a Trotskyite, and that nothing good can be expected of him.'" Moreover, he "'completely ignores the most basic precautions in our work and attracts the attention of surrounding people with his behavior,'" phoning Silverman at work and scheduling meetings during work hours. When his orders were not carried out, he became abusive, screaming and ranting:

"According to A. ["Aileron"/Silverman], when Robert [Silvermaster] was over at A's apartment recently with Dora [Helen Silvermaster] and Pilot [Ullmann], he started rudely scolding A. for his inability to manage his own family in front of A's nineteen-year-old son. The son, outraged by Robert's antics, left the house, having scolded his father for letting R. talk to him like that. R's behavior has frequently led to misunderstandings between A. and his wife. Pilot treats A. the same way R. does. His behavior at A's place of employment has, according to the latter, discredited him in front of other officials, because no one could understand how A's subordinate could talk to him like that. Pilot also attracted the other employees' attention because he did not do any of his work on the official line and acted impudently toward A. in front of other people, as if purposefully ignoring the fact that A. was his superior. According to A., Dora was constantly interfering in A's professional and personal life and occasionally was even more rude than Robert or Pilot."

According to Silverman, the only reason he and several other members of the Silvermaster group had continued to work for the KGB was their recognition of the Soviet Union's wartime needs: "'This is why my friends and I carried out this work under Robert's [Silvermaster's] leadership, despite the persecution and humiliation to which he subjected us. Patience, however, always runs out. In the last several months, we have decided to stop working with Robert. We would rather work on the fraternal [CPUSA] line.'" He added: "'From now on I want to live in dignity, without having to endure the harassment of a madman like Robert.'"[41]

The KGB also learned of another complication about the leadership of the Silvermaster apparatus. Akhmerov had understood that while Gregory Silvermaster was the central figure, Helen Silvermaster and Ludwig

Ullmann functioned as his chief lieutenants in running the group. Ull-mann had been closely associated with the Silvermasters since 1938, when they jointly purchased a house in Washington in which all three lived. But it was not until mid-1945 that Akhmerov realized just how intimate the re-lationship was. In August he reported: "It was learned (and Reed [Harry White] confirmed this) that Robert's wife [Helen Silvermaster] is cohab-iting with Pilot [Ullmann] with Robert's [Gregory Silvermaster's] knowl-edge and consent. 'Without question, these unhealthy relationships be-tween them cannot help but have a negative influence on work and behavior with us.'" The KGB didn't like this news, but inasmuch as it was breaking up the Silvermaster group anyway, it put it aside.[42]

Because so many of the sources in Silvermaster's and Perlo's group worked in the Treasury Department, career rivalries and slights also spoiled relationships. Frank Coe blocked Harold Glasser's transfer to the State Department "ostensibly for business reasons, but actually out of jealousy." Glasser was angry that he was passed over for Harry White's job when the latter moved to the World Bank and blamed it on Silver-master. Silvermaster, in turn, was upset that Glasser was part of Perlo's network and not his. White was reluctant to recommend Glasser for pro-motion because he believed Morgenthau wanted to minimize the num-ber of Jews in high positions. Silverman had long resented the appoint-ment of Silvermaster and Ullmann to run the group since both were relatively late arrivals in the Washington Communist underground.[43]

When it took over the Perlo group in 1944, the KGB discovered that the same pattern existed. Members of the group had come to despise Victor Perlo. Charles Kramer, for example, regarded him as "insufficiently competent as leader for himself." Perlo, in turn, thought Kramer too "'passive'" and had frequent dust-ups with him. Assigned by Anatoly Gorsky to meet with Kramer and resolve the issue, Joseph Katz reported that he sympathized with Kramer's position and thought Perlo should be reporting to Kramer rather than the other way around. Nor was Kramer the only one to resent Perlo. Harry Magdoff told Katz that he didn't get along with him and neither did Ted Fitzgerald, who quarreled with Perlo constantly. Gorsky (then chief of the KGB Washington station) reported to Moscow in early 1945 that "'at the moment they are engaged in their latest quarrel, the roots and substance of which are unknown to us.'" Akhmerov discounted Bentley's diagnosis that Perlo was "'a psychologi-cal case himself'" but only "'because she tells me that most of all our people are psychological cases.'" He did allow that Perlo was "'very ap-prehensive and neurotic.'"[44]

Even spousal relationships had to be handled delicately. Both Harold Glasser and his wife Faye were sources, but she resented her second-class status. One report noted that she "'feels hostility with regard to male chauvinism and explained her period of inactivity not by objective circumstances but by chauvinism on the part of the organization. When the men were presented with gifts, she took the fact that women were excluded from among those who received gifts very badly (this was rectified, and she was convinced that this was only a belated act of gift-giving and was very excited by the gift that was given to her). When, about two months ago, 'Roma' [Faye Glasser] expressed a desire to work, she nevertheless felt unhappy because she will have to work as her husband's 'adjunct,' rather than independently.'"[45]

All of these personal feuds and animosities impinged on the efficiency of the party-based networks because its members worked together so closely and constantly interacted. After the KGB took direct control of the Perlo apparatus, Joseph Katz reported: "'I saw 'Raid' [Perlo] several times and spoke with Magdoff as well, and I believe that I now have an excellent idea of how the group works as a whole. It seems that the group worked exactly like a fellowcountryman [CPUSA] cell. They held meetings at each other's homes, while their wives typed up available reports. Then "Raid" would receive materials from them and pass them on. Taking into account the state of konspiratsia—there is not much that can be done. I urged 'Raid' to stop holding meetings so regularly and to foster individuality in them insofar as it was possible.'" In March 1945, in the midst of the KGB's takeover of the party networks, Gorsky summarized the situation:

"Konspiratsia, both among the members of 'Raid's' [Perlo's] former group and, unfortunately, among oth. info. groups here, leaves a lot to be desired. Moreover, all of them know each other as fellowcountrymen-informers [Communist-informers] and also know what kind of work each of them does. The following serves as an example: When 'X' [Katz] gave 'Tan' [Magdoff] an assignment on oil, the latter replied that Frank Coe could do a better job carrying out this assignment, meaning that he had materials on this subject. Anoth. example—when he received an assignment relating to the conference in San Francisco, 'Raid' said that 'Richard' [Harry White] could do a better job, as could the members of 'Bill's' group (i.e., 'Albert' [Akhmerov]). When he received an assignment on oil, 'Raid' said that a certain David Ramsay from NY was already working on it.

The list of examples could go on. As we already reported earlier, in conversation with me 'Ruble' [Glasser] named more than ten people who are known to him as informants [sources]. 'Raid' gave us a list that included 14 people with ties to groups led by some people named Blumberg and Schimmel (from Congress) and 'Bill' ('Albert'). Once, in conversation with me, 'X' said that conversations with 'Raid,' 'Tan,' et al., left him with the impression that there are almost a hundred illegal informants of this sort in Washington, who know of and about each other. In the course of working with 'Raid,' for instance, it became known that until very recently, his group had represented itself for several years in its work with 'Myrna' [Bentley] as so-called fellowcountryman cells. The members of the cells would get together at each other's apartments every week and discuss which materials should be given to 'Myrna' or her predecessors. At these meetings, they would pick a courier whose job was to get these materials where they needed to go, etc. Naturally, we put an end to all this, but the disclosure connected with it remains a fact."[46]

How dangerous was this? Joseph Katz stated it bluntly: "The whole organization is now in a situation such that if anyone begins so much as a cursory investigation, the whole group with their direct contacts will immediately be exposed." Moscow Center agreed, demanded greater secrecy and a swifter transition from the large, party-based networks to small units under the direction of a KGB professional: "'This will help us eliminate the deeply rooted system in which fellowcountrymen/informants [Communists/informants] not only know about each other's work, but even hold 'production conferences' of a kind regarding the collecting of information. Clearly this situation is abnormal and intolerable, b/c sooner or later, it could have unfortunate consequences for us.'" Moscow Center sent this message to the KGB Washington station in May 1945. The "unfortunate consequences" were six months away.[47]

The Beginning of the End

By early 1945, the KGB had succeeded in taking over the Golos/Bentley networks and agents. However, Moscow Center wanted to make a thorough job of it. Although she was no longer in liaison with the Silvermaster and Perlo networks or the independent agents she had supervised, Bentley remained a security risk. She ran a business linked to both the CPUSA and the Soviet Union. Golos, in fact, had set up the U. S. Service and Shipping Corporation (USSSC) as a vehicle to continue the activities of World Tourists after it was forced to register as the agent of a foreign power, and it was also secretly financed by the CPUSA. Just as World Tourists had brought Golos into the FBI's sights, USSSC might lead to FBI interest in Bentley. Moscow urged Anatoly Gorsky in November

1944 to have Bentley stop her work at USSSC; break her ties to the CPUSA; and go underground with a new identity, fraudulent documents, and a new job. Gorsky himself pointed out several other areas of vulnerability. Bentley had traveled frequently to Washington with no apparent reason, and other employees at USSSC knew she went there for "'special' purposes." She met with sources without taking security precautions, used her own apartment for meetings, and gave some sources her home phone number. The KGB reached an agreement with Browder in December that USSSC "would shift totally to our control," while World Tourists would stay with the CPUSA. Bentley, however, was "to be removed from both companies."[48]

Easing Bentley out of her role as a conduit to the KGB's Washington sources and removing her from both CPUSA and KGB-linked institutions seemed to be a prudent security decision. It turned out to be a personnel disaster. Bentley wrote an autobiography for the KGB that paints a picture of a lonely woman who had found fulfillment only in her relationship with Jacob Golos and his covert work. She wrote of him: "'I loved him very much and lived with him for five years until his death. I was as deeply in love with him when he died as when I first met him, and I still feel the same way, although when I found out certain things after his death about his polit. life, my feelings diminished somewhat. No man has interested me since John [Golos] died.'" After his death, the KGB had destroyed what was left of her one satisfying relationship; it ended the underground work into which he had initiated her, ejected her from the company he had created for her to run, and ordered her to cut ties with the CPUSA, where she had met him and to which both had been devoted.[49]

Bentley's personal frustrations and heavy drinking began to become obvious by the end of 1944, and the KGB paid for her to spend a week at a health resort. Gorsky met her in December to deliver a Christmas present, and she responded by making a pass at him. First, she said he reminded her of her late lover, Golos. "Then she said that it's hard for a young, single woman to live without a man and described her physical suffering as a result of this." Gorsky told Moscow that she needed to be married off but that no suitable candidate had been found. In Moscow, Ovakimyan told Graur to consider the issue, but nothing happened. By mid-1945 Bentley's frustrations had boiled over. Gorsky reported that Rae Elson, a KGB contact who worked with Bentley at USSSC, had informed the KGB

"with great outrage that Myrna [Bentley] had proposed that she become her lover. In this regard "Irma" [Elson] remarked that "M." ["Myrna"] had attempted to establish an intimate relationship with her 'despite the fact that she has a male lover.' This latter fact intrigued us, since M. had always complained in her conversations with me and "X" [Katz] that she had no boyfriend to satisfy her natural needs. We gave "X" a special assignment to have a cautious and tactful chat with M. on this topic. After the usual whining and refusal to admit her guilt "M." told first "X" and then me that in early May she became acquainted with a man in her hotel who was waiting for a room, and on the same day she got into an intimate relationship with him and began to meet with him from time to time. "M." was gushing praise about the man and declared that he would be a perfect husband for her. Then "M's" infatuation apparently began to cool, and she told us a number of details about her lover that left no doubt that he was an agent for the "Hut" [FBI] or for "Arsenal" [Army] counterintelligence, possibly planted especially for "Myrna." We suggested that M. break off the 'affair' and go away for a couple of months on vacation. She did both, but to what extent she left her lover—P. Heller—is hard to say. . . .

As you know, "M." has not been in contact with our probationers [sources] for a long time already. "M.'s" behavior in this whole business was exceptionally bad. For example, she told me at the outset that she had gotten involved with H. [Heller] on "X's" instructions. Yet she told "X" that I was the one who had permitted her to live with H. When both statements were rejected as patent rubbish and nonsense, "M" told us that 'the Amer. fellowcountrymen [Communists] were venal riffraff and all of them, beginning with "Helmsman" [Browder], could be bought and sold for a couple of cents,' whereas she felt very good with H., like someone very close to her.' Later M. apologized for those phrases under the pretext that she said them without thinking, under the influence of wine (she could never be called a teetotaler). In short and on the whole, "M" as of today is a serious and dangerous burden for us here. She should be taken home [Moscow], but to tell the truth, I don't know how to do this, since she won't go illegally."

(Heller, as it turned out, was not with the FBI or Army counterintelligence. He was simply a man taking advantage of an easily available woman.)[50]

Gorsky tried several measures to improve Bentley's mood. Along with several other American agents (Katz, Silvermaster, and Harry Gold) she had received the "Order of the Red Star" for assistance to the Soviet Union. As a morale booster, Gorsky brought an official Soviet certificate and the actual medal to a meeting so she could look at them. She was, of course, not allowed to keep them. He also paid for another vacation, sending her "to a seaside resort for treatment and rest" in late August 1945. Gorsky also suggested once more that she move to another city or country and adopt a new identity, but she categorically refused, demanding to return to her job at USSSC. The KGB considered but rejected allowing her to go back to her old position and then getting her to come to Russia under the pretext of negotiating an agreement with Intourist. A nervous Moscow Center warned Gorsky not to raise the issue again since it might only further alienate her. Instead, it recommended reducing the frequency of meetings with her, keeping her away from her old contacts, finding her another job, and continuing to support her financially. It even considered encouraging her to become publicly active in the CPUSA (also hoping that the party might be able to find her a husband), ensuring she remained tied to the Communist movement but at some distance from illegal work.[51]

None of these palliatives worked. Gorsky met with Bentley in late September after her vacation and reported to Moscow:

"She was half-drunk. When I suggested rescheduling the meeting for another time, she declared that if I broke off the meeting, we wouldn't see her anymore. She said that she had had a drink so as to relate something to me while intoxicated that she couldn't bring herself to relate while sober. This intrigued me, so I stayed for the meeting. "Myrna" [Bentley] asked whether we really don't want to finance the "Complex" [USSSC], enter into a 'human' contract with it, and reduce customs import duties on parcels. I confirmed our decision on this question and declined to discuss the contract with Intourist and other matters.

"Myrna" stated that our refusal to finance the "Complex" 'compels' her not only to break off relations with us but also spurs her and "Scott" [John Reynolds, official owner of USSSC] to resort to assistance from government agencies. "Myrna" showed a story in a newspaper she had with her about the latest summons of Communist Party leaders—Browder and the brother of Cde. Molotov's wife—to appear for questioning before the Un-American Activities Committee. "Myrna" declared threateningly that her and "Scott's" testimony would be very interesting for the committee and American newspapers. When I commented that "Scott's" threats don't scare us, "Myrna" corrected herself, saying that she completely supported him, because he was not only her business partner (I took that to mean that "M." was sleeping with "Scott"), and went on to say: '"So." ["Sound"/Golos] and I created the "Complex" and used it for 10 years for you and against you. Now you're not going to get rid of this business so easily. We have no choice but to liquidate the "Complex," but neither "Scott" nor I will ever again have any dealings with any Russians, because they are all gangsters and care only about Russia.' When I tried to clarify what she meant, M. couldn't say anything that made sense, she just assured me in a drunken monotone that she has hated us for 10 years, but at the same time she 'hasn't sold out and won't sell out' our people, mainly because they are 'Americans.' . . .

Then M. said that a while ago Heller had made her an indirect offer to become an FBI agent for the investigation of the "Complex." Supposedly she rejected the offer. "M." stated that the fact that for 10 years So. had repeatedly told her it was impossible to work honestly with the Russians was not the only thing she had concealed from us. "M." declined to clarify what she meant. During the discussion "M." attempted several times to get into obviously slanderous comments about the Amer. Com. Party ('a band of foreigners'), about "Sound" ('only death prevented him from making an extremely important decision that the whole country would have found out about,' or otherwise 'only death prevented us from moving to South America, where you would have never found us'), about "X" [Katz] ('as soon as I see him, I'll kill him'), about "Albert" [Akhmerov] ('he tried to rape me'), but she said all this in a disjointed and confused manner.

So as not to aggravate relations with M., I turned the conversation to neutral topics, and after a while concluded it altogether. I scheduled the next meeting for the beginning of November; she quietly agreed to this. Our conclusions from the foregoing discussion with "M.":

1. M.'s shenanigans are not accidental, and they attest to the fact that, although she has worked with us for a long time, she is a person who is alien and hostile to us.
2. Judging by her behavior, she hasn't betrayed us yet, but we cannot rely on her. Unfortunately, she knows a great deal about us.
3. The latest 'eruption' occurred as a result of our firm position with regard to the C-plex—the refusal to finance, the 'insulting' (in her words) contract sent by Intourist, the failure to mention in the contract that the C-plex has the exclusive right to send parcels to the Sov. Union and so forth. "M." is dragging in all these extraneous 'arguments' in order to break off with us.
4. Considering that M. won't go anywhere voluntarily, and could cause serious harm to us here, there is only one way left, the most radical one, to get rid of her."[52]

While the KGB's foreign intelligence arm had occasionally assassinated or kidnapped its enemies, such extraordinary measures were rare. KGB head Vsevolod Merkulov replied personally to Gorsky and urged a renewed effort to placate Bentley. Thinking that she might be angling for a better deal for USSSC, he urged another meeting at which Gorsky should calmly reassure her of the KGB's good wishes: "'Point out to her that her many years of productive work with us, which have been appropriately honored with a government award, obligates us to provide her with not only moral but also material support. Tell her that we are prepared to provide necessary financial assistance to her personally (up to 3,000 dollars [$35,000 in 2008 dollars]).'" She also should be informed that "'in appreciation of M's [Myrna/Bentley's] personal work for us, we are prepared, for her personally, to exert possible influence on Intourist in a favorable direction'" for settling a contract with USSSC. If she continued to make threats, "'deflect them firmly and confidently and say that we don't advise her to employ means of that kind, first because the Americans among whom she enjoys such great trust will never forgive her for this, to put it mildly, disloyal act and will stigmatize her for the rest of her life, and second because it's not only not beneficial to her, it's dangerous. Suggest to her at this point that in the current political situation the American government agencies are unlikely to take the step of using M.'s 'exposés' against us. Therefore the consequences of M.'s impetuous act will fall personally on her and the Americans.'" He also instructed Gorsky "'under no circumstances is she to be released from our influence or let out of our field of vision.'"[53]

Gorsky met with Bentley again in late October. This time she was sober and apologized for her prior behavior, although she claimed not to remember anything she had said. She put forward a number of demands on behalf of USSSC. Nevertheless, the conversation was cordial, Bentley accepted $2,000, and they discussed what she would do if the FBI questioned her in the aftermath of Louis Budenz's defection since he might know something about her and Golos's activities.[54]

Catastrophe

The KGB had known for several years that the Golos-Bentley networks had been a disaster waiting to happen but had little choice in order to avail itself of the rich intelligence resources they provided. It had tried to minimize the risk by introducing professional officers into their operations, isolating Bentley, and enforcing more stringent security procedures. But it could not change the fact that dozens of its government sources were veterans of the Washington Communist underground, had worked and socialized together, and knew about each other's activities. If the FBI ever looked closely, most or all would be exposed. And the one person who knew everything about these networks was an embittered, lonely, promiscuous alcoholic. Every effort to neutralize her had backfired badly.

Gorsky went to New York on 21 November 1945 to meet again with

Bentley. She was calm and sober, and they had another discussion about the complex relationship of USSSC with its hidden financier, the CPUSA, and about the possible risks posed by Budenz and her former lover, Peter Heller. Gorsky might have thought the meeting a sign that things had stabilized except that he spotted a car tailing him after he left Bentley. He ducked into the subway, lost it, and returned to Washington. He was sure he had come to the meeting "clean" and that it had been Bentley who had been followed to the rendezvous. It was worse than that. The next day he got a cable from Moscow that Bentley had gone over to the FBI. She had set him up. The KGB had reaped a rich harvest of intelligence from the Golos-Bentley networks. Now it was time to pay the piper.[55]

The KGB's London station had cabled Moscow on 20 November, relaying information from Harold "Kim" Philby, senior officer at the British Secret Intelligence Service (SIS/MI6) and a KGB spy; he had heard that "'the Americans are currently investigating another Soviet intel. organization in the U.S.'" Philby reported that J. Edgar Hoover had told William Stephenson, chief of British Security Coordination (an SIS office operating in America in liaison with the U.S. government) that Bentley had come to the FBI in early November with the story that World Tourists and USSSC had been covers for Soviet intelligence. The FBI had succeeded in identifying some thirty Soviet agents but thus far had given the British only the names of Peter Rhodes and Cedric Belfrage (see chapter 3). And the news only got worse. Bentley completed and signed on 30 November a 108-page typed comprehensive deposition summarizing her career in Soviet espionage and identifying scores of sources that she and Golos had turned over to the KGB. Hoover quickly gave a copy to Stephenson, who dutifully forwarded it to London, where Philby picked it up, and the KGB London station forwarded a summary to Moscow Center on 4 December that listed forty-one Soviet sources Bentley had given to the FBI.[56]

Bentley's defection was by any measure a catastrophe, dismantling in one moment much of what the KGB had constructed from 1942 to 1945. That the KGB got her FBI deposition only five days after she signed it was a partial silver lining that allowed it to contain the damage better than it might have expected. After Philby's warning, Moscow Center ordered Gorsky on 23 November to break off contact with a host of sources, warn them to deny any covert ties to Bentley, destroy compromising documents, arrange passwords for future contacts, issue advance payments to compensated agents, and otherwise prepare to hunker down. Assuming that the FBI had observed and photographed his meeting with Bentley, it ordered Gorsky to settle his affairs and return to Moscow. Having been clearly identified by the FBI as an intelligence officer, his usefulness in America was at an end. It also recalled Akhmerov, chief of the illegal station, and Vladimir Pravdin, chief of the New York station, back to Moscow, and as the extent of Bentley's acquaintance with other officers (or of Golos's acquaintance that might have been conveyed to Bentley) became clear, additional withdrawal orders followed.[57]

Philby's warning allowed the KGB to shut down dangerous or risky operations, alert vulnerable agents, and prepare them for the storm that was about to come. By the time the FBI began to watch them or came to interrogate them, Bentley's American agents had their excuses and cover stories thought out and their cries about political persecution of progressives well rehearsed. With the exception of Louis Budenz, who had already been talking to the FBI, none of the people Bentley named would ever speak honestly about their work for Soviet intelligence or even admit to passing along confidential information to the CPUSA.

Before he left the country, Gorsky raised again the notion of Bentley's "physical liquidation." One option was to use a slow-acting poison: "soak a pillow or handkerchief or food that would be delivered to M's ["Myra's"/ Bentley's] room and left there." But Gorsky didn't have such a poison on hand and had no way to obtain it. He did possess three guns, but they "would be too noisy," and "a car accident or pushing her under a train would be unreliable." He thought that Bentley would be willing to meet with Joseph Katz, who could drop poison in her wine or on her makeup. Alternatively, Katz could use his locksmith skills to break into her room and use: "a cold steel weapon or stage a suicide. That's unreliable, since M. is a very strong, tall and healthy woman and X. [Katz] lately has not felt well." Merkulov put an end to these revenge scenarios, writing that Beria had agreed that assassination was not advisable.[58]

While rapid damage control prevented the FBI from getting sufficient corroboration to bring criminal charges, Bentley's information, reinforced by the Venona decryptions (available in significant quantities starting in 1946), as well as information flowing from other defectors (Budenz, Whittaker Chambers, and Hede Massing), allowed the FBI to neutralize the bulk of the KGB's American sources. Combined with the recall of most of the KGB's experienced officers from America, the lack of active sources crippled the KGB's activities in the United States during the first years of the Cold War. Nor did the damage stop there. Bentley and Chambers testified publicly in 1948, and a series of congressional investigations exposed the CPUSA's assistance to Soviet espionage and irreparably tainted the American Communist movement with treason.

Given the richness of the intelligence the Soviet Union had gained from its use of CPUSA-based networks in World War II, perhaps the trade-off was worth it, but the ultimate price was high.

Failures and Recriminations

Station chiefs Gorsky, Akhmerov, and Pravdin all departed in 1946, along with Leonid Kvasnikov, Anatoly Yatskov, Alexander Feklisov, and other officers with extensive American experience. Their replacements faced daunting problems. Grigory Dolbin, who succeeded Gorsky as the Washington station chief, had a particularly rocky tenure. Gorsky's departure was sudden and unplanned, and Moscow Center had no ready replacement. Dolbin had been preparing for assignment to Japan and was a last-minute choice to head the American station. He complained to Moscow Center:

"Two days before my departure to Japan, to a job for which I had been trained, I unexpectedly received instructions to go to Carthage [Washington]. A country and city which, as I have already said, I did not know. The only training I had received in Center with regard to this country were two brief conversations with Cde. Vetrov [Graur] and Cde. Gennady [Ovakimyan]. These conversations touched on descriptions of the overall situation in the country, and I received virtually no practical advice. I couldn't speak English. Now, one year later, I feel that my grasp of the language has increased significantly. I read English-language newspapers practically without the aid of a dictionary, I translate serious articles from English to Russian, and I can talk to an American about any topic. However, I believe this is not enough, especially when it comes to speaking fluently on everyday topics."

Moscow Center was unsympathetic and responded with a withering, "'Your work abounds in grammatical mistakes and inaccurate wording, as a consequence of insufficient familiarity with facts and a flawed understanding of current events.'" Nor did it respond to his complaints that the officers withdrawn in 1946 had not been replaced and the Washington station had few staff. Moscow Center recalled Dolbin in 1948 after he showed signs of a mental breakdown.[59]

It replaced him with Aleksandr Panyushkin, who was not a professional intelligence officer at all but a senior Soviet Communist Party international affairs adviser and sometime diplomat. He was also the Soviet ambassador to the United States. His appointment as station chief was part of a short-lived reorganization designed to centralize and unify Soviet foreign intelligence. The Kremlin merged the foreign intelligence arm of the Ministry of State Security (predecessor of the KGB) and Soviet military intelligence (GRU) into a new entity, the Committee of Information (KI), with a mandate not only to integrate Soviet intelligence, but also to seamlessly coordinate intelligence with Soviet diplomacy. To that end, Foreign Minister Vyacheslav Molotov, who had spearheaded the campaign to create the KI, became its first chairman. As part of his drive to bring foreign intelligence under the control of his foreign ministry, just as he doubled as foreign minister and head of the KI, Soviet ambassadors doubled as KI station chiefs.

American policymakers had considered similar ideas but rejected them as ultimately unworkable given the conflicting demands of diplomacy and intelligence. The Soviets also soon realized the awkward nature of the arrangement. Andrey Vyshinsky, who succeeded Molotov as foreign minister in 1949, had little interest in intelligence and handed the chairmanship of the KI over to a deputy. Meanwhile, the Soviet military general staff, complaining vehemently that it needed a dedicated intelligence arm, successfully got GRU returned to its control. Everyone soon realized that most Soviet ambassadors were not fit to direct the intelligence station, and the professional officers who served as the deputy station chiefs became the de facto station chiefs but often found themselves in a difficult relationship with their nominal superior, the ambassador. In 1951 the KI experiment ended, and foreign intelligence returned to the Ministry of State Security, itself transformed in 1954 into the Committee of State Security (KGB).

Meanwhile, however, Ambassador Panyushkin doubled as KI station chief in Washington. His tenure coincided with the growing furor over Soviet espionage in the United States. At first, Panyushkin enthusiastically endorsed reactivating the sources who had proven so valuable in the past and had been "put on ice" after Bentley's defection, but by the end of 1948 he had second thoughts. Laurence Duggan's suicide after a recontact and the surge in congressional and FBI investigations convinced him to advise Moscow: "'Continuing to work with old agents and leads in these conditions means giving American counterintelligence the chance to investigate our connections and ourselves even more closely. Furthermore, through old agents and leads, the station could come across new incidents like the one with 'Prince' [Duggan]. . . . We could bring our country to serious harm.'" Moscow did not agree. A report written for the chairman of the Committee of Information scolded, "'The proposal in question is, in our opinion, tantamount to terminating all intelligence work in the USA, b/c the station has not acquired new leads, not to mention valuable new agents in the principal agencies of the USA.'" Gorsky prepared an evaluation of the KGB Washington station work in 1949, concluding: "'In its practical work, the station followed the path of least resistance, either recruiting people widely known for their affiliation with the U.S. Comparty [Communist Party] . . . or trying to use as agents employees of delegations from People's Democracies [East European Communist nations] who are sympathetic toward us but do not have access to information of interest.'" Gorsky did not blame Panyushkin. He dismissed the nominal head of the KGB station as "'busy with his principal work'" as Soviet ambassador and put the blame on the deputy station chief, Georgy Sokolov.[60]

Sokolov had arrived in the United States in November 1948 after stints as station chief in Japan and Brazil and senior positions at Moscow Center. But he did not get along with Panyushkin, who called him "'unsuited to intelligence work.'" And a Moscow Center plan of work for the American station adopted in March 1950 concluded that as a result of "'personal idiosyncrasies,'" Sokolov "'does nothing to establish or develop external connections and has no organizational ability.'" He had made no useful contacts, was unable to manage the station, and "'should be replaced immediately.'"[61]

Moscow Center did replace Sokolov, but not until the end of 1950. And when he got back to Moscow and found out he had been blamed for the station's shortcomings, he wrote a bitter rebuttal. Admitting that his lack of English-speaking ability had hindered his work, he denied other flaws attributed to him, "'namely: cowardice, laziness, ineptitude at organizing the station's work, biding time in the embassy.'" Angry at never being asked "'for an appropriate explanation, or to send someone trustworthy to Washington to check on both the station's and my work, or even to summon me to give a personal explanation,'" he cited his prior good record and wondered how he could have been transformed so quickly "'into a good for nothing piece of shit.'"[62]

Earlier in October 1950 the KGB Washington station had sent a message to Moscow Center. Vassiliev's notebook does not record an author for this message, but given its tone, likely Sokolov, soon on his way back to Moscow, was responsible. It was defiant in its rejection of Moscow's complaints about the paucity of intelligence from America:

"Instead of 'berating' us in every letter, perhaps the authors of these severe and scathing letters could come here themselves and show us by their own example how one would go about acquiring people who work in the State Department and oth. gov't agencies of the country under the current fascist environment in the USA. Yelling, reproaching, and blaming others are the easiest things in the world, but actually solving the concrete issue is considerably harder. For example, in the last two years, Center has neither helped the station by sending over an illegal, nor by transferring agents from European or other countries. . . .

One should not forget that we are working here in a time when the cases of almost 50 agents, who failed [were exposed] long before our time in connection with Myrna's [Bentley's] betrayal, are still under investigation; in a time when Carp and Sima [Valentin Gubichev and Judith Coplon] have failed, when roughly 10 people have failed on X [technical intelligence] line and failures on this line continue, when Vig [Lee Pressman] has chosen to betray us and Vasin [William Weisband] has failed, when surveillance against our people has been heightened as never before, when true Fascism has arisen in this country, and harsh laws are passed both against Communists and against Americans, punishing them for having ties to foreigners with severe penalties —including death.

As for me personally, I insist that you send me replacements as soon as possible, maybe even from among the quick-witted authors of those loud letters, who here could demonstrate their complete understanding of problems and their skill and bravery in solving them."

Both Moscow's complaints and the Washington station's response were vivid illustrations that the golden days of Soviet intelligence in America were over.[63]

The Browder Problem

Bentley's defection was hardly the only issue confounding the KGB's work in America. The Soviet Communist Party had accused Earl Browder of ideological deviance in early 1945 via an article authored by a French Communist leader, Jacques Duclos. American Communists swiftly ousted Browder as their leader in mid-1945 and expelled him from the CPUSA in 1946. The KGB had not been consulted about the decision, and Browder's expulsion presented it with a major problem. Golos and Bentley had thoroughly briefed him on what they were doing and passed on to him much of the intelligence they collected. Further, Browder was aware of and participated in other aspects of the CPUSA's cooperation with Soviet intelligence, personally recommending a number of persons as potential sources.

Moscow had instructed Vladimir Pravdin in August 1945 to "carefully check out all probationers [sources] acquired on H.'s ["Helmsman"/Browder's] recommendation and think over what measures should be taken with regard to these individuals (breaking off contact, temporary deactivation, and so forth)." Late in August Akhmerov bumped into Bill Browder, who asked him if he would pass along a letter from his brother Earl to the KGB. When the KGB checked with the Soviet party, it vetoed the idea, and Moscow Center advised Akhmerov not to accept the letter. Yet when Merkulov sent instructions to Pravdin in early November 1945 on measures to take in response to Bentley's betrayal, one was to brief Bernard Schuster, the KGB's liaison to the CPUSA, and ask him to inform Browder about her defection so he could be forewarned of possible FBI inquiries.[64]

The KGB was reluctant to burn its bridges with Browder because, like Bentley, he knew too much. A Moscow Center memorandum summarized just how damaging he could be:

"Our stations began to use "H.'s" ["Helmsman"/Browder's] capability on the leadership line of the fellowcountryman organization [CPUSA] around 1933. In organizational terms this was done through highly trusted individuals who were personally handpicked by "H." and with whom the heads of our stations maintained illegal contact at various times. "Steve" (a.k.a. "Storm" [Josef Peters]), "H.'s" brother "Bill," and "Sound" [Golos] were used as such trusted representatives.

a) "Steve" was seldom used by our station chiefs until 1936, after which "H." relieved him of this work. "Steve" was used much more actively by GRU operatives. "Steve" had his own group of agents comprised of illegal fellowcountrymen [Communists] working at various govt. agencies, through whom he would receive information both for "H." and for the GRU.

b) "Bill" [Bill Browder] was used sporadically during the periods 1936–1937 and 1942–1944 only by our station chief "Maxim" [Zarubin] for contact with "H."

c) "So." ["Sound"], who was our important group leader of a large group of agents consisting of local citizens, was the principal trusted person for contact with "H." from 1937 until 1940. But he had no relationship with GRU operatives and didn't meet with any of them.

The chiefs of our stations received through the aforementioned trusted representatives of "H.": 1) Persons who had been checked out from among local fellowcountrymen for use as agents, illegal couriers, and illegal group leaders; 2) Background information on persons of interest to us for recruitment; 3) Leads for the purpose of recruitment to so-called illegal fellowcountrymen working at various govt. agencies, private companies, and defense plants and laboratories.

The persons who had been recommended by the fellowcountryman leadership and checked out were used by the stations for various intel. purposes: for infiltration into local Trotskyite organizations, as illegal couriers, owners of apartments for konspiratsia and secret meetings, group leaders for obtaining passports and other citizenship papers, for direct use as agents and, finally, to carry out various special assignments. Through these trusted representatives the stations sporadically also received information, various documents, and other intel. materials.

Note: In certain cases the chiefs of our stations, with special permission from the center, personally met with "H.," in especially secretive conditions, to conduct important discussions."[65]

Browder had been asking for the opportunity to come to Moscow to defend his views, and Merkulov, while avoiding saying anything about the ideological matters at issue, asked Stalin to approve his visit so the KGB could talk with him or, failing that, "'to recommend to the Executive Committee of the CPA [Communist Party of America], under a convenient pretext, that Br. [Browder] be reinstated in the party and that a more tactful line of behavior be adopted toward him.'" This was an extraordinary KGB intervention into a matter of CPSU concern, but Merkulov explained, "'Eighteen people were recruited for agent work on the NKGB USSR line on Br.'s [Browder's] recommendation,'" he knew of another twenty-five secret CPUSA members who were working for the KGB, and he was cognizant of more people whom he had either recruited for GRU or knew were working for it. Merkulov warned that Browder's expulsion from the CPUSA "'may prompt him to turn to extreme means of struggle against the Com. Party and cause harm to our interests.'"[66]

Stalin was sharpening, not relaxing, ideological discipline in the Communist movement, so Browder's reinstatement was off the table. But he was given a visa to visit Moscow. (Moscow's decision to allow Browder's visit shocked CPUSA leaders. After all, they had ousted their long-time leader at Moscow's behest.) When he came to Moscow, Soviet party officials listened to his defense of his ideological views but gave him no encouragement. Separately from his party talks, Browder met with Ovakimyan and Zarubin, both of whom he knew from their days as station chiefs in America. Fitin reported that in this meeting Browder "proposed that both he himself and his contacts be utilized in our work," but given his prominence and their belief that he would face strict scrutiny because of Bentley, "we deem it inadvisable to use him in agent work." Nonetheless, to encourage his continued loyalty, Soviet authorities gave Browder a franchise to market Soviet books in the United States that provided him a modest income. In 1948 a KGB agent also gave him $1,500 to pay for his wife's medical costs. Browder occasionally met with KGB officers, passing along ideological memos (Moscow Center judged them "tendentious"). In July 1949 the KGB Washington station told Moscow Center: "'In the view of friends of the emb. [embassy], Br.'s [Browder's] official connection with Soviet publishing houses is keeping him from making anti-Sov. statements and from disclosing secrets he knows. Our friends don't rule out the possibility that if we officially break with Br., this could prod him in the direction of reactionaries and complete betrayal. Taking this into account, Cde. Panyushkin believes that we should continue to maintain contact with Br. for another year or year and a half, until the spy mania campaign and the uproar over the Com. Party and 'Sov. spy centers' die down.'" To the end of his life, long after he ceased to consider himself a Communist, Earl Browder never said a word about his role in Soviet espionage or the dozens of agents and sources he knew.[67]

Officers Are Human

The flawed agent networks and ideological witch hunts that bedeviled the KGB's operations in America were not the only problems faced by station chiefs or their Moscow bosses. In espionage literature a certain romance has developed about "The Great Illegals," a group of KGB officers of the late 1920s and 1930s who achieved remarkable success moving from country to country, fitting into foreign societies, finding successful cover jobs, and recruiting valuable sources in half a dozen governments. But many of the KGB's officers in America fell short of the sophistication and flair attributed to these legends and had their share of personal problems and human failings.

Station chief Gutzeit glumly reported in 1935 that work infiltrating White Russian organizations had been in abeyance for nearly two months because "Leonid," who oversaw several agents on this line, had suffered a severe heart ailment and been ordered by doctors to refrain from even discussing work. Due to some unspecified breakdown in financial support, one illegal officer, Chivin, was reduced to borrowing money from Gutzeit in 1938 and, as a result of his travails, also suffered a heart attack. Another illegal, "Richard," had come to the United States with his

wife from Harbin in 1939 as tourists on a diplomatic visa. Unable to get
the visa extended and legally barred from working, they had been reduced to penury and forced to take temporary jobs that put them at risk
of deportation. Living with her mother in California, they still had "a
cheerful attitude" but needed immediate help. Another illegal, Leo Helfgott, died of cancer after arriving in the United States.[68]

Moscow Center had worried about the reliability of Valentin Markin's
girlfriend at the time of his death in 1934, and he was not the only KGB
officer whose romantic attachments occasioned concern. Gregory Kheifets, San Francisco station chief, had an affair with Louise Bransten, a
KGB source and a well-known socialite. When Moscow Center sent
Stanislav Shumovsky, a specialist in aviation intelligence, back to the
United States in 1941, it instructed his station chief, Zarubin, "'In the
course of a friendly conversation, Maxim [Zarubin] should warn Blerio
[Shumovsky] to be prudent when meeting with women.'" Presumably,
Moscow Center had a reason for issuing the warning. One KGB source
even had an affair with the Soviet ambassador. Alice Barrows worked for
the U.S. Office of Education in the Interior Department from 1919 to
1942. A secret Communist, she also maintained contact with the KGB,
steering Hede Massing to diplomat Laurence Duggan. The KGB gave
her the cover name "Young Woman." Barrows had an affair with Boris
Skvirsky, an Amtorg employee who served as the USSR's unofficial representative in Washington before the establishment of diplomatic relations. She later took up with Ambassador Aleksandr Troyanovsky, prompting Ovakimyan to complain that she had "'fallen into a kind of habit of
associating with Soviet representatives.'" Barrows gave Troyanovsky some
political information she had obtained from the Justice Department, and
in 1938 the ambassador suggested she be handled by the KGB. The KGB
New York station was agreeable, but Moscow Center thought her links
with the CPUSA were too well known and ordered contact with her severed.[69]

One unstable KGB officer also caused considerable damage. J. Edgar
Hoover received an anonymous letter in Russian in August 1943 that
identified Vasily Zarubin as the chief of KGB operations in the United
States. It also tagged eleven other KGB officers operating under diplomatic cover at Soviet offices in the United States, Canada, and Mexico
and named one American agent, Boris Morros (see chapter 8). The
anonymous author also accused Zarubin of a multitude of sins, including involvement in the Soviet murder of thousands of Polish prisoners of
war at Katyn, and made a bizarre claim that he and his wife were actu-

ally spies for Germany and Japan, urging American authorities to reveal their treachery to Soviet officials. An investigation eventually convinced the Bureau that those identified were, indeed, Soviet intelligence officers. FBI surveillance of those named in the letter led to identification of some of their sources and, in the case of Andrey Shevchenko, turning three of them into double agents (see chapter 6). Boris Morros also agreed to work for the FBI, and his information later resulted in the exposure, prosecution, and imprisonment of members of the Soble spy ring (see chapter 8). And surveillance of Semen Semenov was so obtrusive that he was unable to meet with his sources and returned to Moscow. The FBI was never certain who sent the letter, but internal evidence in the letter suggested it was Vasily Mironov, one of Zarubin's subordinates.[70]

The 1994 memoir of retired KGB general Pavel Sudoplatov first threw light on the mysterious communication. Sudoplatov knew nothing of the anonymous letter to the FBI (not made public until 1995). But he wrote that Mironov sent a letter to Stalin in 1943 denouncing his boss as a double agent for the Axis powers, and after a lengthy investigation, the KGB cleared the Zarubins and arrested Mironov. According to Sudoplatov, Mironov was found to be schizophrenic and hospitalized. Documents in Vassiliev's notebooks discuss Mironov's letter to Stalin in some detail. The overlap between Mironov's letter to Stalin and the anonymous letter to Hoover are such that it is clear that Mironov authored both.[71]

A March 1944 report by Fitin and Ovakimyan to Vsevolod Merkulov explained that a thorough investigation had cleared the Zarubins and "'determined that this matter is a case of far-fetched and false provocation that was instigated by a former worker of the Amer. station, Vasily Dmitrievich Mironov, and his accomplice, a former worker of the Amer. station, Vasily Georgievich Dorogov, who took advantage of their official positions while working abroad, and who blatantly violated the principal rules of konspiratsia and Chekist secrecy.'" Fitin and Ovakimyan recommended firing Mironov, "'send[ing] him to work in one of the far regions of the Soviet Union for a period of 5 years,'" and evicting his family from KGB housing (a perk of the security services). They also wanted Dorogov fired and handed over to the Red Army for assignment to the combat front. To "rehabilitate" (that is, shake up) the American station, they suggested recalling the Zarubins, Semenov, and KGB officer Konstantin Chugunov to Moscow and investigating "'indiscreet behavior by individual employees of the Amer. station, both at work and in private life.'" Merkulov reduced Dorogov's punishment, directing a reprimand, transfer from the prestigious foreign intelligence branch of the KGB to the less desirable internal security branch, and assignment to an "'outlying district with a demotion in rank.'" Nothing more about the incident appears in Vassiliev's notebooks. But KGB archival material brought to the West by Vasili Mitrokhin indicated that Mironov had been sent to a Gulag labor camp and executed in 1945, when he attempted to smuggle out a letter to the U.S. Embassy about the Katyn massacres.[72]

Unstable officers were an exception, but other KGB staff covered the full range from highly skilled to incompetent. Moscow sent Leonid Kvasnikov to New York in 1944 to set up a semi-independent technical intelligence station, and the KGB New York station promptly sloughed off to him two of its ne'er-do-wells, Alexander Feklisov and Anatoly Yatskov. Kvasnikov reported that Feklisov had a poor reputation: he had "heard nothing but low opinions about him as an inept and irresponsible person. For that reason no assignments, especially serious ones, were given to him and he was used, to put it crassly, as an errand boy, without a chance to grow." Given responsibilities and guidance, however, he had flourished: "He is highly responsible in how he approaches assignments that are given and he bleeds for his area of work. He is turning into a fine operative, who can be relied on in his work." Yatskov also had not been highly regarded, although this was partly due to "frequent changes in his area of work; essentially he was working on every line." While concentrating on technical intelligence had greatly improved his work, still "he is somewhat scatterbrained and at times not responsible enough. He can be late to a meeting, fail to check a camera before taking pictures, forget an assignment that has been given, and so forth. For example, after "Goose" [Harry Gold] was transferred to him, he lost him a couple of times, forgot the location of an arranged meeting, missed meetings, and G. was forced after that to travel to G.'s city and establish contact with him." Both Feklisov and Yatskov would in time be regarded as successful KGB field officers, and Feklisov in particular became a senior officer with a distinguished record of work in the United States and Great Britain, eventually returning to the United States as KGB station chief in the 1960s.[73]

Grigory Kheifets, the KGB's station chief in California, earned the scorn of his superiors. In June 1942 Gayk Ovakimyan, by then a senior officer in Moscow, sent the New York station chief a sarcastic evaluation of Kheifets's competence: "'Charon [Kheifets] does not understand his assignments, even though the XY [technical intelligence] is primary in his area. . . . Apparently, what interested him most was studying the climate in his vicinity. Now, apparently, he has looked into it and concluded that the climate is fully acceptable to him and his family—and therefore he asks that they be sent over.'" After Moscow recalled Kheifets in 1944, a report castigated him for having "'failed to organize himself and the station's operative to carry out the task set for them.'"[74]

Junior KGB officer Aleksey Prokhorov, questioned about the operations of the American station after he returned to Moscow in 1944, accused Pavel Pastelnyak, acting station chief in 1941, of periodic drinking binges with Robert Soblen, a KGB illegal. They "'drank together very often; apparently, they could relate through their egos, seeing as both of them liked to talk about themselves. One time it almost ended in a fight outside.'" Prokhorov also confirmed rumors that Moscow Center had heard that Pastelnyak beat his wife. Moreover, "'he thought he was better than everyone else and acted haughtily toward everyone around him,'" demeaning them by saying, "'You don't understand anything, you're still boys, I have experience, I've won awards, and so forth.'" He also failed to effectively oversee Prokhorov's work with Jacob Golos, "'in view of the fact that he didn't know the working conditions, didn't know the network, or home's [Moscow's] requirements.'"[75]

Sometimes KGB officers incurred envy or became too noticeable within the Soviet diplomatic community. Moscow sent a set of instructions that all officers were required to sign in 1943. It complained, "'By their behavior both at work and in private life, our employees abroad are revealing their identities to the Soviet colony and to foreign governments' counterintelligence agencies.'" Some officers had insisted they were too busy to participate in public activities, behaved differently from those holding equivalent jobs who were not in the KGB, "'leased expensive apartments and bought items that exceeded their official financial capabilities and in conversations with other workers did their best to stress that they were 'special' workers.'" In particular, their "'automobiles are frequently of a better make than the ambassador's automobile.'" To deal with these breakdowns in security, officers were instructed to behave in accordance with their cover jobs, eschew special privileges, participate in party and pubic life within the Soviet colony, and recognize the authority of the ambassador when working in their cover jobs, while confining discussion of their KGB business to the station chief and his deputy. Finally, "'the station's automobile should not be of a better make than the car of the ambassador or of other embassy workers who are of equal or higher rank than the station chief.'"[76]

After Zarubin's recall, Moscow sent Anatoly Gorsky to take over as the KGB Washington station chief and as overall head of operations in the United States. Gorsky complained in a letter to Moscow that several of the young KGB officers at the Washington station were still being trained and "'for the time being, they are all completely helpless.'" Having arrived before Gorsky, "'they got it into their heads that they were 'diplomats' and tried in the most serious manner to convince me that it was impossible for 'diplomats' to do anything else. It's up to me to knock this foolishness out of them.'" Gorsky singled out Mikhail Sumskoi and "'his better half,'" presumably his wife, for criticism. Eight months later, things had not improved. In a telegram, Gorsky blamed "'the careless organization of inventories and poor quality of photography of the probationer [source] materials'" on "'the irresponsible attitudes of 'Bogdan' [unidentified] and 'Makar' [Sumskoi], especially 'Bogdan.' Given that this is not the first time 'Bogdan' has damaged valuable materials, we think it necessary to impose a disciplinary penalty on him.'"[77]

KGB officers also varied in their skill and conscientiousness with some basic espionage tradecraft. Legal officers working out of Soviet diplomatic offices in particular had to assume that they were subject to FBI surveillance and were supposed to take elaborate measures to evade tails before meeting with sources. Alexander Feklisov explained in his autobiography how he would take a series of buses and subways, duck in and out of stores, and zigzag around New York, often for an hour or more, to shake any surveillance. Semenov stopped servicing his contacts because he judged he was unable to evade increased numbers of FBI watchers. But other officers were less scrupulous or less competent. Kheifets led the FBI to Amadeo Sabatini and Martin Kamen, while Ovakimyan exposed Jacob Golos and Maurice Cooke. Elizabeth Zarubin was rather blasé about dealing with possible surveillance. Leonid Kvasnikov told Moscow that he had "'major doubts'" about her assertion that she was not being followed, fearing "'that she simply does not notice it.'" Late in 1943 he ran into her while she was on the way to meet Golos and was startled that she was not wearing her glasses, "'without which she sees quite poorly,'" hindering her ability to pick up surveillance. She cavalierly responded that "'people who have been working a long time, such as her, develop a sixth sense, which unerringly lets them know whether or not they are under surveillance.'"[78]

The sometimes swift withdrawal of officers and station chiefs also left problems with the New York station's institutional memory, once with comic results. On station chief Pastelnyak's orders, a KGB officer created a hiding place inside the New York consulate in 1941 "in the upper level of the kitchen next to the Consul General's dining room, in the righthand china cabinet, the fourth or fifth door of the cabinet under the lower shelf counting toward the floor." It contained "explosives, a timer-detonator, poisons, and weapons." Zarubin had the ten pounds of explosives removed and destroyed in 1943. When one officer left New York late in 1944, however, he believed the hiding place still contained "a special Mauser silent pistol with rounds, timer-detonators, poisons, and a sword cane."[79]

Years passed, changes were made in the consulate's interior, and then in 1947 the USSR lost its lease and had to move to a new building. Obviously this material could not be left behind, but the hiding place was too well hidden. The staff could not find it. Pavel Fedosimov, acting chief of the New York station, asked for better directions from Moscow Center, but it replied: "'Our attempts to determine precisely the location of the hiding place, whether the objects in it were removed, by whom and when, have not produced positive results.'" Former station chiefs Zarubin and Apresyan "'supposedly knew only that there was a hiding place, but they don't know when its contents were removed.'" Prokhorov "'has the same information.'" Another operative "'assures us that the poisons and the silent pistol were removed from the hiding place and are kept in your safe. He doesn't know anything about a cane with a sword built into it. As you say, the matter has become extremely confused because of poor organization during the turnover of offices when the managers were replaced. In order to avoid possible trouble as a result of this, check in the closets in which the hiding place cited in the previous cable could be.'" And Moscow asked incredulously, "Boris" (an unidentified KGB officer) "'says that you know about a hiding place located in the equipment room (somewhere in the wall). What kind of hiding place is that?'"[80]

Fedosimov was unable to send good news. Except for a hiding place that Prokhorov had opened when Fedosimov had arrived in New York, "nothing has been found in the kitchen." Prokhorov had given him "a pen-revolver with two cartridges that contained poisoned bullets" in 1944, but he had shipped that to Moscow in February 1947. Fedosimov wanted to know if "this pen-revolver is the specific revolver that was in the hiding place in the kitchen," about which he knew nothing until Moscow had cabled him. The only hiding place of which he was aware was on the sixth floor of the consulate, whose contents he had removed in 1945 and sent to Moscow. Rather unhelpfully, he added that he "cannot report anything regarding the cane." The new tenants of the old Soviet consulate never reported finding any hidden weaponry, so presumably everything had been removed at some point.[81]

Competing Agencies

Even the most competent agents were sometimes stymied by the bureaucratic inefficiencies that frequently interfered with efforts to develop and utilize sources. Peter Gutzeit complained to a colleague at Moscow Center that earlier in 1934 he had asked to be given the "connection" to Jacob Golos and "'received a telegram categorically forbidding a connection with him.'" Four months later, the decision was reversed, and Gutzeit was even authorized "'to forbid his [Golos's] connection'" with another Soviet operative, "Smith," who headed an independent unit. Mystified, Gutzeit complained: "'What does this mean? What compelled you to give such contradictory directives, both in the first case and in the second?'"[82]

Gutzeit's irritation stemmed from Moscow's confusion about how to sort out the multiple Soviet and Communist entities operating covertly in the United States. The KGB's New York station, established in 1933 after diplomatic recognition of the USSR, was its first permanent presence in the United States. But there had been some episodic and limited KGB operations prior to that time. "Smith" was a KGB officer named Chivin, who had contacted Golos in 1930 for assistance in obtaining false American passports, thus beginning Golos's connection to the KGB. Chivin did not report to the New York station, although Gutzeit knew of him, but belonged to a shadowy and semi-autonomous KGB unit headed by Yakov Serebryansky, the "Administration for Special Tasks," which carried out kidnapping and assassination missions, many directed at anti-Bolshevik and anti-Stalinist Russian exiles, and prepared for wartime sabotage missions.[83]

Chivin's mission in the United States is unknown. Alexander Vassiliev did not have access to the files of Serebryansky's group, and it comes into the notebooks only when it brushes up against the KGB New York station, as it did with Chivin and Golos. This mysterious unit also appears in connection with Elizabeth Bentley. Bentley wrote in her KGB autobiography that in 1936 a Communist comrade "'asked whether I would agree to perform 'special' antifascist work. I agreed, and she introduced me to Juliet Stuart Poyntz-Glazer. Juliet spoke about illegal work in Italy, emphasizing the fact that, while doing this work, a woman must often do unpleasant things, such as sleep with men, in order to get information and so forth. I didn't like it. I told her that that didn't interest me.'" Bentley said she met several more times with Poyntz, but eventually they quarreled, with Poyntz accusing her of Trotskyism and threatening violence.[84]

Bentley was a newly minted Communist in 1936 and knew nothing of Juliet Stuart Poyntz (Glazer was a married name). But Poyntz had been a well-known figure in American radical circles. She was director of education for the International Ladies Garment Workers Union in its early years and one of the most prominent women leaders in the Socialist Party and later the CPUSA. She left a prestigious faculty post at Columbia University for full-time radical work in the early 1920s. At various times she directed the party's women's department and the New York Workers School and served on the staff of the Friends of the Soviet Union and International Labor Defense. After more than two decades as one of the nation's leading woman radicals, she dropped out of public political activity in the early 1930s. She disappeared from her New York residence in 1937, leaving behind her personal effects. A police investigation found no traces, and an extensive FBI investigation was equally fruitless. Old friends charged that she had broken with Soviet intelligence and been kidnapped and murdered. Bentley told the FBI in 1945 that Golos told her that Poyntz had been a traitor and was dead. Whittaker Chambers also said that he had heard that Poyntz had been killed for desertion.[85]

Documents in Vassiliev's notebooks fill in more of the story of Poyntz's involvement with Soviet intelligence. After reviewing Bentley's 1944 autobiography, Moscow Center checked on Poyntz and reported some data it had obtained from the Comintern, including the fact that she had worked in Moscow for its trade union arm, the Profintern, from late 1929 to March 1931. In December 1944 the American Department of GRU told Moscow Center she was not in its network "and nothing was known about her." But a second Moscow Center check in 1947 turned up additional information. From 1931 to 1933 Poyntz had worked for Serebryansky's "Administration for Special Tasks," but no details were given about her duties. The 1947 KGB memo also stated: "In Oct. 1934 [Poyntz] was recruited by the RU RKKA [Intelligence Directorate, Red Army—that is, GRU] and in November of that year traveled to the U.S. with an assignment to recruit agents. In November '36 arrived in Moscow and in Feb. '37 returned to the U.S. again. An RU representative met with Poyntz twice before her disappearance in early June 1937. The circumstances of the disappearance are not known to us." This does not solve the mystery of Poyntz's disappearance, but it strengthens suspicions that she met a grim fate at the hands of GRU.[86]

During World War II Akhmerov's illegal station was clearly subordinate to and worked easily with the legal station under Zarubin and Gorsky. But in the 1930s, the illegal station under Bazarov and Akhmerov was semi-autonomous, and occasionally there were communications problems about who was recruiting whom. In 1938 Akhmerov, busy hand-holding a very nervous Laurence Duggan, realized that Gutzeit's legal station had been trying to recruit him as well and waved off its effort. He pleaded with headquarters: "'Please take this into consideration and somehow coordinate it so that a discrepancy like this does not occur in the future.'" Gutzeit, meanwhile, believed that Akhmerov should turn over his operations against Trotskyists to him, lest the separate initiatives lead to "dangerous collisions" because "'Jung [Akhmerov] does not know our agents and we would not know his.'" Ovakimyan of the legal station informed Moscow that the competition between the legal and illegal station for sources had irritated Akhmerov, who intended to "'insist on his rights.'"[87]

The KGB and GRU also jostled against each other, causing occasional problems and jurisdictional issues. Whatever the formal lines of authority, on the ground the two agencies sometimes bumped into each other or were so compartmentalized that the right hand of Soviet espionage sometimes did not know what the left hand was doing. The KGB and GRU both scrambled to recruit Duggan and Noel Field at the State Department in the mid-1930s, with Hede Massing (KGB) and Alger Hiss (GRU) competing for Field's loyalties. Michael Straight (KGB) and Hiss eyed each other a few years later, raising fears that they would be exposed to each other like Duggan, Hiss, and Field had been (see chapter 1). When it considered recruiting Charles Flato, the KGB learned from CPUSA contacts "that he is supposedly connected with one of our other organizations," but "we were unable to verify this, especially as the GRU couldn't tell us for sure whether or not Flato was being used on their line." In the mid-1930s Harold Glasser had been part of Whittaker Chambers's GRU-linked apparatus but had been cut loose after Chambers's 1938 defection. The KGB picked him up in 1944. A year later the KGB grumbled that GRU had tried to contact Glasser and might lead the FBI to him. Gorsky asked that GRU be instructed to leave him alone, especially as he had no military information, but GRU denied it had tried to contact him.[88]

In addition to bureaucratic tussles among its own employees and agencies, Soviet intelligence also had to interact with the CPUSA. The party had created a secret apparatus in the early 1930s on orders from the Comintern. Led at first by Josef Peters, it was responsible for internal security; spied on government and private enemies; infiltrated Trotskyist and Lovestoneist organizations, the Socialist Party, and other rivals on the left; and maintained contact with underground Communists working in the federal government. It also cooperated with Soviet intelligence agencies. While the CPUSA's covert arm performed a variety of tasks for the KGB, greatly enhancing its effectiveness, at times the relationship could prove unwieldy and frustrating. Akhmerov tried to approach Victor Perlo in 1943 through Gerald Graze, who had once belonged to the same party unit, but it precipitated a chain of futility. "The fellowcountryman [CPUSA] leadership had to intervene in order to notify" Perlo that he would be working with Graze. The instructions were supposed to have come from John Abt, who was connected to Perlo via the CPUSA. Earl Browder gave orders to Abt "to meet with his comrades and do what is requested of him," but Abt resisted, insisting that Browder's "instructions to him in this regard were not binding and that he could do something when he had received orders from his superior," Josef Peters. An exasperated Akhmerov wrote: "'We once again took this matter to 'Helmsman' [Browder], but he shrugged and said there was nothing he could do in this situation. There is currently a new fellowcountryman [CPUSA] leader being appointed in Washington, who will be instructed to notify 'Eck' [Perlo] of our interest, and only afterwards will his connection with 'Arena' [Graze] be possible.'" And that was only half of the delay. In March 1943 Zarubin explained that Perlo's recruitment had been "delayed because, according to preliminary information, he had been connected through the fellowcountrymen [CPUSA] to someone with ties to the GRU; it was decided not to take any concrete action until the matter was cleared up. Now it is known for a fact that the GRU has nothing to do with this matter." When Elizabeth Bentley finally met with Perlo's group on Browder's orders, a year after the first futile attempt to contact him, the group members complained that despite their desire to help, they had been neglected for years by the CPUSA.[89]

The CPUSA, of course, had its own view of how the relationship should work. Vasily Zarubin traveled to California in 1942 and met with Steve Nelson, chief of the Communist Party in the San Francisco Bay Area and director of the CPUSA's covert apparatus in the West. Zarubin delivered cash to assist the party's underground work and discussed cooperation between the KGB and the party. The FBI had Nelson's residence bugged and recorded the conversation. While both men were in a cooperative mood, Nelson complained that Soviet intelligence operatives directly approached CPUSA members in California and asked for their help on specific assign-

ments. He was not upset that party members were being used by Soviet intelligence but that CPUSA officials like him, active in the underground apparatus, were being bypassed. The FBI summary of the conversation read:
"Nelson suggested to Zubilin [Zarubin's pseudonym] that in each important
city or State, the Soviets have but one contact who was trustworthy, and to
let that man handle the contact with party members who were to be given
special assignments by the Soviets."[90]

Sometimes the CPUSA political apparatus unknowingly intruded on
the KGB's turf. After Michael Straight returned to the United States in
1938, he began meeting periodically with Akhmerov. Moscow had very
high hopes for him; his wealth and family connections with the Roosevelts
suggested he might be able to secure a position with great potential. No
sooner did he start working at the State Department, however, than
Solomon Adler, a secret Communist at the Treasury Department, began
trying to recruit him for the party's political underground. His reputation
from Britain, and likely his history of extremely generous cash donations
to the British Communist Party, had preceded him. Moscow Center was
upset, warning that "'under no circumstances'" could he be allowed any
ties to the CPUSA and demanded that Browder be asked to call off such
an approach.[91]

Some sources had to juggle their responsibilities to different apparatuses. Charles Kramer, a congressional aide, provided information to
the KGB via the Perlo apparatus and to Albert Blumberg, who supervised legislative work for the CPUSA. After the KGB achieved direct
contact, Joseph Katz reported on Kramer: "'To Blumberg, he gives materials that are of interest to the local Comparty [Communist Party] and
to 'Raid' [Perlo], materials that are of interest to us [KGB]. However,
'Mole' [Kramer] occasionally experiences difficulties and does not know
how to get his bearings. . . . He is completely willing to make adjust-
ments to his work and his intentions in accordance with whatever we
think would be best. The only question he raised had to do with how to
resolve the problem of interrelations with Blumberg and us.'" Kramer
thought it "'unwise for him to break off his connection with Blumberg,'"
both because "'he would end up in a very awkward position'" and because "'he often receives valuable info'" from Blumberg "'about materials given by oth. members of the cell.'" Unable to figure out on the
spot how to disentangle the matter, Katz temporarily advised him "'to
continue working as before and that we would come back to this question in the near future.'"[92]

An Assessment

KGB organizational structure and tradecraft often failed to live up to textbook expectations. Nor should that be surprising. Organizations in practice rarely live up to their myths (or their textbooks). Any large operation, so fraught with secrecy and deception, relying so heavily on often flawed and odd people, was bound to stumble and sometimes fall. The documents in Vassiliev's notebooks demonstrate that how an intelligence agency should operate sometimes bears little resemblance to how it actually did.

Many of the Soviet intelligence officers who served in the United States were well-trained and competent professionals. Some, however, were poorly trained or poorly prepared. Some were shrewd judges of character; others were bullies and boors. Some knew what they were doing, others were the lucky recipients of intelligence windfalls, and a few were comically inept. Moscow suspected some of its most competent operatives of ideological deviation, recalled them, and shot them. Even good officers were sometimes stymied by the complicated bureaucratic structure of Soviet intelligence, exacerbated by the lack of institutional memory occasioned by the purges and the sheer number of players in the intelligence game. Not only did the KGB and GRU and the Naval GRU all have their own apparatuses in the United States, so too did the Communist International. The CPUSA also had its own underground apparatus. All of these secret groups bumped into each other. Operatives from one apparatus tried to recruit agents belonging to another. Poaching on another agency's territory was discouraged, but officers often puzzled over whether someone in whom they were interested belonged to someone else and was off limits or not.

Then there were the agents and sources themselves. They were human beings, prey to all of the emotions and petty grievances all people have. But they were also under enormous pressure and stress from living double lives. They resented some of their fellow spies; sought to inflate their own importance and status; and suffered from personal problems, marital difficulties, and psychological afflictions. Most were Communists, but some of them had doubts about the USSR, particularly during the purge trials and after the Nazi-Soviet Pact. Even true believers sometimes wondered why they needed to expose themselves to danger while the United States and USSR were allies and sometimes resented the demands placed on them. And spying could be personally expensive, necessitating providing support both for expenses and, sometimes, subsidies. KGB officers sometimes had to act as social workers or psychologists, soothing wounded egos and solving lovers' quarrels. While sometimes working out well, not all these therapeutic efforts succeeded.

The KGB was not a ten-foot-tall superman. In the world of intelligence, it was surely a strapping six-footer, but one that tripped over its own shoelaces from time to time and occasionally shot itself in the foot. And in the late 1930s, it turned into a paranoid schizophrenic who heard voices telling it to cut off its limbs, and it proceeded to do just that.

Conclusion

Espionage is a secretive business. It is rare that the agents engaged in it or the agencies they serve speak honestly and openly about what they have done because the incentives to lie, dissemble, and continue to deceive are so strong for all concerned. The tendency to romanticize sometimes dangerous but usually tedious activities also has fed an insatiable public appetite for fictional accounts of spying. Such literature, even when skillfully executed, often cannot match the oddities of the real world, where the best-laid plans of intelligence agencies and their operatives collide with the idiosyncrasies, strengths, and weaknesses of the people on whom they must rely to provide information and the equally human strengths and weaknesses of their adversaries and targets. The documents in Alexander Vassiliev's notebooks open the most complete view we have ever had of how Soviet intelligence functioned, revealing its triumphs, methods, failures, and frustrations as it strove to obtain American secrets during a crucial era of world politics.

The most striking point to emerge from this new information is that a remarkable number of Americans assisted Soviet intelligence agencies. The total exceeds five hundred, only a portion of whom have been discussed in the preceding chapters. There was no shortage of people willing to provide information or assistance to the KGB. Not all of them were classic spies, smuggling secrets out of their government offices or scientific laboratories. Some were talent spotters who suggested friends and colleagues as likely participants, while others facilitated espionage by providing safe houses, serving as couriers, or otherwise aiding and abetting Soviet intelligence operations in the United States.

Soviet spies came in all varieties and from almost all corners of the United States. There were men and women, Jews and gentiles, "old stock" Americans who could trace their lineage to signers of the Declaration of Independence, and those born abroad. (Only one identifiable black American appears as a Soviet agent, Paul Williams, a minor aviation source. Largely excluded from positions of authority or places where they handled secrets in the 1930s and 1940s, blacks were also too conspicuous when interacting with whites to serve as couriers or agent handlers.) Some spies grew up in poverty; others basked in luxury from their childhoods. While many agents had grown up on the sometimes rough streets of New York or Chicago, others were products of rural or small-town America. Some, like Alger Hiss, were graduates of elite prep schools and Ivy League colleges, holding prestigious government jobs where they were entrusted with great responsibilities and pledged to serve the nation's interests but nonetheless cooperated with agents of a foreign power. Others were anonymous people, living quiet lives and struggling with ordinary problems and burdens. Some had been seduced by a visit to the USSR; others only read about the supposed paradise in the USSR and yearned to recreate it in America. A number had been born in Russia and retained a visceral national loyalty. For some it was poverty that had embittered them about capitalism; others feared the rise of fascism and grasped at the Soviet Union as its most resolute foe. Most were energized by ideological zeal; others, however, had no commitment beyond monetary gain. Most had no difficulty working for the American government and pledging loyalty to the American constitution while giving away American secrets to the Soviet Union, believing they were serving a higher cause. A few were tortured by ethical doubts and vacillation, and others feared the consequences of their actions.

And risks there were. Documents recorded in Vassiliev's notebooks contain accounts of the KGB's frantic efforts to exfiltrate such valued sources as Julius Rosenberg and David Greenglass as the net closed in around them and the genuine shock experienced by KGB officers that the Rosenbergs faced the same fate that many thousands of "enemies of the people" had suffered on the basis of far less and usually imaginary evidence in the Soviet Union. (Similarly, since the early 1930s the USSR had been in a permanent state of mobilization against foreign spies, but in their internal communications KGB officers indignantly complained at various times that American "spy mania" was interfering with their management of dozens of, well, spies.) Some agents thrived on the excitement, professing few qualms or fears of exposure and insisted on providing stolen material even during periods when the KGB counseled caution. Others had to be constantly reassured or coaxed to continue. And even ideological sources sometimes worried about exposure or put their own career interests ahead of their work as spies.

Many sources were identified and questioned by the FBI or congressional committees, although relatively few were prosecuted and even fewer convicted and jailed. (The awkwardness and near inability of American criminal law to deal effectively with espionage is a separate matter.) The KGB shut down agents and networks when danger threatened, reducing the chances that its assets would be caught in the act. Only a few of those confronted confessed (Klaus Fuchs in Britain and Alfred Slack in the United States), and even fewer testified against others, most notably Jack Soble, David Greenglass, and Harry Gold. Some, like Amadeo Sabatini, made partial confessions, and one, Nathan Sussman, successfully diverted the Justice Department by admitting Communist membership and testifying about the hidden Communist loyalties of others while concealing years of work as a spy. Most accused agents, however, simply lied or took the Fifth Amendment.

The single most disastrous event in the history of Soviet intelligence in America was Elizabeth Bentley's decision to turn herself in to the FBI in 1945 and tell all she knew. An agent handler, not only did she identify scores of Soviet sources inside the U.S. government and KGB officers with whom she had worked, but her information also led the FBI to focus on Soviet espionage precisely at a time when the end of World War II freed up hundreds of its agents who had been working on German and Japanese counterespionage. Her revelations triggered a wholesale withdrawal of experienced KGB officers that left its American stations woefully unprepared for the opening years of the Cold War; led to the public exposure of links between the American Communist Party and Soviet intelligence that destroyed the former's use as an espionage Fifth Column; and additionally tainted the Communist movement with treason, contributing to its political marginalization.

FBI investigations and voluminous congressional testimony supported Bentley's story. The documents in Vassiliev's notebooks, as well as the KGB cables deciphered by the Venona project, demonstrate un-equivocally that Bentley told the truth. Yet the consensus of several gen-erations of American historians (backed by many journalists and other opinion leaders) routinely mocked, ridiculed, and dismissed her as a fraud and mountebank. Those she named were often defended and even praised as devoted public servants unfairly smeared because of leftist as-sociations. They were, however, guilty.

Bentley's defection was the worst but not the first disaster the KGB faced in America. After the establishment of diplomatic relations in 1933, it had set up a legal station operating out of the Soviet Consulate in New York, as well as an illegal station staffed with officers living covertly under false identities. After a series of successes and the construction of net-works supplying scientific, diplomatic, and political information, much of what had been built was destroyed, but not by indifferent or inept Amer-ican security agencies or defectors. The KGB decapitated its own orga-nization in the late 1930s in an obsessive and murderous search for nonexistent traitors. Stalin's purges of the late 1930s devastated its head-quarters, so much so that in late 1939 a Moscow Center memo noted that illegal officers working covertly in the United States were "unknown to anyone in the department" since everyone who had known them was dead or in the Gulag. Scores of professional field officers were recalled from abroad, accused of being "enemies of the people," and executed, including the chiefs of the American legal and illegal stations. The robust networks created in the 1930s were deactivated and some of the sources lost forever.[1]

When sanity returned in 1941, the KGB's American stations were not entirely starting over, but the reconstruction task was considerable. The Nazi attack on the USSR made the need for intelligence acute, but the crippled American stations had few resources. Fortunately for the short-term needs of the KGB, the American Communist Party maintained large networks of secret party members working in government (managed by Jacob Golos, assisted by Elizabeth Bentley) that it called upon to fill in the gaps while it rebuilt its professional intelligence apparatus. Although it recognized the serious operational deficiencies that the amateurish net-works run by the CPUSA posed, its desperate need for information slowed down its ability to professionalize the operation and sowed the seeds of the disaster that began in 1945 with a series of defections, Bentley chief among them, that ultimately destroyed most of its assets and networks. By the late 1940s, the KGB networks in America were shadows of their former selves, with the dwindling number of sources less able to provide the kinds of information Moscow was demanding. One of the few bright spots for Soviet intelligence in the postwar era was the combination of good luck and skill that placed one man, William Weisband, in a position to warn Moscow in 1948 that the United States was reading its military cipher systems, and that one success ended in 1950, when the FBI, following up clues going back to 1943, tracked him down. Judith Coplon, another valuable postwar sources, was arrested in 1948.

How much damage did these spies do? As evidence of extensive Soviet espionage has mounted in the past decade, some academics and partisans, despite knowing nothing of the substance of what information was passed to Moscow, have simply claimed on the basis of no evidence whatsoever that it was trivial or did little damage to American security. Like most intelligence agencies, the KGB was sometimes disappointed or unimpressed by the quality of information it received from its sources. Some people to whom it devoted much attention produced little. And a few sources turned out to be charlatans or even double agents. But the KGB stations in the United States also produced an extraordinary amount of vital information. The scientific and technical data they transmitted to Moscow saved the Soviet Union untold amounts of money and resources by transferring American technology, which enabled it to build an atomic bomb and deploy jet planes, radar, sonar, artillery proximity fuses, and many other military advances long before its own industry, strained by rapid growth and immense wartime damage, could have developed and fielded them independently. Sources in the American government sometimes provided low-grade intelligence, but they also gave the USSR an unprecedented window on American diplomatic, economic, and political developments and plans. Sources in the world of journalism passed along useful insights into government, the media, and potential recruits. While any intelligence service covets the key document or set of blueprints, it also relies heavily on a stream of less dramatic information that enables it to form a coherent picture of its adversary and provides a check, a second source, on what has been learned from the open media and conventional diplomacy—and the KGB's hundreds of American sources and agents did their best to provide such insights. The evidence is that Soviet espionage in the United States changed history. The espionage-enabled rapid acquisition of the atomic bomb emboldened Stalin's policies in the early Cold War and contributed to his decision to authorize North Korea's invasion of South Korea. Soviet espionage also led to the loss of America's ability to read Soviet military communications and ensured that the Korean invasion was a surprise for which American forces were unprepared.

In addition to enriching our understanding of who worked for the KGB and what information they provided, the documents in Vassiliev's notebooks are a reminder that some KGB sources went on to successful careers, either because they were protected by the American legal system or because they never came under suspicion. Whether it was Bernard Redmont overseeing a distinguished school of journalism; Russell Mc-Nutt building the planned community of Reston, Virginia; David Salmon retiring from the State Department with the government's thanks; or I. F. Stone lecturing intellectuals about truth-telling, the spies who got away with it lived lives built on lies and deception.

The story of KGB espionage in America is not only an account of Soviet infiltration, but also a panorama of individual lives and frustrations, resentments, and dreams that a foreign intelligence agency was able to take advantage of and manipulate. An espionage service is, in part, a social service agency, required to minister to its charges' emotional, financial, and marital woes. The documents in the notebooks include accounts of agent handlers and KGB officers soothing, counseling, and admonishing their recruits, worrying about their physical and mental health, financing vacations at health spas, advising about career moves and matrimonial worries, and fretting about their poor decisions or silly mistakes. The Silvermaster network was one of the KGB's most productive sources of diplomatic and military information, and it also was, to the unease of its officers, a cauldron of unhappy, bitter, and frustrated people, constantly sniping at each other and led by a *ménage à trois.* Even less dysfunctional groups required constant soothing and ego stroking, whether to reassure Julius Rosenberg that he remained highly valued despite the need to reduce his role after the government dismissed him from his job because of Communist connections or to persuade diplomat Laurence Duggan, naively believing the Moscow Trials claims that leading Soviet figures had been in league with Germany, that his fears that these Soviet traitors might have revealed his treachery were baseless.

The notebooks also suggest that the KGB's success, while owing in part to the skills and perseverance of its professional officers, also was the result of a great deal of luck and freely offered gifts. While it took advantage of many of its opportunities, it was not the super-efficient, smoothly running machine of popular myth. It was very lucky to have a committed CPUSA anxious to help, government leaders who largely regarded the Soviet intelligence threat with indifference for many years, and a distracted and sometimes clueless FBI as its foe in the 1930s. And even after the FBI learned the skills needed for counterespionage, it was not until the mid-1940s that the Bureau turned its full attention to the Soviet intelligence threat. But when it did, several key defections, the National Security Agency's decoding of wartime KGB cables, the inherent vulnerability of the party-based networks, and its full-court press against the CPUSA combined to shatter Soviet intelligence in America.[2]

A substantial portion of the KGB's success came from the sources and agents handed to it by the CPUSA. The Silvermaster, Perlo, and Rosenberg rings all came to the Soviets courtesy of leaders of the American Communist Party. Most of its other productive spies were ideological agents whose recruitment was a result of their commitment to communism; indeed several key sources such as atomic spies Theodore Hall and Klaus Fuchs and the engineer spy Julius Rosenberg were not recruited but sought out the KGB and volunteered their services. But the KGB did recruit a number of sources whose chief commitment was money, such as biomedical spy Earl Flosdorf and aviation source Jones York. Some of the sources recruited by the KGB itself turned out to be more trouble than they were worth. Martha Dodd Stern and Victor Hammer, for example, consumed a great deal of time from professional KGB officers but in the end did not deliver very much useful information or, in Hammer's case, anything at all. One KGB recruit, Boris Morros, repeatedly filled the heads of KGB officers with intoxicating tales of his high-level social and business contacts. While he did perform some useful services, in the mid-1940s the FBI turned him into a double agent, and he went on to expose to prosecution members of a Soviet espionage apparatus. Perhaps there was something to Iskhak Akhmerov's observation that having Americans like Silvermaster run the sources made them more productive, that the KGB officers were unable to get the most out of their commitments or accurately assess their motivation. Without the CPUSA, Soviet espionage rings in the United States would have been far, far less effective and widespread. The weakening of Soviet intelligence operations went hand in hand with the weakening of the CPUSA.

Ideological spies present a particularly disturbing challenge in a country where citizenship has never been defined by blood and heritage—with the partial exception of blacks and Indians—but by commitment to a set of democratic ideals. Citizens accused of allegiance to a foreign power have engendered outrage, whether it was Aaron Burr, allegedly seeking to dismember the Union, or German-Americans suspected of disloyalty during World War I. But those who have rejected the principles of the Constitution for another vision of government have earned particular wrath. No era of American life saw so many accusations of espionage and covert activities on behalf of a foreign country as the decade after World War II.

The McCarthy era has long since attained iconic status in American history as the symbol of paranoia about "reds hiding under the beds." Although the postwar attack on the CPUSA preceded Senator McCarthy's rise to prominence, the picture of a relentless governmental persecution of a perhaps annoying but ultimately harmless movement is regularly invoked as an object lesson in the erosion of civil liberties. Most American Communists were not spies; the KGB did not need or want the CPUSA's fifty-to-sixty thousand members as agents. But the documents in Vassiliev's notebooks make crystal clear that the CPUSA's leadership in the 1930s and 1940s willingly placed the party's organizational resources and a significant number of its key cadres at the service of the espionage agencies of a foreign power. The CPUSA as an organized entity was an auxiliary service to Soviet intelligence. Dozens of its members working for the American government or employed in scientific research handed over information, sometimes with the full knowledge that they were serving the Soviet Union, sometimes comforting themselves that they were only informing the CPUSA leadership, and occasionally willfully deceiving themselves about the ultimate destination of the material.

It was no witch hunt that led American counterintelligence officials to investigate government employees and others with access to sensitive information for Communist ties after they became cognizant of the extent of Soviet espionage and the crucial role played in it by the CPUSA, but a rational response to the extent to which the Communist Party had become an appendage of Soviet intelligence. And, as the documents in Vassiliev's notebooks make plain, they only knew the half of it.

Notes

Preface (Klehr and Haynes)

1. William J. Broad, "A Spy's Path: Iowa to A-Bomb to Kremlin Honor," *New York Times*, 12 November 2007.

2. Anatoly Gorsky, "Failures in the USA (1938–48)," December 1948, KGB file 43173, v.2c, pp. 49–55, Alexander Vassiliev, *Black Notebook [2007 English Translation]*, trans. Philip Redko (1993–96), 77–79.

3. Harvey Klehr, John Earl Haynes, and Fridrikh Igorevich Firsov, *The Secret World of American Communism* (New Haven: Yale University Press, 1995); Harvey Klehr, John Earl Haynes, and Kyrill M. Anderson, *The Soviet World of American Communism* (New Haven: Yale University Press, 1998); John Earl Haynes and Harvey Klehr, *Venona: Decoding Soviet Espionage in America* (New Haven: Yale University Press, 1999). NSA released the Russian text of a single Venona decryption, the one discussing the source "Ales" [Alger Hiss]. John R. Schindler, "Hiss in VENONA: The Continuing Controversy," paper presented at Symposium on Cryptologic History, Laural, MD, 2005.

4. Christopher M. Andrew and Vasili Mitrokhin, *The Sword and the Shield: The Mitrokhin Archive and the Secret History of the KGB* (New York: Basic Books, 1999); Christopher M. Andrew and Vasili Mitrokhin, *The World Was Going Our Way: The KGB and the Battle for the Third World* (New York: Basic Books, 2005); V. I. Mitrokhin, *KGB Lexicon: A Handbook of Chekist Terminology* (London and Portland, OR: Frank Cass, 2001); "The Mitrokhin Archive—A Note on Sources," in The Mitrokhin Archive: Cold War International History Project Virtual Archive (2004); "CWIHP Note on the Mitrokhin Archive—A Note On Sources," in The Mitrokhin Archive: Cold War International History Project Virtual Archive (2000). In addition to the segment of Mitrokhin material available at the Cold War International History Project, the SIS gave Mitrokhin's material on Italy to the Italian government, which released the material in 2002. The cables deciphered by the Venona

project are available on the Web at http://www.nsa.gov/venona/index.cfm. Hard copy of the cables is also available at the National Cryptologic Museum (Ft. Meade, MD). Histories of the Venona project includeRobert L. Benson, *The Venona Story* (Ft. Meade, MD: Center for Cryptologic History, National Security Agency, 2001); Robert Louis Benson and Michael Warner, *Venona: Soviet Espionage and the American Response 1939–1957* (Washington, D.C.: National Security Agency, Central Intelligence Agency, 1996).

5. Four books ultimately derived from the original Crown series: John Costello and Oleg Tsarev, *Deadly Illusions* (New York: Crown Publishers, 1993); David E. Murphy, Sergei A. Kondrashev, and George Bailey, *Battleground Berlin: CIA vs. KGB in the Cold War* (New Haven: Yale University Press, 1997); Nigel West and Oleg Tsarev, *The Crown Jewels: The British Secrets at the Heart of the KGB Archives* (New Haven: Yale University Press, 1999); Allen Weinstein and Alexander Vassiliev, *The Haunted Wood: Soviet Espionage in America—The Stalin Era* (New York: Random House, 1999).

6. Information from "Muse," 14 December 1944, KGB file 40935, v.1, p. 99, Alexander Vassiliev, *Yellow Notebook #4 [2007 English Translation]*, trans. Steven Shabad (1993–96), 39; Hayden Peake to John Haynes, 27 April 2006.

Introduction (Vassiliev)

1. Anatoly Gorsky, "Failures in the USA (1938–48)," December 1948, KGB file 43173, v.2c, pp. 49–55, Alexander Vassiliev, *Black Notebook [2007 English Translation]*, trans. Philip Redko (1993–96), 77–79.

2. Allen Weinstein and Alexander Vassiliev, *The Haunted Wood: Soviet Espionage in America—The Stalin Era* (New York: Random House, 1999).

3. Hiss to Volkogonov, 3 August 1992, and Volkogonov to Lowenthal, 14 October 1992, reproduced in Alger Hiss and Dimitri Volkogonov, "In Re: Alger Hiss," *Cold War International History Project Bulletin*, no. 2 (Fall 1992): 33.

4. Kobalzdze to Lowenthal, 30 September 1992, evidence entered into Alexander Vassiliev vs. Frank Cass & Co, HQ 01X03222, the High Court of Justice in London, Queen's Bench Division.

Chapter 1: Alger Hiss

1. The two most thorough studies of the Hiss-Chambers case are Allen Weinstein, *Perjury: The Hiss-Chambers Case* (New York: Random House, 1997), and Sam Tanenhaus, *Whittaker Chambers: A Biography* (New York: Random House, 1997). For a summary, see "The Alger Hiss–Whittaker Chambers Case," chapter 4 in John Earl Haynes and Harvey Klehr, *Early Cold War Spies: The Espionage Trials That Shaped American Politics* (New York: Cambridge University Press, 2006).

2. Alger Hiss and Dimitri Volkogonov, "In Re: Alger Hiss," *Cold War International History Project Bulletin*, no. 2 (Fall 1992): 33. Serge Schmemann, "Russian General Retreats on Hiss," *New York Times*, 17 December 1992. Remarks to the same effect in *Nezavisimaya Gazeta* (Moscow), 24 November 1992, p. 4. On 11 No-

vember 1992, Volkogonov told the researcher Herbert Romerstein that the GRU archives on foreign intelligence were closed and he had not searched them for material on Hiss. Herbert Romerstein and Eric Breindel, *The Venona Secrets: Exposing Soviet Espionage and America's Traitors* (Washington, D.C.: Regnery, 2000), 140.

3. "Nikolay" letter, 3 October 1934, KGB file 36857, v.1, p. 14, Alexander Vassiliev, *Yellow Notebook #2 [2007 English Translation]*, trans. Philip Redko (1993–96), 2.

4. Hede Massing, *This Deception* (New York: Duell, Sloan, and Pearce, 1951); Veronica Anne Wilson, "Red Masquerades: Gender and Political Subversion during the Cold War, 1945–1963" (Ph.D. diss., Rutgers University, New Brunswick, 2002).

5. Mária Schmidt, "Noel Field—The American Communist at the Center of Stalin's East European Purge: From the Hungarian Archives," *American Communist History* 3, no. 2 (December 2004): 228–29. Schmidt's findings in the Hungarian archives were corroborated by Bernd-Rainer Barth and Werner Schweizer, assisted by Thomas Grimm, *Der Fall Noel Field: Schlüsselfigur der Schauprozesse in Osteuropa* (Berlin: BasisDruck, 2005–7), Arte Edition, 2 vols.

6. While Hiss denied participation in the Ware group, in addition to Chambers's testimony, a fellow member of the group, Nathaniel Weyl, later broke with the CPUSA and affirmed his and Hiss's membership. Nathaniel Weyl, "I Was in a Communist Unit with Hiss," *U.S. News and World Report,* 9 January 1953; Nathaniel Weyl, *Encounters with Communism* (Philadelphia: Xlibris, 2004). Chambers provided a detailed account of his covert work in his testimony at the two Hiss perjury trials and in his memoir: Whittaker Chambers, *Witness* (New York: Random House, 1952).

7. Note from "Redhead" appended to a KGB New York letter, 26 April 1936, KGB file 36857, v.1, p. 23 and reverse, Vassiliev, *Yellow #2*, 4.

8. "Nord" to Center, 26 April 1936, KGB file 36857, v.1, pp. 21–22, Vassiliev, *Yellow #2*, 4–5. Emphasis in original. That "Jurist" was a GRU cover name is supported by Chambers's memory that Boris Bykov, the GRU officer who oversaw Chambers's network, referred to Hiss as "Der Advokat," a German word that can be translated as jurist, advocate, or lawyer. Chambers, *Witness,* 414–15.

9. Center to KGB New York, 3 May 1936, KGB file 36857, v.1, p. 24, Vassiliev, *Yellow #2*, 5.

10. "Jung" to Center, 18 May 1936, KGB file 36857, v.1, p. 25, Vassiliev, *Yellow #2*, 5–6.

11. Massing, *This Deception,* 164-78; Chambers, *Witness,* 29–30, 381–82.

12. Noel Field, "Hitching Our Wagon to a Star," *Mainstream,* January 1961; Schmidt, "Noel Field," 243–45.

13. Noel Field statement of 23 September 1954, Noel Field material, Hungarian Historical Institute Archive, cited in Schmidt, "Noel Field," 229–30.

14. KGB New York report, 18 February 1938, KGB file 58380, v.1, p. 51, Alexander Vassiliev, *White Notebook #3 [2007 English Translation]*, trans. Steven Shabad (1993–96), 116. Solomon Adler was a Treasury Department official and secret Communist active in the party's Washington underground. Although he is not known to have assisted Soviet espionage in the 1930s, he was among those identified by Whit-

taker Chambers to Assistant Secretary of State Adolf Berle in September 1939 as covert Communists who were espionage risks. He was an active KGB source in World War II. "Jung" to Center, 28 June 1938, KGB file 58380 ("Nigel"), v.1, pp. 73–74, Vassiliev, *White #3*, 118.

15. "Jung" to Center, 31 July 1938, KGB file 58380, v.1, p. 83, Vassiliev, *White #3*, 119.

16. "Nord" to Center, 28 November 1936; "Nord" letter, 29 November 1936, KGB file 36857, v.1, pp. 49, 51, Vassiliev, *Yellow #2*, 9–10.

17. KGB New York to Center, 14 September 1938, KGB file 35112, v.5, p. 72, Alexander Vassiliev, *Black Notebook [2007 English Translation]*, trans. Philip Redko (1993–96), 152.

18. "List of people who, according to "Raid's" information," 15 March 1945, KGB file 45100, v.1, p. 91, Vassiliev, *White #3*, 78.

19. Chambers, *Witness*, 336, 429–30.

20. "Ruble" biography, December 1944, KGB file 43072, v.1, p. 50, Vassiliev, *White #3*, 48. Vassiliev's notes indicate that the original autobiography was handwritten in English and was located in KGB file 43072, v.1, p. 53, but that his notes were taken from a Russian translation found at pp. 49–50. Karl [Whittaker Chambers], "The Faking of Americans," unpublished essay (Herbert Solow Papers, Hoover Institution on War, Revolution and Peace, Stanford University, Stanford, CA., 1938); Chambers, *Witness*, 336, 429–30. The English names "Carl" and "Karl" are spelled identically in Cyrillic Russian, and under most Cyrillic Russian to Latin English transliteration systems are rendered "Karl" when transliterated into the Latin alphabet.

21. Chambers, *Witness*, 44–48, 55, 365; John W. Berresford, "The Grand Jury in the Hiss-Chambers Case," *American Communist History* 7, no. 1 (June 2008): 27. In interviews with historian Allen Weinstein in 1975 Lieber confirmed that he had been a Communist, participated in the underground and assisted Chambers in the work of his apparatus, knew Josef Peters and Boris Bykov, and had on their instructions attempted to locate Chambers after his defection. Weinstein, *Perjury*, 99, 111–14, 130–31, 138n, 280–81. After the first edition of *Perjury* appeared in 1978, Lieber partially repudiated his statements to Weinstein. Lieber never publicly admitted party membership, although he acknowledged his closeness to the Communist movement in his interviews with Weinstein, but when he fled to Communist Poland in 1954, he filled out forms showing that he had joined the CPUSA in 1929 (he also joined the Polish Communist Party). Maxim Lieber file, IPN BU 1218/8738, Instytut Pamięci Narodowej [Institute of National Remembrance]. The authors thank Włodzimierz Batóg and Leszek Gluchowski for their assistance in locating and reviewing the Lieber file.

22. "Vadim" report to Moscow Center, 18 December 1944; Moscow Center to "Vadim," 22 December 1944; information repeated in Moscow Center report, 2 March 1951, KGB file 43072, v.1, pp. 25–26, 46, Vassiliev, *White #3*, 46, 65. Chambers, *Witness*, 48; Hope Hale Davis, *Great Day Coming: A Memoir of the 1930s* (South Royalton, VT: Steerforth Press, 1994), 98. Josef Peters, a man of many pseudonyms, was also known as Peter, J. Peters, Joseph Peters, Alexander Stevens, Sandor Goldberger, Silver, Isidore Boorstein, Steve, Steve Lapin, and Steve Miller.

23. The Russian translation of Glasser's autobiography rendered Paul in Russian as "Paul'" when transliterated from Cyrillic, with " ' " a transliteration convention for the Russian Cyrillic alphabetic soft sign. Similarly Gorsky's "Pol" in Cyrillic is transliterated as "Pol'" with a soft sign.

24. In 1954, Felix Inslerman, photographer for Chambers's GRU network, told the FBI and testified to a congressional committee that in 1938 Chambers had given him a letter that he delivered to their Soviet contacts warning of exposure if he was harassed. Inslerman copied portions of the letter and gave copies to both the FBI and Permanent Subcommittee on Investigations of the Senate Committee on Government Operations. Felix Inslerman testimony, 20 February 1954, Committee on Government Operations, U.S. Senate Permanent Subcommittee on Investigations, *Subversion and Espionage in Defense Establishments and Industry* (Washington, D.C.: U.S. Govt. Print. Off., 1954–55), pt. 2, 998–1110.

25. "Vladimir" to Moscow Center, 25 December 1948, KGB file 43173, v.4, p. 479; P. Fedotov and K. Kukin report to KI chairman, December 1948, KGB file 43173, v.2c, p. 203, Vassiliev, *Black,* 73. One Hiss defender has advanced the claim that "Karl"/Robert Tselnis was Robert Zelms. There is no evidence for this assertion. Nicholas Dozenberg, a former mid-level CPUSA official, set up business covers for GRU in Europe and Asia in the 1930s. Imprisoned in the United States on a false passport charge, he confessed and in 1948 wrote that he "had recommended for employment with Soviet military intelligence in foreign countries . . . Robert Zelms, Z-e-l-m-s, alias Elmston." A 1944 FBI report noted that Zelms had been arrested in Austria in 1936 for Communist activities and had last been seen in Moscow in 1939. A British MI6 memo regarding an international trading company operating in Asia and Europe and secretly controlled by Soviet intelligence also placed him in Europe in the period 1930–36. Statement of Nicholas Dozenberg, 4 October 1948, U.S. House Committee on Un-American Activities, *Hearings Regarding Communist Espionage* (Washington, D.C.: U.S. Govt. Print. Off., 1951), 3541; "Comintern Apparatus Summary Report," 15 December 1944, serial 3702, p. 189, FBI Comintern Apparatus file 100–203581; Memo to J. A. Cimperman, replying to a letter of 13 January 1949, British Public Records Office, files KV2/1902 and KV2/1655, transcription at www.garethjones.org. There is nothing connecting Zelms to GRU activities in Washington in the mid- to late 1930s or anytime in the 1940s.

26. A. Gorsky, "Failures in the USA (1938–48)," December 1948, KGB file 43173, v.2c, p. 49, Vassiliev, *Black,* 77.

27. Elizabeth Bentley, FBI Deposition, 30 November 1945, serial 220, pp. 52, 55–57, FBI Silvermaster file 65–56402 (cited hereafter as Deposition 1945); "M.'s contacts; list obtained by Vadim," October 1944, KGB file 70545, p. 152, Alexander Vassiliev, *White Notebook #2 [2007 English Translation],* trans. Steven Shabad (1993–96), 10.

28. Venona 195 KGB Moscow to New York, 3 March 1945.

29. Venona 230 KGB San Francisco to Moscow, 4 May 1945; Venona 235–36 KGB San Francisco to Moscow, 5 May 1945; Venona 259 KGB San Francisco to Moscow, 13 May 1945; Venona 312 KGB San Francisco to Moscow, 8 June 1945.

30. Venona 1822 KGB Washington to Moscow, 30 March 1945. The text used

here is John Schindler's 2002 translation. John R. Schindler, "Hiss in VENONA: The Continuing Controversy," paper presented at Symposium on Cryptologic History, Laural, MD, 2005, http://www.johnearlhaynes.org/page61.html.

31. The most thorough examination of Venona 1822, the 30 March 1945 cable, is Eduard Mark, "Who Was 'Venona's 'Ales'? Cryptanalysis and the Hiss Case," *Intelligence and National Security* 18, no. 3 (Autumn 2003).

32. Hiss was indicted for perjury in 1948 for denying supplying State Department documents to Chambers (the statute of limitations precluded an espionage charge). The initial trial ended in a hung jury but with a majority for conviction. A unanimous jury in a second trial convicted Hiss on 21 January 1950. An appeals court affirmed conviction, and the Supreme Court denied appeal in March 1951. A 1952 petition for retrial was similarly rejected by district, appellate, and supreme courts. After serving his prison sentence, Hiss was released and later asked to have his license to practice law restored. The Massachusetts Supreme Judicial Court in 1975 readmitted Hiss to the practice of law, citing his blameless life since prison but adding that "nothing we have said here should be construed as detracting one iota from the fact that . . . we consider him to be guilty as charged." In 1978 Hiss submitted a detailed writ asking that his conviction be overturned. A federal district court in 1982 ruled, "the jury verdict rendered in 1950 was amply supported by the evidence . . . and nothing presented in these papers . . . places that verdict under any cloud." An appeals court and the Supreme Court also rejected Hiss's writ. Weinstein, *Perjury*, 499–502.

33. The defense experts had far more samples of Hiss family typed material to examine than did the prosecution experts. For obvious reasons, the defense did not bring this up at the trial.

34. Weinstein, *Perjury*, 154; "List of people who, according to "Raid's" information," 15 March 1945, KGB file 45100, v.1, p. 91, Vassiliev, *White #3*, 78.

35. Tanenhaus, *Whittaker Chambers*, 519;Weinstein, *Perjury*, 321–22.

36. Weinstein, *Perjury*, 99, 111–14, 130–31, 134, 138n, 171, 204, 273, 280–81, 286, 288, 339, 362, 381, 434, 466.

37. Fitin to Merkulov, 25 April 1945, KGB file 43072, v.1, pp. 96–97, Vassiliev, *White #3*, 58; Bentley, Deposition 1945, 105.

38. "Vadim" to Moscow Center, 5 March 1945, KGB file 43173, v.1, p. 88, Vassiliev, *Black*, 50.

39. "Grew Says World Must Bar Anarchy," *New York Times*, 4 March 1945; "State Department Radio Show Gives 'Oaks' Plan in Plain Talk," *Washington Star*, 4 March 1945.

40. "Vadim" to Moscow Center, 5 March 1945, KGB file 43173, v.1, pp. 88–89, Vassiliev, *Black*, 50–51.

41. Washington Field Office to Director, Re: Harold Glasser, 13 May 1947, serial 2429, FBI Silvermaster file 65–56402. List of "Ruble's" acquaintances, 5 January 1945, KGB file 43072, v.1, p. 133, Vassiliev, *White #3*, 60. Gorsky's 5 March cable is used in Kai Bird and Svetlana Chervonnaya, "The Mystery of Ales," *American Scholar*, Summer 2007, http://www.theamericanscholar.org/su07/ales-birdlong.html #31, to argue that "Ales" was not Hiss and offers Wilder Foote as a replacement can-

didate. The multiple flaws in Bird and Chervonnaya's argument are brought out in John Earl Haynes and Harvey Klehr, "'Ales' Is Still Hiss: The Wilder Foote Red Herring," paper presented at Symposium on Cryptologic History, Center for Cryptologic History, National Security Agency, Ft. Meade, MD, 2007, http://www.john earlhaynes.org/page70.html, and John Ehrman, "Once Again, the Alger Hiss Case," *Studies in Intelligence* 51, no. 4 (December 2007), https://www.cia.gov/library/cen ter-for-the-study-of-intelligence/csi-publications/csi-studies/studies/vol51no4/index .html, as well as in a forthcoming essay on Hiss and "Ales" by Eduard Mark in the *Journal of Cold War Studies* in 2009.

42. "Vadim" to Moscow Center, 2 April 1945, KGB file 43072, v.1, p. 82, Vassiliev, *White #3*, 57. Emphasis in original. Weinstein, *Perjury*, 516.

43. KGB Moscow to "Vadim," 29 May 1945, KGB file 43173, v.2, p. 61, Vassiliev, *Black*, 66.

44. KGB Washington to Moscow Center, 22 June 1945, KGB file 55302, v.1, p. 78, Vassiliev, *White #3*, 98. Emphasis in original.

45. "Vladimir" to Center, 25 December 1948, KGB file 43173, v.4, p. 479, Vassiliev, *Black*, 73. "Vladimir," KGB Washington station chief, was mistaken in his belief that Chambers was German by birth. Chambers was American-born of old-stock American parentage, not German. But he became a skilled German linguist, at times supporting himself with translation work. In 1928 he translated from the original German the first American edition of the childhood favorite *Bambi*. During his years in the Communist underground in the 1930s, he often affected a foreign accent, and some underground Communists with whom he worked gained the impression he was foreign born, possibly a Russian, a German, or a Volga German. In his autobiography, *Witness*, Chambers discussed the usefulness of appearing to be a foreigner in his underground work when he noticed that American Communists were more impressed if they though they were dealing with a Russian or a German than with an ordinary American. Chambers, *Witness*, 350–52.

46. P. Fedotov and K. Kukin report to KI chairman, December 1948, KGB file 43173, v.2c, p. 203, Vassiliev, *Black*, 73. When confronted by the FBI, Wadleigh confessed to espionage and appeared as a prosecution witness in the Hiss trials. Pigman was a professional staff member of the U.S. Bureau of Standards, working on high-technology projects. Under FBI questioning in the late 1940s Pigman denied having delivered material to Chambers but admitted he had met on several occasions in 1936–38 with David Carpenter, Chambers's assistant. Reno was a mathematician at the U.S. Army Aberdeen Proving Grounds, working on advanced military technology. Confronted by the FBI, in 1949 he confessed that he had supplied technical data to Chambers's espionage apparatus in the mid-1930s. In 1952 he pled guilty to perjury and was imprisoned for submitting deceptive information on his federal employment and security applications.

47. Report to KI chairman responding to "Vladimir's" telegram of 25 December 1948, KGB file 43173, v.2c, pp. 33–38, Vassiliev, *Black*, 76.

48. A. Gorsky, "Failures in the USA (1938–48)," December 1948, KGB file 43173, v.2c, pp. 49–50, Vassiliev, *Black*, 77. Note that Chambers was a senior editor at *Time*, not editor-in-chief. Wadleigh's name was Henry Julian Wadleigh—that is,

Henry J. Wadleigh. But there is no "J" in Cyrillic. Why the Cyrillic "A" was substituted is unclear. Chambers identified Alger Hiss, Donald Hiss, Wadleigh, Reno, Collins, Pigman, Peters, Pressman, Carpenter, Inslerman, Field, White, Silverman, and Glasser as involved with his GRU apparatus. While Chambers did not know the name, he identified a source that the FBI determined to be Vladimir V. Sveshnikov. Lester Hutm and Harry Azizov may be spelling garbles for sources that Chambers described, again without remembering the names, that the FBI identified as Lester Huettig and Morris Asimow. No one resembling Peter MacLean is known to be involved with Chambers. Barna Bukov is the GRU officer Chambers identified as "Boris Bykov," pronouncing the name as "boo-koff." Tanenhaus, *Whittaker Chambers,* 548. Chambers's statements about these persons and their background are discussed in Chambers, *Witness;* Weinstein, *Perjury;* and Tanenhaus, *Whittaker Chambers.* On Bukov, also see M. Lurie and V. Kochik, *GRU: Dela i liudi* [GRU: Cases and People] (Moscow: Neva Olma-Press, 2002), 356.

49. "Plan of measures for the 1st Department, 1s Directorate of the KI to improve intelligence work in the USA," approved by S. Savchenko, 16 March 1950, KGB file 43173, v.2c, p. 74, Vassiliev, *Black,* 82. The KGB document referred to "Leonard"/Hiss's State Department status in the present sense, but he had left the State Department in 1946 to take the position as head of the Carnegie Endowment.

Chapter 2: Enormous

1. Pavel Sudoplatov et al., *Special Tasks: The Memoirs of an Unwanted Witness, a Soviet Spymaster* (Boston: Little, Brown, 1994), 172–200; Hans Bethe, "Atomic Slurs," *Washington Post,* 27 May 1994; William J. Broad, "Physicists Try to Discredit Book Asserting Atom Architects Spied," *New York Times,* 1 May 1994; David Streitfeld, "FBI Says Evidence Lacking against A-Bomb Scientists," *Washington Post,* 2 May 1995; Thomas Powers, "Were the Atomic Scientists Spies?" *New York Review of Books,* 9 June 1994.

2. Moscow Center announced the cover name "Enormous" in a message to the KGB New York station, 26 November 1942, KGB file 40159, v.3, p. 222, Alexander Vassiliev, *Black Notebook [2007 English Translation],* trans. Philip Redko (1993–96), 108.

3. In the early 1990s, before the release of the decoded cables of the Venona project, retired KGB officers deliberately spread misleading information about an alleged source in the Manhattan Project with the cover name "Perseus." Vladimir Chikov wrote a lengthy article and a book about Soviet espionage, extolling the contributions of veteran KGB American agents Morris and Lona Cohen. He credited Morris with recruiting "Perseus," described as a physicist whom Morris had known in connection with the International Brigades in the Spanish Civil War. According to Chikov, "Perseus" was a key Soviet atomic spy who had worked at the Metallurgical Laboratory at Chicago and later at Los Alamos. Another retired KGB officer, Anatoly Yatskov, confirmed the story. After the deciphered Venona messages appeared, a number of researchers assumed that Chikov's "Perseus" had been just a minor disguise for the Soviet atomic source "Persian" in Venona (in Russian the cover

name is "Pers"). But several parts of the "Perseus" story didn't fit with Venona's "Persian," including Chikov's claim that "Perseus's" cover name was changed to "Mlad." "Persian" was not changed to "Mlad" in Venona. In any case, "Mlad" was clearly the cover name of Theodore Hall, who did not fit Chikov's description of "Perseus." Eventually, most historians concluded that Chikov and Yatskov had deliberately conflated several different Soviet sources, added outright deception, and created a nonexistent "Perseus." Vladimir Chikov, "How the Soviet Secret Service Split the American Atom," *New Times [Russia]* 16 and 17 (23–30 April 1991); Vladimir Chikov, *Comment Staline a volé la bombe atomique aux Américains: Dossier KGB no. 13676,* assisted by Gary Kern (Paris: R. Laffont, 1996); Michael Dobbs, "How Soviets Stole U.S. Atom Secrets," *Washington Post,* 4 October 1992. On the unraveling of the "Perseus" story, see "The Perseus Myth" in Joseph Albright and Marcia Kunstel, *Bombshell: The Secret Story of America's Unknown Atomic Spy Conspiracy* (New York: Times Books, 1997), 267–77, and Gary Kern, "The PERSEUS Disinformation Operation," *H-HOAC,* 17 February 2006, http://h-net.msu.edu/cgi-bin/logbrowse .pl?trx=lm&list=h-hoac.

4. KGB New York to Moscow Center, 7 February 1944, KGB file 40594, v.6, p. 240; "Agent network as of 1.02.45," 1 February 1945, KGB file 40594, v.7, pp. 24–25, Vassiliev, *Black,* 117–18, 120.

5. *Communist Labor Party News* [Cleveland], no. 3 (November 1919): 2; Testimony of Edward Cassell, 24 August 1940, U.S. House Special Committee on Un-American Activities, *Investigation of Un-American Propaganda Activities in the United States* (Washington, D.C.: U.S. Govt. Print. Off., 1940–44), v.4, 1698–99; Robert Cohen, *When the Old Left Was Young: Student Radicals and America's First Mass Student Movement, 1929–1941* (New York: Oxford University Press, 1993), 234.

6. Cohen, *When the Old Left Was Young,* 234; "Communist Matters—Russell Alton McNutt Gives Results of Interview with M," 14 September 1951, CIA FOIA F–1975–00144. Michael and Anne Sidorovich summary, 29 September 1951, serial 159 (NY 65–15380), FBI Michael and Anne Sidorovich file 65–59294.

7. "Communist Matters—Russell Alton McNutt Gives Results of Interview with M," 14 September 1951, CIA FOIA F–1975–00144, serials 92 and 159, FBI Michael and Anne Sidorovich file 65–59294. Waldo McNutt's interviews in serials 92 and 159 differ on some details about how he first met Julius. Sam Roberts, *The Brother: The Untold Story of Atomic Spy David Greenglass and How He Sent His Sister, Ethel Rosenberg, to the Electric Chair* (New York: Random House, 2001), 174.

8. Moscow Center to "May," 26 April 1944; "'Antenna' made contact," KGB file 40159, v.3, pp. 354, 361, Vassiliev, *Black,* 112; Venona 212 KGB New York to Moscow, 11 February 1944; Venona 854 KGB New York to Moscow, 16 June 1944.

9. Moscow Center to "Anton," "analysis of work in '44," 14 January 1945, KGB file 40159, v.3, p. 457, Vassiliev, Black, 113; Venona 212 KGB New York to Moscow, 11 February 1944; Venona 854 KGB New York to Moscow, 16 June 1944.

10. "Grouping of probationers as of March 1945," KGB file 40594, v.7, p. 97, Vassiliev, *Black,* 135; "Aleksey's first meeting with Persian," 11 March 1945, KGB file

40129, v.3a, p. 380, Alexander Vassiliev, *White Notebook #1 [2007 English Translation]*, trans. Steven Shabad (1993–96), 116.

11. KGB New York to Moscow Center, 5 February 1945, KGB file 82702, v.1, p. 284, Alexander Vassiliev, *Yellow Notebook #1 [2007 English Translation]*, trans. Philip Redko (1993–96), 17. The business may have been Indian Lake Lodge in the Adirondacks, which McNutt purchased in the spring of 1943 with Lee Weiner for $17,000. He later told the FBI that his wife Rose and Sally Weiner ran the lodge during the summer season and he would travel there on weekends to assist.

12. "Anton was informed," 9 February 1945; KGB New York to Moscow Center, 11 May 1945, KGB file 82702, v.1, pp. 284, 310, Vassiliev, *Yellow #1*, 18, 24. Moscow Center to Uglov, 8 June 1948, KGB file 40159, v.5, p. 147, Vassiliev, *Black*, 128.

13. "Russell Alton McNutt," 25 August 1953, CIA FOIA case F-1975–00144; Roberts, *Brother,* 174.

14. *McDowell News,* 7 January 2002; *Washington Post,* 17 November 1974. McNutt obituary, *Fairfax Times,* 1 February 2008. In 2007 Harvey Klehr and John Haynes contacted Mr. McNutt to ask if he wished to comment on the documents we had found about his relationship with Soviet intelligence and sent him background material. He declined an interview.

15. The evidence regarding Robert Oppenheimer's relationship to the CPUSA is thoroughly examined in Gregg Herken, *Brotherhood of the Bomb: The Tangled Lives and Loyalties of Robert Oppenheimer, Ernest Lawrence, and Edward Teller* (New York: Henry Holt, 2002), supplemented by the Web site "The Brotherhood of the Bomb," http://www.brotherhoodofthebomb.com/, which contains a more detailed set of footnotes than the printed book. It also contains a "new evidence" section about documentation available subsequent to publication of the book about Oppenheimer's membership in the CPUSA, particularly the unpublished journal of Barbara Chevalier and the unpublished memoir of Gordon Griffiths. Gordon Griffiths, "Venturing outside the Ivory Tower: The Political Autobiography of a College Professor," Gordon Griffiths Papers (Washington, D.C.: Library of Congress Manuscript Division), 26–28.

16. Oral transcription of interview between Lt. Col. John Landsdale, Jr., and Dr. J. Robert Oppenheimer, 12 September 1943, inserted in U.S. Atomic Energy Commission, *In the Matter of J. Robert Oppenheimer* (Washington, D.C.: U.S. Govt. Print. Off., 1954), hearing of 3 May 1954, 871–86; Herken, *Brotherhood of the Bomb,* pp. 107–15, 160–63.

17. San Francisco FBI report of 1 July 1945–15 March 1947, serial 5421, FBI Comintern Apparatus file. Eltenton moved to England in 1947 and refused to discuss the matter for the rest of his life.

18. Venona 1773 KGB New York to Moscow, 16 December 1944; Venona 580–581 KGB San Francisco to Moscow, 13 November 1945.

19. Venona 259 Moscow to New York, 21 March 1945, deals with the proposal that "Huron" approach "Veksel" and Goldsmith. Vassiliev's notes on Yatskov's report make clear "Veksel" was Fermi. Venona's identification of "Veksel" as Oppenheimer was based on Venona 799 KGB New York to Moscow, 26 May 1945, which had indi-

cated that "Veksel" headed work at Los Alamos. At that time Fermi had moved to Los Alamos for the final phases of the project, and the KGB officer sending Venona 799 apparently made the mistake of assuming Fermi was in charge of the New Mexico facility. Since Oppenheimer directed Los Alamos, that misled NSA/FBI analysts into identifying "Veksel" as Oppenheimer. Arnold Kramish, a physicist who had worked in the Manhattan Project, suggested in 1997 that "Veksel" was not Oppenheimer but Enrico Fermi. Arnold Kramish, "The Manhattan Project and Venona," paper presented at Symposium on Cryptologic History, Ft. Meade, MD, 29–31 October 1997. In addition, Vassiliev's notebooks show that Fermi had the cover name "Vector," and Venona's "Veksel" was likely a decoding garble for "Vector."

20. "Comintern Apparatus Summary Report," 15 December 1944, serial 3702, p. 222, FBI Comintern Apparatus file 100–203581.

21. Moscow Center report on a cable dated 7 December 1942; Moscow Center's 25 January 1943 reply to 7 December 1942 cable, KGB file 82702, v.1, p. 54, Vassiliev, *Yellow #1*, 2.

22. Moscow Center to KGB New York, 1 July 1943; Moscow Center to KGB New York, 22 November 1943, KGB file 40159, v.3, pp. 278, 335–37, Vassiliev, *Black*, 109, 111. Fitin report to Merkulov, 11 August 1943, KGB file 82702, v.1, pp. 192–93, Vassiliev, *Yellow #1*, 14. "Erie" appeared in the Venona decryptions as an unidentified scientific source/agent. A marginal comment by Alexander Vassiliev noted that "Erie" lived in Detroit. This, however, appears to be a confusion with Byron Darling, a Detroit-based physicist and KGB agent. Nahin's cover name "Erie" was later changed to "Ernst," a cover name that applied to Darling for a short time.

23. Ovakimyan and Graur, report to Merkulov on "Enormous," February 1944, KGB file 82702, v.1, p. 143, Vassiliev, *Yellow #1*, 10; Fitin report to Merkulov, July 1944, KGB file 40129, v.3a, p. 148, Vassiliev, *White #1*, 107.

24. Engry on "Charon"; "Memorandum on 'Charon's' work from Dec. '41 through June '44," KGB file 25748, v.2, pp. 88, 115–17, Vassiliev, *White #1*, 136. Assignment for station chief "Gift," March 1944, KGB file 40129, v.3a, pp. 42–43, Vassiliev, *White #1*, 106–7. Moscow Center to KGB New York, 30 June 1944, KGB file 40159, v.3, p. 404, Vassiliev, *Black*, 112.

25. Fitin report to Merkulov, July 1944, KGB file 40129, v.3a, p. 148. The note, "'Chester' was cultivated," is not specifically sourced, but the KGB file page (146) given in the margin suggests it was part of the Fitin to Merkulov report of July 1944. Vassiliev, *White #1*, 107, 118.

26. Fitin, "Plan of Action on 'Enormous,'" 5 November 1944, KGB file 82702, v.1, pp. 223–25, Vassiliev, *Yellow #1*, 15; "Switching 'Callistratus,'" KGB file 40129, v.3a, p. 177, Vassiliev, *White #1*, 109.

27. Moscow Center to "Anton," 10 November 1944, KGB file 40159, v.3, pp. 435–48, Vassiliev, *Black*, 113.

28. Venona 1773 KGB New York to Moscow, 16 December 1944; Moscow Center to KGB New York, 21 December 1944, KGB file 82702, v.1, p. 257, Vassiliev, *Yellow #1*, 17; KGB New York to Moscow Center, 19 March 1945, KGB file 40594, v.7, p. 102, Vassiliev, *Black*, 136; "Anton" to Moscow Center, 19 March 1945, KGB file 40129, v.3a, p. 356, Vassiliev, *White #1*, 116.

29. Semenov, "Background on work on XY line in Western U.S.," July 1945, KGB file 40129, v.3a, p. 415, Vassiliev, *White #1*, 117–18.

30. Semenov, ibid., p. 416, Vassiliev, *White #1*, 117–18.

31. On Apresyan's rocky start at San Francisco, see Herken, *Brotherhood of the Bomb*, 130–31.

32. Memo, Fitin to Merkulov, August 1945; KGB New York to Moscow Center, 20 October 1945, KGB file 82702, v.1, pp. 376, 424–25, Vassiliev, *Yellow #1*, 28, 33–34. "Background sheet from Anton and Arseny re work on Enormous," addressed to Merkulov, 12 September 1945, KGB file 40129, v.3a, p. 458, Vassiliev, *White #1*, 118–19.

33. "Vadim" to Moscow Center, 19 October 1945, KGB file 82702, v.1, pp. 422–43; "Report by 'Mole,'" 22 October 1945, KGB file 82702, v.1, pp. 496–97, Vassiliev, *Yellow #1*, 32–35.

34. Vasilevsky, "Plan of action to expand the agent-oper. cultivation of "En-s," undated, circa October 1945, KGB file 82702, v.1, pp. 403–4, Vassiliev, *Yellow #1*, 31–32.

35. A. Raina, "To Comrade J. v. Stalin, . . . Plan of oper. measures connected with Ch-s's case," 5 February 1950, KGB file 84490, v.3, p. 44, Vassiliev, *Yellow #1*, 91–92. The report refers specifically to Harold Urey, Aristid Grosse, Cyril Smith, George Gamow, Leo Szilard, and Herbert Skinner.

36. Borden to Hoover, 7 November 1953, reproduced in U.S. Atomic Energy Commission, *In the Matter of J. Robert Oppenheimer*, 837–38.

37. Sudoplatov et al., *Special Tasks*, 172–200.

38. An extensive bibliography of essays pro and con on the Sudoplatov atomic espionage controversy is online at "Atomic Espionage and the Sudoplatov Controversy," http://www.johnearlhaynes.org/page94.html.

39. Jerrold L. Schecter and Leona Schecter, *Sacred Secrets: How Soviet Intelligence Operations Changed American History* (Washington, D.C.: Brassey's, 2002), 60–62.

40. Ibid., 49–50.

41. Fitin, untitled note, November 1944; "Report by 'Charon,'" 29 September 1944, KGB file 25748, v.2, pp. 133–39, 148, Vassiliev, *White #1*, 137–38. The Schecters maintain that Kheifets, whom they present as a highly successful KGB officer, was not recalled for inefficiency but as part of the Mironov affair (discussed in chapter 9). Vasily Mironov's charges of misconduct and treason against senior KGB officers in the United States, however, did not include Kheifets, and there was no reason for Moscow to recall him in connection with this matter.

42. Vasilevsky, "Plan of action to expand the agent-oper. cultivation of "En-s," undated, circa October 1945, KGB file 82702, v.1, pp. 403–4, Vassiliev, *Yellow #1*, 31–32.

43. On the contribution of Soviet intelligence to the Soviet atomic bomb project, see V. P. Visgin, ed., "U istokov sovetskogo atomnogo proekta: Rol' rasvedki, 1941–1946 gg. (po materialam arkhiva Vneshnei Razvedki Rossi)" [At the Sources of the Soviet Atomic Project: The Role of Intelligence Operations, 1941–1946 (Based on Material from the Archive of the Foreign Intelligence Service of Russia)], *Vo-*

prosy Istorii Estestvoznaniia i Tekhniki [Questions about the History of Natural Science and Technology], no. 3 (1992); A. A. Yatskov, "Atom i razvedka" [The Atom and Intelligence Gathering], *Voprosy Istorii Estestvoznaniia i Tekhniki*, no. 3 (1992); Alexander Feklisov and Sergei Kostin, *The Man Behind the Rosenbergs*, trans. Catherine Dop (New York: Enigma Books, 2001), 201, 213, 217–19, 238, 258, 260–61; David Holloway, *Stalin and the Bomb: The Soviet Union and Atomic Energy, 1939–1956* (New Haven: Yale University Press, 1994); David Holloway, "Sources for Stalin and the Bomb," *Cold War International History Project Bulletin*, no. 4 (Fall 1994); Richard Rhodes, *Dark Sun: The Making of the Hydrogen Bomb* (New York: Simon and Schuster, 1995).

44. Stalin appointed Lavrenty Beria, commissar general of state security, to take over supervision of the hitherto small Soviet atomic program on 7 August 1945 and tasked him to produce a working Soviet bomb in the shortest time possible. Beria, aware of the quantity and quality of Soviet intelligence on the Manhattan Project, ordered Soviet scientists to stick closely to the proven American design; he also supplied the project with the labor of more than fifty thousand Gulag prisoners and all the industrial resources needed. Thomas B. Cochran, Robert S. Norris, and Oleg A. Bukharin, *Making the Russian Bomb: From Stalin to Yeltsin* (Boulder, CO: Westview Press, 1995); Zhores Medvedev, "Atomnyi gulag" [Atomic Gulag], *Novoye Russkoye Slovo* [New Russian Word], 8 December 1994, 17–18; Zhores A. Medvedev, "Stalin and the Atomic Gulag," in Roy Aleksandrovich Medvedev and Zhores A. Medvedev, *The Unknown Stalin: His Life, Death and Legacy* (Woodstock, NY: Overlook Press, 2004).

45. Kathryn Weathersby, "'Should We Fear This?' Stalin and the Danger of War with America," Working Paper No. 39 (Washington, D.C.: Cold War International History Project, Woodrow Wilson International Center for Scholars, 2002), 9. Among the other reasons Stalin cited were the recent victory of Communist forces in China. See also Evgenii P. Bajanov, "Assessing the Politics of the Korean War, 1949–1951," *Cold War International History Project Bulletin*, no. 6–7 (Winter 1995–96): 54, 87–91.

46. On the frightening and erratic nature of Stalin's final years, see Jonathan Brent and Vladimir Pavlovich Naumov, *Stalin's Last Crime: The Plot against the Jewish Doctors, 1948–1953* (New York: HarperCollins, 2003).

47. Memorandum, Fitin to Merkulov, August 1945, KGB file 82702, v.1, pp. 380–81, Vassiliev, *Yellow #1*, 29.

48. "Vadim" report from London, 22 December 1942, KGB file 82702, v.1, p. 40, Vassiliev, *Yellow #1*, 4–5.

49. "Vadim" letter, 10 March 1943, KGB file 82702, v.1, pp. 77–79, Vassiliev, *Yellow #1*, 5.

50. "Plan for Agent Cultivation of Enormous," 11 August 1943; KGB London to Moscow Center, 30 September 1944; KGB London to Moscow Center, 29 March 1944; all three in KGB file 82702, v.1, pp. 93, 215–17, 158, Vassiliev, *Yellow #1*, 7, 14–15, 11.

51. "Mystery over UK Atomic Spy Solved," 1 March 2007, *BBC News*, http://news.bbc.co.uk/go/pr/fr/-/2/hi/uk_news/6409661.stm; Security Service File ref

KV 2/2349–2354, quoted at "Communists and Suspected Communists: Engelbert Broda," https://www.mi5.gov.uk/output/Page282.html.

52. KGB London to Moscow Center, cable, 29 November 1942, KGB file 82702, v.1, p. 38, Vassiliev, *Yellow #1*, 6.

53. Fitin report to Merkulov, 11 August 1943, KGB file 82702, v.1, p. 193, Vassiliev, *Yellow #1*, 14. On the Allan Nunn May case, see Robert Bothwell and J. L. Granatstein, eds., *The Gouzenko Transcripts: The Evidence Presented to the Kellock-Taschereau Royal Commission of 1946* (Ottawa: Deneau, 1982), 74, 97; U.S. Congress Joint Committee on Atomic Energy, *Soviet Atomic Espionage* (Washington, D.C.: U.S. Govt. Print. Off., 1951), 58; Robert Taschereau and Roy Lindsay Kellock, Royal Commissioners, *The Report of the Royal Commission Appointed under Order in Council P.C. 411 of February 5, 1946, to Investigate the Facts Relating to and the Circumstances Surrounding the Communication, by Public Officials and Other Persons in Positions of Trust, of Secret and Confidential Information to Agents of a Foreign Power. June 27, 1946* (Ottawa: E. Cloutier, 1946).

54. KGB London to Center, 22 June 1945, KGB file 82702, v.1, p. 338, Vassiliev, *Yellow #1*, 25. "Melita Norwood" obituary, 28 June 2005, *The Times* [London]. Citing her advanced age, the British government did not prosecute her.

55. "Luka" to Moscow Center, 24 November 1941; "Vadim" report, 17 December 1941, KGB file 82702, v.1, pp. 25–27, Vassiliev, *Yellow #1*, 1. We are unable to further identify Davrun Wittenberg. Personal reminiscences about Emil Conason can be found in a memoir written by his cousin: William Herrick, *Jumping the Line: The Adventures and Misadventures of an American Radical* (Madison: University of Wisconsin Press, 1998), 39–41.

56. Moscow Center to KGB New York, 27 March 1942, KGB file 40159, v.3, pp. 160–61, Vassiliev, *Black*, 106–7. The last three are unknown. Wittenberg was described as a Urey associate, while Tramm was described as a Van de Graaff assistant.

57. Moscow Center to KGB New York, 27 March 1942; Moscow Center to KGB New York, 26 November 1942; Moscow Center to KGB New York, 1 July 1943; Moscow Center to "Maxim," 22 November 1943, KGB file 40159, v.3, pp. 160, 223–24, 278, 336, Vassiliev, *Black*, 106, 108–9, 111; "Twain" report on "Pike," 5 May 1942, KGB file 40594, v.5, p. 278, Vassiliev, *Black*, 105–6; Ovakimyan and Graur, report to Merkulov on "Enormous," February 1944, KGB file 82702, v.1, p. 144, Vassiliev, *Yellow #1*, 9.

58. Moscow Center to KGB New York, 27 March 1942; Moscow Center to KGB New York, 28 August 1942, KGB file 40159, v.3, pp. 160, 187, Vassiliev, *Black*, 106, 108.

59. Moscow Center to KGB New York, 26 November 1942; Moscow Center to "Maxim," 22 November 1943, KGB file 40159, v.3, pp. 223–24, 264–66, 337, Vassiliev, *Black*, 108–9, 111.

60. KGB New York to Moscow Center, 3 October 1945, KGB file 82702, v.1, p. 398; A. Raina, "Plan of oper. measures connected with Ch-s's case," 5 February 1950, KGB file 84490, v.2, p. 45, Vassiliev, *Yellow #1*, 30, 92.

61. Venona 961 KGB New York to Moscow, 21 June 1943; Venona 972, 979,

983 KGB New York to Moscow, 22–23 June 1943; Venona 1405 KGB New York to Moscow, 27 August 1943.

62. A. Einstein, B. Podolsky, and N. Rosen, "Can Quantum-Mechanical Description of Physical Reality Be Considered Complete?" *Physical Review* 47 (1935).

63. Moscow Center to KGB New York, 27 March 1942, KGB file 40159, v.3, p. 160, Vassiliev, *Black,* 106; KGB New York to Moscow Center, 8 May 1943, KGB file 82702, v.1, p. 90, Vassiliev, *Yellow #1,* 6–7.

64. KGB New York to Moscow Center, 8 May 1943, KGB file 82702, v.1, p. 90, Vassiliev, *Yellow #1,* 6–7.

65. Venona 961 KGB New York to Moscow, 21 June 1943.

66. Venona 972, 979, 983 KGB New York to Moscow, 22–23 June 1943.

67. Moscow Center to "Maxim," 1 July 1943; Moscow Center to KGB New York, 22 November 1943, KGB file 82702, v.1, pp. 87–88, 106, Vassiliev, *Yellow #1,* 6–7.

68. Testimony of Clarence Hiskey, 9 September 1948, U.S. House Committee on Un-American Activities, *Excerpts from Hearings Regarding Investigation of Communist Activities in Connection with the Atom Bomb* (Washington, D.C.: U.S. Govt. Print. Off., 1948), 1–9.

69. "Chap" report on Clarence Hiskey, 28 March 1942, KGB file 82702, v.1, pp. 69–71, Vassiliev, *Yellow #1,* 2–3.

70. Moscow Center to KGB New York, 27 March 1942, KGB file 40159, v.3, p. 160, Vassiliev, *Black,* 106.

71. Moscow Center report based on KGB New York cable of 1 April 1942; Moscow Center to KGB New York, 5 April 1942, KGB file 82702, v.1, pp. 32, 34, Vassiliev, *Yellow #1,* 1–2.

72. "Chap" report, 24 April 1942, KGB file 82702, v.1, p. 72, Vassiliev, *Yellow #1,* 4.

73. Report based on a KGB New York cable of 22 October 1943, KGB file 82702, v.1, p. 96, Vassiliev, *Yellow #1,* 7.

74. Moscow Center to "Luka," 28 October 1943; Moscow Center to KGB New York, 22 November 1943, KGB file 82702, v.1, pp. 98, 104–5, Vassiliev, *Yellow #1,* 8.

75. Venona 912 KGB New York to Moscow, 27 June 1944; Venona 1403 KGB New York to Moscow, 5 October 1944; Venona 1429 KGB New York to Moscow, 9 October 1944; Venona 164 Moscow to New York, 20 February 1945; Venona 259 Moscow to New York, 21 March 1945. A. Gorsky, "Failures in the USA (1938–48)," December 1948, KGB file 43173, v.2c, p. 49, Vassiliev, *Black,* 79; Background on Active Sources on XY for 1943, KGB file 40129, v.3a, pp. 72–73, Vassiliev, *White #1,* 107; Semenov to Fitin, 29 November 1944, KGB file 40129, v.3a, pp. 203–4, Vassiliev, *White #1,* 110; Agent network as of 1 February 1945, KGB file 40594, v.7, p. 32, Vassiliev, *Black,* 121; Testimony of Byron Darling, 12 March 1953, U.S. House Committee on Un-American Activities Executive Session Testimony, Box 21, Center for Legislative Archives, National Archives and Records Administration.

76. Moscow Center to KGB New York, 29 January 1944; Ovakimyan and Graur, report to Merkulov on "Enormous," February 1944, KGB file 82702, v.1, pp. 123, 139–42, 231, Vassiliev, *Yellow #1,* 9–10; Moscow Center to "May" and "Anton," 29 January 1944, KGB file 40159, v.3, p. 359, Vassiliev, *Black,* 112.

77. KGB New York to Moscow Center, 6 March 1944, KGB file 82702, v.1, p. 152, Vassiliev, *Yellow #1*, 11.

78. Venona 619 KGB New York to Moscow, 4 May 1944; KGB New York to Moscow Center, 20 July 1944, KGB file 82702, v.1, p. 176, Vassiliev, *Yellow #1*, 12.

79. Venona 1020 KGB New York to Moscow, 20 July 1944; KGB New York to Moscow Center, 4 May 1944; Moscow Center to KGB New York, 25 July 1944, KGB file 82702, v.1, pp. 163–64, 176, Vassiliev, *Yellow #1*, 12; The 20 July message referred to the delivery to Hiskey of letters from "Rose Willen" and "Willy," whereas earlier the letters were described as being from Rose Olsen and "Victor." Likely there were simply alternative designations for the same persons.

80. Venona 1332 KGB New York to Moscow, 18 September 1944; Venona 1715 KGB New York to Moscow, 5 December 1944.

81. KGB New York to Moscow Center, letter entitled "Problems in our work," 19 March 1945; KGB New York to Moscow Center, 3 July 1945; Moscow Center to KGB New York, 28 August 1945, KGB file 82702, v.1, pp. 307, 345, 369, Vassiliev, *Yellow #1*, 23, 27–28. Moscow Center to "Anton," 28 August 1945, KGB file 40159, v.3, p. 550, Vassiliev, *Black*, 115. The 19 March 1945 letter can also be found at KGB file 40594, v.7, pp. 102–3, Vassiliev, *Black*, 136. The two citations to messages of 28 August 1945 may be notes on the same message but found in two different files.

82. "Chap" entries, KGB file 40594, v.7, pp. 257, 346, Vassiliev, *Black*, 138.

83. U.S. House Committee on Un-American Activities, *Excerpts from Hearings . . . Atom Bomb;* U.S. House Committee on Un-American Activities, *Testimony of James Sterling Murray and Edward Tiers Manning Regarding Clarence Hiskey and Arthur Adams. Hearings, Eighty-First Congress, First Session. August 14 and October 5, 1949* (Washington, D.C.: U.S. Gov. Print. Off., 1950), 877–99; Serials 3392, 3428, 3641, and 3702, FBI Comintern Apparatus file 100–203581. Vladimir Lota, in a hagiographic book about GRU, presents Arthur Adams as a peerless GRU intelligence officer who recruited a source at the Metallurgical Laboratory who delivered over three thousand pages of documents and samples of pure uranium and scarce "heavy water" before illness ended contact. The source, given the pseudonym Martin Kemp by Lota, appears to be an exaggerated amalgam of Hiskey, Manning, and Chapin, with the fact left out that all three were uncovered and neutralized by the FBI because it had Adams under surveillance. Vladimir Lota, *GRU i atomnaya bomba* (Moscow: OLMA Press, 2002).

84. Venona 259 Moscow to New York, 21 March 1945; "Aleksey" report on the meeting with "Huron," 1 April 1945, KGB file 40594, v.7, p. 159, Vassiliev, *Black*, 137.

85. Herken, *Brotherhood of the Bomb*, 96–97; U.S. House Committee on Un-American Activities, *Report on Atomic Espionage: (Nelson-Weinberg and Hiskey-Adams Cases)* (Washington, D.C.: U.S. Govt. Print. Off., 1949).

86. Herken, *Brotherhood of the Bomb*, 107–9.

87. Background sheet from Anton and Arseny re work on Enormous," addressed to Merkulov, 12 September 1945, KGB file 40129, v.3a, p. 458, Vassiliev, *White #1*, 118–19.

88. KGB New York to Moscow Center, "Anton's report," KGB file 82702, v.1, pp. 424–25, Vassiliev, *Yellow #1*, 33–34.

89. "Arseny" report, 24 October 1945, KGB file 82702, v.1, pp. 427–28, Vassiliev, *Yellow #1*, 34.

90. AAUP Committee A Case Files–Ohio State University–Darling 1953, located in George Washington University Gelman Library, Box 106, "Transcript of Closed Hearing of the Case of Byron Thorwell Darling, Associate Professor of Physics and Astronomy, Ohio State University, before President Howard Bevis," 2 and 4 April 1953. Ellen Schrecker, *No Ivory Tower: McCarthyism and the Universities* (New York: Oxford University Press, 1986), 207–8. Schrecker termed Darling's dismissal "perhaps the most egregious" of the era. David Caute, *The Great Fear: The Anti-Communist Purge under Truman and Eisenhower* (New York: Simon and Schuster, 1977), 416–17.

91. Report by "Charon," 20 September 1944, KGB file 25748, v.2, 135–36, Vassiliev, *White #1*, 137–38.

92. Testimony of Martin Kamen, 14 September 1948, U.S. House Committee on Un-American Activities, *Excerpts from Hearings . . . Atom Bomb*, 11–49; Martin David Kamen, *Radiant Science, Dark Politics: A Memoir of the Nuclear Age* (Berkeley: University of California Press, 1985).

93. KGB New York to Moscow Center, 17 February 1945, KGB file 40594, v.7, p. 31, Vassiliev, *Black*, 121.

94. Alfred Slack statement, serial 80, FBI Slack file 65–59183.

95. Moscow Center to KGB New York, 28 August 1944, KGB file 82702, v.1, p. 190, Vassiliev, *Yellow #1*, 13.

96. Christopher M. Andrew and Vasili Mitrokhin, *The Sword and the Shield: The Mitrokhin Archive and the Secret History of the KGB* (New York: Basic Books, 1999), 117.

97. The most complete biography of Klaus Fuchs is Robert Chadwell Williams, *Klaus Fuchs, Atom Spy* (Cambridge, MA: Harvard University Press, 1987). See also Ruth Werner [Ursula Kuczynski], *Sonya's Report* (London: Chatto and Windus [Random Century Group], 1991); Norman Moss, *Klaus Fuchs: The Man Who Stole the Atom Bomb* (New York: St. Martin's Press, 1987).

98. "Memorandum on K. F. from the GRU," circa 1950, KGB file 84490, v.2, pp. 127–28, Vassiliev, *Yellow #1*, 86.

99. KGB London to Moscow Center, 3 November 1943; Ilichev to Fitin, 29 November 1943, KGB file 84490, v.1, pp. 17, 22, Vassiliev, *Yellow #1*, 67.

100. GRU report on Fuchs, 21 January 1944, KGB file 84490, v.1, pp. 25–29, Vassiliev, *Yellow #1*, 67–68.

101. Moscow Center to KGB New York, 29 January 1944, KGB file 82702, v.1, p. 119–21, Vassiliev, *Yellow #1*, 8–9; Moscow Center to "May" and "Anton," 29 January 1944, KGB file 40159, v.3, pp. 354–56, Vassiliev, *Black*, 111–12.

102. "'Goose's' report on a meeting with 'Rest,'" 5 February 1944, KGB file 84490, v.1, pp. 31–32, Vassiliev, *Yellow #1*, 68–69.

103. Moscow Center report on KGB New York to Moscow Center, 25 February 1944; KGB New York to Moscow Center, 22 March 1944, KGB file 82702, v.1, pp. 150, 154, Vassiliev, *Yellow #1*, 11. "Goose's" report on meeting on 11 March 1944, KGB file 84490, v.1, p. 48, Vassiliev, *Yellow #1*, 69–70.

104. "Goose's" reports of meetings on 28 March 1944, 4 May 1944, 9 June 1944, 15 June 1944, KGB file 84490, v.1, pp. 48–49, Vassiliev, *Yellow #1*, 70; KGB New York to Moscow Center, 15 June 1944, KGB file 82702, v.1, p. 171, Vassiliev, *Yellow #1*, 12; Venona 645 KGB New York to Moscow, 8 May 1944; Venona 850 KGB New York to Moscow, 15 June 1944.

105. Moscow Center to "May," 28 July 1944, KGB file 40159, v.3, p. 416, Vassiliev, *Black*, 112–13.

106. KGB New York to Moscow Center, 29 August 1944, with Ovakimyan annotation of 30 August 1944, KGB file 40129, v.3a, p. 154, Vassiliev, *White #1*, 108. KGB New York to Moscow Center, 19 October 1944, KGB file 86194, v.2, p. 19, Vassiliev, *Yellow #1*, 103.

107. Venona 1345 KGB New York to Moscow, 22 September 1944; Venona 1606 KGB New York to Moscow, 16 November 1944. KGB New York to Moscow Center, 16 November 1944, KGB file 82702, v.1, p. 240, Vassiliev, *Yellow #1*, 16; "Arno" reports on visits to Kristel Heineman on 24 October 1944, 2 November 1944, and 7 December 1944, KGB file 84490, v.1, pp. 68–71, Vassiliev, *Yellow #1*, 70–71. See also "Anton" to Moscow Center, 17 February 1945, KGB file 40594, v.7, p. 59, Vassiliev, *Black*, 134–35.

108. KGB New York to Moscow Center, 19 March 1945; "Aleksey" report on meeting with "Arno," 22 January 1945, KGB file 40594, v.7, pp. 75, 79, Vassiliev, *Black*, 122. (This later memo's dating of 22 January 1945 is likely in error. Gold did not meet with Fuchs until mid-February.) Report on visit to Fuchs, 21 February 1945, KGB file 84490, v.1, pp. 79–82; KGB New York to Moscow Center, 23 February 1945, KGB file 82702, v.1, p. 286, Vassiliev, *Yellow #1*, 18, 72–74.

109. Venona 349 KGB Moscow to New York, 10 April 1945. "Anton" to Moscow Center, 2 March 1945, KGB file 84490, v.1, p. 74; Moscow Center to KGB New York, 27 February 1945, KGB file 82702, v.1, pp. 286, 292, Vassiliev, *Yellow #1*, 18–19, 72.

110. "Aleksey" on the meeting with "Arno," with Graur annotation, 22 January 1945; "Aleksey" response, KGB file 40594, v.7, pp. 81–82, 144, Vassiliev, *Black*, 123–24.

111. "Aleksey's" report on a meeting with "Arno," 8 March 1945, KGB file 84490, v.1, p. 76; entries to KGB file 84490, v.1, pp. 84, 90, Vassiliev, *Yellow #1*, 74. KGB New York to Moscow Center, 13 June 1945, KGB file 86192, v.1, p. 30, Vassiliev, *Yellow #1*, 40. "Report by Arno on the meeting with Ch. 20.06.45" (although dated 20 June 1945, other evidence indicates that this was an error for 2 June 1945), KGB file 82702, v.1, p. 363, Vassiliev, *Yellow #1*, 27.

112. KGB New York to Moscow Center, 26 June 1945, KGB file 40594, v.7, p. 131, Vassiliev, *Black*, 136.

113. KGB New York to Moscow Center, 12 September 1945, and Moscow Center approval of New York station request, KGB file 82702, v.1, 386–87, Vassiliev, *Yellow #1*, 29. KGB New York to "Arseny" at Moscow Center, 17 October 1945; Report on visit to "Charles" on 19 September 1945, KGB file 84490, v.1, pp. 99, 104–6, Vassiliev, *Yellow #1*, 76. Report of "Arno" meeting with "Charles" on 19 September 1945, KGB file 40594, v.7, pp. 251–52, Vassiliev, *Black*, 124–25.

114. "Aleksey's" report on meeting with "Arno," 12 November 1945, KGB file 40594, v.7, pp. 317–19, Vassiliev, *Black,* 125. Kvasnikov's report, 27 September 1946, KGB file 84490, v.1, p. 117; "Due to complications," KGB file 84490, v.1, p. 115, Vassiliev, *Yellow #1,* 77. "Bob's" cable with "Sohnchen's" information, 20 November 1945, KGB file 70545, p. 393, Alexander Vassiliev, *White Notebook #2 [2007 English Translation],* trans. Steven Shabad (1993–96), 27.

115. KGB New York to Moscow Center, 20 September 1944; Moscow Center to KGB New York, 3 October 1944, KGB file 40129, v.3a, pp. 168–69, Vassiliev, *White #1,* 108; Venona 1340 KGB New York to Moscow, 21 September 1944; Venona 1549 KGB New York to Moscow; Moscow Center to "Anton," 10 November 1944, KGB file 40159, v.3, pp. 442, 447, Vassiliev, *Black,* 113.

116. Venona 1600 KGB New York to Moscow, 14 November 1944. "Liberal" report on "Wasp," 5 December 1944, KGB file 86191, v.1, p. 16, Vassiliev, *Yellow #1,* 54–55. Julius's report differs from Ruth's later testimony that she had initially balked at Julius's proposal although was ultimately persuaded.

117. KGB New York to Moscow Center, 15 December 1944, KGB file 82702, v.1, p. 253, Vassiliev, *Yellow #1,* 16–17; Venona 1773 KGB New York to Moscow, 16 December 1944; KGB New York to Moscow Center, 15 December 1944, KGB file 86192, v.1, p. 20, Vassiliev, *Yellow #1,* 39.

118. Moscow Center to KGB New York, 21 December 1944, KGB file 82702, v.1, p. 257; report and list of questions for "Caliber," 8 January 1945, KGB file 86192, v.1, pp. 21, 23, Vassiliev, *Yellow #1,* 17, 39–40; Venona 28 KGB New York to Moscow, 8 January 1945; memo to Fitin for period from 1 January through 13 February 1945, KGB file 40129, v.3a, p. 333, Vassiliev, *White #1,* 116; KGB New York to Moscow Center, 17 February 1945, KGB file 40594, v.7, pp. 48–49, Vassiliev, *Black,* 134; Ronald Radosh and Joyce Milton, *The Rosenberg File: A Search for the Truth* (New York: Holt, Rinehart, and Winston, 1983), 69; Feklisov and Kostin, *Man Behind,* 154.

119. Venona 1749–1750 KGB New York to Moscow, 13 December 1944; Moscow Center to "Anton," 23 February 1945, KGB file 40159, v.3, pp. 472–74, Vassiliev, *Black,* 114; "Anton requested," KGB file 40129, v.3a, p. 380, Vassiliev, *White #1,* 116; Ronald Radosh and Joyce Milton, *The Rosenberg File* (New Haven: Yale University Press, 1997), 68–70.

120. "Arno's report on visits to Wasp and Caliber on 2 and 3 June 1945," KGB file 84490, v.1, p. 92, Vassiliev, *Yellow #1,* 74–75.

121. KGB New York to Moscow Center, 13 June 1945, KGB file 86192, v.1, p. 28; KGB New York to Moscow Center, 4 July 1945, KGB file 86192, v.1, p. 30; "'Caliber's' materials," KGB file 86192, v.1, p. 45, Vassiliev, *Yellow #1,* 40. KGB New York to Moscow Center, 26 June 1945, KGB file 40594, v.7, p. 131, Vassiliev, *Black,* 136.

122. Background sheet from Anton and Arseny re work on "Enormous," addressed to Merkulov,12 September 1945, KGB file 40129, v.3a, p. 458; Moscow Center to KGB New York, 21 September 1945, KGB file 40129, v.3a, p. 468, Vassiliev, *White #1,* 118–19. KGB New York to Moscow Center, 12 September 1945, KGB file 82702, v.1, pp. 386, 393, Vassiliev, *Yellow #1,* 29. KGB New York to Moscow

Center, 19 October 1945, KGB file 40594, v.7, pp. 250–51, Vassiliev, *Black*, 137–38. "Tuballoy" was a Manhattan Project technical term for refined uranium (uranium ore with impurities removed).

123. KGB New York to Moscow Center, 19 October 1945, KGB file 40594, v.7, pp. 250–51, Vassiliev, *Black*, 137–38. "Petrov" to KGB New York, 27 October 1945, KGB file 82702, v.1, p. 430; Report on "Caliber," 3 June 1946, KGB file 86192, v.1, p. 46, Vassiliev, *Yellow #1*, 34, 40.

124. "Report by 'Callistratus' on his trip to the U.S.," 27 February 1947, KGB file 40129, v.3a, p. 377, Vassiliev, *White #1*, 120.

125. Michael Dobbs, "Unlocking the Crypts: Most Spies Code Revealed Escaped Prosecution," *Washington Post*, 25 December 1995; Michael Dobbs, "Code Name 'Mlad,' Atomic Bomb Spy," *Washington Post*, 25 February 1996, 1, 20–21; Albright and Kunstel, *Bombshell*. In our discussion of Hall in John Earl Haynes and Harvey Klehr, *Venona: Decoding Soviet Espionage in America* (New Haven: Yale University Press, 2000), pp. 314–17, we mistakenly wrote that he received a commission after he was drafted.

126. KGB New York to Moscow Center, "Beck's" report on Theodore Hall, 7 December 1944, KGB file 82702, v.1, pp. 287–89, Vassiliev, *Yellow #1*, 19–22. Earlier accounts have Saville Sax making the initial contact with Napoli and Kurnakov, but Kurnakov's memo, while a bit unclear, strongly suggests it was Hall. See Albright and Kunstel, *Bombshell*, 93.

127. KGB New York to Moscow Center, "Beck's" report on Theodore Hall, 7 December 1944, KGB file 82702, v.1, pp. 287–89, Vassiliev, *Yellow #1*, 19–22.

128. KGB New York to Moscow Center, "Beck's" report on Theodore Hall, 7 December 1944, KGB file 82702, v.1, pp. 287–89, Vassiliev, *Yellow #1*, 19–22.

129. KGB New York to Moscow Center, 11 November 1944, KGB file 82702, v.1, p. 237; KGB New York to Moscow Center, 7 December 1944, KGB file 82702, v.1, pp. 290–91, Vassiliev, *Yellow #1*, 16, 22–23.

130. KGB New York to Moscow Center, 11 November 1944; Moscow Center to KGB New York, 16 November 1944; KGB New York to Moscow Center, "Beck's" report on Theodore Hall, 7 December 1944, KGB file 82702, v.1, pp. 237, 287–89, Vassiliev, *Yellow #1*, 15–16, 19–22. Venona 1585 KGB New York to Moscow, 12 November 1944.

131. Venona 1699 KGB New York to Moscow, 2 December 1944; KGB New York to Moscow Center, 7 December 1944, KGB file 82702, v.1, pp. 290–91; memo, KGB file 82702, v.1, p. 262; KGB New York to Moscow Center, 23 January 1945, KGB file 82702, v.1, p. 272, Vassiliev, *Yellow #1*, 17, 22; Venona 94 KGB New York to Moscow, 23 January 1945; Agent network, 1 February 1945, KGB file 40594, v.7, pp. 29–30, Vassiliev, *Black*, 121. While it seems less likely, it is possible that the KGB British sources provided information on plutonium.

132. Moscow Center ("Victor") to KGB New York ("Anton"), 23 February 1945, KGB file 40159, v.3, pp. 475–76, Vassiliev, *Black*, 133. KGB New York to Moscow Center, 21 March 1945; Moscow Center to KGB New York, 24 March 1945, KGB file 82702, v.1, pp. 298–99, Vassiliev, *Yellow #1*, 23.

133. KGB New York to Moscow Center, 11 May 1945, KGB file 82702, v.1,

p. 309, Vassiliev, *Yellow #1,* 23–24; Venona 799 KGB New York to Moscow, 26 May 1945; KGB New York to Moscow Center, 26 June 1945, KGB file 40594, v.7, pp. 130–31, Vassiliev, *Black,* 136. Albright and Kunstel suggest that Sax traveled to meet Hall in New Mexico in the late fall of 1944 and that Lona Cohen made the spring 1945 trip. Alexander Vassiliev's notebooks establish that Sax, not Cohen, traveled to Albuquerque in April 1945 and suggest there was no earlier trip. Albright and Kunstel, *Bombshell,* 112, 135.

134. KGB New York to Moscow Center, 30 June 1945, KGB file 82702, v.1, p. 342, Vassiliev, *Yellow #1,* 25–26.

135. Moscow Center to KGB New York, 4 July 1945, KGB file 82702, v.1, p. 343, Vassiliev, *Yellow #1,* 26.

136. Venona 709 Moscow to New York, 5 July 1945; Albright and Kunstel, *Bombshell,* 143.

137. KGB New York to Moscow Center, 12 September 1945, KGB file 40594, v.7, pp. 212–14, Vassiliev, *Black,* 137. "Anton was asked," 7 August 1945, KGB file 82702, v.1, p. 349; "Intelligence only learned," KGB file 82702, v.1, p. 351; "Anton was asked," 18 August 1945, KGB file 82702, v.1, p. 362; KGB New York to Moscow Center, 25 August 1945, KGB file 82702, v.1, p. 367; KGB New York to Moscow Center, 12 September 1945, KGB file 82702, v.1, p. 386, Vassiliev, *Yellow #1,* 26–28. Background sheet from Anton and Arseny re work on "Enormous," addressed to Merkulov, 12 September 1945, KGB file 40129, v.3a, p. 458, Vassiliev, *White #1,* 118–19.

138. Moscow Center to KGB New York, 28 August 1945, KGB file 82702, v.1, pp. 369–70, Vassiliev, *Yellow #1,* 28.

139. "Petrov" to KGB New York, 27 October 1945, KGB file 82702, v.1, p. 430, Vassiliev, *Yellow #1,* 34.

140. Moscow Center to "Anton," 28 August 1945, KGB file 40159, v.3, pp. 548–51, Vassiliev, *Black,* 115.

141. Report and memo from Fitin to Merkulov, August 1945, KGB file 82702, v.1, p. 375, Vassiliev, *Yellow #1,* 28.

142. Moscow Center to KGB New York, 29 January 1947, KGB file 40159, v.5; Moscow Center to KGB New York, 12 April 1948, KGB file 40159, v.5, p. 86; Moscow Center to Uglov, 8 June 1948, KGB file 40159, v.5, pp. 146–47; Moscow Center to "Vladimir," 18 October 1948, KGB file 40159, v.5, pp. 247, 249, Vassiliev, *Black,* 127–28, 130.

143. Moscow Center to Uglov, 8 June 1948; "Larry conducted," KGB file 40159, v.5, pp. 148, 249, Vassiliev, *Black,* 128, 130.

144. Moscow Center to Uglov, 8 June 1948, KGB file 40159, v.5, p. 147, Vassiliev, *Black,* 128.

145. Moscow Center to "Bob," 28 October 1948, KGB file 40159, v.5, pp. 238–39, Vassiliev, *Black,* 130.

146. U.S. House Committee on Un-American Activities, *Report on Atomic Espionage: (Nelson-Weinberg and Hiskey-Adams Cases).* Kai Bird and Martin J. Sherwin, *American Prometheus: The Triumph and Tragedy of J. Robert Oppenheimer* (New York: A. A. Knopf, 2005), 454–61.

147. U.S. House Committee on Un-American Activities, *Report on Atomic Espionage: (Nelson-Weinberg and Hiskey-Adams Cases);* San Francisco FBI report of 1 July 1945 through 15 March 1947, serial 5421, FBI Comintern Apparatus file 100–203581; F. David Peat, *Infinite Potential: The Life and Times of David Bohm* (Reading, MA: Addison Wesley, 1997).

148. "Charon" report, 20 September 1944, KGB file 25748, v.2, p. 135, Vassiliev, *White #1,* 137.

149. Marshak to Lawrence, 28 March 1952, folder 36, Alfred Marshak file, Ernest O. Lawrence papers, Bancroft Library, University of California, Berkeley. We thank Gregg Herken for providing background on Marshak and the quoted material from the 1952 letter.

150. Moscow Center to "Claude," 19 April 1948; Moscow Center to "Claude," 27 April 1948, KGB file 40159, v.5, pp. 107, 118, Vassiliev, *Black,* 127. Albright and Kunstel, *Bombshell,* 174.

151. Moscow Center to "Bob," 5 October 1948, KGB file 40159, v.5, pp. 208–11, Vassiliev, *Black,* 129.

152. Albright and Kunstel base their story of Hall's recruiting two sources at Hanford on a book by retired KGB officer Vladimir Chikov and on confidential Moscow sources. Chikov, however, was not always reliable, and Albright and Kunstel elsewhere demonstrate his mythmaking in the "Perseus" legend. Albright and Kunstel, *Bombshell,* 193–94; Chikov, *Comment Staline,* 200, 205.

153. Hall's 1997 statement is reproduced in Albright and Kunstel, *Bombshell,* 288–89.

154. August 1946 note on lack of knowledge of Fuchs's location; "Erofey's" report on Hans Siebert's report, 30 September 1946, KGB file 84490, v.1, pp. 114, 130–32, Vassiliev, *Yellow #1,* 77. KGB New York to Moscow Center, cables of 11, 12, and 18 December 1946; KGB New York to Moscow Center, 27 December 1946; "Aleksey's" addenda to the Center's questions; "Who knew whom by what name" chart; "CY's failure," KGB file 86194, v.2, pp. 103–5, 108, 113–14, 142, 169, Vassiliev, *Yellow #1,* 104–6. KGB New York to Moscow Center, 27 December 1946, KGB file 84490, v.1, p. 174, Vassiliev, *Yellow #1,* 80.

155. "Igor" of KGB London to Moscow Center, 26 September 1946; "Erofey's" report on Hans Siebert's report, 30 September 1946; Moscow Center to KGB London, 30 September 1946, KGB file 84490, v.1, pp. 126, 128, 130–32, Vassiliev, *Yellow #1,* 77. "Report on Jurgen Kuczynski 'Karo,'" undated, KGB file 84490, v.1, pp. 138–42, Vassiliev, *Yellow #1,* 78–79.

156. "We decided," KGB file 84490, v.1, pp. 154; "'Marta' met with," KGB file 84490, v.1, p. 227; "Martha's" report, KGB file 84490, v.1, 235; "We instructed Callistratus," KGB file 84490, v.1, p. 244, Vassiliev, *Yellow #1,* 79–80.

157. "We instructed Callistratus," KGB file 84490, v.1, p. 244; "On the meeting with Ch.," KGB file 84490, v.1, pp. 264–71, Vassiliev, *Yellow #1,* 80–81. An "operational car" was kept inside embassy grounds to prevent it from being "bugged" or having other tracking devices attached by counterintelligence.

158. Report on "Charles," 19 April 1948; P. Fedotov and M. Vorontsov to Molotov and Beria, June 1948; "Addendum to a letter to London dated 5.4.48 (handwrit-

ten by Arseny),'' KGB file 84490, v.1, p. 316, 332–33, 336–37, 383–84, Vassiliev, *Yellow #1*, 81–82. Feklisov and Kostin, *Man Behind*, 219. "Arseny's" [Raina's] note uses a masculine ending in reference to Fuchs's recruiter, but this is likely a matter of linguistic style. Alexander Vassiliev's annotation indicated that the recruiter was Ursula Kuczynski, and she wrote of the incident in her autobiography. Werner [Ursula Kuczynski], *Sonya's Report*, 278–79. See also "Memorandum on K. F. from the GRU," KGB file 84490, v.2, pp. 127–29, Vassiliev, *Yellow #1*, 86–87.

159. "Ch. arrived," 10 July 1948; Meeting, 25 October 1948; Report on meeting, 12 February 1949; Moscow Center to KGB London, 12 March 1949; Report on meeting, 10 July 1948; Report on meeting, 1 April 1949; next meetings note, KGB file 84490, v.1, pp. 343, 345, 356, 393, 408–9, 424–26, 468, Vassiliev, *Yellow #1*, 82–84.

160. A. Raina report on "Charles," 6 February 1950, KGB file 84490, v.2, pp. 119–25, Vassiliev, *Yellow #1*, 85–86. "Vladimir reported"; notes regarding "Arno," 18 and 27 July 1949; "Photon" report on meetings with "Arno" on 10 and 29 September 1949; Moscow Center to KGB New York, 19 October 1949, KGB file 86194, v.2, pp. 166, 169, 185, 188, 190, 219–22, 224–28, 236–38, 241, Vassiliev, *Yellow #1*, 106–8.

161. A. Raina report on "Charles," 6 February 1950, KGB file 84490, v.2, pp. 119–25, Vassiliev, *Yellow #1*, 85–86. Station's notes; Report on meeting of 24 October 1949; "Bob" report, 4 February 1950; "Bob" order, 5 February 1950; KGB New York to Moscow Center, 6 February 1950; Moscow Center to KGB New York, 23 February 1950, KGB file 86194, v.2, pp. 232, 241, 246, 257, 260, 263–64, Vassiliev, *Yellow #1*, 107–9.

162. Zorin to Stalin, 5 February 1950; memo on "Charles's" case, KGB file 84490, v.3, pp. 27–30, 32–33, Vassiliev, *Yellow #1*, 91.

163. A. Raina report on "Charles," 6 February 1950; "Memorandum on K. F. from the GRU"; "Possible reasons for failure," February 1950; "S. Savchenko ordered," 28 February 1950; Kvasnikov report to Savchenko, 15 March 1950; "'Sonya' flew"; "Anatoly met," 18 March 1950, KGB file 84490, v.2, pp. 119–25, 127–29, 151–53, 168–75, 205, 278–79, Vassiliev, *Yellow #1*, 85–89. Moscow Center to KGB New York, 23 February 1950, KGB file 86194, v.2, pp. 263–64, Vassiliev, *Yellow #1*, 109. On Field, see chapter 4.

164. "Refutation of TASS," 8 March 1950, KGB file 84490, v.2, p. 245; Kvasnikov report to Savchenko, 15 March 1950, KGB file 84490, v.2, pp. 274–75; Moscow Center to KGB London, 6 April 1950, KGB file 84490, v.2, p. 292; A. Raina, "Addendum to the plan of oper. measures with regard to Ch-s's case," 21 February 1950, KGB file 84490, v.2, 47–50; Moscow Center to Ross, "On improving the polit. and oper. education of agents," 6 April 1950, KGB file 84490, v.2, pp. 288–90; Zorin to Savchenko, 25 February 1950, KGB file 84490, v.2, p. 46; Vassiliev, *Yellow #1*, 87–90, 93.

165. Zorin to Stalin, 29 May 1950, KGB file 84490, v.3, pp. 129–30, Vassiliev, *Yellow #1*, 94.

166. Draft from Panyushkin to Kruglov, December 1953, KGB file 84490, v.5, pp. 329–33; Kvasnikov decision, 18 December 1953, KGB file 84490, v.5, p. 329, Vassiliev, *Yellow #1*, 56–57. Feklisov and Kostin, *Man Behind*, 240.

167. Kvasnikov comment on KGB London to Moscow Center, 22 December 1950, KGB file 84490, v.3, pp. 153–54, Vassiliev, *Yellow #1*, 95.

168. Kvasnikov, "Report on a meeting with "Bras," 28 May 1960; Shelepin to N. S. Khrushchev, 25 June 1960, KGB file 84490, v.6, pp. 43–48, Vassiliev, *Yellow #1*, 63–66.

169. Feklisov to Sakharovsky, 19 April 1965; Shebarshin note of 16 June 1989, KGB file 84490, v.6, pp. 71–72, 77, 79–80, Vassiliev, *Yellow #1*, 66–67.

170. Moscow Center to "August," 1 March 1948; KGB New York to Moscow Center, 2 August 1948; KGB New York to Moscow Center, 21 September 1948; note on U-238, KGB file 86192, v.1, p. 50–51, 55, 56, 58, Vassiliev, *Yellow #1*, 41–42. When David Greenglass later confessed and cooperated with the FBI, he never mentioned providing the KGB with a U-238 sample.

171. KGB New York to Moscow Center, 18 December 1948; KGB New York to Moscow Center, 30 June 1949; KGB New York to Moscow Center, 1 September 1949, KGB file 86192, v.1, pp. 59–60, 70–71, Vassiliev, *Yellow #1*, 42–44.

172. Report on a meeting between "August" and "Liberal," 11 October 1949; KGB New York to Moscow Center (with Moscow Center annotation), 13 January 1950, KGB file 86192, v.1, pp. 77–78, 82–83, 85–87, Vassiliev, *Yellow #1*, 44–45.

173. Moscow Center to KGB New York, 17 September 1949; Excerpt from a KGB New York to Moscow Center report, 13 February 1950, KGB file 86192, v.1, pp. 75, 92, Vassiliev, *Yellow #1*, 44–45.

174. Excerpt from a KGB New York to Moscow Center report, 13 February 1950; "Line of conduct for C. and W.," KGB file 86192, v.1, pp. 92, 94, Vassiliev, *Yellow #1*, 45. In fact, the FBI interview with Greenglass had been routine, a hunt for some missing uranium hemispheres. Later, after his arrest on espionage charges, Greenglass stated that he had had one of the hemispheres, that they were of low-radioactivity uranium, and that many of the workers, including Greenglass, had kept them as souvenirs. After the FBI inquiry in January, 1950, he said he had thrown it in the river. Radosh and Milton, *Rosenberg File* (1983), 75–76. It is unclear if this is a confusion on Greenglass's part with the plutonium noted as having been thrown in the East River in a 1948 KGB document.

175. Venona 1340 KGB New York to Moscow, 21 September 1944; Venona 1657 KGB New York to Moscow, 27 November 1944; Venona 628 KGB New York to Moscow, 5 May 1944; Venona 736 KGB New York to Moscow, 22 May 1944; Venona 845 KGB New York to Moscow, 14 June 1944; Venona 911 KGB New York to Moscow, 27 June 1944; Venona 976 KGB New York to Moscow, 11 July 1944; Venona 1053 KGB New York to Moscow, 26 July 1944; Venona 1251 KGB New York to Moscow, 2 September 1944; Venona 1314 KGB New York to Moscow, 14 September 1944; Venona 1327 KGB New York to Moscow, 15 September 1944; Venona 491 KGB New York to Moscow, 22 October 1944; Venona 1600 KGB New York to Moscow, 14 November 1944; Venona 1609 KGB New York to Moscow, 17 November 1944; Venona 1715 KGB New York to Moscow, 5 December 1944; Venona 1749–1750 KGB New York to Moscow, 13 December 1944; Venona 1773 KGB New York to Moscow, 16 December 1944; Venona 1797 KGB New York to Moscow, 20 December 1944; Venona 28 KGB New York to Moscow, 8 January 1945;

Venona 200 KGB Moscow to New York 6 March 1945; Venona 325 Moscow to New York 5 April 1945.

176. Moscow Center to KGB New York, 10 April 1950, KGB file 86192, v.1, p. 97, Vassiliev, *Yellow #1*, 46.

177. KGB New York to Moscow Center, 25 April 1950, KGB file 86192, v.1, pp. 103, 107, Vassiliev, *Yellow #1*, 46–47.

178. Report on meeting with "King," 23 May 1950; KGB New York to Moscow Center, 25 May 1950; Moscow Center to KGB New York, 25 May 1950; Moscow Center to "Ilya" at KGB Mexico City, 25 May 1950; Moscow Center to KGB Stockholm, 25 May 1950; Moscow Center to "Bob" at KGB New York, 26 May 1950, KGB file 86192, v.1, pp. 109–10, 113–14, 116–18, Vassiliev, *Yellow #1*, 47–49.

179. KGB New York to Moscow Center, 30 June 1950, Report by "Kirillov" on 9 June meeting with "King," KGB file 86192, v.1, pp. 130–31, Vassiliev, *Yellow #1*, 49–50.

180. Moscow Center to KGB New York, 13 July 1950; KGB New York to Moscow Center, 14 July 1950; Moscow Center to KGB New York, 15 July 1950; Moscow Center to KGB New York, 18 July 1950; KGB New York to Moscow Center, 6 April 1951, with Yatskov comment of 7 April 1951, KGB file 86192, v.1, pp. 140–41, 143, 145, 159, Vassiliev, *Yellow #1*, 50–51.

181. KGB New York to Moscow Center, "Proposal to organize assistance for King," 14 April 1951, KGB file 86192, v.1, pp. 161–65, Vassiliev, *Yellow #1*, 51–53.

182. Ibid.

Chapter 3: The Journalist Spies

1. Prudnikov, "Report on intelligence in the USA," 12 April 1941, KGB file 35112, v.1, pp. 68–69, Alexander Vassiliev, *Black Notebook [2007 English Translation]*, trans. Philip Redko (1993–96), 172–73.

2. Robert C. Cottrell, *Izzy: A Biography of I. F. Stone* (New Brunswick: Rutgers University Press, 1992), 44. See also Myra MacPherson, *All Governments Lie: The Life and Times of Rebel Journalist I. F. Stone* (New York: Scribner, 2006).

3. Cottrell, *Izzy*, 63.

4. Herbert Romerstein, "The KGB Penetration of the Media," *Human Events*, 6 June 1992, 5–6; Andrew Brown, "The Attack on I. F. Stone," *New York Review of Books* 39, no. 16 (8 October 1992): 21; Oleg Kalugin and Fen Montaigne, *The First Directorate* (New York: St. Martin's Press, 1994), 74.

5. Venona 1172–1173 GRU New York to Moscow, 19 July 1943; Venona 1313 KGB New York to Moscow, 13 September 1944; Venona 1506 KGB New York to Moscow, 23 October 1944; Venona 1805 KGB New York to Moscow, 23 December 1944. Sections of the 23 October message could not be deciphered by Venona code breakers.

6. Eric Alterman, "Redbaiting Stone," *Nation*, July 1998; MacPherson, *All Governments Lie*, 311.

7. Paul Berman, "The Watchdog," *New York Times*, 1 October 2006; Alterman, "Redbaiting Stone"; Paul Berman, "Confound It," *American Prospect*, 4 Octo-

ber 2006, http://www.prospect.org/cs/articles?articleId=12081; Eric Alterman, "All Governments (and Some Journalists) Lie," *Nation,* 18 September 2006.

8. KGB New York to Moscow Center, 13 April 1936; KGB New York to Moscow Center, 20 May 1936, KGB file 35112, v.5, pp. 212, 283, Vassiliev, *Black,* 23.

9. KGB New York to Moscow Center, 20 May 1936, KGB file 35112, v.5, p. 285, 287; KGB New York to Moscow Center, 1 August 1936, KGB file 3463, v. 2, pp. 41–42, Vassiliev, *Black,* 23–24.

10. "Agents: (3rd qtr. of '38)," KGB file 40159, v.1, p. 253; "Report on "Dan," 8 June 1948, KGB file 43173, v.6, p. 75, Vassiliev, *Black,* 90, 101. "Biography of V. Perlo" by "Vadim," 29 December 1944; "Vadim" to Moscow Center, 20 and 21 March 1945, KGB file 45100, v.1, pp. 45, 97, Alexander Vassiliev, *White Notebook #3 [2007 English Translation],* trans. Steven Shabad (1993–96), 73, 76.

11. Moscow Center to "Sergey," 1 June 1945, KGB file 35112, v.2, p. 135, Alexander Vassiliev, *White Notebook #1 [2007 English Translation],* trans. Steven Shabad (1993–96), 56.

12. Peter Moreira, *Hemingway on the China Front: His WWII Spy Mission with Martha Gellhorn* (Washington, D.C.: Potomac Books, 2006), 193.

13. "Glan" to Moscow Center, 19 August 1941; "Report from "Sound" dated 2.X-41," KGB file 35112, v.4a, pp. 481, 776, Vassiliev, *White #1,* 25, 29. Hemingway's China trip was January–May 1941, and the "2.X-41" on Golos's report is a misdating or a mistake in note taking (possibly 2.X-40, 2 October 1940). "Glan's" report of August 1941 noted sending a Golos report on Hemingway and was stated in the past tense, "when he left for China we let you know the terms of communicating with him in China."

14. Herbert Mitgang, *Dangerous Dossiers: Exposing the Secret War against America's Greatest Authors* (New York: D. I. Fine, 1988), 42–50; Moreira, *Hemingway on the China Front,* 193–95.

15. Moscow Center to "Maxim," 27 November 1941, KGB file 35112, v.6, p. 9, Vassiliev, *White #1,* 30. Report on "Argo," 8 June 1948, KGB file 43173, v.6, pp. 41–42, Vassiliev, *Black,* 89. In context, the dating of the contact in London as June 1943 may be an error for June 1944. "List of agents," 23 December 1949, KGB file 43173, v.2c, p. 67, Vassiliev, *Black,* 81.

16. Moscow Center to KGB Washington, 3 July 1950, KGB file 43173, v.11, pp. 187–88, Vassiliev, *Black,* 95.

17. "Ludwig Lore," in *Biographical Dictionary of the American Left,* ed. Bernard K. Johnpoll and Harvey Klehr (Westport, CT: Greenwood Press, 1986), 252–53.

18. "Plan of work for "Davis's" station for the 2nd half of 1934," Moscow Center to KGB New York, KGB file 17643, v.1, pp. 20–22, Vassiliev, *Black,* 35–36. The first public identification of "Leo" as Lore was by retired KGB general Julius Kobyakov, "ALES/Hiss," 22 March 2004, H-Diplo (http://h-net.msu.edu/cgi-bin/log browse.pl?trx=lm&list=H-Diplo).

19. The various versions of Markin's death are summarized in Gary Kern, *A Death in Washington: Walter G. Krivitsky and the Stalin Terror* (New York: Enigma Books, 2003), 40–41. There is nothing in Vassiliev's notebooks lending support to some suggestions in espionage literature that Markin died at the hands of a Soviet

agency. Grafpen to Berman, 27 November 1934, KGB file 17643, v.1, pp. 39–42, Vassiliev, *Black,* 37–38.

20. "Nikolay" to Moscow Center, 22 September 1934, KGB file 17643, v.1, p. 33, Vassiliev, *Black,* 37. KGB New York to Moscow Center, 8 September 1936; Moscow Center to "Nord," 13 February 1937; "Nord" to Moscow Center, February 1937, KGB file 36857, v.1, pp. 37–39, 58, 60, Alexander Vassiliev, *Yellow Notebook #2 [2007 English Translation],* trans. Philip Redko (1993–96), 8, 12.

21. Moscow Center to "Nord," 2 October 1936; "Nord" to Moscow Center, 18 October 1936; Moscow Center to "Nord," 13 February 1937, KGB file 36857, v.1, pp. 41, 45, 58, Vassiliev, *Yellow #2,* 8–9, 12.

22. Moscow Center to "Nord," 2 April 1937; Grafpen to Slutsky, 25 September 1936; Report on advice to "Nord," 4 February 1937; "Nord" reply to No. 313, 8 February 1937, KGB file 36857, v.1, pp. 40, 55–56, 63, Vassiliev, *Yellow #2,* 8, 11–13. Hede Massing, *This Deception* (New York: Duell, Sloan, and Pearce, 1951), 199–205. Notes on A. E. Vassiliev and A. A. Koreshov, *Station Chief Gold,* Andropov Red Banner Institute, 1984, Vassiliev, *Black,* 140.

23. Whittaker Chambers, *Witness* (New York: Random House, 1952), 389–92, 412–13.

24. "Robert S. Allen, Political Columnist," *New York Times,* 25 February 1981, p. B6; Oliver Ramsay Pilat, *Drew Pearson: An Unauthorized Biography* (New York: Harper's Magazine Press, 1973), 5–9, 86, 119.

25. KGB New York to Moscow Center, 27 January 1933, KGB file 17517, v.3, p. 46, Alexander Vassiliev, *Yellow Notebook #4 [2007 English Translation],* trans. Steven Shabad (1993–96), 24–25.

26. "Information from Sh/147 re various domestic and foreign-policy issues," 27 January 1933; Sh/147 on "various issues," 20 January 1933; Sh/147 report, 19 February 1933; Copy of Raymond Moley message, KGB file 17517, v.3, pp. 28–29, 47–49, 57–59, 69, Vassiliev, *Yellow #4,* 25–27. Allen joined the army when World War II broke out and served as a colonel with General George Patton. He lost an arm in combat in 1945 and spent a year recuperating at Walter Reed Hospital. His journalistic partnership with Pearson had become precarious, Pearson bought his share of the column for $45,000, and Allen resumed a career as an independent syndicated writer. In 1981, suffering from cancer, he shot himself.

27. John Louis Spivak, *A Man in His Time* (New York: Horizon Press, 1967).

28. "Tommy" to Moscow Center, 2 May 1930; "Tommy" to Moscow Center, 15 May 1930; "Re Amer. fabrications," 12 September 1930, and sample copies of Amtorg forgeries, KGB file 1186, v.1, pp. 76–94, Vassiliev, *Yellow #4,* 73–76.

29. "Charlie, Taras, and the source 'Grin,'" circa 1934, KGB file 3461, v.1, p. 117; A. Gorsky, "Failures in the USA (1938–48)," December 1948, KGB file 43173, v.2c, p. 54, Vassiliev, *Black,* 10, 79.

30. "Report by 'Grin' on Nazi activities," 3 October 1935; "'Grin's' line," with handwritten note from "Nikolay," July 1935, KGB file 3461, v.1, pp. 140, 153, 155–57, Vassiliev, *Black,* 11, 13–14.

31. "'Grin's' line," July 1935, KGB file 3461, v.1, pp. 155, 158–60; "Work on 'Grin's' line," circa late 1935, KGB file 3461, v.1, p. 241; "'Grin' was," circa late 1935,

KGB file 3461, v.2, p. 165; "Center views 'Grin's,'" 14 September 1935, KGB file 3460, v.2, pp. 1–3, 9; "'Grin's' information," KGB file 3460, v.2, pp. 29, 32; Vassiliev, *Black*, 14–15, 17, 18, 21.

32. "Political and Diplomatic Intelligence Work in the USA," circa 1943, KGB file 43173, v.1, pp. 36–37; Prudnikov, "Report on intelligence in the USA," 12 April 1941, KGB file 35112, v.1, p. 68, Vassiliev, *Black*, 46, 173.

33. Elizabeth Bentley, FBI Deposition, 30 November 1945, serial 220, pp. 29–30, 66, FBI Silvermaster file 65–56402. Spivak discussed Panama, Mexico, and California at the end of the 1930s in connection with his exposés of Japanese and German espionage in Spivak, *A Man in His Time*. Venona 600 KGB New York to Moscow, 2 May 1944; Venona 694 KGB New York to Moscow, 16 May 1944; Venona 601 KGB New York to Moscow, 2 May 1944.

34. Ronald Radosh and Joyce Milton, *The Rosenberg File: A Search for the Truth* (New York: Holt, Rinehart, and Winston, 1983), 366–72; Herbert Romerstein and Eric Breindel, *The Venona Secrets: Exposing Soviet Espionage and America's Traitors* (Washington, D.C.: Regnery, 2000), 252; Spivak, *A Man in His Time*, 466.

35. James Maurer et al., *Russia after Ten Years: Report of the American Trade Union Delegation to the Soviet Union* (New York: International Publishers, 1927); "15,000 Here Object to Rift with Reds," *New York Times*, 26 February 1935; "15,000 at Garden Protest on Relief," *New York Times*, 21 November 1935.

36. "Nikolay" to Moscow Center, 3 October 1935, KGB file 3461, v.1, pp. 137–38; Moscow Center, "General working principles," 3 September 1935, KGB file 3460, v.2, p. 21, Vassiliev, *Black*, 10–11, 21.

37. "'Liberal' gave information," circa 1935, KGB file 3461, v.1, pp. 109, 111–12, Vassiliev, *Black*, 10.

38. "Former sources in the USA," circa 1933–34, KGB file 17407, v.1, p. 90; A. Gorsky, "Failures in the USA (1938–48)," December 1948, KGB file 43173, v.2c, p. 51, Vassiliev, *Black*, 6, 78. Absent from the 1948 list of Soviet sources exposed by Budenz's defection was Owen Lattimore. Budenz never identified Lattimore as a Soviet agent but stated that senior CPUSA officers had described him as a secret Communist. Senator Joseph McCarthy, however, went much farther, identifying Lattimore, an Asian scholar and occasional government adviser, as a "top Russian spy." There is no mention of Lattimore in Vassiliev's notebooks. On Budenz, Lattimore, and McCarthy, see David M. Oshinsky, *A Conspiracy So Immense: The World of Joe McCarthy* (New York: Free Press, 1983).

39. "Former sources in the USA," circa 1933–34, KGB file 17407, v.1, p. 90, Vassiliev, *Black*, 6.

40. J. B. Matthews, *Odyssey of a Fellow Traveler* (New York: Mount Vernon Publishers, 1938), 259–68. See also Lawrence B. Glickman, "The Strike in the Temple of Consumption: Consumer Activism and Twentieth-Century American Political Culture," *Journal of American History* 88, no. 1 (2001): 99–128.

41. "Charlie, Taras, and the source "Grin" (1932)," KGB file 3640, v.1, p. 117; "Center views," 14 September 1935, KGB file 3460, v.2, pp. 1–9, Vassiliev, *Black*, 10, 18.

42. "Mail," 2 June 1937, KGB file 3465, v.2, p. 320; Pudnikov, "Report on intel-

ligence in the USA," 12 April 1941, KGB file 35112, v.1, p. 68; "We traced 'Liberal,'" circa June 1942, KGB file 43173, v.1, p.11, Vassiliev, *Black*, 34, 44, 77, 172–73.

43. FBI memo, 12 May 1952, serial 132; FBI memo, 27 May 1952, serial 139, FBI Bernard Schuster file 100–1556. FBI memo on Frank Palmer, FBI Frank Palmer file 100–34853 (NY file 100–82937); FBI memo on Frank Palmer, serial 236, FBI Thomas Black file 65–4332.

44. George Seldes, *You Can't Print That!: The Truth behind the News, 1918–1928* (Garden City, NY: Garden City Publishing, 1929); George Seldes, *Witness to a Century: Encounters with the Noted, the Notorious, and the Three SOBs* (New York: Ballantine Books, 1987).

45. Testimony of George Seldes, 1 July 1953, U.S. Senate Committee on Government Operations, *Executive Sessions of the Senate Permanent Subcommittee on Investigations of the Committee on Government Operations* (Washington, D.C.: U.S. Govt. Print. Off., 2003), v.2, 1206–11.

46. KGB New York to Moscow Center, 19 April 1940, KGB file 35112, v.5a, p. 512, Vassiliev, *Black*, 164.

47. "Report on Bruce Minton was received from Sound," 9 October 1940, KGB file 55298, pp. 21–22, Vassiliev, *White #3*, 1.

48. "Note by Albert," "Information on Robert," 7 July 1945, KGB file 55298, p. 253, Vassiliev, *White #3*, 23; Richard Bransten section, Silvermaster summary report, 3 January 1946, serial 621, pp. 444–45, FBI Silvermaster file 65–56402.

49. "Undated report by Sound on Bruce Minton," circa 1940–41, KGB file 55298, p. 20, Vassiliev, *White #3*, 1. Reports from "Informator," 21 July 1941, 5 August 1941, 11 August 1941, 25 August 1941, 1 September 1941, 28 September 1941, 6 October 1941, KGB file 35112, v.4a., pp. 408–21, 625, 627–29, Vassiliev, *White #1*, 21–22, 26. Several other reports listed as from "Pal"/Silvermaster were likely via "Informator"/Minton.

50. Moscow Center to "Maxim," 27 November 1941, KGB file 35112, v.6, pp. 8–9, Vassiliev, *White #1*, 30.

51. Moscow Center to "Maxim," 10 January 1942, KGB file 35112, v.6. pp. 100, 102, Vassiliev, *White #1*, 34–35.

52. Don S. Kirschner, *Cold War Exile: The Unclosed Case of Maurice Halperin* (Columbia: University of Missouri Press, 1995), 279–80, 286; Bentley, Deposition 1945, 32–34, 39, 79–80.

53. Moscow Center to KGB New York, 27 July 1943, KGB file 35112, v.6, p. 483; KGB New York to Moscow Center, 18 August 1942, KGB file 35112, v.7, p. 94, Vassiliev, *White #1*, 42, 44; "Plan of assignments for 'May,'" 16 December 1943, KGB file 35112, v.1, p. 303a, Vassiliev, *Black*, 182.

54. Bentley, Deposition 1945, 15–17, 33–35, 39, 43–44, 53–54, 71, 74. FBI Charlotte to Director, 4 April 1946, serial 557, FBI Silvermaster file 65–56402. Butkov to Prudnikov, 11 April 1941, KGB file 35112, v.1, pp. 85, 87; Vassiliev, *Black*, 174–76.

55. "'Sound' passed along," 5 November 1941; KGB New York to Moscow Center, 5 November 1941, KGB file 35112, v.4a, pp. 443, 662–63; Moscow Center to "Maxim," 17 March 1942, KGB file 35112, v.6, p. 131, Vassiliev, *White #1*, 22, 28, 36.

Butkov to Prudnikov, 11 April 1941, KGB file 35112, v.1, pp. 85, 87; Vassiliev, *Black,* 174–76.

56. Moscow Center to "Maxim," 28 August 1942, KGB file 35112, v.6, p. 263, Vassiliev, *White #1,* 38.

57. Bentley, Deposition 1945, 34–36, 40, 52, 57, 78–80. FBI memo, 16 November 1945, serial 108; FBI memo, 26 December 45, serial 356; Lieutenant Colonel Duncan C. Lee memo, serial 464; Ladd to Director, 21 February 1946, serial 573, FBI Silvermaster file 65–56402. "Biography of "Koch," received from "Sound,"" 8 September 1942; "Maxim" to Moscow Center, 22 September 1942, KGB file 40457, v.1, pp. 7–9, Vassiliev, *White #3,* 102; Bentley, Deposition 1945, 34–35.

58. "Maxim" to Moscow Center, 12 October 1942, KGB file 35112, v.7, p. 180, Vassiliev, *White #1,* 48; KGB Washington to Moscow Center, 2 November 1944, KGB file 40457, v.1, p. 38, Vassiliev, *White #3,* 104–5.

59. "Maxim" to Moscow Center, 14 April 1943, "Maxim" to Moscow Center, 30 October 1943, KGB file 35112, v.7, pp. 386, 492, Vassiliev, *White #1,* 50, 52. Venona 868 KGB New York to Moscow, 8 June 1943.

60. "Maxim" to Moscow Center, 30 October 1943, KGB file 35112, v.7, pp. 492–93, Vassiliev, *White #1,* 52. Bentley, Deposition 1945, 43. Ladd memo, 15 December 1945, serial 367; Scheidt to Director, 31 January 1947, serial 1976; FBI Washington Field Office memo, 29 May 1947, serial 2540; Michael Greenberg statement, 1947, serial 2583, FBI Silvermaster file 65–56402. Earl Latham, *The Communist Controversy in Washington: From the New Deal to McCarthy* (Cambridge, MA: Harvard University Press, 1966), 306–7.

61. "Message from 'Myrna' re 'Helmsman,'" 11 December 1944, KGB file 70545, pp. 284–85, Alexander Vassiliev, *White Notebook #2 [2007 English Translation],* trans. Steven Shabad (1993–96), 18; Bentley, Deposition 1945, 77, 80, 91, 94–95; Elizabeth Bentley and Hayden B. Peake, *Out of Bondage: The Story of Elizabeth Bentley* (New York: Ivy Books, 1988), 136–38.

62. KGB New York to Moscow Center, 8 March 1944; KGB New York to Moscow Center, 31 March 1944, KGB file 35112, v.8, pp. 126, 133, Vassiliev, *White #1,* 59–60.

63. Bernard S. Redmont, *Risks Worth Taking: The Odyssey of a Foreign Correspondent* (Lanham, MD: University Press of America, 1992).

64. Bentley, Deposition 1945, 47–50, 79–80; Redmont, *Risks,* 61–62.

65. Gary May, *Un-American Activities: The Trials of William Remington* (New York: Oxford University Press, 1994), 59.

66. Redmont, *Risks,* 58–60.

67. "M.'s contacts; list obtained by Vadim," October 1944; "List of M.'s contacts (prepared by her)," 25 January 1945; "Bob" to Moscow Center, 4 December 1945; "Bob from London," KGB file 70545, pp. 140, 143, 303, 447, Vassiliev, *White #2,* 9, 19, 33; Anatoly Gorsky, "Failures in the USA (1938–48)," KGB file 43173, v.2c, p. 53, Vassiliev, *Black,* 79. "Mon" appeared as an unknown cover name in two 1943 KGB cables deciphered by the Venona project, one as a source on Latin American matters and the other so badly broken that little can be deduced. Venona 1019, 1021, 1024, 1034 KGB New York to Moscow, 29 June 1943; Venona 1056 KGB New York to Moscow, 3 July 1943.

68. "Nikolay" to Moscow Center, 2 August 1938, KGB file 34194, pp. 181–85, Vassiliev, *White #1*, 125–26. Edward T. Folliard, "Hottest Primary in Half Century Embroils Nearby Virginia," *Washington Post*, 31 July 1938; Edward T. Folliard, "Virginians Reject New Deal Supporter by Wide Margin," *Washington Post*, 3 August 1938.

69. KGB New York to Moscow Center, 2 March 1939; KGB New York to Moscow Center, 2 March 1939, KGB file 35112, v.5, pp. 166–67, 169, 186–87; KGB New York to Moscow Center, 13 December 1939, KGB file 35112, v.5a, pp. 452–55; Butkov to Prudnikov, 11 April 1941, KGB file 35112, v.1, p. 84, Vassiliev, *Black*, 158, 160, 163–64, 174.

70. Butkov to Prudnikov, 11 April 1941; "Expense estimate for 'Stephan's' station," January 1941; "Plan of Operations," January 1941, KGB file 35112, v.1, pp. 41, 47, 89, Vassiliev, *Black*, 170, 172, 175. "Glan" to Moscow Center, 21 August 1941; KGB New York to Moscow Center, 5 November 1941, KGB file 35112, v.4a, pp. 444, 644, Vassiliev, *White #1*, 23, 27.

71. Moscow Center to "Maxim," 10 January 1942, KGB file 35112, v.6, pp. 96–97, Vassiliev, *White #1*, 33.

72. Testimony of William E. Dodd, Jr., 5 April 1943, U.S. House Special Committee on Un-American Activities, *Investigation of Un-American Propaganda Activities in the United States (Executive Hearings)* (Washington, D.C.: U.S. Govt. Print. Off., 1940–43), v.7, 3366–82; Testimony of William E. Dodd, Jr., 9 April 1943, U.S. House Special Subcommittee of the Committee on Appropriations, *Hearings [Kerr Commission]* (Washington, D.C.: U.S. Govt. Print. Off., 1943), 120, 258; Stephen C. Mercado, "FBIS against the Axis, 1941–1945," *Studies in Intelligence*, no. 11 (Fall–Winter 2002): 33–43.

73. "Maxim" to Moscow Center, 1 September 1943, KGB file 35112, v.7, pp. 438–39, Vassiliev, *White #1*, 51.

74. United States v. Lovett, 328 U.S. 303 (1946). Moscow Center memo, 9 June 1945; Moscow Center to "Vadim," 14 June 1945, KGB file 43173, v.1, pp. 126, 129, Vassiliev, *Black*, 53. "President" and "Lisa herself," circa 1945, KGB file 35112, v.9, pp. 73, 94, Vassiliev, *White #1*, 76. "Report on 'President,'" KGB file 43173, v.5, pp. 103–4, Vassiliev, *Black*, 86.

75. "Political and Diplomatic Intelligence Work in the USA," circa 1943, KGB file 43173, v.1, pp. 35–36, Vassiliev, *Black*, 45–46.

76. Ibid.; Butkov to Prudnikov, 11 April 1941; Prudnikov, "Report on intelligence in the USA," 12 April 1941, KGB file 35112, v.1, pp. 68–69, 85, 87, Vassiliev, *Black*, 172–76.

77. "On the meeting with 'Sound,'" 18 October 1941, KGB file 35112, v.6, p. 783, Vassiliev, *White #1*, 29; Bentley, Deposition 1945, 37–38, 87; Venona 1221 KGB New York to Moscow, 26 August 1944. Emphasis in the original.

78. FBI New York office memo, 3 December 1945, serial 292; FBI Washington office memo, 1 November 1946, serial 464; Scheidt to Hoover, 31 January 1947, serial 1976, FBI Silvermaster file 65–56402. Son [Rudy Baker] to Comintern, 22 February 1940, Archive of the Secretariat of the Executive Committee of the Communist International: Coded Correspondence with Communist Parties (1933–1943),

Russian State Archive of Socio-Political History (RGASPI) 495–184–4 (1939–1940 file).

79. Venona 851 KGB New York to Moscow, 15 June 1944; Venona 928 KGB New York to Moscow, 1 July 1944; Venona 1154 KGB New York to Moscow, 12 August 1944; Venona 1198 KGB New York to Moscow, 23 August 1944; Venona 433 KGB San Francisco to Moscow, 11 August 1945; Venona 483–484 KGB San Francisco to Moscow, 13 September 1945. "Glan" to Moscow Center, 19 August 1941; "Sound knows"; Report from probationer "Yun," 12 November 1941, KGB file 35112, v.4a, pp. 478, 570–71, 657, Vassiliev, *White #1*, 24–25, 28. Moscow Center to "Maxim," 27 November 1941, KGB file 35112, v.6, p. 13, Vassiliev, *White #1*, 30.

80. "Maxim" to Moscow Center, 9 February 1943, KGB file 35112, v.7, p. 253, Vassiliev, *White #1*, 49; Venona 851 KGB New York to Moscow, 15 June 1944; Venona 928 KGB New York to Moscow, 1 July 1944; Venona 1154 KGB New York to Moscow, 12 August 1944; Venona 1198 KGB New York to Moscow, 23 August 1944; Venona 433 KGB San Francisco to Moscow, 11 August 1945; Venona 483–484 KGB San Francisco to Moscow, 13 September 1945. John Earl Haynes and Harvey Klehr, *Venona: Decoding Soviet Espionage in America* (New Haven: Yale University Press [Nota Bene], 2000), 237–38.

81. "Political and diplomatic intelligence work in the USA," circa 1943, KGB file 43173, v.1, pp. 35–36, Vassiliev, *Black*, 45–46. Haynes and Klehr, *Venona* (2000), 76–77; FBI memo, "Existing Corroboration of Bentley's Overall Testimony," reproduced in Bentley and Peake, *Out of Bondage*, 254–55, 327; Winston Burdett testimony, 29 June 1955, U.S. Senate Internal Security Subcommittee, *Strategy and Tactics of World Communism, Recruiting for Espionage—Part 14* (Washington, D.C.: U.S. Govt. Print. Off., 1955), 1324–81; Venona 823 KGB New York to Moscow, 7 June 1944; Venona 881 KGB New York to Moscow, 20 June 1944.

82. Testimony of Louis Budenz, 23 September 1953, U.S. Senate Committee on Government Operations, *Executive Sessions of the Senate Permanent Subcommittee on Investigations of the Committee on Government Operations*, v.3, 1915; Raymond Arthur Davies and Andrew J. Steiger, *Soviet Asia, Democracy's First Line of Defense* (New York: Dial Press, 1942); Henry Agard Wallace, *Soviet Asia Mission*, in collaboration with Andrew J. Steiger (New York: Reynal and Hitchcock, 1946); Whitman Bassow, *The Moscow Correspondents: Reporting on Russia from the Revolution to Glasnost* (New York: W. Morrow, 1988), 146.

83. Moscow Center to Gennady, 26 April 1941, KGB file 35112, v.4, pp. 406–7; KGB New York to Moscow Center, 5 November 1941, KGB file 35112, v.4a, p. 661, Vassiliev, *White #1*, 21, 28. Venona 939 KGB New York to Moscow, 18 June 1943; Venona 823 KGB New York to Moscow, 7 June 1944; Venona 881 KGB New York to Moscow, 20 June 1944; Venona 905 KGB New York to Moscow, 26 June 1944; Venona 1275 KGB New York to Moscow, 7 September 1944; Venona 1403 KGB New York to Moscow, 5 October 1944; Venona 275 KGB Moscow to New York, 25 March 1945; Venona 656 KGB New York to Moscow, 9 May 1944. Emphasis in the original.

84. "Plan of measures," March 1949, KGB file 43173, v.2c, p. 23, Vassiliev, *Black*, 74. "His papers were not issued for oper. reasons" indicates that Epstein did not receive official Soviet citizenship papers for "operational reasons"—that is, the KGB

did not want a paper record of his Soviet citizenship to exist that might compromise his intelligence work.

85. Moscow Center to "Maxim," 15 March 1943, KGB file 35112, v.6, pp. 424–26, Vassiliev, *White #1*, 41; Venona 823 KGB New York to Moscow, 7 June 1944; Venona 881 KGB New York to Moscow, 20 June 1944. "Pacific Institute" was likely the Institute for Pacific Affairs. Emphasis in the original.

86. "Plan of work with agents of the Washington Station for 1950," KGB file 43173, v.2c, p. 59, Vassiliev, *Black*, 80; Sidney Rittenberg, *The Man Who Stayed Behind*, assisted by Amanda Bennett (New York: Simon and Schuster, 1993), 252, 273; Douglas Martin, "Israel Epstein, Prominent Chinese Communist, Dies at 90," *New York Times*, 2 June 2005.

87. Stephen R. MacKinnon and Oris Friesen, *China Reporting: An Oral History of American Journalism in the 1930s and 1940s* (Berkeley: University of California Press, 1987).

88. References to Krafsur/"Ide" in Vassiliev, *Black*, 72, 75, 80; Vassiliev, *White #1*, 56, 74. Venona messages on Krafsur/"Ide" are in Appendix A, Haynes and Klehr, *Venona* (2000).

89. References to Belfrage/"Charlie" in Vassiliev, *Black*, 65 and 79; Vassiliev, *White #1*, 7; Vassiliev, *White #2*, 9, 10, 28, 33. Venona messages about Belfrage are in Appendix A, Haynes and Klehr, *Venona* (2000). Cedric Belfrage, *The Frightened Giant: My Unfinished Affair with America* (London and New York: Secker and Warburg, 1957); Cedric Belfrage, *The American Inquisition, 1945–1960* (Indianapolis: Bobbs-Merrill, 1973); Cedric Belfrage and James Aronson, *Something to Guard: The Stormy Life of the National Guardian, 1948–1967* (New York: Columbia University Press, 1978).

90. References to Lauterbach/"Pa" in Vassiliev, *White #1*, 74. Venona messages about Lauterbach/"Pa" are in Appendix A, Haynes and Klehr, *Venona* (2000).

91. Moscow Center to Stalin, Molotov, and Beria, 5 July 1945, KGB file 224, v.2, pp. 68–69, Alexander Vassiliev, *Yellow Notebook #4 [2007 English Translation]*, trans. Philip Redko (1993–96), 123; Venona 734 KGB New York to Moscow, 21 May 1944; Venona 1039–1041 KGB New York to Moscow, 24–25 July 1944; Venona 1393 KGB New York to Moscow, 3 October 1944; Venona 1814–1815 KGB New York to Moscow, 23 December 1944.

92. References to Setaro/"Express Messenger" in Vassiliev, *Black*, 79; Vassiliev, *Yellow #2*, 88. Venona messages about Setaro/"Express Messenger" are in Appendix A, Haynes and Klehr, *Venona* (2000).

93. References to Scott/"Fir" in Vassiliev, *Black*, 46, 51, 189; Vassiliev, *White #1*, 2, 30. Venona messages about Scott/"Fir" are in Appendix A, Haynes and Klehr, *Venona* (2000).

94. References to MacLean/"101st" in Vassiliev, *Black*, 77. "MacLean" has not been identified, and the exact English spelling of the name is uncertain.

95. References to Carpenter/"103rd" in Vassiliev, *Black*, 77.

96. References to "Bough" in Vassiliev, *White #1*, 72. Venona messages about "Bough" (transliterated as "Suk") are in Appendix A, Haynes and Klehr, *Venona* (2000).

97. "Plan of measures," March 1949; Gorsky to Savchenko, 23 December 1949, KGB file 43173, v.2c, pp. 21, 47, Vassiliev, *Black*, 74, 77.

98. Frances Stonor Saunders, *The Cultural Cold War: The CIA and the World of Arts and Letters* (New York, New Press, 2000).

Chapter 4: Infiltration of the U.S. Government

1. Gorsky, "Failures in the USA (1938–48)," KGB file 43173, v.2c, pp. 49–55, Alexander Vassiliev, *Black Notebook [2007 English Translation]*, trans. Philip Redko (1993–96), 77–79.

2. "Plan of work for Davis's station for the 2nd half of 1934"; Grafpen to Berman, 27 November 1934, KGB file 17643, v.1, pp. 20, 40, 42, Vassiliev, *Black*, 35, 37–38.

3. "Plan of work for Davis's station for the 2nd half of 1934," KGB file 17643 v.1, p. 20, Vassiliev, *Black*, 35.

4. "Salmon, David Alden" entry, U.S. Department of State, *Register of the Department of State, July 1, 1934* (Washington, D.C.: U.S. Govt. Print. Off., 1934). William V. Nessley, "State Department Keeps a Finger on the Pulse of World Affairs," *Washington Post*, 4 June 1939; Robert C. Albright, "Investigators Decide to Call 12 Witnesses," *Washington Post*, 9 December 1948.

5. Letter to "Davis," No. 006, 25 March 1934, KGB file 17643, v.1, pp. 17–19, Vassiliev, *Black*, 34–35.

6. "Ludwig Lore," in *Biographical Dictionary of the American Left*, ed. Bernard K. Johnpoll and Harvey Klehr (Westport, CT: Greenwood Press, 1986), 252–53. Grafpen to Berman, 27 November 1934, KGB file 17643, v.1, pp. 39–42, Vassiliev, *Black*, 37–38.

7. "Jung" to Moscow Center, 26 October 1934, KGB file 17643, v.1, pp. 53–54, Vassiliev, *Black*, 38.

8. Grafpen to Berman, 27 November 1934; "Nikolay" to Moscow Center, 22 September 1934; "Work plan for Nord's station," December 1934, KGB file 17643, v.1, pp. 33, 39–42, 70, Vassiliev, *Black*, 37–39. KGB New York to Moscow Center, 8 September 1936; Moscow Center to "Nord," 13 February 1937; "Nord" to Moscow Center, February 1937, KGB file 36857, v.1, pp. 37–39, 58, 60, Alexander Vassiliev, *Yellow Notebook #2 [2007 English Translation]*, trans. Philip Redko (1993–96), 8, 12.

9. Moscow Center to "Nord," 2 April 1937; Grafpen to Slutsky, 25 September 1936; Report on advice to "Nord," 4 February 1937; "Nord" reply to No. 313, 8 February 1937, KGB file 36857, v.1, pp. 40, 55–56, 63, Vassiliev, *Yellow* #2, 8, 11–13. Hede Massing, *This Deception* (New York: Duell, Sloan, and Pearce, 1951), 199–205. Notes on A. E. Vassiliev and A. A. Koreshov, *Station Chief Gold*, Andropov Red Banner Institute, 1984, Vassiliev, *Black*, 140. Chapter 3 has a more detailed discussion of the KGB-Lore relationship.

10. KGB New York to Moscow Center, 3 March 1937, KGB file 3465, v.1, pp. 230–32, 237; "M. is glad," KGB file 3465, v.2, pp. 61, 307, Vassiliev, *Black*, 32–33.

11. Department of Justice Investigative Files, Part III: "The Use of Military

Force by the Federal Government in Domestic Disturbances, 1900–1938," Lexis-Nexis/UPA microfilm, 19 reels. The "Glasser Files" are part of General Records of the Department of Justice, Record Group 60.3.5, National Archives and Records Administration, College Park, MD. "Gennady" to Moscow Center, 25 January 1938, KGB file 35112, v.5, pp. 5, 8, Vassiliev, *Black*, 146–47; "Gennady" letter, 25 January 1938, KGB file 3591, v.5, p. 1, Alexander Vassiliev, *Yellow Notebook #4 [2007 English Translation]*, trans. Stephen Shabad (1993–96), 111.

12. "Gennady" to Moscow Center, 13 April 1938, KGB file 35112, v.5, pp. 16–17, Vassiliev, *Black*, 147.

13. Harvey Klehr, *The Heyday of American Communism: The Depression Decade* (New York: Basic Books, 1984), 274.

14. "Based on Morris's material," circa 1937, KGB file 70994, p. 51, Alexander Vassiliev, *White Notebook #1 [2007 English Translation]*, trans. Steven Shabad (1993–96), 141.

15. "Nikolay's account of Brit's disappearance," 24 May 1938, KGB file 34194, p. 161, Vassiliev, *White #1*, 125; "Nikolay" to Moscow Center, 29 June 1938; Moscow Center to "Gennady," 5 August 1939, KGB file 35112, v.5, pp. 48, 358, Vassiliev, *Black*, 149, 154.

16. Moscow Center to "Gennady," 9 November 1939, KGB file 35112, v.5a, p. 408, Vassiliev, *Black*, 161–62.

17. Fitin to Beria, January 1941, KGB file 35112, v.1, p. 38, Vassiliev, *Black*, 170. "Glan" to Moscow Center, 21 August 1941; "Glan" to Moscow Center, 23 August 1941, KGB file 35112, v.4a, pp. 446, 455, Vassiliev, *White #1*, 23–24.

18. Summary of Feldman statement, 5 August 1941, serial 638; Feldman summary, 23 June 1942, serial 743; Ladd to Director, 25 April 1946, serial 821x, FBI Feldman file 61–7574.

19. Glasser to Arnold, 25 May 1941, Box 3, Rutgers University, School of Law, Committee of Review, Transcripts of the Hearings Regarding the Suspension of Abraham Glasser, May–June 1953, Special Collections and University Archives, Rutgers University Libraries RG N7/G2/03. Jackson to McGuire, 17 June 1941; Alexander Holtzoff to McGuire, "Re Abraham Glasser," 23 July 1941, in U.S. House Committee on Un-American Activities, *Communist Methods of Infiltration (Education)* (Washington, D. C.: U.S. Govt. Print. Off., 1953–54), part 2, 197–200.

20. Murray Marder, "Once Cleared, Teacher Balks at Red Probe," *Washington Post*, 19 March 1953. Ugo Carusi, "Memorandum for the records. In re: Abraham Glasser," 6 November 1941, U.S. House Committee on Un-American Activities, *Infiltration (Education)*, part 2, 200–202.

21. Attorney General James McGranery to OPA Deputy Administrator Thomas Emerson, 7 July 1944; H. A. Bergsom memo with McGranery concurrence, "Subject: Abraham Glasser's request for reemployment," U.S. House Committee on Un-American Activities, *Infiltration (Education)*, part 2, 217–20. Abraham Glasser testimony, 2 June 1953, Transcripts of the Hearings Regarding the Suspension of Abraham Glasser.

22. U.S. House Committee on Un-American Activities, *The Shameful Years: 30 Years of Soviet Espionage in the United States* (Washington, D.C.: U.S. Govt. Print.

Off., 1951). Testimony of Abraham Glasser, 18 March 1953, U.S. House Committee on Un-American Activities, *Infiltration (Education)*, part 2, 179–221; Testimony of Abraham Glasser, 2 June 1953, Transcripts of the Hearings Regarding the Suspension of Abraham Glasser. On Stone's own history as a KGB agent, see chapter 3.

23. Testimony of Abraham Glasser, 3, 5, and 30 June 1953, Transcripts of the Hearings Regarding the Suspension of Abraham Glasser.

24. Transcripts of the Hearings Regarding the Suspension of Abraham Glasser, May–June 1953; Glasser obituary, *New York Times*, 15 December 1976; *Report to the Committee on Academic Freedom and Tenure by the Subcommittee to Study and Report on the Case of Professor Abraham Glasser of Rutgers University*, 1955 Association of American Law School Program and Reports of Committees; "AAUP censure of the Administration of Rutgers University," 1955, Records of the Rutgers University Board of Governors Special Committee on Academic Freedom and Tenure, 1952–58, v.1, Collections and University Archives, Rutgers University Libraries, RG 02/C1.

25. Floyd Jones, Silvermaster summary memo, 13 December 1945, serial 234; Director to Attorney General, 16 September 1946, serial 155, FBI Silvermaster file 65–56402. Another FBI Silvermaster case summary, serial 446, February–March 1946, has a seven-page discussion of Wahl entirely redacted. The only extended attention to Wahl is in M. Stanton Evans, *Blacklisted by History: The Untold Story of Senator Joe McCarthy and His Fight against America's Enemies* (New York: Crown Forum, 2007), 7–8, 131, 142, 332, 336, 395.

26. Testimony of David Wahl, 8 April 1943, U.S. House Special Committee on Un-American Activities, *Investigation of Un-American Propaganda Activities in the United States (Executive Hearings)* (Washington, D.C.: U.S. Govt. Print. Off., 1940–43), v.7, 3438–53.

27. "Plan of measures for the 1st Department," 16 March 1950; "Pink," KGB file 43173, v.2c, pp. 99, 162–63, Vassiliev, *Black*, 83–84. On Aronberg and Dozenberg, see "Comintern Apparatus Summary Report," 15 December 1944, serial 3702, FBI Comintern Apparatus file 100–203581; Harvey Klehr, John Earl Haynes, and Fridrikh Igorevich Firsov, *The Secret World of American Communism* (New Haven: Yale University Press, 1995), 42, 46–49; and John Earl Haynes and Harvey Klehr, *Venona: Decoding Soviet Espionage in America* (New Haven: Yale University Press [Nota Bene], 2000), 164–66.

28. Moscow Center to "Vadim" and "Sergey," June 1945; Moscow Center to "Vadim," 25 September 1945; "Vadim" to Moscow Center, 1 October 1945; "Vadim is exploring" and "Graur's decision," KGB file 43173, v.1, pp. 128, 150, 153, Vassiliev, *Black*, 53, 55, 57.

29. "Grigory" to Moscow Center, 1 July 1947; Moscow Center to "Grigory," 3 July 1947, KGB file 43173, v.2, p. 176, 178–79, Vassiliev, *Black*, 62–63.

30. KGB Washington to Moscow Center, 18 July 1947; "Grigory" to Moscow Center, 10 July 1947; "'Pink' goes to"; "Received information"; "Grigory" to Moscow Center, 1 August 1947, KGB file 43173, v.2, pp. 182–84, 209–11, 213, 219–20, Vassiliev, *Black*, 63.

31. KGB Washington to Moscow Center, 19 August 1948; "'Pink' was in-

structed," 16 November 1948, KGB file 43173, v.4, pp. 369, 373–74, 454, Vassiliev, *Black,* 71.

32. "Vladimir" to Moscow Center, 25 December 1948, KGB file 43173, v.4, p. 478; "Plan of measures for the 1st Department"; "Pink," 16 March 1950, KGB file 43173, v.2c, pp. 99, 162, Vassiliev, *Black,* 72, 83–84.

33. Feinberg obituary, *New York Times,* 7 December 1998; Michael I. Karpin, *The Bomb in the Basement: How Israel Went Nuclear and What That Means for the World* (New York: Simon and Schuster, 2006).

34. Report on "Vick," 28 October 1948, KGB file 43173, v.6, pp. 302–3, Vassiliev, *Black,* 90–91; Claudia Levy, "Henry H. Ware, 90, Dies," *Washington Post,* 27 May 1999; FBI New York report, 16 August 1948, serial 1474, FBI Silvermaster file 65–56402.

35. Report on "Vick," 28 October 1948, KGB file 43173, v.6, pp. 302–3, Vassiliev, *Black,* 90–91. Zarubin to Merkulov, "Memorandum (on the station's work in the country)," 30 September 1944, KGB file 35112, v.1, p. 396; Moscow Center to "Maxim," 15 March 1943, KGB file 35112, v.6, p. 417, Vassiliev, *White #1,* 3, 40.

36. Zarubin to Merkulov, "Memorandum (on the station's work in the country)," 30 September 1944, KGB file 35112, v.1, pp. 396, 402–4, Vassiliev, *White #1,* 3, 6. There is one KGB cable deciphered by the Venona project that refers to "Vick," but it is badly broken and largely unintelligible. "Vick" was not identified by NSA/FBI analysts. Venona 959 KGB New York to Moscow, 21 June 1943.

37. Report on "Vick," 28 October 1948, KGB file 43173, v.6, pp. 302–3, Vassiliev, *Black,* 90–91.

38. FBI New York report, 16 August 1946, serial 1474; FBI Washington report, 19 July 1946, serial 1447; FBI Washington report, 19 November 1946, serial 1909, p. 171, FBI Silvermaster file 65–56402. Ware obituary, *Washington Post,* 27 May 1999.

39. "Source Sh-142"; "A. is a lieutenant," "War Preparations by W. A., 7 January 1933," KGB file 17517, v.3, pp. 9, 51–53, 95, Vassiliev, *Yellow #4, English Translation,* 23–24.

40. "Jung" to Moscow Center, 5 July 1937; "Jung" to Moscow Center, 26 October 1938, KGB file 59264, v.1, pp. 9, 26–28, Vassiliev, *Yellow #2,* 70, 72.

41. "Jung" to Moscow Center, 5 July 1937; Moscow Center to "Jung," 27 November 1937; Moscow Center to "Jung," 8 January 1938; Note by "Granite," KGB file 59264, v.1, pp. 9, 15a, 16–17, Vassiliev, *Yellow #2,* 70–71.

42. Report on "Arena," 14 November 1940; Report, April 1942, KGB file 59264, v.1, pp. 30, 36, Vassiliev, *Yellow #2,* 73.

43. Zarubin to Merkulov, "Memorandum," 30 September 1944, KGB file 35112, v.1, p. 419; Moscow Center to "Gennady," 24 February 1941, KGB file 35112, v.4, pp. 113–14; Moscow Center to "Maxim," 27 November 1941, KGB file 35112, v.6, p. 11, Vassiliev, *White #1,* 13–14, 17, 31. Report on Graze, circa 1945; Handwritten "P.S." July 1943 addition to Report, April 1942; Report, October 1946, KGB file 59264, v.1, pp. 36, 44–45, 53, Vassiliev, *Yellow #2,* 72–75. Entries regarding "Arena"/Graze can be found in Vassiliev, *Yellow #2,* 40–61, 66, 70–75, 77–78; Vassiliev, *Black,* 51, 78, 89, 95, 173, 175–76; Vassiliev, *White #1,* 10–14, 17, 30–31;

Alexander Vassiliev, *White Notebook #3 [2007 English Translation]*, trans. Steven Shabad (1993–96), 66–71, 74, 76, 79–80, 120.

44. "Vadim" to Moscow Center, 7 December 1944; Report, circa 1945; "Vadim" to Moscow Center, April 1945; Report by "X," 16 November 1944, KGB file 59264, v.1, pp. 43–45, 48, 57–58, Vassiliev, *Yellow #2*, 73–75. "Vadim" to Moscow Center, 20–21 March 1945, KGB file 45100, v.1, pp. 97–98, Vassiliev, *White #3*, 76.

45. "Jung" to Moscow Center, 13 April 1939; "Jung" to Moscow Center, 3 June 1939; "Mer" to Moscow Center, 1 December 1942; "Permission granted in Dec. 1942"; "Mer" to Moscow Center, 9 March 1943; "Maxim," 30 March 1943; KGB New York to Moscow Center, 8 May 1943; "Report by Gorsky," 4 May 1944; "Mer" to Moscow Center, 13 May 1944, KGB file 45100, v.1, pp. 1–3, 7, 8–10, 12–14, Vassiliev, *White #3*, 66–68. Zarubin to Merkulov, "Memorandum (on the station's work in the country)," 30 September 1944, KGB file 35112, v.1, pp. 412–13, Vassiliev, *White #1*, 10–11. Elizabeth Bentley, FBI Deposition, 30 November 1945, serial 220, pp. 51–57, 78–79 ; FBI New York memo, 16 January 1947, serial 1936, FBI Silvermaster file 65–56402.

46. Moscow Center to "Vadim," 23 November 1945, KGB file 70545, p. 405, Alexander Vassiliev, *White Notebook #2 [2007 English Translation]*, trans. Steven Shabad (1993–96), 30; "In 1948, X," KGB file 59264, v.1, p. 81, Vassiliev, *Yellow #2*, 75; Remarks of Senator Joseph McCarthy, *Congressional Record*, 20 February 1950. To confuse matters, McCarthy sent a written list to the Tydings Committee with slightly different numbering. Gerald Graze was number twenty-six on that list. McCarthy's Tydings Committee list and the earlier "Lee List" from which it was drawn can be found in Evans, *Blacklisted by History*, 246–62. Gerald Graze obituary, *Washington Post*, 31 March 1999.

47. Allen Weinstein, *Perjury: The Hiss-Chambers Case* (New York: Random House, 1997), 269. Arthur Schlesinger, Jr., "The Party Circuit," *New Republic,* 29 May 1995, 39. The object of Schlesinger's ire was Klehr, Haynes, and Firsov, *Secret World.*

48. "Report by source S-17," circa 1934; "Nikolay" letter, 3 October 1934, KGB file 36857, v.1, pp. 11–12, 14, Vassiliev, *Yellow #2*, 1–2. "S-17" was unidentified, but his report indicated he was a native Russian speaker whose vocabulary was pre-Soviet.

49. "Nord" to Moscow Center, 30 November 1935; "Personal data regarding Helen Boyd (wife of '19')," 1935; "Note by 'Redhead' about Helen Boyd," circa 1935, KGB file 17407, v.1, pp. 16, 19–20 and reverse, Vassiliev, *Yellow #2*, 2–3.

50. David P. Hornstein, *Arthur Ewert: A Life for the Comintern* (Lanham, MD: University Press of America, 1993), 200–202, 207, 267–77; Fernando Morais, *Olga,* trans. Ellen Watson (New York: Grove Weidenfeld, 1990), 56, 61–62, 65, 82, 94, 108–11, 123–24, 129–33.

51. "Report by 'Nord' regarding the trip to '19,'" circa 1936, KGB file 36857, v.1, p. 30, Vassiliev, *Yellow #2*, 6–7. Whittaker Chambers testimony, 28 December 1948, U.S. House Committee on Un-American Activities, unpublished executive session testimony; Sam Tanenhaus, *Whittaker Chambers: A Biography* (New York: Random House, 1997), 334.

52. "Report by 'Nord' regarding the trip to '19,'" circa 1936, KGB file 36857, v.1, p. 30, Vassiliev, *Yellow #2*, 6–7.

53. "Report by 'Granite,'" 8 March 1948, KGB file 36857, v.1, pp. 258–61, Vassiliev, *Yellow #2*, 34–35.

54. KGB New York to Moscow Center, 8 September 1936; Grafpen to Slutsky, 25 September 1936; Moscow Center to "Nord," 14 November 1936, KGB file 36857, v.1, pp. 36–37, 40, 46, Vassiliev, *Yellow #2*, 8–9.

55. KGB New York to Moscow Center, 8 September 1936; "Excerpted letters from 'Nord' from February 1937"; "Nord" report, 18 December 1936; "Granite" report on meeting with Duggan, 12 October 1936; "Nord" report with attached annotation by the chief of the INO, 19 December 1936, KGB file 36857, v.1, pp. 37–38, 43–44, 53–54, 60, Vassiliev, *Yellow #2*, 8–9, 10–12.

56. "Nord" to Moscow Center, 1 June 1937, KGB file 36857, v.1, p. 71–72, Vassiliev, *Yellow #2*, 14.

57. Moscow Center to "Nord," 14 May 1937; "On the meeting between Granite and 19," 29 May 1937, KGB file 36857, v.1, pp. 67–70, Vassiliev, *Yellow #2*, 13–14.

58. "Jung" to Moscow Center, 15 August 1937, KGB file 36857, v.1, p. 86, Vassiliev, *Yellow #2*, 18. Report from "19," circa 1937; "People's Commissar of Internal Affairs Yezhov sent," 14 May 1937; report on "Carp Export and Import Corporation," circa 1937, KGB file 3587, v.2, pp. 185, 192, 199, 202, 240, Vassiliev, *Yellow #2*, 38. "Recent trends in German competition," 5 July 1938; "Memorandum on Italian," November 1938, KGB file 3587, v.7, pp. 36, 154, Vassiliev, *Yellow #2*, 39.

59. "Jung" to Moscow Center, 5 July 1937; "Granite" report on meeting Duggan, 2 July 1937; "Jung" to Moscow Center, 10 July 1937, KGB file 36857, v.1, pp. 74–77, 80, Vassiliev, *Yellow #2*, 14–17.

60. Part of the text of Poretsky's letter to Stalin is in Gary Kern, *A Death in Washington: Walter G. Krivitsky and the Stalin Terror* (New York: Enigma Books, 2003), 128–29. Also see Elisabeth K. Poretsky, *Our Own People: A Memoir of "Ignace Reiss" and His Friends* (Ann Arbor: University of Michigan Press, 1970). Chambers discussed the influence of Poyntz, Poretsky (Riess), and Krivitsky on his decision to defect in *Witness*, pp. 36, 47, 59, 204, 439, 457–63.

61. "Jung" to Moscow Center, 15 August 1937, KGB file 36857, v.1, p. 84, Vassiliev, *Yellow #2*, 18.

62. Noel Field statement of 23 September 1954, Noel Field material, Hungarian Historical Institute Archive, quoted in Mária Schmidt, *Battle of Wits—Beliefs, Ideologies and Secret Agents in the 20th Century* (Budapest: XX. Század Intézet, 2007), 119–20; Mária Schmidt, "Noel Field—The American Communist at the Center of Stalin's East European Purge: From the Hungarian Archives," *American Communist History* 3, no. 2 (December 2004): 231.

63. Moscow Center to "Jung," 11 September 1937, KGB file 36857, v.1, p. 87, Vassiliev, *Yellow #2*, 18.

64. Poretsky, *Our Own People*; "Sergey," "Work in illegal conditions," circa 1944, KGB file 35112, v.8, p. 233, Vassiliev, *White #1*, 61; *Les crimes du Guépéou: Documents sur les assassinats d'Ignace Reiss et de Rudolf Klement* (Paris: Centre d'études et de recherches sur les mouvements trotskyste et révolutionnaires internationaux,

1985); Moscow Center to "Jung," 11 September 1937, KGB file 36857, v.1, pp. 87–88, Vassiliev, *Yellow* #2, 18–19.

65. "June" to Moscow Center, 25 September 1937, KGB file 36857, v.1, pp. 90–93, Vassiliev, *Yellow* #2, 19–20.

66. Moscow Center to "Jung," 23 October 1937, KGB file 36857, v.1, p. 97, Vassiliev, *Yellow* #2, 21.

67. "Jung" to Moscow Center, 9 November 1937, KGB file 36857, v.1, p. 99, Vassiliev, *Yellow* #2, 21. Technically, Lowry was Browder's half-niece, the daughter of Bessie Browder Lowry, his half-sister.

68. "Jung" report, 2 December 1937; "Jung" report, 7 January 1938; "Jung" report on Duggan meeting, 3 January 1938, KGB file 36857, v.1, pp. 100–102, Vassiliev, *Yellow* #2, 21.

69. "Jung" to Moscow Center, 7 March 1938, KGB file 36857, v.1, pp. 108–9, Vassiliev, *Yellow* #2, 22–23.

70. "Jung" to Moscow Center, 28 June 1938; "Jung did not meet," KGB file 36857, v.1, pp. 114, 116, Vassiliev, *Yellow* #2, 23. Additional reports about material Duggan delivered in 1938 and 1939 in Vassiliev, *Yellow* #2, 23–25.

71. "Jung" to Moscow Center, 5 October 1939, KGB file 36857, v.1, p. 152, Vassiliev, *Yellow* #2, 25. Adolf Berle, "Underground Espionage Agent [Transcription of Berle's notes of 2 September 1939 interview with Whittaker Chambers]," in U.S. Senate Internal Security Subcommittee, *Interlocking Subversion in Government Departments [Hearings]* (Washington, D.C.: U.S. Govt. Print. Off., 1953), part 6, pp. 329–30. The other six were Alger and Donald Hiss, Julian Wadleigh, Noel Field (who by that time had left DOS for the League of Nations), Leander Lovell, and Richard Post. Adolf Augustus Berle, *Navigating the Rapids, 1918–1971: From the Papers of Adolf A. Berle,* ed. Beatrice Bishop Berle and Travis Beal Jacobs (New York: Harcourt Brace Jovanovich, 1973), 249–50.

72. "Jung" to Moscow Center, 5 October 1939, KGB file 36857, v.1, pp. 156–58, Vassiliev, *Yellow* #2, 25–26; Moscow Center to Gennady, 9 November 1939, KGB file 35112, v.5a, pp. 395–96, Vassiliev, *Black,* 161.

73. Moscow Center to KGB New York, 11 April 1940; "Jung" to Moscow Center, 1 December 1938, KGB file 36857, v.1, pp. 134, 161, Vassiliev, *Yellow* #2, 24, 26.

74. "Glan called 19," 21 October 1940; "He called again," 4 November 1940; "Information (evidently November 1940) from a report from Center," KGB file 36857, v.1, pp. 167–68, Vassiliev, *Yellow* #2, 27. "Hull Aide Stresses Hemisphere Unity," *New York Times,* 3 November 1940.

75. Report by "Glan," November 1940, KGB file 36857, v.1, pp. 170–78, Vassiliev, *Yellow* #2, 27–28.

76. Moscow Center to "Maxim," 27 November 1941; Moscow Center to "Maxim," 10 January 1942, KGB file 35112, v.6, pp. 10, 95–96, Vassiliev, *White* #1, 31–33.

77. KGB New York to Moscow Center, 25 February 1942; "Mer" to Moscow Center, 17 November 1942, KGB file 36857, v.1, pp. 185, 193, Vassiliev, *Yellow* #2, 28–29. "Polit. and dip. line of work (Plan)," 6 April 1942, KGB file 43173, v.1, p. 8a, Vassiliev, *Black,* 43. "Mer's letters to C. through Zarubin," 29 July 1942, KGB file 35112, v.7, p. 106, Vassiliev, *White* #1, 45.

78. Moscow Center to "Mer," 26 November 1942; "'Granite's' letter to 19," 25 November 1942; "Mer" to Moscow Center, 2 February 1943; "Mer" to Moscow Center, 4 February 1943; "Report on 19," KGB file 36857, v.1, pp. 196a–198, 200–205, 219–22, Vassiliev, *Yellow #2*, 29–33.

79. Venona 1025, 1035–36, KGB New York to Moscow, 30 June 1943; Venona 380 KGB New York to Moscow, 20 March 1944; Venona 744 and 746 KGB New York to Moscow, 24 May 1944; Venona 916 KGB New York to Moscow, 17 June 1944. Zarubin to Merkulov, "Memorandum (on the station's work in the country)," 30 September 1944, KGB file 35112, v.1, pp. 418–19, Vassiliev, *White #1*, 13.

80. "Albert" to Moscow Center, 10 July 1944, KGB file 36857, v.1, p. 229, Vassiliev, *Yellow #2*, 34. Venona 1015 KGB New York to Moscow, 22 July 1944; Venona 1613 KGB New York to Moscow, 18 November 1944; Venona 1636 KGB New York to Moscow, 21 November 1944. "Report on 'Prince' (a.k.a. 19)," 7 May 1948, KGB file 43173, v.5, p. 267, Vassiliev, *Black*, 88.

81. "Report by 'Granite,'" 8 March 1948, KGB file 36857, v.1, p. 262, Vassiliev, *Yellow #2*, 35.

82. Moscow Center to "Vladimir," 7 May 1948, KGB file 36857, v.1, pp. 263–64, Vassiliev, *Yellow #2*, 36. The phrase "not to reveal our worker's identity" does not mean that Striganov was not to use his name but that he should take care not to reveal his identity *as a KGB agent*.

83. Report by "Saushkin," July 1948; KGB Washington to Moscow Center, 25 November 1948; "'Saushkin' called Pr.," 15 December 1948, KGB file 36857, v.1, pp. 271–72, 282, 284, Vassiliev, *Yellow #2*, 36–37.

84. Massing, *This Deception*. FBI interview with Hede Massing, 7–8 December 1948; Letter to Director, 9 February 1949, no serial, in Tanenhaus, *Whittaker Chambers*, 578n.

85. John Danahy and William McCarthy, 10 December 1948 interview with Laurence Duggan, "Re: Laurence Duggan," FBI file 65–14920, no serial; Whittaker Chambers testimony, 28 December 1948, U.S. House Committee on Un-American Activities, unpublished executive session testimony; Weinstein, *Perjury*, 22, 175; Tanenhaus, *Whittaker Chambers*, 334.

86. "Vladimir" to Moscow Center, 25 December 1948, KGB file 43173, v.4, pp. 477–78, Vassiliev, *Black*, 72.

87. "Excerpt from a report by 'Madchen' (Burgess)," January 1937; Excerpt to "Madchen's" report from a letter from "Man," 29 January 1937; "Madchen's" report in "Man" to Moscow Center, 16 February 1937, KGB file 58380, v.1, pp. 12, 13, 14, Vassiliev, *White #3*, 81.

88. "Madchen's" report in "Man" to Moscow Center, 16 February 1937; "In April 1937, N. gave us a report," KGB file 58380, v.1, p. 17, Vassiliev, *White #3*, 111–12.

89. "In April 1937, N. gave us a report," KGB file 58380, v.1, pp. 27–32, Vassiliev, *White #3*, 112.

90. "Stephan" on "Nigel," 9 July 1937; "Stephan" report, KGB file 58380, v.1, pp. 33–34, 39, Vassiliev, *White #3*, 114.

91. Moscow Center to "Jung," 11 September 1937; Moscow Center to "Jung," 23

October 1937; "Jung" to Moscow Center, 13 November 1937; Moscow Center to "Jung," circa November 1937; "Jung" to Moscow Center, 9 November 1937, KGB file 58380, v.1, pp. 40, 43–46, Vassiliev, *White #3*, 115.

92. "Jung" to Moscow Center, 9 November 1937; Moscow Center to "Jung," circa November 1937; "$2,000 were," KGB file 58380, v.1, pp. 46–49, Vassiliev, *White #3*, 115–16.

93. Michael Whitney Straight, *After Long Silence* (New York: W. W. Norton, 1983).

94. Report on Straight with Moscow Center annotation, 18 February 1938; "Jung" to Moscow Center, 25 January 1938; "Jung" to Moscow Center, 28 June 1938; "Jung" to Moscow Center, 28 February 1938, KGB file 58380, v.1, pp. 51–53, 73–74, Vassiliev, *White #3*, 116, 118.

95. "Jung" to Moscow Center, 25 January 1938; Moscow Center to "Jung," 26 March 1938; Moscow Center to "Jung," 22 April 1938; "Jung" to Moscow Center, 6 April 1938; "Jung" to Moscow Center, 28 June 1938, KGB file 58380, v.1, pp. 53, 59–62, 73, Vassiliev, *White #3*, 116–18.

96. "Jung" to Moscow Center, 24 May 1938; "Jung" to Moscow Center, July 1938; "N. often meets with Yost"; "Jung" to Moscow Center, October 1938; "Jung" to Moscow Center, 1 December 1938; "Jung" to Moscow Center, 1 March 1939; Moscow Center to "Jung," 29 March 1939; Moscow Center to "Jung," 15 November 1938, KGB file 58380, v.1, pp. 67–68, 71, 81, 86–87, 92–94, 96–97, 113, 117–22, Vassiliev, *White #3*, 118–20.

97. "Jung" report, 8 September 1939; "Jung" letter, 5 October 1939; "Jung" to Moscow Center, 25 October 1939; "Stopped receiving"; "'Chap' met with N.," 15 July 1941, KGB file 58380, v.1, pp. 142–44, 146–48, 165–67, Vassiliev, *White #3*, 120–22. Moscow Center to Gennady, 9 November 1939, KGB file 35112, v.5a, p. 395, Vassiliev, *Black*, 161.

98. Moscow Center to "Maxim," 27 November 1941; Moscow Center to "Maxim," 10 January 1942, KGB file 35112, v.6, pp. 10, 94–95, Vassiliev, *White #1*, 30–32.

99. "Mer's" letters to Moscow Center, 1942, KGB file 35112, v.7, pp. 106, 110, 112, Vassiliev, *White #1*, 45, 47–48.

100. Zarubin to Merkulov, "Memorandum (on the station's work in the country)," 30 September 1944, KGB file 35112, v.1, p. 418, Vassiliev, *White #1*, 13.

101. "Work with him," KGB file 43173, v.5, p. 68, Vassiliev, *Black*, 85; "The magazine," circa 1948, KGB file 14449, v.2, p. 50, Vassiliev, *White #2*, 70.

102. John Earl Haynes, "Speak No Evil, Michael Straight: *After Long Silence*," *Chronicles of Culture* 7, no. 11 (1983).

103. Roland Perry, *Last of the Cold War Spies: The Life of Michael Straight—The Only American in Britain's Cambridge Spy Ring* (Cambridge, MA: Da Capo Press, 2005), makes the claim that Straight's espionage career extended into the 1970s. There is not only nothing in Vassiliev's notebooks that supports this thesis, but also the documents cited directly refute it.

104. KGB New York to Moscow Center, 19 April 1940, KGB file 35112, v.5a, p. 512, Vassiliev, *Black*, 164.

105. Conroy to Headquarters, 16 November 1945, serial 26; memo on Robert Miller, 26 December 1945, serial 356, FBI Silvermaster file 65–56402.

106. Fahy and Gregg's espionage activities are discussed in John Earl Haynes and Harvey Klehr, *Venona: Decoding Soviet Espionage in America* (New Haven: Yale University Press, 1999), 111, 113–14, 186–88, 207.

107. Bentley, Deposition 1945, 16–17, 45–46. Ladd to Director, 14 November 1945, serial 21; FBI memo, 26 December 1945, serial 356; Ladd to Director, "Underground Soviet Espionage Organization (NKVD) in Agencies of the United States Government," 21 February 1946, serial 573; summary memo to Ladd, 21 February 1946, serial 999x; Scheidt to Director, 31 January 1947, serial 1976; Bentley interview, 10 March 1947, serial 2154; FBI Washington Field Office report, 21 April 1947, serial 2349; FBI Washington Field Office to Director, 21 April 1947, serial 2436; Hottel to Director, 28 February 1947, serial 2437; FBI memo on Robert Talbott Miller, III, 24 January 1948, serial 3085, FBI Silvermaster file 65–56402.

108. A. Gorsky, "Failures in the USA (1938–48)," December 1948, KGB file 43173, v.2c, p. 53, Vassiliev, *Black*, 79. KGB New York to Moscow Center, 5 November 1941, KGB file 35112, v.4a. p. 645, Vassiliev, *White #1*, 27. "M.'s contacts; list obtained by Vadim in Oct. '44," KGB file 70545, p. 143; "List of M.'s contacts (prepared by her, 25.1.45)," KGB file 70545, p. 303, Vassiliev, *White #2*, 9, 19. Venona 842 KGB New York to Moscow, 3 June 1943; Venona 1179 KGB New York to Moscow, 20 July 1943; Venona 1625 KGB New York to Moscow, 3 October 1943; Venona 1681 KGB New York to Moscow, 13 October 1943. In Haynes and Klehr, *Venona* (2000), we suggested Charles Page as a possibility for "Mirage," but Vassiliev's notebooks establish "Mirage" as Miller.

109. Martin Dies statement, *Congressional Record*, 1 February 1943, 504–16; FBI memo, 17 June 1946, serial 1364, FBI Silvermaster file 65–56402.

110. *Daily Worker*, 17 October 1938. Hottel to Director, 28 February 1947, serial 2437; Memo on Fahy, 17 April 1946, serial 1364, FBI Silvermaster file 65–56402. Jack Fahy testimony, 8 April 1943, U.S. House Special Committee on Un-American Activities, *Investigation of Un-American Propaganda Activities in the United States* (Washington, D.C.: U.S. Govt. Print. Off., 1940–44), v.7, 3453–65; Kerr Commission report, 14 May 1943, box 856, Clinton Anderson Papers, Library of Congress. Venona 115 Naval GRU Moscow to Washington, 20 January 1943; Venona 360 Naval GRU Moscow to Washington, 26 February 1943; Venona 366 Naval GRU Moscow to Washington, 28 February 1943; Venona 849 Naval GRU Washington to Moscow, 20 April 1943; Venona 901 Naval GRU Washington to Moscow, 27 April 1943; Venona 393 Naval GRU Moscow to Washington, 5 March 1943; Venona 427 Naval GRU Moscow to Washington, 11 March 1943.

111. FBI Washington Field Office report, Memo on Joseph Gregg, 11 March 1946, serial 674, FBI Silvermaster file 65–56402.

112. Bentley, Deposition 1945, 45–46.

113. "Mer" message, 12 April 1944, KGB file 70545, pp. 79–80, Vassiliev, *White #2*, 3. "Report by 'Vadim,' no date (excerpt) (evidently January 1945)," KGB file 45100, v.1, p. 73, Vassiliev, *White #3*, 74. Zarubin to Merkulov, "Memorandum (on

the station's work in the country)," 30 September 1944, KGB file 35112, v.1, p. 405, Vassiliev, *White #1*, 7. The blank in the quotation ""Gor" is Joseph . . ."" is in the original document. Leaving the family name blank was a common intelligence agency security practice to prevent typists from knowing a source's identity. The document author would then write in the name by hand on the copy sent to the intended recipient, but this was often not done on additional copies and file copies.

114. Bentley, Deposition 1945, 18–28, 34, 40, 45, 52, 56, 74–75, 80, 91, 94, 104–5. "Albert," "Information on Robert," 7 July 1945, KGB file 55298, pp. 253–54, Vassiliev, *White #3*, 22–23. "George Harrison" was actually Harrison George; reversing of his family and given names was a common error. For a listing of the numerous deciphered KGB cables regarding Silvermaster, see Appendix A, Haynes and Klehr, *Venona* (2000).

115. White is discussed in KGB documents found at Vassiliev, *White #1*, 5, 14, 26–27, 30, 34, 38, 43–44, 54–56, 65, 67–74, 154; Vassiliev, *White #2*, 31, 33; Vassiliev, *Yellow #4*, 123, 126, 128, 131; Vassiliev, *Black*, 77, 174–76.

116. Malcolm Hobbs, "Confident Wallace Aides Come Up with Startling Cabinet Notions," Overseas News Service dispatch, 22 April 1948, reprinted in U.S. Senate Internal Security Subcommittee, *Interlocking Subversion in Government Departments [Hearings]*, part 30, 2529–30.

117. Whittaker Chambers, *Witness* (New York: Random House, 1952), 429–30. Zarubin to Merkulov, "Memorandum (on the station's work in the country)," 30 September 1944, KGB file 35112, v.1, p. 401; Moscow Center to "Maxim," 26 November 1942, KGB file 35112, v.6, p. 314, Vassiliev, *White #1*, 5, 38.

118. "Maxim on Mer's first conversation with Pal," circa mid-1944, KGB file 35112, v.4, p. 148, Vassiliev, *White #3*, 16. Venona 1119–1121 KGB New York to Moscow, 4–5 August 1944. The "new course" referred to a policy of American accommodation of Soviet foreign policy goals. Venona 1388–1389 KGB New York to Moscow, 1 October 1944.

119. Venona 328 KGB Moscow to New York, 6 April 1945; Venona 230 KGB San Francisco to Moscow, 4 May 1945; Venona 235–236 KGB San Francisco to Moscow, 5 May 1945; Venona 259 KGB San Francisco to Moscow, 13 May 1945. Moscow Center to KGB New York, 29 May 1945, KGB file 35112, v.9, p. 200, Vassiliev, *White #1*, 65.

120. KGB New York to Moscow Center, 29 October 1945, KGB file 35112, v.9, p. 143, Vassiliev, *White #1*, 73.

121. Bentley, Deposition 1945, 20, 25–27, 55; Moscow Center to "Sergey," 23 November 1945, KGB file 70545, p. 407, Vassiliev, *White #2*, 31.

122. Testimony of Elizabeth Bentley, 31 July 1948; Testimony of Whittaker Chambers, 3 August 1948; Testimony of Harry Dexter White, 13 August 1948, U.S. House Committee on Un-American Activities, *Hearings Regarding Communist Espionage in the United States* (Washington, D.C.: U.S. Govt. Print. Off., 1948), 503–84, 877–906.

123. Berle, "Underground Espionage Agent"; Bentley, Deposition 1945, 20, 25, 43.

124. Lauchlin Currie interview, 31 July 1947, serial 2787, FBI Silvermaster file

65–56402; Lauchlin Currie testimony, 13 August 1948, U.S. House Committee on Un-American Activities, *Hearings Regarding Communist Espionage*, 851–77.

125. Robert Louis Benson and Cecil Philips, "History of Venona," unpublished classified manuscript (Fort George Meade, MD: National Security Agency, 1995), 37–38 (declassified).

126. Venona 928 KGB New York to Moscow, 30 June 1943; Venona 1317 KGB New York to Moscow, 10 August 1943; Venona 1431 KGB New York to Moscow, 2 September 1943; Venona 900 KGB New York to Moscow, 24 June 1944; Venona 1243 KGB New York to Moscow, 31 August 1944; Venona 1463, KGB New York to Moscow, 14 October 1944; Venona 1634 KGB New York to Moscow, 20 November 1944; Venona 143 KGB Moscow to New York, 15 February 1945; Venona 253 KGB Moscow to New York, 20 March 1945.

127. Zarubin to Merkulov, "Memorandum (on the station's work in the country)," 30 September 1944, KGB file 35112, v.1, p. 402, Vassiliev, *White #1*, 5–6.

128. Venona 1634 KGB New York to Moscow, 20 November 1944; Venona 143 KGB Moscow to New York, 15 February 1945; Venona 253 KGB Moscow to New York, 20 March 1945. Roger J. Sandilands, *The Life and Political Economy of Lauchlin Currie: New Dealer, Presidential Adviser, and Development Economist* (Durham, NC: Duke University Press, 1990); Roger J. Sandilands, "Guilt by Association? Lauchlin Currie's Alleged Involvement with Washington Economists in Soviet Espionage," *History of Political Economy* 32, no. 3 (2000): 474–515; James M. Boughton and Roger J. Sandilands, "Politics and the Attack on FDR's Economists: From the Grand Alliance to the Cold War," *Intelligence and National Security* 18, no. 3 (Autumn 2003). One of the deciphered cables, Venona 1463, had Currie meeting directly with the KGB illegal officer Iskhak Akhmerov, but inasmuch as Vassiliev's notebooks indicate that Akhmerov often presented himself as a covert American Communist linked to the KGB rather than a Soviet officer, Currie may not have known he was delivering information directly to a KGB operative rather than indirectly via the CPUSA.

129. Lauchlin Currie interview, 31 July 1947, serial 2787, FBI Silvermaster file 65–56402; Report on "L.C.," October 1945, KGB file 61512, v.2, p. 101, Vassiliev, *Yellow #2*, 58; "Expense account for Vadim," January 1945," KGB file 43173, v.1, p. 73, Vassiliev, *Black*, 49–50.

130. Butkov to Prudnikov, 11 April 1941, KGB file 35112, v.1, p. 87; "Polit. and dip. line of work (Plan)," 6 April 1942, KGB file 43173, v.1, p. 8, Vassiliev, *Black*, 43, 175. "Pal" report, 3 November 1941, KGB file 35112, v.4a, p. 637; Moscow Center to "Maxim," 27 November 1941; Moscow Center to "Maxim," 10 January 1942, KGB file 35112, v.6, pp. 8, 100, Vassiliev, *White #1*, 27, 30, 34.

131. N. Gregory Silvermaster, "Memorandum for General Strong," 9 June 1942; Report by "Sound," 23 June 1942, KGB file 55298, pp. 83–85, 369 (in the envelope), Vassiliev, *White #3*, 6–12. In testimony to the House Committee on Un-American Activities in 1948 Currie called his intervention "routine" and continued to insist he had no reason to doubt Silvermaster's denials of Communist links. Lauchlin Currie testimony, 13 August 1948, U.S. House Committee on Un-American Activities, *Hearings Regarding Communist Espionage*, 851–77; File card of Patterson contacts

in regard to Silvermaster, Box 203, Robert P. Patterson Papers, Library of Congress; General Bissell to General Strong, 3 June 1942; Silvermaster reply to Bissell memo, 9 June 1942; Robert P. Patterson to Milo Perkins of BEW, 3 July 1942–all reprinted in U.S. Senate Internal Security Subcommittee, *Interlocking Subversion,* part 30, pp. 2562–67. On Baldwin's secret Communist allegiances, see John Gates to Joseph Starobin, undated, Box 10, folder 2, Philip Jaffe Papers, Emory University, Atlanta, Georgia.

132. "Maxim" to Moscow Center, 1 September 1943; "Maxim" to Moscow Center, 9 October 1943, KGB file 35112, v.7, pp. 437, 471a, Vassiliev, *White #1,* 50, 52. Ladd to Director, 21 February 1946, serial 573; Silvermaster background memo, serial 464, FBI Silvermaster file 65–56402.

133. Moscow Center to KGB New York, 14 January 1945, KGB file 35112, v.9, p. 167, Vassiliev, *White #1,* 64; "Report on L. C.," October 1945, KGB file 61512, v.2, p. 101, Vassiliev, *Yellow #2,* 58.

134. Moscow Center to "Vadim," 23 November 1945, KGB file 70545, p. 405, Vassiliev, *White #2,* 30.

135. Report by "Ted" on Bela Gold, 15 March 1945, KGB file 40624, v.1, pp. 44–46, Vassiliev, *Yellow #2,* 63–64.

136. Ibid.; Zarubin to Merkulov, "Memorandum (on the station's work in the country)," 30 September 1944, KGB file 35112, v.1, pp. 402–3, Vassiliev, *White #1,* 6; Report on Silvermaster, 8 January 1946, KGB file 55298, p. 337, Vassiliev, *White #3,* 42.

137. Venona 918 KGB New York to Moscow, 28 June 1944; Venona 12–13–15–16 KGB New York to Moscow, 4 January 1945; Venona 18–19 KGB New York to Moscow, 4 January 1945; Venona 79 KGB New York to Moscow, 18 January 1945. Report on a meeting with "Aileron," 3 October 1945; Note by "Albert," 12 November 1945, KGB file 55298, pp. 298, 304–5, Vassiliev, *White #3,* 34, 37–38.

138. Bentley, Deposition 1945, 25, 27–28; Moscow Center to "Vadim," 23 November 1945, KGB file 70545, pp. 405–8, Vassiliev, *White #2,* 30–31. FBI Washington Field Office report, 21 April 1947, serial 2349; Branigan to Belmont, 19 August 1954, serial 4087, FBI Silvermaster file 65–56402. Testimony of Bela and Sonia Gold, 13 August 1948, U.S. House Committee on Un-American Activities, *Hearings Regarding Communist Espionage,* 906–15.

139. Bentley, Deposition 1945. On Taylor's charges and the FBI response, see FBI, "'Existing Corroboration of Bentley's Overall Testimony,' 6 May 1955," serial 4201, FBI Silvermaster file 65–56402, and Hayden B. Peake, "Afterword," in Elizabeth Bentley and Hayden B. Peake, *Out of Bondage: The Story of Elizabeth Bentley* (New York: Ivy Books, 1988). Moscow Center to KGB New York, 14 January 1945, KGB file 35112, v.9, p. 169, Vassiliev, *White #1,* 64; Report on Silvermaster, 8 January 1946, KGB file 55298, p. 337, Vassiliev, *White #3,* 42; A. Gorsky, "Failures in the USA (1938–48)," KGB file 43173, v.2c, pp. 51–54, Vassiliev, *Black,* 78–79; Zarubin to Merkulov, "Memorandum (on the station's work in the country)," 30 September 1944, KGB file 35112, v.1, pp. 381–445, Vassiliev, *White #1,* 1–15. For a summary of the Remington trials, see John Earl Haynes and Harvey Klehr, *Early Cold War Spies: The Espionage Trials That Shaped American Politics* (New York:

Cambridge University Press, 2006), 73–79, 90. Before the availability of the Vassiliev notebooks, Gary May, *Un-American Activities: The Trials of William Remington* (New York: Oxford University Press, 1994), suggested that Remington did give perjured testimony about his Communist links but was skeptical of his involvement in espionage.

140. Zarubin to Merkulov, "Memorandum (on the station's work in the country)," 30 September 1944, KGB file 35112, v.1, pp. 381–445, Vassiliev, *White #1*, 1–15.

141. On the Perlo group, see Bentley, Deposition 1945, 40, 51–57, 78–80, 105; Klehr, Haynes, and Firsov, *Secret World*, 312–15; Appendix A, Haynes and Klehr, *Venona* (2000).

142. "Biography of V. Perlo," via "Vadim," 29 December 1944, KGB file 45100, v.1, pp. 44–45, Vassiliev, *White #3*, 72–73.

143. Victor Perlo testimony, 9 August 1948, U.S. House Committee on Un-American Activities, *Hearings Regarding Communist Espionage*, 677–89, 693–701; Victor Perlo, "Imperialism—New Features," *Political Affairs*, May 1981, 3.

144. Klehr, Haynes, and Firsov, *Secret World*, 312–15; Bentley, Deposition 1945, 52, 55–57; Chambers, *Witness*, 430. Venona 1195 KGB New York to Moscow, 21 July 1943; Venona 1206 KGB New York to Moscow, 22 July 1943; Venona 588 KGB New York to Moscow, 29 April 1944; Venona 769 and 771 KGB New York to Moscow, 30 May 1944; Venona 79 KGB New York to Moscow, 18 January 1945; Venona 179–180 KGB Moscow to New York, 25 February 1945; Venona 1759 KGB Washington to Moscow, 28 March 1945; Venona 3598 KGB Washington to Moscow, 21 June 1945; Venona 3600 KGB Washington to Moscow, 21 June 1945; Venona 3645 KGB Washington to Moscow, 23 June 1945; Venona 3688 KGB Washington to Moscow, 28 June 1945.

145. "Ruble"/Harold Glasser's biography, circa December 1944; Faye Glasser biography, KGB file 43072, v.1, pp. 49–51, Vassiliev, *White #3*, 47–49. Vassiliev's notes indicate that Harold Glasser's original autobiography was handwritten in English and was located in KGB file 43072, v.1, at p. 53, but that his notes were taken from a Russian translation found at pp. 49–50.

146. "Ruble" biography, December 1944, KGB file 43072, v.1, p. 50, Vassiliev, *White #3*, 48–49. Transcripts of Glasser's promotions and job rating forms signed by Coe, Ullmann, and White, U.S. Senate Internal Security Subcommittee, *Interlocking Subversion*, part 2, 81–82, 98–99; Hottel to Hoover, 14 January 1947, serial 2028, FBI Silvermaster file 65–56402.

147. Report, 27 February 1943; "Mer" to "Maxim," 5 January 1944; "Vardo" report on "Ruble," 11 November 1944, KGB file 43072, v.1, pp. 11, 21, 36, Vassiliev, *White #3*, 44–45. Venona 1169 GRU New York to Moscow, 19 July 1943; Venona 1258–1259 GRU New York to Moscow, 31 July 1943; Venona 1350 GRU New York to Moscow, 17 August 1943.

148. Moscow Center to "Vadim," 16 December 1944; "Vadim" to Moscow Center, 24 December 1944; "Vadim" to Moscow Center, 31 December 1944, KGB file 43072, v.1, pp. 39, 54, 57–60, Vassiliev, *White #3*, 47, 49, 51–52.

149. "Albert" note, 16 January 1945, Moscow Center to "Vadim," 3 January 1945;

"Vadim" letter, 6 March 1945, KGB file 43072, v.1, pp. 62–63, 66, 76, Vassiliev, *White #3*, 52–53, 56.

150. "Ruble's" informational telegrams; "Vadim was informed," 27 April 1945; Moscow Center to "Vadim," 29 May 1945, KGB file 43072, v.1, pp. 84, 86, 134–54, Vassiliev, *White #3*, 57–58, 61–65. "To S, M, B—memorandum," 17 June 1945; "To S, M, B," 29 June 1945, KGB file 49701, v.1, pp. 54–67, Vassiliev, *Yellow #4*, 123. Moscow Center to "Vadim," 23 November 1945, KGB file 70545, p. 405, Vassiliev, *White #2*, 30.

151. Ladd to Director, 1 May 1947, serial 2380; FBI Washington Field Office to Director, Re: Harold Glasser, 13 May 1947, serial 2429, FBI Silvermaster file 65–56402.

152. Testimony of Harold Glasser, 14 April 1953, U.S. Senate Internal Security Subcommittee, *Interlocking Subversion,* part 2, 53–100; Testimony of Harold Glasser, 20 October 1953, U.S. Senate Committee on Government Operations, Permanent Subcommittee on Investigations, *Hearings, Transfer of Occupation Currency Plates—Espionage Phase, Part 1* (Washington, D.C.: U.S. Govt. Print. Off., 1953), 17.

153. Testimony of Charles Kramer, 6 May 1953, U.S. Senate Internal Security Subcommittee, *Interlocking Subversion,* part 6, 327–81; Patterson had been discreetly allied to the CPUSA since the late 1930s. Klehr, *Heyday,* 271–72, 403.

154. Nathaniel Weyl, *Encounters with Communism* (Philadelphia: Xlibris, 2004), 31; "Raid" report on "Mole," 23 February 1945, KGB file 55302, v.1, p. 24, Vassiliev, *White #3*, 86; Hope Hale Davis, *Great Day Coming: A Memoir of the 1930s* (South Royalton, VT: Steerforth Press, 1994), 68–74.

155. Berle, "Underground Espionage Agent"; Bentley, Deposition 1945, 51–52, 54, 56, 105; Hoover to George Allen, 31 May 1946, serial 1160; Ladd to Director, 5 September 1947, serial 2787, FBI Silvermaster file 65–56402; Testimony of Charles Kramer, 12 August 1948, U.S. House Committee on Un-American Activities, *Hearings Regarding Communist Espionage,* 818–35. Venona 588 KGB New York to Moscow, 29 April 1944; Venona 687 KGB New York to Moscow, 13 May 1944; Venona 1015 KGB New York to Moscow, 22 July 1944; Venona 1163 KGB New York to Moscow, 15 August 1944; Venona 3612 KGB Washington to Moscow, 22 June 1945; Venona 3640 KGB Washington to Moscow, 23 June 1945; Venona 3655 KGB Washington to Moscow, 25 June 1945; Venona 3706 KGB Washington to Moscow, 29 June 1945; Venona 3709 KGB Washington to Moscow, 29 June 1945; Venona 3710 KGB Washington to Moscow, 29 June 1945.

156. "Mer" memo, 29 April 1944; KGB New York to Moscow Center, 13 May 1944, KGB file 70545, pp. 83–84, Vassiliev, *White #2*, 4. Bentley, Deposition 1945, 51; Moscow Center to KGB New York, 1 June 1944; "Mole" autobiography, received 25 March 1945, KGB file 55302, v.1, pp. 14, 35–46, Vassiliev, *White #3*, 86, 88–90.

157. KGB Washington to Moscow Center, 10 April 1945; "Raid" report on meeting with "Mole," 14 April 1945; Moscow Center to KGB Washington, 14 April 1945; Moscow Center to KGB Washington, 8 May 1945, KGB file 55302, v.1, pp. 49–53, Vassiliev, *White #3*, 90–91.

158. "X" report on meeting with "Mole," 13 May 1945, KGB file 55302, v.1, pp. 55–60, Vassiliev, *White #3*, 91–93.

159. Fitin to Vyshinsky, "Background on the new U.S. secretary of state, Byrnes," 25 August 1945, KGB file 40935, v.1, pp. 158–65; "To S, M, B—memo from "Mole" on the activities of a group of liberal Democratic senators," 16 August 1945; "To S, M, B Memo re the domestic polit. situation in the U.S., prepared by 'Mole,'" 13 September 1945; "To S, M, B The domestic political situation in the U.S. from 'Mole,'" 21 September 1945, KGB file 49701, v.1, pp. 133–42, 228, 248, Vassiliev, *Yellow #4,* 40, 126–27, 130. "Bogdan" report on meeting with Kramer, 6 July 1945; "Vadim reported," 5 July 1945; Moscow Center to KGB Washington, 27 October 1945, KGB file 55302, v.1, pp. 74–75, 82, 84–85, 88, Vassiliev, *White #3,* 96, 98. Moscow Center to "Vadim," 23 November 1945, KGB file 70545, p. 405, Vassiliev, *White #2,* 30.

160. "Record of conversations between the 1st Secretary of the Soviet Embassy in Washington, M. S. Vavilov, and Kramer on 1 and 5 July 1947," KGB file 55302, v.1, pp. 103–14, Vassiliev, *White #3,* 99–101.

161. Moscow Center to "Grigory," 16 July 1947, KGB file 55302, v.1, p. 98, Vassiliev, *White #3,* 99. "Pepper Lauds Kramer's Work," *New York Times,* 13 August 1948. As Pepper feared, his reputation as pro-Soviet became an electoral liability. In 1950 he lost the Democratic primary for renomination to the Senate to George Smathers, a Cold War Democrat.

162. Note by "X," 11 January 1945; Report, 21 August 1950, KGB file 40623, v.1, pp. 22, 45, Vassiliev, *Yellow #2,* 66–67; Bentley, Deposition 1945, 51, 54, 56; Klehr, Haynes, and Firsov, *Secret World,* 312–15; Magdoff appeared in the Venona decryptions under his cover names "Kant" and "Tan," but FBI/NSA analysts were only able to identify "Kant" as Magdoff. Appendix A, Haynes and Klehr, *Venona* (2000).

163. "Report by "Ted," 17 February 1945; "List of materials from 'Ted,'" KGB file 40624, v.1, pp. 31, 36, 37, 50, Vassiliev, *Yellow #2,* 63, 65.

164. Report, 21 August 1950, KGB file 40624, v.1, p. 51, Vassiliev, *Yellow #2,* 64. Bentley, Deposition 1945, 51, 53–54, 56, 80; Appendix A, Haynes and Klehr, *Venona* (2000); Klehr, Haynes, and Firsov, *Secret World,* 312–15. Testimony of Edward J. Fitzgerald, 1 May 1953, U.S. Senate Internal Security Subcommittee, *Interlocking Subversion,* part 5, 241–86. U.S. v. Fitzgerald 235 F.2d 453 (2d cir.) *cert. denied* 352 U.S. 842 (1956).

165. On the "Brown scare" of the 1930s, see Leo Ribuffo, *The Old Christian Right: The Protestant Far Right from the Great Depression to the Cold War* (Philadelphia: Temple University Press, 1983), and chapter 2 of John Earl Haynes, *Red Scare or Red Menace?: American Communism and Anticommunism in the Cold War Era* (Chicago: Ivan R. Dee, 1996).

166. KGB New York to Moscow Center, 20 July 1937, KGB file 15428, pp. 54–65, Vassiliev, *White #2,* 82–85.

167. KGB New York to Moscow Center, with Slutsky annotation, 14 December 1937; KGB New York to Moscow Center, 25 May 1938, KGB file 15428, pp. 1–2, 9–13, Vassiliev, *White #2,* 83–85.

168. KGB New York to Moscow Center, 25 May 1938; "Gennady" to Moscow Center, 5 November 1939; Memo on "Crook," 13 August 1939, KGB file 15428, pp. 13–14, 122–26, 147, Vassiliev, *White #2,* 86, 97–99.

169. "Judith Coplon: The Spy Who Got Away with It," in Haynes and Klehr,

Early Cold War Spies, and Marcia Mitchell and Thomas Mitchell, *The Spy Who Seduced America: Lies and Betrayal in the Heat of the Cold War: The Judith Coplon
Story* (Montpelier, VT: Invisible Cities Press, 2002).

170. A number of deciphered KGB cables deal with Coplon and her recruitment. Venona 1014 KGB New York to Moscow, 20 July 1944; Venona 1050 KGB
New York to Moscow, 26 July 1944; Venona 1385 KGB New York to Moscow, 1 October 1944; Venona 1587 KGB New York to Moscow, 12 November 1944; Venona
1637 KGB New York to Moscow, to Victor, 21 November 1944; Venona 1714 KGB
New York to Moscow, 5 December 1944; Venona 1845 KGB New York to Moscow,
31 December 1944; Venona 27 KGB New York to Moscow, 8 January 1945; Venona
55 KGB New York to Moscow, 15 January 1945; Venona 76 KGB New York to
Moscow, 17 January 1945; Venona 992 KGB New York to Moscow, 26 June 1945;
Venona 1053 KGB New York to Moscow, 5 July 1945; Venona 268 KGB Moscow to
New York, 24 March 1945; Venona 284 and 286, KGB Moscow to New York, 28
March 1945.

171. "Sergey met with Sima," 4 January 1945; KGB New York to Moscow Center, 27 July 1945, KGB file 35112, v.9, pp. 5, 62–63, Vassiliev, *White #1,* 77–79.

172. KGB New York to Moscow Center, 1 March 1945; KGB New York to
Moscow Center, 17 October 1945, KGB file 35112, v.9, pp. 13, 131, 138, Vassiliev,
White #1, 66, 78–79. Memo on "Sound," KGB file 70994, pp. 37–38, Vassiliev, *White
#1,* 154. "Letter from 'Sergey,'" 9 October 1945, KGB file 55298, p. 291; KGB New
York to Moscow Center, 27 December 1948, KGB file 45100, v.1, p. 160, Vassiliev,
White #3, 33, 84. "Source—Sima," 26 October 1945, KGB file 82702, v.1, p. 320,
Vassiliev, *Yellow #1,* 24.

Chapter 5: Infiltration of the Office of Strategic Services

1. Henry Lewis Stimson and McGeorge Bundy, *On Active Service in Peace
and War* (New York: Harper, 1948), 188. In 1940 Stimson became secretary of war.
By that point he recognized that the world had changed and supported the Army's
increasingly effective code-breaking operations.

2. Robert Hayden Alcorn, *No Bugles for Spies: Tales of the OSS* (New York: D.
McKay, 1962), 134; John Earl Haynes and Harvey Klehr, *Venona: Decoding Soviet Espionage in America* (New Haven: Yale University Press [Nota Bene], 2000), 194.

3. When the KGB found out about the arrangement, via the Comintern, it ordered the CPUSA to shut down the effort, mistakenly fearing that Donovan might attempt to use the arrangement to develop sources in the Communist underground. Harvey Klehr, John Earl Haynes, and Fridrikh Igorevich Firsov, *The Secret World of
American Communism* (New Haven: Yale University Press, 1995), 260–80; John Earl
Haynes and Harvey Klehr, "The Myth of 'Premature Antifascism,'" *New Criterion* 21,
no. 1 (September 2002); Peter N. Carroll, *The Odyssey of the Abraham Lincoln Brigade:
Americans in the Spanish Civil War* (Stanford, CA: Stanford University Press, 1994),
254. There were other International Brigade veterans who served with the OSS, such
as Irving Fajans and Manuel Jiminez, but it is not clear they came via Wolff.

4. Zarubin to Merkulov, "Memorandum (on the station's work in the country),"

30 September 1944, KGB file 35112, v.1, p. 383, Alexander Vassiliev, *White Notebook #1 [2007 English Translation]*, trans. Steven Shabad (1993–96), 1.

5. Semenov to P. Fitin, 29 November 1944, KGB file 40129, v.3a, p. 215, Vassiliev, *White #1*, 113.

6. "Report on Americans," 27 September 1937, *RGASPI* 545–3–453. Pavel Fitin to Georgi Dimitrov, 23 February 1943; Dimitrov to Fitin, 27 March 1943, *RGASPI* 495–74–485.

7. Report, 9 February 1945, KGB file 40457, v.1, pp. 49–50; "List of OSS employees," circa September 1944, KGB file 40457, v.2, p. 16, Alexander Vassiliev, *White Notebook #3 [2007 English Translation]*, trans. Steven Shabad (1993–96), 106–7, 110. One KGB cable partially deciphered by the Venona project likely was about Goff. The June 1943 cable refers to a letter received by the wife of a KGB agent with a cover name Venona cryptanalysts could never decode and that was simply listed as "UCN/6" (unidentified cover name #6). In the portions of the cable cryptanalysts could read it appears that "UCN/6" was writing from Algeria and made a reference to Milton Felsen. Felsen was also an International Brigades veteran, Communist, and OSS officer. He had been part of Goff's OSS unit in North Africa, but by the time of the cable he had been wounded in combat and captured by German forces. Very likely "UCN/6" was "Tyazh"/Goff. Venona 884 New York KGB to Moscow, 8 June 1943.

8. On the OSS's investigation of Goff's use of OSS assets to assist Italian Communists, see Klehr, Haynes, and Firsov, *Secret World*, 279–80.

9. "Jung" to Moscow Center, 1 March 1939, KGB file 59264, v.1, p. 28a, Alexander Vassiliev, *Yellow Notebook #2 [2007 English Translation]*, trans. Philip Redko (1993–96), 72. Murray Illson, "8 Teachers Are out for Balking Query on Communist Ties," *New York Times*, 1 February 1952; Murray Illson, "7 Teachers Ousted at Stormy Session," *New York Times*, 9 January 1953.

10. "Brothers' Timing Varies but Result Is the Same," *New York Times*, 14 October 1952; "Lie Acts on 12 in U.N. Silent on Red Link," *New York Times*, 23 October 1952; Testimony of Stanley Graze, 13 October 1952, U.S. Senate Internal Security Subcommittee, *Activities of United States Citizens Employed by the United Nations* (Washington, D.C.: U.S. Govt. Print. Off., 1952), 52. Meeting, 10 August 1955, KGB file 61512, v.2, p. 46 (in envelope), Vassiliev, *Yellow #2*, 54.

11. "Mer" to Moscow Center, 7 June 1943; "Vadim" to Moscow Center, 20 March 1945, KGB file 61512, v.1, pp. 13–14, 40, Vassiliev, *Yellow #2*, 40, 44.

12. "Vadim" to Moscow Center, 6 August 1945, KGB file 61512, v.1, p. 19, Vassiliev, *Yellow #2*, 41.

13. "Vadim" to Moscow Center, 4 September 1945, KGB file 61512, v.1, p. 22, Vassiliev, *Yellow #2*, 41.

14. "Vadim" to Moscow Center, 4 September 1945; Report on the meeting with "Dan," 23 September 1945, KGB file 61512, v.1, pp. 22, 27–29, Vassiliev, *Yellow #2*, 41–43.

15. Reports on meetings on 23, 24, and 29 September, 3 and 10 October 1945; "Vadim" to Moscow Center, 29 October 1945, KGB file 61512, v.1, pp. 27, 32–48, Vassiliev, *Yellow #2*, 43–45.

16. Report on "Dan," 8 June 1948, KGB file 43173, v.6, pp. 73–83, Alexander Vassiliev, *Black Notebook [2007 English Translation]*, trans. Philip Redko (1993–96), 89–90. "In 1948, there"; Vladimirov report, November 1950; KGB New York to Moscow Center, 1 March 1951; "Jour" report on 20 and 26 February, 19 and 26 March 1951 meetings; Moscow Center to KGB New York, 13 June 1951; "Jour" report, 15 June 1951, KGB file 61512, v.1, pp. 51, 82–83, 99, 104, 106–8, 110, 123–25, Vassiliev, *Yellow #2*, 45–49.

17. KGB New York to Moscow Center, 7 October 1952; Report on "Dan," 30 July 1953, KGB file 61512, v.1, pp. 225, 291, Vassiliev, *Yellow #2*, 50–51.

18. Moscow Center to KGB New York, 2 April 1955; "'Alan's' account," 22 June 1955; meeting report, 10 August 1955, KGB file 61512, v.2, pp. 24, 33–39, 46 (in the envelope), Vassiliev, *Yellow #2*, 51–54.

19. Moscow Center to KGB New York, 16 November 1955, KGB file 61512, v.2, p. 61, Vassiliev, *Yellow #2*, 56.

20. "Draft of an appeal to the CC CPSU (April–May 1959)"; "At the end," KGB file 61512, v.2, pp. 97–98, 122–25, Vassiliev, *Yellow #2*, 57–59.

21. Robert A. Hutchison, *Vesco* (New York: Praeger, 1974), 247–49.

22. Ibid., 255–56, 260–61, 272, 280, 298.

23. Ibid., 310; Scott Schmedel, "SEC Files Against," *Wall Street Journal*, 28 November 1972; "Vesco Trial Witness," *Wall Street Journal*, 21 March 1973; "Vesco Is Indicted," *Wall Street Journal*, 15 January 1976.

24. "Malov" to Moscow Center, 3 October 1976, KGB file 61512, v.2, pp. 131–32, Vassiliev, *Yellow #2*, 59.

25. Moscow Center to KGB San Jose, 12 October 1976; KGB San Jose to Moscow Center, 18 October 1976; KGB San Jose to Moscow Center, 21 October 1976; KGB file 61512, v.2, pp. 134, 141–42, 144–45, Vassiliev, *Yellow #2*, 60.

26. "'Izra's' autobiography," 30 January 1945, KGB file 45049, v.2, pp. 33, Vassiliev, *White #3*, 129.

27. Ibid., pp. 33–40, Vassiliev, *White #3*, 129–30; *People's Weekly World*, 23 November 2002; FBI background memo on Donald Wheeler, serial 3291, FBI Silvermaster file 65–56402.

28. "'Izra's' autobiography," 30 January 1945, KGB file 45049, v.2, p. 37, Vassiliev, *White #3*, 130; Testimony of Emile Despres, 5 August 1948, U.S. House Committee on Un-American Activities, *Hearings Regarding Communist Espionage in the United States* (Washington, D.C.: U.S. Govt. Print. Off., 1948), 627; U.S. Senate Internal Security Subcommittee, *Interlocking Subversion in Government Departments [Hearings]* (Washington, D.C.: U.S. Govt. Print. Off., 1953), part 30, xxviii. Marzani transferred to the State Department after the OSS's dissolution. The government charged him with perjury for falsely signing a security form denying Communist allegiance. The Justice Department had evidence that he had worked as a CPUSA organizer under the name Tony Wales, and he was convicted and imprisoned in 1947. *The United States of America v. Carl Aldo Marzani, alias Tony Whales* [Transcript of proceedings, 12–22 May 1947, in the District Court of the United States for the District of Columbia, exhibits, briefs and papers]. After his jail term, Marzani headed a left-wing publishing house. A former KGB officer in 1994 identified Marzani as a

contact and recipient of KGB subsidies for his publishing house in the 1960s. Oleg Kalugin and Fen Montaigne, *The First Directorate* (New York: St. Martin's Press, 1994), 48–60.

29. KGB New York to Moscow Center, 8 May 1943; KGB New York to Moscow Center, 3 August 1943, KGB file 45049, v.1, pp. 9, 12, Vassiliev, *White #3*, 131; memo on Donald Wheeler, 12 July 1948, serial 3291, FBI Silvermaster file 65–56402.

30. "'Raid'—on 'Izra,'" circa 1945, KGB file 45049, v.2, p. 32, Vassiliev, *White #3*, 128. Elizabeth Bentley, FBI Deposition, 30 November 1945, serial 220, pp. 40, 53–57, 78–80, 105; FBI New York memo, 16 January 1947, serial 1936, FBI Silvermaster file 65–56402. Venona 588 KGB New York to Moscow, 29 April 1944; Venona 687 KGB New York to Moscow, 13 May 1944; Venona 769 and 771 KGB New York to Moscow, 30 May 1944. "Mer" to Moscow Center, 13 May 1944; "Mer" to Moscow Center, 30 May 1944, KGB file 4510, v.1, pp. 14, 17, Vassiliev, *White #3*, 68.

31. "'Raid'—on 'Izra,'" circa 1945, KGB file 45049, v.2, p. 32; Allakhverdov to Graur, circa mid-1944, KGB file 45049, v.2, p. 8; Moscow Center to KGB New York, 3 September 1944, KGB file 45049, v.1, p. 16; Moscow Center to "May," 1 June 1944, KGB file 45100, v.1, p. 18, Vassiliev, *White #3*, 68, 125, 128, 131. Bentley, Deposition 1945, 52, 54–55, 57. Venona 769 and 771 KGB New York to Moscow, 30 May 1944.

32. "Albert" to Moscow Center, 17 September 1944, KGB file 45049, v.1, p. 22; "Albert" to Moscow Center, 17 September 1944, KGB file 45100, v.1, p. 28, Vassiliev, *White #3*, 71, 131.

33. "'Raid'—on 'Izra,'" circa 1945, KGB file 45049, v.2, p. 32, Vassiliev, *White #3*, 128. George Wheeler later worked for the American military occupation government in Germany and was accused of attempting to manipulate occupation labor policies in the American zone to block unions aligned with the German Social Democratic Party and give preference to Communist-controlled labor formations. Paul R. Porter, "Conflict within American Military Government Concerning the Revival of German Trade Unions," unpublished essay, 15 November 1983, Paul R. Porter Papers, Harry Truman Presidential Library. George Wheeler later defected to Communist Czechoslovakia and became a propagandist authoring books and essays praising the Communist regimes of Eastern Europe and blaming the United States for the Cold War division of Germany and Europe.

34. Letter from "Albert," 21 September 1944, KGB file 40457, v.1, pp. 43–44; "List of OSS employees who allegedly," circa 1944, KGB file 40457, v.2, p. 16; "Koch" report, 12 September 1944, KGB file 45049, v.1, p. 18, Vassiliev, *White #3*, 106, 110, 131. Venona 1325–1326 KGB New York to Moscow, 15 September 1944; Venona 954 KGB Moscow to New York, 20 September 1944.

35. "Vadim" Report, 31 December 1944; List of "Ruble's" acquaintances, 5 January 1945, KGB file 43072, v.1, pp. 58, 133, Vassiliev, *White #3*, 51, 60. When Glasser supplied the KGB with a list of people he knew in the CPUSA underground previously but didn't see now, he included "Wheeler (2)," meaning that he had known both Donald and George Wheeler. Report by "X," 26 March 1945; Report by "Raid," 24 March 1945, KGB file 45100, v.1, pp. 104, 106, Vassiliev, *White #3*, 78, 80.

"Vadim" to Moscow Center, April 1945, KGB file 59264, v.1, p. 48, Vassiliev, *Yellow #2*, 74.

36. Moscow Center to KGB Washington, 28 March 1945, KGB file 45100, v.1, p. 109, Vassiliev, *White #3*, 80; Moscow Center to KGB Washington, 29 May 1945, KGB file 43173, v.2, pp. 60–61, 65, Vassiliev, *Black*, 66–67.

37. "Vadim" to Moscow Center (marked 27 April 1945 but may be in error because the text refers to events in May); Report by "Raid," 17 June 1945; KGB New York to Moscow Center, 13 July 1945, KGB file 45049, v.2, pp. 10–12 Vassiliev, *White #3*, 125–26. The spelling of Voosling's name has not been verified.

38. "Vadim" to Moscow Center, 1 September 1945, KGB file 45100, v.1, p. 67, Vassiliev, *White #3*, 132.

39. "Izra" report, "Prospects for the State Dep's Interim Intelligence Org.," 20 November 1945, KGB file 45049, v.2, p. 23, Vassiliev, *White #3*, 127. See multiple reports by Wheeler in Vassiliev, *White #3*, 127–28.

40. Kvasnikov to Graur, October 1946, KGB file 45049, v.2, p. 20, Vassiliev, *White #3*, 127.

41. Moscow Center to "Vadim," 21 October 1945, KGB file 43173, v.1, p. 162, Vassiliev, *Black*, 57. Moscow Center to "Vadim," 23 November 1945, KGB file 70545, p. 405, Alexander Vassiliev, *White Notebook #2 [2007 English Translation]*, trans. Steven Shabad (1993–96), 30. *People's Weekly World*, 23 November 2002. Wheeler's son Tim became an editor of the CPUSA's newspaper, the *People's Weekly World*.

42. Don S. Kirschner, *Cold War Exile: The Unclosed Case of Maurice Halperin* (Columbia: University of Missouri Press, 1995), 130–31, 314–16.

43. "Memorandum from Myrna re her contacts," November 1944, KGB file 70545, p. 143, Vassiliev, *White #2*, 9. Moscow Center to Maxim, 26 November 1942; Moscow Center to Maxim, 15 March 1943, KGB file 35112, v.6, pp. 313, 416–17, Vassiliev, *White #1*, 38, 40.

44. Venona 880 KGB New York to Moscow, 8 June 1943; Venona 887 KGB New York to Moscow, 9 June 1943; Venona 921, 922, 924 KGB New York to Moscow, 16 June 1943; Venona 931 KGB New York to Moscow, 17 June 1943; Venona 993 KGB New York to Moscow, 24 June 1943; Venona 1019, 1021, 1024, 1034 KGB New York to Moscow, 29 June 1943; Venona 1106 KGB New York to Moscow, 8 July 1943; Venona 1162 KGB New York to Moscow, 17 July 1943; Venona 1189 KGB New York to Moscow, 21 July 1943; Venona 206 KGB New York to Moscow, 10 February 1944; Venona 611 KGB New York to Moscow, 3 May 1944; Venona 694 KGB New York to Moscow, 16 May 1944; Venona 748 KGB New York to Moscow, 26 May 1944; Venona 993 KGB New York to Moscow, 13 July 1944; Venona 1214 KGB New York to Moscow, 25 August 1944; Venona 1325–1326 KGB New York to Moscow, 15 September 1944; Venona 1333 KGB New York to Moscow, 18 September 1944; Venona 1437 KGB New York to Moscow, 10 October 1944; Venona 1438 KGB New York to Moscow, 10 October 1944; Venona 1453 KGB New York to Moscow, 12 October 1944; Venona 1484 KGB New York to Moscow, 19 October 1944; Venona 954 KGB Moscow to New York, 20 September 1944.

45. "Maxim re Vardo's meeting with Helmsman," 19 December 1943, KGB file

70545, p. 69, Vassiliev, *White #2,* 2; "Report by 'Vadim,' no date (excerpt) (evidently, Jan. 1945)," KGB file 45100, v.1, p. 73, Vassiliev, *White #3,* 74; Zarubin to Merkulov, "Memorandum (on the station's work in the country)," 30 September 1944, KGB file 35112, v.1, p. 404, Vassiliev, *White #1,* 7. Other references to Halperin can be found in Vassiliev, *White #1,* 48–49; Vassiliev, *Black,* 65–66, 79, 92; Vassiliev, *White #2,* 9, 19, 33.

46. Moscow Center to "Vadim," 23 November 1945, KGB file 70545, p. 405; Korneev report, circa 1957, KGB file 14449, v.2, p. 175, Vassiliev, *White #2,* 30, 76. On Halperin's later life, see Kirschner, *Cold War Exile.*

47. Bentley, Deposition 1945, 34–36, 40, 52, 57, 78–80. Testimony of Duncan Lee, 10 August 1948, U.S. House Committee on Un-American Activities, *Hearings Regarding Communist Espionage,* 715–25, 733–59.

48. Duncan Lee interview report, 4 June 1947, serial 2530; Washington Field Office report, "Lieutenant Colonel Duncan C. Lee," 11 January 1946, serial 464; Washington Field Office report, "Re: Lt. Col. Duncan C. Lee," 28 January 1946, serial 466, FBI Silvermaster file 65–56402. Nor did Lee disclose that he and Ishbel Gibb, who became his wife, toured the Soviet Union in the mid-1930s. Ishbel Petri, *Not a Bowl of Cherries* (County Durham, U.K.: Petland Press [privately printed], 1997). Venona 782 KGB New York to Moscow, 26 May 1943; Venona 880 KGB New York to Moscow, 8 June 1943; Venona 887 KGB New York to Moscow, 9 June 1943; Venona 830 KGB New York to Moscow, 9 June 1944; Venona 1325–1326 KGB New York to Moscow, 15 September 1944; Venona 1354 KGB New York to Moscow, 22 September 1944 (does not mention Lee by name but is a follow-up to Venona 1325–1326); Venona 1353 KGB New York to Moscow, 23 September 1944; Venona 1437 KGB New York to Moscow, 10 October 1944; Venona 954 KGB Moscow to New York, 20 September 1944.

49. "Biography of 'Koch,' received from 'Sound,'" 8 September 1942; "Koch" report, 24 November 1943; "Koch" report, 26 June 1944; "INFO assessed," KGB file 40457, v.1, pp. 7, 26, 34, 49, and "Koch" report, 24 January 1944, KGB file 40457, v.2, p. 8, Vassiliev, *White #3,* 102, 104, 106, 109.

50. Bentley, Deposition 1945, 34–36. Chugunov report, 9 February 1945; "Vadim" to Moscow Center, 20 March 1945; "Center asked," 7 April 1945; "K. was," 23 November 1945, KGB file 40457, v.1, pp. 50, 54–55, 57–58, Vassiliev, *White #3,* 107–9.

51. It is unclear if "Mary" was a joint cover name for Paul and Hede Massing or only one of them. Venona 846 KGB New York to Moscow, 3 June 1943; Venona 854 KGB New York to Moscow, 5 June 1943; Venona 880 KGB New York to Moscow, 8 June 1943; Venona 917 KGB New York to Moscow, 15 June 1943. There is also a "Ruff" in a 1945 KGB message, but that is clearly a different person from "Ruff" of 1943. Venona 876 KGB New York to Moscow, 6 June 1945. Report on "Ruff," circa 1942; "Report by 'Mary,'" August 1942, KGB file 28734, v.1, pp. 7–8, Vassiliev, *White #3,* 133.

52. KGB New York to Moscow Center, 3 April 1943, KGB file 28734, v.1, p. 15, Vassiliev, *White #3,* 134.

53. "R. does," circa late 1943; "Information based on a report by 'Mary,'" 6 Jan-

uary 1944; "Maxim" report based on "Mary's" report of 13 June 1944," KGB file 28734, v.1, pp. 16, 20, 23, Vassiliev, *White #3*, 134–36.

54. Report, 17 July 1944; Report, 4 April 1945, KGB file 28734, v.1, pp. 24, 27, Vassiliev, *White #3*, 136.

55. Bentley, Deposition 1945, 38–41, 71, 79, 80, 84. Entries regarding "Muse"/Tenney can be found at Vassiliev, *Black*, 51, 67, 79; Vassiliev, *Yellow #2*, 78; Vassiliev, *White #1*, 7, 58, 132; Vassiliev, *White #3*, 74, 80; Vassiliev, *White #2*, 9, 19, 30, 32–33; Alexander Vassiliev, *Yellow Notebook #4 [2007 English Translation]*, trans. Steven Shabad (1993–96), 39. Venona 756 KGB New York to Moscow, 27 May 1944; Venona 769 and 771 KGB New York to Moscow, 30 May 1944; Venona 940 KGB New York to Moscow, 4 July 1944; Venona 1118 KGB New York to Moscow, 4 August 1944; Venona 1352 KGB New York to Moscow, 23 September 1944. On Tenney's espionage career, see Haynes and Klehr, *Venona* (2000), 111–13, 396n5.

56. "Vadim" to Moscow Center, 3 December 1945, KGB file 70545, pp. 432–33, Vassiliev, *White #2*, 32–33.

57. Strickland memo on Tenney, 6 June 1946, serial 1195; Ladd to Director, 15 January 1947, serial 2081; Scheidt to Hoover, 12 February 1947, serial 2407; Ladd to Hoover, 6 June 1947, serial 2547, FBI Silvermaster file 65–56402. Elizabeth Bentley and Hayden B. Peake, *Out of Bondage: The Story of Elizabeth Bentley* (New York: Ivy Books, 1988), 209–10. Testimony of Helen Tenney, 16 June 1953, U.S. Senate Internal Security Subcommittee, *Interlocking Subversion*, part 12, 772–86.

58. "Glan" to Moscow Center, 7 August 1941, KGB file 35112, v.4a, pp. 549–50, Vassiliev, *White #1*, 25.

59. "Maxim" to Moscow Center, 14 April 1943; "Maxim" to Moscow Center, 23 December 1943, KGB file 35112, v.7, pp. 308, 498, Vassiliev, *White #1*, 50–53.

60. "Maxim" to Moscow Center, 3 August 1943, KGB file 35112, v.7, p. 419, Vassiliev, *White #1*, 50; "Myrna" contact list, October 1944, KGB file 70545, p. 143, Vassiliev, *White #2*, 9.

61. Bentley, Deposition 1945, 30–32, 79–80, 84. Venona 880 KGB New York to Moscow, 8 June 1943; Venona 1464 KGB New York to Moscow, 14 October 1944; Venona 1454 KGB New York to Moscow, 13 October 1944.

62. Julius Joseph testimony, 26 May 1953, U.S. Senate Internal Security Subcommittee, *Interlocking Subversion*, part 10, 615.

63. Venona 325 KGB Moscow to New York, 17 May 1942; Venona 726–729 New York to Moscow, 22 May 1942; Venona 1234 New York to Moscow, 29 August 1944.

64. Excerpts from Mary Jane Keeney's diary and from the Keeneys' correspondence, serials 1938 and 2661, FBI Silvermaster file 65–56402. One factor identifying Kurnakov as Thomas was that the diary records Colonel Thomas leaving the United States to return to his homeland at the same time that Kurnakov returned to the Soviet Union. The FBI also photographed a handwritten note from Thomas indicating that around 10 January 1946 he would be going home. Kurnakov left the United States in January 1946.

65. Venona 82 KGB New York to Moscow, 18 January 1945.

66. Excerpts from Mary Jane Keeney's diary and from the Keeneys' correspondence, serials 1938 and 2661, FBI Silvermaster file 65–56402.

67. Ibid.

68. Ibid.

69. "Grigory" to Moscow Center, 1 July 1947, KGB file 43173, v.2, p. 176; Letter to Moscow Center, 19 August 1948, KGB file 43173, v.4, pp. 370–71, Vassiliev, *Black*, 62, 71.

70. Background memoranda of Philip and Mary Jane Keeney, serial 2127, FBI Silvermaster file 65–56402; U.S. House Committee on Un-American Activities, *Testimony of Philip O. Keeney and Mary Jane Keeney and Statement Regarding Their Background: Hearings* (Washington, D.C.: U.S. Govt. Print. Off., 1949), 221–77; Arthur Edson, "Ex-U.S. Aide Tells," *Washington Post*, 10 June 1949; John Fisher, "Reveal Ex-Aid Tried," *Chicago Tribune*, 10 June 1949.

71. "Grigory" to Moscow Center, 1 July 1947, KGB file 43173, v.2, p. 176; Letter of Moscow Center, 19 August 1948, KGB file 43173, v.4, pp. 370–71, Vassiliev, *Black*, 62, 71; Background memoranda of Philip and Mary Jane Keeney, serial 2127, FBI Silvermaster file 65–56402; "Lie Won't Rehire," *New York Times*, 26 September 1951; Testimony of Mary Jane Keeney, 18 February 1952, U.S. Senate Committee on the Judiciary, *Institute of Pacific Relations* (Washington, D.C.: U.S. Govt. Print. Off., 1951–52), part 8, 2773–2380; "List of Accused U.S. Employees on U.N. Payroll," *Chicago Tribune*, 2 June 1953; "Ex-Aide of U.S.," *New York Times*, 18 March 1953; "Mrs. Keeney Freed," *New York Times*, 5 April 1955. The authors thank Louise S. Robbins for generously sharing her background material on the Keeneys.

72. Zarubin to Merkulov, "Memorandum (on the station's work in the country)," 30 September 1944, KGB file 35112, v.1, p. 396, Vassiliev, *White #1*, 3; Memo, 26 July 1957, KGB file 14449, v.2, p. 346, Vassiliev, *White #2*, 80; KGB Vienna to Moscow Center, 18 April 1953, KGB file 30595, v.4, p. 199, Alexander Vassiliev, *Yellow Notebook #3 [2007 English Translation]*, trans. Philip Redko (1993–96), 94. Venona 854 KGB New York to Moscow, 16 June 1942; Venona 958 KGB New York to Moscow, 21 June 1943; Venona 1025, 1035–1936 KGB New York to Moscow, 30 June 1943; Venona 769 and 771 KGB New York to Moscow, 30 May 1944. Foster's espionage career is discussed in John Earl Haynes and Harvey Klehr, *Venona: Decoding Soviet Espionage in America* (New Haven: Yale University Press, 1999), 119, 272–73.

73. Jane Foster, *An Unamerican Lady* (London: Sidgwick and Jackson, 1980).

74. Zarubin to Merkulov, "Memorandum (on the station's work in the country)," 30 September 1944, KGB file 35112, v.1, p. 383, Vassiliev, *White #1*, 1; "Vadim" to Moscow Center, 1 September 1945, KGB file 45100, v.1, p. 67, Vassiliev, *White #3*, 132. Venona 1397 KGB New York to Moscow, 4 October 1944; Venona 726–729 New York to Moscow, 22 May 1942. Venona 387 New York to Moscow, 12 June 1942, deals with Scott but is badly garbled. On Scott's background and Communist ties, see Haynes and Klehr, *Venona* (2000), 194–95.

75. Haynes and Klehr, *Venona* (2000), 181–83, 192–94. Examples of Communists who passed beyond Donovan's willingness to tolerate included Leonard Mins

and Stephen Dedijer, fired for displaying excessive Communist partisanship. Mins was, in fact, a GRU source. The plans for a formal OSS-KGB relationship are discussed and citations from the notebooks are provided in Allen Weinstein and Alexander Vassiliev, *The Haunted Wood: Soviet Espionage in America—The Stalin Era* (New York: Random House, 1999), 238–48.

Chapter 6: The XY Line

1. "On the tasks of the USA station," April 1934, KGB file 17407, v.1, pp. 75–76; Prudnikov, "Report on intelligence in the USA," 12 April 1941, KGB file 35112, v.1, pp. 68–69; "XY network," 1 May 1943, KGB file 40594, v.6, p. 134, Alexander Vassiliev, *Black Notebook [2007 English Translation]*, trans. Philip Redko (1993–96), 4, 117, 172–73.

2. "May" to Moscow Center, 2 September 1944, KGB file 35112, v.2, p. 54, Alexander Vassiliev, *White Notebook #1 [2007 English Translation]*, trans. Steven Shabad (1993–96), 55; "Agent network," 1 February 1945, KGB file 40594, v.7, pp. 17–18, Vassiliev, *Black,* 119. Emphasis in the original. Venona 863 KGB New York to Moscow, 16 June 1944; Venona 1251 KGB New York to Moscow, 2 September 1944; Venona 1657 KGB New York to Moscow, 27 November 1944; Venona 200 Moscow to KGB New York, 6 March 1945; Venona 325 Moscow to KGB New York, 5 April 1945. Steven Usdin in 2005 suggested Sussman as a candidate for "Nil." Steven Usdin, *Engineering Communism* (New Haven: Yale University Press, 2005), 296.

3. John J. O'Conner, "TV: 'Rosenberg-Sobell Revisited' Offers New Thinking on Spy Case," *New York Times,* 19 June 1978; Morton Sobell, *On Doing Time* (San Francisco: Golden Gate National Parks Association, 2001).

4. "Agent network," 1 February 1945, KGB file 40594, v.7, p. 23, Vassiliev, *Black,* 120. Other references to Sobell's espionage are found at: Moscow Center to "Anton," 14 January 1945; Moscow Center ("Victor") to "Anton," 23 February 1945, KGB file 40159, v.3, pp. 461, 473, Vassiliev, *Black,* 113, 132. Moscow Center to KGB New York, 12 March 1948; Moscow Center to "Uglov," 8 June 1948, KGB file 40159, v.5, pp. 50–51, 147, Vassiliev, *Black,* 127–28. "Agent network," 1 February 1945; "Grouping of probationers as of March 1945"; "Callistratus" report on a meeting with "Meter," KGB file 40594, v.7, pp. 14–15, 97–98, 353, Vassiliev, *Black,* 119, 125, 135–36. Semenov to Fitin, 29 November 1944; "Memo to Fitin for period from 1.01 through 13.02.45," KGB file 40129, v.3a, pp. 205, 350, 354, Vassiliev, *White #1,* 110–11, 116. Venona 976 KGB New York to Moscow, 11 July 1944, mentioned a Soviet source with the cover name "Relay," and here the NSA/FBI footnote said, "Possibly Morton Sobell." But this tentative identification was withdrawn in Venona 1251 KGB New York to Moscow, 2 September 1944, which stated that "Relay's" cover name had been changed to "Serb," with the NSA/FBI footnote stating, "RELAY has been tentatively identified as Morton Sobell. However, the only other reference to SERB is in New York's no. 50 of 11 January 1945 and would not appear to refer to Sobell." In this latter message "Serb" was designated as unidentified by NSA/FBI analysts. One other message dealt with "Relay"/"Serb": Venona 943 KGB New York to Moscow,

4 July 1944, mentioned "Relay," and the NSA/FBI footnote has "Relay" as unidentified. This message noted that "Relay" had an artificial leg. In a theatrical display, Sobell ignored the NSA's withdrawal of the tentative identification of "Relay" as Sobell and pretended that he had been identified as "Relay" by NSA/FBI analysts. At a public conference he pulled up his pants to demonstrate that he did not have an artificial leg and pronounced this proof that no identification in Venona could be trusted. The reasonable way to consider the identification of "Relay"/"Serb" is to look at all four messages, not just one. NSA/FBI analysts had "Relay" or "Serb" unidentified in two messages, had a third in which "Relay" was "possibly Morton Sobell," but then had a fourth in which they explicitly withdrew their tentative Sobell identification. That NSA/FBI did not conclude "Relay" or "Serb" was Sobell was clear to any reasonable researcher. Sobell's objection was a contrivance. Morton Sobell, "An Examination of the Authenticity of the Venona 'Intercepts'" (http://rosenbergtrial.Org/doc sobven.html) (2002). Sam Roberts, "Figure in Rosenberg Case Admits to Spying," *New York Times*, 11 September 2008.

5. Robert Meeropol, *An Execution in the Family: One Son's Journey* (New York: St. Martin's Press, 2003), 224; Usdin, *Engineering Communism*, 42–43; Moscow Center to KGB New York, 12 September 1942, KGB file 40159, v.3, p. 195, Vassiliev, *Black*, 108; Elizabeth Bentley, FBI Deposition, 30 November 1945, serial 220, p. 106, FBI Silvermaster file 65–56402; Ronald Radosh and Joyce Milton, *The Rosenberg File* (New Haven: Yale University Press, 1997), 176.

6. "Conversation with Leonid about work in the station," 12 September 1944, KGB file 35112, v.1, p. 347, Vassiliev, *Black*, 187–88. Prokhorov's/"Leonid's" debriefing has closing quotes but not opening ones, but in the context the latter are clearly intended and are inserted here. Zarubin to Merkulov, "Memorandum (on the station's work in the country)," 30 September 1944, KGB file 35112, v.1, pp. 407–8, Vassiliev, *White #1*, 8.

7. Semenov to Fitin, 29 November 1944; KGB New York to Moscow Center, 20 September 1944, KGB file 40129, v.3a, pp. 168, 205–7, Vassiliev, *White #1*, 108, 110–11. Venona 1340 New York to Moscow, 21 September 1944.

8. "Report by 'Callistratus' on his trip to the U.S.," 27 February 1947, KGB file 40129, v.3a, p. 354, Vassiliev, *White #1*, 120; Alexander Feklisov and Sergei Kostin, *The Man Behind the Rosenbergs*, trans. Catherine Dop (New York: Enigma Books, 2001).

9. Venona 1600 KGB New York to Moscow, 14 November 1944; Venona 1609 KGB New York to Moscow, 17 November 1944; Memo to Fitin for period from 1 January through 13 February 1945, KGB file 40129, v.3a, p. 350, Vassiliev, *White #1*, 116.

10. "Agent network," 1 February 1945, KGB file 40594, v.7, pp. 15–20, 23–26, 48–49, Vassiliev, *Black*, 119–22. Emphasis in the original. "Mutterperl" was William Perl's birth name.

11. "Report by 'Callistratus' on his trip to the U.S.," 27 February 1947, KGB file 40129, v.3a, pp. 380–81, Vassiliev, *White #1*, 121–22.

12. Venona 717 KGB New York to Moscow, 10 May 1944; Venona 732 KGB New York to Moscow, 20 May 1944; Venona 854 KGB New York to Moscow, 16

June 1944; Venona 1048 KGB New York to Moscow, 25 July 1944; Venona 1251 KGB New York to Moscow, 2 September 1944; Venona 1314 KGB New York to Moscow, 14 September 1944; Venona 1491 KGB New York to Moscow, 22 October 1944; Venona 1536 KGB New York to Moscow, 28 October 1944; Venona 1797 KGB New York to Moscow, 20 December 1944; Venona 954 Moscow to KGB New York, 20 September 1944; Venona 154 Moscow to KGB New York, 16 February 1945; Venona 224 Moscow to KGB New York, 13 March 1945; Venona 305 Moscow to KGB New York, 1 April 1945. Feklisov and Kostin, *Man Behind,* 137–47.

13. "Victor" to "Anton," 23 February 1945, KGB file 40159, v. 3, pp. 472–74, Vassiliev, *Black,* 132–33.

14. "Grouping of probationers as of March 1945"; KGB New York to Moscow Center, 26 June 1945, KGB file 40594, v.7, pp. 97, 134, Vassiliev, *Black,* 124, 135. Closing quote supplied after "using our password."

15. Moscow Center to "Vadim," Moscow Center to "Sergey," 22 November 1945, KGB file 70545, pp. 402–3, Alexander Vassiliev, *White Notebook #2 [2007 English Translation],* trans. Steven Shabad (1993–96), 30; "Callistratus's" report on the meetings with "Meter" and "Liberal," circa December 1945, KGB file 40594, v.7, pp. 352–55, Vassiliev, *Black,* 125–26. Opening single quote supplied for "No, I am waiting. . . ." The original notebook has "Helen" and "Helene."

16. Bentley, Deposition 1945, 106; Radosh and Milton, *Rosenberg File* (1997), 176; Usdin, *Engineering Communism,* 58–59, 294.

17. "Petrov" to KGB New York, 27 October 1945, KGB file 82702, v.1, p. 430, Alexander Vassiliev, *Yellow Notebook #1 [2007 English Translation],* trans. Philip Redko (1993–96), 34.

18. Moscow Center to KGB New York, 12 March 1948; Moscow Center to "Stepan" and "August," 6 May 1948; Moscow Center to Uglov, 8 June 1948; Moscow Center to Uglov, 7 July 1948, KGB file 40159, v.5, pp. 50–51, 128, 147–48, 173, Vassiliev, *Black,* 127–28. Moscow Center to "August," 1 March 1948, KGB file 86192, v.1, pp. 50–51, Vassiliev, *Yellow #1,* 41.

19. Moscow Center to "Bob," 28 October 1948; Moscow Center to "Bob," 7 December 1948, KGB file 40159, v.5, pp. 238, 278, 282–83, Vassiliev, *Black,* 130–31. On Finestone, see Ronald Radosh and Joyce Milton, *The Rosenberg File: A Search for the Truth* (New York: Holt, Rinehart, and Winston, 1983), 307–14. "Plumb" in 1944 was Charles Kramer. Cover names were reused from time to time, and this "Plumb" was a different person.

20. The story of Barr and Sarant in the Soviet Union is told in Usdin, *Engineering Communism.* On Sobell and Perl, see Radosh and Milton, *Rosenberg File* (1997), and John Earl Haynes and Harvey Klehr, *Early Cold War Spies: The Espionage Trials That Shaped American Politics* (New York: Cambridge University Press, 2006).

21. New York Special Agent memo "Re: Nathan Sussman," 6 December 1950, serial 975; FBI New York teletype to FBI Washington "Re: Nathan Sussman," 17 January 1951, serial 1055; FBI New York teletype to FBI Washington "Re: Nathan Sussman," 18 January 1951, serial 1060; FBI New York teletype to FBI Washington, 21 March 1951, serial 1489, FBI Julius Rosenberg file 65–15348.

22. Statement of Nathan Sussman, 30 October 1953, U.S. Senate Committee

on Government Operations, *Executive Sessions of the Senate Permanent Subcommittee on Investigations of the Committee on Government Operations* (Washington, D.C.: U.S. Govt. Print. Off., 2003), v.4, 106–11; Nathan Sussman testimony, 8 December 1953, U.S. Senate Committee on Government Operations, *Army Signal Corps—Subversion and Espionage* (Washington. D.C.: U.S. Govt. Print. Off., 1954), part 1, 57–59.

23. "Agent network," 1 February 1945, KGB file 40594, v.7, pp. 27–28, Vassiliev, *Black*, 120. Prior to "Block," Urewich had the cover name "Fisherman." Venona 1052 KGB New York to Moscow, 26 July 1944.

24. "Agent network," 1 February 1945, KGB file 40594, v.7, pp. 21–22, Vassiliev, *Black*, 120; Venona 50 KGB New York to Moscow, 11 January 1945; Venona 1052 KGB New York to Moscow, 26 July 1944; Semenov to Fitin, circa 1944, KGB file 40129, v.3a, p. 204, Vassiliev, *White #1*, 110.

25. Venona 1405 KGB New York to Moscow, 27 August 1943; Venona 1403 KGB New York to Moscow, 5 October 1944; Venona 1509 KGB New York to Moscow, 23 October 1944. KGB New York to Moscow Center, 8 February 1943, KGB file 40594, v.6, p. 43; Moscow Center to "Vadim," "Work on the XY line," 25 June 1945, KGB file 43173, v.2, p. 83, Vassiliev, *Black*, 69, 115.

26. "James Herbert Hibben," *Journal of the Washington Academy of Sciences* 49, no. 6 (1959): 196.

27. Stuart G. Hibben, *Aristocrat and Proletarian: The Extraordinary Life of Paxton Pattison Hibben* (Tamarac, FL: Llumina Press, 2006).

28. Expense estimate for the NY station for the 2nd quarter of 1937, KGB file 3464, v.1, p. 84; "Agents: (3rd qtr. of '38)," KGB file 40159, v.1, p. 253; Moscow Center to KGB New York, 27 March 1942; "Station in Washington," circa 1943; Moscow Center to KGB New York, 1 July 1943, KGB file 40159, v.3, pp. 161, 331, 285; KGB New York to Moscow Center, 8 February 1943, and KGB New York to Moscow Center, 15 April 1943; "XY network as of," 1 May 1943, KGB file 40594, v.6, pp. 115, 134; "Agent network," 1 February 1945; "Grouping of probationers as of March 1945," KGB file 40594, v.7, pp. 14, 97; Moscow Center to "Anton," 14 January 1945, KGB file 40159, v.3, p. 465; "Task plan for 'Vadim,'" 10 August 1944, KGB file 43173, v.1, p. 58; "In Washington: Frank's new source," circa 1937, KGB file 3465, v.2, p. 80, Vassiliev, *Black*, 27, 33, 49, 101, 107, 110–11, 116–17, 119, 135.

29. "'Twain' went to Wash.," 6 October 1942, KGB file 40594, v.5, pp. 316–17; KGB New York to Moscow Center, 8 February 1943; KGB New York to Moscow Center, 15 April 1943, KGB file 40594, v.6, pp. 43–44, 115, Vassiliev, *Black*, 105–6, 115–16.

30. Moscow Center to "Anton," 14 January 1945, and Moscow Center to KGB New York, 27 March 1942; Moscow Center to KGB New York, 1 July, 1943, KGB file 40159, v.3, pp. 161, 465, 285, Vassiliev, *Black*, 107, 110, 114. Semenov to Fitin, 29 November 1944, KGB file 40129, v.3a, p. 208, Vassiliev, *White #1*, 111.

31. SAC Charlotte to Director, 4 April 1946, serial 557, p. 6398, FBI Silvermaster file 65–56402.

32. "Network," circa 1933, KGB file 17407, v.1, p. 42; "Letter," KGB New York to Moscow Center, 20 January 1937, KGB file 3465, v.7, p. 28, Vassiliev, *Black*, 1, 31.

33. KGB New York letter to Moscow Center, 10 March 1939, KGB file 40594, v.2, pp. 67–68; "Center approved," KGB file 40159, v.2, p.109, Vassiliev, *Black*, 101.

34. FBI Washington Field Office, interview with Paul Elisha Williams, 3 February 1955, serial 2735, FBI Julius Rosenberg file 65–15348; Report by John O'Donoughue, 7 August 1950, serial 38, FBI Michael and Anne Sidorovich file 65–59294. Williams told the FBI that over the years the *Daily Worker* and the CPUSA promoted numerous myths about him. Among the inventions was the claim that he had attended Carnegie Technological Institute, that his company had designed a light bomber for the government, and that he had been a naval officer. Williams's own account of his biography given to the FBI differs significantly from that provided in Danny Duncan Collum, ed., assisted by Victor A. Berch, *African Americans in the Spanish Civil War: "This Ain't Ethiopia, but It'll Do"* (New York: G. K. Hall, 1992), 96–97.

35. "'Talent's' sub-source," circa 1939–1940, KGB file 40594, v.2, p. 438; Moscow Center to KGB New York, 25 June 1942, KGB file 40159, v.3, pp. 169–71, Vassiliev, *Black*, 102, 107. The latter was a June 1942 message, and at that point Rosenberg was a source for Jacob Golos, but it was not until later in the year that the KGB assumed direct contact with him, thus the reference to Rosenberg as "unaffiliated with us."

36. *New York Times*, 1 May 1958; *Philadelphia Bulletin*, 30 April 1958; *Philadelphia Inquirer*, 1 May 1958; *Philadelphia Bulletin*, 7 May 1958.

37. Moscow Center to KGB New York, 13 February 1937, KGB file 3464, v.1, p. 31, Vassiliev, *Black*, 26.

38. "Expense estimate for the NY station for the 2nd quarter of 1937," KGB file 3464, v.1, p. 84; Moscow Center to KGB New York, 1 July 1943, KGB file 40159, v.3, p. 284, Vassiliev, *Black*, 27, 110. Thomas Black interview in June and July 1950, transcribed 1 August 1951, serial 1–B–17, pp. 102–5, 245–29, 260, 315–32, FBI Thomas Black file 65–4332.

39. Moscow Center to "Maxim," 27 November 1941, KGB file 40159, v.3, pp. 124–25, Vassiliev, *Black*, 106. William Welte, Jr., memo, "Unknown Subject, was Roberts, Rabinowitz, Mr. Rich," 2 August 1950, no serial (filed after serial 262), FBI Thomas Black file 65–59181. Flosdorf's name is misspelled "Flosdorff" in the letter, and "Rabinovitch" is a variant spelling usually appearing as "Rabinovich." It is not clear if the "5/7/42" follows the American convention of the era (May 7, 1942) or the Russian (5 July 1942). Rabinovitch was also known in the United States as Gregory Rabinowitz, Dr. Schwartz, and Mr. Rich. He was recalled to Moscow in 1939.

40. Moscow Center to "Maxim," 20 October 1943, KGB file 40159, v.3, pp. 330–31, Vassiliev, *Black*, 110–11. *New York Times*, 1 May 1958; *Philadelphia Bulletin*, 30 April 1958, p. 1; *Philadelphia Inquirer*, 1 May 1958; *Philadelphia Bulletin*, 7 May 1958.

41. KGB New York to Moscow Center, 17 July 1941; KGB New York to Moscow Center, 7 January 1942, KGB file 40594, v.5, pp. 134, 201, 203, Vassiliev, *Black*, 103; Moscow Center to KGB New York, 25 June 1942, KGB file 40159, v.3, p. 169, Vassiliev, *Black*, 107.

42. "In the past," circa 1942, KGB file 40594, v.5, p. 278; Moscow Center to

KGB New York, 26 November 1942, KGB file 40159, v.3, p. 223, Vassiliev, *Black*, 105, 108–9.

43. KGB New York to Moscow Center, 27 March 1943, KGB file 40594, v.6, p. 119, Vassiliev, *Black*, 117.

44. Venona 622 KGB New York to Moscow, 4 May 1944.

45. Venona 1706 KGB New York to Moscow, 4 December 1944; Venona 1680 KGB New York to Moscow, 30 November 1944; Venona 1755 KGB New York to Moscow, 14 December 1944. Moscow Center to "Anton," 14 January 1945, KGB file 40159, v.3, p. 464, Vassiliev, *Black*, 113–14.

46. Albert Glinsky, *Theremin Ether Music and Espionage* (Urbana: University of Illinois Press, 2000), 162.

47. Report by "Grin" on Nazi activities with note by "Nikolay," 3 October 1935, KGB file 3461, v.1, pp. 140–42, Vassiliev, *Black*, 11. In that era, the term "hermaphrodite" was often used for women with a bisexual orientation as well as for persons with dual or ambiguous sexual organs.

48. "Frenchman developed," circa 1935, KGB file 3461, v.1, pp. 32–33, Vassiliev, *Black*, 11–12.

49. "Frenchman developed," circa 1935, KGB file 3461, v.1, pp. 33–34, Vassiliev, *Black*, 12.

50. Glinksky, *Theremin*, 271–73. Among the leading Soviet scientists who were imprisoned and worked in sharashkas were Andrey Tupolev, among the USSR's leading aircraft designers; Sergey Korolyov, a rocket engineer who was later the chief designer for the Soviet space program; and Georgy Langemak, a co-inventor (with Korolyov) of the highly effective Katyusha military rocket launcher.

51. The instrument used in *Good Vibrations* was not a Theremin per se but an "Electro-Theremin," an instrument that produced a similar sound but with a different control mechanism.

52. Although "Gapon" initially declined recruitment in 1935, he was providing information by 1937. Report on "Blerio's trip to California," 5–15 November 1935, KGB file 3461, v.1, pp. 50–58; "Expense estimate for the NY station for the 2nd quarter of 1937," KGB file 3464, v.1, p. 84, Vassiliev, *Black*, 9–10, 27.

53. "About 'Needle,'" circa 1936, KGB file 3461, v.2, pp. 176–77, Vassiliev, *Black*, 24. KGB New York to Moscow Center, 2 January 1936; KGB New York to Moscow Center, 13 April 1936; "Needle has," KGB file 3463, v.1, pp. 90, 128, 236, Vassiliev, *Black*, 23. "Letter," 23 October 1937; "Letter," 27 November 1937, KGB file 3464, v.1, pp. 217, 246, Vassiliev, *Black*, 30.

54. KGB New York to Moscow Center, 29 June 1938, KGB file 40594, v.1, p. 319; KGB New York to Moscow Center, 28 July 1939, KGB file 40594, v.2, pp. 230–31, Vassiliev, *Black*, 99, 102. Venona 446 KGB San Francisco to Moscow, 31 October 1943; Venona 457 KGB San Francisco to Moscow 2 November 1943; Venona 1266 KGB New York to Moscow, 6 September 1944; Venona 1523 KGB New York to Moscow, 27 October 1944. Jones York statement of 6 October 1953 in William Wolf Weisband background memo, 27 November 1953, Office of Security, National Security Agency, reproduced in Robert Louis Benson and Michael Warner, *Venona: Soviet Espionage and the American Response 1939–1957* (Washington,

D.C.: National Security Agency; Central Intelligence Agency, 1996), 167–69. Hood to Director, 11 April 1950, serial 53, FBI York file 65–2223.

55. "Background on 'Needle,'" 10 February 1947, KGB file 40129, v.4, pp. 255–58, Vassiliev, *White #1*, 119–20. York identified Zalmond Franklin as the KGB liaison he knew as "Werner." Belmont to Ladd, 12 July 1951, serial 91, FBI York file 65–2223.

56. Moscow Center to KGB New York with annotation, 23 June 1940, KGB file 40594, v.2, p. 386, Vassiliev, *Black*, 102. York came to the FBI's attention in early 1939, when the Office of Naval Intelligence forwarded a report of his having come into its investigation of Shumovsky's activities. The FBI's investigation of his finances and activities suggested involvement in espionage, but his interview with the FBI in 1940 on his return to California provided little exploitable information, and his case was put aside. FBI Los Angeles summary report, 23 August 1940, serial 5, FBI York file 65–2223.

57. "Background summary on 'Lever,'" 6 January 1944, KGB file 40129, v.3a, p. 26, Vassiliev, *White #1*, 106.

58. Ibid.; "'Blerio's' contact," circa 1935, KGB file 3461, v.1, p. 90; "Cover names of agents on X line," KGB file 3461, v.2, p. 95; "Expense estimate for the NY station for the 2nd quarter of 1937," KGB file 3464, v.1, p. 84, Vassiliev, *Black*, 10, 17, 27.

59. KGB New York to Moscow Center, 20 January 1937, KGB file 3465, v.1, pp. 45–46, Vassiliev, *Black*, 31–32.

60. "Between the 20th and 30th of Sept. '38"; "The Source "Goose,"" KGB file 40594, v.3, pp. 209–10, 290–92, Vassiliev, *Black*, 99–100.

61. KGB New York to Moscow Center, 16 March 1940; KGB New York to Moscow Center, 14 November 1940, KGB file 40594, v.4, pp. 167–68, 214–15; Moscow Center to KGB New York, 20 October 1943, KGB file 40159, v.3, p. 331; KGB New York to Moscow Center, 1 March 1938, KGB file 40594, v.1, p. 144; KGB New York to Moscow Center, 10 March 1939, KGB file 40159, v.2, pp. 56–57, 115, 148, 150; KGB New York to Moscow Center, 9 October 1942, KGB file 40594, v.5, p. 306; Moscow Center to "Maxim," 27 October 1941, KGB file 40159, v.3, pp. 134, 178, Vassiliev, *Black*, 98, 101–2, 105–6, 111.

62. "Meeting with 'Goose,'" 16 February 1941; KGB New York to Moscow Center, 29 July 1942, KGB file 40594, v.5, pp. 14, 268, Vassiliev, *Black*, 102, 104. Background summary on "Lever," 6 January 1944, KGB file 40129, v.3a, p. 26, Vassiliev, *White #1*, 106. Radosh and Milton, *The Rosenberg File* (1983), 466.

63. Robert J. Lamphere and Tom Shachtman, *The FBI-KGB War: A Special Agent's Story* (Macon, GA: Mercer University Press, 1995), 166–67; Haynes and Klehr, *Early Cold War Spies*, 157; Radosh and Milton, *Rosenberg File* (1997), 465–67.

64. "Agent network," 1 February 1945, KGB file 40594, v.7, pp. 14, 33–43, Vassiliev, *Black*, 119, 121–22. Andrey Ivanovich Shevchenko likely was the pseudonym used by Andrey Ivanovich Raina when in the United States.

65. Memo on Leona and Joseph Franey, 5 August 1944, serial 2919; Memo on Leona and Joseph Franey, 21 August 1944, serial 2989; FBI memo on Shevchenko, 30 October 1944, serial 3379; FBI memo on Shevchenko, 9 December 1944, serial

3612, FBI Comintern Apparatus file 100–203581. Venona 941 KGB New York to Moscow, 4 July 1944; Venona 1048 KGB New York to Moscow, 25 July 1944; Venona 1403 KGB New York to Moscow, 5 October 1944; Venona 1559 KGB New York to Moscow, 6 November 1944; Venona 305 Moscow to KGB New York, 1 April 1945. Leona Franey testimony and Joseph Franey testimony, 6 June 1949, U.S. House Committee on Un-American Activities, *Soviet Espionage Activities in Connection with Jet Propulsion and Aircraft* (Washington, D.C.: U.S. Govt. Print. Off., 1949).

66. Venona 1607–1608 KGB New York to Moscow, 16 November 1944; Loren Haas testimony, 6 June 1949, U.S. House Committee on Un-American Activities, *Soviet Espionage . . . Jet.*

67. Thomas Black interview in June and July 1950, transcribed 1 August 1951, serial 1–B–17, pp. 1, 4, FBI Thomas Black file 65–4332; FBI Albany office to Washington teletype, 20 June 1950, serial 146, FBI Thomas Black file 65–59181.

68. Thomas Black interview in June and July 1950, transcribed 1 August 1951, serial 1–B–17, pp. 15–18, FBI Thomas Black file 65–4332. "Ovakimian" is a variant transliteration of Ovakimyan. The plural "we" refers to Black and his friend Fred Heller. KGB New York to Moscow Center, 3 October 1935, KGB file 86194, v.1, p. 16, Vassiliev, *Yellow #1*, 99. There are numerous references to "Black" throughout Alexander Vassiliev's notebooks.

69. Thomas Black interview in June and July 1950, transcribed 1 August 1951, serial 1–B–17, pp. 318–319, FBI Thomas Black file 65–4332.

70. SAC New York to Director, 16 June 1950, serial 21, FBI Thomas Black file 65–59181; Thomas Black testimony, 17 May 1956, U.S. Senate Internal Security Subcommittee, *Scope of Soviet Activity in the United States* (Washington, D.C.: U.S. Govt. Print. Off., 1956), part 21.

71. Report Re: Alfred Dean Slack, FBI Newark office, 28 June 1950, serial 228; SAC Knoxville to Director, 5 July 1950, serial 281; Report Made at Albany, NY, 30 June 1950, serial 298, FBI Alfred Slack file 65–59183.

72. KGB New York to Moscow Center, 1 March 1938, KGB file 40594, v.1, p. 110, Vassiliev, *Black*, 98. "Report Made at Albany, NY," 30 June 1950, serial 298, FBI Slack file 65–59183.

73. KGB New York to Moscow Center, 29 July 1942, KGB file 40594, v.5, p. 252, Vassiliev, *Black,* 104. Interview of Stanley Glass, 15 September 1950, serial 608, FBI Slack file 65–59183; "Report Made at Pittsburgh," 5 August 1950, serial 302, FBI Slack file 65–59183.

74. Report Made at Pittsburgh, 5 August 1950, serial 302, FBI Slack file 65–59183.

75. KGB New York to Moscow Center, 19 April 1942, KGB file 86194, v.1, p. 350, Vassiliev, *Yellow #1*, 102.

76. KGB New York to Moscow Center, 29 July 1942, KGB file 40594, v.5, p. 253; Moscow Center to "Maxim," 20 October 1943, KGB file 40159, v.3, p. 330, Vassiliev, *Black,* 104, 110.

77. FBI New York Report, 20 June 1950, serial 97; Slack statement after arrest, serial 200, FBI Slack file 65–59183; Katherine A. S. Sibley, *Red Spies in America: Stolen Secrets and the Dawn of the Cold War* (Lawrence: University Press of Kansas,

2004), 110; Lamphere and Shachtman, *FBI-KGB War,* 167–68. KGB New York to Moscow Center, 5 April 1943, KGB file 50594, v.6, p. 116, Vassiliev, *Black,* 116.

78. FBI Report, 15 June 1950, serial 200, FBI Slack file 65–59183.

79. Moscow Center to "Vadim," "Work on the XY line," 25 June 1945, KGB file 43173, v.2, p. 84, Vassiliev, *Black,* 69.

80. "Agents in the USA station," 15 December 1933; "On the tasks of the USA station," April 1934, KGB file 17407, v.1, pp. 42, 76; Vassiliev, *Black,* 1, 5. "Memorandum on the Feldman case," circa 1945, KGB file 70994, pp. 367–68, Vassiliev, *White #1,* 155; Feldman background memos, serial 734, FBI Armand Labis Feldman file 61–7574.

81. "Nikolay's account of Brit's disappearance," 24 May 1938, KGB file 34194, pp. 158–59; "Memorandum on the Feldman case," circa 1945, KGB file 70994, p. 368, Vassiliev, *White #1,* 125, 155. On Feldman/Volodarsky's involvement with the Woolwich Arsenal case, see William E. Duff, *A Time for Spies: Theodore Stephanovich Mally and the Era of the Great Illegals* (Nashville: Vanderbilt University Press, 1999), 123–31.

82. Thomas Black interview in June and July 1950, transcribed 1 August 1951, serial 1–B–17, pp. 195–205, 257, 260; Francis Zangle report, 1, 10–13 August 1950, serial 240, FBI Thomas Black file 65–59181.

83. KGB New York to Moscow Center, 9 October 1942, KGB file 40594, v.5, p. 299; "Grouping of probationers as of March 1945," KGB file 40594, v.7, p. 97, Vassiliev, *Black,* 105, 135. Thomas Black interview in June and July 1950, transcribed 1 August 1951, serial 1–B–17, pp. 195–205, 257, 260, FBI Thomas Black file 65–59181.

84. Venona 1403 KGB New York to Moscow, 5 October 1944; Venona 1429 KGB New York to Moscow, 9 October 1944; Venona 1557 KGB New York to Moscow, 6 November 1944; Venona 1818 KGB New York to Moscow, 26 December 1944. Interview with Thomas Black, 20 June 1950, serial 1–B–17, pp. 195–205, 257–60, FBI Thomas Black file, 65–4332; Ladd to Director, 28 February 1951, "This memorandum is designed," page 19 of the FBI FOIA "Venona" released to Daniel P. Moynihan, part 1, http://foia.fbi.gov/foiaindex/venona.htm. Stapler is likely the source Feklisov gives the cover name "Khvat" or "Vulture" in Feklisov and Kostin, *Man Behind,* 55–56.

85. "Memorandum on the Feldman case," circa 1945, KGB file 70994, pp. 367–68, Vassiliev, *White #1,* 155; FBI Report, 23 June 1942, serial 743, FBI Feldman file, 61–7574. "On the tasks of the USA station," April 1934, KGB file 17407, v.1, p. 76, Vassiliev, *Black,* 4.

86. FBI New York report, 1 February 1940, serial 40; FBI New York report, 29 June 1940, FBI Feldman file 61–7574; "Aleksey" at Moscow Center to KGB New York, 14 May 1937, KGB file 3464, v.1, p. 133; "Agents in the USA station," 15 December 1933, KGB file 17407, v.1, p. 9, Vassiliev, *Black,* 1, 29.

87. "On the tasks of the USA station," April 1934, KGB file 17407, v.1, p. 76, Vassiliev, *Black,* 4; Venona 917 KGB New York to Moscow, 28 June 1944; Interview of Armand Feldman, 3 August 1950, serial 942, p. 9, FBI Feldman file 61–7574.

88. KGB New York to Moscow Center, 12 September 1936, and KGB New York

to Moscow Center, 21 October 1936, KGB file 3463, v.2, pp. 99–100, 121; KGB New York to Moscow Center, 16 August 1940, KGB file 40594, v.4, pp. 144–45, Vassiliev, *Black,* 25, 102.

89. "The work of Doctor Goddard, received from S-2," circa 1935, KGB file 3460, p. 36, Vassiliev, *Black,* 9; Slutsky memo, June 1935, KGB file 3469, v.12, pp. 37–38, Alexander Vassiliev, *Yellow Notebook #4 [2007 English Translation],* trans. Steven Shabad (1993–96), 102.

90. FBI Report, 23 June 1942, serial 743; Director to Arnold, 14 July 1942, serial 749; serial 768, FBI Feldman file 61–7574.

91. Prudnikov, "Report on intelligence in the USA," 12 April 1941, KGB file 35112, v.1, p. 68; KGB New York to Moscow Center, 8 August 1941, KGB file 40594, v.5, p. 158, Vassiliev, *Black,* 103, 172–73.

92. Venona 801 KGB New York to Moscow, 28 May 1943; Venona 1054 KGB New York to Moscow, 5 July 1945. KGB New York to Moscow Center, 26 June 1945, KGB file 40594, v.7, pp. 248–49, Vassiliev, *Black,* 124.

93. "Vadim" to Moscow Center, 20 September 1945, KGB file 43173, v.1, p. 149, Vassiliev, *Black,* 54–55. Emphasis in the original.

94. Bentley, Deposition 1945, 66, 106; Testimony of 5 March and 21 March 1947, U.S. House Committee on Un-American Activities, *Investigation of Un-American Propaganda Activities in the United States. (Regarding Leon Josephson and Samuel Liptzen) Hearings* (Washington, D.C.: U.S. Govt. Print. Off., 1947); FBI memo, "John Loomis Sherman Background and Personal History," serial 3221, FBI file 65–14920. GRU would take an authentic American passport such as Kagan's and modify it (new photograph or other changes) for use by one of its operatives.

95. "Communist Infiltration of Radiation Laboratory" in "Summary Report," serial 3702, pp. 25–28, FBI Comintern Apparatus file 100–203581; Alfred Bergens to F. Brown, 10 July 1935, CPUSA records, RGASPI 515–1–3816; "Minutes of Meeting of Party Group of Anglo-American Secretariat," 17 February 1937, Anglo-American Secretariat of the Executive Committee of the Communist International, RGASPI 495–72–281; "Marcel Scherer," in *Biographical Dictionary of the American Left,* ed. Bernard K. Johnpoll and Harvey Klehr (Westport, CT.: Greenwood Press, 1986), 349–50.

Chapter 7: American Couriers and Support Personnel

1. Moscow Center to "Maxim," 27 July 1943, KGB file 35112, v.6, p. 482, Alexander Vassiliev, *White Notebook #1 [2007 English Translation],* trans. Steven Shabad (1993–96), 42.

2. KGB New York to Moscow Center, 3 September 1945, KGB file 35112, v.9, p. 112, Vassiliev, *White #1,* 71.

3. "Maxim" to Moscow Center, 19 April 1942, KGB file 35112, v.7, p. 23, Vassiliev, *White #1,* 43.

4. Venona 1491 KGB New York to Moscow, 22 October 1944; Venona 1536 KGB New York to Moscow, 28 October 1944; Venona 1609 KGB New York to Moscow, 17 November 1944; Venona 1797 KGB New York to Moscow, 20 Decem-

ber 1944; Venona 210 Moscow to KGB New York, 9 March 1945; Venona 224 Moscow to KGB New York, 13 March 1945.

5. Moscow Center to KGB Washington, 29 May 1945, KGB file 45100, v.1, p. 121, Alexander Vassiliev, *White Notebook #3 [2007 English Translation]*, trans. Steven Shabad (1993–96), 82; "Vadim" to Moscow Center, 5 March 1945, KGB file 43173, v.1, p. 95, Alexander Vassiliev, *Black Notebook [2007 English Translation]*, trans. Philip Redko (1993–96), 51.

6. Igor Damaskin, assisted by Geoffrey Elliott, *Kitty Harris: The Spy with 17 Names* (London: St Ermin's, 2001), 143–99.

7. "Vadim" to Moscow Center, circa January 1945; Moscow Center to KGB Washington, 28 March 1945, KGB file 45100, v.1, pp. 73–74, 107, Vassiliev, *White #3*, 74, 80.

8. Zarubin to Merkulov, "Memorandum (on the station's work in the country)," 30 September 1944, KGB file 35112, v.1, p. 420, Vassiliev, *White #1*, 14; "Vadim" to Moscow Center, 20–21 March 1945, KGB file 45100, v.1, p. 99, Vassiliev, *White #3*, 76–77.

9. KGB Washington to Moscow Center, 19 August 1948, KGB file 43173, v.4, p. 369, Vassiliev, *Black*, 71.

10. Robert Louis Benson, "Weisband," paper presented at Symposium on Cryptologic History, Maritime Institute, MD, 2003); Robert Louis Benson to Harvey Klehr, 20 June 2007. "'Zero' was handed over to 'Link,'" circa 1936, KGB file 3461, v.2, p. 165; "Expense estimate for the NY station for the 2nd quarter of 1937," KGB file 3464, v.1, p. 84; "Agents: (3rd qtr. of '38)," KGB file 40159, v.1, p. 253, Vassiliev, *Black*, 17, 27, 101. Raymond J. Batvinis, "Is Counterintelligence an Affair of State or Justice? The Bureaucratic Struggle over Responsibility in Two Wars," paper presented at the Society for Historians of American Foreign Relations annual meeting, Chantilly, Virginia, 2007.

11. KGB New York to Moscow Center, 17 July 1941, KGB file 40594, v.5, p. 126, Vassiliev, *Black*, 103; FBI Washington Field Office report, Jones York deposition, 6 October 1953, reproduced in Robert Louis Benson and Michael Warner, *Venona: Soviet Espionage and the American Response 1939–1957* (Washington, D.C.: National Security Agency; Central Intelligence Agency, 1996), 167–70; "Background on 'Needle,'" 10 February 1947, KGB file 40129, v.4, p. 257, Vassiliev, *White #1*, 120; Hood to Director, 11 April 1950, serial 53; Hood to Director, 4 April 1950, serial 57, FBI Jones Orin York file 65–2223.

12. Venona 981 KGB New York to Moscow, 23 June 1943; Venona 1239 KGB New York to Moscow, 30 August 1944; Venona 154 Moscow to KGB New York, 16 February 1945. Semenov to Fitin, circa 1944, KGB file 40129, v.3a, pp. 212–13, Vassiliev, *White #1*, 112–13; "Victor" to "Anton," 23 February 1945, KGB file 40159, v.3, p. 474, Vassiliev, *Black*, 133.

13. Semenov to Fitin, 29 November 1944, KGB file 40129, v.3a, p. 213, Vassiliev, *White #1*, 113; Moscow Center to "Vadim," 21 October 1945, KGB file 43173, v.1, p. 162, Vassiliev, *Black*, 57.

14. On the NSA background to the Weisband story, see "Who Was William Weisband?" in Benson and Warner, *Venona*, xxviii; Laura Sullivan, "Spy's Role

Linked to U.S. Failure on Korea," *Baltimore Sun,* 29 June 2000; Benson, "Weisband"; John Schindler, "Weisband," paper presented at Symposium on Cryptologic History, Maritime Institute, MD, 2003.

15. "Plan of measures," March 1949, KGB file 43173, v.2c, p. 25, Vassiliev, *Black,* 75.

16. "Plan of measures," March 1949, KGB file 43173, v.2c, pp. 25, 27, Vassiliev, *Black,* 75.

17. "'Zhora' is asking," circa 1948, KGB file 43173, v.4, p. 230; "In Dec. '48," KGB file 43173, v.7; "Vasin signed," circa 1950, KGB file 40159, v.2, p. 101; "We consent," circa 1950, KGB file 43173, v.11, p. 87, Vassiliev, *Black,* 70, 91, 95–96.

18. "At a meeting," 16 July 1949, KGB file 43173, v.11, p. 85, Vassiliev, *Black,* 91.

19. "Pavel's" lines, KGB file 43173, v.2c, pp. 26–27; "Materials from," 13 September 1949, KGB file 43173, v.7, p. 100; "On the days," circa 1949, KGB file 43173, v.7, p. 114; Moscow Center to KGB Washington, 28 February 1950, KGB file 43173, v.2c, p. 70; Moscow Center to KGB Washington, 28 March 1950, KGB file 43173, v.11, p. 51, Vassiliev, *Black,* 75, 81, 91, 94.

20. "The stations' info," circa 1948, KGB file 43173, v.8, p. 84; Moscow Center to "Vladimir," 3 January 1950, KGB file 43173, v.11, pp. 11–12, Vassiliev, *Black,* 92, 94.

21. FBI Washington Field Office report, Jones York deposition, 6 October 1953, reproduced in Benson and Warner, *Venona,* 167–70; Hood to Director, 11 April 1950, serial 53, and Hood to Director, 4 April 1950, serial 57, FBI Jones Orin York file 65–2223. In a very belated response to the problem of defense lawyers thwarting espionage prosecutions by threatening to subpoena or use discovery motions to obtain government secrets and expose them in open court, in 1980 the Congress passed the Classified Information Procedures Act (CIPA), establishing procedures for handling classified information in criminal trials. CIPA provided that government prosecutors could request that a judge review classified information demanded by a defense attorney under discovery procedures both *in camera* (nonpublicly, in judicial chambers) and *ex parte* (presented by only one side, the government, without the presence of defense attorneys). The judge would then rule on what classified information necessarily had to be disclosed in order for the defendant to present an adequate defense, and the act included an option of substituting unclassified summaries for the sensitive materials. CIPA called upon judges to balance the need of the government to protect intelligence information and the right of a defendant to a fair trial. CIPA reduced but did not eliminate the "graymail" problem in espionage and terrorism cases because a large element of individual judicial discretion (arbitrariness) remained.

22. Harold Kennedy FBI New York report, 14 December 1945, serial 236; Harold Kennedy FBI New York report, 7 December 1945, serial 248, FBI Silvermaster file 65–56402.

23. Autobiography of "Don," circa 1937; autobiography of "Carmen," circa 1937; Report by "Jung," November 1936; "Jung" to Moscow Center, 5 July 1937, KGB file 40132, v.1, pp. 16–17, 20–24, 26–27, Alexander Vassiliev, *Yellow Notebook #2 [2007 English Translation],* trans. Philip Redko (1993–96), 81–82.

24. Moscow Center to "Jung," 21 June 1937; "Jung" to Moscow Center, 5 July 1937, pp. 25, 27, Vassiliev, *Yellow #2*, 82–83.

25. Adolf Berle, "Underground Espionage Agent [Transcription of Berle's notes of 2 September 1939 interview with Whittaker Chambers]," in U.S. Senate Internal Security Subcommittee, *Interlocking Subversion in Government Departments [Hearings]* (Washington, D.C.: U.S. Govt. Print. Off., 1953), part 6, pp. 329–30; Whittaker Chambers, "Statements to the Federal Bureau of Investigation," January–April 1949, pp. 58–59; Harvey Klehr, John Earl Haynes, and Fridrikh Igorevich Firsov, *The Secret World of American Communism* (New Haven: Yale University Press, 1995), 25–26; Harvey Klehr, John Earl Haynes, and Kyrill M. Anderson, *The Soviet World of American Communism* (New Haven: Yale University Press, 1998), 111; Richard H. Tourin, *Memoirs and Adventures* (New York: privately published, 2003), in the Richard H. Tourin Papers, Manuscript Division, Library of Congress; Herbert Romerstein and Eric Breindel, *The Venona Secrets: Exposing Soviet Espionage and America's Traitors* (Washington, D.C.: Regnery, 2000), 120; Gary Kern, *A Death in Washington: Walter G. Krivitsky and the Stalin Terror* (New York: Enigma Books, 2003), 232, 235, 393, 416, 445; "Report on Rosenbliett," 23 October 1947, KGB file 40132, v.1, pp. 133–34, Vassiliev, *Yellow #2*, 86–87.

26. Venona 1636 KGB New York to Moscow, 21 November 1944. "Albert" report, 2 March 1943; "Berg went," 22 September 1944; Moscow Center to "Sergey," 20 April 1945, KGB file 40132, v.1, pp. 47, 60, 86, 92, Vassiliev, *Yellow #2*, 83–84. Moscow Center to KGB Washington, 28 March 1950, KGB file 43173, v.11, p. 52, Vassiliev, *Black*, 94.

27. "Albert" to Moscow Center, 10 October 1944; Moscow Center to KGB New York, 20 October 1944; Moscow Center to "May," 9 December 1944; "Albert" to Moscow Center, 9 January 1945; Moscow Center to "Sergey," 20 April 1945; "'Julia' met with 'Art,'" 25 November 1945; "As of Jan. 1st, 1937," KGB file 40132, v.1, pp. 63–65, 73, 78, 85, 127, Vassiliev, *Yellow #2*, 82, 84, 86.

28. Note by "Albert," 12 November 1945, KGB file 40132, v.1, pp. 122–25, Vassiliev, *Yellow #2*, 85–86.

29. "'Albert's' meeting with 'Sergey' and 'Peter,'" 23 June 1945, KGB file 40132, v.1, p. 100, Vassiliev, *Yellow #2*, 84–85.

30. Venona 337 Moscow to KGB New York, 8 April 1945. "They were deactivated," 23 November 1945; "'Julia' met with 'Art,'" 25 November 1945, KGB file 40132, v.1, pp. 126–27, Vassiliev, *Yellow #2*, 86.

31. Ladd to Director, 12 December 1945, serial 235; Harold Kennedy FBI New York report, 7 December 1945, serial 248; Scheidt FBI New York report, 9 June 1947, serial 2558; Alexander Koral interview summary, 9 June 1947, serial 2571; Francis O'Brien FBI New York report with Koral statement, 11 June 1947, serial 2608; FBI memo, "Existing Corroboration of Bentley's Overall Testimony," 6 May 1955, serial 4201, FBI Silvermaster file 65–56402.

32. Francis O'Brien FBI New York report with Koral statement, 11 June 1947, serial 2608, FBI Silvermaster file 65–56402.

33. Scheidt FBI New York report, 9 June 1947, serial 2558; Alexander Koral interview summary, 9 June 1947, serial 2571; Scheidt FBI New York report, Helen

Koral interview, 14 June 1947, serial 2593; Scheidt FBI New York report, Alexander Koral interview, serial 2595; Francis O'Brien FBI New York report with Koral statement, 11 June 1947, serial 2608; Francis O'Brien FBI New York report, Helen Koral interview, 25 June 1947, serial 2630, FBI Silvermaster file 65–56402.

34. Graur to Kukin, September 1947; KGB New York to Moscow Center, 13 October 1947; "Alex. Koral is testifying," circa 1948, KGB file 40132, v.1, pp. 135–38, 141, 143, Vassiliev, *Yellow #2*, 87–88. Testimony of Alexander Koral, 9 August 1948, U.S. House Committee on Un-American Activities, *Hearings Regarding Communist Espionage in the United States* (Washington, D.C.: U.S. Govt. Print. Off., 1948), 674–75, 704–11; Report addressed to the Chairman of the KI in view of Vladimir's cipher telegram dated 25.12.48, KGB file 43173, v.2c, pp. 36–38, Vassiliev, *Black*, 76.

35. Anatoly Gorsky, "Failures in the USA (1938–48)," December 1948, KGB file 43173, v.2c, pp. 54–55, Vassiliev, *Black*, 79.

36. Venona 1234 KGB New York to Moscow, 29 August 1944. Andrew and Mitrokhin mention in passing that "Grigulevich's couriers to New York included the Chilean Communist Eduardo Pecchio." Christopher M. Andrew and Vasili Mitrokhin, *The Sword and the Shield: The Mitrokhin Archive and the Secret History of the KGB* (New York: Basic Books, 1999), 591, n61. Given the multiple translations involved (Spanish, Russian, and English), it is possible that Andrew and Mitrokhin's "Pecchio" is Vassiliev's "Pequeño." The exact spelling of "Teacher"/Leah Melamed's name is uncertain. *Melamed* occurs in Vassiliev, *Black*, 79. A second spelling, *Melament*, appears in *White #1*, p. 58, where "Teacher" is identified as Leah *Melament*, along with her father, Joseph *Melament* ("Old Man"), and it is noted that Joseph was born in 1874 in Ukraine in the Russian Empire. Boris Morros, assisted by Charles Samuels, in *My Ten Years as a Counterspy* (New York: Viking Press, 1959), 47, 50, 55, also described an espionage contact of his in New York as Lea *Melament*. However, the 1930 census showed a third spelling, with Leah *Melement* living in Bronx, New York, with her father, Joseph, who was noted as having been born in Russia in 1874. Moscow Center to "May," 28 July 1944, KGB file 35112, v.8, p. 99, Vassiliev, *White #1*, 58. Zarubin to Merkulov, "Memorandum (on the station's work in the country)," 30 September 1944, KGB file 35112, v.1, p. 384, Vassiliev, *White #1*, 2. On Sylvia's relationship to Helen, Alan Koral to Harvey Klehr, 7 April 2007. Venona 1791 KGB New York to Moscow, 20 December 1944.

37. Interview with Marjorie Brockman, "Student Voices from World War II and the McCarthy Era," http://www.ashp.cuny.edu/oralhistory/brockmanscript.html; "3 Seized as Vandals in Furniture Factory," *New York Times*, 20 October 1951.

38. Biographical information can be found in FBI Amadeo Sabatini file 100–244909, particularly FBI Los Angeles report, 5 October 1944, serial 5; FBI Los Angeles report, 22 July 1950, serial 59; FBI Los Angeles report, 26 July 1950, serial 99. This file, including Sabatini's confession, is heavily redacted so that very few details about his activities are available. References to his work as a Comintern courier can be found in Comintern radio messages deciphered by the "Mask" project. In 1997 the Government Communications Headquarters (GCHQ), the British equivalent of the American NSA, released for public access thousands of these messages. GCHQ's 1930s predecessor had intercepted the broadcasts during 1934 to 1937 and broken

the Comintern's code in a project given the name "Mask." Radio messages regarding Sabatini can be found in Mask 1959/H, Comintern Moscow to Amsterdam 13, 5 January 1935, and Mask 3760/H, Comintern Moscow to Amsterdam 326, 3 September 1935, Mask collection, National Cryptologic Museum, Ft. Meade, MD.

39. Roster and assignment list of American Communists with the International Brigades, Archive of the International Brigades, RGASPI 545–6–846; FBI memo, "Existing Corroboration of Bentley's Overall Testimony," 6 May 1955, serial 4201, FBI Silvermaster file 65–56402; Arthur H. Landis, *The Abraham Lincoln Brigade* (New York: Citadel Press, 1967), 305, 311; FBI New York report, 15 September 1953, serial 14x1, FBI Thomas Black file 65–61847.

40. Details about the Krivitsky surveillance operation are in FBI Los Angeles SAC to Director, 17 November 1959, serial 111, FBI Amadeo Sabatini file 100–244909. Butkov to Prudnikov, 11 April 1941, KGB file 35112, v.1, p. 91, Vassiliev, *Black,* 176.

41. Larry Kerley testimony, 15 September 1949, U.S. Senate Subcommittee on Immigration and Naturalization, *Communist Activities among Aliens and National Groups* (Washington, D.C.: U.S. Govt. Print. Off., 1950), part 2, 811. FBI Los Angeles to FBI Washington, 18 November 1943, serial 2; Hoover memo for Attorney General, 15 November 1943, serial 3; FBI Los Angeles report, 5 October 1944, serial 5; FBI Los Angeles report, 22 July 1950, serial 59, FBI Amadeo Sabatini file 100–244909. Venona 1220 KGB New York to Moscow, 26 August 1944. The source Sabatini met was identified as "Engineer" in Venona 1220, but the details, particularly the reference to a lost report, corresponded to Jones York, who in other documents had the cover name "Needle." It is possible that his code name had been changed.

42. Venona 942 KGB New York to Moscow, 4 July 1944; Venona 1015 KGB New York to Moscow, 22 July 1944; Venona 1087 KGB New York to Moscow, 30 July 1944; Venona 1220 KGB New York to Moscow, 26 August 1944; Venona 1266 KGB New York to Moscow, 6 September 1944; Venona 1313 KGB New York to Moscow, 13 September 1944; Venona 1370 KGB New York to Moscow, 27 September 1944; Venona 1523 KGB New York to Moscow, 27 October 1944; Venona 1649 KGB New York to Moscow, 25 November 1944; Venona 29 KGB New York to Moscow, 8 January 1945; Venona 130 Moscow to KGB New York, 11 February 1945; Venona 446 KGB San Francisco to Moscow, 31 October 1943; Venona 55 KGB San Francisco to Moscow, 8 February 1944; Venona 298 KGB San Francisco to Moscow, 13 July 1944.

43. Moscow Center to Vladimir, 18 October 1948, KGB file 40159, v.5, p. 249, Vassiliev, *Black,* 130. FBI memo Belmont to Ladd, 15 May 1950; FBI memo Ladd to Director, 28 February 1951, in Venona-related FBI documents released to Senator Daniel P. Moynihan. FBI Los Angeles SAC to Director, 26 September 1948, serial 27; FBI Los Angeles report, 22 July 1950, serial 59, FBI Amadeo Sabatini file 100–244909.

44. FBI New York report, 21 November 1946, serial 1980, FBI Silvermaster file 65–56402.

45. Ovakimyan and Graur, report to Merkulov on "Enormous," February 1944, KGB file 82702, v.1, p. 142, Alexander Vassiliev, *Yellow Notebook #1 [2007 English Translation]*, trans. Philip Redko (1993–96), 9. Louis Budenz affidavit, 11 November 1950, U.S. House Committee on Un-American Activities, *American Aspects of Assassination of Leon Trotsky* (Washington, D.C.: U.S. Govt. Print. Off., 1951), part 1, v–ix; Louis F. Budenz, *Men without Faces: The Communist Conspiracy in the USA* (New York: Harper, 1950), 123–26.

46. "Glan" to Moscow Center, 21 August 1941; "Glan" to Moscow Center, 23 August 1941; KGB New York to Moscow Center, 5 November 1941, KGB file 35112, v.4a, pp. 444, 455, 644, Vassiliev, *White #1*, 23–24, 27. "Chap" report on Clarence Hiskey, 28 March 1942, KGB file 82702, v.1, pp. 69–71, Vassiliev, *Yellow #1*, 2–3; Moscow Center to KGB New York, 27 March 1942, KGB file 40159, v.3, p. 160, Vassiliev, *Black*, 106.

47. "Maxim" to Moscow Center, 9 February 1943, KGB file 35112, v.7, p. 234, Vassiliev, *White #1*, 49.

48. Venona 749 KGB New York to Moscow, 26 May 1944; Venona 1523 KGB New York to Moscow, 27 October 1944.

49. Klehr, Haynes, and Firsov, *Secret World*, 205–26; Browder to Comintern, 15 January 1943, RGASPI 495–184–7, 1943 file; "Veterans of International Brigades," circa 1940, KGB file 35112, v.1, p. 22, Vassiliev, *Black*, 168. Emphasis in the original. The Cohens are discussed extensively in Joseph Albright and Marcia Kunstel, *Bombshell: The Secret Story of America's Unknown Atomic Spy Conspiracy* (New York: Times Books, 1997).

50. KGB New York to Moscow Center, 17 February 1945, KGB file 40594, v.7, p. 21, Vassiliev, *Black*, 120. Although the message says that Chmilevski was recruited by "Volunteer" in August 1942, Morris was already in the Army by that time, so presumably his initiation of the recruitment took place earlier. Moscow Center to "Bob," 5 October 1948, KGB file 40159, v.5, p. 208, Vassiliev, *Black*, 129; Albright and Kunstel, *Bombshell*, 71–74; Venona 1239 KGB New York to Moscow, 30 August 1944.

51. Semenov to Fitin, circa 1944, KGB file 40129, v.3a, pp. 212–13, Vassiliev, *White #1*, 112–13.

52. Venona 50 KGB New York to Moscow, 11 January 1945; "Victor" to "Anton," 23 February 1945, KGB file 40159, v.3, p. 474, Vassiliev, *Black*, 133.

53. Moscow Center to "Claude," 19 April 1948; Moscow Center to "Claude," 27 April 1948, KGB file 40159, v.5, pp. 107, 118, Vassiliev, *Black*, 127. The Cohens' relationship with Hall is discussed in Albright and Kunstel, *Bombshell*.

54. The FBI investigation of the Cohens can be followed in FBI Morris and Lona Cohen file 100–406659.

55. Report by "Callistratus" on his trip to the U.S., 27 February 1947, KGB file 40129, v.4, p. 353, Vassiliev, *White #1*, 120. Feklisov also discussed his work with the radio in Alexander Feklisov and Sergei Kostin, *The Man behind the Rosenbergs*, trans. Catherine Dop (New York: Enigma Books, 2001), 28–31.

56. Handwritten and typescript notes in John Barron Papers, Hoover Institu-

tion, Stanford University, Box 2, Folders 4 and 5, derived from FBI New York SAC to Director, 26 September 1952.

57. Report by "Callistratus" on his trip to the U.S., 27 February 1947, KGB file 40129, v.4, p. 377–79, Vassiliev, *White #1*, 121.

58. KGB Washington to Moscow Center, 1 October 1950, KGB file 43173, v.12, pp. 201–3, 216, Vassiliev, *Black*, 97.

59. Gilbert J. Gall, *Pursuing Justice: Lee Pressman, the New Deal, and the CIO* (Albany: State University of New York Press, 1999); Gilbert J. Gall, "A Note on Lee Pressman and the FBI," *Labor History* 32, no. 4 (Fall 1991); Gilbert J. Gall, To the Editor, *Labor History* 33, no. 2 (Spring 1992); Earl Latham, *The Communist Controversy in Washington: From the New Deal to McCarthy* (Cambridge, MA: Harvard University Press, 1966), 107–8; Joseph P. Lash, *Dealers and Dreamers: A New Look at the New Deal* (New York: Doubleday, 1988), 218, 316, 434–37; Steve Rosswurm, "The Wondrous Tale of an FBI Bug: What It Tells Us about Communism, Anti-Communism, and the CIO Leadership," *American Communist History* 2, no. 1 (June 2003).

60. KGB Washington to Moscow Center, 23 August 1950, KGB file 43173, v.12, p. 181, Vassiliev, *Black*, 96; Testimony of Lee Pressman, 20 August 1948, U.S. House Committee on Un-American Activities, *Hearings Regarding Communist Espionage*, 1022–28.

61. Lee Pressman testimony, 28 August 1950, U.S. House Committee on Un-American Activities, *Hearings Regarding Communism in the United States Government* (Washington, D.C.: U.S. Govt. Print. Off., 1950), pt. 2, 2844–2901.

62. "A report from 'Raid,'" September 1949; "Raid was given," October 1949, KGB file 45100, v.1, pp. 171, 214, Vassiliev, *White #3*, 84; Report, 2 March 1951, KGB file 43072, v.1, p. 159, Vassiliev, *White #3*, 65. Bruslov, "Measures for improving the work of the Washington station," 21 January 1950, KGB file 43173, v.2c, p. 59, Vassiliev, *Black*, 80.

63. Report, 2 March 1951, KGB file 43072, v.1, p. 159, Vassiliev, *White #3*, 65; Gall, *Pursuing Justice,* 256–58; Hans Moses, "The Case of Major X [*Studies in Intelligence* 18, 1 (1974)]," in *Inside CIA's Private World: Declassified Articles from the Agency's Internal Journal, 1955–1992,* ed. H. Bradford Westerfield (New Haven: Yale University Press, 1995).

64. Gorsky, "Failures in the USA (1938–48)," KGB file 43173, v.2c, p. 49, Vassiliev, *Black*, 77.

65. Berle, "Underground Espionage Agent"; Whittaker Chambers, *Witness* (New York: Random House, 1952), 436; Lee Pressman testimony, 28 August 1950, U.S. House Committee on Un-American Activities, *Hearings Regarding Communism*, pt. 2, 2844–2901.

66. Bentley autobiography, circa 1944; NKGB sent an inquiry, December 1944, KGB file 70545, pp. 242–43, 1193–94, Alexander Vassiliev, *White Notebook #2 [2007 English Translation]*, trans. Steven Shabad (1993–96), 13–14. Elizabeth Bentley, FBI Deposition, 30 November 1945, serial 220, pp. 5–9; Michael Endelman interview on 2 June 1947 in Washington Field Office report, 7 June 1947, serial 2583; Washington Field Office report based on FBI New York report of 3 January 1946, serial 329, FBI Silvermaster file 65–56402.

Chapter 8: Celebrities and Obsessions

1. Meeting with "Chap," 1 October 1941, KGB file 14449, v.1, pp. 75–76, Alexander Vassiliev, *White Notebook #2 [2007 English Translation]*, trans. Steven Shabad (1993–96), 56–58.

2. Moscow Center to "Arkhip," 28 March 1934; "Emir's" report on meeting with "L," 16 January 1936; Memorandum on M. D., circa 1936, KGB file 14449, v.1, pp. 13, 17–20, 25, Vassiliev, *White #2*, 46–47.

3. From "A's" letter, 5 June 1935; Memo on M. D., circa 1936; Memo re "Liza," 1937; Dodd to Soviet government, 14 March 1937; Letter from "Alexander," 21 March 1937; "Alexander" to Moscow Center, 5 November 1937; "Alexander" to Moscow Center, 12 November 1937; "M. D. took," KGB file 14449, v.1, pp. 15, 25, 33, 37, 45–46, 50–51, Vassiliev, *White #2*, 46–47, 49–50, 52–53.

4. Slutsky to Yezhov containing Dodd statement, 28 March 1937; Yezhov to Stalin, 29 March 1937, KGB file 14449, v.1, pp. 38–44, 48, Vassiliev, *White #2*, 50–53.

5. Moscow Center to "Jung," 8 January 1938, KGB file 14449, v.1, p. 52, Vassiliev, *White #2*, 54. "Gennady" to Moscow Center with annotations, 13 April 1938; KGB New York to Moscow Center, 25 May 1938, KGB file 35112, v.5, pp. 23–24, 30, Alexander Vassiliev, *Black Notebook [2007 English Translation]*, trans. Philip Redko (1993–96), 147–48. "Luisa" is likely a garble for "Liza."

6. "Nikolay" to Moscow Center, 29 June 1938; KGB New York to Moscow Center, 14 September 1938, KGB file 35112, v.5, pp. 45, 76, Vassiliev, *Black*, 148, 152. Letter from M. D. to B. V., 9 July 1938; Memo re "Liza," 1938, KGB file 14449, v.1, pp. 56–57, Vassiliev, *White #2*, 54–55.

7. KGB New York to Moscow Center, 14 September 1938; KGB New York to Moscow Center, 1 December 1938, KGB file 35112, v.5, pp. 76, 101–2, 117–18, Vassiliev, *Black*, 152–53.

8. Martha Dodd, *Through Embassy Eyes* (New York: Harcourt, Brace, 1939); William Edward Dodd, *Ambassador Dodd's Diary, 1933–1938*, ed. William Edward Dodd, Jr., and Martha Dodd (New York: Harcourt, Brace, 1941). John Fox presents evidence suggesting that significant portions of the published version of Ambassador Dodd's diaries were faked by Martha and Bill Dodd to conform to their pro-Soviet political views. John Francis Fox, Jr., "'In Passion and in Hope': The Pilgrimage of an American Radical, Martha Dodd Stern and Family, 1933–1990" (PhD diss., University of New Hampshire, 2001). Moscow Center to "Gennady," 23 September 1939, KGB file 35112, v.5, p. 388; Butkov to Prudnikov, 11 April 1941, KGB file 35112, v.1, pp. 84, 89, Vassiliev, *Black*, 154, 174–75.

9. "Stephan was supposed," circa 1941, KGB file 35112, v.1, pp. 47–48, Vassiliev, *Black*, 172; KGB New York to Moscow Center, 21 August 1941, KGB file 35112, v.4a, p. 444, Alexander Vassiliev, *White Notebook #1 [2007 English Translation]*, trans. Steven Shabad (1993–96), 23; "Chap" re meeting with Martha, 24 September 1941, KGB file 14449, v.1, pp. 70–73, Vassiliev, *White #2*, 55–56.

10. Meeting with "Chap," 1 October 1941; Memo re "Liza"; Moscow Center to "Sergey," 29 October 1941, KGB file 14449, v.1, pp. 61, 75–77, 86, Vassiliev, *White #2*, 55–58.

11. KGB New York to Moscow Center, 5 November 1941, KGB file 35112, v.4a, p. 644, Vassiliev, *White #1,* 27; Message from "Liza," 26 December 1941, KGB file 14449, v.1, pp. 106–7, Vassiliev, *White #2,* 58–59.

12. Moscow Center to "Maxim," 10 January 1942, KGB file 35112, v.6, pp. 96–99, Vassiliev, *White #1,* 33–34.

13. "Liza," 5 February 1942, KGB file 14449, v.1 (in envelope), Vassiliev, *White #2,* 63–64.

14. "Liza," 11 March 1942, KGB file 14449, v.1 (in envelope), Vassiliev, *White #2,* 65–66.

15. "Liza," 19 March 1942, KGB file 14449, v.1 (in envelope), Vassiliev, *White #2,* 67.

16. "Maxim" to Moscow Center, 19 April 1942, KGB file 35112, v.7, pp. 23, 28–29, Vassiliev, *White #1,* 43–44.

17. Moscow Center to "Maxim," 24 June 1942; Moscow Center to "Maxim," 26 November 1942, KGB file 35112, v.6, pp. 177, 313, Vassiliev, *White #1,* 37–38; Plan of assignments for "May" approved by Merkulov, 16 December 1943, KGB file 35112, v.1, p. 303a, Vassiliev, *Black,* 182; Venona 854 KGB New York to Moscow, 16 June 1942.

18. "Maxim" report, 30 September 1944; KGB New York to Moscow Center, 19 March 1945, with "Peter's" report; "Vadim" report, circa 1945; Moscow Center to "Vadim," 14 June 1945, KGB file 30595, v.1, pp. 97–106, 110–11, Alexander Vassiliev, *Yellow Notebook #3 [2007 English Translation],* trans. Philip Redko (1993–96), 17–20, 22. Report, 9 June 1945, KGB file 43173, v.1, p. 126; "Plan of measures," March 1949, KGB file 43173, v.2c, p. 22, Vassiliev, *Black,* 53, 74.

19. "Plan of measures," March 1949, KGB file 43173, v.2c, pp. 21–23, Vassiliev, *Black,* 74; "Vladimir" to Moscow Center, 4 February 1948; Moscow Center to "Vladimir," 12 February 1948; "Snegirev" reports on 10 and 27 January, 18 March, and 10 May 1948 meetings with Martha Dodd Stern, KGB file 14449, v.2, pp. 17–72, Vassiliev, *White #2,* 69–70.

20. "Vladimir" to Moscow Center, 12 August 1948; Moscow Center to KGB Washington, 14 August 1948; KGB Washington to Moscow Center, circa 1948; Report on meeting, 6 October 1948, KGB file 14449, v.2, pp. 76–79, Vassiliev, *White #2,* 71. "Liza" report, 14 May 1948, KGB file 43173, v.4, p. 154, Vassiliev, *Black,* 70.

21. Report on meetings with "Liza" and "Louis," 16 October 1948, KGB file 14449, v.2, pp. 81–82, Vassiliev, *White #2,* 71–72.

22. "Liza" gave "Snegirev," 30 June 1949; "Kostrov" established, 26 August 1949; Gorsky memo, 8 December 1949; Memo, October 1953, KGB file 14449, v.2, pp. 87–111, Vassiliev, *White #2,* 72–73. "Kostrov" report, 12 May 1950, KGB file 43173, v.2c, p. 111; "During a reception," 7 November 1949, KGB file 43173, v.7, p. 122, Vassiliev, *Black,* 84, 91.

23. "Decided to reactivate," March 1955; Moscow Center to KGB Mexico City, 14 May 1956; "Ostap" report, 8 June 1957; Moscow Center to "Ostap," 11 June 1957; "Ostap" report, 18 June 1957; "Ostap" report, 9 July 1957; "Ostap" report, 13 July 1957; "Peshekhonov" to Moscow Center, 5 August 1957; Korneev report on the Sterns, circa 1957; KGB file 14449, v.2, pp. 117, 129, 137–38, 142–45, 148, 150,

152–53, 165, 170–71, 173–75, 177, 179, 184, Vassiliev, *White #2*, 73–76. The government of Paraguay later repudiated its diplomat's action.

24. Korneev report, 17 August 1957; Korneev report, 22 August 1957; KGB petitioned, 28 August 1957; Vakhrushev report on the Sterns, September 1957; Sterns decided, September 1957; Stern letter, "After careful," 11 October 1957; Stern sent, 29 October 1957, KGB file 14449, v.2, pp. 186–89, 205–6, 210–11, 227–44, 278–80, 282–89, Vassiliev, *White #2*, 77–80.

25. China; Reply from Peking, 31 August 1957; KGB Prague to Moscow Center, 14 October 1975; Moscow Center to KGB Prague, 14 October 1975, KGB file 14449, v.2, pp. 177, 179, 212, 362–63, 365, Vassiliev, *White #2*, 76–78, 81. For a view of the Sterns as innocent victims of anti-Communist paranoia and suggesting there was no substance to charges of their participation in espionage, see Katrina vanden Heuvel, "Martha Dodd Stern," *Nation*, 24 September 1990, and Katrina vanden Heuvel, "Grand Illusions," *Vanity Fair* 54, no. 9 (September 1991). The one comprehensive scholarly study of the Sterns depicted them as having cooperated with Soviet intelligence. Fox, "'In Passion.'"

26. "Nikolay" to Moscow Center, "On Morros," 1934, KGB file 30595, v.1, pp. 13–17, Vassiliev, *Yellow #3*, 1–3.

27. Center took an interest, circa 1934; Moscow Center to "Nikolay," 5 October 1934; KGB New York to Moscow Center, 24 October 1934; KGB New York to Moscow Center, 26 October 1934, KGB file 30595, v.1, pp. 18, 21, 25–26, Vassiliev, *Yellow #3*, 3–4.

28. KGB New York to Moscow Center, 20 July 1935; "Nikolay" to Moscow Center with "Archimedes'" report, KGB file 30595, v.1, pp. 27, 35–38, Vassiliev, *Yellow #3*, 4–7.

29. Report by "Betty," 8 June 1938, KGB file 30595, v.1, pp. 44–47, Vassiliev, *Yellow #3*, 9–10.

30. KGB New York to Moscow Center, 3 November 1940; Moscow Center to KGB New York, 15 February 1941; Moscow Center to KGB New York, circa 1941, KGB file 30595, v.1, pp. 62–64, Vassiliev, *Yellow #3*, 12.

31. "Maxim" report, 28 December 1941; KGB New York to Moscow Center, 4 April 1942; Moscow Center to KGB New York, 16 April 1942; Report, 1 September 1942; "F. has been receiving letters"; "Charon" to Moscow Center, 30 September 1943, KGB file 30595, v.1, pp. 65–71, 74, 76–79, Vassiliev, *Yellow #3*, 12–14.

32. Relatives, 14 October 1946, KGB file 30595, v.1, pp. 113–15, Vassiliev, *Yellow #3*, 23–24. Article 58–10 criminalized anti-Soviet agitation, while Article 193–17 punished neglect of duty by Red Army personnel.

33. "Maxim's" report, 30 September 1944, KGB file 30595, v.1, pp. 93–99, Vassiliev, *Yellow #3*, 15–17.

34. Venona 1824 KGB New York to Moscow, 27 December 1944; Venona 4–5 KGB New York to Moscow, 3 January 1945; Venona 11 KGB New York to Moscow, 4 January 1945; Venona 18–19 KGB New York to Moscow, 4 January 1945. Report, 9 June 1945, KGB file 43173, v.1, p. 126, Vassiliev, *Black*, 53. "Maxim" report, 30 September 1944; KGB New York to Moscow Center, 19 March 1945, with "Peter's" report; "Vadim" report, circa 1945; Moscow Center to "Vadim," 14 June 1945;

"Vadim" to Moscow Center, 27 June 1945; Moscow Center to "Sergey," 30 June 1945; "Vadim" report, 9 June 1945, KGB file 30595, v.1, pp. 97–110, Vassiliev, *Yellow #3*, 17–22.

35. Moscow Center to "Vadim," 14 June 1945; "Czech" report, 18 December 1945, KGB file 30595, v.1, pp. 111–12, Vassiliev, *Yellow #3*, 22–23.

36. "Czech" on "Frost," 18 August 1947, KGB file 30595, v.1, pp. 119–23, Vassiliev, *Yellow #3*, 24–25; Report, 9 June 1945, KGB file 43173, v.1, p. 126, Vassiliev, *Black*, 53.

37. "Czech" reports: March 1948, 6 May 1948, 4 May 1948, 14 June 1948, 27 July 1948, KGB file 30595, v.1, pp. 129–52, Vassiliev, *Yellow #3*, 26–30.

38. Boris Morros, assisted by Bill Davidson, "My Ten Years as a Counterspy," *Look Magazine* 21, nos. 24 and 25 (26 November 1957); Boris Morros, assisted by Charles Samuels, *My Ten Years as a Counterspy* (New York: Viking Press, 1959). "Czech" on "Frost," 18 August 1947, KGB file 30595, v.1, pp. 119–23, Vassiliev, *Yellow #3*, 24–25.

39. "Czech" reports: 4 and 6 May 1948; Korotkov to Moscow Center, 25 August 1948; Moscow Center to KGB Bern, 27 August 1948; Korotkov record of 2nd meeting with "John," 10 September 1948, KGB file 30595, v.1, pp. 131–34, 166–84, Vassiliev, *Yellow #3*, 26, 33–40.

40. Korotkov record of 2nd meeting with "John," 10 September 1948, KGB file 30595, v.1, pp. 180–86, Vassiliev, *Yellow #3*, 40–41.

41. On "John" and his audience with the Pope, September 1948; "Czech" report, 25 June 1949; provisions for "Czech's" work, 28 July 1949, KGB file 30595, v.1, pp. 195–200, 206–13, Vassiliev, *Yellow #3*, 42–48.

42. Record of a conversation with "John," 20 January 1950 (conducted by Korotkov and Kovalenok); Conversation with "John," 27 January 1950 (conducted by Pavlov and Kovalenok); Conversation with "John," 28 January 1950 (conducted by Pavlov and Kovalenok); Conversation between Kovalenok and "John," 4 February 1950; Assignments for "John," KGB file 30595, v.3, pp. 63–81, 93–99, Vassiliev, *Yellow #3*, 54–56, 61–62.

43. Moscow Center to KGB New York, 11 November 1952, KGB file 30595, v.4, pp. 142–47, Vassiliev, *Yellow #3*, 89–90. Closing quote mark inserted.

44. "Czech" report, 11 September 1950; "Klim's" meeting with "John," 4 September 1950, KGB file 30595, v.3, pp. 273, 279–81, Vassiliev, *Yellow #3*, 71–72. Plan of action regarding "Czech's" station, 21 December 1951; Moscow Center to Yakov, 30 January 1952; KGB Vienna to Moscow Center, 2 September 1952; "John's" report at 8 September 1952 meeting, with Savchenko annotation, KGB file 30595, v.4, pp.84, 90–93, 119, 123–29, Vassiliev, *Yellow #3*, 82–87.

45. Moscow Center to KGB New York, 11 November 1952, KGB file 30595, v.4, pp. 142–46, Vassiliev, *Yellow #3*, 89–90.

46. KGB Vienna to Moscow Center, 18 April 1953; Moscow Center to KGB Vienna, 21 April 1953; KGB Vienna to Moscow Center, 27 July 1953; KGB Vienna to Moscow Center, 6 August 1953; KGB Vienna to Moscow Center, 2 October 1953; KGB Vienna to Moscow Center, 19 December 1953; Korotkov's resolution, 28 December 1953, KGB file 30595, v.4, pp. 198–99, 201, 207, 210, 230–32, Vassiliev, *Yel-*

low #3, 94–96. Venona 777–781 KGB New York to Moscow, 26 May 1943; Venona 893 KGB New York to Moscow, 10 June 1943.

47. "Yakov" on "John" report at 6 May 1954 meeting; KGB Vienna to Moscow Center, 1 June 1954; Moscow Center to KGB Vienna, 3 July 1954; Pavlov to Panyushkin, 24 July 1954; KGB Vienna to Moscow Center, 12 August 1954; Moscow Center to KGB Vienna, 9 November 1954; Moscow Center to KGB Vienna, 12 November 1954; Aksenov's report on a conversation with "John," 10 November 1954, KGB file 30595, v.4, pp. 247, 250–51, 254, 259, 269–72, 291, 297–300, 320–44, Vassiliev, *Yellow #3,* 97–101. KGB Vienna to Moscow Center, 31 March 1955; Moscow Center to KGB Vienna, 5 April 1955, KGB file 30595, v.5, pp. 43–47, Vassiliev, *Yellow #3,* 102–4.

48. For a summary of the Soble and Soblen trials, see John Earl Haynes and Harvey Klehr, *Early Cold War Spies: The Espionage Trials That Shaped American Politics* (New York: Cambridge University Press, 2006).

49. Biographical material is drawn from Steve Weinberg, *Armand Hammer: The Untold Story* (Boston: Little, Brown, 1989), and Edward Jay Epstein, *Dossier: The Secret History of Armand Hammer* (New York: Random House, 1996).

50. Epstein, *Dossier,* 41.

51. Epstein, *Dossier,* 63–64, 80–82, 91.

52. Harvey Klehr, John Earl Haynes, and Fridrikh Igorevich Firsov, *The Secret World of American Communism* (New Haven: Yale University Press, 1995), 26–30; Harvey Klehr, John Earl Haynes, and Kyrill M. Anderson, *The Soviet World of American Communism* (New Haven: Yale University Press, 1998), 132–35.

53. Epstein, *Dossier,* 69.

54. Memo re Yuly Yakovlevich Hammer; Memoranda on agents "Physician," "Sonny," and "Lyudmila," 23 June 1951, KGB file 77273, pp. 49, 245–47, Vassiliev, *White #2,* 105, 137–38; "Re Trotskyites, Max Eastman and his work and contacts with Trotsky," 25 March 1932, KGB file 15359, p. 1, Alexander Vassiliev, *Odd Pages [2008 English Translation],* trans. Steven Shabad (1993–96), 1.

55. Memoranda on agents "Physician," "Sonny," and "Lyudmila," 23 June 1951, KGB file 77273, pp. 245–47, Vassiliev, *White #2,* 137; Memo re Trotsky's connection with the U.S.; Bredis memo re agent file no. 14127 on concessionaire Yuly Yakovlevich Hammer, KGB file 15359, pp. 8–11, Vassiliev, *Odd Pages,* 4–5.

56. Statement by Dr. Yuly Yakovlevich Hammer, KGB file 15359, pp. 3–7, Vassiliev, *Odd Pages,* 1–4. Closing quote missing from the notebook and inserted here.

57. Memoranda on agents "Physician," "Sonny," and "Lyudmila," 23 June 1951, KGB file 77273, pp. 245–47, Vassiliev, *White #2,* 137–38.

58. Memo from OGPU agent, 10 July 1931; Memo re "Victor Yuliyevich Hammer," KGB file 77273, pp. 3–9, 13, Vassiliev, *White #2,* 100.

59. Memoranda on agents "Physician," "Sonny," and "Lyudmila," 23 June 1951; Memo re A. V. Hammer, circa 1941, KGB file 77273, pp. 125–26, 245–47, Vassiliev, *White #2,* 113–14, 137–38.

60. Memo from OVIR, 7 October 1942; Ovakimyan request, 30 January 1943; Moscow Center to KGB New York, 29 January 1943; Moscow Center to KGB New York, 20 August 1943, KGB file 77273, pp. 16 (reverse), 18, 20, 23, Vassiliev, *White #2,* 101–2.

61. Ovakimyan request, 26 February 1943; Agent memo, December 1942; Memo based on the file/data sheet no. 8859; Sharapov and Zaporozhchenko agent memo, 29 May 1945, KGB file 77273, pp. 15, 24, 27 (and reverse), 49–50, Vassiliev, *White #2*, 100–106.

62. Sharapov and Zaporozhchenko agent memo, 29 May 1945, KGB file 77273, pp. 27 (reverse), Vassiliev, *White #2*, 103.

63. Moscow Center to KGB New York, 21 May 1945, KGB file 77273, p. 53, Vassiliev, *White #2*, 107.

64. Memo re V. D. Hammer, 13 October 1950; Memo re A. V. Hammer, KGB file 77273, pp. 84–85, 125–26, Vassiliev, *White #2*, 109, 113–14.

65. Gorsky request, 12 August 1950; Savchenko request, 15 August 1950; Memo re V. D. Hammer, 13 October 1950; KGB New York to Moscow Center, 25 December 1950; "Levin" report, 2 February 1951; Utekhin to Pitovranov, June 1951, KGB file 77273, pp. 55–56, 84–85, 127–31, 136–38, Vassiliev, *White #2*, 107–9, 114–15.

66. Sharapov and Mishakov, background report re Varvara Hammer, 22 December 1950; Memo re A. V. Hammer; Gorsky memo, December 1952, KGB file 77273, pp. 98–105, 125–26, 257–58, Vassiliev, *White #2*, 110–14, 139.

67. KGB New York to Moscow Center, 7 February 1952; Gorsky, Memo re A. V. Hammer, 8 June 1951; KGB New York to Moscow Center, 7 February 1952; KGB New York to Moscow Center, re "Miron" meeting with "Sonny" on 8 February 1952; Moscow Center to KGB New York, 23 February 1952, KGB file 77273, pp. 110, 147–51, 157, 161, Vassiliev, *White #2*, 113, 115–19.

68. Moscow Center to KGB New York, 23 February 1952; Moscow Center to KGB New York, 17 May 1952; KGB New York to Moscow Center, 29 May 1952; KGB New York to Moscow Center, 20 June 1952; Report on meeting of 19 June 1952, KGB file 77273, pp. 157, 168–69, 174, 177–79, 182–83, Vassiliev, *White #2*, 118, 120–22.

69. Moscow Center to KGB New York, 27 September 1952; Reports on meeting on 25 and 28 October 1952, KGB file 77273, pp. 185–87, 194–97, Vassiliev, *White #2*, 122–24.

70. Report on meeting of 25 November 1952; "Tikhon" to Pavlov, reply to letter of 27 September 1952; Gorsky annotation, 30 December 1952; Moscow Center to KGB New York, 13 January 1953, KGB file 77273, pp. 188–93, 198, Vassiliev, *White #2*, 124–26.

71. KGB New York to Moscow Center, 13 January 1953; Moscow Center to "Tikhon," 6 February 1953; unsent Moscow Center letter to KGB New York, circa 1953, KGB file 77273, pp. 203–6, 210–11, Vassiliev, *White #2*, 126–27.

72. Moscow Center to KGB New York, 15 April 1953; KGB New York to Moscow Center re meeting of 3 April 1953, KGB file 77273, pp. 212–18, Vassiliev, *White #2*, 131–32.

73. KGB New York to Moscow Center, 28 April 1953; KGB New York to Moscow Center, 27 May 1953; Report of meeting on 29 October 1953; Moscow Center to KGB New York, 21 November 1953; Tishkov to Voronin, 21 November 1953, KGB file 77273, pp. 222–24, 234–39, Vassiliev, *White #2*, 133–37.

74. Memo, 29 September 1955, KGB file 77273, pp. 282, Vassiliev, *White #2,* 141. Victor Hammer's second wife was Irene Wicker, an actress and radio performer.

75. "Operational contact"; Moscow Center to Vlasov, 18 August 1956; Agent report from "Negro," 19 July 1956; Agent report from "Negro," 22 July 1956, KGB file 77273, pp. 307–8, 310–19, Vassiliev, *White #2,* 142–46.

76. KGB New York to Moscow Center, 9 January 1957, KGB file 77273, pp. 324–28, Vassiliev, *White #2,* 147–48.

77. KGB New York to Moscow Center with Feklisov annotation, 2 May 1957; KGB New York to Moscow Center, 31 May 1957; Moscow Center to KGB New York, 12 August 1957; Memo with Feklisov concurrence, 20 August 1957, KGB file 77273, pp. 332–38, Vassiliev, *White #2,* 148–50.

78. Plan for agent-operative action to re-establish an agent relationship with agent "Screw," May 1965; Shaytukhov memo, 8 June 1965; Shaytukhov memo, 20 December 1965; Shaytukhov memo, May 1966, KGB file 77273, pp. 340–45, 353–54, Vassiliev, *White #2,* 150–54.

79. Yeliseyev and Kondrashov to Ivanov, 13 June 1966, with Maslov outline of conversation, 12 June 1966, KGB file 77273, pp. 346–50, Vassiliev, *White #2,* 153–54.

80. Weinberg, *Hammer,* 413; Epstein, *Dossier,* 27, 349.

81. Epstein, *Dossier,* 112–13. Memo re Armand Hammer, 8 September 1972, KGB file 77273, p. 359, Vassiliev, *White #2,* 155.

82. Fitin, Sudoplatov, and Zarubin, "Plan for the organization of the illegal station," 17 April 1940; "Stephan" was supposed; Butkov to Prudnikov, 11 April 1941, KGB file 35112, v.1, pp. 19, 47–48, 89, Vassiliev, *Black,* 167, 172, 175.

83. Max Eastman to Corliss Lamont, *New International* 4, no. 4 (April 1938): 122.

84. Testimony of Louis Budenz, 30 January 1953, U.S. Senate Committee on Government Operations, *Executive Sessions of the Senate Permanent Subcommittee on Investigations of the Committee on Government Operations* (Washington, D.C.: U.S. Govt. Print. Off., 2003), v.3, 1917; Corliss Lamont executive session testimony, 28 January 1953, in U.S. Senate Committee on Government Operations, *Hearings before the Permanent Subcommittee on Investigations, Communist Infiltration in the Army* (Washington, D.C.: U.S. Govt. Print. Off., 1953), 1–19; Edward S. Shapiro, "Corliss Lamont and Civil Liberties," *Modern Age* 42, no. 2 (April 2000): 158–75; Corliss Lamont, *A Lifetime of Dissent* (Buffalo, NY: Prometheus Books, 1988).

85. Work on Trotskyites, KGB file 3461, v.1, pp. 104–5, 117, Vassiliev, *Black,* 10. On Miller's anti-Trotsky work, see John Earl Haynes and Harvey Klehr, *Venona: Decoding Soviet Espionage in America* (New Haven: Yale University Press [Nota Bene], 2000), 263–66, 276.

86. "We now have," circa 1937; "Your latest," circa 1937, KGB file 3464, v.1, pp. 113–14, 119–20, Vassiliev, *Black,* 28.

87. Thomas Black testimony, 17 May 1956, U.S. Senate Internal Security Subcommittee, *Scope of Soviet Activity in the United States* (Washington, D.C.: U.S. Govt. Print. Off., 1956), part 21, pp. 1113–1124.

88. Entries of Callen as "Satyr" and "Rita" are in Vassiliev, *Black*, 78, 101, 161, 176, and Vassiliev, *White #1*, 18, 49, 55. Also see John Earl Haynes and Harvey Klehr, *Venona: Decoding Soviet Espionage in America* (New Haven: Yale University Press, 1999), 261–63.

89. KGB New York to Moscow Center, 25 May 1938; KGB New York to Moscow Center, 14 September 1938, KGB file 15428, pp. 13, 31, Vassiliev, *White #2*, 85–86, 89. "Gennady" to Moscow Center, 5 November 1939, KGB file 28554, v.1, pp. 19–21, Alexander Vassiliev, *Yellow Notebook #4 [2007 English Translation]*, trans. Steven Shabad (1993–96), 113–14. Moscow Center to "Jung," 31 July 1937; "Jung to Moscow Center, 28 September 1937, KGB file 36857, v.1, pp. 83, 94, Alexander Vassiliev, *Yellow Notebook #2 [2007 English Translation]*, trans. Philip Redko (1993–96), 17, 20. "Regarding Trotsky's activities," 1937, KGB file 3591, v.6, pp. 36–41; Memo, 5 April 1937, KGB file 16695, v.12, p. 40, Vassiliev, *Yellow #4*, 98, 112.

90. Butkov to Prudnikov, 11 April 1941; Report to Beria, KGB file 35112, v.1, pp. 5, 87, 90, Vassiliev, *Black*, 165, 175–76. Pavel Sudoplatov et al., *Special Tasks: The Memoirs of an Unwanted Witness, a Soviet Spymaster* (Boston: Little, Brown, 1994), 65–69.

91. "Existing Corroboration of Bentley's Overall Testimony," 6 May 1955, serial 4201, FBI Silvermaster file 65–56402; Venona 1160 KGB New York to Moscow, 17 July 1943; Sudoplatov et al., *Special Tasks*, 73–74.

92. Albert Glotzer, *Trotsky: Memoir and Critique* (Buffalo, NY: Prometheus Books, 1989), 307n11.

93. Christopher M. Andrew and Vasili Mitrokhin, *The Sword and the Shield: The Mitrokhin Archive and the Secret History of the KGB* (New York: Basic Books, 1999), 87–88; E. M. Primakov, *Ocherki istorii rossiiskoi vneshnei razvedki, t.3: 1933–1944* [Outline of the History of Russian External Intelligence, v.3: 1933–1941] (Moscow: Mezhdunarodnye otnosheniia, 1995), 98, 100–101. Moscow Center to "Gennady," 9 November 1939, KGB file 35112, v.5a, pp. 394–95, Vassiliev, *Black*, 161; Sudoplatov et al., *Special Tasks*, 74.

94. Louis Budenz affidavit, 11 November 1950, U.S. House Committee on Un-American Activities, *American Aspects of Assassination of Leon Trotsky* (Washington, D.C.: U.S. Govt. Print. Off., 1951). American Communists were also intimately involved with the KGB's efforts to free Mercader from a Mexican prison. Haynes and Klehr, *Venona* (2000), 279–83.

95. Moscow Center to "Gennady," 27 January 1941; Moscow Center to "Gennady," 24 February 1941, KGB file 35112, v.4, pp. 66–67, 115–17, Vassiliev, *White #1*, 16–18.

96. Moscow Center to "Maxim," 26 October 1942, and Moscow Center to "Maxim," 20 August 1943, KGB file 35112, v.6, pp. 280–81, 507; Moscow Center to "May," 29 May 1944, KGB file 35112, v.8, p. 76, Vassiliev, *White #1*, 39–40, 42, 57.

97. "Informer's" conversation with "Echo," circa 1943, KGB file 35112, v.7, p. 494, Vassiliev, *White #1*, 53; "Maxim" to Moscow Center, circa 22 October 1943, KGB file 82702, v.1, p. 97, Alexander Vassiliev, *Yellow Notebook #1 [2007 English Translation]*, trans. Philip Redko (1993–96), 8.

Chapter 9: The KGB in America

1. "Press Release Issued by the Department of State, 25 August 1935, U.S. Department of State, *Foreign Relations of the United States: Diplomatic Papers: The Soviet Union, 1933–1939* (Washington, D.C.: U.S. Govt. Print. Off., 1952), 250–51; "In Washington," circa 1935, KGB file 3460, v.2, p. 26, Alexander Vassiliev, *Black Notebook [2007 English Translation]*, trans. Philip Redko (1993–96), 21.

2. Moscow Center to KGB New York, 31 August 1934; Moscow Center to KGB New York, 9 September 1934; KGB New York to Moscow Center, 10 September 1934; "Jung" to Moscow Center, 2 October 1934, KGB file 17643, v.1, pp. 29–31, 38, Vassiliev, *Black*, 36–37; "Jung" to Moscow Center, 5 July 1937, KGB file 40132, v.1, p. 27, Alexander Vassiliev, *Yellow Notebook #2 [2007 English Translation]*, trans. Philip Redko (1993–96), 83.

3. Shorthand record of Iskhak Akhmerov lecture, KI KGB archive, 1954, reproduced in A. E. Vassiliev and A. A. Koreshkov, *Station Chief Gold*, Andropov Red Banner Institute, 1984, pp. 31–32, Vassiliev, *Black*, 139.

4. SAC New York to Director, 11 March 1963, serial 811; SAC New York to Director, 15 March 1963, serial 813; SAC New York to Director, 15 April 1963, serial 829, FBI Iskhak Akhmerov file 65–57905. Zarubin to Merkulov, "Memorandum (on the station's work in the country)," 30 September 1944, KGB file 35112, v.1, pp. 415–17; "Mer" to Moscow Center, 28 July 1942, KGB file 35112, v.7, p. 107, Alexander Vassiliev, *White Notebook #1 [2007 English Translation]*, trans. Steven Shabad (1993–96), 12, 45. Fitin, Sudoplatov, and Zarubin, "Plan for the organization of the illegal station," 17 April 1940; Prudnikov, "He arrives," June 1941, KGB file 35112, v.1, pp. 18, 46, Vassiliev, *Black*, 66, 172.

5. "Mer" to Moscow Center, 28 July 1942, KGB file 35112, v.7, pp. 107–9, Vassiliev, *White #1*, 46.

6. "Nikolay" personal file, KGB file 9995, pp. 11–12, Vassiliev, *White #1*, 132.

7. "Nikolay" to Moscow Center, 28 June 1938, KGB file 35112, v.5, pp. 40–41, Vassiliev, *Black*, 151–52.

8. "To the CC of the VKP(b), Cde. Vasilyev," circa 1938, KGB file 9995, p. 40, Vassiliev, *White #1*, 132.

9. "Kurt's" report, 13 December 1938, KGB file 34194, pp. 305–6, Vassiliev, *White #1*, 128–29. "Kurt's" identity is unclear, possibly Andrey Graur or Vasily Mironov.

10. "Gennady" to "Reggie," 21 January 1939, KGB file 34194, pp. 129–30, Vassiliev, *White #1*, 125.

11. Report by Graur, 7 April 1939; "Memorandum from "Yuz," 30 January 1939, KGB file 34194, pp. 225–35, 497, 555; "Smith," 15 August 1940, KGB file 70994, p. 257, Vassiliev, *White #1*, 127–28, 131, 148. Feldman is discussed in chapter 4. Graur's cover name in the United States is unknown, and it is possible that he was the unidentified "Kurt." But there were other unidentified officers as well, such as "Glan."

12. Fitin to Beria, 25 September 1939, KGB file 35112, v.1, pp. 5–10, Vassiliev, *Black*, 165–66.

13. Butkov and Graur report on Ovakimyan, September 1939, KGB file 34194, pp. 1–6; Ilya Lvovich Durmashkin testimony, 10 July 1938, KGB file 70994, p. 181, Vassiliev, *White #1*, 122–24, 147.

14. Butkov and Graur report on Ovakimyan, September 1939, KGB file 34194, pp. 1–6, Vassiliev, *White #1*, 122–24.

15. Fitin to Beria, 27 October 1939; Moscow Center to "Luka," KGB file 34194, pp. 266, 396, Vassiliev, *White #1*, 128–29. Pavel Pastelnyak used the pseudonym of "Pavel Klarin" in the United States.

16. "Gennady was supposed"; "Luka" to Moscow Center, 20 April 1940, KGB file 34194, pp. 354, 385, Vassiliev, *White #1*, 128–30.

17. KGB New York to Moscow Center, May 1941; Decision by Merkulov, 9 May 1941; "Gennady" file entries, KGB file 34194, pp. 423–25, 430–31, 433, 438, Vassiliev, *White #1*, 131. Dismissed in 1947 in another Stalin initiated shake-up of the security services, Ovakimyan became a Soviet chemical industry administrator.

18. Lovestone to the Central Committee, VKP(b), circa 1922–1923, Stetsenko, "Background on Golos from the IKKI," September 1939, KGB file 70994, pp. 10, 125, Vassiliev, *White #1*, 140, 144–45.

19. "Sound," 26 January 1937; "We wanted"; Stetsenko, "Background on Golos from the IKKI," September 1939, KGB file 70994, pp. 7, 26, 125, 128, Vassiliev, *White #1*, 139–40, 144–45.

20. Report by "Harry," December 1939, KGB file 70994, p. 141, Vassiliev, *White #1*, 145. "Nikolay" to Moscow Center, 28 June 1938, KGB file 35112, v.5, p. 38, Vassiliev, *Black*, 151.

21. "Nikolay" to Moscow Center, May 1937; Moscow Center to "Nikolay," 14 May 1937; "Sound" file entries, KGB file 70994, pp. 48–49, 71–72, 76, 95, Vassiliev, *White #1*, 141–42.

22. "Was known to individuals arrested by us," 19 April 1938; "Testimony of arrestee P. Gutzeit," circa 1939; "Memorandum on Sound without a date or author," circa 1939; "Arrestee Durmashkin," 3 September 1939, KGB file 70994, pp. 9, 97–99, 101–2, 105–6, 114, Vassiliev, *White #1*, 139, 142–44.

23. P. Pshenichny, "Memorandum on Sound," 9 September 1939; P. Pshenichny, "An investigation conducted," 14 September 1939, KGB file 70994, pp. 120–21, 124–25, Vassiliev, *White #1*, 143–44.

24. "Gennady" report, 20 October 1939; Gennady to Moscow Center, 21 October 1939; "Gennady fears," KGB file 70994, pp. 115, 130, 138, Vassiliev, *White #1*, 143, 145.

25. Moscow Center to "Gennady," 23 October 1939; "Gennady" report, 9 January 1940, KGB file 70994, pp. 131, 146, Vassiliev, *White #1*, 145–46.

26. "Luka" to Moscow Center, 20 April 1940, KGB file 34194, pp. 385–86, Vassiliev, *White #1*, 129–30.

27. Ilya Lvovich Durmashkin testimony, 10 July 1938; Memo on "Sound," 19 July 1940; "Gennady" to Moscow Center, 30 June 1940; "Gennady" report, 11 July 1940; "Word was sent," 12 July 1940; "Gennady" report, 24 August 1940; Golos's son's cable of 26 July 1940, KGB file 70994, pp. 173–74, 181–88, 191, 196, 235–36, 292, Vassiliev, *White #1*, 147–48.

28. Prudnikov, "Report on intelligence in the USA," 12 April 1941, KGB file 35112, v.1, pp. 69–79, Vassiliev, *Black*, 173.

29. "Plan for reinforcing," circa 1943, KGB file 43173, v.1, p.33, Vassiliev, *Black*, 45.

30. Fitin, Sudoplatov, and Zarubin, "Plan for the organization of the illegal station,"17 April 1940; Butkov to Prudnikov, 11 April 1941; Fitin to Beria, with Sudoplatov annotation of Beria's approval, 20 January 1941; Kropachev, "Plan of Operation," 23 May 1941, KGB file 35112, v.1, pp. 18–21, 38, 43–44, 83, Vassiliev, *Black*, 166–68, 170–71, 174.

31. "Sound was transferred," 10 April 1941; "Leonid" to "Luka," Meeting with "Sound," 27 June 1941, KGB file 35112, v.4, pp. 352, 354–57, Vassiliev, *White #1*, 19–20.

32. "Leonid's" report to Fitin, 9 September 1944, KGB file 35112, v.1, p. 336, Vassiliev, *Black*, 184.

33. Zarubin to Merkulov, "Memorandum (on the station's work in the country)," 30 September 1944, KGB file 35112, v.1, pp. 395–96, Vassiliev, *White #1*, 3.

34. Ibid., pp. 398–99, Vassiliev, *White #1*, 4.

35. Ibid., pp. 407–9, Vassiliev, *White #1*, 8–9; "Myrna," "My relationship with Sound," received through "X," 11 December 1944, KGB file 70545, pp. 281–82, Alexander Vassiliev, *White Notebook #2 [2007 English Translation]*, trans. Steven Shabad (1993–96), 16–17.

36. Zarubin to Merkulov, "Memorandum (on the station's work in the country)," 30 September 1944, KGB file 35112, v.1, pp. 409–10; Messages from "Mer," December 1943, KGB file 70994, pp. 318–25, Vassiliev, *White #1*, 9–10, 152. "Mer's" account of his meeting with "Clever Girl," 29 November 1943, KGB file 70545, pp. 26–28, 32, 35–37, Vassiliev, *White #2*, 1–2.

37. "Maxim" re "Vardo's" meeting with "Helmsman," 19 December 1943; Cipher cable, 20 March 1944; Note from "Mer," 5 January 1944; Message from "Mer," 25 April 1944, KGB file 70545, pp. 65–69, 74–75, 77, 79–80, Vassiliev, *White #2*, 2–3.

38. Memo from "Mer," 29 April 1944; Moscow Center to "Maxim," 13 May 1944; "Maxim" to Moscow Center, 23 May 1944, KGB file 70545, pp. 82, 85–89, Vassiliev, *White #2*, 3–4. KGB New York to Moscow Center, 28 August 1945, KGB file 35112, v.9, p. 109, Vassiliev, *White #1*, 70.

39. "Mer" re "Clever Girl," 15 June 1944; Fitin to Graur, circa mid-1944, KGB file 70545, pp. 95, 98–100, 103, Vassiliev, *White #2*, 5–6.

40. Note by "Albert," 19 August 1945; Note by "Albert," 27 September 1945, KGB file 55298, pp. 268–72, 286, Alexander Vassiliev, *White Notebook #3 [2007 English Translation]*, trans. Steven Shabad (1993–96), 24–26, 31. Emphasis in the original.

41. Report on the meeting with "Aileron" (apparently by "Sergey"), 1 October 1945, KGB file 55298, pp. 295–96, Vassiliev, *White #3*, 33–34.

42. KGB New York to Moscow Center, 28 August 1945, KGB file 35112, v.9, p. 108, Vassiliev, *White #1*, 70.

43. "Vadim" report, 20 February 1945; "Vadim" to Moscow Center, 29 October

1945; Note by "Albert," 22 February 1945; Note by "Albert," 11 March 1945, KGB file 43072, v.1, pp. 70–72, 75, 77–78, 102, Vassiliev, *White #3*, 53–56, 59.

44. KGB Washington to Moscow Center, 10 April 1945; Report by "Raid" on his meeting with "Mole," 14 April 1945; KGB Washington to Moscow Center, 8 May 1945; Report by "X" on the meeting with "Mole," 13 May 1945, KGB file 55302, v.1, pp. 49–50, 53–60, Vassiliev, *White #3*, 90–93. "Mer's" note regarding "Raid," 10 June 1944; "Albert" to Moscow Center, 17 September 1944, KGB file 45100, v.1, pp. 21, 28–29, Vassiliev, *White #3*, 69, 71. Note by "X," 11 January 1945, KGB file 40624, v.1, p. 22, Vassiliev, *Yellow #2*, 66.

45. "Roma," circa 1945, KGB file 45100, v.1, p. 147, Vassiliev, *White #3*, 83.

46. Note by "X," 28 January 1945; "Vadim" to Moscow Center, 20–21 March 1945, KGB file 45100, v.1, pp. 80, 100–101, Vassiliev, *White #3*, 76–77.

47. Message from "X" re "M.'s" work, 7 December 1944, KGB file 70545, pp. 288–89, Vassiliev, *White #2*, 18. Moscow Center to "Vadim," 29 May 1945, KGB file 43173, v.2, p. 61, Vassiliev, *Black*, 66.

48. Moscow Center to "Vadim," 24 November 1944; "Vadim" to Moscow Center, 4 December 1944; "Agreement with 'Helmsman,'" December 1944, KGB file 70545, pp. 178–79, 184, 246, Vassiliev, *White #2*, 10–11, 15.

49. Autobiography, Elizabeth Terrill Bentley, circa 1944, KGB file 70545, pp. 233–34, Vassiliev, *White #2*, 12.

50. "In Dec. 1944"; "Vadim met," with Ovakimyan annotation, 25 December 1944; "Vadim" to Moscow Center, 27 June 1945, KGB file 70545, pp. 247, 249, 338–40, Vassiliev, *White #2*, 15, 20–21.

51. "Vadim" to Moscow Center, 4 July 1945; "Vadim" to Moscow Center, 1 September 1945; "Vadim" to Moscow Center, 10 September 1945; Moscow Center to "Vadim," 14 September 1945, KGB file 70545, pp. 351, 353, 358–62, Vassiliev, *White #2*, 21–22. Vladimir Pozniakov, "A NKVD/NKGB Report to Stalin: A Glimpse into Soviet Intelligence in the United States in the 1940's," *Cold War International History Project Bulletin*, no. 10 (March 1998).

52. "Vadim" to Moscow Center, 27 September 1945, KGB file 70545, pp. 363–67, Vassiliev, *White #2*, 23–24.

53. Merkulov to "Vadim," 11 October 1945, KGB file 35112, v.1, pp. 368–71, Vassiliev, *White #2*, 24–25.

54. "Vadim" to Moscow Center, 29 October 1945, KGB file 35112, v.1, pp. 387–90, Vassiliev, *White #2*, 26.

55. Moscow Center to "Vadim," 22 November 1945; "Vadim" to Moscow Center, 25 November 1945, KGB file 70545, pp. 402, 410–14, Vassiliev, *White #2*, 30–31.

56. "Bob" to Moscow Center, 20 November 1945; "Bob" to Moscow Center, 4 December 1945, KGB file 70545, pp. 393–96, 446–48, Vassiliev, *White #2*, 27–28, 33.

57. Moscow Center to "Vadim," 23 November 1945; Moscow Center to "Sergey," 23 November 1945; Moscow Center to "Vadim," 26 November 1945, KGB file 70545, pp. 405–8, 415, Vassiliev, *White #2*, 30–32.

58. "Vadim" to Moscow Center, with Merkulov annotation and note of reply to "Vadim," 27 November 1945, KGB file 70545, pp. 420–24, Vassiliev, *White #2*, 32.

59. "Grigory" to Moscow Center, 11 March 1947; Moscow Center to "Grigory," 29 March 1947, KGB file 43173, v.2, pp. 130, 134–36, Vassiliev, *Black,* 62; Christopher M. Andrew and Vasili Mitrokhin, *The Sword and the Shield: The Mitrokhin Archive and the Secret History of the KGB* (New York: Basic Books, 1999), 143.

60. "Vladimir" to Moscow Center, 25 December 1948, KGB file 43173, v.4, pp. 477–78; "Report addressed to the Chairman of the KI in view of Vladimir's cipher telegram dated 25.12.48, KGB file 43173, v.2c, p. 33, Vassiliev, *Black,* 72, 76.

61. "Plan of measures," 16 March 1950, KGB file 43173, v.2c, p. 78, Vassiliev, *Black,* 82.

62. "Explanation by G. Sokolov," 27 January 1951, KGB file 43173, v.2c, pp. 309–10, Vassiliev, *Black,* 85.

63. KGB Washington to Moscow Center, 1 October 1950, KGB file 43173, v.12, pp. 201–3, 216, Vassiliev, *Black,* 97.

64. Moscow Center to "Sergey," 23 November 1945, KGB file 70545, pp. 407–8, Vassiliev, *White #2,* 31. Moscow Center to "Sergey," 7 August 1945; Memo, 1 September 1945; Panyushkin to Fitin, 11 September 1945; Moscow Center to "Sergey," 14 September 1945, KGB file 70548, pp. 69, 73, 75–76, Vassiliev, *White #2,* 38–39.

65. Memo, circa 1946, KGB file 70548, pp. 149–50, Vassiliev, *White #2,* 41–42.

66. Merkulov to Stalin, circa 1946, KGB file 70548, pp. 152–54, Vassiliev, *White #2,* 42–43.

67. KGB interview with Solomon Lozovsky regarding his meeting with Browder; Fitin to Abakumov, 18 June 1946; Panyushkin to Gromyko, 5 July 1949; other entries regarding Browder's activities in Moscow in 1946 and his relationship with the KGB later, KGB file 70548, pp. 155–56, 163, 165, 170–72, 175–76, 265, 272, 283, 300, 323, 344, 375, Vassiliev, *White #2,* 43–45. Closing quote after "die down" missing in the notebook and supplied here.

68. "Nikolay" to "Duche," 1 October 1935, KGB file 17690, p. 3; KGB New York to Moscow Center, 14 September 1938, KGB file 35112, v.5, p. 105; KGB New York to Moscow Center, 5 October 1939, KGB file 35112 v.5a, pp. 410–12, 414, Vassiliev, *Black,* 141, 152, 162. Serial 642, FBI Armand Labis Feldman file 61–7574.

69. Moscow Center to KGB New York, 27 November 1941, KGB file 40159, v.3, p. 139; "Young Woman"; "Gennady" to Moscow Center, 1 December 1938; "Gennady" to Moscow Center, 2 February 1939, KGB file 35112, v.5, pp. 26, 111, 171, Vassiliev, *Black,* 106, 155.

70. Anonymous Russian letter to Hoover, 7 August 1943, reproduced in Robert Louis Benson and Michael Warner, *Venona: Soviet Espionage and the American Response 1939–1957* (Washington, D.C.: National Security Agency; Central Intelligence Agency, 1996), 51–54.

71. Pavel Sudoplatov et al., *Special Tasks: The Memoirs of an Unwanted Witness, a Soviet Spymaster* (Boston: Little, Brown, 1994), 196–97; Ben Fischer, "'Mr. Guver': Anonymous Soviet Letter to the FBI," *Newsletter of the Center for the Study of Intelligence,* no. 7 (Winter–Spring 1997): 10–11.

72. Fitin and Ovakimyan to Merkulov, with Merkulov annotation, 30 March 1944, KGB file 35112, v.1, pp. 310–11, Vassiliev, *Black,* 182–83; Andrew and Mitrokhin, *Sword and the Shield,* 124.

73. "Switching 'Callistratus,'" KGB file 40129, v.3a, p. 177, Vassiliev, *White #1,* 109.

74. "Gennady" to "Maxim," 25 June 1942, KGB file 40159, v.3, p. 185, Vassiliev, *Black,* 107; "Memorandum on "Charon's" work from Dec. '41 through June '44," KGB file 25748, v.2, p. 115, Vassiliev, *White #1,* 136.

75. "Conversation with Leonid," 18 September 1944, pp. 366–67, 372, Vassiliev, *Black,* 190.

76. "On the behavior of our workers abroad," 6 March 1943, KGB file 35112, v.1, pp. 314–17, Vassiliev, *Black,* 183–84.

77. "Vadim" to Boyarsky, 20 February 1945; "Vadim" to Moscow Center, 29 October 1945, KGB file 43173, v.1, pp. 81, 165, Vassiliev, *Black,* 50, 57.

78. "Anton" to Moscow Center, 1 June 1944, KGB file 35112, v.1, p. 327, Vassiliev, *Black,* 184.

79. Prudnikov to Korotkov, 2 June 1947, KGB file 35112, v.3, p. 185, Vassiliev, *White #1,* 83.

80. Moscow Center to "Stepan," 26 July 1947, KGB file 35112, v.3, p. 185, Vassiliev, *White #1,* 83.

81. "Stepan" to Moscow Center, 5 August 1947; "Stepan received," KGB file 35112, v.3, p. 185, Vassiliev, *White #1,* 84.

82. "Nikolay" to "Jack," September 1934, KGB file 17571, v.2, p. 10, Vassiliev, *Black,* 41.

83. On Serebryansky, see Andrew and Mitrokhin, *Sword and the Shield,* 41, 69, 73, 75–76, 85–86. Pavel Sudoplatov later headed the Administration for Special Tasks.

84. Bentley "Autobiography," circa 1944, KGB file 70545, pp. 240–41, Vassiliev, *White #2,* 13.

85. Dorothy Gallagher, *All the Right Enemies: The Life and Murder of Carlo Tresca* (New Brunswick, NJ: Rutgers University Press, 1988), 170–76; Elizabeth Bentley, FBI Deposition, 30 November 1945, serial 220, pp. 3–4, FBI Silvermaster file 65–56402; Whittaker Chambers, *Witness* (New York: Random House, 1952), 36. Elizabeth Bentley and Hayden B. Peake, *Out of Bondage: The Story of Elizabeth Bentley* (New York: Ivy Books, 1988), 108, 176–77; FBI Juliet Poyntz file 100–206603.

86. Memo on Poyntz, KGB file 70545, pp. 198–208, Vassiliev, *White #2,* 14. Possibly Poyntz disappeared on her own, but in view of the subsequent absence of any known contact with family and close friends, this seems unlikely.

87. "Nikolay" to Moscow Center, 26 June 1938; "Gennady" to Moscow Center, 25 January 1938, KGB file 35112, v.5, pp. 4, 32, Vassiliev, *Black,* 146, 149. "Jung" to Moscow Center, 28 June 1938, KGB file 36857, v.1, pp. 116, 121–22, Vassiliev, *Yellow #2,* 23.

88. KGB New York to Moscow Center, 9 or 13 October 1943, KGB file 41988, v.1, pp. 12, 15, Vassiliev, *Yellow #2,* 77–78; KGB Washington to Moscow Center, 10 November 1945, KGB file 43072, v.1, pp. 104–5, Vassiliev, *White #3,* 59.

89. KGB New York to Moscow Center, 8 May 1943; Gorsky report, 4 May 1944, KGB file 45100, v.1, pp. 12–13, Vassiliev, *White #3,* 67. For a discussion of the

CPUSA's secret apparatus, see Harvey Klehr, John Earl Haynes, and Fridrikh Igorevich Firsov, *The Secret World of American Communism* (New Haven: Yale University Press, 1995), 71–187.

90. FBI summary of Nelson/Cooper [Zarubin] conversation, 22 October 1944, serial 3515, FBI Comintern Apparatus file 100–203581. The FBI summary of the recorded conversation is found in U.S. Senate Internal Security Subcommittee, *Interlocking Subversion in Government Departments [Hearings]* (Washington, D.C.: U.S. Govt. Print. Off., 1953), part 15, 1050–51. See also "COMRAP—Vassili M. Zubilin" and J. Edgar Hoover to Harry Hopkins, 7 May 1943, reproduced in Benson and Warner, *Venona,* 49–50, and FBI report, "Soviet Espionage Activities," 19 October 1945," attached to Director to Vaughan, 19 October 1945, President's Secretary's Files, Harry S. Truman Library, Independence, Missouri.

91. Report on "Nigel," 18 February 1938, KGB file 58380, v.1, pp. 51–52, Vassiliev, *White #3,* 116.

92. Report by "X" on the meeting with "Mole," 13 May 1945, KGB file 55302, v.1, pp. 56, 58, Vassiliev, *White #3,* 92–93.

Conclusion

1. Fitin to Beria, 25 September 1939, KGB file 35112, v.1, p. 8, Alexander Vassiliev, *Black Notebook [2007 English Translation],* trans. Philip Redko (1993–96), 165.

2. On the sometimes awkward evolution of FBI counterintelligence, see Raymond J. Batvinis, *The Origins of FBI Counterintelligence* (Lawrence: University Press of Kansas, 2007).

Index